M000317791

Should Race Matter?
Unusual Answers to the Usual Questions

In this book, philosopher David Boonin attempts to answer the moral questions raised by five important and widely contested racial practices: slave reparations, affirmative action, hate speech restrictions, hate crime laws, and racial profiling. Arguing from premises that virtually everyone on both sides of the debates over these issues already accepts, Boonin arrives at an unusual and unorthodox set of conclusions, one that is neither liberal nor conservative, color conscious nor color blind. Defended with the rigor that has characterized his previous work but written in a more widely accessible style, this provocative and important new book is sure to spark controversy and should be of interest to philosophers, legal theorists, and anyone interested in trying to resolve the debate over these important and divisive issues.

David Boonin is a Professor of Philosophy at the University of Colorado. He is the author of the book *Thomas Hobbes and the Science of Moral Virtue* (1994) and the prize-winning books *A Defense of Abortion* (2002) and *The Problem of Punishment* (2008), all of which were published by Cambridge. He is also the author of a number of articles on issues in applied ethics and the co-editor of the popular applied ethics textbook *What's Wrong?* (2009).

Should Race Matter?

Unusual Answers to the Usual Questions

DAVID BOONIN

University of Colorado

CAMBRIDGE
UNIVERSITY PRESS

CAMBRIDGE UNIVERSITY PRESS
Cambridge, New York, Melbourne, Madrid, Cape Town,
Singapore, São Paulo, Delhi, Tokyo, Mexico City

Cambridge University Press
32 Avenue of the Americas, New York, NY 10013-2473, USA

www.cambridge.org
Information on this title: www.cambridge.org/9780521149808

First published 2011

Printed in the United States of America

A catalog record for this publication is available from the British Library.

Library of Congress Cataloging in Publication data
Boonin, David,
Should race matter? : unusual answers to the usual questions/David Boonin.
p. cm.
Includes bibliographical references and index.
ISBN 978-0-521-76086-7 (hardback) – ISBN 978-0-521-14980-8 (paperback)
1. Race relations. 2. Slavery. 3. Reparations for historical injustices.
4. Affirmative action programs. 5. Hate crimes. I. Title.
HT1521.B634 2011
305.8–dc22 2011003648

ISBN 978-0-521-76086-7 Hardback
ISBN 978-0-521-14980-8 Paperback

For my parents, my wife, and my children

Contents

Preface

Several years ago, a student suggested that our department introduce a course focusing on applied ethics issues that involve race. This struck me as a good idea. I wondered how much work would be involved if I wanted to put such a course together myself, and so I started to make a list of all of the issues I had covered, in well over a decade of teaching a variety of applied ethics courses, that were strongly connected to race. It didn't take long for me to realize that there weren't any. That's when I decided to write this book.

I decided to write this book because I wanted to be able to teach a course on applied ethics and race and because I knew that committing myself to a new book project on the subject would motivate me to do the research necessary to get such a course up and running. I began by looking into the popular and the academic literature on a number of issues that my teaching had previously ignored and ended up deciding to focus on five controversies that struck me as particularly important: the debates over slave reparations, affirmative action, hate speech restrictions, hate crime laws, and racial profiling. With the help of a teaching reduction that was funded by a course development grant from the Institute for Ethical and Civic Engagement at the University of Colorado, I then began to put together a series of documents that would serve both as tentative lecture notes and as preliminary chapter drafts. Although the grant was awarded to help me develop the course and not the book, I would like to express my gratitude here for the support that the grant indirectly provided as my various ideas for the book began to take shape through the process of creating the course.

I set out to write a book that, like the course that I wanted to teach, would consider nonacademic as well as academic writings. And I hoped that, as a result, it would be of interest to both nonacademic and academic readers. Because of this, I made an attempt to solicit feedback from members of both potential audiences as I began to work on the manuscript itself. Of the nonacademic readers who gave me feedback, I would especially like to thank Irving Kagan, Dan Urist, Andy Strom, and Kurt Nordback for their detailed and often challenging comments, and Robert Astle, for helping me figure out the best way to present and find a readership for the final product. Of the academic philosophers who commented on parts or all of the manuscript, I would like to thank Mike Huemer, Dan Korman, Hugh LaFollette, Graeme Forbes, Brad Monton, Chris Heathwood, and, especially, Eric Chwang, Michael Levin, Stephen Kershnar, and Lionel McPherson. I learned a great deal from their responses and have done my best to address them here.

My greatest debt, however, is to two sets of students whose critical feedback was indispensible in writing and revising this book. The first is the set of undergraduates who took the course once I began to offer it. Their detailed questions forced me to make countless clarifications in the way that I presented the material, and their enthusiastic contributions to class discussion gave me an opportunity to test out many of the arguments and objections that eventually made their way into the manuscript.

The second is the reading group that a number of graduate students participated in as the project was nearing its end. These students all dedicated a good part of one summer to reading the entire manuscript in detail and to meeting weekly to discuss it and to provide me with detailed questions, comments, and concerns. For all the help and encouragement that this provided, I would like to thank Cory Aragon and Barrett Emerick for organizing the group and all of their fellow participants: Michaela McSweeney, Duncan Purves, Jennifer Kling, Scott Wisor, Emma Kobil, Amber Arnold, Jason Hanna, and Amandine Catala, who also served as a research assistant on the project.

Finally, I would like to thank my family for their love and support throughout my work on this project and in everything else. This book is for them.

I

Thinking in Black and White

An Introduction to the Moral Questions that America's Past Raises about Its Present

Two facts about black and white people in the United States give rise to a number of important moral questions. This book attempts to answer five of them. The two facts are that for much of our nation's history, black people as a group were treated worse than were white people as a group and that by many uncontroversial measures of human well-being, black Americans on average aren't doing as well today as white Americans are doing. The five moral questions that arise from these facts, and that constitute the subject of this book, concern the moral status of slave reparations, affirmative action, hate speech restrictions, hate crime laws, and racial profiling.

One way to respond to these five practices would be to focus on something they all have in common. All five practices involve treating racial distinctions, in one way or another, as morally relevant. Someone might claim that racial distinctions should never be treated as morally relevant, and so oppose all five practices. Or someone might claim that racial distinctions may always be treated as morally relevant, and so think that there's nothing wrong in principle with any of them.

Attempting to reach a moral conclusion about these five issues by appealing to either of these general principles, though, is implausible. Despite much talk about the prevalence of color-blind or color-conscious thinking, no one really believes that racial distinctions should never matter or that they may always matter. Supporters of affirmative action who think that racial distinctions should matter when the post office is deciding who to hire, for example, don't think that such distinctions should matter when the post office is deciding how much to charge people for stamps. They think that the postal service's stamps should be distributed in a color-blind manner, that is, but they don't think that its jobs should be. Similarly, opponents of affirmative action who think that racial distinctions shouldn't matter when a public hospital is deciding which doctors to hire don't insist that such distinctions shouldn't matter when those doctors are deciding how to diagnose or treat their patients. They think that the doctors' jobs should be distributed in a color-blind manner, that is, but if the race of a patient proves to be relevant to diagnosing or treating a particular medical condition, they don't think that the medical care the doctors provide should be. The attempt to resolve any particular racial controversy by insisting that racial distinctions should never matter or that they may always matter is therefore bound to fail.

A second way to respond to these five issues would be to focus on the distinction between conferring a positive benefit on someone because of their race and imposing a sanction on someone because they targeted a person for unwelcome treatment because of that person's race. Slave reparations and affirmative action would go hand in hand, on this account, since both involve preferential treatment according to race. And hate speech restrictions, hate crime laws and a ban on racial profiling would stand or fall together, too, since all involve penalizing someone for targeting people by race for unwelcome treatment. But there would be no reason to treat all five cases as being morally on a par. One might consistently oppose affirmative action programs on the grounds that they use race to favor some people over others, for example, while at the same time supporting hate crime laws on the grounds that criminals who select their victims by race do something worse than criminals who don't.

This second way of approaching these five practices is a bit more promising. But it, too, is ultimately unsatisfactory. There's no reason to view all cases that involve preferential treatment by race as being morally on a par. Nor is there reason to view all cases that sanction those who target people by race for unwelcome treatment as being morally on a par. The moral status of targeting a person by race for unwelcome treatment, for example, might turn out to depend in part on the moral status of the kind of unwelcome treatment in question. Insulting a person in nonracial contexts is objectionable but it isn't prohibited by legal or academic regulations. Committing a crime against someone in nonracial contexts is objectionable and is also prohibited by the law. A cop pulling someone over for speeding in nonracial contexts is neither objectionable nor prohibited by the law. Whether the targeting of a person by race for unwelcome treatment makes the act in question more objectionable or more worthy of sanction than it would otherwise be, then, might depend in part on whether the act would be objectionable or worthy of punishment if it were performed in a purely nonracial context. Since insulting people, committing crimes against them, and pulling them over for speeding in nonracial contexts each differ from the other two in terms of their moral status, their legal status, or both, we might well be led to reach substantially different conclusions about the moral status of targeting people by race for each of these forms of treatment or about the moral status of imposing sanctions on people who target people by race in these different ways.

And while slave reparations and affirmative action each involve conferring benefits on some people because of their race, there's no reason to assume that these two practices must go hand in hand morally, either. One could support reparations while opposing affirmative action, for example, if one thought that the latter but not the former involved a certain kind of rights violation. And one might support affirmative action while opposing slave reparations if one's support for affirmative action arose from considerations, such as the importance of promoting diversity, that are independent of claims about compensation and reparation. Trying to reach a moral conclusion about these five cases by considering them in presumptively comparable groups, then, is bound to fail as well.

This leaves a third possibility: considering these five issues one at a time, on their own individual merits, recognizing that the most reasonable conclusions might entail support for some, opposition to others, and perhaps at times positions that lie somewhere between embrace and condemnation. That is the approach that I've tried to take in this book, and it's led me to a somewhat eclectic set of conclusions that as a whole can't readily be characterized as left or right, color blind or color conscious: support for slave reparations, a position on affirmative action that lies between that of its supporters and its opponents, opposition to hate speech restrictions but support for hate crime laws, and a limited but nonetheless substantive defense of the permissibility of racial profiling, at least under certain sorts of conditions. Taken as a whole, these positions may seem not just eclectic but downright inconsistent: how could one oppose hate speech restrictions without also opposing hate crime laws? Who could endorse slave reparations, widely dismissed as the most radical of racial practices, while also supporting racial profiling, almost universally reviled as the most reactionary? Why maintain that practicing affirmative action is morally permissible but then maintain that not practicing affirmative action is morally permissible, too?

Virtually everyone who reads this book, I suspect, will initially agree with at least some of the positions I defend here. Virtually no one who reads this book, I suspect, will initially agree with all of them. In the chapters that follow, though, I'll try to show that they should agree with all of them. And I'll try to show this by appealing to assumptions that virtually everyone who reads this book, regardless of their initial views about these various issues, already accepts. In this way, I hope to show that my apparently unusual combination of positions does, in fact, offer a coherent and defensible response to some of the most difficult and controversial moral problems raised by the use, and the misuse, of race in this country.

WHAT'S BLACK AND WHITE AND CONTESTED ALL OVER?

I've started out by writing as if it's clear what it means to say that someone is black or white. It isn't. Some people treat the line between black and white as essentially a matter of biology. Birds come in different varieties, dogs come in different breeds and, on this account, people come in different races. We recognize a line between white people and black people on this view because nature itself has drawn this line. Others treat race as something that's a fundamentally social construction. Nature doesn't tell us whether to call Pluto a planet, for example. We decide whether to call it a planet. And if we decide not to call it a planet, this isn't because it "really isn't" a planet. Rather, it really isn't a planet because we've decided not to call it one. In the same sort of way, many people have argued, truths about racial identity are created rather than discovered. It isn't that a man with three Swedish grandparents and one African grandparent is called black because he "really is" black. Rather, he's black because that's what we call him.[1]

This debate about the reality of race is a confusing one in part because the people who engage in it often seem to mean different things when they use the word "race." As a result, it's often unclear whether those who claim that race is real and those who claim that it isn't are really disagreeing with each other about anything. Consider, for example, two recent books that, at least on the face of it, defend diametrically opposed views about the reality of race: *Race: the Reality of Human Differences* by anthropologist Vincent Sarich (written with journalist Frank Miele) and *The Race Myth: Why We Pretend Race Exists in America*, by evolutionary biologist Joseph Graves Jr., both published in 2005. Graves sets out to demonstrate that "The traditional concept of race as a biological fact is a myth" and that "The fact is that no biological races exist in modern humans."[2] Sarich and Miele, on the other hand, set out to show that race is real and that denying this is no more than political correctness run amok. Both sides have impressive scientific credentials and both appeal to plenty of scientific data to support their positions. One would therefore expect to find a powerful clash of positions.

But a careful study of both books reveals that, in this case at least, the two sides of the debate are talking entirely past each other. And this is so precisely because the two sides are using the term "race" to mean fundamentally different things. When Graves attacks the claim that race is real, for example, he describes himself as attacking the claim that "biological races can be unambiguously identified within the human species, and that these races have an innate essence that distinguishes them from other races."[3] On this use of the term, a race is a subset of the human species that has some fixed, immutable essence that's shared by every human being who is a member of the subset and by no human being who is not. But when Sarich and Miele argue that race is real and not a mere social construction, they are equally clear that by "race" they mean something very different: a group of humans who have largely similar ancestry in terms of how recently their ancestors migrated from sub-Saharan Africa and in terms of where they ended up settling when they first left.[4]

While each of the two books defends the truth of its own claim about the reality of "race" when the word is used in one sense, moreover, neither of the books denies the truth of the claim about the reality of race made by the other book when "race" is used in the other sense. Referring to some of the facts that have been cited in favor of the claim that race is real, for example, Graves writes that "All this data really does is allow us to get a better handle on the past migratory history of our species, as opposed to identifying or assigning individuals to discrete racial categories."[5] While denying the reality of "race" in his Platonic sense of the term, that is, Graves acknowledges the reality of race in the genealogical sense of the term employed by Sarich and Miele. And the arguments that Sarich and Miele stress in favor of the view that race is real just as clearly apply to their sense of the term "race" but not to the sense used by Graves. As an important argument for their thesis, for example, Sarich and Miele cite the case of a 2003 investigation into a series of killings in and around Baton Rouge, Louisiana. In March of that year, as they report the story, Tony Frudakis of DNAPrint Genomics told the task force working on the case that it should shift its focus away from white suspects and toward "an African American of average skin tone, because his analysis indicated the perpetrator had 85 percent sub-Saharan African and 15 percent Native American ancestry. The seventy-three-marker DNAPrint, which became sufficiently developed for this type of investigation only in early 2003, determines an individual's proportion of East Asian, Indo-European, Native American, and sub-Saharan African ancestry and then compares these proportions against a database of 300 to 400 people already typed to produce a comparable skin tone."[6] Sarich and Miele take this as evidence that objective biological facts about a person's genetic makeup can be used to determine which race the person belongs to precisely because by race they mean facts about the person's ancestral history and not some eternal, immutable essence that he shares with all and only other members of his group. The police were looking for a white person, that is, objective DNA analysis told them to look for a black person, and when the killer was finally identified he did, in fact, turn out to be black. Or, at least, he turned out to be "black" given what Sarich and Miele mean by that term: a person with a sufficiently high proportion of relatively recent sub-Saharan African ancestry. Sarich and Miele don't claim that he (or anyone else) was black in the sense of having a fixed and essential quality that links him to all and only black people.

So is race real? A reasonable response to the debate between Graves on the one hand and Sarich and Miele on the other would seem to be: yes and no. Race is real in the sense that there really are physical differences between different human populations grouped together by genetic ancestry. Race is not real in the sense that there really are no natural fault lines that perfectly divide the world into a discrete number of groups each bound together by its own eternal essence. The subtitle of Kenan Malik's excellent 2008 book on the subject, *Strange Fruit*, is "Why Both Sides Are Wrong in the Race Debate." But a more charitable assessment of the situation, and one that seems equally consistent with Malik's own analysis, is that both sides are right.[7] Each side makes a claim about the reality of race that turns out to be correct given what it means by the term. Neither side offers an argument that undermines the claim about the reality of the race made by the other side given what the other side means by the term.

Whether this conclusion about the debate between Graves on the one hand and Sarich and Miele on the other can successfully be extended to the vast literature on the subject as a whole is a deep and vexing question. But for the purposes of this book, answering this particular question won't be necessary. The reason for this is simple. In order for any theory of race or of racial identity to be successful, it must produce results that are accurate across a broad range of cases about which virtually everyone agrees. Abraham Lincoln and Jefferson Davis, for example, were white. Frederick Douglass and Harriet Tubman were black. Will

Smith and Denzel Washington are black; Russell Crowe and George Clooney are white. Hillary Clinton is white. Condoleezza Rice is black. Any theory of racial identity that fails to produce the correct results in such cases is unacceptable for that very reason. And for the purposes of this book, all we really need to assume is that these particular kinds of judgment are generally correct.

The problems I want to discuss in this book, after all, arise because of the two facts that I mentioned at the outset: that for much of our nation's history, black people on the whole were treated significantly worse than were white people as a whole, and that by many current indicators of basic human welfare, black Americans today are doing considerably worse on average than are white Americans. In order to affirm that these two basic claims are true, we need to be able determine which people should be counted as black and which should be counted as white when we look at such questions as who was legally entitled to vote prior to the Civil War or who is more likely to graduate from college today. But while we do need to be able to say who is black and who is white for these sorts of purposes, we don't need to be able to say what theory best explains why the black people are black and the white people are white. Any theory that gets it right in the clear, uncontroversial cases will be as good as any other. And so, for the purposes of this book, I'll simply assume that we by and large agree about which people are black and which people are white, even if we don't agree about what exactly this means or about what theory best accounts for our agreement. What ultimately explains the nature of racial differences is a widely contested topic. But it won't be contested here.

BEYOND BLACK AND WHITE

In assuming that we generally agree about who is black and who is white, though, it may seem that I also mean to be assuming that everyone is one or the other. I don't mean to be assuming this. In the first place, some people might most reasonably be characterized as simply falling in between these two categories. In the United States, we no longer use such terms as "mestizo," "mulatto," "creole," and "quadroon," all of which were once commonly used to designate people who were neither "fully black" nor "fully white."[8] We tend instead to consider people to be black if it seems clear to us that they are at least partly black. Tiger Woods, for example, tried for a while to refer to himself as "Cablinasian," as a way of acknowledging his Caucasian, African, (American) Indian, and Asian ancestry, but when most Americans looked at him, they simply saw a black man. In other countries, however, it continues to be common to make more fine-grained judgments than simply dividing people into black and white, and the project of this book in no way depends on the assumption that this alternative approach is mistaken. If it proves in the end to make more sense to refer to a particular individual as half-black and half-white, for example, this need pose no problem for the various questions I will want to raise or the various conclusions I will want to draw. It will simply follow that what I say about black people will apply to this person to the extent that he is counted as black, and not to the extent that he is not. Since we Americans do tend to push most people of mixed ancestry into one category or the other, though, and since this is a book about a distinctly American problem written primarily for an American audience, I will largely follow the current American convention of calling most of the people I refer to either black or white.

There's a second and much more obvious reason, of course, for not assuming that everyone is either black or white: a great number of people are neither black nor white nor partly both. They are Asian or Latino, Maori or Inuit, or many other things besides. It may also seem, then, that by carving the world up into black and white for the purposes of this book, I am diminishing the importance of these further groups. But the point of this book is not to catalog humanity in all of its racial or ethnic diversity, or to suggest that some groups matter more than others. The point is simply to focus on one particular set of questions that Americans have found, and continue to find, particularly vexing. These questions involve the line between black and white Americans, in particular, because much of what is distinctive of our national history and current racial demography involves the relationship between black and white people in particular. This is the reason that I will discuss the practices that I focus on here primarily by thinking of ethics in terms that are black and white.

While the explicit focus of most of what follows will be presented in black and white, however, this doesn't mean that what I have to say isn't relevant to many other important groups. What I say about slave reparations in Chapters 2 and 3, for example, is likely to apply to Native Americans as well. What I conclude about affirmative action in Chapters 4 and 5 probably goes for many other groups, including Hispanics and women. My discussion of hate speech restrictions in Chapters 6 and 7 and of hate crime laws in Chapters 8 and 9 could plausibly be extended to cases involving bias against gay people, and my argument about racial profiling in Chapters 10 and 11 almost certainly has implications for the treatment of Arabs and people perceived to be Muslim.[9] While all of these other groups of people are obviously important, however, I will generally leave it to the reader to consider how readily, if at all, the arguments I develop here can be made to apply to them. The arguments themselves can best be developed if they remain narrowly focused. And so, for the reasons already mentioned, I will treat the moral problems with which this book is concerned as issues that can most clearly be seen in black and white.

DON'T KNOW MUCH ABOUT (BLACK) HISTORY

February is Black History Month. It's also the shortest month. It's easy enough to joke about this, to anticipate the predictable complaint that there isn't a White History Month, and the equally predictable rejoinder that every month is White History Month. It's less easy to know how to initiate a responsible discussion of the moral problems that this book is concerned with given that Black History

Month exists largely because so many Americans don't know that much about black history in the first place. In order to understand the background that gives rise to the various questions that I want to address in this book, though, and in order to think fairly and responsibly about the different positions that can be taken in response to them, it's necessary to have a clear and explicit grasp of some basic, and regrettable, facts about the history of black people in America. So while there's a great deal to celebrate and to be grateful for in our nation's history, and while there's surely much more to the history of black people in America than a tale of victimization, I will focus in this section exclusively on identifying some of the important ways in which the United States hasn't always been so good to black people.

The point of this brief exercise, I should emphasize, is not to insist that the ways in which America has been bad to black people are more important or more representative than are the ways in which it has been good to black people. Nor is it to insist that black Americans should care about or identify with the negatives more than the positives, or that they should not, on the whole, be happy and proud to live here. The point, rather, is simply to make clear those particular circumstances that in one way or another give rise to the questions I want to discuss in the chapters that follow. If a man used to beat up his neighbor once in a while and steal from him on occasion, for example, it is these specific incidents that would require clarification in order to determine what, if anything, he now owed his neighbor in response to his past wrongdoings. Facts about all of the other times that he was perfectly nice to his neighbor, left his neighbor alone, or even went out of his way to do favors for his neighbor would be considered irrelevant. In the same way, and for the same reason, what matters for the purposes of understanding the problems to be addressed in this book, for better or worse, is the worse and not the better of the history of black people in the United States. With this understanding of the limited purpose of this section in mind, then, it's important to take account of the following facts about the past before we begin to consider what we should say about their moral implications, if any, for the present.[10]

As far as we can tell, the first black people to settle in the English Colonies that were later to become the United States arrived in 1619. They came neither as free people nor as slaves. Like many of the white people who lived in the New World at the time, the first black Americans came as servants. They entered the country as part of a larger system in which workers were compelled to serve for a predetermined amount of time, typically four or five years, after which they would gain their freedom. Some servants found themselves in this position involuntarily, as a result of their having been convicts or prisoners of war. Others freely consented to take on their roles as apprentices or indentured servants, usually in exchange for passage to their new home and some kind of professional training. But regardless of how they found themselves to be servants in the New World, the defining feature of their servitude was that it was temporary, and there is no evidence that black people were treated differently from white people in this respect, at least in the first few years in which there were black people in the Americas.[11]

While black people may therefore have been treated in the same way as white people when they first arrived on this continent, however, this equality of the races didn't last long. In 1625, a mere six years after the earliest known arrival of black people in America, a Virginia court was called upon to settle the case of three indentured servants who had escaped and fled to Maryland before being captured and returned. Two of the men were white, and they were each sentenced to four years of additional service. But the third, a black man named John Punch, was ordered to "serve his said master or his assigns for the time of his natural life here or elsewhere."[12] Punch, in effect, became the first American slave. And while the black population remained relatively small through the middle of the 1600's, the number of black people who were burdened with permanent servitude began its slow and steady rise.[13]

This enslavement of black laborers in America was not initially authorized by any legal statutes, but it was quickly accepted and enforced by the courts nonetheless. And before long, the Colonies began the formal process of adopting laws to officially recognize slavery: Massachusetts in 1641, followed by Connecticut in 1650, Virginia in 1661, and Maryland in 1663.[14] Near the beginning of this series of events, it may be worth noting, a small number of people attempted to enslave some members of the Native American population as well, but this was a largely isolated and generally unsuccessful practice. By 1675, at least, as the numbers involved continued to increase, American slavery had become, for all intents and purposes, black slavery. It would continue to be so until its abolition nearly two hundred years later.[15] By the time the Colonies finally declared their independence in 1776, moreover, all thirteen of them had positive laws on the books permitting and regulating the practice of slavery.[16]

The country we live in today was born in 1776, but the government we live under today came into existence in 1789, when the Constitution was officially ratified. When calculating the population of a given state for the purposes of determining the size of its representation in Congress, the Constitution counted each slave as three-fifths of a person, but when calculating his importance for the purposes of determining his legal rights, a slave counted as no person at all. So far as the Constitution was concerned, slaves were property. Indeed, Article IV, Section 2 of that document contained the explicit stipulation that a slave who escaped from his master was to be treated as property that would simply be "delivered up" to his master regardless of what the law said in the state to which he escaped.[17] And Article I, Section 8 authorized Congress to use the state-based militias to "suppress insurrections," a provision that was clearly understood at the time to be aimed at preventing slaves from rebelling against their masters.[18]

The active role that the federal government thereby played in protecting the rights of slave owners in the ownership of their slaves was reinforced by the Fugitive Slave Act of 1793, a law that was later strengthened even further in the revised version that came to be known as the Compromise of 1850.[19] This latter version of the law, in particular, helped slave owners to get around various obstacles that some Northern states had attempted to erect in the years between. Some Northern states, for example, which had since outlawed slavery within their borders, also passed laws guaranteeing a fugitive slave's right to a hearing in the court of the state to which the slave had escaped. But the revised federal statute of 1850 mandated that a slave owner merely had to go to the court in his own (of course, slaveholding) state in order to be granted a legal document authenticating his right to recover the slave in question. And at that point, the return of the slave became a federal matter to be carried out by federal officials. From the very moment of the creation of our national government, then, the state played an active role in maintaining the system of slavery, and while a number of individual states retreated from this practice in the years leading up to the Civil War, the government of the nation as a whole stepped in to fill the void. Slavery, in short, wasn't simply a bad thing that happened in America, the way that poverty, disease, or crime are bad things that sometimes happen. Rather, it was a bad thing that was authorized, facilitated, and protected by the United States government.

Not all of the black people who lived in the newly created United States of America were slaves, of course, but even those who are often referred to as "free blacks" were subject to important restrictions that didn't apply to white people. In the first place, no black people in the United States were citizens. The first Federal Naturalization Act, passed in 1790, explicitly restricted citizenship to "free white persons."[20] All black people in America, free or not, were prohibited from voting and from holding public office. An 1810 law even forbade them from working for the Post Office.[21] In addition, in the years leading up to the Civil War, the federal government actively enforced the rights of individual states to impose even further limits on what free blacks could do. South Carolina, for example, was one of several states to pass a Negro Seaman Act, the point of which was to ensure that black sailors arriving from abroad couldn't spread any dangerous ideas by making contact with black people in America. When a ship originating from a foreign country arrived at a South Carolina port, the law required all the black people on board to be arrested and jailed until the ship was ready to depart. John Berrien, the Attorney General under President Andrew Jackson, explicitly confirmed in his statement about this case that the United States government recognized and protected "the general right of a State to regulate persons of color within its own limits."[22] Even Northern states imposed severe legal limits on what free blacks could do, including in some cases prohibiting them from serving on juries, testifying in court, carrying guns, and attending public schools.[23] And black Americans in the North lived in constant fear of being kidnapped and enslaved, especially as the market value of American slaves reached new heights in the early part of the nineteenth century and Congress continued to reject calls for federal antikidnapping legislation or improved protection in the fugitive slave laws.[24]

The Civil War brought an end to the practice of slavery in America.[25] Whether fought for that reason or not, the result was that, in one enormously important respect, life got better for a large number of black people in the United States almost instantly. During the period of Reconstruction that followed from the end of the war in 1865 to the final withdrawal of federal troops from the South in 1877, however, black people in the South continued to suffer various forms of treatment that their white counterparts were spared. At the beginning of this period, President Andrew Johnson imposed relatively mild restrictions on the Southern states as conditions for their return to the Union. The states were free to develop their own new state constitutions, at conventions attended entirely by white delegates, provided only that they repealed their articles of secession, accepted the end of slavery that was brought about by the Thirteenth Amendment, and declared their loyalty to the United States. Johnson justified his decision to largely allow the Southern states to police their treatment of the recently freed black population by themselves by saying that the South "would treat the negro with greater kindness than the North if it were let alone and not exasperated."[26] But the result was that Southern states were largely free to continue their efforts to deny black people most of the fundamental rights of free citizens: the rights to vote, hold office, serve on juries, and so forth, and they proved to be quite determined in these efforts.

Even the familiar offer of "forty acres and a mule," frequently remembered as a form of compensation that black Americans enjoyed toward the end of the war, proved far less helpful to the recently liberated black population than is sometimes now assumed. At the conclusion of his famous March to the Sea, General Sherman issued Special Field Order #15 which, among other things, granted former slaves the right to forty acres of the land abandoned by slave owners on Georgia's offshore islands and parts of its corresponding coastal land for a distance of up to thirty miles inland. But a mere two months later, Congress dramatically weakened the force of this benefit, reducing it to the mere offer that freed blacks could have the right to lease the land for three years with an option to purchase it at the end of that time – provided, of course, that they could come up with the required money. While there is no doubt that the abolition of slavery was a tremendous step toward racial equality in the United States, then, there is also no question that this advance was not completed by the mere adoption of the Thirteenth Amendment.

As the period of Reconstruction ended with the withdrawal of federal troops from the South in 1877, moreover, the Southern states began to try to roll back the rights of their black inhabitants even further. Most states almost immediately enacted prohibitions on interracial marriages, and required their schools to be racially segregated. By 1884, less than a decade after the Northern troops had left, most of the Southern states had accomplished at least this much, either by law or by amendment to their state constitutions. The rise of the so-called Jim Crow laws during this period, named for a stereotypical figure common in minstrel shows, continued so that by 1890 it was common to find legal segregation of such facilities as public transportation, hospitals, restaurants, orphanages, and public drinking fountains.[27] A law passed that year in Louisiana, for example, required trains traveling within the state to provide "separate but equal" accommodations for black and white passengers, and despite the fact that separate was plainly not equal, that law was upheld six years later in the landmark Supreme Court decision *Plessy v. Ferguson.*[28] Racial segregation worked its way into every aspect of public life. Oklahoma mandated separate telephone booths for black and white customers. Florida and North Carolina prohibited schools from providing white students with textbooks that had been used by black students. Macon County, Georgia, even considered providing two sets of public roads, one for white drivers and one for black drivers. As Stephan and Abigail Thernstrom put it in their meticulous 1997 study, *America in Black and White*, "By the early twentieth century the two races were as rigidly separated by law in the South as they later would be under apartheid in South Africa."[29]

The Fifteenth Amendment, meanwhile, had been adopted in 1870. It declared that "The right of citizens of the United States to vote shall not be denied or abridged by the United States or by any State on account of race, color, or previous condition of servitude." This made it difficult for the Southern states to prevent black people from voting, but not impossible. In the years that followed Reconstruction, these states devised a variety of ingenious ways to circumvent the intention of the Amendment and to keep black people off the voting rolls. They could not explicitly require that a person be white in order to register to vote, for example, but they could impose a number of other requirements and then selectively enforce them on black but not white people, especially since enforcement was left entirely to local officials. Thus rules about such things as having a proper mailing address, passing something presented as a literacy test, or paying a tax in order to register were used to prevent black people from having a significant impact at the polls. A number of Southern states amended their constitutions to exempt potential voters from the new requirements if their grandfathers had been eligible to vote prior to Reconstruction. This ensured that white people could continue to vote even if they were unable to pass the literacy tests that were used to keep many black people from voting.[30] In addition, even those black Southerners who did manage to register to vote were often prevented from actually having their votes counted. Some were turned away on Election Day by officials and others were given inadequate instructions on how to cast their ballots so that their votes were ruled invalid. By the time the twentieth century was fully underway, black people in the American South had, in practice if not in principle, essentially been disenfranchised.[31]

During the first half of the twentieth century, racial segregation and the stigma that accompanied it began to work its way from the governments of individual Southern states into the laws of other states like Oklahoma and Maryland,[32] and into the structure of the federal government itself. By 1913, for example, segregated work areas, eating areas and restrooms were common in a wide variety of federal buildings.[33] When the National Recovery Administration established national wage standards as a part of the New Deal a few decades later, it excluded almost three quarters of the black workforce from its requirements by exempting domestic servants and farm workers, an exemption that was designed to satisfy legislators from the South.[34] When the Social Security system was established during the same period of time, it initially excluded these two classes of workers as well.[35] And as late as the Second World War, the United States military was officially segregated by race. Over four hundred thousand black Americans served in the military during this period, and they were not provided with the same standard of care that their white counterparts enjoyed. Indeed, because of the arcane voting restrictions still on the books in most Southern states, many of these black soldiers could fight and die for their country, but could not legally vote. A federal bill called the Soldiers' Vote Act, first introduced in 1942 and then again in 1943, would have secured the right of everyone serving in the military to vote, but its passage was blocked by the opposition of Southern lawmakers. The bill that was finally passed merely encouraged states to allow members of the armed services to vote.[36]

The second half of the twentieth century saw the beginning of the end of official racial segregation in the United States and the rise of the civil rights movement. Some of this history is well known. Many Americans, for example, know that when Rosa Parks refused to move to the back of the bus, she sparked a boycott that ultimately helped to end the segregation of buses in Montgomery, Alabama. But many of the details of this important period are already largely forgotten and, along with them, we have lost a genuine understanding of just how little Parks and her fellow protestors actually demanded, and just how much racial segregation even they still expected to endure as the price for living in the United States. When Parks got on that now famous bus on December 1, 1955, the front section was reserved for white people and black people were forced to sit in the back. Parks, like all of the other black riders that day, dutifully took a seat behind the white people. When the bus was filled and another white person got on board, the driver ordered Parks and three other black riders in her row to stand and move further to the back so that the white passenger could sit. This is what she refused to do.[37] But the demand that Parks and her fellow activists subsequently made was not that black people should be allowed to sit anywhere on the bus they wanted. Even they, in 1955, didn't really think to demand such complete desegregation. Instead, they accepted the idea that black passengers should start filling the bus from the back and white ones from the front, and asked only that once a bus was full, no one would be forced to give up a seat for anyone else. Even Parks and her fellow protestors, that is, agreed that black people could be forced to sit in the back of the bus, just as long as they could keep their seat in the back once they had sat down. And while they also wanted black people to be allowed to apply for jobs driving the buses, they only wanted this for those buses that primarily served black neighborhoods.[38] This is how deeply entrenched the practice of legal racial segregation was in this country just a little over fifty years ago.

In this context, it would be hard to overstate the importance of the pivotal ruling in *Brown v. Board of Education* in 1954, when the U.S. Supreme Court

officially struck down the practice of providing black Americans with public schools that were "separate but equal."[39] Separate but equal, of course, had
always meant separate in order to be unequal. In a famous study of the segregated public schools in Atlanta conducted by W. E. B. Du Bois in 1945, to take just
one of many such cases, it was determined that there was one building for every
855 white children while there was only one for every 2,040 black children. The
local authorities spent $2,156 on land and facilities for each student at the white
schools, but only $877 per student at the black ones. White students attended
school for six and half hours per day while black students went for three and half
hours. The black children had no kindergarten.[40] And this was consistent with a
long-standing pattern in the South in particular. In 1890, for example, only 0.39
percent of black children in the South went to high school, and in 1910 the figure was only 2.8 percent. At that time, there was only one public high school for
black students in Georgia, and only four in the South as a whole.[41]

The Court's ruling in *Brown*, perhaps not surprisingly, did not make state-
sanctioned racial discrimination disappear overnight. When the Court considered the question of putting its decision into practice a year later in what came
to be widely referred to as *Brown II*, it explicitly declined to set any timetables
that states and school districts would have to follow. Most jurisdictions took
advantage of this fact, and many found creative ways to avoid integration more
than a decade after the initial ruling had been handed down. In Charlotte, North
Carolina, for example, the school boards deliberately located school buildings
not in response to population growth but according to established patterns of
residential segregation, with the result that toward the end of the 1960's, the
schools there were still racially segregated in practice, even if not in principle.[42]
Indeed, many studies have suggested that our nation's public schools have continued to be largely segregated in fact if not in theory in the years that have since
passed. One study, for example, found that in 1984, one-third of all black students
were attending schools that consisted of at least 90 percent minority students.[43]
And a 1992 Harvard study concluded that the nation's public schools as a whole
were more segregated than they had been at any point since 1967.[44] The importance of the fact that officially sanctioned race-based discrimination began its
demise over half a century ago should not be underestimated. *Brown v. Board*
was a turning point in the history of the treatment of black people in the United
States. At the same time, we should not overlook the fact that long after the
Court handed down its decision, the consequences of decades of government-
sponsored discrimination were still being felt.

A second great change that came about in the second half of the twentieth century concerned access to the ballot. At the end of 1956, only 20,000 of the 497,000
black people of voting age in Mississippi were registered to vote. In Alabama, the
numbers were 53,000 out of 516,000; in Georgia, 163,000 out of 633,000. A Civil
Rights Act was passed as early as 1957 in order to address this concern, but in
the two years that followed its enactment, it resulted in only three cases in which
the Justice Department charged officials in Southern states with interfering with

the right of black people to register to vote. The Civil Rights commission created by the Act filed a report in September 1959, concluding that deliberate acts of white officials in Southern states remained the single greatest obstacle to black voter registration. In the South as a whole, there were sixteen counties in which a majority of the population was black and in which not a single black person was registered to vote. Forty-six more counties had registered fewer than five percent of the black people who were old enough to be eligible.[45]

While a subsequent version of the Civil Rights Act, passed in 1960, produced relatively few improvements, the same cannot be said of the 1964 Civil Rights Act and 1965 Voting Rights Act. In 1964, just a year before the passage of the Voting Rights Act, nearly eighty percent of the black people of voting age in Alabama were still not registered to vote.[46] When Martin Luther King Jr. arrived in Selma to help launch his famous voting rights campaign at the start of 1965, it was part of a county in which fewer than 250 of the 15,000 black residents of voting age were registered.[47] Within just five months of the Act's passage, nearly a quarter of a million additional black voters were added to the rolls. And within just five years, the rate of black voter registration in the South had nearly equaled that of white voter registration.[48] Official segregation of public facilities came to a similarly sudden end as a result of the passage of the Civil Rights Act. While historical change happens slowly and drawing lines is generally difficult, it seems fair to say that 1964 and 1965 marked a crucial turning point in the end of official, state-sanctioned discrimination against black people in the United States.

There is, of course, much more that could be said about the history of the treatment of black people in America up to 1965. The shameful history of lynching, for example, merits space that I can't devote to it here, and the consequences of the long-standing practice by which white Americans, especially in the South, refused to dignify black Americans with the titles of "Mr." or "Mrs." and referred to grown men as "boy" deserve more attention than is commonly recognized.[49] There is also much that could be added about the treatment of black people in America since 1965. Many people have argued that the law continues to discriminate against black people in the context of capital punishment, for example, in jury selection,[50] and in the disenfranchisement of felons which disproportionately removes black voters from the rolls,[51] or that the slow federal response to Hurricane Katrina was in part due to the racial demography of the areas most severely damaged. And, of course, as I emphasized at the outset of this brief exercise, the story I'm relating here omits all of the positive things that black people have been able to enjoy and to achieve in this country. What I have provided here is meant not as a balanced overview of the black experience in America, but rather as a brief summary of the primary negative parts of American history that generate the moral questions to be addressed in the chapters that follow, a kind of "Oppression of Black People by the United States Government from Colonization to 1965 For Dummies."

For the purposes of this book, though, this should be enough. When I refer in some of the discussion that follows to the legacy of "slavery and its aftermath," what I will mean by that expression is the series of actions taken by the U.S. government from its exclusion of black people from citizenship and its protection of the slave trade at its inception to the various forms of official segregation and discrimination that persisted until the passage of the Voting Rights Act in 1965. Whether other bad things were also done to black people during this period and since shouldn't affect the basic outline of the arguments that will be considered. And whether all of the good things that have been done for black people in America should be enough to render these bad things morally irrelevant can be considered in due course. For now, we can simply conclude that from the very beginning of this country's existence until a little less than fifty years ago, the U.S. government treated black people in a variety of ways that were different from, and worse than, the way it treated white people. If someone denies that this is true or denies that we can now see that this was wrong, the problems to be discussed in this book will remain largely invisible for them. But on the assumption that it is true and that it was wrong, we should be in a better position to see what gives rise, in one way or another, to the moral questions that this book attempts to answer.

THE STATE OF THE UNION(S)

If the lives of black Americans today were going about as well on the whole as the lives of white Americans, it's not clear how much this history of official injustice in the United States would matter morally. What was done in the past would remain a terrible wrong, of course, but if the wrongs of the past seemed to leave no trace in the present, it seems plausible to suppose that many of the moral problems about race that currently divide us simply would not arise. But the unfortunate fact is that, by a good number of basic, uncontroversial measures of human well-being, black Americans today, on average, are not doing as well as white Americans are. An extensive survey of young Americans conducted in 2007 by the Associated Press and MTV, to take just one of many recent examples, found that 72 percent of the white respondents said they were "happy with life in general" while this was true of only 56 percent of the black respondents. And while the size of the difference varied somewhat from subject to subject, the existence of the difference was consistent throughout: young white Americans were more likely than young black Americans to wake up happy in the morning, feel happy about their relationships with their parents and their friends, be happy about their jobs, their grades, their financial status, even their sex lives.[52]

White Americans aren't always inclined to acknowledge this fact. A 1995 national survey, for example, found that a majority of white Americans believed that black people in the United States do "as well as or better than the average white in such specific areas as jobs, education and health care."[53] This despite the fact that incarceration rates for black Americans are roughly eight times higher than for white Americans and that black men who were in their mid-thirties around the time the survey was taken were almost twice as likely to have prison records as to have college degrees.[54] It's therefore important to devote a bit of space to a brief summary of some of the main facts about contemporary American life that, when placed in the context of past acts of racial injustice, help to generate the moral problems that the rest of this book seeks to address. As with the brief historical overview presented in the previous section, the point here is not to provide a complete or balanced picture of black life in America today. Rather, the point is to focus on a few of the most basic features of the current racial landscape that in part give rise to the moral questions that are the focus of this book.

One thing that's relatively uncontroversial is this: it's helpful to have money. Some poor people, of course, are happier than some rich people. But, on the whole, having money makes it easier to satisfy one's needs and desires. In this respect, what matters is not simply the wages that a person earns, but the total income that a person has available, including such additional sources of money as pensions, welfare payments, capital gains and disability benefits. And while it would be inaccurate and insulting to ignore the very significant rise of the black middle class that has occurred in this country since the end of the Second World War, the fact that a large number of black people are now doing quite well in the United States doesn't alter the fundamental fact that, on average, things are still going significantly better economically for white Americans than for black Americans.[55] The results from the most recently available national census, in 2000, for example, show that when year-round, full-time workers are compared, there's a significant difference between the median for black income – the line where half the people are above it while the other half are below it – and the median for white income. For white families in 2000, the median income was $56,442. For black families, it was $34,192. For white male workers, the median was $42,224. For black male workers, it was $30,886. For white female workers, the median was $30,777, while for black female workers it was $25,736.[56] One way to think of such figures is to say that, for example, the mid-point for white families is $22,250 higher than is the mid-point for black families. Another way to think of it is that the mid-point for black families is only 60 percent of the mid-point for white families. But however the numbers are ultimately framed, it's hard to avoid the conclusion that, on the whole, white Americans on average are doing better economically than are black Americans on average.

When the focus is placed on young people, moreover, the figures are often even starker. The percentage of black men in America with zero annual earnings was 16 in 1969, 23 in 1979, and 23 again in 1984. The figures for white men in America during these years were 8, 7, and 9.[57] The youth unemployment rates in 1990 were 36.7 percent for black men and 40.5 percent for black women, but only 9.4 percent for white men and 9.9 percent for white women.[58] In 2004, the poverty rate for black Americans was 24.7 percent while for white Americans it was 8.6 percent. The poverty rate for black American children was 33.6 percent while for white American children it was 10.5 percent.[59] And when attention turns to the total value of all the wealth that people have accumulated – their total assets rather than just their total income – the figures often become even more striking still. In 1993, for example, the median wealth for black households was $4,418 while the median for white households was over ten times greater: $45,740.[60]

Two more measures of basic human well-being are also relatively uncontroversial: health and education. In both cases, in general, the more of it you have, the better things go for you. And in both of these cases, in general, the numbers are again quite consistent and clear: on the whole, things are going considerably better for white Americans on average than for black Americans on average. The infant mortality rate for black Americans, for example, is more than twice that for white Americans.[61] Black women in America on average die six and a half years sooner than do white women. Black men live seven years less than white men. A black man is nine times more likely to die of AIDS than is a white man, and black men in general are likely to sleep less, weigh more, and suffer from hypertension more than their white counterparts.[62] Black Americans are less likely to have health insurance than are white Americans, are less likely to have vaccinations, and are less likely to have a regular source of health care.[63]

Turning to the subject of education, schools tend to spend more money per student when most of the students are white than when most of the students are black.[64] High schools with mostly white students are far more likely to offer Advanced Placement courses than are schools where most of the students are black.[65] Only 15 percent of black adults have college degrees while nearly 30 percent of white adults do.[66] Black Americans make up approximately 13 percent of the population but less than 5 percent of those who receive a PhD.[67] And so on and so on.

Statistics, of course, can be misleading. Black families, for example, make less money on average than do white families. But a greater number of white families have husbands contributing to their total income. So perhaps the issue is not really black families versus white families, but rather one-parent homes versus two-parent homes. It wouldn't be at all surprising, after all, to learn that two-parent homes tend to generate more income than do one-parent homes. And so if that's all that's going on when black families earn less on average than white families, then it might not seem to justify the same kind of conclusion about the gap between black and white America. The problem with this kind of analysis, though, is that black men themselves earn less on average than do white men. And so even if the numbers are adjusted to see what would happen if black families and white families had two-parent households at the same rate, the result would still be that black families would earn less than white families: $817 for every $1,000 by one calculation.[68]

Similarly, black workers make less money on average than do white workers. But black workers on average also have less education than do white workers. So perhaps the gap isn't so much about black people versus white people, but rather about people with less education versus people with more education. Again, it wouldn't be particularly surprising to learn that people with more education tend to earn, on average, more than people with less education. And so, again, if that's all that's going on when white workers earn more than black workers, then it won't seem to justify the same kind of conclusion about the gap between black and white Americans. But here, too, adjusting the numbers fails to eliminate the gap. Looking again at figures from the year 2000 that focus on individuals who worked full-time throughout the year, we can compare black and white workers who have the same educational level. When we do that, we see that black men who finished high school earn $799 for every $1,000 earned by white men who finished high school, that black men with a bachelors degree earn $784 for every $1,000 earned by white men with such a degree, and that black men with a master's degree earn $778 for every $1,000 earned by white men with that degree. Black men get college degrees at about half the rate that white men do, and this is surely part of the cause of the gap between what black men earn and what white men earn. But even when black men do graduate from college, their degree only gives them about half the earnings benefit that a white man who graduates from college receives.[69]

There is, in any event, a more fundamental problem with these sorts of attempts to get beyond the basic facts about black and white inequality in America. For suppose it really did turn out that black families with two parents were doing just as well on average as white families with two parents, that black men with college degrees were doing just as well on average as white men with college degrees, and so on. If all of this were true, then it would turn out that black Americans were considerably worse off than white Americans only because they lagged so far behind white Americans in terms of such measures as level of education and stability of family structure. But even if all of this turned out to be true, black Americans would still be considerably worse off than white Americans nonetheless. In 2004, for example, close to 25 percent of black Americans were living in poverty, roughly three times the percentage for white Americans.[70] Getting into the technical details of which particular discrepancies are most responsible for the fact that black Americans are worse off on average than white Americans, then, does nothing to cast doubt on the fundamental fact that they *are* worse off. And, for the purposes of understanding the various moral problems that this book seeks to address, that's all that really matters.

The comedian Chris Rock uses this line in his stand-up act: "There ain't no white man in this room that will change places with me – and I'm rich! That's how good it is to be white."[71] While the line itself may be an exaggeration, it nonetheless captures something true: that black people in the United States today, on the whole, are disadvantaged relative to white people. A middle-class white American man reading this book might be willing to trade places with a wealthy, successful young black American man, but that's not really the question. The question is whether he would rather trade places with a randomly selected white American or a randomly selected black American. As long as he agrees that he's likely to do better by taking the place of the randomly selected white American, he agrees that things are going better on average for white Americans than for black Americans. And as long as he agrees that this is so, he accepts the basic facts that give rise to the questions to be addressed in this book: compared to white Americans as a whole, black Americans as a whole were mistreated in the past and are disadvantaged in the present. In one way or another, these facts play a part in the moral debates over slave reparations, affirmative action, hate speech restrictions, hate crime laws, and racial profiling. Before turning to the debates themselves, though, I want to conclude this introductory chapter by saying a few words about the method I propose to use in attempting to resolve them.

WHAT WOULD SOCRATES DO?

So how should we go about trying to morally evaluate these controversial practices? The answer, I think, is simple: start with assumptions that most people on both sides of the debate over a particular practice already accept, then try to use those assumptions to ground an argument in favor of a particular conclusion about that practice. Most people, for example, regardless of their views about slave reparations, agree that a country's obligation to honor the terms of a treaty it signs doesn't disappear when the people who signed the treaty on its behalf die. The case of treaty obligations, then, provides at least one instance in which virtually everyone already agrees that the currently living generation of Americans can be obligated to do something because of the acts of other Americans who are no longer living. If an argument could show that failing to make reparations for slavery would be like failing to live up to the terms of such a treaty, then, it would provide a powerful argument for slave reparations on terms that supporters and opponents of reparations alike already accept. Regardless of their views on race-based affirmative action programs, to take another example, most people agree that it's morally permissible for a university to admit a qualified white student from North Dakota over a somewhat more qualified white student from New York if doing so would enhance the regional diversity that its students would enjoy. This geographical form of affirmative action is widespread and widely accepted, and so if an argument could show that if geography-based affirmative action is morally permissible then so, too, is race-based affirmative action, it would be a powerful argument for this view on terms that supporters and opponents of race-based affirmative action already accept.

My point in mentioning these examples, I should emphasize, is not to insist that they should be persuasive on their own. It would be odd to think that in the span of a few sentences one could resolve the debate over both affirmative action and slave reparations. My point is simply to explain that this is the kind of argument that I'll attempt to employ in the chapters that follow. When we set aside our stated opinions about the various racial controversies that divide us, we find that there are many other basic claims about which virtually all of us – black or white, liberal or conservative, young or old – agree. The method I will attempt to use in this book involves trying to argue from these uncontroversial assumptions about non-racial matters to conclusions about the racial issues that we can all therefore have reason to accept.

I've adopted this argumentative strategy for two reasons. One reason is tactical: I would like my arguments to be convincing. If my arguments started from assumptions that I found reasonable but that most people rejected, the arguments would have little chance of changing anyone's mind. But if my arguments start from assumptions that most people already endorse, people should find it more difficult to resist the conclusions that I've come to, even if the conclusions are at odds with their current beliefs. If your position turns out to be objectionable from my point of view, after all, this may not seem to give you a reason to abandon it. But if your position turns out to be objectionable even from your own point of view, then it's hard to see how you could do anything but consider changing your mind. In this respect, the inspiration for the method that I've attempted to employ in this book is fundamentally Socratic. Socrates was a pest, but he was an effective pest.

Proceeding as Socrates would have proceeded by arguing with people on their own terms is especially important when trying to convince people to accept conclusions about controversial racial matters. This is because polls have consistently revealed deep and seemingly intractable differences between the views of black and white Americans on many of the issues with which this book is concerned. A 1986 National Election Study, for example, showed that 49.3 percent of black Americans but only 4.9 percent of white Americans "strongly" favored the "preferential hiring and promotion of blacks" while 62.9 percent of white Americans but only 19.7 percent of black Americans "strongly" opposed it.[72] A compilation of such studies from 1986, 1988, and 1992 showed that 79.7 percent of black Americans but only 29.7 percent of white Americans supported "college quotas" and that 74.6 percent of black Americans but only 17.6 of white Americans agreed that the government should "increase federal spending on programs that assist blacks."[73] A 2002 poll showed that 55 percent of black Americans believed the government should make monetary payments to descendants of slaves, while only 10 percent of white Americans believed this,[74] while a 2003 study reported an even greater disparity with 67 percent of black Americans supporting slave reparations and only 4 percent of white Americans doing so.[75] By trying to follow the model of Socrates when considering these questions, reasoning carefully from starting points that virtually everyone, black or white, liberal or conservative, already accepts, I hope to contribute to bridging this divide by developing arguments that virtually everyone, black or white, liberal or conservative, can find convincing.

The second reason I've adopted this approach to the questions this book addresses is more philosophical: I'd like the answers I defend in it to be true. There's no guarantee that my approach will lead to the truth, of course. I might be wrong in thinking that most people will accept a particular assumption, I might make a mistake in reasoning from a particular assumption to a particular conclusion, and even when I'm right in supposing that most people would accept a particular assumption, they might turn out to be mistaken in doing so. But while the approach that I've adopted here can't promise to produce the morally correct results, I don't know of any alternative method that has a better claim to pointing us in the right direction. Every argument has to start somewhere, and it's hard to know where a more reasonable place to start would be than at points which virtually everyone already finds reasonable.

The approach I've tried to take here, I should add, doesn't assume that these starting points are infallible. If an initially promising account of why we'd have a certain kind of obligation in a certain kind of situation seems to run into problems, for example, we may be forced to revise our opinions about the particular case or about the more general principle. My approach allows for this possibility and, I exploit it at a number of points in the discussions that follow. In this respect, the approach I've tried to take in this book owes at least as much to Rawls as it does to Socrates. To the extent that some form of reflective equilibrium is the most promising method for arriving at moral truths, then, I hope that the arguments that follow can make a fair claim to being enlightening, and not simply convincing.

Since the method of starting with generally uncontroversial assumptions may itself prove to be somewhat controversial, though, and since I'd like my approach to be as uncontroversial as possible, let me conclude these preliminary comments by briefly addressing two concerns that might be raised before we turn to the task of putting the approach into practice. First, some people might object that while the approach that I've described here seems reasonable enough as a general matter, it will prove insufficiently reliable when applied to racial issues in particular. The problem, they may say, is that the moral views that most people have come to accept have themselves been tainted by the pernicious influence of racism, past or present.

This is a reasonable concern to raise. But I've attempted to respond to it in the chapters that follow by resting my arguments specifically on beliefs about matters that don't involve race. Here, for example, are five specific claims that I'll appeal to at one point or another in the chapters that follow, one each in the course of arguing for a particular claim about slave reparations, affirmative action, hate speech restrictions, hate crime laws, and racial profiling: If I vandalize your car, I incur a moral obligation to compensate you for the damage I wrongfully caused you. If I have to hire a company to fix a hole in my roof, it's morally permissible for me to select one simply because I like its name the best. Telling your brother you hate him shouldn't be a crime. It's appropriate for the law to treat first-degree murder as a more serious offense than negligent homicide. It's morally permissible for airport security officials to search the luggage of every passenger who's boarding a plane.

Most people on both sides of the debates in question will accept these claims. And since the claims themselves make no reference to race, it's hard to see how any form of racism, subtle or otherwise, could be responsible for their being so widely and deeply shared. Indeed, even in the relatively rare instances where I appeal to beliefs about cases that do involve race, it's hard to see how they could be the product of racist thinking. In a few contexts in the chapters that follow, for example, I appeal to the claim that it would be morally permissible for a director to take race into account when casting actors to portray Abraham Lincoln and Frederick Douglass. Virtually no one would disagree with this claim, and it's hard to see why we should think that more people would disagree with it if they had been raised in a perfectly nonracist or antiracist society. If at any particular point in the arguments that follow you nonetheless think that a particular assumption I rely on is widely accepted only because of the contaminating influence of racism, though, you should certainly ignore whatever support that assumption would otherwise provide to my argument. But in the absence of a credible explanation of how a particular assumption has been tainted in this particular way, the mere fact of racism past or present does not justify rejecting the application of the methodological approach I've described here to the particular questions that this book seeks to answer.

A second concern might be raised not about applying this method to racial issues in particular, but about the method itself in general. On this view, the fact that most people accept a certain belief is simply irrelevant to deciding whether it should be accepted. "It matters to me that I find a given claim to be a reasonable one," such a critic might say, "but I don't care what other people think. If a claim seems reasonable to me, that's good enough for me. If a claim seems reasonable to everyone but me, that's their business, not mine."

I'm inclined to be skeptical of this sort of skepticism. It's hard to see why the fact that virtually everyone else finds a certain claim to be reasonable shouldn't count in favor of your accepting it, at least in cases where you have no independent reason to think that you're in a better position to judge the matter than everyone else is. But for the purposes of engaging with the particular arguments that I develop in the chapters that follow, we can set this more general question aside. If you reject the methodological approach that I attempt to employ in this book as a general matter, then at each of the points in the discussions that follow where I say something like "virtually everyone on both sides of the debate over this issue agrees that the following claim is true," you should feel free to ignore these words and simply focus on asking yourself whether you think the claim is true. Since I'm confident that virtually everyone will accept the claim in question, I'm confident that you will, too. And even if you put no weight on the fact that virtually everyone else will accept the claim, as long as you yourself accept the claim, that will be good enough. Or, at least, that should be good enough for you.

2

Repairing the Slave Reparations Debate

How I Got into an Argument with Myself about David Horowitz and Lost

Suppose that a white American kidnapped a black American and forced him to work in his home. Virtually everyone would agree that this was wrong of him and that the white American would owe the black American some kind of compensation as a result. If the original perpetrators and victims of American slavery were alive today, then, I suspect that there would be little dispute about the claim that the former would owe a debt of some kind to the latter. But slavery in the United States ended well over a hundred years ago, and none of the original participants remain. The contemporary debate over slave reparations, then, is not about whether wrongdoers owe debts to those they unjustly exploit – surely they do – but rather about whether such debts can meaningfully be passed down through the generations. Do white Americans today owe something to their black contemporaries because some white Americans in the past enslaved some of their ancestors?

In the spring of 2001, the writer and political activist David Horowitz entered this debate in memorable fashion by attempting to take out an ad in seventy-one college newspapers across the country. The message of the ad was reflected in its clear and simple title: "Ten Reasons Why Reparations for Slavery Is a Bad Idea – and Racist Too."[1] Although polls at the time indicated that roughly three out of four Americans agreed with Horowitz's assessment, the ad set off a series of events that generated national attention.[2] Forty-three of the newspapers that Horowitz solicited refused to run the ad, and many of those that did run it were attacked for doing so. Copies of some papers were stolen and destroyed by protesters. Horowitz was called a racist.[3] And, somewhat suddenly, the issue of slave reparations was moved closer to the center of the American debate about race.

I remember my first reaction to reading Horowitz's ad. I agreed with it. Not only did I agree with it, in fact, I didn't even think he needed ten reasons to prove his point. Reason number four, reproduced here in its entirety, seemed good enough all by itself:[4]

IV
Most Living Americans Have No Connection (Direct or Indirect) to Slavery.

The two great waves of American immigration occurred after 1880 and then after 1960. What logic would require Vietnamese boat people, Russian refuseniks, Iranian refugees, Armenian victims of the Turkish persecution, Jews, Mexicans[,] Greeks, or Polish, Hungarian, Cambodian and Korean victims of Communism, to pay reparations to American blacks?

My own family seemed a perfect case in point. My maternal and paternal grandparents came to the United States during the first of the two waves of immigration that Horowitz refers to. My ancestors played no role in sustaining the institution of American slavery. They had nothing to do with it whatsoever. Why, then, should I have to pay for the harm that it had caused? Even if the sins of the father can somehow be visited upon the son, my father, and his father, were untainted by this particular sin. So what was there for me to pay for? Horowitz's position seemed to me to be not simply correct, but obviously correct.

At around this same time, I was looking for one or two new topics to add to an undergraduate course that I regularly teach on contemporary moral problems. I thought that the Horowitz piece might be a good one to add. But his basic argument seemed so compelling to me that I worried that I would have nothing to say in class on behalf of the other side and that I would therefore be unable to teach the issue in a sufficiently even-handed manner. So I went looking for a defense of slave reparations and came across a short piece called "America's Debt to Blacks" that had been published in *The Nation* the previous year by the author and activist Randall Robinson, widely considered to be the most prominent defender of slave reparations. I have to admit that I was not greatly impressed by Robinson's piece the first time I read it. Claims were made but not defended, assumptions seemed required but were not explicitly stated. I tried to produce a diagram of Robinson's essay, outlining each of the steps that it contained, and when I was finished, the result was a set of claims that did not seem sufficient to support his position.

What I took to be the basic idea behind Robinson's argument was intriguing, though, and so over the next few days and weeks I found myself repeatedly returning to the diagram I had produced. I tried to play devil's advocate and put myself in the quite unfamiliar position of someone who wanted to defend slave reparations, a position I found extremely implausible and had no real interest in occupying. I asked myself what the best way would be to fill in the gaps I found in Robinson's presentation. My goal was to see if there was any version of an argument for reparations that could be teased out of Robinson's text and that was strong enough to be worth presenting in class as a kind of counterpoint to what struck me as Horowitz's clearly superior reasoning. Slowly, gradually, a fuller and more satisfying argument began to emerge as I tried to picture ways that the loose ends in Robinson's piece might be tied up. And when I was finished, something unexpected happened: I found that I had inadvertently converted myself into a supporter of the slave reparations position. I had challenged myself to a debate on the subject, that is, and I had lost.

My goal in this chapter and the chapter that follows is to explain how I came to see the slave reparations position as a perfectly reasonable one. I should probably start, then, by saying a few things about what I take the slave reparations position to be. So for the purposes of these two chapters, whenever I refer to "the slave reparations position," or "the reparations position," what I will mean is the claim that the U.S. government has a moral obligation to benefit the current generation of African Americans because of the wrongful harms that were inflicted on past generations of Africans and African Americans by the institution of slavery and its aftermath.

A few comments about this formulation of the reparations position may be helpful before we proceed. First, I'm limiting myself here to a claim about an obligation that is properly attributed to the federal government. Similar claims have been made about obligations that might be attributed to state governments, private corporations, universities, and even individual families, and I will simply set those claims to the side. If my case for reparations at the federal level succeeds, then it may well turn out to provide a model for defending some or all of these further claims, but I'll leave that question for others to consider. My claim here is not that the federal government is the only entity that owes reparations for the harms that arose from slavery and its aftermath or that the federal government owes reparations for all of the harms that were wrongfully caused by these practices. To the extent that others were responsible for causing some portion of these harms, then others may well prove to be obligated to make reparations as well, and this in turn may reduce the total amount of reparations that the federal government is obligated to provide.[5] My claim is simply that the federal government does owe at least some reparations to the current generation of black Americans and that this is in virtue of the wrongful harms that were caused by slavery and its aftermath.

Second, I'm focusing here exclusively on the claim that the government is under a moral obligation to make reparations. In doing this, I'm setting aside the question of whether it is under any legal obligation to do so. Some people have argued that the case for reparations can be made by appealing to various legal precedents,[6] and a number of lawsuits have been filed, so far unsuccessfully, on this basis. But my argument in these chapters will not depend on this kind of support. People can have moral obligations without having any corresponding legal obligations and my focus here will be entirely on the claim that the U. S. government has a moral obligation to make reparations, regardless of whether it also has a legal obligation.

Third, although I'm following much of the literature in referring to the position as "the slave reparations position," strictly speaking the position arises in response to wrongful harms that include many that were inflicted after slavery was abolished. When I refer to the aftermath of slavery, I mean the various forms of legalized segregation and discrimination that persisted from the end of

Reconstruction until the middle of the 1960s, and that were briefly summarized in Chapter 1.

And finally, in maintaining that the U.S. government has a moral obligation to benefit the current generation of African Americans, the slave reparations position as I understand it does not take any particular stance with respect to the question of how, precisely, this could most effectively be achieved. Some people would argue that more government money should be spent on job training for black Americans, or on public schools in the inner city, or on government contracts for minority-owned businesses. Others have suggested that the government should establish a large trust fund from which money could be drawn by black Americans in the form of such benefits as college scholarships, interest-free mortgages and small business loans. Still others would maintain that policies such as reforming welfare, providing parents with school vouchers, or encouraging business investment in black neighborhoods through the use of enterprise zones would do more to improve the lot of black America. Yet others have argued for a national monument or museum to the legacy of slavery and its aftermath, and others still have claimed that nothing short of a separate political state for black Americans or even financial support for repatriation back to Africa would do the trick. And while relatively few defenders of the reparations position have endorsed the merits of simply making monetary payments to individual black Americans, despite the fact that the popular debate often treats the issue as if this is the only option, this is nonetheless a still further possibility.[7] The defender of the slave reparations position need not settle this further debate. The claim put forward by the advocate of slave reparations is that the government owes a debt to the current generation of black Americans. We can try to show that the debt really exists without insisting that we know the best way to pay it off.[8]

THE UNJUST ENRICHMENT ARGUMENT

The primary challenge for any defender of the slave reparations position is to explain why white Americans like me should have to contribute to making reparations for slavery when we played no role in causing slavery to occur in the first place. The most common strategy for meeting this challenge has involved shifting the focus of the debate from the harm that was inflicted on the slaves to the benefits that were reaped from their labors. Even if I didn't do anything to cause slavery to occur, after all, I might still be benefiting in some way from the fact that it happened. And if I'm profiting from the legacy of slavery and its aftermath, then it might be fair to make me give the profits back, if not to the original victims of the injustice then at least to their descendants, even if it's not my fault that slavery occurred in the first place.

Why the Argument Isn't So Bad

This kind of argument for slave reparations appeals to the idea of "unjust enrichment," the principle at the center of a number of lawsuits that have been filed against corporations that benefited from slavery,[9] as well as at the foundation of most of the defenses that have been offered of the reparations position itself, including the most prominent popular work, Randall Robinson's book *The Debt: What America Owes to Blacks*, and most of the defenses provided by the most prominent philosophers who have written on the subject, such as Bernard Boxill and Howard McGary.[10] Robinson himself cites the following formulation of the idea as a legal doctrine: "the principle of unjust enrichment: In law if a party unlawfully enriches himself by wrongful acts against another, then the party so wronged is entitled to recompense,"[11] but the principle is typically understood as the more general claim that one person should not be unjustly enriched at the expense of another.[12]

Here's a simple example. Suppose that you're an artist and you go on an extended vacation. While you're away, I break into your house, steal a bunch of your paintings, display them in my art gallery, and charge people money to view them. In this example, I'm wrongfully profiting from your labor, and the unjust enrichment principle would dictate that I would not be entitled to keep the profits that I made. I would have to hand my earnings over to you. And in this case, at least, I assume that the principle's verdict would be uncontroversial. Virtually everyone, that is, regardless of their views on slave reparations, would agree that I would owe you the money that I earned by unjustly enriching myself from your labor in the case where I stole your paintings in order to display them in my art gallery. If an argument could show that the case of slave reparations really is analogous to the case of the art gallery, then it would provide a very strong defense of reparations on terms that most people, including most opponents of slave reparations, already accept.

The art gallery case, though, seems to be very different from the slave reparations case in at least two potentially important respects. First, in the art gallery case, I do a wrongful act and then I profit from it. But in the slave reparations case, even if it turns out to be true that contemporary white Americans like me are somehow profiting today from the legacy of slavery and its aftermath, we didn't do the wrongful acts that we're now profiting from. Other people in the past did the wrongful acts, and we're profiting from their immorality, not from our own. Second, in the art gallery case, the person whose labor I unjustly benefit from is still alive. But in the slave reparations case, even if it turns out that white Americans like me are benefiting from the fact that other people were wrongfully harmed in the past, those people are now dead. In the former case, the money can simply be returned to its rightful owner, but in the latter case, it can't. And these two differences seem to undermine the claim that slave reparations can be justified by appealing to the principle of unjust enrichment.

But proponents of the unjust enrichment argument don't think that these two differences matter. As long as you're unjustly profiting from the labor of another, they maintain, you're not entitled to keep the profits even if you're not the one who did the unjust act that led to your profiting. And if you can't pay your debt because the person you owe it to is dead, they add, that doesn't mean the debt is cancelled either. It simply means that you have to pay it to the person's descendants. I'm inclined to agree with the defenders of the unjust enrichment argument on both of these points, and so while in the end I don't find the argument to be convincing, I'm inclined to think that it isn't as easy to defeat as it might at first seem.

One way to determine whether or not the unjust enrichment argument is strong enough to overcome these two potentially powerful worries is to consider what happens to our moral intuitions if we make changes in the story about the art gallery to take the two differences into account. Let's start with the first difference: in the art gallery case, I did the wrongful act that I profit from while in the slave reparations case, someone else did the wrongful act that I profit from. We can try to figure out whether or not this difference between the cases makes a moral difference by changing the story about the art gallery so that someone else does the unjust act that I profit from in that case, too. So suppose again that you're an artist away on vacation, but suppose this time that a shadowy figure breaks into your house and steals your paintings. He then brings them to my gallery, tells me that the paintings are his, and offers to let me display them and charge admission for people to come and view them. He seems to have impeccable documentation to demonstrate that the paintings are his and so, in this version of the story, I can't be blamed for behaving immorally when I display what in fact turn out to be your paintings and charge people money to look at them.

By changing the art gallery story from one in which I benefit from my immoral behavior to one in which I benefit from the immoral behavior of someone else, we make the art gallery case more like the slave reparations case. So let's now consider the question of whether I would be morally obligated to turn the profits over to you in this "shadowy figure" version of the story. When you come back from your vacation and discover that I've been making money by charging people to view your paintings, that is, will you be entitled to recover the money I've taken in, as you clearly were in the original version of the story? Or will the fact that I didn't realize that I was profiting from your labor without your consent mean that I should get to keep the money this time? If we think that you would still be entitled to the money even though it isn't my fault that I was enriching myself by displaying your paintings, then this first objection to the unjust enrichment argument will be defeated. The difference between the original art gallery case and the case of slave reparations will prove to be morally irrelevant. But if we think that I would be entitled to keep the money for myself in this version of the story even though I earned it as a result of someone else's immoral treatment of you, then the objection to the unjust enrichment argument will succeed and the argument itself will have to be rejected. The fact that I would owe you the money in the version of the story where I profit from my own immoral behavior will no longer provide support for the claim that white Americans who are benefiting from the immoral behavior of others are obligated to restore those benefits to their rightful owners in the case of the debate over slave reparations.

My own reaction to the shadowy figure version of the story is pretty clear: you would still have the right to the money. And the reason for this reaction is pretty simple: it's still the case that the money was generated by your labor without your permission, and money that's generated by your labor is rightfully yours unless you agree to let someone else have it. If this is your reaction to the shadowy figure story, too, then you should agree that this first objection to the unjust enrichment argument is unsuccessful. I suspect that many people, regardless of their view of slave reparations, will have the same reaction to the story that I have. And so for those people, this should count as a sufficient response to this first objection to the unjust enrichment argument. It seems plausible to suppose, though, that a good number of other people will respond differently. They will agree that you have the right to the money in the original version of the story, but will maintain that I nonetheless have the right to keep it in the shadowy figure version. Why might they think that?

One reason for thinking that I should get to keep the money in the shadowy figure story simply appeals to the fact that I can't be blamed for having done anything wrong by showing the paintings in that version of the story. A critic of the unjust enrichment argument, that is, might say that I can keep the money in this case precisely because people can only be obligated to return enrichment that they've acquired if they themselves did something unjust in acquiring it. And, indeed, the very formulation of the principle of unjust enrichment that Robinson himself cites seems clearly to be limited to cases where the person who is unjustly enriched is enriched by doing the wrongful act himself: "the principle of unjust enrichment: In law if a party unlawfully enriches himself *by wrongful acts against another*, then the party so wronged is entitled to recompense."[13] If the scope of the principle of unjust enrichment is restricted in this way, then it clearly can't be made to apply to the case of the shadowy figure, and it just as clearly can't be made to apply to the case of slave reparations. Even if it turns out to be true that I've benefited from the slave labor of others, after all, I clearly didn't do any of the wrongful acts involved in enslaving and extracting the labor from them.

While this might at first seem to be a good reason to deny that I would owe you the money I earn by displaying your paintings in the shadowy figure version of the story, though, it turns out to have implications that virtually everyone, regardless of their view of slave reparations, will surely find unacceptable. This is because the principle of unjust enrichment is widely accepted as the more general claim that one person should not be unjustly enriched at the expense of another. And understood in this broader sense, the law uncontroversially recognizes a wide variety of cases in which a person can be required to give up a benefit to which he is not fairly entitled despite the fact that, as in the case of the shadowy figure story and the case of the contemporary beneficiaries of the legacy of slavery, he did nothing wrong in acquiring it.[14] If you mistakenly pay a debt to the wrong store, for example, you're entitled to recover your money from the store you paid even if the clerk who accepted your money was blameless in accepting it in the first place. If you mistakenly pay a debt to the right store but after both of you and the clerk at the store forget that you've already paid it, you're again entitled to recover the money from the store despite the fact that the store is again blameless for having acquired the money it isn't entitled to. If someone steals a watch from you and then gives the watch to me, you're entitled to recover the watch from me even though I did nothing wrong in acquiring it. If I'm given some books from my uncle's estate because his will declaring that they were intended for you was wrongfully suppressed without my knowledge, you're entitled to recover the books from me once his will is revealed even though I did nothing wrong in acquiring them in the first place. If as a result of an honest mistake I accidentally take your coat home from the office rather than mine and then donate it to Goodwill, I would owe you money to replace the coat even though my behavior in taking and donating the coat was blameless. In all of these sorts of cases, and many more, the law maintains that a person can be legally obligated to return something he has blamelessly acquired or to compensate its rightful owner if returning it is no longer possible, despite the fact that he's legally blameless for having acquired it in the first place. And in all of these sorts of cases, and many more, virtually everyone on both sides of the reparations debate will agree that morally speaking a person can be obligated to return something he has blamelessly acquired or to compensate its rightful owner if returning it is no longer possible, despite the fact that he's morally blameless for having acquired it in the first place.

Indeed, the shadowy figure story itself provides an uncontroversial counterexample to the claim that you can't be obligated to return enrichment that you have blamelessly acquired. Even those who might initially be inclined to think that I'm allowed to keep the money I make in the shadowy figure story, after all, will surely agree that I'm not allowed to keep the paintings themselves. Virtually everyone, that is, regardless of their view of slave reparations, will agree that at the very least, I have to give the paintings back to you once I discover what the shadowy figure has done. But I was blameless in acquiring the paintings, after all, just as I was blameless in acquiring the money I charged people in order to view them. And so if it's really true that I'm entitled to keep enrichment that I acquired without doing anything immoral, then it would also have to be true that I'm entitled to keep your stolen paintings because I didn't act immorally in acquiring them, either. Since it's clear that I would not, in fact, be entitled to keep your paintings, it should again be clear that the fact that I acquired something in a blameless manner doesn't mean that I should be entitled to keep it. So the fact that I acquire the money from people who view your paintings in a blameless manner in the shadowy figure story provides no reason to deny that I would still owe you the money in that version of the story. And if I would still owe you the money in that version of the story, then the first objection to the unjust enrichment argument must be rejected. The fact that I'm blameless for receiving whatever benefits I've received from the legacy of slavery and its aftermath can't, by itself, show that I have the right to keep them.

Some people, though, might point to a second feature of the shadowy figure story as a way of trying to justify the claim that I should be allowed to keep the money. The important point, they might suggest, isn't simply that I behaved blamelessly in the story, but that I invested my own time and resources in displaying the paintings. Had I known that the paintings were stolen property, I would instead have committed my time and resources to displaying some other paintings and would most likely have profited from doing so. If I'm forced to give you the money that I got from showing your paintings, then, I'll end up losing money overall. Since I acted blamelessly in showing the paintings, this doesn't seem fair. And so, on this account, I have the right to keep the money I made from showing your paintings in the shadowy figure story after all.

While this attempt to revive the first objection to the unjust enrichment argument may initially seem reasonable, though, it, too, proves to have implications that virtually everyone on both sides of the reparations debate will ultimately find unacceptable. Indeed, it has implications that are unacceptable in the very same sorts of cases that undermine the initial response to the case of the shadowy figure. Suppose, for example, that after someone steals your watch and gives it to me, I invest a good deal of money in purchasing a fancy new watch band for it. Or when the books that my uncle bequeathed to you are wrongfully given to me before his will is discovered, I devote a great deal of time to building custom-sized bookshelves to use in holding them. In these cases, forcing me to give you the watch or the books means that I will end up having wasted some of my own valuable time or money. But while I might therefore be entitled to compensation from the wrongdoer who stole your watch or suppressed my uncle's will, virtually everyone will nonetheless agree that I would have no right to hold on to the watch or books that are rightfully yours. If someone steals your watch and then sells it to me, for that matter, you would have the right to recover your watch from me even though I would then be out the money that I had unwittingly paid to the thief. And, indeed, a slightly modified version of the story of the shadowy figure itself can again provide a clear counterexample, this time to the claim that people may permissibly hold on to the enrichments they acquire so long as they act blamelessly in acquiring them and will end up losing time or money overall if they return them. Suppose, after all, that when the shadowy figure gives me your paintings, I invest a good deal of time and money in making custom frames for them, frames that will be useless to me if I'm forced to return your paintings. In this case, not only will I lose out if I have to give you the money that I earned showing your paintings, but I'll lose out if I have to give you back the paintings themselves. But virtually everyone will agree that this doesn't mean that I get to keep the paintings. And so, in order to be consistent, they must agree that it doesn't mean that I get to keep the money either. I'm not aware of any other differences between my original art gallery story and the shadowy figure version that might be used to justify the claim that you'd have the right to recover the money in the former case but not in the latter. And so, in the end, I can see no good reason to think that I should get to keep the money I earn from displaying your paintings in the shadowy figure case, and thus no good reason to accept the first objection to the unjust enrichment argument.

Let's now turn to the second objection to the argument, the one that appeals to the second difference between the two cases: in the art gallery case, the money's rightful owner is still alive, while in the slave reparations case, the money's rightful owners are now dead. We can again determine whether or not this difference matters morally by making a parallel change to the art gallery case and seeing whether or not it changes our moral beliefs about the case. So suppose again that a shadowy figure breaks into your house and steals your paintings, and that I unwittingly profit from the theft by charging admission to see them in my gallery. I have agreed that I'm not entitled to keep this money and am about to return it to you, when I learn that you have suddenly died. Does this mean that I now get to keep my inadvertently ill-gotten gains? It seems to me that it does not mean this. In particular, it seems reasonable to insist that I simply owe the money to your estate. If when you died you owed the money to someone else, for example, then I should have to pay them the money that you owed them. It was, after all, your money, not mine. You were entitled to it and I was not entitled to it, and since you owed it to someone else, then the person you owed it to should get the money, not me. If when you died you had no such debts, on the other hand, then your money would presumably go to your descendants. In this case, it seems reasonable to insist that I would have to give the money to them. Again, the money was rightfully yours rather than mine, and had it been where it rightfully belonged when you died, it would have gone to your children not to me. If this is correct, then even if we change the art gallery case to make it just like the slave reparations case with respect to the two differences that I've identified here, it still turns out that I would have to pay up. And, if I would have to pay up in the suitably revised version of the art gallery case, and if the suitably revised version of that case really is morally on a par with the case of making reparations to the descendants of slaves and other victims of racial injustice, then the unjust enrichment argument for slave reparations would seem to survive both of these objections.

Why the Argument Isn't So Good, Either

The unjust enrichment argument is by far the most popular argument for slave reparations. And that, I think, is the problem. Because while I don't think the unjust enrichment argument is a particularly bad argument, I also don't think it's a particularly good one. As long as supporters of the slave reparations movement follow people like Robinson in focusing their energies on advancing this particular strategy, then, I suspect that the movement will fail. Indeed, if the unjust enrichment argument were the only argument for the reparations position available, I would remain unconvinced by the reparations position to this day. Before explaining how an importantly different argument ultimately persuaded me to become an advocate of the reparations position, then, I want first to explain why

I remain unconvinced by the unjust enrichment argument. Repairing the reparations debate, in my view, will involve abandoning the popular unjust enrichment argument in favor of this less familiar alternative, and then seeing that a variety of apparent objections to this alternative approach can be satisfactorily answered. Before turning to that alternative approach, then, let me first explain why I remain unconvinced by the unjust enrichment argument.[15]

The first problem with the unjust enrichment argument is that it rests on a factual assumption that can reasonably be called into question. The assumption is that white Americans like me are benefiting today from the consequences of slavery and its aftermath. This assumption is essential to the argument. If there's no enrichment, then there's no unjust enrichment. And if there's no unjust enrichment, then there can be no unjust enrichment argument. My objection to this feature of the argument isn't that I think that the factual assumption is obviously false. It could certainly turn out to be true. My objection, rather, is that it simply isn't clear that the assumption is true, and that without a good reason to think that it is, there's no good reason to accept the argument that's based on it. Proponents of the unjust enrichment argument appeal to two kinds of consideration in supporting the claim that white Americans today are profiting unjustly from the legacy of slavery and its aftermath. But I don't find either of these considerations to be convincing. My skepticism on this point, moreover, is hardly unusual. As the editor's introduction to an important collection of papers by economists and other specialists on the subject of the present value of benefits from past injustices notes, there's simply "no final consensus" among those experts who have studied the matter in detail, "as to whether real unjust enrichments have currently resulted from past discriminatory practices."[16] And since it's hard to be confident in the argument's foundational assumption that such enrichments currently exist, it's hard to be confident in the argument that's based on it.

The first kind of support that defenders of the unjust enrichment argument typically provide for the claim that white Americans like me are benefiting from the legacy of slavery and its aftermath emphasizes the various important respects in which slave labor contributed to developing the infrastructure of the early United States. It's common, for example, for defenders of the reparations position to point out that slave labor was used to clear much of the land for the building of the city of Washington, DC, and in the construction of the White House and the Capitol Building,[17] to note the pivotal role that slave labor played in developing such important parts of the nation's infrastructure as its nascent railroad system,[18] and to emphasize that money generated by taxation on slavery played an important role in funding the Revolutionary War and the War of 1812, as well as in such further investments as the Louisiana Purchase.[19] To the extent that the nation today benefits from these various fruits of slavery and others, and to the extent that white Americans like me benefit from living in this nation, white Americans like me are benefiting from the labor of slaves. Second, proponents of the unjust enrichment argument appeal to the many ways in which white Americans were given an unfair advantage over black Americans for many years even after slavery was abolished. To the extent that the legacy of slavery and subsequent forms of segregation and discrimination have left black Americans today educationally disadvantaged on average relative to white Americans, for example, and to the extent that white Americans like me benefit from the reduced competition for admission to elite schools and for opportunities for attractive employment, white Americans like me are again benefiting from the legacy of slavery and its aftermath. And if we're profiting from this history of injustice, the argument claims, we owe reparations as a result.

I don't find either of these kinds of considerations to be particularly convincing. The first kind of consideration points to some social benefits that were produced by slavery, but ignores the corresponding social costs, including the costs involved in preventing slaves from escaping and the opportunity costs involved in not investing resources in other and potentially more efficient ways. The mere fact that a practice is profitable for those who engage in it, after all, is hardly evidence that it's beneficial for society as a whole. Consider the case of crack dealers. And while economic historians generally agree that slavery was a profitable practice for many of the slaveholders who engaged in it, the claim that it was profitable for the South as a whole is far less widely accepted precisely because of its various social costs.[20] If for these reasons slavery was less economically efficient on the whole than a free labor system would have been, then the country as a whole would have developed more rapidly if slavery had never been brought to its shores. And if this is true, then white Americans like me are not better off today because of the history of slavery. We, like everyone else, are worse off because the country as a whole is worse off.

More importantly, and from the point of view of the unjust enrichment argument, more problematically, the practice of slavery ultimately led to the Civil War, and the Civil War, in turn, was devastating to the country in general, and to the South in particular. In fact, it's been estimated that 60 percent not just of the slave-related wealth in the South but of the total wealth in the South was destroyed as a result of the War.[21] Even if slavery initially produced significant benefits that were handed down to later generations, then, it also led to a cataclysmic conflict that caused tremendous harms that were passed down as well. This makes it seem plausible to suppose that the total costs that slavery ultimately imposed on this country significantly outweighed whatever social benefits, if any, it may temporarily have produced. As University of Illinois economist Stanley H. Masters has put it, "Many white planters made great fortunes, based partly on their ownership of slaves. In the long run, however, it is doubtful that either the planter class or the South as a whole benefited from slavery. The costs of the Civil War most likely outweighed the previous gains."[22] And if this is true then, again, slavery on the whole produced a net loss for this country and white Americans, like all Americans, are worse off today, and certainly not better off, as a result of its legacy.

Finally, the Civil War in turn led to a dramatic increase in the size and power of the federal government. Some people would argue that this has been a good thing, of course, but many others would argue that it has made things worse on the whole than they would otherwise have turned out to be. If that's true, then it seems even more clear that the country as a whole today would be in much better shape if it had never practiced slavery. And if that's true, then there's no enrichment for white Americans like me to be unjustly enjoying today. I don't mean to insist that it's obvious that we're worse off today because of the history of slavery in this country, though it seems quite plausible to think that we are. Maybe the short-term benefits that were produced by slavery were great enough to outweigh all of the long-term costs that its legacy ultimately imposed on us. But, without a sufficiently uncontroversial argument to demonstrate that this is so, the unjust enrichment argument is left without a secure foundation to build from.

The second kind of consideration given in favor of the claim that white Americans like me are benefiting today from the legacy of slavery and its aftermath appeals instead to the various ways in which black Americans were systematically disadvantaged relative to white Americans from the founding of the Republic until the rise of the modern civil rights movement. As a white American, for example, it's easier for me on average to win a competition with a black American for a job, or for admissions to a particular school, or even for a ride in a taxi cab, than it would be if black and white Americans had been treated as equals from the very beginning. Since I benefit from these various competitive advantages, and since these advantages can be traced back to the practice of slavery and its aftermath, it again turns out that I'm benefiting from the practice of slavery and its aftermath. This kind of consideration is often presented in terms of the language of "white privilege," an idea that's vividly and forcefully developed in Tim Wise's popular book, *White Like Me: Reflections on Race from a Privileged Son*.

The problem with appealing to white privilege as a way of supporting the unjust enrichment argument, though, is that it confuses two importantly different kinds of claims: claims about a person's relative well-being, and claims about a person's absolute well-being. Suppose, for example, that there are a hundred people living in my apartment building and that about half of them are healthier than me and about half of them are less healthy than me. A madman then poisons the building's water supply and this makes everyone sick. Because different people are affected differently by the poison, some people are made sicker than others. I get pretty sick, but many people get much sicker than I do. As a result, after the poisoning occurs, I'm less healthy than I was before, but I'm now healthier than almost all of the people in my building, while before the poisoning occurred, I was healthier than I am now, but was only healthier than about half of the others. In the case of the apartment building and the madman, the poisoning that occurs makes me better off in a relative sense. Before the poisoning, lots of people in the building were healthier than me but after the poisoning I'm healthier than almost all of them. I've "moved up" in the health ranks. But the poisoning nonetheless makes me worse off in an absolute sense. When I focus only on my own well-being, that is, and not on how I compare to others, it's clear that I'm worse off after the poisoning than before.

Now, in the case of the poisoned water supply, it should be clear that it is absolute rather than relative well-being that matters when we ask if someone has been benefited by an action. It would be absurd to claim that the madman benefited me by poisoning the water. Clearly, he harmed me, even though he didn't harm me as much as he harmed many other people. But if that's right, and surely people on both sides of the reparations debate would agree that that it is, then the second consideration appealed to by defenders of the unjust enrichment argument is ineffective as well. The legacy of slavery and its aftermath has exerted a poisonous influence on this country. The fact that it's left white Americans better off than black Americans in terms of relative well-being doesn't mean that it hasn't also left white Americans worse off than they would otherwise be today in terms of absolute well-being. The fact that white Americans like me currently enjoy a variety of competitive advantages over black Americans is certainly consistent with the conclusion that the legacy of slavery and its aftermath has absolutely benefited white Americans like me. But it's just as consistent with the conclusion that it has harmed white Americans like me, while harming black Americans even more.[23]

As with the first consideration invoked by supporters of the unjust enrichment argument, I don't mean to suggest that it's simply obvious that white Americans today are worse off in absolute terms than they would otherwise be because of the legacy of slavery and its aftermath. But, again as with the first consideration, I don't find it any more obvious that white Americans are better off in absolute terms than they would otherwise be as a result of it, either. As Masters has noted, arguments that move directly from the claim that past discrimination has benefited white Americans in a relative sense to the conclusion that white Americans are better off in absolute terms are based on the assumption that the past wrongful acts didn't have an effect on the size of "the total economic pie" that's available for black and white Americans to compete for. "By underutilizing black abilities and increasing racial conflict," as he puts it, "discrimination probably reduces the size of the pie. Thus, it is not clear whether, on balance, whites have gained from discrimination."[24] White Americans on average presumably enjoy a larger share of the economic pie than they would have enjoyed had slavery and its aftermath never occurred, that is, but a larger share of a smaller pie can still be smaller than a smaller share of a larger pie. So the existence of white privilege does not, by itself, provide a reason to conclude that white Americans today are benefiting from the legacy of slavery and its aftermath. And without a good reason to believe that white Americans today are better off as a result of the legacy of slavery and its aftermath, there's no good reason to accept the factual assumption that lies at the foundation of the unjust enrichment argument.

My first objection to the unjust enrichment argument raised a worry about whether or not white Americans really have been unjustly enriched by the legacy of slavery and its aftermath. A second and more troubling objection focuses on the question of which currently living black Americans would actually be entitled to reparations on the assumption that unjust enrichment really is taking place. So let's now go ahead and suppose, at least for the sake of the argument, that white Americans like me today really are the inheritors of the unjust profits that slaves and other victims of racial injustice produced in the past. Does that mean that every black American who is a descendant of these victims would be owed reparations by white Americans like me? No, it doesn't. It means only that descendants of those particular victims who were used profitably would be owed reparations. And this limitation on the scope of the unjust enrichment argument has implications that virtually everyone, including virtually every supporter of slave reparations, will surely find unacceptable.

Consider, for example, the case of a plantation owner who had two large groups of slaves. Year after year, he forced one group to work in the cotton fields and year after year he forced the other to work at raising sugar cane. His cotton crops were consistently successful, but he never managed to produce a viable growth of sugar cane. As a result, he consistently made a profit from growing cotton and consistently incurred a loss from trying to grow sugar cane. Now consider two currently living black Americans. John is descended from slaves who were in the owner's first group of slaves, while Paul is descended from slaves who were in the owner's second group. If slave reparations really are to be justified by appealing to the unjust enrichment argument, then it follows that while John is owed reparations, Paul is not. John's ancestors produced wealth that others unjustly enjoyed at the expense of his descendants, after all, but Paul's ancestors did not. Or consider a second and even more disturbing version of this worry. A second plantation owner also had two groups of slaves. One group he treated relatively well and, as a result, they remained healthy enough to do productive labor for many years. The other he mistreated terribly, inflicting such savage abuse on them that they soon became incapable of doing anything useful for him at all. This owner profited from the first group of slaves but he lost a great deal of money on the second group. The unjust enrichment argument, therefore, would imply that descendents of the relatively well-treated group of slaves are owed reparations, since their ancestors produced wealth that is rightfully theirs, but that descendants of the savagely-abused group are owed nothing since their ancestors produced no wealth that unjustly enriched anyone. And this implication should again be extremely difficult for defenders of reparations to accept.[25]

These two objections should give proponents of slave reparations serious doubts about the wisdom of continuing to rest their case for reparations on the unjust enrichment argument. But even if both of these objections can successfully be overcome, there's a third and final problem with the unjust enrichment argument that runs even deeper. This more fundamental problem has to do with applying the principle of unjust enrichment to slave reparations in the first place, and so is perhaps best understood by first returning to the case of the artist and the art gallery. So suppose that I profit from charging people money to view paintings in my art gallery and that it turns out, due to no fault of my own, that these paintings had been stolen from you. As I noted earlier, it seems reasonable to me to say that you would still be entitled to the money I had earned from your labor, and the defender of the unjust enrichment argument maintains that this is sufficiently like the case of slave reparations to justify reparations in that case as well. But there's an important difference between the two cases that we have not yet considered. And this further difference generates a final and serious problem for the unjust enrichment argument.

The difference I have in mind has to do with the way in which one person profits from the injustice committed against another in each of the two cases: the case where the gallery owner profits from the injustice committed against the artist and the case where white Americans like me profit from the injustices committed against the slaves. The significance of this difference becomes clear if we start with yet one more story. So setting aside the case of slave reparations for a moment, suppose this time that I own a coffee shop next door to an art gallery. For months, business has been very slow. But then, one day, a new exhibit opens up at the gallery next door and crowds of people come streaming in. They are all there to see the works of a previously unknown artist, and when they leave the exhibit, many of them stop by my shop for a cup of coffee. Indeed, the new exhibit draws so many more people to the area, that my profits are five times greater now that the exhibit is on than they were before it opened.

With this further story in mind, let's start with an assumption and a question. The assumption is that the gallery owner in this case does have the artist's permission to display her paintings and that the two of them have agreed to the terms by which he will compensate her for showing the paintings. The question is whether, given this assumption, I as the owner of the coffee shop who benefits from the art exhibit next door, would be morally obligated to share some of my earnings with the artist. To this question, I suspect, virtually everyone would reply with the same answer: no. I don't have to give the artist some of the money I earn just because the exhibit of her work in the gallery next door drew customers to my coffee shop. It's true that I benefited from her art being exhibited next door to me, of course, and it's true that I never asked her permission to benefit from her work in this manner. But all business owners benefit whenever anyone does anything that attracts more potential customers to their area. And virtually everyone, regardless of their views about slave reparations, will agree that this can't be enough by itself to render the owners obligated to share their profits with the people whose actions drew more business to their neighborhood. When one store has a big sale, for example, and when the people it draws to the area end up spending some of their money at a second store next door, no one insists that the owner of the second store has to give some of his profits to the owner of the first store just because the second store benefited from the sale held by the first store. So it should be clear, in this first case, that I would owe nothing to the artist despite the fact that my coffee shop earned extra profits as a result of the display of her paintings in the art gallery next door.

Now let's make the story about my coffee shop a bit more complicated. Let's suppose that after the exhibit at the art gallery next door closes, a startling discovery is made: the gallery owner, without realizing it, had been exhibiting stolen paintings, and, as a result, the woman who had painted them had not received a single penny from him, despite the fact that he had earned a great deal of money from charging people admission to view her works. As I've already noted, it seems reasonable to me to say that the art gallery owner would owe the artist the money he earned from showing her paintings in this case. But my question here is a different one: would I, as the owner of the coffee shop next door who earned more money while the exhibit was on, have to give the extra money that I earned to the artist? Would the discovery that the artist had not given the gallery owner permission to display her work mean that I as the coffee shop owner next door would have to pass along my extra profits to her?

Although this question is a bit more complicated, it should be just as clear, at least upon reflection, that the answer must again be no. If I don't owe money to the artist in the case where my coffee shop has more customers because the gallery owner next door has paid her to display her paintings in his gallery, then I don't owe money to the artist in the case where my coffee shop has more customers because the gallery owner next door displayed her paintings without her permission. This should be clear because virtually everyone, regardless of their view of slave reparations, should accept the following more general claim: if the artist has her work displayed without her permission, then she should be entitled to collect precisely those profits that she would have been entitled to collect if the work had been displayed with her permission. But even if she had given the art gallery owner permission to display her art, she still would not have been entitled to any money from me as the owner of the coffee shop next door whose sales went up during her exhibit. So I would not owe her any money for profiting from the display of her work in the case where the gallery owner had failed to secure her consent and had not compensated her for her labor, either.

The lesson of the two versions of the coffee shop case can be used to generate a final problem for the unjust enrichment argument. This is because if white Americans like me really are benefiting today from the labor that slaves performed without consent and compensation in the past, the way in which we are benefiting from it is more like the way the coffee shop owner benefits from the exhibit of the artist's stolen paintings than it is like the way that the art gallery owner himself benefits from exhibiting them. Suppose, for example, that the value of my property is higher today than it would have been had slave labor not contributed to some of the early infrastructure of the United States. This would be like a case where I own a house near the art gallery and the value of my house goes up as the neighborhood becomes more attractive due to the flourishing of the art gallery. In that case, I wouldn't owe any money to the artist whose stolen work helped increase the value of my house, any more than the coffee shop owner would owe any money to the artist whose stolen work increased his profits. And so I would owe no money in virtue of the fact that my property is worth more today because of the contribution that slave labor made to the early infra-structure of the United States. Or suppose that my wages are higher today than they would otherwise be because of factors that can successfully be traced back to the practice of slavery and its aftermath. This would be like a case where I work at the coffee shop next door to the art gallery and where increased business in the area leads to increased competition which forces the coffee shop owner to give me a raise if he wants to keep me from taking a job with a rival coffee shop. In that case, my salary goes up because the art gallery owner displayed the artist's work in his gallery without her permission. But since I wouldn't have to give the artist my extra salary earnings if the gallery displayed her work with her permission, I wouldn't have to give it to her if it displayed her work without her permission. And since this would be like the case where my salary today is higher because slave owners in the past wrongfully extracted labor from their slaves, I wouldn't have to give up my extra salary earnings for that reason either. Finally, suppose that my life is going better today because I'm enjoying the benefits of public goods that were purchased with tax money that was raised from taxing the institution of slavery. This would be like a case where the extra money the gallery owner makes generates enough tax revenue to construct a new bike path that I enjoy using. But since I wouldn't have to give the artist any money because I enjoy using the bike path in the case where the path is paid for by taxes raised when the gallery displays her work with her permission, I wouldn't have to give her any money when I enjoy using the bike path in the case where the path is paid for by taxes raised when the gallery displays her work without her permis-sion. And since this would be like the case where I benefit from public goods that were paid for by taxes on slavery, I wouldn't owe any money in that case either.

While the unjust enrichment argument is in some respects better than it might at first appear, then, in the end it suffers from some serious problems. I'm inclined to think that the first of the three objections that I've raised provides a sufficient reason to refrain from endorsing the argument and that the second and third objections each provide sufficient reasons to reject it outright. But even if it remains possible that a satisfactory response to all three of these objections might be developed, the reparations position would surely be in better shape if it could be justified by a different kind of argument that could avoid them altogether.[26] And there is, in fact, a very different argument that does precisely that.

THE COMPENSATION ARGUMENT

The unjust enrichment argument is grounded in the claim that slave owning was a profitable enterprise for those who engaged in it. Its focus on the benefit to the owners, rather than on the harm to the slaves, is extremely common among those who endorse the reparations position. Robinson, for example, argues that "As Germany and other interests that profited owed reparations to Jews follow-ing the holocaust of Nazi persecution, America and other interests that profited owe reparations to blacks following the holocaust of African slavery."[27] As noted earlier, it's common for defenders of the reparations position to point to such facts as that slave labor was used to clear the land for the building of the city of Washington, DC, and in the construction of the Capitol Building, forms of labor from which we are all presumed to have benefited. And, indeed, the title of Robinson's book, by far the most prominent case for slave reparations to date, itself clearly refers to this kind of argument: "black people worked long, hard, killing days, years, centuries – and they were never *paid*," Robinson writes. "The value of their labor went into others' pockets.... Where *is* the money? There is a debt here."[28]

This focus on the profitability of slavery, although widespread among defenders of the reparations position, has always struck me as peculiar. Why should it matter if a slave was forced to pick valuable cotton all day rather than to carry heavy rocks pointlessly from one end of a field to another and then back again? Why should it matter if the labor he performed produced value that went into someone else's pocket rather than producing nothing of value to anyone at all? Either way, forcing the slave to do difficult work against his will would unjustly harm him, and either way, being unjustly harmed seems to be a perfectly suitable basis for making a reparations claim regardless of whether anyone else benefited from it. If I steal your car and destroy it, after all, I would presumably owe you some kind of debt to make up for the harm I imposed on you regardless of whether I benefited from stealing your car, say by charging other people money to drive it before it was destroyed, or was ultimately harmed by it, say by being seriously injured in the accident that destroyed it.[29] What matters in generating your claim to reparations in the case where I destroy your car, at least, seems simply to be the harm to you, not the profit, or lack of profit, to me. Why not try, then, to develop a defense of slave reparations along similar lines?

Indeed, the very analogy that Robinson himself repeatedly offers to support the slave reparations position provides a powerful reason to reject the persistent focus on profits that seems to be so common among advocates of the reparations position. Suppose, for example, that during the Second World War, the Nazis confiscated two factories owned by Jews, burned one to the ground and used the other to produce valuable supplies during the remainder of the war. It's hard to see how what the Nazis did with the factories after they unjustly seized them could affect the merits of the claim for reparations that the factories' original owners would have against them. If each original factory owner had a currently living descendant, then it seems plausible to suppose that the descendant of each owner could justly claim to have been made worse off by the Nazis' wrongful actions, and thus to have a reasonable basis for making a claim for reparations. This suggests a second and fundamentally different kind of argument for slave reparations, an argument based entirely on considerations having to do with wrongful harm. I will refer to this in what follows as the compensation argument. It is the compensation argument, rather than the unjust enrichment argument, that I slowly teased out of Robinson's short essay in the *Nation* when I first started looking into the slave reparations debate.[30] And it was my attempt to develop the compensation argument in a much fuller form than Robinson presented it that, in the end, inadvertently converted me into a defender of the reparations position. I'll therefore devote the rest of this chapter and all of the chapter that follows to explaining how this happened and to arguing that none of the objections that have been raised against the reparations position in general provide a good reason to reject the compensation argument for reparations in particular.

Step One: The Compensation Principle

The argument that I wish to defend here begins with a simple principle that I will call "the compensation principle." This principle says that if someone wrongfully harms another person, then he incurs a moral obligation to compensate his victim for the harms that he has wrongfully caused. If I wrongfully damage your car by vandalizing it, for example, then I incur a moral obligation to repair the damage that I caused or pay the costs involved in having someone else repair it on my behalf.

This compensation principle serves as the foundation of the compensation argument for slave reparations. Since my goal here is to defend this argument, it might seem fair to ask me to provide a defense of the principle that the argument depends on. But I'm not going to do that. The reason I'm not going to do that is simple: virtually everyone, regardless of their views about slave reparations, already accepts it. As I explained near the end of Chapter 1, my goal in this book is to try to resolve a variety of race-related debates by arguing from claims that people on both sides of those debates already accept. Since most people on both sides of the slave reparations debate already accept the compensation principle, it's fair to begin an argument about slave reparations by simply assuming that it's true. And so that's what I'll do.

Step Two: Applying the Compensation Principle to the Past

Accepting the compensation principle is the first step in accepting the compensation argument in defense of slave reparations. The second step involves taking this very general principle and applying it to the specific case at hand. To do this, we simply take the principle and fill in the blanks, as it were, with the original perpetrators and the original victims of slavery and its aftermath. Instead of talking about me wrongfully harming you by vandalizing your car, for example, we will instead talk about previous generations of American citizens wrongfully harming previous generations of Africans and African Americans through the institution of slavery and its aftermath. Regardless of their views on slave reparations, after all, virtually everyone today agrees that slavery did occur, that it was harmful, and that it was wrong. They agree, in addition, that up until the middle of the 1960s, black Americans were harmed through various forms of legalized segregation and discrimination, and they agree that this, too, was wrong. So virtually everyone already accepts the compensation principle and virtually everyone already accepts the historical claim that previous generations of Americans wrongfully harmed previous generations of Africans and African Americans through the institution of slavery and its aftermath.

This is an important start. But, just by themselves, these two claims don't get us very far. If you apply the compensation principle to the historical claim, what you get is simply this: some people in the past wrongfully harmed some other people in the past and so if they were still around today, the people in the past who caused the harm would owe something to the people in the past who suffered the harm. If there were any former slave owners still alive today, for example, and if any of their former slaves were still around, too, then the owners would owe some kind of compensation to their slaves. This is an extremely modest conclusion, and I doubt that many opponents of slave reparations would resist it. It is, in any event, of purely academic interest since there are, in fact, no such survivors remaining. The slave reparations position is about a debt that is supposed to be owed by one group of currently living people to another group of currently living people, but it seems that all we can get by applying the compensation principle to the historical claim is a much weaker conclusion about a debt that would be owed by one group of formerly living people to another group of formerly living people if both groups of formerly living people were still alive.

What the defender of the compensation argument for slave reparations needs to do here, then, is two things. First, he has to explain how the fact that black Americans who lived in the past would have been owed something supports the claim that black Americans who are alive today are owed something. This is what I will refer to as the move from "past claimants" – those Africans and African Americans who were directly harmed by slavery, Jim Crow laws, and so on – to "present claimants" – the current generation of black Americans who are supposed to be owed something as a result of these past harms. Second, the proponent of reparations has to explain how the fact that some white Americans in the past would have owed something to these claimants supports the claim that white Americans like me in the present owe them something. I will refer to this as the move from "past debtors" – those who were responsible for harming Africans and African Americans via the institution of slavery, Jim Crow laws, and so on – to "present debtors" – the white Americans like me who are supposed to help foot the bill even though we didn't cause any of these harms. Neither of these moves seems at all obvious. Indeed, both, on the face of it, seem quite implausible. This, I suspect, is why the slave reparations position ultimately strikes so many people as unreasonable. It certainly made the reparations position seem unreasonable to me when I first became aware of it. But I now think that there is, in fact, a way to justify both of these moves. Robinson hints at how both of these moves can be defended in his article and in his book, but more needs to be said to fill in the details. Doing so will be the principal goal of the next two steps of the argument.

Step Three: From Past Claimants to Present Claimants

The third step in the compensation argument maintains that the debt that would be owed to previous generations of black Americans if they were still alive can be transferred to the current generation of black Americans. The key to this step of the argument is the idea that an act that harms the members of one generation can in turn have lingering consequences that impose costs on subsequent generations. In some contexts, this idea is pretty straightforward. Suppose, for example, that I wrongfully harm you by dumping toxic waste in your neighborhood. The hazardous effects of my polluting might well continue to make people in the area sick for generations to come. In this kind of case, at least, it seems clear that I would owe a debt not just to the people who got sick right away, but to the people my act caused to suffer later on. Virtually everyone, I suspect, regardless of their views of slave reparations, would accept such a claim in this kind of case. If it can be shown that slavery and its aftermath involved wrongful acts that, in effect, "polluted" race relations in this country in ways that continue to cause harmful consequences for the current generation of black Americans, then the move from the uncontroversial debt to past claimants to the more controversial debt to present claimants would be secured on terms that even most opponents of slave reparations already accept.[31]

It's clear from Robinson's writings that he means to support this third step in the argument in just this way. In his article in *The Nation*, for example, he writes that "the black living suffer real and current consequences as a result of wrongs committed by a younger America." And in his book, *The Debt*, he refers to "the savage time-release social debilitations of American slavery," says that "slavery, with its sadistic patience, asphyxiated memory, and smothered cultures, has hulled empty a whole race of people with inter-generational efficiency," and writes that slavery "produces its victims *ad infinitum*, long after the active stage of the crime has ended."[32] Even in the context of the more specific harms that he discusses in his book, such as the fact that a 1998 study showed that the two counties in Maryland with the highest concentration of black students placed at the very bottom in the state's standardized public school tests, Robinson explains things by saying that "Blacks scored behind in the two counties because of slavery's lasting legacy to them."[33]

We can summarize the sort of claim that Robinson makes in passages such as these as follows: the acts by which previous generations of American citizens wrongfully harmed previous generations of Africans and African Americans continue to cause harmful consequences for black Americans today. Since this is a claim about the effects that past acts continue to cause in the present, I will refer to it here as "the causal claim." This causal claim is absolutely essential to making the compensation argument work. If the past wrongful acts involving slavery and its aftermath are not currently exerting any harmful influence on the present generation of black Americans, after all, then the compensation principle won't entitle the present generation of black Americans to any compensation because there won't be any damages to compensate them for. If these past wrongful acts do continue to exert a harmful influence on the present, then the current generation of black Americans is indeed being harmed by the very same acts that harmed black Americans in the past, and so the move from a debt to past claimants to a debt to present claimants will therefore seem to be firmly established. Whether or not the defender of slave reparations is in a position to justify reparations on compensatory grounds, then, depends on whether or not we have reason to accept this causal claim.

And this is one of the places where Robinson's case for slave reparations breaks down entirely. For while it seems clear that the compensation argument turns crucially on the causal claim, and while it seems equally clear that Robinson means to endorse this claim, he does nothing, in his book or in his article in the *Nation*, to justify it.[34] We need some reason to accept the causal claim, that is, and Robinson simply fails to provide one. It's possible, of course, that Robinson simply assumes that his intended readers will accept the causal claim without argument. Maybe it just seems obvious to him. But if proponents of the reparations position wish to construct a defense of slave reparations on grounds that most people already accept, they can't start by simply assuming that the causal claim is true. Most opponents of slave reparations, after all, won't begin by simply assuming that the causal claim is true. If anything, they're likely to be inclined to presume that it's false.

The problem of justifying the causal claim was one of the things that prevented me from accepting Robinson's argument when I first looked into the debate over slave reparations. After a while, though, it became clear to me that while Robinson himself offered no solution to the problem, the problem itself could be approached by backing up and starting with a claim that virtually everyone on both sides of the debate does already accept.[35] This is the purely factual claim that by a large number of relatively uncontroversial measures of human well-being, black people in the United States on the whole are doing considerably less well today than are white people in the United States on the whole. As I noted toward the end of Chapter 1, for example, when we look at such factors as health, life expectancy, education, and income, it's hard to resist the conclusion that, on average, white Americans are doing better than black Americans. The key to trying to justify the causal claim, then, is to start with this essentially uncontested set of data and then to ask the following question: what is the best explanation of it?

When we look at the problem of justifying the causal claim from this perspective, a compelling strategy for vindicating the claim seems naturally to emerge. For, at least on the face of it, there seem to be only two kinds of explanation available to account for the current discrepancy between black and white levels of well-being in this country: either genetic differences between black and white Americans account for the discrepancy, or there is some difference between the social environments that the two groups inhabit that makes it more difficult for black Americans to flourish. The first possibility seems to have been thoroughly discredited within the relevant scientific communities. If this is so, then there's no reason to believe that black people are genetically disposed to be less intelligent than white people, or to rank lower in terms of other characteristics that seem clearly relevant to one's ability to flourish. If that's right, then if black and white Americans were placed on a level playing field, we would expect to see them faring at least roughly equally in terms of common measures of human well-being. Since we don't see this happening, the argument maintains, and if genetic differences can't be used to account for the fact that we don't see it happening, then the fact that we don't see it happening supports the conclusion that the other possible explanation must be correct: there must be some significant difference between the social environment that white Americans occupy and the social environment that black Americans occupy, and that difference must be one that makes it more difficult, on average, for black Americans to flourish. The most obvious candidate for such a difference by far is the existence of the legacy of slavery and its aftermath. And so the most reasonable conclusion to draw, on this account, is that slavery and its aftermath do, in fact, continue to exert a negative influence on the lives of black Americans. As the political scientist Andrew Hacker has put the view that underlies this kind of defense of the causal claim, "despite more than a century of searching, we have no evidence that any ... pools of race-based genes has a larger quotient of what we choose to call intelligence or organizational ability or creative capacities. So if more members of some races end up doing better in some spheres, it is because more of them grew up in environments that prepared them for those endeavors."[36]

I will discuss some objections that might be raised against this argument for the causal claim in some detail in the next chapter, including objections based on the claim that there really are important genetic differences between black and white people and on the claim that cultural differences provide a superior alternative to both the biological and the historical accounts. But for now, at least, and setting aside possible objections, the appeal to the claim that environmental differences between current black and white Americans provide the most plausible explanation of well-being differences between current black and white Americans seems to vindicate the causal claim. And by doing so, it vindicates the third step in the compensation argument by appealing to considerations that most people on both sides of the slave reparations debate already accept.

The result of adding the causal claim to the historical claim and the compensation principle, however, is not that currently living white Americans like me owe anything to currently living black Americans. It is instead the much weaker claim that if any of the early Americans who wrongfully harmed previous generations of Africans and African Americans were still alive today, *they* would owe compensation, not just to any surviving members of their own generation who had been wrongfully harmed by their acts, but also to those members of the current generation of black Americans who continue to be harmed by the lingering effects of those early actions. And that claim, too, falls short of the claim made by defenders of slave reparations. The claim made by the reparations position isn't that the dead white men of the past would owe something to currently living black Americans if they were still alive, but that currently living white Americans like me owe them something. To tie this debt to people like me, then, a fourth step is needed.

Step Four: From Past Debtors to Present Debtors

The fourth step in the compensation argument attempts to move us from the claim that the dead white men of yesterday would owe something to currently living black Americans to the claim that contemporary white Americans like me owe something to currently living black Americans. This seems to be the most difficult step in the argument to defend. Even if we agree that some of the harms that contemporary black Americans currently suffer can be traced to the wrongful acts of these dead white men, after all, it's simply not my fault that those dead white men did what they did. And if it's not my fault that these wrongful acts occurred in the past, then how can I and other Americans like me be held responsible for repairing the harms that they continue to cause in the present?

This is a very good question. For a long time, it was one of the main reasons that the reparations position struck me as deeply implausible. But I now think that this very good question has a very good answer. The answer consists of two parts. The first part points out that many of the wrongful acts in question were committed not by private citizens acting in their capacity as individuals, but rather by representatives of the United States government, acting in their official capacities as judges, congressmen, police officers, militia members, presidents, and so on. The second part maintains that there's a morally important difference between the debts that are generated by private acts and the debts that are generated by public acts. Both parts of this answer can be sustained simply by appealing to claims that virtually everyone, regardless of their views on slave reparations, already accepts.

The first part of answering the challenge to the justification of step four involves establishing a series of factual claims. Since these have already been identified and documented in Chapter 1, I will treat them briefly here. The relevant facts are ones such as these: slavery was not simply a private vice. It was a legally recognized, legally protected, and legally facilitated practice. When a slave escaped to a free state in the North, for example, the federal government actively enforced the legal right of the slave owner to have his property returned to him.[37] After slavery was ended, moreover, the federal government actively protected the legal rights of state officials to devise voting requirement tests even though it was clear that their purpose was to prevent black people from voting in significant numbers. Up until the landmark ruling of *Brown v. the Board of Education*, the federal government protected the rights of states to segregate their public schools in a manner that clearly disadvantaged black schoolchildren. In short, and as Robinson emphasized in his article in the *Nation*, "Federal and state governments were active participants not only in slavery but also in the exclusion and dehumanization of blacks that continued legally up until the passage of key civil rights legislation in the sixties." The historical facts that this claim rests on are essentially uncontested, and so virtually everyone, regardless of their views on slave reparations, will accept them.

The second part of answering the challenge to step four involves a moral claim. The claim is that there's an important difference between the moral debts that are created by private acts and the moral debts that are created by public ones. More specifically, the claim is that while private moral debts may be cancelled by the death of the individual whose act created them, the same can't be said of public moral debts. When a private citizen does something in his capacity as a private individual, if his act generates a moral obligation, he incurs that obligation as a private individual. When he dies, it's at least plausible to suppose that the moral obligation dies with him. But when a representative of the federal government, acting in his official capacity as an agent of the state, does something that generates an obligation, it's not that he himself incurs the obligation, but rather that the government does. And once the government has incurred this moral obligation, the obligation doesn't cease to exist simply because the official in question ceases to exist. We might call this the "surviving public obligation principle": If a government incurs a moral obligation as a result of the authorized actions of some of its public officials, then this obligation doesn't cease to exist when the officials in question die. If we accept the surviving public obligation principle, and if we recognize that many of the acts that generated a debt to the original victims of slavery and its aftermath were acts done by public officials acting in their official capacities as agents of the U.S. government, then we will be in a position to justify the fourth step in the compensation argument: since it is the U.S. government itself that would have incurred an obligation to currently living black Americans, and not simply the particular individuals whose acts originally generated this obligation, then the obligation will continue to exist today despite the fact that the individuals whose acts generated the obligation don't. White Americans like me will be obligated to contribute to reparations to black Americans today, therefore, not because the past wrongs that continue to harm them were our fault, but because they were the fault of our government and because, as its citizens, we're obligated to help our government live up to its responsibilities.

It's quite clear that Robinson believes in this surviving public obligation principle. As he puts it at one point, "The life and responsibilities of a nation are not limited to the life spans of its mortal constituents."[38] But, as with the causal claim that I discussed in the context of step three of the argument, while it's clear that this principle is needed in order for the compensation argument to succeed, and while it's clear that Robinson means to endorse the principle, he again fails to provide an argument in its defense. And without a good reason to accept the surviving public obligation principle, the case for reparations will again be at risk of collapsing.

Fortunately for the defender of the reparations position, a satisfactory defense of the surviving public obligation principle is available. And, once again, the principle can be grounded simply by starting with claims that virtually everyone, regardless of their views about slave reparations, already accepts. Consider, for example, the case of those obligations that are generated when a country signs an international treaty. A number of years ago, for example, the United States signed a treaty that resulted in the creation of the North Atlantic Treaty Organization (NATO). As a result of this fact, it incurred certain obligations that it would not otherwise have incurred, such as the obligation to come to the defense of other NATO countries that find themselves under attack. If France is invaded, for example, and if the treaty commits NATO members to coming to its defense under such circumstances, then even if the United States doesn't feel like helping it out, it would be wrong for it to refuse to help because refusing to help would violate it treaty obligations.

But now imagine that someone offered the following argument in an attempt to justify the claim that it would be okay for the United States to ignore its obligation to live up to the terms of the NATO treaty: "all of the Senators who voted to ratify the NATO treaty are now dead. The president who signed the NATO treaty is dead. All of the government officials who were responsible for generating the obligation to follow the NATO treaty are dead. And since they're all dead, the obligation that their actions generated is dead, too. It's true that we have to follow the terms of the treaties that our country agrees to as long as the officials who agree to the treaties are still alive, but as soon as they die, we can do what we want. The obligation to follow the agreement dies with them." Surely in this case virtually everyone, regardless of their view of slave reparations, would see right through this attempted rationalization. They may believe that under some circumstances, perhaps even under many circumstances, a country can justify violating a treaty it has agreed to. But virtually no one will say that a country can lose whatever treaty obligations it has simply because the individuals who originally signed the treaty die. And this means that virtually everyone will accept the surviving public obligation principle: when a government acquires a set of obligations because of the official acts of some of its representatives, the government doesn't lose these obligations simply because those representatives die.[39]

The same lesson, moreover, arises when we consider the case of government obligations that are generated by legislation. The Social Security Act, for example, generated an obligation on the part of the government to make payments of a certain sort to a certain group of people. Now imagine, again, that a critic points out that all of the congressmen who voted for the act, as well as the president who signed it into law, are now dead, and that this critic then claims as a result that the government is no longer obligated to honor the terms of the law that it had enacted. Again, virtually everyone on both sides of the reparations debate will recognize that this is an unacceptable argument. If a law raises the national speed limit, the speed limit doesn't go back down after the president who signs the law dies and the same goes for any other right or obligation generated by legislation. Indeed, it's hard to imagine what things would be like otherwise. The death of every former president would instantly void all of the legislation that he had signed into law.

And finally, since I'm ultimately interested in applying the surviving public obligation principle to the problem of slave reparations, it's important to note that virtually nobody succumbs to this kind of flawed reasoning in those cases of government reparations that are relatively uncontroversial. Few people, for example, objected when the federal government made reparations in the amount of about $1.6 billion to approximately eighty thousand Japanese-Americans who had been unjustly interned by the government during the Second World War. Yet if we believed that a government's obligations die when the person whose acts created the obligations dies, then it would have been a simple matter to prove that reparations for these victims were unjustified. The internment camps, after all, were created as a result of an executive order signed by President Franklin Roosevelt, and Roosevelt died long before the reparations were paid. Most opponents of slave reparations seem to accept the justice of reparations to specific victims of the internment camps. Even Horowitz doesn't complain about them and the law putting them into effect was signed by none other than Ronald Reagan. As a result, even most opponents of slave reparations are already committed to the view that a government's obligations – *including those obligations to make reparations that arise from the wrongful acts of some of its officials in the past* – do not die with the death of the person or persons whose acts generated the obligations. And to accept this is to accept the surviving public obligation principle that's needed to sustain step four of the compensation argument.

The point of appealing to the examples that I've discussed here, it's important to emphasize, is not to insist that once a government has incurred an obligation it must be burdened by that obligation indefinitely. Legitimate procedures may be in place by which a government can repeal a law that it has enacted, amend a constitution that it is ruled by, withdraw from a treaty it has agreed to, and so forth. The point is simply to say that in cases in which such procedures have not yet been followed – cases, that is, in which the obligation that a government has incurred has not yet been fully discharged or eliminated – the mere fact that the people whose official acts created the obligation have died can't in and of itself render the government's obligation null and void. Once we consider the implications of denying this claim, it's extremely difficult to see how we could avoid accepting it, and so it's extremely difficult to see how we could avoid accepting the surviving public obligation principle. And since it's difficult to see how we could do anything but accept the surviving public obligation principle, it's difficult to see how, in the end, we could do anything but accept step four of the compensation argument. If it really is true that past wrongful acts by officials of the U.S. government generated an obligation on the government's part to make reparations to those harmed by the acts, including those subsequently harmed by the acts in later generations – as the first three steps of the argument maintain – then the fact that those officials are now dead can't mean that the government no longer has this obligation. The move from a debt that would have been owed in the past to a debt that is owed in the present is thus vindicated and, along with it, so is step four of the compensation argument.

Step Five: Checking the Balance

If the first four steps of the compensation argument are accepted, then the case for slave reparations is almost complete. Step one establishes the general obligation to repair harms that are wrongfully caused, step two specifies that slavery and its aftermath did wrongfully cause harm, step three maintains that the wrongful acts of the past continue to cause harmful effects to black Americans in the present, and step four claims that the obligation to repair these harms that the government incurred a long time ago hasn't disappeared simply because the individuals whose acts generated the obligation have long since died. If all of this is true, then the present American government has indeed inherited a debt to the present generation of black Americans. All that remains to secure the case for slave reparations, then, is to consider whether or not this debt has already been paid. If the debt has, in fact, been paid, then the argument for reparations, although technically sound, is practically moot. But if the debt has not yet been paid, then the argument really does secure the case for slave reparations, and on grounds that virtually everyone, including virtually every opponent of slave reparations, already accepts.

Many of those who reject the reparations position, of course, will balk at precisely this point. Yes, they will agree, the U.S. government did mistreat black Americans in the past, and yes, they will admit, this did give rise to a responsibility on the part of the government to make things right. But, they will then add, the government has already lived up to this responsibility. It ended slavery, abolished segregation, protected voting rights, adopted various forms of affirmative action and created other social programs that benefit black Americans as well. And so, they will conclude, while the federal government may once have incurred a debt to black Americans because of the wrongful harms inflicted by slavery and its aftermath, that debt has since been paid off and the reparations position must be rejected for this reason.

The response to this objection to the reparations position is a simple one: if reparations had, in fact, already been made, then black Americans today would, in fact, be doing at least roughly as well, on the whole, as white Americans are doing. But they aren't, so they haven't. Unless we believe that genetic differences between black and white Americans account for the sizeable gap between current black and white average levels of well being, that is, the best explanation of the current discrepancies between black and white levels of well-being is that black Americans are, in fact, still continuing to suffer negative consequences as a result of the legacy of slavery and its aftermath. And if they are continuing to suffer the harms, then they have not yet been fully compensated for them. We might refer to this result as the "unpaid balance claim," and it constitutes the fifth step in the compensation argument: the United States government has not yet fully compensated the currently living generation of black Americans for the harms they continue to suffer as a result of slavery and its aftermath.

This fifth step is the final step needed to secure the compensation argument. The argument is therefore complete. And, although I strongly resisted the reparations position when I first encountered it, and although I continued to resist it as I debated the issue with myself, I'm now inclined to think that the argument is not simply complete, but sound. From assumptions that even opponents of slave reparations generally concede, the compensation argument makes a cogent case for the slave reparations position. As a result, I now think that the argument itself, and the reparations position that it defends, should simply be accepted.

Not everyone will agree with this assessment, of course. And so the next task is to consider the various objections that have been raised against the reparations position, including the ten objections raised in Horowitz's famous ad. Many of these objections continue to strike me as perfectly reasonable. But what I can now see, and was unable to see when I first looked into this debate, is that while they may be good objections to at least some arguments for the reparations position, they all fail as objections to the compensation argument in particular.

Before going through all of these objections, though, it may first be useful to have available a brief summary of the compensation argument as a whole. And since it became clear as the argument unfolded that in order to justify a conclusion about a debt owed by the U.S. government in particular, its early steps must refer to the U.S. government in particular and not just to Americans in the past in general, I will present those steps here in a more specific version than the versions I used in introducing them. For the purposes of the remaining discussion in this chapter and the chapter that follows, then, the compensation argument refers to the claim that the reparations position is justified by the following five steps:

Step one – the compensation principle: if a government wrongfully harms someone as a result of the authorized actions of some of its public officials, then it incurs a moral obligation to compensate its victim for the harms that it has wrongfully caused.

Step two – the historical claim: in the past, the U.S. government wrongfully harmed previous generations of Africans and African Americans by supporting the institution of slavery and subsequent forms of legalized segregation and discrimination.

Step three – the causal claim: the acts by which the U.S. government wrongfully harmed previous generations of Africans and African Americans by supporting the institution of slavery and subsequent forms of legalized segregation and discrimination in the past continue to cause harmful consequences for the currently living generation of black Americans today.

Step four – the surviving public obligation principle: if a government incurs a moral obligation as a result of the authorized actions of some of its public officials, then this obligation doesn't cease to exist when the officials in question die.

Step five – the unpaid balance claim: the U.S. government has not yet fully
compensated the currently living generation of black Americans for the
harmful consequences they continue to incur as a result of slavery and its
aftermath.

It seems to me that all five of these steps must be accepted, and on grounds
that opponents of slave reparations themselves already accept. It also seems to
me that if all five of these steps must be accepted, then the reparations position
itself must be accepted: the first two steps justify an obligation on the part of
the past government to past black Americans, the third justifies extending the
obligation from one owed to past black Americans to one owed to present black
Americans, the fourth justifies extending the obligation from one owed by the
past government to one owed by the present government, and the fifth justifies
the conclusion that the present government's obligation has not yet been fully
discharged. Since each of the steps taken individually seem to be justified, and
since all of the steps taken together seem to justify the conclusion, the conclusion
itself seems to be justified: the U.S. government does indeed have a moral obligation to benefit the currently living generation of black Americans because of the
wrongful harms that were inflicted on past generations of Africans and African
Americans by the institution of slavery and its aftermath.

DAVE'S TOP TEN LIST OF OBJECTIONS TO SLAVE REPARATIONS

I've now explained what the compensation argument says and why it seems reasonable to me. The question that remains is whether there is nonetheless a good
reason to reject it. David Horowitz remains the most prominent opponent of
slave reparations writing these days, so it seems appropriate to start with his
famous list of ten reasons for rejecting the reparations position. As I mentioned
at the start of this chapter, my initial reaction to reading Horowitz's widely discussed ad was that his position was surely correct. But this was before I had
taken the time to carefully distinguish between the unjust enrichment argument
and the compensation argument, and before I had tried to work out ways to
reinforce the compensation argument in the places where it seemed to be in need
of support. Now that I've come to understand the important differences between
the two arguments and to see how the compensation argument can be strengthened, my reaction to Horowitz's ten reasons is very different: I still think that his
ad includes some good reasons for rejecting some arguments for slave reparations, but I now see that it contains no good reason to reject the compensation
argument in particular. And since I now see that the compensation argument is
the best argument for the reparations position, this means that Horowitz's arguments provide no good reason to reject the reparations position itself. I'll focus
in the rest of this chapter on explaining why I no longer find any of Horowitz's
ten reasons for rejecting reparations to be convincing, and I'll devote the chapter that follows to responding to some still further objections to the reparations

position, including some that Horowitz endorses elsewhere, and some that have been raised by other writers.

White Slaves, Black Masters, Arab Traders

Horowitz's first objection to slave reparations consists of two parts. The first part points to the fact that white Americans were not the only people responsible for slavery in America. The second points to the fact that not all slaves in America were black and not all slave owners were white. In each case, Horowitz suggests that in light of these facts the reparations position has implications that are unacceptable.

The text of this first objection in his ad runs as follows:[40]

I
There Is No Single Group Responsible For The Crime Of Slavery.

Black Africans and Arabs were responsible for enslaving the ancestors of African-Americans. There were 3,000 black slave-owners in the ante-bellum United States. Are reparations to be paid by their descendants too? There were white slaves in colonial America. Are their descendents going to receive payments?

And in his subsequent book on the subject, Horowitz presses the first part of this objection even more forcefully. He cites sources to support the claim that three to ten million Africans were purchased by Muslim slave traders as a part of an African internal slave trade between the years 650 and 1600, and evidence to the effect that more African slaves were exported even to the small island nation of Cuba than were ever sent to the United States.[41] "America's role in the global tragedy of slave systems involving Africans," Horowitz concludes, "while bad enough, was relatively minor compared with the roles of Arabs, Europeans and Africans themselves."[42]

Part of Horowitz's complaint here is surely irrelevant. Whether other groups did or didn't play a bigger role in slavery worldwide than the United States played doesn't have any bearing on whether the United States nonetheless owes a debt of reparations in virtue of the particular role that it did play. If I vandalize your car, after all, the fact that my act plays a tiny role in the global problem of car vandalism doesn't make me owe you any less compensation for the harm that I wrongfully caused you. But part of Horowitz's complaint here does seem to raise a legitimate question: if debts of compensation really can be passed down from generation to generation, after all, then why shouldn't the descendants of the particular Africans and Arabs who were involved in the slave trade be held responsible for the sins of their ancestors, too? And if currently living Americans really can be entitled to compensation based on the wrongs that were committed against previous generations, then why shouldn't every descendent of a slave claim such entitlement, even if the slave in question was white?[43]

I was inclined to think that this was a good objection when I first read Horowitz's ad, and I'm still inclined to think that it's a good objection. But while

I was initially inclined to think that it was a good objection to the reparations position itself, I can now see it for what it really is: a good objection to one particular kind of argument for the reparations position. This is the kind of argument that operates along bloodlines: if your biological ancestors owed a debt of compensation to my biological ancestors, on this kind of account, then you will have inherited a debt to me as a result of it. Horowitz's observations here do seem to show that this kind of argument has the kind of unwelcome implications he identifies, and so they do seem to show that a defender of the slave reparations position shouldn't appeal to considerations having to do with obligations being passed down through the generations according to bloodlines.

But the compensation argument, it's important to emphasize, doesn't operate according to bloodlines. It claims that currently living black Americans are owed reparations not because they're biologically descended from the victims of slavery and its aftermath, but because they continue to suffer the negative consequences of slavery and its aftermath. And it claims that the current United States government owes such reparations not because its officials are biologically descended from the people responsible for slavery and its aftermath, but rather because they represent the very government that was responsible for it, a government whose moral obligations outlive the particular individuals whose actions generated those obligations. Since the compensation argument doesn't depend on the claim that the biological descendants of wrongdoers owe reparations to the biological descendents of their victims, and since Horowitz's first objection only applies to arguments that depend on this assumption, Horowitz's first objection provides no reason to reject the compensation argument.

The Legacy of Slavery – Everyone's a Winner!

Horowitz's second objection turns on the claim that if the United States has profited from slave labor, then everyone in the country has profited from it, including those African Americans whose ancestors were compelled to provide the labor in the first place. As he puts this objection in his ad:[44]

II
There Is No Single Group That Benefited Exclusively from Slavery.

The claim for reparations is premised on the false assumption that only whites have benefited from slavery. If slave labor has created wealth for Americans, then obviously it has created wealth for black Americans as well, including the descendants of slaves. The GNP of black America makes the African-American community the tenth most prosperous "nation" in the world. American blacks on average enjoy per capita incomes in the range of twenty to fifty times that of blacks living in any of the African nations from which they were kidnapped.

Horowitz develops this objection in more detail in his book on slave reparations[45] and repeats it in a second ad, called "The Debt," that he submitted to eight additional school newspapers after the controversy provoked by his initial ad.[46] And the basic point that most black Americans today are better off than most black Africans has been taken as a problem for the reparations position by a number of other writers as well.[47] If black Americans are better off for being here, after all, then what could they be owed reparations for?

Like his first objection, Horowitz's second objection raises a real problem for a particular kind of defense of the reparations position. In this case, the defense is the one provided by the unjust enrichment argument. That argument does seem to depend on the assumption that white Americans today are being unjustly enriched by slavery in a way that black Americans aren't. So if that assumption turns out to be mistaken, then the unjust enrichment argument would seem to be in trouble.

But, again like his first objection, Horowitz's second objection does nothing to undermine the compensation argument for slave reparations. The compensation argument, after all, depends on the claim that black Americans today are owed compensation for the adverse effects they suffer from the legacy of slavery and its aftermath. And the legitimacy of a claim for compensation for harm isn't undermined by the fact that a victim of wrongful harm has also been a recipient of significant benefits, even if they received the benefits from the one responsible for the harm.

Suppose, for example, that a white American businessman goes to an impoverished African country, meets an impoverished young African man, and persuades him to come to America to work for his company. For many years, the African is happily and profitably employed by the company and earns, let's say, fifty times more money each year than he would have earned had he remained in Africa. One day, though, he suffers a minor injury in a factory accident that was caused by his employer's negligently failing to replace a faulty part in a machine. It may well be true that, on the whole, this African man is much better off as a result of his having left Africa to work for the white businessman's company. But this doesn't mean that the company wouldn't owe him compensation for his injury. Virtually everyone, regardless of their view of slave reparations, agrees that a company owes compensation to an employee who is injured as a result of its negligence even if the employee is, on the whole, much better off than he would have been had he not come to work for the company in the first place. Similarly, it may well be true that, on the whole, black Americans are much better off today as a result of their ancestors having been forcibly taken from Africa, but this doesn't mean that the government owes them no compensation for the harms they nonetheless suffer today as a result of its wrongful actions in the past. Horowitz's second objection, then, like the first, provides no reason to reject the compensation argument for the reparations position.

The Few and the Many

Horowitz's third objection appeals to a pair of additional claims: that a relatively small number of white Americans actually owned slaves and that a relatively large number of white Americans made great sacrifices to free the slaves. In his ad, the objection is stated as follows:[48]

III

Only A Minority Of White Americans Owned Slaves, While Others Gave Their Lives To Free Them.

Only a tiny minority of Americans ever owned slaves. This is true even for those who lived in the antebellum South where only one white in five was a slaveholder. Why should their descendants owe a debt? What about the descendants of the 350,000 Union soldiers who died to free the slaves? They gave their lives. What morality would ask their descendants to pay again? If paying reparations on the basis of skin color is not racism, what is?

And in his book, the second part of this objection is put like this: "More than 350,000 Americans lost their lives in the northern armies that vanquished the slave power. Was this not a form of atonement?"[49]

Once again, Horowitz's objection succeeds in identifying a genuine problem for a particular kind of argument for slave reparations. This time, we are back to the kind of bloodlines argument that proved to be relevant to his first objection. If the argument for slave reparations depends on the claim that each of us is responsible for discharging the unfulfilled obligations of our biological ancestors, then Horowitz is right to insist that even those white Americans who can trace their family lineage back to the American Revolution will often find that their records are clean, if not positively praiseworthy, with respect to the practice of slavery.

But, once again, while Horowitz's attack poses a problem for a certain kind of argument for slave reparations, it poses no problem for the compensation argument in particular. The compensation argument, it should by now be clear, simply doesn't depend on the claim that moral obligations can be inherited biologically. It maintains, instead, that our government continues to have the obligations it has even after the death of the public officials whose acts originally generated those obligations. And for this particular kind of argument for slave reparations, the number of people initially involved in generating the obligation is simply irrelevant.

Consider, for example, the obligations that were generated by the American ratification of the NATO treaty. Prior to ratification, the United States did not stand under a special obligation to come to the defense of NATO countries. After the ratification, it did stand under such an obligation because it had committed itself to providing such defense. Yet it takes only two-thirds of the Senate and the signature of the president for such a treaty to be ratified. The acts of a tiny handful of public officials, then, were enough to put the entire country under a substantial new moral obligation. The vast majority of currently living Americans are not directly descended from any of the senators who voted in favor of the NATO treaty, nor are they directly descended from the president who signed the treaty. But this fact is clearly irrelevant to the claim that their government is nonetheless obligated to fulfill the obligations that arose from the acts of those officials even if all of those officials are now dead. In the same way, and for the same reason, the fact that most Americans today are not directly descended from any of the public officials who were involved in protecting and facilitating the practice of slavery is irrelevant to the claim that their government is nonetheless obligated to fulfill the obligations that arose from the acts of those officials even though all of those officials are now dead.

If some of my tax money is used to help to defend a NATO ally, it would be absurd for me to complain that this is unfair to me because none of my ancestors were involved in the ratification of the NATO treaty. If some of my tax money is used to help to make reparations for slavery, it would be no more reasonable for me to complain that this is unfair to me because none of my ancestors were involved in the legal protection and facilitation of the practice of slavery. It's true, of course, that the acts of the government officials in question in the two cases are very different – signing a treaty in one case, wrongfully facilitating the practice of slavery in the other – and it's also true that the ways in which such acts generate a moral obligation are very different as well – acquiring an obligation by making a promise in one case, acquiring an obligation by wrongfully harming someone in the other. But what kind of acts they were and how they generated a moral obligation is not the question. The question is whether, once a government has incurred a moral obligation because of some sort of act of some of its officials, it matters that the obligation was generated by the acts of a relatively small number of people. The NATO case shows that the answer to this question must be no. The Japanese-American internment case, in which the relevant act was an executive order signed by a single individual, shows that the answer is no, too. And if the answer is no, then the fact that the obligation to make reparations for slavery was generated by the acts of a relatively small number of people doesn't matter in that case either.

What about the second part of Horowitz's third objection? Horowitz puts a great deal of weight on the fact that so many Americans paid such a great price to help put an end to slavery. And from the point of view of the bloodlines approach to reparations, this focus is again understandable. If your obligations relating to slavery really are determined by your biological genealogy, after all, and if your ancestors died in order that the slaves could be freed, then it seems plausible to say that you don't owe anyone anything as a result of the legacy of slavery. Your biological bloodline has already paid more than its fair share. But from the point of view of the compensation argument, the fact that many Americans made great sacrifices to end slavery again proves to be irrelevant to the claim that the United States has an obligation to repair the harms that slavery and its aftermath continue to cause. Suffering greatly in order to stop doing something wrong, after all, doesn't get you off the hook for paying for the damages that your wrongful behavior has already caused.

Suppose, for example, that I steal your car and leave it at the bottom of a cliff, where the rocks that frequently fall from the cliff will eventually destroy it. After a number of rocks have fallen onto the car and caused it several hundred dollars worth of damage, I begin to have some regrets about my behavior and go back to try to protect your car from any further harm. Just as I am about to move the car out of the way, however, I am hit by a rock and am seriously injured as a result. Clearly, in this case, I have suffered a great deal in trying to discontinue my wrongful behavior. But, just as clearly, this fact doesn't mean that I owe you nothing for the damage my wrongful behavior has already caused to your car. Virtually everyone, regardless of their view of slave reparations, would agree with that. Yet in just the same way, and for just the same reason, the fact that the United States suffered a great deal in order to put an end to the practice of slavery doesn't mean that it has no obligation to try to repair the damage that its past wrongful behavior continues to cause. Horowitz's third objection to the reparations position, then, like the two that come before it, may work against some arguments for slave reparations, but it doesn't work against the compensation argument.

The Immigrant's Complaint

Horowitz's fourth objection is essentially an extension of his third. The third objection appealed to the case of contemporary Americans whose ancestors lived in America during the period before the Civil War but who owned no slaves and perhaps even fought to end slavery. The fourth objection appeals to a different set of contemporary Americans whose ancestors also owned no slaves: those whose families came to America after the practice of slavery had been abolished. As Horowitz puts it in his famous ad:[50]

IV

Most Living Americans Have No Connection (Direct or Indirect) to Slavery.

The two great waves of American immigration occurred after 1880 and then after 1960. What logic would require Vietnamese boat people, Russian refuseniks, Iranian refugees, Armenian victims of the Turkish persecution, Jews, Mexicans[,] Greeks, or Polish, Hungarian, Cambodian and Korean victims of Communism, to pay reparations to American blacks?

As I noted near the beginning of this chapter, this fourth objection struck me as strong enough to make the case against slave reparations all by itself when I first read Horowitz's ad.[51] But, as with the other objections I've discussed to this point, I can now see that while the objection may work against some arguments for slave reparations, it fails to pose a problem for the compensation argument in particular. Indeed, since the fourth objection ultimately amounts to a variation on the third objection, it fails to undermine the compensation argument for precisely the same reason that the third objection failed to undermine it: the compensation argument doesn't depend on the claim that moral obligations can be inherited biologically and the fourth objection, like the third, is relevant only to arguments that rely on this assumption.

To see that this is so, it may help once again to consider the case of the obligations generated by the ratification of the NATO treaty. Imagine a recent immigrant to the United States who is indignant at the thought that any of his hard-earned money should be used to help America fulfill its NATO obligations. "My family," he complains, "came to this country well after the United States ratified the NATO treaty. What logic would require me to help pay the costs involved in fulfilling obligations that resulted from actions taken long before my family came to these shores?" I doubt very much that anyone, regardless of their views on slave reparations, would have much sympathy with this immigrant's complaint. The answer to his question should be obvious: the logic that requires the recent immigrant to bear his fair share of the burdens involved in America's fulfilling its obligations is simply the logic of citizenship. When you freely choose to become a citizen of a country, that is, you incur a duty to help your country fulfill all of its obligations, including those obligations that it incurred before you arrived. This includes having some of your tax money go to paying off a national debt that you had nothing to do with generating, paying to fund programs that were adopted before you were born, and so on.[52] But given that this is so, the logic of citizenship provides a cogent answer to the question at the heart of Horowitz's fourth objection to slave reparations. Why must the recent immigrant contribute to reparations for harms that were committed long before he came to America? Because accepting the burden of helping your country to fulfill its obligations, even those that it incurred long before you were born, is part of what it is to be a citizen. If the fact that the government harmed past generations of black Americans means that it has an obligation to benefit the current generation of black Americans, then, the fact that the harms occurred long before the recent immigrant arrived will provide no reason to think that the recent immigrant would not be obligated to pay his fair share of the costs involved in the government's discharging that obligation.

Faulty Precedents

Horowitz's fifth objection maintains that there's a morally relevant difference between uncontroversial cases of reparations in general and the controversial case of slave reparations in particular. In the uncontroversial cases, such as the reparations that the United States eventually made to Japanese Americans who were wrongfully detained during the Second World War, the reparations benefits were given to the direct victims of the wrongful treatment or to the victims' immediate families. This would not be so in the case of slave reparations, and Horowitz maintains that this fact deprives the reparations position of its credibility. As he put the point in his ad:[53]

V

The Historical Precedents Used to Justify the Reparations Claim Do Not Apply, and the Claim Itself Is Based on Race Not Injury.

The historical precedents generally invoked to justify the reparations claim are payments to Jewish survivors of the Holocaust, Japanese-Americans and African-American victims of racial experiments in Tuskegee, or racial outrages in Rosewood and Oklahoma City. But in each case, the recipients of reparations were the direct victims of the injustice or their immediate families. This would be the only case of reparations to people who were not immediately affected and whose sole qualification to receive reparations would be racial. During the slavery era, many blacks were free men or slave-owners themselves, yet the reparations claimants make no attempt to take this fact into account. If this is not racism, what is?

Once again, Horowitz seems to succeed in identifying a problem with a certain kind of defense of slave reparations.[54] In this case, the argument in question appeals to the claim that slave reparations should be made because they are suitably analogous to other cases in which the legitimacy of reparations is widely accepted. We might call this the argument from historical precedent: since Holocaust reparations are widely accepted, for example, then if slave reparations are relevantly like Holocaust reparations, then slave reparations should be accepted, too. This represents yet another popular argument among defenders of the reparations position.[55]

Horowitz's fifth objection to slave reparations clearly poses a problem for the argument from historical precedent. Since it identifies a significant difference between slave reparations, on the one hand, and less controversial cases of reparations, on the other, we can't in good faith conclude that reparations are justified in the former case merely because they are justified in the latter cases. But, once again, Horowitz's objection still fails to pose a problem for the compensation argument. None of the steps in the compensation argument invoke historical precedents as a justification for the argument's conclusion. So even if Horowitz is correct in maintaining that the examples he cites are poor precedents for slave reparations, this fact does nothing to undermine the compensation argument.

In addition, the compensation argument explicitly accounts for the fact that slave reparations would go to people who were not the direct victims of slavery and its aftermath. The third step in the argument, what I referred to as "the causal claim," justifies the move from a debt to the original victims to a debt to currently living black Americans by maintaining that the acts by which previous generations of Africans and African Americans were wrongfully harmed through the institution of slavery and its aftermath continue to cause harmful consequences for black Americans today. This causal claim, of course, could be challenged. Indeed, as we will see in his sixth objection, Horowitz finds the claim unconvincing. But given that the causal claim is in fact a part of the compensation argument, the compensation argument need not depend on the claim that the case of slave reparations is just like the less controversial cases of reparations that involve compensation to the immediate victims of past wrongdoing. And since the compensation argument need not depend on such comparisons, it can't be undermined by Horowitz's fifth objection.

Before moving on to Horowitz's sixth objection, it's worth making two final observations about his fifth. The first is that at the very end of the objection, he manages to squeeze in an additional and seemingly unrelated point: that many black people in America during the era of slavery were not slaves. Horowitz complains that defenders of the reparations position make no attempt to take this fact into account. But there is no need for the compensation argument to take this fact into account. The argument depends on the claim that slavery and its aftermath was pervasive enough to have caused lingering harms to the currently living generation of black Americans. And that claim is consistent with the fact that many black people in America during the era of slavery were not slaves – although it's well worth remembering the many respects in which they were also not the legal equal of white people in America.

The second point is that although he does not explicitly say so in his fifth objection, Horowitz seems plainly to accept that reparations are in fact justified in cases, such as those involving Japanese Americans who were wrongly detained during the Second World War, in which the reparations are aimed directly at the immediate victims of the wrongful treatment. But given what Horowitz himself says about slave reparations in his fourth objection, this apparent concession should seem quite surprising. If his fourth objection to slave reparations is accepted, after all, then it would seem that a recent immigrant to the United States would be entitled to make the following complaint: "My family came to this country well after the United States wrongly detained Japanese Americans during the Second World War. What logic would require me to help pay the costs involved in making reparations for harms that occurred long before my family came to these shores?" But even Horowitz doesn't seem to think that this would count as a reasonable objection to Japanese-American reparations. And given that this is so, it's hard to see how even Horowitz could think that his fourth objection could count as a reasonable objection to slave reparations.[56]

In any event, Horowitz's fifth objection clearly poses no problem for the compensation argument in particular. And so halfway through Horowitz's ten famous objections to slave reparations, the result is that we have three reasons to reject the bloodlines argument, one reason to reject the unjust enrichment argument, one reason to reject the argument from historical precedent, but no reason at all to reject the compensation argument.

Failures of Individual Character

My strategy so far has been to show that while Horowitz's objections to slave reparations may count as good reasons to reject other arguments for slave reparations, they aren't relevant to the compensation argument that inadvertently turned me into an advocate of the reparations position. This approach, however, won't work in the case of Horowitz's sixth objection. His sixth objection, unlike any of the first five, is aimed directly at a key component of the compensation argument itself: the claim that past acts that caused wrongful harms to previous generations of Africans and African Americans continue to have lingering negative consequences for the currently existing generation of black Americans. This is what I referred to as step three of the compensation argument, the causal claim that justifies the move from past claimants to present claimants. Horowitz's sixth objection attempts to raise a doubt about this step in the argument, and if the doubt is sustained, then the compensation argument must be rejected. If currently living black Americans are not suffering the lingering consequences of the past wrongful acts involved in slavery and its aftermath, after all, then there's nothing associated with those past acts for them to be compensated for.

When I first introduced the causal claim as step three of the compensation argument, I attempted to provide support for it by appealing to two relatively uncontroversial claims: that black Americans, on average, are not doing as well as are white Americans, on average, and that there's no credible explanation for this discrepancy that involves appealing to genetic racial differences. If black Americans aren't doing as well as white Americans and if genetic differences don't account for this fact, I suggested, then it seems that the best explanation for the fact that black Americans are doing less well on average must be that they inhabit a more hostile social environment than do white Americans on average. And since the most plausible explanation of this difference in social environments seems clearly to involve the legacy of slavery and its aftermath, I concluded, this seems to show that the past wrongful acts committed by our nation's government do, indeed, continue to exert a powerful negative influence on the lives of its present black citizens.

Horowitz, however, can be understood as rejecting this kind of argument for the causal claim by proposing an alternative explanation of the difference between white and black average levels of well-being: it isn't because black people are genetically inferior to white people that they lag behind them, on his account, but neither is it because black Americans are hampered by the legacy of slavery and its aftermath. Many black Americans today are doing just fine, he points out, and so the best explanation for why others are not isn't that they're being held back by their genes or that they're being held back by their history, but rather that they're being held back by what he calls "failures of individual character." As Horowitz puts it:[57]

VI

The Reparations Argument Is Based on the Unsubstantiated Claim That All African-Americans Suffer from the Economic Consequences of Slavery and Discrimination.

No scientific attempt has been made to prove that living individuals have been adversely affected by a slave system that was ended nearly 150 years ago. But there is plenty of evidence that the hardships of slavery were hardships that individuals could and did overcome. The black middle class in America is a prosperous community that is now larger in absolute terms than the black underclass. Its existence suggests that present economic adversity is the result of failures of individual character rather than the lingering after-effects of racial discrimination or a slave system that ceased to exist well over a century ago. West Indian blacks in America are also descended from slaves but their average incomes are equivalent to the average incomes of white (and nearly 25 percent higher than the average incomes of American-born blacks). How is it that slavery adversely affected one large group of descendants but not the other? How can government be expected to decide an issue that is so subjective?

The key claim here is that the "present economic adversity" in question is the result of "failures of individual character" rather than of the "lingering after-effects" of slavery and its aftermath.[58] And the key argument for the truth of this claim is that the existence of a thriving black middle class "suggests" that the claim is true.

The problem with Horowitz's objection here is simple. The existence of a flourishing black middle class by itself provides no reason to deny that black Americans on the whole continue to be harmed by the lingering effects of slavery and its aftermath. Even if it's true that the existence of successful black Americans counts as evidence that those black Americans who fail to thrive do so because of a failure of individual character, the appeal to character flaws as an explanation for their "present economic adversity" fails to provide a genuine alternative to the two explanations for such adversity that we've already considered: the explanation that appeals to genetic differences between black and white people and the explanation that claims that black Americans are continuing to suffer from the lingering effects of slavery and its aftermath. Instead of providing such an alternative explanation, in fact, Horowitz's proposal simply pushes the question back a step. If his suggestion is correct, after all, if black Americans on the whole really are doing considerably less well than are white Americans on the whole because so many black Americans suffer from failures of individual character, then it must be the case that black Americans suffer from failures of individual character at a considerably higher rate than do white Americans. And if this is really true, then an explanation of the current disparity between black and white American average levels of well-being that appeals to failures of individual character will have to provide an answer to this question: why do black Americans suffer from failures of individual character at a considerably higher rate than do their white counterparts?

It's hard to see how we could answer this further question without appealing to one or the other of the two kinds of explanation that we started with and to which Horowitz's proposal was supposed to provide an alternative: either the account will have to maintain that black Americans have character flaws at a disproportionately higher rate than white Americans because black people are genetically more disposed to have such flaws, or it will have to maintain that they do so for reasons that can be traced to differences in their social environment – differences which, in turn, can be traced to the damaging legacy of slavery and its aftermath. If so many black Americans are unsuccessful because they're too lazy to overcome the burdens that successful black Americans have overcome, for example, then Horowitz's account will have to insist that black people are genetically more prone to such laziness than white people, or it will have to appeal to claim that the legacy of slavery and its aftermath has exerted a more discouraging effect on black Americans than it has on white Americans. Horowitz clearly does not mean to be appealing to claims about genetic differences between black and white people. But given that this is so, and given that he provides no other explanation for why so many more black Americans would suffer from what he considers to be failures of individual character, we seem to be left with only one reasonable conclusion: if black Americans really are more likely to suffer from failures of individual character than are white Americans, this discrepancy must be due to the lingering and discouraging consequences of slavery and its aftermath.

As for the question of why the American descendants of those who were enslaved in West India don't seem to be disadvantaged by the legacy of slavery today in the same way that the American descendants of Africans who were enslaved in America seem to be, there are a number of possible answers. Slavery was abolished in the British empire several decades before it was abolished in the United States, for example, and after it was abolished, West Indians enjoyed a wide range of voting rights and other freedoms that were denied to most black Americans during the long reign of Jim Crow.[59] Recent immigrants from the West Indies, that is, come from a background much further removed from slavery and legalized segregation and discrimination than do black Americans. There were, in addition, important differences between the way that slavery was typically practiced in the United States and the way that it was typically practiced in the West Indies. In the United States, for example, the amount of food that slaves received was usually unrelated to the value of the goods that they helped to produce. In the West Indies, on the other hand, although slaves were also required to provide the requisite labor, they were able to market the crops they grew by themselves.[60] The culture of slavery as practiced in the West Indies, that is, rewarded slaves for greater productivity in a way that the culture of slavery as practiced in the United States didn't. This, too, might help to account for the differences in the way that the legacy of slavery has affected the two populations. And the West Indians who came to this country were those with the ambition and resources to freely immigrate, another factor that may help to explain the differences between present-day American descendants of the two groups.[61]

There is, in fact, a sizeable literature on this very question containing a number of additional possible answers. But a defender of the compensation argument need not choose between them in order to successfully respond to this final element of Horowitz's sixth objection. All that needs to be said is that Horowitz's own suggestion, that in the case of black Americans of African descent it is failures of individual character that are to blame for their lagging behind West Indian immigrants rather than the legacy of slavery in America and its aftermath, leads us right back to the same problem with his objection: if Horowitz's position is to depend on the claim that African Americans display such character flaws so much more frequently than do American immigrants from the West Indies, then his position will require an account of why this is so. And there will again seem to be only two possible answers: either Horowitz will have to claim that people of African descent are genetically prone to have such defects at a higher rate than are people of West Indian descent, or he will have to appeal to the existence of some difference in the social backgrounds of the two groups that accounts for the difference. Horowitz again is clearly not maintaining that there are genetic differences between the two groups that account for the differences. But given that this is so, and given that he provides no other explanation for why so many more Americans of African descent would suffer from what he considers to be failures of individual character relative to the rate at which Americans of West Indian descent would suffer them, we seem to be left with only one reasonable conclusion: if Americans of African descent really are more likely to suffer from failures of individual character than are Americans of West Indian descent, this discrepancy must be because differences between the slave experience in America and the slave experience in the West Indies are responsible for the differences in the legacies they have left even if we can't say precisely which differences are responsible.

When Horowitz suggests that the current problems facing black America are caused by failures of individual character "rather than" by the lingering consequences of slavery and its aftermath, then, he appeals to a false dichotomy. The correct explanation for the current state of affairs need not appeal to one factor rather than the other. It can appeal to both. And, indeed, the most plausible version of the explanation that appeals to the former factor is plausible only to the extent that it in turn appeals to the latter factor. Without some such explanation, after all, it would remain utterly mysterious why black Americans should suffer these failures of character at a higher rate than white Americans. In the end, then, Horowitz's sixth objection provides no good reason to reject the causal claim that constitutes the third step in the compensation argument for slave reparations, and thus no good reason to reject the argument itself.

The Victimization Message

Horowitz's seventh objection maintains that the slave reparations position generates a harmful message about black Americans:[62]

VII

The Reparations Claim Is One More Attempt to Turn African-Americans into Victims. It Sends a Damaging Message to the African-American Community and to Others.

The renewed sense of grievance – which is what the claim for reparations will inevitably create – is not a constructive or helpful message for black leaders to send to their communities and to others. To focus the social passions of African-Americans on what some other Americans may have done to their ancestors 50 or 150 years ago is to burden them with a crippling sense of victim-hood. How are the millions of non-black refugees from tyranny and genocide who are now living in America going to receive these claims, moreover, except as demands for special treatment – an extravagant new handout that is only necessary because some blacks can't seem to locate the ladder of opportunity within reach of others, many of whom are less privileged than themselves?

Horowitz also presses this point in the follow-up ad he took out in several papers, and it has been made by a number of other critics of the reparations position as well.[63]

This objection to the reparations position turns on a factual claim about what the overall effects of demanding reparations will be on the black American state of mind. It's hard to know how to determine whether or not the factual claim is true. It could be that the demand for reparations will on the whole have a negative effect on black self-esteem, as critics of reparations like Horowitz maintain. But it could also be that the demand for reparations will on the whole have a liberating and cathartic effect on the black American psyche, as defenders of reparations such as Robinson and McGary maintain.[64] Most likely, it will have some positive effects for those black Americans who will welcome the demand with relief and some negative effects for those who will resist the demand with resentment. If assessing the merits of the reparations position requires us to answer this difficult empirical question, then, the debate over reparations might well reach a stalemate at this point. Indeed, in his otherwise generally insightful point-by-point response to Horowitz's original advertisement, the maverick social critic Christopher Hitchens, who is rarely at a loss for words, offers a simple one-word reply to Horowitz's seventh objection: "Undecidable."[65]

Fortunately for the defender of the reparations position, however, Hitchens's uncharacteristic retreat to agnosticism is premature. For while the factual claim that Horowitz appeals to in pressing his seventh objection might turn out to raise difficulties for some arguments in favor of slave reparations, it does nothing to undermine the compensation argument in particular. And so the defender of the reparations position who bases his acceptance of the reparations position on the compensation argument can simply set aside the question of whether or not the factual claim underlying Horowitz's seventh objection is true.

Since the claim that the demand for reparations will have this unwanted victimizing effect seems to constitute one of the most widespread and deeply contested aspects of the reparations debate, my suggestion that in the end the claim is essentially irrelevant may seem a bit surprising. So let me point to a few reasons for thinking that this suggestion is nonetheless correct.

One way to confirm that Horowitz's seventh objection is irrelevant to the compensation argument is to remember that the compensation argument consists of five specific steps. If all five steps in the argument are accepted, then the conclusion that the reparations position is correct follows as a simple matter of logic. In order for an objection to the compensation argument to succeed, therefore, it must give us a reason to reject at least one of these five steps. Horowitz's sixth objection, for example, did pose a potential problem for the compensation argument because it threatened to undermine step three of the argument, the causal claim. And so a simple way to test the relevance of Horowitz's seventh objection is to go back through each of the five steps in the compensation argument and, after reviewing each step, ask whether Horowitz's seventh objection gives any reason to doubt that the step in question is true. If you follow this procedure carefully, it should be clear that Horowitz's seventh objection fails this test each time. Even if everything he says in the seventh objection is true, that is, it provides no reason to deny the compensation principle (step one), the historical claim (step two), the causal claim (step three), the surviving public obligation principle (step four) or the unpaid balance claim (step five). But if the objection provides no reason to doubt any of the steps in the compensation argument, then it provides no reason to doubt the compensation argument itself.

A second way to see that Horowitz's seventh objection is irrelevant to the compensation argument is to notice that there is a difference between the claim that the United States does, in fact, have an obligation to make reparations to the currently living generation of black Americans, and the claim that it would be a good idea for black Americans to devote their time and energy to demanding such reparations. The compensation argument offers a defense of the first claim, while Horowitz's seventh objection is directed only at the second claim. But even if the second claim turned out to be false, this would provide no reason to deny that the first claim is true. The fact that it would be a bad idea for someone to ask for something, after all, does not by itself establish that they are not entitled to receive it. If a vicious bully stole your bicycle, for example, it might be a bad idea for you to demand that he return it, but surely you would have a right that he return it nonetheless. And so, again, even if what Horowitz says in his seventh objection turns out to be correct, it will do nothing to undermine the compensation argument.

Finally, it may help to focus for a moment on a specific example that illustrates the problem underlying Horowitz's seventh objection. So suppose that you're a member of the jury in a medical malpractice case. It's clear to you from all of the evidence and testimony that the doctor in question is, indeed, responsible for having negligently caused his patient to lose one of his legs and that the patient has, indeed, incurred a variety of costs as a result. Taking into account the costs of the additional medical treatment that was subsequently required, of the prosthetic leg he was eventually forced to buy, the loss of future wages resulting from his disability and other relevant costs, you've been convinced that the patient has incurred a million dollars in overall harm as a result of the doctor's negligent actions. But it has also become clear to you over the course of the trial that the patient has developed a terrible victim complex and that voting to award him the damages will only serve to reinforce this self-image. If the jury finds that the doctor did nothing wrong, that is, this will convince the patient that the incident was just the result of bad luck, but if the jury finds that the doctor was negligent, this will convince the patient that he was a victim of a real injustice. And he will find it much harder to get on with his life if he is convinced that his disability was the result of a real injustice. You have come to believe, in short, that awarding the patient compensation for the damages that you think the doctor wrongfully caused him will itself be damaging to the patient's psyche.

People might respond to this case in one of two ways, but either of them will suffice to bring out the problem with Horowitz's seventh objection. The most straightforward response would be to say that you must vote to award damages to the plaintiff. This strikes me as the correct response, and I suspect that many people, regardless of their view of slave reparations, would agree. If the doctor really is responsible for the costs that the patient has incurred, on this account, then justice requires that the patient be awarded the compensation even if this will in turn have the unfortunate consequence of validating his identification of himself as a victim. And if this is the appropriate response to the malpractice case, then it should be clear precisely why Horowitz's seventh objection is unsuccessful: if black Americans today really are owed compensation for the harms that they have wrongfully suffered as a result of previous injustices, then justice requires that they be awarded the compensation owed to them even if this will have a damaging effect on their self-esteem. The compensation argument provides good reason to believe that black Americans today really are owed such compensation, and since if they really are owed such compensation then justice will require that they receive it even if this will increase their sense of victimhood, Horowitz's seventh objection will therefore provide no reason to reject the compensation argument.[66]

But a number of people may respond to the case differently. If the damage that would be caused by reinforcing the patient's sense of victimhood would be sufficiently great, they may well insist that it would be wrong to make the doctor pay for the costs that the patient incurred. If, in particular, awarding damages to the patient would leave him even worse off in the end than would voting not to award damages, they may maintain that the right thing to do would be to vote against awarding damages. And if one believed that the sense of grievance at the heart of Horowitz's seventh objection would be sufficiently harmful to black Americans, they might then think that the right thing to do would be to oppose slave reparations for the same reason.

But even if one responds to the malpractice case by concluding that the doctor should not be made to compensate his patient for the harms the he wrongly caused his patient to incur, this response will not help to salvage Horowitz's seventh objection to the reparations position. This is because the claim that the doctor should not be made to compensate his patient in the case where doing so will ultimately harm the patient does nothing to undermine the claim that the doctor nonetheless does have a genuine obligation to compensate his patient in this case. Indeed, this second response to the case is much more plausibly understood as arising from the belief that the doctor does have an obligation to make his patient better off, but that due to the unfortunate circumstances surrounding the case, there is no way for him to meet this obligation.

Suitably applied to the case of slave reparations, then, this second response to the malpractice case implies that the federal government really does have a moral obligation to benefit black Americans today because of the wrongful harms that were inflicted by slavery and its aftermath, but that the prospective costs of increasing the sense of victimhood among the black American community are so high that there is simply no way for the government to meet this obligation. The claim that the prospective costs associated with trying to make reparations make it literally impossible for the government to improve the lives of black Americans on the whole strikes me as extremely implausible. And Horowitz has certainly offered no evidence for it. But even if it does turn out to be true, this will at most establish that there is no way for the government to meet the obligation that it has to benefit the present generation of black Americans, not that the government has no such obligation. And since the claim made by the reparations position is the claim that the United States government has a moral obligation to benefit the current generation of black Americans because of the wrongful harms that were inflicted on past generations of Africans and African Americans by the institution of slavery and its aftermath, this concession, even if Horowitz could find some way to force the defender of reparations to make it, would do nothing to undermine the reparations position itself.[67]

The Check's Already in the Mail

Horowitz's eighth objection to slave reparations is like his sixth objection and unlike the seventh and the first five in that it does, indeed, challenge a particular step in the compensation argument. This is step five, what I called the unpaid balance claim, the claim that the U.S. government has not yet fully compensated the currently living generation of black Americans for the harms that they continue to suffer as a result of the legacy of slavery and its aftermath. Pointing to the advent of affirmative action and to the vast amounts of money that have been spent on various social programs since the successes of the civil rights movement in the first half of the 1960s, Horowitz simply denies that this is true:[68]

VIII

Reparations To African Americans Have Already Been Paid.

Since the passage of the Civil Rights Acts and the advent of the Great Society in 1965, trillions of dollars in transfer payments have been made to African-Americans in the form of welfare benefits and racial preferences (in contracts, job placements and educational admissions) – all under the rationale of redressing historic racial grievances. It is said that reparations are necessary to achieve a healing between African-Americans and other Americans. If trillion-dollar restitutions and a wholesale rewriting of American law (in order to accommodate racial preferences) is not enough to achieve a "healing," what is?

In his book on the subject, Horowitz supports this characterization of the money that has already been spent by the federal government by quoting from Lyndon Johnson's famous 1965 commencement address at Howard University. In that speech, Johnson said that the problems facing black America "are solely and simply the consequence of ancient brutality, past injustice, and present prejudice" and argued that "they must be faced and they must be dealt with and they must be overcome." From this, Horowitz concludes that "nearly forty years ago the American government set out on exactly the path of repairing the wrong of slavery and its legacies, an effort that Robinson and the reparationists stubbornly deny was ever attempted."[69]

But as supporters and opponents of reparations alike should surely agree, the question is not whether the government has ever "attempted" to make "an effort" to provide reparations, but whether it has actually succeeded in making reparations. If I vandalize your car and then try valiantly but unsuccessfully to repair the damage I have caused, after all, then I continue to owe you compensation for the harm even if I've already spent a great deal of time and money in my failed attempts to fix the damage. And this is where Horowitz's objection to the fifth step in the compensation argument becomes quite puzzling. For while he points to all of the money that has been spent on various social programs as evidence for the claim that "reparations to African Americans have already been paid," he also maintains in his book that these programs have been dismal failures: "welfare programs devised by well-intentioned social reformers," he writes, "not only did not reduce black poverty, but exacerbated and deepened it."[70] Horowitz's considered position, then, seems to be that while the United States government has tried to make things better for black Americans in recent decades, it has in fact made things worse. But this means that while the government has attempted to make reparations to black Americans, it has not yet succeeded in doing so. And if it has not yet succeeded in doing so, then step five of the compensation argument must be accepted, and Horowitz's eighth objection must be rejected.[71]

This assessment of the merits of Horowitz's eighth objection, moreover, stands regardless of whether one accepts Horowitz's claim that welfare programs have ultimately failed to help the people they have aimed to benefit. If, as Horowitz maintains, such programs do more harm than good, then it's clear that reparations have not yet been made. But even if such programs ultimately do more good than harm for those they aim to benefit, it still doesn't follow that reparations have thereby been made. It follows that, through a variety of transfer payment programs, the federal government has done a good deal to help a good number of black Americans in need. But it also follows that the very same programs have also done a good deal to help a good number of white Americans in need. Since the aim of reparations is to compensate the current generation of black Americans by reducing the gap between black and white average levels of well-being, welfare programs that help poor black Americans but also help poor white Americans can't count as forms of reparations, even if they are successful, unless they direct resources in a significantly disproportionate manner toward black Americans. Otherwise, it would make as much sense to say that reparations to black Americans have been made because black Americans benefit greatly from the services provided by the United States Postal Service, the armed forces, the space program, or the National Parks.

Horowitz may simply be assuming that welfare benefits mostly go to black Americans, but he provides no evidence that this is so, and the evidence that's available seems clearly to indicate that they don't, in fact, significantly close the gap between black and white average levels of well-being. A study by poverty experts Sheldon Danziger and Peter Gottschalk, for example, found that "nonwhites are more likely to be pretransfer poor and hence eligible for income transfers. However, conditional on their demographic group and pretransfer poverty, they are only slightly more likely than whites to receive transfers. Moreover, despite the fact that their pretransfer incomes are further below their poverty line than those of whites, they receive smaller amounts of cash transfers on average" and concluded: "Thus, transfer programs are not reallocating resources disproportionately to the nonwhite poor."[72] Whether ultimately successful or unsuccessful in benefiting those they aim to help, then, the fact that the government has spent a lot of money on a variety of welfare programs fails to support the claim that the government has already made reparations to the current generation of black Americans.

Finally, even if it turned out that federal money spent on welfare programs was significantly closing the gap between black and white levels of average well-being, this still would not be enough to show that reparations had already been made. Federal welfare programs are intended and carried out as needs based, after all, and helping people because they need help doesn't by itself count as a form of compensation even if some of the people that you end up helping are people you previously harmed. If I donate some money to a soup kitchen, for example, and if some of the people my money ends up helping to feed are people whose cars I previously vandalized, the benefits they received as a result of my donation would not count toward the compensation that I would owe them for vandalizing their cars.[73] In the end, then, Horowitz's eighth objection also proves to be unsuccessful.

White Sacrifice, Black Ingratitude

Horowitz's ninth objection attempts to turn the tables on the reparations position, focusing not on what America owes to its black citizens, but on what its black citizens owe to America:[74]

IX
What about the Debt Blacks Owe to America?

Slavery existed for thousands of years before the Atlantic slave trade, and in all societies. But in the thousand years of slavery's existence, there never was an anti-slavery movement until white Anglo-Saxon Christians created one. If not for the anti-slavery beliefs and military power of white Englishmen and Americans, the slave trade would not have been brought to an end. If not for the sacrifices of white soldiers and a white American president who gave his life to sign the Emancipation Proclamation, blacks in America would still be slaves. If not for the dedication of Americans of all ethnicities and colors to a society based on the principle that all men are created equal, blacks in America would not enjoy the highest standard of living of blacks anywhere in the world, and indeed one of the highest standards of living of any people in the world. They would not enjoy the greatest freedoms and the most thoroughly protected individual rights anywhere. Where is the acknowledgment of black America and its leaders for those gifts?

Defenders of the reparations position, on this account, have simply gotten things backward.[75]

While it's easy to understand the point that Horowitz is raising here, it's hard to see how it could pose a problem for the compensation argument. Black Americans on the whole do, indeed, have much to be grateful for. But so do many people who are nonetheless entitled to compensation for the wrongful harms that they have incurred. Consider, for example, a worker who is fortunate enough to work for the very best company in his profession. His salary and benefits are tops in the field, his working conditions are the envy of his peers, and he genuinely loves what he does. One day, though, it's discovered that the company has been negligent in allowing a modest amount of some banned chemical substance to circulate in the air in his office, and that this is responsible for the occasional nausea and headaches that he has experienced over the past several years. This worker is, on the whole, extremely fortunate to work for this company. Even taking into account the occasional nausea and headaches, his overall quality of life is considerably higher than it would be if he worked anyplace else. Still, as both supporters and opponents of slave reparations would surely agree, this fact doesn't mean that the company owes him no compensation for the harms that it's responsible for having caused him to suffer. Being the best place to work overall doesn't insulate a company from liability for whatever wrongful harms it might nonetheless be responsible for causing. And so the same must be true in the case of the controversy over slave reparations. Even if it's true that black people on the whole enjoy a higher standard of living in America than they do anywhere else and that they should be grateful for this fact, the fact itself does nothing to undermine the claim that America nonetheless owes reparations for whatever harms black Americans on the whole continue to suffer as a result of the legacy of slavery and its aftermath. Horowitz's ninth objection, then, like the first eight, gives no reason to reject the compensation argument for slave reparations.

They Hate Us, They Really Hate Us

Last but not least – well, actually, last and, in addition, least – Horowitz's tenth objection strikes an uncharacteristically low blow, aiming not so much at any particular argument in favor of slave reparations as at the people like me who find the arguments for the reparations position to be persuasive ones. The charge, simply put, is that those people who are pro-reparations are for that reason anti-American. As he puts it in his famous ad's concluding paragraphs:[76]

X

The Reparations Claim Is A Separatist Idea That Sets African-Americans against the Nation That Gave Them Freedom.

Blacks were here before the Mayflower. Who is more American than the descendants of African slaves? For the African-American community to isolate itself from America is to embark on a course whose implications are troubling. Yet the African-American community has had a long-running flirtation with separatists, nationalists and the political left, who want African-Americans to be no part of America's social contract. African-Americans should reject this temptation.

For all America's faults, African-Americans have an enormous stake in this country and its heritage. It is this heritage that is really under attack by the reparations movement. The reparations claim is one more assault on America, conducted by racial separatists and the political left. It is an attack not only on white Americans, but on all Americans – especially African-Americans.

America's African-American citizens are the richest and most privileged black people alive, a bounty that is a direct result of the heritage that is under assault. The American idea needs the support of its African-American citizens. But African-Americans also need the support of the American idea. For it is the American idea that led to the principles and created the institutions that have set African-Americans – and all of us – free.

And in his second ad, the point is, if anything, put even more bluntly. Horowitz there writes that "a personal hostility towards the United States" is "what animates the reparations movement"[77] and he characterizes the movement as a whole as one that arises from "an irrational fear and hatred of America."[78]

This final objection to the reparations position strikes me as unsuccessful for two reasons. First, the claim that people who favor slave reparations hate the United States is unfounded. No one insists that people who supported Japanese American reparations hated America, for example, and I see no reason to treat the two cases differently in this respect. The slave reparations position, like the Japanese American reparations position, amounts not to an attack on our nation's heritage as a whole, but rather to a principled response to a part of our nation's heritage that is genuinely shameful. Just as it takes a big person to admit a mistake and attempt to make amends for it, so it takes a great country to admit a past wrong and attempt to make reparations for it. It therefore seems reasonable to view the reparations position as arising from a laudable concern that America find an honorable way to close the book on a dishonorable chapter of its past, rather than from a spiteful disdain for America itself. It's because some people care about this country and identify with it that they want very much to see it do right by those it has wronged. That, at least, is why the reparations position makes sense to me.

But suppose for the sake of the argument that I'm mistaken about this, and that every single defender of the reparations position, myself included, is driven by a pathological hatred for the United States. Even if this is true, it still provides no reason to reject the compensation argument for reparations, or any other argument for reparations, for that matter. The reason for this is simple: You can't judge the quality of an argument by looking at the quality of the person offering it. Kind, well-meaning people can end up misguidedly endorsing unsound arguments, and cruel, hateful people can end up adopting surprisingly sound arguments despite themselves. The question that ultimately matters, then, is not whether defenders of slave reparations are bad people, but whether they have been appealing to bad arguments. And since Horowitz's tenth and final objection does nothing to address any of the arguments for reparations, it does nothing to suggest that any of the arguments for reparations, the compensation argument or any other, are unsound.

We've now taken a careful look at all ten of David Horowitz's famous objections to slave reparations. If my analysis has been correct, then while a number of Horowitz's objections may well pose problems for a number of arguments in defense of the reparations position, none of them in the end provide a reason to reject the compensation argument that eventually turned me into a believer in the reparations position. The question that remains, then, is whether there are any other objections to the compensation argument that might succeed where Horowitz's objections all turn out to fail. I will turn to that question in Chapter 3.

3

Advancing the Slave Reparations Debate

Bonus Objections, Bonus Responses, and a Modest Proposal

In Chapter 2, I tried to help repair the reparations debate. I argued that too many defenders of the reparations position devote too much of their energies to defending the unjust enrichment argument, and that while that argument isn't as bad as some people think it is, it isn't good enough to justify the reparations position either. And I argued that a better alternative was available in what I called the compensation argument, an argument that's strong enough to overcome all ten of David Horowitz's famous objections to slave reparations. In this chapter, I want to try to advance the debate further by turning to the question of whether there are any other objections to the compensation argument that might succeed where Horowitz's objections fail. Since the compensation argument consists of five steps, it seems plausible to suppose that if there is such an objection, it will be one that gives us a reason to reject one of these five steps. As a result, I'll begin my consideration of additional objections to the reparations position in this chapter by going back through these five steps in order before turning to some further objections that can't be readily understood as objections to any one step of the argument in particular.

GOVERNMENTS AREN'T PEOPLE

Step one of the compensation argument endorses what I called the compensation principle. When I first introduced this principle, I presented it in general terms by saying that if someone wrongfully harms another person, then he incurs a moral obligation to compensate his victim for the harms that he has wrongfully caused. Horowitz didn't raise any doubts about this step in the argument and, so far as I am aware, neither have any other critics of the reparations position. People on both sides of the reparations debate generally accept the view that when you wrongfully harm someone, you owe them some kind of compensation as a result. And so, I concluded, step one of the compensation argument is perfectly secure.

In order to apply the compensation principle to the case of the United States government in particular, though, I was later forced to specify that the principle applies not just to cases in which individual people wrongfully harm others, but also to cases in which governments, through the authorized acts of their public officials, do. And a critic of the compensation argument might complain that this subtle shift in the discussion amounts to an objectionable kind of sleight of hand. Just because the version of the principle that I started out with is uncontroversial, this critic might object, doesn't mean that the version I ended up with is uncontroversial as well. Not every principle that applies to private individuals, after all, applies to governments. Governments are not people. And so perhaps step one of the compensation argument should be rejected after all, if not in its initial generic formulation, then at least in the more specific formulation that's required in order for the compensation argument as a whole to be successful.

There is some merit to this complaint. By introducing the compensation principle in terms of cases like the one in which I wrongfully damage your car and now uncontroversially owe you compensation, I took advantage of the fact that the simplest cases often yield the strongest intuitions. And moral principles that apply to individual people don't always apply, or apply in the same way, to national governments. But while this complaint is therefore certainly worth airing, in the end it poses no real problem for the compensation argument. If necessary, I can simply modify the kind of defense I offered the principle to take this difference into account, and the result will still be a claim that virtually everyone on both sides of the slave reparations debate will surely accept. If the President signed an executive order which authorized the FBI to vandalize your car, for example, virtually everyone would agree that the government would owe you compensation as a result. Indeed, it's hard to imagine anyone who would be content with a state of affairs in which the government could wrongfully harm people at will without then having to do anything to repair the damage it caused. And as I noted at several points in the previous chapter, even most opponents of slave reparations accept the legitimacy of reparations that the government made to the specific Japanese-American victims of the internment camps in the Second World War. Even when step one of the compensation argument is formulated to make more clear that it includes governments and not just private individuals within its scope, then, the result should still prove to be acceptable to people on both sides of the reparations debate.

FORGIVE THE FOUNDING FATHERS, FOR THEY KNEW NOT WHAT THEY DID

The second step in the compensation argument strikes me as equally uncontroversial. This is what I referred to as the historical claim, the claim that previous generations of Americans wrongfully harmed previous generations of Africans and African Americans through the institution of slavery and its aftermath and that, more specifically, the United States government wrongfully harmed previous generations of Africans and African Americans by supporting the institution of slavery and subsequent forms of legalized segregation and discrimination.

None of Horowitz's ten objections attack this step in the compensation argument either, and, in general, other opponents of slave reparations have conceded it as well. The fact that slavery and the various forms of public segregation and discrimination that followed did in fact exist and were in fact harmful is a matter of public record, after all, and very few people today would deny that these practices were morally wrong. Still, I'm aware of two ways in which at least some opponents of slave reparations might be understood as denying this second step in the compensation argument. I will therefore consider them in turn.

The first way of attacking step two of the compensation argument involves appealing to the claim that while we now know that slavery was wrong, the people who participated in it didn't know it at the time. This point is seldom raised in the literature on the subject, but it often comes up when the issue is discussed in class. Students who would never think to excuse Hitler or Stalin or Mao as a product of their times frequently try to accommodate Washington, Jefferson, and Franklin in just this way. Yes, they owned slaves, these critics acknowledge, and, yes, we now understand that owning slaves is wrong, but people didn't know that at the time and so they shouldn't be blamed for it. And if they shouldn't be blamed for what they did, of course, then how can we owe compensation for what they did as a result?

There are two problems with this "product of their times" objection to the compensation argument. The first problem is that it's not really true that slavery was generally considered to be an acceptable form of behavior at the time that the United States was founded. As the distinguished Yale historian David Brion Davis has noted, "By the eve of the American Revolution, there was a remarkable convergence of culture and intellectual development which at once undercut traditional rationalizations for slavery and offered new ways of identifying with its victims."[1] When they declared their independence in 1776, after all, the American Colonists were subjects of the British Empire, and England had abolished the practice of slavery on its shores several years earlier when Lord Mansfield, chief justice of the King's Bench, had ruled in the case of James Somersett, an African slave who had been brought by his master from Virginia to England, that "as soon as any slave sets foot upon English territory, he becomes free."[2] Certainly the Colonists understood this fact. Moreover, by the time that the United States Constitution was ratified in 1789, most of the Northern states had abolished slavery as well. Indeed, this was precisely the reason that slavery was such a contentious issue at the Constitutional Convention. In addition, many of the Founding Fathers privately or publicly expressed deep reservations about the practice, despite the fact that many of them participated in it. In a personal letter to a prominent abolitionist, for example, Patrick Henry wrote that he admired the Quakers "for their noble effort to abolish slavery. It is equally calculated to promote moral and political good."[3] Referring to the prospect that adopting the Constitution would preserve the institution of slavery, Virginian George Mason warned that "Providence punishes national sins by national calamities."[4] And Thomas Jefferson himself, in an early draft of the Declaration of Independence, denounced the slave trade. Although the passage was later voted out by the Continental Congress, Jefferson deliberately saved it in his personal papers and included it in the autobiography he was working on.[5] By nonetheless adopting a constitutional form of government in which they agreed to guarantee the rights of slave owners in the Southern states to secure the return of those slaves who escaped to the North, then, the Founding Fathers acted to protect and support an institution that many people at the time clearly understood to be wrong. Indeed, Horowitz himself, at one point in his book, inadvertently comes to the defense of the reparations position on this particular point, maintaining that the men who drafted the language of the Constitution deliberately used wording that avoided the terms "slave" and "black" to hammer out this agreement precisely because "the Framers believed that slavery was a dying and immoral institution."[6] And if they really did believe this, of course, then the factual claim underlying the "product of their times" objection is simply false.

But there's a second and more fundamental problem with this objection. For suppose that the people who endorsed a Constitution that legally protected slavery, who actively enforced the Fugitive Slave Acts, and so on, honestly had no idea that what they were doing was wrong. Even if this is so, it would still fail to undermine the compensation argument. The reason for this can be seen by simply looking back at what the compensation principle says. It doesn't say that if someone wrongfully harms another person, then he incurs a moral obligation to compensate his victim as long as he knows that what he is doing is wrong. It says that he owes compensation if his harmful act is wrong, period. This, moreover, is precisely as it should be. If I wrongfully harm you, after all, then I owe you compensation for the harm that I wrongfully cause you even if I honestly believed that my action wasn't wrong when I did it.

Suppose, for example, that I take your nice, new coat and shred it to pieces. This would clearly be wrong of me and I would clearly owe you compensation as a result. But now suppose that when I ripped your coat up, I honestly had no idea that what I was doing was wrong. Maybe I mistakenly confused your coat for one that I had bought last year at a thrift shop, or mistakenly believed that you had given up your right to ownership of the coat. No matter why I mistakenly believed I had the right to do what I did, I would still owe you compensation for having done it. This is a claim that virtually everyone on both sides of the slave reparations debate would surely accept. My ignorance of the wrongness of my behavior might be relevant to the question of whether I should be punished for it, or whether you should think poorly of me because of it, but it isn't relevant to the question of whether you're entitled to have me compensate you for the loss of your coat. The fact that a person sincerely believes that he has the right to do something doesn't mean that he has the right to do it. Again, people on both sides of the slave reparations debate surely accept at least this much. And if I didn't have the right to do what I did, then you have the right to expect me to compensate you for the losses that I wrongfully imposed on you. But if all of this is true in the case of me wrongfully destroying your coat, then the same must be true of the previous generations of Americans whose actions wrongfully harmed previous generations of Africans and African Americans. Even if they sincerely believed that they had the right to do what they did, this doesn't mean that they did have the right to do what they did, and if they didn't have the right to do what they did, then their ignorance can't be used to undermine the compensation argument for slave reparations.

COULDN'T HAVE DONE OTHERWISE

A more subtle and less common way of attacking the second step of the compensation argument has been forcefully pressed by the philosopher George Schedler. The objection begins with the principle that "ought implies can." If I ought to perform some particular action, that is, then it must at least be possible for me to perform it. Given that it's not possible for you to draw a square circle, for example, you can't be morally obligated to draw one. The objection then attempts to apply this principle to the slave reparations debate by raising a question that participants on both sides of the debate rarely pause to consider: given the circumstances at the time of the founding of the Republic, was it really possible for the Colonists to have established a U.S. government that prohibited slavery? Could the delegates at the Constitutional Convention really have succeeded in getting the Constitution ratified if the Constitution had guaranteed full citizenship and equality for black Americans? To these questions, Schedler plausibly suggests that the answers are most likely no. But given the principle that ought implies can, this seems to have disastrous results for the second step of the compensation argument. If the Founding Fathers truly could not have adopted a Constitution that prohibited slavery, after all, and if once the Constitution was ratified, it effectively prevented the Congress and the president from doing anything about it either, then the Founding Fathers were not obligated to do anything to prevent slavery in the first place. And as Schedler then puts the problem that this poses for the reparations position, "if [the United States] could not have [abolished slavery] at certain times in American history, then it does not owe compensation for failing to do so from that time period (on the principle that one is obligated to do only what one can do)."[7]

There are three problems with this "ought implies can" objection to the compensation argument. The first is that the objection is too quick to conclude that the United States could not have been founded as a slavery-free country. At least some of the Southern colonies would almost certainly have refused to join if the Constitution had prohibited slavery, but most if not all of the rest of the colonies would probably have agreed to form a new, independent country. The United States would likely have had fewer states, at least at the beginning, but it could still have been successfully founded, and founded without slavery. In addition, it doesn't seem right to say that it would have been literally impossible for those who believed in slavery to be convinced to change their mind. It was highly unlikely that this would happen, of course, but that is not enough to justify appealing to the ought implies can principle. Every time that someone very strongly wants to do something wrong, for example, it's highly unlikely that they will refrain from doing it, but surely that can't be enough to justify denying that they ought to refrain from doing it. The principle says "ought implies can," after all, not "ought implies not very difficult to do." So strictly speaking, it doesn't seem right to say that it was impossible, in a strong enough sense of that term, for the country to be founded without permitting slavery.

A second problem with the "ought implies can" objection is that it neglects the possibility that the Founding Fathers could simply have decided not to start a new country in the first place. Suppose, after all, that my neighbors and I decide that we want to start a new neighborhood association. We find that we can only get enough people in the area to join if we agree that the association will sponsor monthly cross burnings on the lawns of the few black families who live in the neighborhood. Suppose, that is, that the only possible choices available to us really are these: fail to form a neighborhood association at all, or form one that sponsors monthly cross burnings. If we form the neighborhood association and someone then criticizes the association for engaging in monthly cross burnings, it would plainly be unsatisfactory for us to respond by pointing out that the association couldn't have come into existence in the first place if it hadn't agreed to sponsor the cross burnings. If it really was impossible for us to form the association without its engaging in monthly cross burnings, then forming the association was itself a wrongful act. And since it was clearly possible not to form the association in the first place, the rule that ought implies can will do nothing to shield us from criticism for having formed it. In the same way and for the same reason, then, if the only options available to the Founding Fathers really were to have their territories remain colonies of England, which by this point had abolished slavery, or to form a new government that would permit and facilitate slavery, then it was wrong for them to start a new country in the first place. And, again, since it was clearly possible for them to remain subjects of the Crown – and, in fact, a good number of people preferred this option – the ought implies can principle will do nothing to undermine the claim made by the second step of the compensation argument: that they did something wrong by forming a government that permitted and facilitated the practice of slavery.

Finally, there's a more fundamental problem with the objection as a whole. The objection proceeds on the assumption that if it really was impossible for the Founding Fathers to avoid doing what they did, then we can't say that it was wrong for them to do what they did. But the claim made in step two of the compensation argument, the claim that previous generations of Americans acted *wrongly* when they harmed previous generations of Africans and African Americans, can be understood in two importantly different ways. And while the "ought implies can" objection seems to refute the claim in one of these two senses, it doesn't refute it in the other sense. And it is the other sense that's required in order for the compensation argument to succeed.

This final problem with the objection arises from the fact that we can use the word "wrong" to mean at least two different things. One thing we might mean by calling person's act wrong is that they should be morally blamed or criticized for having done it. Let's call this the "blame" sense of wrongness. In the blame sense of wrongness, the rule that "ought implies can" really does seem to establish that what the Founding Fathers did was not wrong if they had no alternative to doing it. It doesn't seem to make sense to blame or criticize someone for doing something that they couldn't help but do. But another thing we might mean by calling a person's act wrong is that, objectively speaking, they didn't have the moral right to do what they did. We can call this the "objective" sense of wrongness. In the objective sense of wrongness, the rule that "ought implies can" doesn't really show that what the Founding Fathers did wasn't wrong. It doesn't really show that the Founding Fathers actually had a right to enslave Africans, for example, because if they really did have the right to enslave Africans then the Africans would not have had the right to resist their enslavement. And surely people on both sides of the reparations debate will agree that the Africans did, in fact, have the right to resist their enslavement. So while the "ought implies can" principle seems to work in one sense of the word "wrong" it doesn't work in the other sense. The question, then, is which is the sense that matters.

The way to answer this question is to go back for a moment to the first step in the compensation argument, the compensation principle. That principle maintains that if someone wrongfully harms another person, then he incurs a moral obligation to compensate his victim for the harms that he has wrongfully caused. The question about which sense of "wrong" is the one that matters in the second step of the argument can be answered by figuring which is the sense of "wrong" that matters in the first step. If the compensation principle requires wrongness in the "blame" sense, then since it seems wrong to say that we should blame the Founding Fathers for doing what they couldn't help doing, the "ought implies can" objection to the compensation argument will succeed if we really think that they could not have avoided doing what they did: since we shouldn't blame the Founding Fathers for what they did, on that assumption, what they did would not be able to generate a legitimate claim of compensation. But if the compensation principle only requires wrongness in the "objective" sense, then since what the Founding Fathers did was still wrong in that sense – they didn't really have the right to enslave Africans even if they weren't really blameworthy for doing so – the objection will fail: even if we shouldn't blame the Founding Fathers for doing what they had no right to do, that is, the fact that they did what they had no right to do will still generate a legitimate claim of compensation. The "ought implies can" objection is important, then, because it forces us to go back and be more clear about what we should mean by the compensation principle.

How should we decide which version of the compensation principle is the more reasonable? We should proceed in the same way that I've tried to decide other potentially difficult questions up to this point: by working from considerations that people on both sides of the slave reparations debate already accept.

So suppose that I'm driving my car down your block when suddenly the steering column locks up and I find myself unable to steer away from a path leading directly to your car, which is parked in your driveway. I immediately hit the brakes, only to discover that they, too, have failed, with the result that I collide with, and destroy, your car. Clearly in this case it would be unfair to aim moral blame at me for destroying your car. I really couldn't help it. But, just as clearly, this doesn't mean that I had a right to destroy your car. If you had been able to move your car out of the way in time, for example, you would clearly have had the right to do so. So the case of my car smashing into your car is a good test case for the competing possible versions of the compensation principle.

And it seems clear, at least to me, that this test case reveals that the version of the compensation principle that appeals to wrongness in the objective sense is superior to the version that appeals to wrongness in the blame sense. It seems clear, that is, that you would, in fact, be entitled to compensation from me in this case, even though you would not be entitled to aim moral criticism at me. It's not my fault that I ended up doing something I had no right to do, but I did something that I had no right to do all the same, and so I must incur the costs of repairing the damage that I caused. And most people, I suspect, would concur with this judgment, regardless of their views of slave reparations. If neither of us had car insurance, for example, I doubt very much that you'd feel obligated to incur the costs yourself. But if this is true, then it doesn't really matter whether the Founding Fathers could have avoided creating a government that permitted and facilitated the practice of slavery. It would matter if we were trying to figure out whether or not we should blame or punish them for what they did, but it doesn't matter in trying to figure out whether what they did generated a legitimate claim of compensation. What matters in trying to figure that out is simply whether or not they really had a right to engage in the practice of slavery. Since they clearly did not have this right, the second step of the compensation argument is true in the only sense in which the argument requires it to be true. For a third and final time, then, the "ought implies can" objection fails to undermine the reparations position. And since I know of no other reason that might be given to reject the second step of the compensation argument, the second step in the argument, like the first, should simply be accepted.

IT'S A BLACK THING – YOU WOULDN'T UNDERSTAND

What about the third step? The third step of the compensation argument is what I referred to as the causal claim, the claim that the acts by which previous generations of American citizens wrongfully harmed previous generations of Africans and African Americans through the institution of slavery and its aftermath continue to cause harmful consequences for black Americans today. This may well be the most controversial step in the argument and the one most likely to lead people to reject the reparations position. A great many black Americans are doing quite well, after all, and it's not as if you can simply look at a contemporary black

American and watch the lingering effects of state-supported slavery, segregation and discrimination exert a negative influence on his life prospects. The evidence for the causal claim is instead essentially indirect: something is clearly keeping the average level of black American well-being below the average level of white American well-being, and unless one is prepared to endorse the claim that genetic differences between black and white people account for the difference, it's hard to imagine what that something could be if not the lingering effects of slavery and its aftermath. And since the argument for the causal claim depends on this kind of indirect reasoning, it leaves itself vulnerable to the response that it's really something other than the legacy of slavery and its aftermath that's responsible for the present difficulties of contemporary black Americans.

This is the kind of problem that Horowitz pointed to in his sixth objection to the reparations position, the objection that claimed that the current discrepancies between black and white average levels of well-being in America were due to failures of individual character. As I pointed out in that context in Chapter 2, Horowitz's particular version of this kind of objection proved to be unsuccessful because it simply pushed the question back a step: if black Americans really do suffer from such individual failings at a high enough rate to account for the differences between black and white levels of well-being in this country, then the explanation that appeals to this fact would have to say something about why this is so. And if it's not so because black people are genetically disposed to suffer a higher rate of such failings than are white people, then it will remain difficult to see how to avoid concluding that this discrepancy itself is ultimately due to the harmful legacy of slavery and its aftermath. But while Horowitz's particular version of this kind of objection must be rejected for this reason, this doesn't prove that no other version of this kind of objection will succeed. And, in fact, one of the most common objections to the reparations position is precisely a more detailed and nuanced version of this very kind of concern.

What I have in mind here is the position that has been defended at some length by such writers and social critics as Shelby Steele, John McWhorter, and Dinesh D'Souza.[8] On the account that they favor, the causes of the present difficulties faced by contemporary black Americans are neither biological nor historical, but rather cultural. There is a distinctive "black culture" in America, on this account, and this culture has features that render it harmful to black Americans in a way that the cultures of other American groups are not harmful to their members. If this cultural explanation ultimately proves to be a more plausible analysis of the cause of the discrepancy between black and white average levels of well-being than the historical explanation, then the case for the causal claim will be defeated and, along with it, so too will be the compensation argument for slave reparations.

I claim no particular competence in assessing the accuracy of any given description of black American culture. But as a philosopher, I can claim a certain kind of competence in assessing the cogency of arguments, including arguments that are based on such descriptions. What I want to do in this section, then, is describe the picture of black American culture and its negative consequences that is painted by critics such as Steele, McWhorter, and D'Souza, and then explain why I think that even if their accounts are correct, they pose no problem for the causal claim that makes up the third step of the compensation argument.

The details of the accounts of black culture offered by these critics vary somewhat from writer to writer, but the basic story remains the same. First, this analysis maintains, there is indeed a distinctive black culture in this country. Virtually every black American is exposed to it and feels at least some pressure to belong to the community that it represents. The distinctively black culture exerts this pull not just on poor black Americans living in predominantly black neighborhoods, but on middle-class and affluent black Americans as well, including those who live and work in places where virtually nobody else is black. All of them are made to feel that they must embrace this culture in order to be "authentically black" and all are made to fear that they will be criticized and shunned for "acting white" if they reject it.

Second, on this account, the distinctively black American culture encourages and celebrates patterns of thought and behavior that make it more difficult for people to flourish in a modern, complex, market society. To thrive in a capitalist order, for example, one must have confidence in one's power and autonomy. But this culture encourages black Americans to view themselves as passive victims of forces beyond their control. To prosper, one must seek to integrate oneself into, and thus take advantage of the resources possessed by, the larger social order, but the separatist strain in this culture discourages this kind of outlook. To succeed in this country, one must develop the personal virtues that we associate with people like Ben Franklin: temperance, modesty, patience, and the kind of self-control that enables one to make sacrifices now in order to enjoy greater rewards in the future. But contemporary black culture, these critics charge, celebrates the opposite of these essential character traits: flamboyance, bravado, impulsiveness, and instant gratification. And, perhaps most important, while it's widely recognized that those who take full advantage of the educational opportunities made available to them have a better chance of flourishing in this society, the black American culture that these critics are concerned with is anti-intellectual and looks down on black academic achievement as a sign of "acting white."

John McWhorter, for example, taught linguistics for many years at the University of California at Berkeley. Even at this distinguished and selective school, McWhorter reports experiencing a discouraging pattern among the black student body as a whole: "The sad but simple fact," he observes in his book, *Losing the Race: Self-Sabotage in Black America*, "is that while there are some excellent black students, on the average, black students do not try as hard as other students." And in trying to account for this unhappy phenomenon, McWhorter appeals neither to a biological nor to an historical explanation: "The reason they do not try as hard is not because they are inherently lazy, nor is it because they are stupid ... [the reason] is that all of these students belong to a culture infected with an Anti-intellectual strain, which subtly but decisively teaches them from birth not to embrace schoolwork too wholeheartedly."[9] Indeed, as he puts the point even more forcefully in the preface to his book, "these defeatist thought patterns have become part of the bedrock of black identity."[10]

Shelby Steele offers a similar diagnosis in his influential book, *The Content of Our Character: A New Vision of Race in America.* There he affirms that it "is no doubt correct that black students, like the ones I regularly see, internalize a message of inferiority that they receive from school and the larger society around them" and he maintains that this phenomenon, rather than currently existing forms of white racism, is largely responsible for the respects in which black Americans on average lag behind white Americans.[11] And in *The End of Racism*, Dinesh D'Souza says much the same thing. "*Is racism the main problem facing blacks today?*," he asks near the beginning of his book. "No. The main contemporary obstacle facing African Americans is neither white racism, as many liberals claim, nor black genetic deficiency, as Charles Murray and others imply. Rather it involves destructive and pathological cultural patterns of behavior." And near the end of the book he reaffirms that black people in the United States "seem to have developed what some scholars term an 'oppositional culture' which is based on a comprehensive rejection of the white man's worldview.... Today black culture has become an obstacle, because it prevents blacks from taking advantage of rights and opportunities that have multiplied in a new social environment."[12]

When writers such as McWhorter, Steele, and D'Souza make these sorts of claims about the nature and consequences of contemporary black American culture, they at times appeal to their own impressions from personal experience. But there also seems to be a striking amount of empirical research available to lend support to their fundamental contentions. In 1997, for example, the distinguished anthropologist John Ogbu and a team of researchers from the University of California at Berkeley spent nine months conducting an extensive study of the disparities between black and white academic achievement in Shaker Heights, Ohio. Shaker Heights is an affluent community. The public schools are among the best in the country, and 1990 census data showed that half of its white households and a third of its black households enjoyed incomes of over $50,000 per year. Even under these very promising circumstances, though, Ogbu and his team documented significant disparities in the levels of black and white academic performance. Where the average grade point average for black students was 1.9, a little below a C, the average for white students was 3.45, close to the line between a B+ and an A–. 78 percent of the white students had a grade point average of 3.0 or higher, while only 2.5 percent of the black students did. Over a three-year period, black students constituted 295 of the 325 students to graduate in the bottom 20 percent of their class.[13] Ogbu's study concluded that the primary cause of these disparities lay in cultural differences between the two groups and, in particular, in differences between black and white attitudes among parents toward the importance of education. The research discovered, for example, that middle-class black parents spent considerably less time helping their children with homework and interacting with their children's teachers than did middle-class white parents.[14] University of Illinois education professor Danny Martin reached similar conclusions in his broader study of mathematics education in black communities.[15] And Harvard economist Ronald Ferguson, focusing more on the attitudes of the students than of their parents, studied the patterns of academic achievement in several Texas school districts and concluded that black pressure not to "act white" played a significant role in accounting for the lower average grades of black students, especially in the case of boys, who were subject to what he called a kind of "antiachievement" pressure.[16] All of this does seem to lend empirical support to the thought that critics such as McWhorter, Steele, and D'Souza are onto something.

So let's go ahead and assume, at least for the sake of the argument, that this picture of the nature and consequences of contemporary black American culture is by and large an accurate one. If it is, would this pose a problem for the compensation argument for slave reparations? On the face of it, at least, it seems that it would. The causal claim that makes up the third step of the argument, after all, maintains that the legacy of slavery and its aftermath continues to have harmful consequences for the currently living generation of black Americans. But if this picture of black American culture is correct, then it is black American culture itself that is responsible for the various difficulties that modern black Americans face. This would imply that the causal claim is false and that the compensation argument is therefore unsound. This seems to be a common reaction to this critique of black American culture.

But this assessment of the situation is premature. As was the case with Horowitz's sixth objection, the account that appealed to failures of individual character, an argument that appeals to the negative consequences of black American culture instead of the negative consequences of slavery and its aftermath rests on a false dichotomy. Indeed, appealing to the harmful effects of contemporary black American culture again simply pushes the question back a step: if black Americans really have embraced a dysfunctional culture while other American groups haven't, then why has this happened? And, once again, it's difficult to see how we could avoid reverting at this point to one of the two sorts of more basic explanations that we seemed to be stuck with all along: genetics and environment, nature or nurture. If black American culture rejects the value of learning while other American cultures cherish it, for example, then this must either be because black people are genetically less disposed to enjoy developing their intellectual abilities or because historical circumstances have conspired to thrust this rejection of learning upon them. And so, yet again, unless one is prepared to endorse the genetic explanation, the view that black American culture is to blame for contemporary black America's problems ultimately boils down to the view that, at its very foundation, it is the legacy of slavery and its aftermath that is to blame for contemporary black America's problems.

And this is precisely where the writings of McWhorter, Steele, and D'Souza all turn out to provide unexpected, and presumably unintended, support for the reparations position. For all three of these writers recognize that the appeal to a dysfunctional black American culture as a cause of contemporary black American difficulties in turn demands an explanation of the cause of the dysfunctional culture itself, and all three of them explicitly endorse the claim that the American legacy of slavery and its aftermath is at least in part to blame for the rise of a dysfunctional black American culture.[17]

Here, for example, is McWhorter, who at one point refers to the dysfunctional aspects of black American culture as the "direct consequences of the abrupt unshackling of a crippled race":[18]

Centuries of abasement and marginalization led African Americans to internalize the way they were perceived by the larger society, resulting in a postcolonial inferiority complex.[19]

As the common cold is caused by the rhinovirus, black students do so poorly in school decade after decade not because of racism, funding, class, parental education, etc., but because of a virus of Anti-intellectualism that infects the black community. This Anti-intellectual strain is inherited from whites having denied education to blacks for centuries, and has been concentrated by the Separatist trend, which in rejecting the 'white' cannot help but cast school and books as suspicious and alien, not to be embraced by the authentically "black" person.[20]

Blacks were almost all brutally relegated to the margins of society and denied education for centuries. Generations and generations of blacks lived and died in a cultural context in which books and learning were actively withheld or lent only grudgingly. Because of both of these historical factors, black American culture emerged in contexts that could not emphasize the ways of thinking necessary to scholarly success.[21]

And here is Shelby Steele:

Oppression conditions people *away* from all the values and attitudes one needs in freedom – individual initiative, self-interested hard work, individual responsibility, delayed gratification, and so on. In oppression these things don't pay off and are therefore negatively reinforced. It is not that these values have never had a presence in black life, only that they were muted and destabilized by the negative conditioning of oppression.[22]

One of the worst aspects of oppression is that it never ends when the oppressor begins to repent. There is a legacy of doubt in the oppressed that follows long after the cleanest repentance by the oppressor, just as guilt trails the oppressor and makes his redemption incomplete.[23]

The accusation black Americans have always lived with is that they are inferior – inferior simply because they are black. And this accusation has been too uniform, too ingrained in cultural imagery, too enforced by law, custom, and every form of power not to have left a mark. Black inferiority was a precept accepted by the founders of this nation; it was a principle of social organization that relegated blacks to the sidelines of American life. So when young black students find themselves on white campuses surrounded by those who have historically claimed superiority, they are also surrounded by the myth of their inferiority.[24]

And Dinesh D'Souza:

Slavery placed enormous pressure on the monogamous family. Because men had no special responsibility or ability to provide for others, the black family was never as patriarchal as the white family.... Ever since [Du Bois's 1900 estimate that the black illegitimacy rate was 25 percent while the white rate was 2 percent], single-parent and illegitimacy rates for black families have always been higher than those for white families. Who can deny that this is partly a consequence of slavery?[25]

Black cultural traits may well be the product of centuries of oppression.[26]

Skepticism toward the values of whites may be a cultural stance that served blacks well in the past: it was a technique for refusing to be defined by the categories of the oppressor.... Also blacks in the past who did try to assimilate in white society often found themselves rebuffed and scorned. So now an attitude of rejection seems to have set in, and values identified as white are spurned by many blacks.[27]

All three writers, moreover, are clear in acknowledging that black Americans today are not to be blamed for the existence of the cultural forces that hinder their progress. Steele writes that "You cannot be raised in a culture that was for centuries committed to the notion of your inferiority and not have some doubt in this regard – doubt that is likely to be aggravated most in integrated situations."[28] McWhorter describes his black students as being "caught in a cultural holding pattern they cannot help" and later adds that "It is not the *fault* of black Americans that they have inherited Anti-intellectualism from centuries of disenfranchisement, followed by their abrupt inclusion in American life before they had time to shed the internalization of their oppressor's debased view of them."[29] And D'Souza refers to what he calls "cultural dysfunctionalities in the black community" as "cultural traits that they did not freely choose, and that were to some extent imposed on them."[30] The upshot of all of this, then, is as follows: contemporary black American culture imposes significant harms on black Americans and contemporary black American culture was caused, at least in part, by the legacy of slavery and its aftermath. It follows from this that the legacy of slavery and its aftermath does, indeed, continue to impose significant harms on the currently living generation of black Americans. It does so precisely through the harmful effects it has exerted on the formation of contemporary black American culture.

Before turning to a very different kind of challenge that can be raised against the third step of the compensation argument, it's worth pausing to consider one objection that is likely to be raised at this point against my response to the cultural challenge. The objection is based on the claim, popular with many of the sorts of critics who press the cultural challenge to the causal claim, that in a number of important respects, things have gotten worse for black Americans since the 1960s. If things have gotten worse over the last few decades as slavery and its aftermath have receded further and further into the past, on this account, then slavery and its aftermath can't be the cause of the problems that confront contemporary black Americans. As Dinesh D'Souza, for example, has put this argument:

The civilizational crisis of the black community is not the result of genes and it is not the result of racism. This can be shown indisputably by the fact that this crisis did not exist a generation ago. In 1960, 78 percent of all black families were headed by married couples; today that figure is less than 40 percent. Similarly in the 1950s, black crime rates were higher than those for whites, but they were vastly lower than they are today. During that period the black gene pool has not changed substantially, and racism was far worse, especially in its ability to deny blacks access to basic rights and opportunities. The conspicuous pathologies of blacks are the product of catastrophic cultural change that poses a threat both to the African American community and to society as a whole. These pathologies are far more serious than the fact that, for whatever reason, there are too few black math professors and nuclear physicists.[31]

There are two problems, though, with the attempt to use the difficulties that have befallen black Americans since the 1960s as a reason to deny that black Americans today continue to suffer harmful consequences as a result of the legacy of slavery and its aftermath. The first problem is that the claim made by the third step of the compensation argument is not the claim that *all* contemporary black American problems can be traced to slavery and its aftermath. It is the claim that *some* such problems can be so traced. And the claim that things have gotten worse for black Americans in some important respects since the 1960s is fully consistent with this claim. D'Souza notes, for example, that the percentage of black children born out of wedlock has increased substantially since 1960 and concludes from this that "high black illegitimacy rates cannot be blamed on slavery or segregation."[32] But the fact is that the percentage of white children born out of wedlock has increased substantially during this period as well. The black rate rose from 22 percent in 1960 to 70 percent in 1994, while the white rate rose from 2 percent in 1960 to 25 percent in 1994.[33] And the claim made by the third step of the compensation argument doesn't entail that the entire contemporary black illegitimacy rate can be attributed to slavery and its aftermath. Plenty of white Americans have children out of wedlock, too, after all, and they don't live in the shadow of a long history of slavery and discrimination against white people. The claim, rather, is that to the extent that something like illegitimacy is on average a greater problem for black Americans today than for white Americans, this disparity itself is most plausibly explained by the lingering effects of slavery and its aftermath. The claim isn't that were it not for slavery and its aftermath black Americans would have no problems at all. The claim is that were it not for slavery and its aftermath black Americans would have roughly the same amount of problems as white Americans. To the extent that black Americans on average tended to have more problems than white Americans before the 1960s and have tended to continue to have more problems than white Americans since the 1960s, then, the claim is not affected by whether or not things have gotten worse in various respects for black Americans – and for white Americans – since the 1960s. The fact that things have gotten worse for black Americans in some important respects since the 1960s, in short, doesn't mean that black Americans no longer have worse problems on average than do white Americans. And so the claim that things have gotten worse for black Americans since the 1960s does nothing to undermine the third step of the compensation argument. Far from establishing his thesis "indisputably," as he claims, the facts that D'Souza appeals to in its support are simply irrelevant to it.

The second problem with appealing to the claim that things have gotten worse for black Americans since the 1960s as a way of trying to undermine the causal claim is that this strategy, too, ultimately does no more than push the crucial question back a step. The 1960s, after all, were a tumultuous period for all Americans, not just for black Americans. If the upheaval of those years led to the development of a highly dysfunctional black American culture without producing an equally dysfunctional white American culture, then this fact itself calls for an explanation. And, once again, it seems hard to avoid the conclusion that this explanation, in the end, will have to appeal to either biological reasons or historical reasons. Unless we're prepared to endorse the claim that black Americans are genetically more prone to such dysfunctional behavior as violence and illegitimacy, then, we must conclude that the most plausible explanation of whatever damage to the black community was wrought by the culture that emerged from the 1960s involves ultimately tracing it back to the legacy of slavery and its aftermath.

And, once again, whenever the cultural critics of this sort stop to consider just why black American culture developed in the way that it did, they reach precisely this conclusion. In *Winning the Race: Beyond the Crisis in Black America*, for example, his 2005 followup to *Losing the Race*, John McWhorter discusses at great length the nature, consequences, and origins of what he calls the culture of "therapeutic alienation" that, on his account, has gripped and crippled black America since the 1960s.[34] McWhorter is clear and explicit in arguing that the best explanation of "the descent of a previously dignified people into a violent, feckless underclass" appeals to the fact that a "new culture emerged of white-hot, unfocused animus against mainstream culture" and that the "explicit aim [of his book] is to argue that poor blacks indeed have been waylaid by a culture of poverty."[35] And he is equally clear and explicit in emphasizing that, on his account, the central question is "why therapeutic alienation acquired such a hold on black America only in the sixties."[36] The answer McWhorter provides to this question is twofold: this dysfunctional black culture came to dominance in the 1960s because of the "rise of a hostile, anti-establishment ideology as mainstream opinion" in America as a whole, and the "expansion of [government provision of] welfare such that it could provide a passable living indefinitely."[37] And since neither of these developments can be blamed on slavery or Jim Crow, McWhorter characterizes his position as one that is antithetical to the reparations position.[38]

But if McWhorter is right that contemporary black American problems can largely be traced to the emergence of a dysfunctional black American culture in the 1960s, and if he is also right that the emergence of that culture can largely be traced to changes in the welfare laws and cultural norms that characterized the country as a whole at that time, then we are once again back to the very question that undermined the cultural critique of the causal claim in the first place. White Americans, after all, were equally exposed to the cultural upheaval of the 1960s, and the expansion of welfare that made it possible for poor black Americans to make a "passable living" without getting a job made it equally possible for poor white Americans to do so. If these two conditions led black Americans to adopt a substantially more dysfunctional cultural identity than white Americans adopted, as McWhorter's account maintains, then there must be an explanation for this. And, indeed, McWhorter provides such an explanation, the very explanation that defenders of slave reparations like Robinson appeal to in justifying the causal claim that makes up the third step of the compensation argument: things turned out worse for black Americans than they did for white Americans, even on McWhorter's own analysis, because of the legacy of slavery and its aftermath.

In the introduction to his book, for example, McWhorter writes that "Centuries of slavery and segregation left a stain on the black American psyche" and that "insecurity about being black is why this kind of [therapeutic] alienation for its own sake – curiously exaggerated, melodramatic, and heedless of reason – is so attractive to so many black Americans today. It assuages a person who is quietly unsure that they are worthy or okay, by giving them something or someone to always feel better than. They seek this because slavery and segregation left black America with a hole in its soul – and why would it have not?"[39] And the narrative that follows is frequently peppered with such observations as that "the ideology spread fast, among a people left so susceptible to it by a hideous past," and that an "open-ended wariness of whites became a bedrock of black identity, among a people deprived by history of a more positive, individual source of security and purpose. If this had not led black kids to start turning away from school as 'white,' it would have been surprising."[40] Indeed, when at one point he argues that "too many black students and their parents are not driven enough to foster scholastic success – and to an extent much more than white kids," he adds: "And if this traces to the demoralization and alienation created by slavery and segregation, then we are now right back at, essentially, my argument."[41]

Which brings me back, essentially, to *my* argument. The causal claim that constitutes the third step of the compensation argument maintains that black Americans today continue to suffer harmful consequences as a result of the legacy of slavery and its aftermath. The argument for this claim rests on the idea that the current discrepancies between black and white average levels of well-being in this country must either be explained biologically or historically, and that on the assumption that biological accounts have been thoroughly discredited within the relevant scientific communities, the best explanation for the disparity is that black Americans today continue to be harmed by the consequences of slavery and its aftermath. The cultural challenge attempts to undermine this argument by providing a third alternative explanation, one that appeals to culture rather than to biology or history. In the end, though, its claim that contemporary black problems are largely caused by contemporary black culture simply pushes the question back a step: is contemporary black culture a product of black biology or of black history? Again on the assumption that the biological account has been discredited, it follows that the black culture that causes black problems can in turn be traced to slavery and its aftermath, with the result that the cultural challenge actually helps to support, rather than to defeat, the causal claim.

The 1960s variant of the cultural challenge attempts to avoid this problem by emphasizing the respects in which this dysfunctional black American culture is a relatively recent development. If it emerged out of distinctive historical circumstances of the 1960s rather than out of the distinctive circumstances of slavery and Jim Crow, the argument maintains, then the culture that causes contemporary problems for black America can't be traced to slavery and its aftermath. But the 1960s variant of the cultural challenge ends up suffering from precisely the same problem that defeats the original version: if the circumstances of the 1960s produced a more dysfunctional culture for black Americans than it did for white Americans, then this too must be explained either biologically or historically. And so once again, even on McWhorter's own account, the ultimate explanation for the current gaps between black and white average levels of well-being lies largely in the history of slavery and its aftermath. The critique of contemporary black American culture as a dysfunctional source of contemporary black American problems, then, even when it focuses on cultural developments of the last four or five decades, in the end gives us no reason to reject the causal claim that constitutes the third step in the compensation argument. Indeed, if anything, by identifying the mechanism through which the legacy of slavery continues to exert its destructive influence, the cultural critique associated with such writers as Steele, McWhorter, and D'Souza gives us all the more reason to accept it.[42]

FISHING FOR ANSWERS IN THE GENE POOL

Unless one is willing to endorse the claim that black people are genetically inferior to white people, then, it's hard to see how one can coherently reject the third step in the compensation argument. How else could one account for the undeniable discrepancies that continue to exist between black and white average levels of well-being in this country? Because most people aren't willing to endorse the claim that black people are genetically inferior to white people, I have to this point been taking this feature of the argument to provide a powerful defense of the causal claim. But in order to provide a truly comprehensive treatment of the objections that can be raised against the reparations position, it's necessary in the end to acknowledge the uncomfortable fact that a number of people are, in fact, willing to endorse the claim that black people are genetically inferior to white people. If accepted, this claim poses a potentially serious threat to the compensation argument. If genetic differences successfully explain why black Americans on average aren't doing as well as are white Americans on average, after all, then the existence of differences in black and white average levels of well-being will no longer provide support for the causal claim. And without the causal claim, the compensation argument will collapse. Although I would prefer to avoid the distressing subject of race differences and genetics altogether, then, and while I genuinely regret the discomfort and even offense that I may cause simply by attempting to discuss the issue in a dispassionate manner, it seems to me that we have no choice but to address the writings of those who have maintained that black people are genetically inferior to white people in terms of such potentially relevant characteristics as native intelligence. Some people have argued that a convincing objection to the compensation argument can be developed by appealing to this claim, and intellectual honesty requires us to address their position and to give it a fair hearing rather than pretend that it doesn't exist.

The natural place to focus such a discussion is the highly controversial book, *The Bell Curve: Intelligence and Class Structure in American Life*, which was first published in 1994 by Richard J. Herrnstein and Charles Murray. Although only a relatively small portion of the book's 845 pages were devoted to the subject of race and intelligence, this part of the book generated an immediate uproar and a ferocious amount of discussion because of its provocative claim that genetic differences between the races play a significant role in explaining differences in intelligence as measured by various standardized tests. Just a few years later, in 1997, the philosopher Michael Levin defended the same claim in a book called *Why Race Matters: Race Differences and What They Mean*. Levin's book received considerably less attention, in part because it was directed toward a more academic audience and in part simply because it appeared in the shadow of *The Bell Curve*. But Levin's book actually devotes considerably more space to arguing for this claim about genetic differences than does the book by Herrnstein and Murray, and Levin's arguments are generally developed with more rigor and depth. I will therefore refer to his book as well as *The Bell Curve* in the discussion that follows. As in the previous section of this book, on the argument about the role of black culture in causing difficulties for contemporary black Americans, I will not take the time here to critically evaluate the merits of the arguments offered by Herrnstein, Murray, and Levin. There is already an enormous literature devoted to the task of responding to such arguments and I would have little of interest to add to that discussion. Instead, I will simply present the arguments offered by these writers and the conclusions that they are used to support, and then explain why I think that, even if their arguments are accepted, they fail to undermine the causal claim and thus provide no reason to reject the compensation argument or the reparations position.

The position defended by Herrnstein, Murray, and Levin begins with two foundational claims. The first is that there really is such a thing as general intelligence. Although it's difficult to provide a precise definition of just what exactly this thing is, it is something like general cognitive ability: the ability to learn, process information, solve problems, and so on. The second foundational claim is that general intelligence can be measured in a reasonably reliable manner. Although people often refer to an "IQ test" as if this refers to a specific exam in the way that the SAT does, there are in fact a wide variety of tests that are commonly used to try to measure general intelligence. The tests differ from one another in a variety of respects, but they are all statistically normed so that a score of 100 represents the average score for any particular exam.[43] This makes it possible to compare the IQ scores of different people who have taken different versions of an IQ test, and the commonly recognized framework for assessing people in this manner makes use of the following scale: 130 is outstanding, 115 is high, 100 is average, 85 is poor, and 70 indicates borderline mental retardation.[44]

To these two foundational assumptions, the three writers add an empirical claim: that when such IQ tests are administered over a large range of cases, a fairly consistent and not insignificant difference emerges between the average score of white people and the average score of black people. The difference is said to amount to approximately 15 points – enough, for example, to make the difference between "high" and "average" or "average" and "poor." Herrnstein and Murray, for example, cite a compilation of 156 studies conducted between 1918 and 1990, on which the average result was a difference of approximately 16 IQ points.[45] Levin cites a National Academy of Science study that concluded that such a gap exists "between blacks and whites on all given tests and at all grade levels.... Differences of approximately this magnitude were found at the sixth, ninth and twelfth grades."[46] Both books cite a number of further sources as well. And while, as we will see in a moment, the best explanation of the persistence of this gap is a subject of fierce debate, the existence of the gap itself seems to be generally accepted by those who have studied the matter. Even Stephen Jay Gould, for example, the widely acclaimed Harvard paleontologist and science writer, and one of the sharpest and most vocal critics of the position defended by Herrnstein, Murray and Levin, concedes that the roughly 15-point gap is "an undisputed fact."[47]

The claim that there's a significant difference between average black and white IQ scores, moreover, is said to remain true even when other differences between black and white people are taken into account. For students taking the SAT in 2001–2002, to take just one example, the average score for a white student was 1060 while the average score for a black student was 857, a difference of just over 200 points. White students, on average, come from families with a higher income, and students from families with a higher income, on average, have access to a higher-quality education. And so it might be thought that the test score gap in this case is essentially a function of class differences rather than race differences. But when the numbers are broken down by family income level, much, though not all, of the gap between black and white test scores appears to remain:[48]

Family Income Level	Average Score of Black Student	Average Score of White Student	Gap
$20,000–$30,000	830	992	162
$40,000–$50,000	873	1022	149
$60,000–$70,000	897	1041	144
$80,000–$100,000	934	1075	141

The gap at each income level is lower than the 203-point gap that appears before the numbers are adjusted to take income into account, and the gap becomes somewhat smaller as income level rises, but even at its lowest, the gap is still considerably more than half of what it was before income was taken into account. This, again, suggests that there is a significant difference between black and white scores and this, again, is something that seems to be widely accepted by both sides of the debate over books like *The Bell Curve*. The figures used here, for example, are taken from the second edition of Andrew Hacker's book *Two Nations*, and Hacker, like Gould, is a pointed critic of Herrnstein and Murray's position.

If IQ tests really do measure something worth measuring, and if they really do consistently reveal a significant gap between black and white levels of what is measured, then it becomes important to answer the question of just why this gap appears. And this is where the position taken by Herrnstein, Murray, and Levin becomes so controversial. Writers such as Gould and Hacker maintain that the answer to this question lies in differences between the social, and perhaps even natural, environments of the two groups. If black people on average were raised under the circumstances that white people on average enjoy, that is, they would end up on average with the same IQ scores that white people achieve. But the authors of *The Bell Curve* and *Why Race Matters* insist that this environmental account is mistaken and argue for the importance of genetic differences between black and white populations. Because I will later want to explain why I think that their arguments provide no reason to reject the compensation argument even if they are accepted, it is important to be clear about what their arguments are, even if the prospect of considering them in a fair and impartial manner is taken to be distressing or even offensive. So here is a brief summary.

The most important and commonly cited evidence for the genetic account defended by writers such as Herrnstein, Murray, and Levin arises from the study of twins. Thomas Bouchard and his colleagues at the University of Minnesota's Center for Twin and Adoption Research, in particular, have conducted an exhaustive long-term study on over one thousand sets of twins, and both Levin[49] and Herrnstein and Murray[50] cite this research in support of their position.

The basic idea behind the argument based on twin studies is a simple one: compare the IQ scores of those fraternal twins who were raised in the same household with the IQ scores of those identical twins who were raised separately. If environmental conditions are mostly responsible for the development of an individual's IQ, then one would expect that the average difference between the IQs within each pair of fraternal twins would be relatively small, as members of each pair in the sample were raised in the same environment, whereas the average difference between the IQs within each pair of the identical twins would be relatively large, as the members of each pair in the sample were raised in different environments. If, instead, an individual's genetic endowment is what primarily determines his IQ, then one would expect precisely the opposite result: the average difference between the IQs within each pair of identical twins would be relatively small, as the members of each pair would have precisely the same DNA, and the average difference between the IQs within each pair of fraternal twins would be relatively large, as the members of each pair would have significantly different DNA.[51] And, in fact, the result of the Bouchard study to this point has been that the gap between the IQ scores of identical twins remains quite small even when the twins are raised in different environments, while the gap between the IQ scores of fraternal twins is notably larger even when the twins are raised in the same environment. Based on a statistical analysis of the relevant figures, Bouchard himself calculates that the results reveal that fully 70 percent of the differences in IQ scores within the groups are due to genetic differences and 30 percent are due to environmental differences.[52] Writers such as Herrnstein, Murray, and Levin then infer from these results that there's good reason to conclude the same sort of thing about the differences in black and white average IQ scores. Although the authors of the two books cite a somewhat different range of particular numbers,[53] the bottom line remains the same: since genetic differences play the primary role in explaining the differences between the IQs of different individuals, they must also play the primary role in explaining the differences between the IQs of different groups of individuals. Because there is a significant difference between the IQs of white people and black people as a whole, this must primarily be due to genetic differences between white people and black people as a whole.

Defenders of the genetic account appeal to other sources of evidence as well. Herrnstein and Murray, for example, cite data from studies involving transracial adoptions that seem to indicate that black children raised by white parents end up with about the same IQ levels as black children raised by black parents.[54] Levin also puts a good deal of weight on such studies and appeals to statistics involving the average brain and skull sizes of black and white people as well, citing various studies suggesting a correlation between such sizes and IQ levels.[55] And Herrnstein and Murray, in particular, seem impressed by the so-called "digit span test," one component of the widely accepted Wechsler intelligence tests. In one part of the digit span test, the test-taker is read a series of numbers and is then asked to repeat them in the order in which they were read. In the other part, the test-taker is asked to repeat a series of numbers in the reverse order from the order in which they were read. The backward portion of the test seems to be the more intellectually demanding of the two, and Herrnstein and Murray are struck by evidence that indicates that the gap between black and white scores tends to be about twice as great on this portion as on the forward portion.[56] They also seem especially impressed by the results of studies conducted by Arthur Jensen that attempt to measure, in effect, mental speed.[57] In one of these "reaction time tests," for example, the subject sits in front of a series of eight lights. When one of the lights is activated, the subject pushes the button corresponding to it. Two time measurements are made: the first recording the time from when the light goes on to when the subject first lifts a finger to move it, the second recording the time from when the finger first moves to when it hits the button. The studies that Herrnstein and Murray cite seem to indicate that average reaction time is faster for white people in the first stage but faster for black people in the second stage, and they appeal to evidence that claims that the first reaction time correlates well with overall IQ scores.

Finally, and to some extent most important, both Herrnstein and Murray in their book and Levin in his maintain that it is this 15-point gap in IQ scores, with its fundamentally genetic basis, that accounts for the basic discrepancies between average black and white levels of well-being. Fifteen points may not sound like a lot, but this is where the idea of the "bell curve" becomes so important. IQ scores, like many other things, seem to be distributed in such a way that a relatively large number of people score relatively close to the middle and relatively few score at either of the extremes. This is what generates the familiar bell curve shape: when the results are plotted on a graph with scores being represented along the horizontal axis and the number of people achieving a given score being measured along the vertical axis, the result is a kind of hill with a crest near the middle and slopes going down in a roughly symmetric pattern on either side. This matters because if the middle of the "black curve" is about 15 points to the left of the middle of the "white curve," the implications will be greatly amplified as one moves further and further from the middle of the test score spectrum: even if the black and white populations are of identical size, that is, white people will be far more likely than black people to be represented at the extreme high end of the spectrum, and black people will be far more likely than white people to be represented at the extreme low end of the spectrum. Indeed, as Dinesh D'Souza points out in his sympathetic though ultimately critical discussion of Herrnstein and Murray, when looked at from this point of view, the 15-point gap in average scores is enough to place the average white test score all the way up in the eighty-fifth percentile of all black test scores and to place the average black test score all the way down at the fifteenth percentile of all white scores. And the numbers become even more striking as they approach the extreme ends of the scoring spectrum: only 2 percent of black test scores fall in the 110–20 range, whereas 18 percent of white test scores do, and a full 13 percent of white test scores are at 120 or higher, whereas only 0.32 percent of black test scores reach that level.[58]

All of this is true, moreover, even under the assumption that the black and white populations are the same size. When one then adds to all of this the fact that in the United States, black people make up a considerably smaller portion of the population than do white people, the imbalance will be magnified still further: there will be, by an even greater margin, far more white Americans than black Americans at the high end of the IQ spectrum.

Why does all of this matter? It matters, on the accounts offered by Herrnstein and Murray and by Levin, because human intelligence is closely tied to human well-being. In general, those with more of it will tend to do better than will those with less of it, especially in a complex market society such as the contemporary United States. And so if it's true that intelligence is distributed in this manner and that this is fundamentally due to facts about human genetics that are beyond our control, then this will explain why black Americans on average continue to do considerably less well than do white Americans on average. The fault, on this view, lies not in our past, but in our genes.

And, in fact, both Herrstein and Murray in their book[59] and Levin in his[60] cite the work of the sociologist Linda Gottfredson in an attempt to establish precisely this point. Gottfredson has argued that when statistics comparing black and white representation in various high-paying professions versus black and white representation in the population as a whole are adjusted to take into account differences in average IQ levels between the two groups, the result is that black people are not, in fact, underrepresented in the fields in which they are often believed to be underrepresented. Doctors and engineers, for example, tend to come from the population of people whose IQ scores are in the range of 114 and higher. 23 percent of white Americans but only 1.1 percent of black Americans fall into this category. Given the current ratio of black to white people in America, then, it follows on this account that one would expect there to be roughly 0.05 black Americans for every white American holding such jobs. Gottfredson, with Herrstein, Murray, and Levin then following her, cites evidence that in most cases there are at least that many black Americans holding such positions. If analyses of these sorts are generally sound then, to put the point bluntly, black Americans on the whole are doing just about as well as you would expect them to be doing given how intelligent they tend to be. As Herrnstein and Murray put the point, "A Latino, black, and white of similar cognitive ability earn annual wages within a few hundred dollars of one another."[61] And if that's the case, then there's apparently no justification for claiming that slavery and its aftermath are continuing to exert any harmful consequences on the currently living generation of black Americans. Black Americans are doing just fine as it is, given their natural cognitive limitations.

Herrnstein and Murray don't address the implications of this analysis for the compensation argument in particular, but Levin is quite explicit about it:

Since the heart of the compensation argument is ... a theory of the cause of the race gap [what I have referred to as step three, the causal claim], a more plausible account of the gap in terms of factors other than white misdeeds would annul black rights to a remedy [if the causal claim turns out to be false, that is, then since past wrongs would not be responsible for present inequalities, there would be no present harm for black Americans to be owed compensation for]. Such an account can acknowledge past wrongs; it need only deny that current black limitations are among their effects. Innate race differences in intelligence and time preference offer such an alternative.[62]

And, indeed, Levin is even more clear and direct than this: "whites owe blacks no compensation in any form because the limitations of blacks are by-products of genetic differences, not injuries done by whites," he writes at one point.[63] "No damages are owed when no damage has been done," he adds at another, "and the difficulty blacks have in competing in a white world are not the legacy of past wrongs – however regrettable those wrongs may have been – but a result of biology for which whites are not to blame."[64] The bottom line of this somewhat long and tangled story, then, is a seemingly simple one: genetic differences are responsible for intelligence differences, intelligence differences are responsible for differences in well-being, and so genetic differences are responsible for differences in well-being. The causal claim maintains that the legacy of slavery and its aftermath are responsible for differences in well-being, and so the causal claim must be false. The compensation argument depends on the causal claim, and so the compensation argument must be rejected.

The objection to the compensation argument that arises from claims about race differences and genetics can be challenged in a variety of ways. Some people are skeptical about the very idea that there is such a thing as "intelligence" that can be measured in the first place. Others believe that intelligence exists, but that IQ tests are biased in various ways that render the results they produce misleading and unreliable. Still others have raised doubts about the various statistical methods employed in the debate, especially in response to Herrnstein and Murray's book. And a number of more specific problems have been raised in the context of the use made of a variety of particular studies that are appealed to in both *The Bell Curve* and *Why Race Matters*. Gould, for example, famously objected that the prominent argument based on twin studies is flawed because it overlooks the distinction between differences within a group and differences between groups.[65] If you compare the heights of different people within the group of those who are poor, to take Gould's example, and then compare the heights of different people within the group of those who are rich, you'll see that height is largely a genetically inherited trait. The taller people in the poor group will tend to have parents who were among the taller people in the poor group, that is, and the taller people in the rich group will tend to have parents who were among the taller people in the rich group. But while genes clearly play a large role in determining relative height *within* these two groups, Gould pointed out, it would be a mistake to conclude from this that genes play any such role in explaining the average height difference *between* the two groups. Here it could well be the case that the rich group is taller on average than the poor group not because of genetic differences between rich people and poor people, but rather because on average the rich people get more nutrition than do the poor people. Similarly, Gould maintained, even if genetic differences are largely responsible for IQ differences *within* different groups, as the twin studies seem to indicate, it would not follow that such differences account for IQ differences *between* different groups, such as the group of black Americans and the group of white Americans.[66]

Relatedly, worries can be raised about the use of other kinds of studies to which writers such as Herrnstein, Murray, and Levin appeal. Studies involving transracial adoption, for example, may fail to isolate genetic from environmental factors since a black child raised by white parents still faces many of the environmental burdens faced by black children raised by black parents (as well as some that are unique to them). Men have larger brains than women do, on average, but there seem to be no significant differences between male and female average IQ scores, raising doubts about the relevance of evidence based on claims about the average brain sizes of black and white people.[67] And similar doubts can be raised about the importance of the digit span and reaction time tests that Herrnstein and Murray, in particular, put a great deal of weight on.

But let's suppose that all the critics are wrong. Let's suppose that there really is such a thing as general intelligence, that black people really do on average have less of it than white people, and that the various studies that are cited by writers such as Herrnstein, Murray, and Levin really are relevant to determining the role that genetics play in explaining this fact in just the way that these writers claim them to be. Even if all of this is true, it would still fail to undermine the causal claim that makes up step three of the compensation argument. The reason for this is that the causal claim does not depend on the insistence that *all* of the gap between black and white well-being in this country is due to the legacy of slavery and its aftermath. In claiming that slavery and its aftermath continue to cause harmful consequences for African Americans today, it depends only on the claim that at least *some* of the gap in black and white levels of well-being is a result of previous wrongs committed by the U.S. government. And this more modest claim is not threatened by any of the arguments made by Herrnstein and Murray or by Levin even if their arguments are accepted at face value. The causal claim, that is, would be threatened only if we had reason to believe that the *entire* gap between black and white well-being in this country could be traced to genetic differences. If that were the case, then we would have no reason to think that slavery and its aftermath continue to generate negative consequences for black Americans today. But none of the studies cited by these writers can be used to support this much stronger claim even if the reliability and relevance of the studies is taken to be precisely as they claim it to be.

In the famous twin studies appealed to both by Herrnstein and Murray and by Levin, for example, Thomas Bouchard himself concludes that genetic differences account for 70 percent of the differences in intelligence levels while environmental factors account for 30 percent. This means that even if Gould is mistaken and Bouchard's findings really can unobjectionably be applied to the case of racial differences, nearly a third of the gap between black and white IQ scores will still be due to environmental rather than genetic differences. And none of the arguments based on the other sorts of studies that these writers appeal to justify a conclusion any stronger than this. Even if the arguments based on transracial adoptions, cranium size, or digit span and reaction time test scores are just as cogent as Herrnstein and Murray and/or Levin claim them to be, that is, they would establish, at the most, only that some significant portion of the differences between black and white IQ scores are due to genetic differences. They would not justify the conclusion that the gap is entirely due to genetic differences.

And, in fact, Herrnstein and Murray are quite explicit in acknowledging this feature of their arguments. Referring to the large amount of data surveyed in their book, they write that "half a century of work, now amounting to hundreds of empirical and theoretical studies, permits a broad conclusion that the genetic component of IQ is unlikely to be smaller than 40 percent or higher than 80 percent."[68] "Cognitive ability is substantially heritable," they write at another point, "apparently no less than 40 percent and no more than 80 percent,"[69] an estimate that they deem "beyond significant technical dispute."[70] They are clear, moreover, that this is not just their own view, but is the view of others who are convinced by the sorts of arguments that they find compelling: "Those who argue that genes might be implicated in group differences," they emphasize, "do not try to argue that genes explain everything."[71] And for the purposes of their own discussion, they "adopt a middling estimate of 60 percent heritability."[72]

Indeed, even Levin himself is generally careful to make this point about his own work clear and explicit, except when he's attacking the compensation argument. When he's attacking the compensation argument in particular, he writes as if his book has shown that the gap between black and white is due to genetic differences *instead of* environmental differences: "whites owe blacks no compensation in any form," he insists, because the limitations of blacks are by-products of genetic differences, *not* injuries done by whites."[73] And when appealing to the principle that "No damages are owed when no damage has been done," he argues that "the difficulty blacks have in competing in a white world are *not* the legacy of past wrongs – however regrettable those wrongs may have been – *but* a result of biology for which whites are not to blame."[74] Yet when Levin is actually discussing and developing his various arguments for the genetic claim upon which his attack on the compensation argument is based, he is far more careful to acknowledge that even on his own account, just as on that of Herrnstein and Murray, genes and environment both play a significant role in explaining current inequalities between the races. The "hereditarian" position that he is concerned to defend, as he clearly explains near the outset of his book, claims only that the race differences he is concerned with are "*significantly* genetic in origin.... This position – not that genetic factors explain all of the black/white difference, but that they explain a *significant* proportion – is 'hereditarianism'."[75] And throughout the book he is generally consistent in characterizing his view in this more limited and qualified way: "genes contribute *significantly* to race differences,"[76] "genes *matter* to intelligence and personality,"[77] "genes are *important* determinants of the human psyche,"[78] the difference between black and white IQ scores "is due *significantly* to genes,"[79] "On average, blacks are less intelligent than whites and more impulsive, for *largely* biological reasons,"[80] and so on.

Why does the difference between the qualified and the unqualified version of Levin's position matter so much? An analogy may be of some use at this point. So suppose that a big corporation has been found to have been secretly burying large amounts of toxic waste in predominantly black neighborhoods across the country for many years. Suppose also that this kind of waste is known to cause a certain form of cancer, and that black Americans seem to suffer from this form of cancer at a higher rate than do white Americans. Taking into account the apparent difference in cancer rates and the size of the relevant populations, let's say that each year ten thousand more black Americans die from this form of cancer than would die if the black cancer rate were as low as the white cancer rate is. On the face of it, at least, we would have the makings of a powerful class-action lawsuit: the corporation acted wrongfully in the past, and these past wrongful acts continue to have harmful consequences for black Americans in the present.

People on both sides of the slave reparations debate would surely agree that the corporation would owe compensation for the harms that it was responsible for having wrongfully caused in this case.

But now imagine that lawyers for the besieged corporation hire expert witnesses who testify to the fact that black people are genetically disposed to suffer from this form of cancer at a higher rate than are white people. The fault, they maintain, lies not in the victims' wrongfully polluted environment – regrettable as that may be – but in the victims' genes. In trying to determine whether or not this testimony was sufficient to rebut the claim that the corporation owes compensation in this case, it would be absolutely essential to determine whether or not the genetic difference between black and white people explained all of the difference between the black and white cancer rates, or only some part of it, even some significant part. If the genetic difference accounted for the entire difference in the cancer rates, this would mean that black people were dying from cancer at precisely the rate they would be dying from it if the corporation had not buried the toxic waste in the first place. The corporation's act would therefore not be currently causing any harm to anyone, and so no one would have a claim to compensation as a result of it. But if the reported genetic difference between black and white people only accounted for part of the difference between black and white cancer rates, even a quite significant part, then this fact would fail to undermine the compensation claim. If, for example, to follow the figure that Herrnstein and Murray settle on in the case of the IQ debate, a full 60 percent of the difference in cancer rates was correctly attributed to genetic differences, this would mean that a very substantial 40 percent of the extra ten thousand deaths per year were still due to environmental differences. On the assumption that the buried toxic waste constituted the most obviously salient environmental difference between black and white Americans in this example, it would follow that the corporation would still be responsible for wrongfully causing a significant amount of harm. Forty percent of a very significant amount of harm, after all, is still a significant amount of harm. Indeed, even if we adopt the very highest figure that Herrnstein, Murray, or Levin cite in the context of race and IQ and propose that a full 80 percent of the difference in this case is attributable to genetic differences, it would still be the case that a far from trivial 20 percent of the difference in cancer rates would be the fault of the corporation. Unless we were convinced that the entire gap between black and white levels of well-being in this case were attributable to genetic differences, then, the existence of genetic differences between black and white people would give us no reason to reject the claim that the corporation owed compensation for the harms that it was responsible for having wrongfully caused. The claim that genetic differences played a significant role in the differences in cancer rates would be relevant to determining the total amount of damages that the corporation would owe, to be sure, but while it would be relevant to determining how much compensation the corporation would owe, it would not be relevant to determining whether or not the corporation did, in fact, owe compensation.

But everything that I've said about the case involving the corporation's past wrongful acts and current differences in black and white cancer rates is just as true in the case of the government's past wrongful acts and current differences in black and white levels of well-being, even if we assume that levels of well-being are closely tied to levels of intelligence. Unless the hereditarian thesis maintains that genetic differences account for the entire gap in average levels of intelligence, the thesis gives us no reason to reject the claim that differences in social environment are responsible for part of the difference between black and white average levels of well-being, and thus no reason to reject the causal claim that makes up step three of the compensation argument. In the end, then, Levin's objection to the compensation argument is undone by an unwarranted overgeneralization that creeps in when he moves from his claims about race, genes and intelligence in general, to an application of those claims to the compensation argument in particular. If genetic differences are only *partly* responsible for intelligence differences, then even if intelligence differences in turn are *entirely* responsible for well-being differences, it won't follow that genetic differences are entirely responsible for well-being differences. And as long as environmental differences still play a significant role in explaining well-being differences, the hereditarian position will provide no reason to reject the causal claim[81] or the compensation argument that depends on it.

I've spent a fair amount of time here addressing an objection to the compensation argument that arises from the positions taken in *The Bell Curve* and *Why Race Matters*. A number of people may think that this has been a misguided enterprise, not because they agree with the views of Herrnstein, Murray, and Levin, but because they disagree with them so strongly that they deem them unworthy of discussion. Indeed, some people may well object at this point that by taking their views seriously here and trying to treat them in a fair and impartial manner, I've done nothing but lend undeserved credibility to the noxious claim that black people are genetically inferior to white people.

I would certainly have preferred to ignore their writings entirely. The subject itself is a distressing one, and some people consider it offensive and even racist simply to describe and consider the implications of the views held by people such as Herrnstein, Murray, and Levin. But while it's therefore tempting to avoid any consideration of their views when critically evaluating the objections that can be raised against the reparations position, in the end this would be an irresponsible form of evasion. Whether we like it or not, the claim that genetic differences between black and white people play at least some role in explaining the differences between black and white IQ scores is not an uncommon one. In a 1988 survey of over six hundred psychologists and educators with some knowledge of the subject, for example, only 15 percent endorsed the view that such IQ differences are entirely due to environmental differences, whereas 45 percent expressed the belief that the difference is a result of some combination of both environmental and genetic factors.[82] A defense of the reparations position that simply ignores objections based on claims about genetic differences, therefore, strikes me as disingenuous and dangerously incomplete.

In trying to defend the causal claim in previous sections, I said that one would have to accept this third step in the compensation argument unless one was willing to endorse the claim that black people are genetically inferior to white people. Having taken the time to examine the kinds of arguments offered by Herrnstein, Murray, and Levin, though, I can now conclude this section by making an even stronger claim: one must accept the causal claim that makes up the third step in the compensation argument *even if* one is willing to endorse the claim that black people are genetically inferior to white people, unless one is also willing to endorse the extraordinarily strong claim that the genetic differences between the races account for *all* of the contemporary differences between the races in terms of levels of intelligence and well-being. But virtually no one, not even the authors of *The Bell Curve* or *Why Race Matters*, has endorsed this extreme claim. And so virtually no one, in the end, is in a position to consistently deny step three of the compensation argument.

BETTER THAN NOTHING

For most people, I think, the results of the previous two sections should be clear: regardless of your views of black culture and regardless of your views of black genetics, you have no good reason to reject the causal claim. The third step of the compensation argument, that is, like the two that come before it, should simply be accepted. But philosophers aren't like most people. They tend to see problems where other people don't. And so there's a further objection to this third step in the compensation argument that I suspect will occur to many philosophers although it may not occur to anyone else. This further objection arises from a puzzle that has received a good deal of attention in a number of philosophical journals over the last few decades under the name of "the non-identity problem." And while I'm not sure how many people other than philosophers have even heard of the non-identity problem, at least a few philosophers have not only heard of it, but have pointed out that it can be used to raise a potentially serious concern about the reparations position.[83] The non-identity problem is somewhat abstract and esoteric, and so my discussion of it in this section is likely to seem a bit unusual, if not simply downright bizarre, to people who aren't used to reading contemporary academic moral philosophy. But for those who are willing to tolerate this sort of thinking, or maybe even to enjoy it, I'll try briefly to explain what the non-identity problem is and why it seems to pose a difficulty for the compensation argument before explaining why, in the end, I think this appearance turns out to be mistaken.

The non-identity problem arises from the fact that in certain kinds of cases, people's actions can affect not only the quality of life that subsequent generations will enjoy in the future, but also the very identity of the people who will exist in the future to enjoy it. In these often unusual sorts of cases, the application of moral principles that seem relatively uncontroversial in more familiar contexts can yield results that most people find intuitively unacceptable. Suppose, for example, that a factory was illegally dumping chemical waste into a city's water supply, and that the waste caused young children who lived in the city to become irreversibly blind. In this case, it would be clear that the company that owned the factory had wrongfully harmed these children and that it would owe them compensation as a result. But now consider a second and more complicated example. In this case, the chemical waste that's dumped into the water doesn't harm any children who already exist. Instead, when couples who live in the city try to have children, the chemical in the water supply causes it to take them two months longer than it would otherwise take to successfully conceive, and it causes the child who is eventually conceived to be born irreversibly blind.

For most people, it seems clear that there's no morally relevant difference between the two cases. In both cases, after all, the company wrongfully dumps chemical waste into the city's water supply, and in both cases, this causes an increase in irreversible blindness among children. If the company owes compensation in the first version of the story, our moral common sense tells us, then it owes compensation in the second and more complicated version as well. But the argument that gives rise to the non-identity problem seems to show that this is not the case, and it seems to show this simply by appealing to claims that virtually everyone already accepts. Since this feature of the argument can perhaps best be understood by focusing on the details of a particular couple in each version of the story, let's suppose that in the first example, Arnold and Alice had a child named Alex who became irreversibly blind when he was exposed to the toxic waste at the age of three, and that in the second example, Bob and Betty had difficulty having a child because of the presence of the waste in their water but eventually conceived Bill, who was born irreversibly blind. The argument then proceeds as follows.

First, while in the first example, the company's actions clearly caused Alex to be worse off than he would otherwise have been, in the second example, the company's actions did not, in fact, make Bill worse off than he would otherwise have been. If the company hadn't dumped its chemical waste into the water supply in the first example, Alex would now exist and would be sighted rather than blind. Because it's worse to exist and be blind than to exist and be sighted, the company's acts thus made Alex worse off than he would otherwise have been. But if the company hadn't dumped its chemical waste into the water supply in the second and more complicated example, Bill would not be better off than he is today because Bill would not exist today. This is because if the company hadn't dumped its waste into the water, Bob and Betty would have conceived two months earlier than they did, and thus would have created a child from a different sperm and egg than the ones that gave rise to the existence of Bill. From the point of view of Bill, then, unlike from the point of view of Alex, the choice is not between existing and being blind or existing and not being blind. Rather, the choice is between existing and being blind or not existing at all. Existing and being blind is not worse than not existing at all. No one really thinks, when they see a blind person, that the blind person would have been better off never existing. And so it turns out that the company's act of dumping the chemical waste in the city's water supply did not, in fact, make Bill worse off than he would otherwise have been.

To this foundational claim about the effects of the company's act in the more complicated version of the story, the argument that generates the non-identity problem adds a few more steps. First, it maintains, to harm someone is to make them worse off than they would otherwise have been. Since the company's actions did not make Bill worse off than he would otherwise have been, the company's actions did not harm him. Second, it claims, if an act doesn't harm someone, it doesn't wrong them. Since the company's actions apparently did not harm Bill, it follows that they did not wrong Bill either. Finally, the argument points out, if an act doesn't wrong someone, then it can't be used to ground a claim of compensation.[84] And from all of this it thus seems to follow that while the company would owe compensation for causing blindness to exist in children in the first case, it would not owe compensation for causing blindness to exist in children in the second case. Because this conclusion seems unreasonable, and since the argument that gives rise to it seems to rely only on steps that, when looked at one at a time, each seem to be reasonable, the argument that the steps give rise to generates a problem. And since the argument turns crucially on the fact that in the second case, unlike in the first case, the child who ends up existing and being blind is not identical to the sighted child who would have existed otherwise, the problem is called the non-identity problem.

Now what, it might well be asked at this point, does this esoteric philosophical puzzle have to do with slave reparations? The answer is that black Americans today, like the blind children in the second version of the story about the polluting factory, seem to owe their very existence to the fact that wrongful acts took place before they were conceived. Indeed, they seem to owe their existence to precisely those wrongful acts that the compensation argument appeals to in making the case for slave reparations. And if this feature of the situation is enough to undermine the claim for compensation in the second factory case, as the argument behind the non-identity problem seems to establish, then it would seem to be enough to undermine the claim for compensation in the slave reparations case as well. The causal claim will be defeated, that is, because the black people who live in America today aren't really worse off than they would have been had slavery and its aftermath never occurred. They aren't really worse off precisely because if slavery and its aftermath had never occurred, they would not have existed in the first place.

Here, again, it may be useful to focus on a specific example in order to see how the non-identity problem arises. So suppose that several generations ago, a small plantation owner in Georgia purchased a male slave from one part of Africa and a female slave from another part of Africa. These two slaves went on to have three children together. John, a typical black teenager living today in Detroit, is one of their descendants. If the U.S. Constitution had prohibited slavery, it is virtually certain that these two slaves would never have met. Before they were captured, they lived in isolated areas in different parts of Africa, spoke different languages, knew nothing of each other's communities. And even if, by some miraculous coincidence, they would have met at some point in Africa had they not both been enslaved and sent to Georgia, it's virtually certain that they would not have conceived three children at exactly the same moments that they conceived their three offspring on a small plantation in Georgia. In short, if slavery had been abolished in the United States in 1789, then at least one of John's ancestors would never have existed. And if at least one of John's ancestors would never have existed, then John himself would never have existed. John is here today only because some of his ancestors were wrongfully enslaved.

With this example in mind, we can see how the non-identity problem really does seem to pose a difficulty for the compensation argument and, more specifically, how it seems to undermine the causal claim that makes up the third step of the argument. The compensation argument depends crucially on the claim that black Americans like John are being wrongfully harmed today as a result of wrongful acts that were committed in earlier times by the U.S. government. John faces obstacles in school, for example, that black teenagers in Detroit wouldn't be facing today were it not for the legacy of slavery and its aftermath. This causal claim is essential to the compensation argument because if John isn't being harmed by the past wrongful acts that were committed by the United States, then there's nothing for John to be compensated for. And the fact about the contingency of John's very existence seems clearly to undermine this claim: if there had never been slavery, legalized segregation, and discrimination in the United States, after all, then while black teenagers in Detroit would presumably be doing better today than they're currently doing, John would not be one of them. To harm someone, as the argument underlying the non-identity problem points out, is to make him worse off than he would otherwise have been. But John is not, in fact, worse off than he would otherwise have been. If slavery had not occurred, then John would not have been at all. Beacuse John is not worse off than he would have been had slavery not occurred, he has not been harmed by the fact that slavery did occur. And because he has not been harmed by the fact that slavery occurred, he can't be owed anything to compensate him for the fact that it occurred.

This objection to the causal claim depends on the claim that the case of John is suitably analogous to the case of Bill. There are therefore two ways in which a defender of the causal claim might attempt to respond. One would be to agree that the two cases are analogous and to insist that compensation is owed in both cases rather than in neither. The other would be to concede that no compensation is owed in the case of Bill but to maintain that even if this is so, the case of John is sufficiently different to warrant the appropriateness of compensation in that case nonetheless.

I suspect that most people will be satisfied by the first kind of response. Most people, after all, will surely believe that a company that dumps toxic waste into a city's water supply owes compensation for the blindness that results even if the blindness only occurs in children who would not have been conceived had the waste not been dumped in the first place. Most people who are exposed to the non-identity problem, that is, while certainly puzzled by the problem, are not really convinced by the argument that generates it. Even if they can't explain precisely where the argument goes wrong, they're convinced that it must go wrong somewhere. Because I think this is true of most people regardless of their views of slave reparations in particular, and since my goal here is to defend the compensation argument on terms that most people on both sides of the reparations debate accept, I think it's reasonable to appeal to this first kind of response in defending the compensation argument from the objection based on the non-identity problem. Because most people will agree that the company owes compensation in the case of Bill despite the fact that Bill would not exist had the company not wrongfully polluted the city's water supply, that is, the fact that John would not exist had slavery not occurred in the United States will give them no reason to deny that the United States owes John compensation in that case either.

But let's suppose that most people are wrong about this. Let's suppose that Bill has not been harmed by the company's wrongful acts and that as a result of this, the company really would owe nothing to Bill in the form of compensation. Even if all of this is true, the non-identity problem still fails to give us a reason to reject the compensation argument. This is because there turns out to be a crucial difference between the case of Bill and the case of John.[85]

To appreciate the difference between these two cases, it may help to begin by considering yet another variation on the story of the company that dumps toxic waste into a city's water supply. So let's suppose that on this third version of the story, as in the version about Bill, the presence of the waste in the water supply causes couples to take two months longer than it would otherwise take to conceive and that it causes the children that they do conceive to be born blind. But let's suppose that in this third version of the story, unlike in the second version, the blindness is not irreversible. And let's suppose, in particular, that the lingering effects of the waste having been dumped in the water supply several years ago continue to impede the ability of the young children to recover from their blindness. Claude and Carol end up having a little boy named Charlie. Charlie is born blind. If the air did not contain traces of the toxic waste that was dumped in the water, his vision would gradually clear up. But because the air does continue to contain such traces, he continues to suffer from vision problems.

In this third version of the toxic waste story, as in the second version, the children who are made blind by the company's wrongful actions would not exist at all if the company hadn't dumped the toxic waste into the water in the first place. So it is as true of Charlie as it was of Bill – however true that turns out to be – that being born blind is not, in itself, a harm to him, given that being blind isn't worse than never being born at all. But in this third version of the story, unlike the second version, the children who are born blind continue to be subjected to harmful exposure to the lingering consequences of the toxic waste well after their birth. Once Bill is born, that is, he is no worse off living in an environment that continues to contain traces of the waste than living in a cleaner environment, because either way he will continue to be irreversibly blind. But after Charlie is born, he is made worse off by living in the polluted environment than he would be if he were living in a cleaner one, because the lingering effects of the toxic waste being dumped into the water cause him to continue to have vision problems that he would not continue to have if the waste were cleaned up.

This third version of the story seems to be importantly different from the second. Even if we find ourselves unable to resist the argument that generates the non-identity problem, and even if we therefore insist that the company would owe nothing to Bill for causing him to be conceived in the way that he was conceived in the second version of the story, it would not follow from this that the company would owe nothing to Charlie in the third version of the story. Even if Charlie was not harmed by the company's causing him to be conceived in the way that he was conceived, after all, now that he exists he is clearly being harmed by the continuing presence of the toxic waste in the environment. The presence of the waste is clearly the result of the company's wrongful act, and so the company would owe it to Charlie to clean up the remaining waste or to compensate him in some other way for the vision problems that the remaining waste causes him to continue to suffer. It's true, of course, that the act that now causes Charlie these harms took place before he was conceived, but this in itself provides no reason to doubt that the company would owe compensation to Charlie even if it wouldn't owe compensation to Bill. If the company had planted a bomb under Claude and Carol's house several years before Charlie was conceived, after all, this would do nothing to undermine the claim that it would owe compensation to Charlie if the bomb later exploded and caused Charlie to lose his vision.

It seems to me, then, that even if someone is willing to accept the very counterintuitive conclusion endorsed by the argument behind the non-identity problem, they will still have no reason to deny that the company would owe compensation to Charlie as a result of its having wrongfully damaged the environment that Charlie finds himself growing up in. And this result is important because, in the end, the case of John the black teenager in Detroit is more like the case of Charlie than it is like the case of Bill. It is as true of John as it is of Bill, of course, that he would not now exist had certain previous wrongful acts not occurred. But like Charlie, and unlike Bill, John finds himself growing up in an environment that makes things more difficult for him than it would be were he growing up in an environment that did not suffer the lingering aftereffects of those previous wrongful actions. The lingering aftereffects are there because of earlier wrongs committed by the U.S. government and, as in the case of Charlie, it doesn't matter that these wrongful acts took place before John was conceived. What matters is that now that John exists, he is harmed by those features of his environment that impede his progress, and that it is the fault of the U.S. government that the acts that led to those features took place. Even those who think that the polluting company would owe no compensation to Bill in the second version of the story should still think it would owe compensation to Charlie in the third version.

And since the case of John the black teenager in Detroit is more like the case of Charlie than it is like the case of Bill, they should therefore agree that compensation is owed to John even if they resist the claim that it is owed to Bill. Not only should people accept the third step of the compensation argument regardless of what they think about black culture and black genetics, then, but they should accept it regardless of what they think (if they think anything at all) about the non-identity problem. Put simply, people should accept the third step of the compensation argument.

COMPENSATION COMPLICATIONS

I've argued so far that we should accept the first three steps of the compensation argument. Before considering objections that might be raised against either of the two remaining two steps, though, it's important to acknowledge one final kind of worry that might arise at this point. For after having considered my defenses of the first and third steps of the argument individually, some readers may be left with the nagging suspicion that even if I've succeeded in rendering each of the steps fairly plausible on their own, I've overlooked a problem with formulating one of the two steps that only becomes apparent once we consider the prospect of combining them as part of a larger argument. In particular, they might complain, now that it's become clear precisely what's involved in defending the causal claim, we should become more skeptical about precisely what the compensation principle should say.

One version of this worry concerns the level of confidence we can reasonably have in the causal claim. A critic of the reparations position might acknowledge that my responses to the various objections to that claim succeed in making it seem more plausible than its denial, but the critic might still worry that I haven't really established that it's true beyond any reasonable doubt. It's still possible, the critic might say, that the biological explanation of contemporary differences in black and white average levels of well-being will eventually be vindicated, that some version of the cultural explanation of the differences could be devised that doesn't simply lapse into the biological explanation, or that some entirely different and better explanation of the contemporary data might be uncovered. And while simply being pretty confident that the causal claim is true might be good enough for purely speculative purposes, the critic might then add, it isn't good enough if we're going to use the claim as the basis for making potentially significant demands on the federal government. For that, the critic might insist, we would really require proof.

I'm perfectly happy to acknowledge that I haven't proved the truth of the causal claim beyond a reasonable doubt. But I'm just as happy to insist that this is an unreasonable standard to apply to the issue at hand. In a civil suit, after all, a plaintiff doesn't have to prove beyond a reasonable doubt that he was injured by the defendant's act. He merely has to establish that the claim is more likely true than not, that his claim is supported by a simple preponderance of the evidence.

Even if it's only a little bit more likely than not that his injury really was due to the culpable behavior of the defendant, that is, that's enough to warrant a judgment in his favor. There's no reason to treat the parallel moral claim any differently, and so no reason to reject the compensation argument on the grounds that the causal claim is merely more than likely to be true. Although I passed over the issue of the appropriate level of burden of proof when I introduced and later modified step one of the compensation argument, then, we can go ahead and make the appropriate level of burden of proof explicit now. Rather than maintaining that a government incurs a moral obligation to compensate its victim for the harms that it has wrongfully caused only if it's known beyond a reasonable doubt to have wrongfully harmed someone as a result of the authorized actions of some of its public officials, the principle should be understood as saying that a government incurs a moral obligation to compensate its victim for the harms that it has wrongfully caused if it's more reasonable to believe than to deny that it has wrongfully harmed someone as a result of the authorized actions of some of its public officials. And with this reasonable understanding of step one of the argument in mind, our lack of genuine certainty about step three provides no reason to reject the argument itself.

A second version of this general worry also concerns our degree of confidence in the causal claim. On this second account, though, the worry isn't about how confident we are in the general claim that the government's past wrongful acts continue to have negative consequences today, but rather about how confident we are in any specific claim that a given individual is one of the particular people who has suffered these negative consequences. Even if we're sufficiently confident that black Americans as a whole on average are doing less well today than black Americans would be doing in the absence of a long history of slavery and legalized segregation and discrimination, that is, the critic might still worry that we can't be as confident about identifying precisely which black Americans are doing worse off as a result and which ones aren't. Even if we believe that every black American is confronted by a sort of adverse social environment that no white American faces, for example, some people might turn out to flourish more in the face of adversity than they would have under more comfortable circumstances. And this, too, might be thought to pose a problem for applying the causal claim to the compensation principle. If the causal claim can't tell us precisely which individuals are being adversely affected, that is, and if the compensation principle is only plausible when it requires this level of specificity, then while each of the two steps in the argument will continue to seem reasonable on their own terms, we won't be able to combine them in the way that the compensation argument requires them to be combined.

This second worry is understandable. But as with the first worry, it can be satisfactorily addressed by appealing to the parallel case of tort law.[86] Suppose, for example, that there's sufficient evidence that a corporation's negligence in allowing some of its toxic waste to leak into a city's public water supply was responsible for a twenty percent increase in the incidence of cancer in the city.

Even if the evidence can't demonstrate which particular cancer sufferers got their cancer as a result of the corporation's act, it should be clear that this would not be enough to get the corporation off the hook. Although there's room for reasonable disagreement about how the suitable form of compensation could best be determined in such a case, it's hard to believe that anyone on either side of the slave reparations debate would think that the company would owe absolutely nothing as a result. If funding a new cancer unit in the local hospital would help to take care of the increase in cancer cases, for example, then even though there would be no way of ensuring that all and only the patients whose cancer was caused by the corporation's negligence would benefit from the funding, it's hard to believe that anyone would think it more just to have the corporation pay nothing at all than to have it fund the new cancer unit, at least on the assumption there was no more effective way available of directing resources to all and only the patients whose cancer was caused by the corporation. And if the uncertainty about the identity of the particular victims wouldn't be enough to void an obligation to make compensation in the case of the corporation and the toxic waste, it should be clear that it wouldn't be enough to do so in the case of slave reparations either. If there's no way for the federal government to direct compensatory benefits to all and only those black Americans who really are being adversely impacted by the lingering effects of slavery and Jim Crow, that is, this is a reason to conclude that the government is obligated to simply do the best it can to benefit those who are entitled to it rather than a reason to think it isn't obligated to do anything at all.

Two other features of the causal claim may also seem to reveal previously unnoticed worries about the compensation principle. They arise not from concerns about our degree of confidence in the causal claim, but from features of the content of the claim itself. One is that the particular mechanisms by which the claim maintains that slavery and its aftermath causally contributed to the difficulties of contemporary black American life would have been extremely difficult for anyone in the past to have foreseen. The compensation principle maintains that if the government wrongfully harms someone, then it incurs a moral obligation to compensate its victim, but it should presumably include at least some sort of condition requiring that the harm be in some sense a reasonably foreseeable consequence of the government's act. And this might seem to suggest that a suitably qualified version of the principle would not, in fact, apply in the case of slave reparations, given the complex nature of the causal claim. But this worry can easily be set aside. A standard that required a person to be able to anticipate precisely how his actions could lead to future harm would be far too strict to be reasonable. A person who wrongfully dumped an unmarked container of chemicals into the public water supply, for example, would be able to evade responsibility by pointing out that he was unable to foresee exactly what effect his action would have. A standard that requires that a person be able to recognize that his act is the kind of act that has the potential to cause significant harm, by contrast, is a more reasonable one. But there is no reason to think that it is not met in the case of the wrongful acts of slavery and Jim Crow. When George Mason warned that "Providence punishes national sins by national calamities,"[87] he was far from the only person to see that the course the nation had set for itself was likely to have devastating consequences.

The other feature of the causal claim that might seem to suggest a further problem with the compensation principle concerns the fact that the causal chain it appeals to runs from the acts of the initial wrongdoers through the acts of subsequent people before it reaches the harmful consequences to contemporary black Americans. The acts of those who facilitated slavery and Jim Crow, that is, set into motion a chain of events, but the events have only had an impact on contemporary black Americans because they impacted the behavior of those who lived between then and now, and the actions of those people in turn impacted the lives of contemporary Americans. As with the issue of foreseeability, this feature of the causal claim suggests that the compensation principle requires an additional qualification. A standard on which a person is held responsible for all of the indirect harmful consequences of his behavior would again be unreasonable. If I wrongfully vandalize your car and this makes you angry and your anger leads you to beat your spouse, for example, my act indirectly causes harm to your spouse but it would be unreasonable to say that I would owe your spouse compensation as a result.[88] But, again as with the issue of foreseeability, this need not pose a problem for the compensation argument. There are plenty of cases in which it is perfectly reasonable to hold a person responsible for the harms that their wrongful acts cause by influencing the behavior of others. If my libelous article about your restaurant causes your customers to take their business elsewhere, for example, virtually everyone on both sides of the reparations debate would agree that it's fair to hold me responsible for the harm you suffer, even though my article only causes harm to you because it influences other people to behave in ways that are bad for you. If I steal from you and as a result you are unable to pay your child's medical bills, virtually everyone would agree that it's fair to hold me responsible for the harm your child suffers even though my act only harms your child because it has an impact on the level of benefits you are able to pass along to him. These cases involve causal connections that are more like the connections involved in the causal claim that constitutes the third step of the compensation argument. And so even if we are unable to say precisely how the compensation principle should be formulated in terms of foreseeability or the role of intervening agents, we can say enough to show that its most reasonable formulation will enable it to successfully apply to the causal claim. In the end, then, there is no reason to reject the first three steps of the compensation argument either individually or when combined.

What about the final two steps of the argument? Step four of the compensation argument is what I called the "surviving public obligation principle," the claim that if a government incurs a moral obligation as a result of the authorized actions of some of its public officials, then this obligation doesn't cease to exist when the officials in question cease to exist. The NATO Treaty, for example,

didn't stop generating obligations for Americans when the president and senators whose actions caused it to be ratified died. And the United States didn't
stop owing reparations to Japanese Americans who were confined to internment
camps during the Second World War when President Roosevelt died. I'm not
aware of any opponent of slave reparations who has opposed this principle and
am not even sure how many opponents of slave reparations have recognized that
the principle plays a crucial role in justifying the reparations position in the first
place.[89] It is, in any event, extremely difficult to imagine any credible objection
that could be raised against this step in the argument. Virtually everyone on both
sides of the slave reparations debate accepts the legitimacy of reparations in the
internment camp case, for example, and it's hard to see how reparations in that
case could be justified if the surviving public obligation principle were rejected.
In addition, virtually everyone on both sides of the debate agrees that what the
principle says is true in the case of the various rights that we claim today. If the
government sought to ban newspapers or prevent people from attending religious
services, for example, no one would take seriously a justification for such actions
based on the fact that all of the public officials who ratified the First Amendment
died a long time ago. But if we're perfectly happy to claim legal rights that were
generated by the acts of our Founding Fathers, on what basis could we refuse
to accept legal obligations that were generated by their acts? Because I haven't
encountered any objections to this fourth step of the compensation argument in
the works I've read on the subject and since I haven't been able to think of any
on my own, I conclude that the fourth step, like the first three, should simply be
accepted, and that it, again like the others, should be accepted on grounds that
people on both sides of the reparations debate already accept.

This brings us, finally, to step five. The fifth step in the compensation argument is what I called the "unpaid balance claim," the claim that the U.S. government has not, in fact, fully compensated the currently living generation of
black Americans for the harms they continue to suffer as a result of slavery and
its aftermath. This step is needed because even if it's true that the past wrongful acts of the government had generated a debt, the debt would not exist today
if it had already been paid. As we saw in the discussion of his eighth objection
to slave reparations, Horowitz does seem to reject this final step in the argument. The United States, he points out, has already implemented various forms
of affirmative action and has spent a tremendous amount of money on a variety
of social programs, and these actions were designed, at least in part, to alleviate
the harmful consequences of earlier injustices. But, as we also saw in that discussion, Horowitz himself also believes that these attempts have been unsuccessful
and even counterproductive, and to the extent that they have been beneficial
they have benefited poor white Americans and not just poor black Americans.
This means that while it may be true that the government has tried to make
reparations, it is not true that it has succeeded in making reparations, and that
even if it has helped a number of black Americans, it hasn't done so in a way
that significantly addresses the continuing disparities between black and white

average levels of well-being that are the contemporary legacy of slavery and its aftermath.

In order to deny the fifth step of the compensation argument, then, one would have to insist not merely that the government has attempted to repair the harms that continue to linger from past injustices, but that it has succeeded in doing so. One would have to insist, in short, that black Americans on the whole today are doing at least roughly as well as one would expect black Americans on the whole to be doing if our nation's history hadn't included a long period of legalized slavery followed by a long period of legalized segregation and discrimination. But as we saw in our discussion of the third step of the argument, no one really believes this. People such as McWhorter, Steele, and D'Souza, who think that contemporary black American culture is largely to blame for contemporary black American problems agree that slavery and its aftermath played a crucial role in giving rise to that culture, and people such as Herrnstein, Murray, and Levin, who think that genetic racial differences play a significant role in explaining contemporary black American problems agree that the genetic account does not provide a complete explanation of those problems and that part of the source of the problems lies in the way that black Americans have historically been treated. Since no one really doubts that black Americans today on the whole would be doing at least somewhat better were it not for the legacy of slavery and its aftermath, no one should doubt the fifth and final step of the compensation argument either.

AMERICA 2.0

I've argued that all five steps of the compensation argument should be accepted, and that they should be accepted on grounds that people on both sides of the reparations debate already admit. If I've been right about this, then there are only two more ways in which a critic of the reparations position might respond. One would be to agree that all of the steps in the argument should be accepted but to deny that the conclusion that we should accept the reparations position follows from them. The other would be to admit that no flaw has been found in the compensation argument, but to insist that there is some problem with the argument's conclusion that is so great that it proves that there must be a flaw in the argument somewhere, even if we can't figure out precisely where the flaw is. I will conclude my examination of the objections that might be raised against the compensation argument by considering these two approaches in turn.

On the face of it, at least, there seems to be no room to press the first kind of objection to the compensation argument. If the steps of the argument are examined slowly and carefully, it should seem clear that if all five of the steps are accepted, then the reparations position itself must be accepted as well: the first two steps of the argument establish a debt that the U.S. government in the past would have owed to black Americans in the past, the third justifies extending the debt from one owed to past black Americans to one owed to present black Americans, the fourth justifies extending the debt from one owed by the past government to one owed by the present government, and the fifth justifies the conclusion that this debt of the current government to current black Americans still exists because it has not yet been fully paid. There is, however, one kind of objection to the reparations position that can be understood as claiming that this conclusion doesn't really follow even if all of the steps in the argument are accepted.

The objection that I have in mind maintains that the compensation argument as a whole commits the fallacy of equivocation. Here's a simple example. Suppose that I say that Bill wrongfully damaged my car, that when someone wrongfully damages someone else's car, they incur a moral obligation to compensate their victim for the harm they have wrongfully caused, and that Bill has therefore incurred a moral obligation to compensate me for the harm that he has wrongfully caused. This looks like a well-constructed argument. If the two claims that it makes are true, then the conclusion that Bill has incurred an obligation to compensate me seems clearly to follow as a simple matter of logic. But now suppose that when I said "Bill" the first time, I was referring to Bill Clinton, and that when I said "Bill" the second time, I was referring to Bill Gates. Suppose, that is, that my argument was claiming that because Bill Clinton wrongfully damaged my car, Bill Gates now owes me compensation. Now it doesn't look like such a good argument. The reason the argument initially appears to be a valid one is that the reader assumes that the name "Bill" refers to the same person in both cases. If the name really does refer to the same person, then the argument really does work. But the reason the argument turns out to be faulty is that I am in fact using the name "Bill" in a manner that involves equivocation. If a term appears at different stages in an argument, it has to be used consistently in order for the parts of the argument to mesh successfully as a whole.

Here's why this might seem to pose a problem for the compensation argument for slave reparations. Some of the steps in the compensation argument refer to "the U.S. government" and the conclusion refers to it as well. If the expression, "the U.S. government" is used to refer to one and the same entity at each stage, then this will pose no problem for the argument. The government that caused the harms in the past will be the same as the government that now owes compensation as a result in the present. This will be like the case where the Bill who damaged my car in the past is the same person as the Bill who is now said to owe me compensation, and not some entirely different person who just happens to have the same first name. But if the expression "the U.S. government" refers to one entity when talking about things that happened in the past and a second and distinct entity when talking about debts of compensation that are owed in the present, then the compensation argument will break down. Saying that "the United States government" owes compensation now because "the United States government" wrongfully caused harm in the past will be like saying that Bill Gates owes me compensation now because Bill Clinton wrongfully caused me harm in the past. And at least a few people have objected to the compensation argument in just this way. The U.S. government that used to exist doesn't exist anymore, on this account, and the U. S. government that exists now did not exist back in the days of slavery and Jim Crow. And so the government that exists today, according to this objection, doesn't owe compensation in response to the wrongful harms that were inflicted by the government that existed in the regrettable past.

In order to respond to the complaint that the compensation argument is guilty of equivocation, it's important to begin by getting clearer about just what, precisely, this complaint amounts to. When the critic acknowledges that there was a national government in the past that enforced the fugitive slave laws, for example, he isn't insisting that it was the government of some other country, like France or Spain, that helped Georgia plantation owners recover their slaves when they escaped to New York. He agrees that it was the government of the United States that did this. And when he denies the conclusion of the compensation argument, the claim that the government today owes compensation to the currently living generation of black Americans, he doesn't pretend that that the argument is making a conclusion about the government of some other country at that point either, either. He agrees that the defender of reparations is, again, talking about the government of the United States. And it's not as if the critic is under the impression that there are two different countries with the same name, one of which practiced slavery in the past and one of which didn't, in the way that there are two different people named Bill, one of whom vandalized my car in the past and one of whom didn't. The critic understands that there is and has been only one country called the United States of America.

But while the critic recognizes that there is only one country called the United States, he maintains that the differences between the government that rules that country today and the government that ruled it back in the bad old days are so fundamental that it doesn't really make sense to think of them as one and the same government. Rather, on this analysis, it makes more sense to think that there was one government ruling this country back then and a very different government ruling this country today. And if that's right, then the compensation argument is guilty of the fallacy of equivocation. Even if all of the steps of the argument are correct, they will still fail to justify the reparations position.

The reasons given for thinking that we are really talking about two different governments here and not just one are varied. Sometimes the point made is that the country is much larger today than it was at the outset. The federal government, that is, rules a much greater territory than it did prior to the Civil War. A second and perhaps more significant difference concerns the breadth and depth of the power of the federal government. In the early years of the Republic, the federal government was relatively weak and much more power was vested in the individual states. The original vision of America, that is, pictured the United States as a federation of largely autonomous individual states. As more and more power has been concentrated in the hands of the federal government in the years that have passed, the critic then points out, the very nature of the federal government has significantly changed. Finally, and perhaps most importantly, the proponent of this kind of objection to the compensation argument appeals to the many substantive Constitutional and legislative changes that have been made since the end of the Civil War, especially those that pertain to the right of black Americans to equal treatment under the law.[90] If the government of old was in many ways an unjust government, then at least in these respects, the government of today is undeniably a much better one.

The result of all of this, the critic then concludes, is that the country today is not really being ruled by the same government that enforced the fugitive slave laws. That earlier government was, in effect, the alpha version of the federal government and we now live under the beta version, a sort of America 2.0. And if that's the case, then the government we live under today owes no compensation for the harms that were caused by slavery and its aftermath in the past because those harms were caused by some other government. And since that other government no longer exists, there is no one else to owe the compensation either.

With this understanding of the equivocation objection in mind, we are now in a better position to see just what is wrong with it. The problem can be discerned from a few different angles, but in each case the flaw is fundamentally the same: it's much more reasonable to picture the changes that have occurred over the years as changes that have happened within one and the same government than to try to construe them as changes that resulted in the destruction of one government and the creation of another.

One way to see this problem with the equivocation objection is to consider the effects that these sorts of changes have on our judgments regarding the changes that occur in people over time, rather than in governments. So suppose that you have an uncle – let's call him Sam – who has changed a great deal over the past twenty-five years. When he was a younger man, he was physically frail, wielded very little influence over others, and was a virulent racist. Now that he's reached middle age, he's virtually unrecognizable to those who haven't seen him during the intervening decades. He's made himself far stronger in both body and in mind, holds enormous power over a great number of people by virtue of the sheer force of his personality and the vast personal fortune that he has amassed, and is now a leading figure in the modern civil rights movement, having long ago tearfully repented for his youthful infatuation with racial hatred.

In cases such as this, where a person evolves greatly over time or undergoes some kind of radically transformative experience such as a religious conversion, we often speak of them as if they were "a whole different person." But it's important to recognize that we don't really mean this literally. We don't mean that your Uncle Sam has literally ceased to exist, for example, and that some truly different person, one who did not exist when Sam did, has now taken his place. We mean that he is still Sam, the very same person he was a quarter century ago, but that he – Sam, and not someone other than Sam – is now very different from the way that he, Sam, was before. If your Uncle Sam took out a thirty-year mortgage on his house twenty-five years ago, for example, he could not get out of paying the remaining balance on his loan by insisting to the bank that he is now a completely different person from the person who took out the loan. In one sense of the word, he is indeed a very different person, but in the sense that matters in determining whether or not he's still the person who is obligated to pay the debt that he incurred twenty-five years ago, he's exactly who he was before. He is the very same Sam who signed the papers agreeing to make his monthly payments for thirty years and not someone other than that Sam. When a person who incurs a long-term obligation goes on to become much bigger, better, and more power-ful than he was before, this doesn't get him off the hook by making him literally a different person. And this fact creates a powerful presumption in favor of the view that we should say precisely the same thing about governments. If the gov-ernment of the United States is now much bigger, better, and more powerful than it was when it first incurred a debt to its black citizens, this fact doesn't get it off the hook by making it literally some government other than the one that still owes something in virtue of its own past injustices.

A second way to see this problem with the equivocation objection involves looking at things from a somewhat more theoretical point of view. In the case of your Uncle Sam, for example, we can try to reflect on the more philosophical question of *why* Sam is still the same person he was before, why the changes that take place in the story involve changes happening to a particular person rather than changes that cause one person to turn into a second and distinctly different person. Although it's difficult to give a precise answer to this question, at a very general level the best explanation seems to be clear: while many things about Sam have changed over the years, whatever it is that we think made Sam the particular person that he was and not some other person in the first place have not really changed. Philosophers who think about these sorts of questions disagree quite sharply about just what it is that constitutes a particular person. Some would say that Sam is essentially a particular human organism: as long as that organism continues to exist, then so does Sam, and as long as you are point-ing to that particular organism you are pointing to Sam and not to someone else. Others would say that Sam is essentially a particular mind, or psyche, or perhaps soul: as long as that mind or psyche or soul continues to exist, then so does Sam, and as long as you are speaking of that particular mind or psyche or soul you are speaking of Sam and not of someone else. But whatever it is that ultimately makes Sam the particular person that he is and not some other person at the beginning of the story, the point remains that that something (that organism, per-haps, or that mind) continues to exist at the end of the story, and that this is why the story involves a change happening within Sam's life rather than a catastrophe in which Sam's life ends and the life of some other truly different person begins.

The general lesson of the story of the changes that took place in Sam's life can then be applied to the case of the great changes that have taken place in our nation's government. If we want to know whether the government that rules the United States today is the same government as the one that ruled the United States two hundred years ago, we must start by asking just what it was that con-stituted that government in the first place. When the U.S. government was first created, that is, what exactly made it a national government, and what made it the

U.S. government in particular, and not, say, the French government or the Spanish government? And while the question of what constitutes a distinct human person has proved to be a deeply puzzling one, the question of what constitutes a distinct national government seems to have a relatively straightforward answer, at least in the case of a national government like that of the United States: what constitutes the government is, as its name suggests, the Constitution. When the individual states that originally composed the United States agreed to the terms of the U.S. Constitution, they thereby created a national sovereign authority to rule over them. As long as that authority continues to reside in that Constitution, then that national authority continues to exist, even if more states agree to join and submit themselves to it, even if it becomes more powerful, even if the people who wield it become more enlightened, even if the Constitution itself is amended, as long as the amendments are made in accordance with procedures that the Constitution itself requires. As long as the U.S. government continues to be constituted by the U.S. Constitution, in short, it remains the very same government that first came into being when the Constitution was first ratified.[91] And since the U.S. government today does, in fact, continue to be constituted by the United States Constitution, the best theoretical understanding of what it is for a government to continue to exist over time confirms what the analogy with your Uncle Sam already strongly suggested: that although the U.S. government has changed in a great many ways over the years, it is nonetheless the very same government that has ruled the United States since well before the Civil War.[92] The compensation argument, as a result, is not subject to the equivocation objection.

Finally, the claim that the equivocation objection appeals to, the claim that the government that rules the United States today is literally not the same government as the one that ruled the United States two hundred years ago, must be rejected because it has implications that virtually everyone, regardless of their view of slave reparations in particular, will surely reject as unacceptable. Consider, for example, the practice of buying government bonds. If you buy a savings bond for a certain amount of money today, you can redeem it from the government for a significantly greater value a number of years later. And the United States has been engaging in this practice since the very beginning of its existence. Now imagine a family that has been in this country since the year the Constitution was ratified. Every year, a member of this family has bought one new thirty-year bond, and every time one of the bonds has matured, a member of the family has cashed it in. If the U.S. government today is not the same government that ruled the United States over two hundred years ago, then there must be some point at which one of the members bought a U.S. Savings Bond and then found, when it went to cash it in, that the government would not accept it because the government that issued the bond no longer existed.[93] But virtually everyone, regardless of their views of slave reparations, would recognize this scenario as absurd. Even if we look at one of the greatest periods of change in our nation's history, say from five years before the Civil War began to twenty years after it ended, it should be clear that any bond issued by the U.S. government at the beginning of that period would still be good at the end of it. The same, for that matter, goes for postage stamps. The post office will deliver your mail as long as you have put the appropriate amount of postage on it. If you put a bunch of new French stamps on your letter, that won't count. But if you put a bunch of American stamps on it, even if the stamps are very old, it will. And this is because, again, the U.S. government today is the very same government as the one that has been ruling this country since the Constitution was ratified over two hundred years ago. And since it is, the equivocation objection to the compensation argument must, once again, be rejected. The government that the compensation argument refers to in any one part of the argument is precisely the same as the government that it refers to in any other. And so if all of the steps in the argument are, indeed, accepted, then the conclusion must be accepted as well.[94]

PAYING THE BILL

I've now argued that all five steps of the compensation argument should be accepted and that if all five steps are accepted then the truth of the reparations position follows as a matter of elementary logic. Let's now assume that I've been correct about both of these claims. Does this mean that the reparations position has now, at last, been vindicated? Not quite. Sometimes you can find yourself confronted by an argument where the assumptions all seem clearly true, the conclusion seems clearly to follow from the assumptions, but the conclusion itself is so hard to believe that it's more reasonable to conclude that the argument must contain a mistake somewhere that you overlooked than to concede that the argument's conclusion really should be accepted. In these somewhat unusual circumstances, you may well be entitled to continue to reject an argument's conclusion even though you have no idea what's wrong with the argument that leads to it.

If the compensation argument has implications that are sufficiently objectionable, then, perhaps it's reasonable to reject the argument even if we can't see precisely where the argument goes wrong. The question, then, is whether critics of the reparations position have succeeded in identifying any problems with the position that would be serious enough to warrant rejecting the argument given that the argument itself seems now to have been fully vindicated.

One such possible problem is often posed as a question: if the United States is going to make reparations for slavery and its aftermath, who's going to pay for it? This is a question that my students invariably raise in class whenever I present readings on the subject. Whenever they ask this, I always suggest what seems to be a fairly straightforward answer: the same people who pay for anything else the government does – the taxpayers. But this answer rarely strikes everyone as satisfactory. There are usually at least a few students who are bothered by the fact that black people pay taxes, too. Isn't it a problem for the reparations position, they ask, if it says on the one hand that black people should be benefited by being given reparations but then says on the other that black people should be burdened by being taxed in order to pay for it?

While this feature of the reparations position can seem a bit peculiar at first, it should become clear after a bit of reflection that it doesn't really pose a problem. The same thing is true, after all, of veteran's benefits: the government makes various benefits available to veterans, the benefits are paid for by taxpayer money, and veterans are among the people who pay taxes. Indeed, this feature that raises doubts about the reparations position in some people's minds is really a feature of every instance in which an American citizen receives benefits from the government: federal employees, farmers who receive subsidies, plaintiffs who successfully sue the government for damages, and so on. No one on either side of the reparations debate really thinks it's objectionable that park rangers, for example, are paid by the government and also pay taxes to the government. And so, in the end, no one should really think that this feature of the reparations position provides any reason to reject it either.

WHOSE STRIFE IS IT, ANYWAY?

The question of who's supposed to pay for reparations, then, doesn't raise any real difficulties. What about the question of who's supposed to receive them? Many people seem to think that this question generates a serious problem for the defender of the reparations position, too.

One reason that some people think this is a problem has to do with the question of who, exactly, has been made worse off by the legacy of slavery and its aftermath. This objection is sometimes raised by asking whether each black American would have to prove that he or she is directly descended from slaves in order to qualify for receiving reparations benefits. When put this way, the question may well turn out to pose practical problems for some defenses of the reparations position. But, as has proved to be the case throughout this discussion, it poses no problem for the reparations position itself because it poses no problem for the compensation argument for that position in particular. On that argument, it's important to remember, compensation is owed not to the biological offspring of particular victims of previous injustices, but rather to black Americans who continue to suffer the lingering effects of slavery and its aftermath. Black Americans who trace their family lineage to free black ancestors inhabit the same difficult racial environment that black Americans descended from slaves inhabit. And so the practical difficulty of determining which black Americans are descended from slaves and which are not can simply be passed over. If the compensation argument is accepted, reparations are owed to all black Americans.

Of course, saying that reparations are owed to all black Americans quickly generates a second version of the worry about who should receive reparations: which Americans, exactly, count as black? As the conservative columnist and talk show host Armstrong Williams has put the concern, "what percentage of black blood would entitle a citizen to reparations?"[95] This question, I have to admit, can't be answered so easily.[96] But the fact that it doesn't have an easy answer provides no reason to reject the reparations position itself. In cases involving complex, widespread harms, after all, it's almost always difficult to determine precisely who the victims are and precisely how much harm they have wrongfully suffered. But this fact itself is never taken to show that those responsible for the harms have no obligation to do the best they can to distribute benefits to those who are entitled to them.

Consider, for example, the extremely complicated and large-scale lawsuits that have been filed against a number of tobacco companies in recent years. Let's assume, at least for the sake of the argument, that the suits have merit and that the tobacco companies are liable for having wrongfully caused harm to large numbers of people. Now suppose that an opponent of tobacco reparations raised the following objection: "it's true that the tobacco companies acted wrongfully in the past and it's true that there are a large number of people suffering as a result of this in the present, but it's impossible to figure out precisely which people have been harmed by smoking, second-hand smoke, *in utero* exposure to smoking and so on. Therefore, the companies shouldn't have to do anything to make reparations to anyone." Whatever people think about the merits of the slave reparations position, I doubt that anyone would find this a persuasive objection to the tobacco reparations position. In the case of the tobacco lawsuits, it should be clear, the impossibility of determining precisely who has been harmed by a company's past wrongful actions doesn't mean that the company owes nothing to anyone. Instead, it simply means that while the company can't provide perfectly proportioned compensation to all and only those who deserve it, it must distribute the benefits that it's obligated to provide in a way that will, as much as possible, result in the people who have been harmed the most receiving the most compensation. If the money taken from a tobacco company was used to build a new hospital that would specialize in treating patients with those conditions most likely to have been caused by smoking and exposure to smoking, for example, then many of the people who would benefit from the hospital would be victims of the company's past wrongful acts, but some of the people who would benefit would not be. Similarly, many of the people who would not benefit from the new hospital would not be victims of its past wrongful acts, but some of them would be. Still, if building such a hospital were the most practical way of ensuring that people harmed by the effects of the tobacco company's past wrongful actions received some sort of compensating benefits, I doubt that anyone would object to the claim that the company should be required to help fund the hospital.

But what's true of the tobacco case is equally true of the slavery case. The practical impossibility of reaching a consensus on who counts as black in this country means that it would be practically impossible for the United States to provide reparations to each and every black American just as it would be practically impossible for the tobacco company to provide compensation to each and every person who ended up being made worse off as a result of the company's past wrongful actions. But just as building a hospital specializing in conditions most likely to have been caused by smoking might prove to be a reasonable solution to the practical difficulty in the tobacco case, the United States could spend money in a

variety of ways as a reasonable solution to the practical difficulty in the slave reparations case. Without being able to determine who is black and who isn't in every
single case, for example, the government could uncontroversially determine that
some neighborhoods or schools are predominantly black, that some crimes have
victims that are predominantly black, that some organizations have members that
are predominantly black, and so forth. Aiming benefits at such areas or institutions would not be a perfect way of ensuring that all and only black Americans be
made better off. But if that turned out to be the best that could be done, then that
would be the right thing to do. And certainly the fact that we could not do better
would be no excuse not to at least do as much as we could.

Finally, it may be worth noting that an even closer parallel arises in the case
of Holocaust reparations. Most people, including most people who oppose slave
reparations, accept the validity of Holocaust reparations. Some of the money
that was spent by Germany after the war was intended to compensate particular
Jews who had been wrongfully harmed, but some was also aimed at attempting
to help restore the welfare of the Jewish people as a whole. Now the question of
who counts as Jewish is at least as complicated as the question of who counts as
black. But the impossibility of arriving at a definitive answer to the question of
who counts as Jewish didn't prevent Germany from paying some money to the
state of Israel as a part of its attempt to make amends for its past. Certainly not
everyone who benefits from Israel's flourishing is a Jew and not every Jew benefits from Israel's flourishing. But, once again, if something along these lines was
the most practical way for Germany to direct benefits toward the Jewish people
as a whole, then most people would agree that it was a perfectly appropriate way
to proceed. The difficulty of determining who is a Jew, in short, provided no reason to reject a claim of reparations to the Jewish people as a whole. And so the
difficulty of determining precisely who is a black American provides no reason
to reject the claim of reparations to black Americans as a whole.

REPARATIONS FOR EVERYONE?

There's one final way, though, in which the question of who merits reparations
might seem to pose a serious problem for the defender of the reparations position. The problem, on this account, lies not in determining who's been harmed
by the legacy of slavery and its aftermath in particular but, rather, in recognizing
that many other groups have been wrongfully harmed in the past by many other
injustices as well. If the claim that black Americans are owed reparations implies
that many other groups are owed reparations as well, and if this further claim is
rejected as unacceptable, then the claim that black Americans are owed reparations must be rejected as unacceptable, too. Even if we're unable to detect a flaw
in the compensation argument, that is, we'll be justified in concluding that there
must be a flaw in it somewhere.

Although the structure of organization that I've adopted in this chapter makes
it natural to consider this objection at the end of the discussion, it's often one

of the first that's raised in popular discussions of the subject. Students almost always raise this concern in class and it frequently appears in opinion pieces on the issue. Armstrong Williams, for example, again puts a widespread objection to the reparations position well, asking: "Would American Indians be able to stake a similar claim? How about the various religious groups that the Puritan settlers persecuted? Would modern-day members of the occult be entitled to reparations, to make up for the fact that our founding fathers regularly burned their relatives at the stake?"[97] And to this list of potential problem cases, for that matter, he might well have added groups such as Irish, Polish, or Chinese immigrants, all of whom suffered various injustices when they first came to this country, not to mention women, who were, among other things, denied the vote until early in the twentieth century. It can start to seem, then, that reparations for black Americans implies reparations for virtually everyone else, which in turn seems to provide a good reason to reject the case for reparations for black Americans in the first place.

The objection based on the worry that the reparations position has such implications takes the form of a *reductio ad absurdum*. Rather than identifying a problem with a particular step in a particular argument for the reparations position, that is, the objection attempts to take the position itself and reduce it to absurdity by demonstrating that it has implications that are unacceptable. There are therefore two distinct ways in which a defender of the reparations position can attempt to respond to the objection: deny that the position has the implication in question, or agree that the position has the implication but attempt to show that the implication isn't an unacceptable one. There are differences between the various examples that proponents of this objection appeal to, but for any particular example that comes up, the defender of the reparations position can successfully employ one or the other of these two strategies in rebutting the objection that the example is meant to sustain.

Take the case of Native Americans, for example. Here it does seem quite plausible to suppose that the case for reparations for black Americans implies a case for reparations for Native Americans as well. Native Americans in the past, like black Americans in the past, were the victims of serious, persistent, harmful injustices that were committed or facilitated by the U.S. government. Native Americans in the present, like black Americans in the present, are clearly doing less well, on average, than the rest of the population by a number of commonly accepted measures of human well-being. And in the case of Native Americans, as in the case of black Americans, there seems clearly to be some kind of causal connection between the first set of facts and the second set of facts. Because these are the considerations that the compensation argument appeals to in making the case for reparations for black Americans, it seems right to say that if they do justify reparations for black Americans, then they also justify reparations for Native Americans.

But it's odd to think of this implication as posing a problem for the reparations position, let alone a sufficiently powerful problem to warrant rejecting the position if the compensation argument otherwise seems to make a compelling case for it. The U.S. government, after all, makes a variety of attempts to aim benefits at the current generation of Native Americans precisely because of these regrettable facts. Indeed, the Department of the Interior has an entire branch, the Bureau of Indian Affairs, dedicated to overseeing millions of acres of land that are held in trust by the government for Native Americans and it provides vital educational services to many Native American students as well. While people may disagree about the effectiveness of various government programs in improving the lives of contemporary Native Americans, it seems relatively uncontroversial to say that the government owes it to them to do something to make things go better for them. And since it seems relatively uncontroversial to say that this is so, it seems to be no real problem for the slave reparations position that it implies that it is so. Indeed, if anything, the fact that the compensation argument for slave reparations yields an intuitively satisfying justification for a view about our obligations to contemporary Native Americans that most people already accept, the fact that it has this implication seems to provide a further reason to believe that the slave reparations position is correct.

In the case of many other groups, though, the implication that contemporary members of the group are entitled to reparations in virtue of wrongs that were committed against their predecessors is likely to strike most people as objectionable. Many Americans today, for example, are followers of Wicca, and many Wiccans consider themselves to be witches, the contemporary representatives of those who were persecuted and killed as witches in the early days of this country's history. But few people, I suspect, would accept the claim that the government owes reparations to contemporary Wiccans. If the case for reparations for black Americans entails reparations for Wiccan Americans as well, therefore, this will seem to be a bigger problem for the case for reparations for black Americans.

But I see no reason to think that the compensation argument for slave reparations entails reparations for Wiccan Americans. There is substantial evidence, after all, that black Americans on the whole are doing considerably less well than are white Americans on the whole, and substantial reason to believe that this is at least in part due to the grave injustices that were committed against black Americans for a very substantial part of our nation's history. But as far as I know, there's no evidence to suggest that Wiccan Americans today are doing any less well than the next person or that they are impaired in any way by the lingering effects of wrongs that were committed against people who were thought to be witches a long time ago. There's no reason, for example, to think that Wiccan American SAT scores are lagging behind those of non-Wiccans with comparable family assets, or that Wiccans are doing less well in terms of annual income, unemployment rates, or life expectancy. Because these are the sorts of considerations that the compensation argument appeals to in justifying reparations for black Americans, and since these considerations don't seem to apply to the case of Wiccan Americans, there's no reason to think that the case for reparations for black Americans entails reparations for Wiccan Americans.

Native Americans and Wiccan Americans, of course, are just two of many possible examples. But the problems with appealing to either of them as a basis for accepting this "reparations for everyone" objection to the slave reparations position seem sufficient, at least to me, to warrant rejecting the objection itself. For most such groups, after all, there will be little reason to suspect that their contemporary members are being adversely impacted by the lingering consequences of earlier wrongful acts committed by the federal government. Although Irish and Italian and Polish immigrants certainly suffered in many ways from a variety of private forms of wrongful treatment, for example, they were not victims of sustained, multigenerational injustices caused or facilitated by the United States government in the way that black Americans and Native Americans were. Even if it turns out that the current generations of some of these groups are doing less well than they would otherwise be, then, this will give little reason to conclude that they are suffering the lingering consequences of wrongs committed by the federal government in particular. And while some other groups, such as Chinese Americans, can point to specific acts of the federal government that targeted them, as in the case of immigration restrictions that picked out people from China in particular, it's considerably less clear that the depth and persistence of any wrongs that the government might have committed would have sufficed to leave a lasting impact on the current generation. So in the case of most other groups, I suspect, there will be relatively little reason to think that the compensation argument for black Americans implies reparations for the group in question.

If, however, there are other groups besides Native Americans where the case for reparations for black Americans really does turn out to entail reparations for members of that group as well, this will have to be because the members of the group in question really are suffering from the consequences of previous wrongful acts committed by the government. Perhaps, for example, Chinese Americans today really are being harmed by the legacy of earlier restrictions on immigration. If there really do prove to be such cases, then the slave reparations position will indeed support reparations for the other group. But since the other group will by hypothesis truly be suffering as a result of wrongful acts of the government, I see no reason to think that this implication will be objectionable. Indeed, as with the case of reparations for Native Americans, this feature of the compensation argument for slave reparations seems to me if anything simply to reinforce it. Someone who initially finds it absurd to think that the government owes something to contemporary Chinese Americans because the government used to restrict immigration from China, that is, probably does so either because they think that the immigration restrictions were not really unjust or because they think that they are not really causing any harm to currently living Chinese Americans. If they became convinced that the government's past acts were unjust and that current Chinese Americans are doing less well as a result of those acts, I see no reason to think that they would view the case any differently from the way most people view the case of Native Americans. They would come to find the claim that Chinese Americans are owed some form of compensation to be a reasonable one and this implication of the compensation argument would again help rather than hinder it.

Even if the compensation argument does imply that reparations are owed to a number of these further groups, however, and even if this implication does not in fact help to reinforce the argument in the way that I've suggested, there are still two additional reasons to conclude that, at the very least, the implication should not be taken as undermining the argument. First, it's hard to understand how harming one group of people could justify compensation to that group while harming many groups of people would justify compensation to no group at all. Suppose, for example, that you're on a jury in a case in which a large corporation is being sued for wrongfully harming a particular group of people. The evidence in the case has seemed very strong to you and so you are on the verge of voting to find that the corporation does, indeed, owe compensation to this group of people. At the last minute, though, the lawyers for the corporation excitedly approach the judge and announce, "Your Honor, we'd like to introduce evidence that conclusively demonstrates that our clients have actually wrongfully harmed *hundreds* of groups of people." In this case, it should be clear, the fact – if it is a fact – that the corporation has wrongfully harmed hundreds of other groups of people should do nothing to undermine your belief that it owes compensation to this particular group of people. Whether it owes something to this group can't really be determined by whether or not it also owes something to other groups. In the same way, and for the same reason, the fact – if it is a fact – that many groups of Americans besides black Americans are suffering the negative consequences of prior wrongful acts by the U.S. government should do nothing to undermine your belief that the government U.S. owes compensation to black Americans in particular.

The second reason that the implication that many other groups are owed compensation can't be used to justify rejecting the compensation argument for slave reparations has to do with the case of compensation for Native Americans in particular. As I've already noted, most people, regardless of their views of slave reparations, seem to accept the claim that the U.S. government has a special obligation to do something on behalf of the current generation of Native Americans. People like Horowitz who protest forcefully against slave reparations, for example, don't make a point of insisting that the government abolish the Bureau of Indian Affairs. But if the "reparations for everyone" objection is a good objection to reparations for black Americans, then it's an equally good objection to reparations for Native Americans. If reparations for black Americans opens the door to reparations for many other groups, after all, then so does reparations for Native Americans. But no one really seems to think that this fact suffices to justify rejecting reparations for Native Americans. And so no one should really think that it suffices to justify rejecting reparations for black Americans either.

The "reparations for everybody" objection, then, can succeed only if it identifies a case where reparations for black Americans clearly implies reparations for another group and where reparations for this other group is clearly objectionable.

But, in the end, there seems to be no such group for the critic of reparations to appeal to. And so, in the end, neither this objection nor any other that I am aware of seems able to provide a good enough reason to reject the reparations position. There's no good reason to deny any of the five steps in the compensation argument, no good reason to deny that the reparations position follows from these five steps, and no good reason to think that any implications of the argument provide sufficient reason to reject it given that the five steps are reasonable and that the connection between them and the conclusion is logical. Although it took me some time to realize it, and although I had to defeat myself in a one-person debate along the way in order to do so, I now recognize that the reparations position in the end should simply be accepted. The U.S. government really does have a moral obligation to benefit the currently living generation of black Americans because of the wrongful harms that were inflicted on past generations of Africans and African Americans by the institution of slavery and its aftermath.

A PROPOSAL

When I first became aware of the reparations position, it struck me as radical and wrongheaded. Now it doesn't. Part of the reason for this is that I can now see that the truth of the reparations position follows from a series of steps each one of which we have good reason to accept. Indeed, since one would have to commit oneself to a quite extreme claim in order to deny any of the steps in the compensation argument, it now seems to me that it is those who reject the reparations position who must hold a radical view. But the reparations position no longer strikes me as radical or wrongheaded for another reason as well. This is because I can now see more clearly than before the difference between the reparations position itself and the particular remedies that have been proposed by particular advocates of the reparations position. As I mentioned at the start of Chapter 2, I understand the reparations position to maintain that the U.S. government owes a debt to its current black citizens but I also understand it to be neutral with respect to the question of how, precisely, this debt could most effectively be paid off. This means that the reparations position itself need not be saddled with what might prove to be unreasonable assertions made by particular proponents of the position about the magnitude of the debt or about the specific steps that the government is obligated to take in order to eliminate it.

Because many people may nonetheless remain inclined to view the claim defended in this chapter and the one that preceded it as a rather extreme one, though, it may be worth developing this last point a bit further by way of concluding this long discussion. So consider one final analogy. Suppose that a long time ago, the federal government wrongfully helped a number of companies and private individuals to bury a large amount of toxic waste in a residential neighborhood and that as a result of this wrongful behavior, the people who live there today have, on average, cholesterol levels that are significantly higher than those of people elsewhere in the country, and that are high enough to pose considerable risks to their health. In this case, I take it, it would be clear that the government's past wrongful actions would raise three fundamentally different questions: is the federal government now obligated to help these people lower their cholesterol levels? If it is obligated to help them to lower their cholesterol levels, how much lower is it obligated to help make the levels go? And, if it is obligated to help them lower their cholesterol levels by a certain amount, then what, specifically, should it do in order to help them to accomplish this?

The second and third questions in this case would be complicated for a number of reasons. For one thing, it would be difficult to determine precisely what the cholesterol level of the people living in the area would have been had the toxic waste not been buried in the first place. We might assume that it would be the same as the average cholesterol level of the rest of the country, but that assumption might turn out to be mistaken. If people's cholesterol levels are partly determined by their age, their education, their past eating habits, their genetic dispositions, and so on, then depending on the demographics of the neighborhood, it might turn out that this particular group of people would still have had cholesterol levels that are somewhat higher than the national average even if the government had not helped to bury the waste near their homes. As a result, reasonable people might well end up disagreeing about just how much lower the cholesterol levels would have to go before the people in the neighborhood were as well off as people in the neighborhood would have been had the waste not been wrongfully dumped in the first place.

In addition, even if it were clear exactly how much harm the residents of the neighborhood were currently suffering as a result of the past wrongful dumping of toxic waste, there would be room for reasonable disagreement about precisely what proportion of this total harm could legitimately be attributed to the government's wrongful behavior in particular. Some people might argue that while the government would bear some of the responsibility for helping to cause the harm, more would be borne by the companies or individuals involved. Helping someone else do something wrong, they might argue, is not as bad as actually doing the wrong thing, and so merely helping someone else to do something wrong makes you less responsible for the harms that result than actually doing the wrong thing yourself. And they might add that the magnitude of the government's obligations could be diminished to the extent that it would have been difficult for the government to foresee how deep and long-lasting the consequences of its wrongful acts would turn out to be at the time that they took place. Others would argue that since the companies and individuals would not have been able to bury the waste without the government's facilitating their behavior in the first place, the results were almost entirely the government's fault, and they might add that since governments have a special obligation to protect their citizens that companies and private individuals don't have, this makes the government more responsible for the harm that resulted than anyone else. And even if agreement were reached about precisely what proportion of the harm could justly be attributed to the government's wrongful actions, further disagreement might arise about whether it would be fair to make the government also take responsibility for any harms that would properly be attributed to companies that were no longer around to be sued.

Finally, even if everyone agreed about precisely how low the cholesterol levels would have to get before the government had repaired the harm that it in particular was responsible for having wrongly caused, it would be a difficult matter to determine precisely the best way to achieve that level. Should it rely primarily on providing free medication? If so, which one, and in what dosage? Should it instead do something to enable the people in question to change their diets? If so, what sorts of changes would be best, and what would be the most effective ways of making the changes stick? Should it do something to get the people to exercise more? If so, what kind of exercise would be best, and how much of it, and how could the government most effectively make sure that the exercises would really get done? As a result of all of this, it seems unlikely that everyone would agree on the optimal course of action.

But while answering the second and third questions would be extremely difficult in the case of the buried toxic waste and resulting high cholesterol levels, the difficulty of answering them would pose no difficulties for answering the first question. The fact that we could not determine precisely how much lower the cholesterol levels should go or precisely how best to get them there, that is, would do nothing at all to undermine our confidence in the belief that the government would, in fact, be obligated to at least do *something* to help get them lower.[98] Any particular proposal about how best to proceed would inevitably be at least somewhat controversial, but the basic proposition that the government would be obligated to do something to help these people get their cholesterol levels at least somewhat closer to the norm would surely be accepted by virtually everyone. The claim that the government would owe nothing to the current residents at all simply because it was too difficult to say precisely how much harm they had incurred or precisely how much of that harm was the government's fault would persuade virtually nobody. Regardless of what they think about the slave reparations issue in particular, no one really believes that compensation is owed only in cases where it's clear exactly how much harm has been wrongfully caused or exactly what needs to be done in order to repair it.

But if what I've said about the compensation argument in these two chapters has been correct, then we should say precisely the same thing about the case of reparations for the wrongful harms caused by the long years of slavery followed by the long years of official segregation and discrimination. Any particular view about the precise magnitude of the debt that has resulted from these past injustices is bound to be controversial, as is any particular view about how, precisely, the government could most effectively respond to it, but the basic claim that the government is obligated to do at least something to help black Americans as a result should be recognized and accepted by everyone. Part of the way that we can repair the reparations debate in this country is to shift our attention away from arguments that appeal to claims about unjust enrichment, debts that are passed down to biological descendants and so on, and to focus instead on the considerations raised by the compensation argument. But part of the way that we can repair the debate is by acknowledging that the question of whether the United States owes reparations for slavery and its aftermath and the question of what, exactly, it should do if it does owe such reparations, are two fundamentally different questions.[99]

In the end, then, people like Horowitz, who oppose slave reparations entirely, and people like Robinson, who support slave reparations but seem inflexibly wedded to a particular set of views about what kinds of reparations are owed, should abandon the extreme positions they hold and come together to occupy a more just and reasonable middle ground. From this starting point, it would simply be a matter of common decency to say that the U.S. government should apologize for the role it played in facilitating the wrongful harms inflicted by slavery and its aftermath, and to acknowledge that it has a special responsibility to do something to help improve the average level of quality of life of its black citizens. We could then set aside the acrimonious debate over slave reparations and get on with the difficult but necessary work of determining how best to live up to that responsibility.

4

One Cheer for Affirmative Action

Why There's Nothing Wrong with Abandoning Racial Preferences

A white candidate and a black candidate submit an application for a position. Both want to be admitted to the same university, hired at the same automobile plant, or promoted from their current jobs within the same police department. Both candidates are suitably qualified for the position. If either of them were the only one to submit an application, the organization in question would offer the position to that candidate without hesitation. The white applicant, though, is at least a little bit better qualified than the black applicant. His grades and test scores are a little bit higher, he has slightly stronger letters of recommendation, or he has a little bit more experience on the job. If the organization didn't know the race of either of the applicants, it would select the white applicant over the black applicant for this reason. But the organization does know the race of both applicants. And it has a policy that leads it to select the black applicant over the white applicant, despite the fact that the white applicant is at least a little bit better qualified, precisely because the white applicant is white and the black applicant is black.

Supporters of policies that give an advantage to black applicants over white applicants in this way tend to refer to such policies as a form of "affirmative action." It's hard to oppose taking action that's "affirmative," after all, without sounding, well, negative.[1] Opponents of such policies, on the other hand, tend to refer to them as "racial preferences."[2] If the advantage that's given to black candidates over white candidates is merely a matter of "preference" after all, rather than of sound moral reasoning, then such policies seem to be simply a matter of imposing one's whim on others, like insisting that since you prefer chocolate ice cream to vanilla, everyone else should, too. I'm not particularly fond of either label. Something like "race-based prioritization" strikes me as a more accurate and less question-begging term to use. I'll mostly stick with the term "affirmative action" in this chapter and the chapter that follows, though, since that's the closest thing we have to an official title.

Affirmative action, in turn, can usefully be divided into two categories: "weak" and "strong." Weak affirmative action involves taking positive steps to ensure that minority candidates are made aware of positions that are open and are encouraged to apply for them, but it then treats the applications that are submitted in an entirely race-neutral manner. In addition to doing whatever it would normally do to publicize a new opening, for example, a company that has a weak affirmative action policy might take out ads in magazines with a primarily black readership or on radio or television stations with a primarily black audience. It might send representatives to recruit at minority job fairs, make funding available to help black applicants fly in for interviews, and so on. But after doing all of this, a company that practices weak affirmative action would do nothing to give preference to black applicants over white applicants once all of the applications had been received. Potential black applicants would receive extra attention in the initial stage of the process, that is, when the company was trying to round up applications, but no extra attention in the final stage, when the applications it received were being evaluated. The people making the final decisions, for example, might not be given information about the race of the different candidates.

Strong affirmative action, on the other hand, goes beyond weak affirmative action by giving at least some sort of preference to minority candidates when the applications are actually being evaluated. In addition to assigning points to each applicant based on his grade point average and SAT score, for example, a college that has a strong affirmative action policy might add some points to the total evaluation score of each black applicant. A black applicant might then end up with a higher total evaluation score than an otherwise comparable white applicant who had at least somewhat higher grades or test scores. Or the college might set aside a certain number of places in its freshman class for minority students and take its target numbers into account when examining its applicant pool. Either way, its policy of strong affirmative action would make it possible for a qualified black student to be admitted ahead of an otherwise better qualified white student precisely because the black student is black and the white student is white.

Weak affirmative action is relatively uncontroversial. It simply involves making an effort to ensure that qualified minority candidates are identified and considered. Few people, if any, are opposed to it. But strong affirmative action is quite controversial. My focus in this chapter and the chapter that follows will therefore be on it. Unless noted otherwise, when I use the expression "affirmative action" in what follows, I will mean "strong affirmative action." Strong affirmative action is controversial in a number of respects. People disagree about its practicality, its morality, its legality, and its constitutionality. My focus here will be on the moral question posed by affirmative action policies, though I will at times make use of other sorts of arguments insofar as they help to clarify, advance, or critically evaluate some of the moral arguments. And while affirmative action policies can be used to target a variety of groups for special consideration, I will focus here on cases involving black and white candidates. Most people agree that if affirmative action is justified in any cases, it is at least justified in these sorts of cases. The central question that this chapter and the chapter that follows will address, then, is this: what is the moral status of strong race-based affirmative action?

I have to admit that I've never found this to be a particularly interesting question. For as long as I can remember being aware of the existence of such policies, I've always thought that the question had a pretty simple answer. And for as long as I can remember thinking this, I always thought that the answer was a pretty mundane, straightforward, commonsense one. I don't remember ever reading anything about affirmative action or talking about it with anyone, but I guess I always assumed that most people thought that the correct answer was the answer that I always thought was the correct one. The answer itself didn't strike me as particularly interesting or controversial, so I never really thought much about it. I certainly never contemplated writing about it.

When I first decided that I wanted to be able to teach a course on ethics and race, though, I began to look into the literature on the subject in some detail: books and articles by academics and media pundits, letters to the editor, and so on. And I discovered something surprising: it seemed that virtually no one was defending the view that I always thought was the sort of obvious view to hold. What I want to do in these two chapters, then, is explain what my answer to the question is and how it differs from what seem to be the two more common answers to the question, give a simple argument to establish a presumption in favor of my simple answer, and then respond to a number of objections that might be raised by defenders of either of the two more common positions. When I looked into the literature on slave reparations, I came to see that my initial view of that issue had been wrong. But the more I've looked into the literature on affirmative action, the more it's come to seem to me that almost everyone else is wrong.

Let's start by getting clear about what most people seem to think about affirmative action. Virtually everyone who writes or protests about it seems to fall into one or the other of two camps, what I'll call the "pro" camp and the "anti" camp. Most people in the pro camp, those who support affirmative action, don't just think that it's nice to do black people a favor by adopting affirmative action policies. They think that having an affirmative action policy is a matter of justice, not a matter of charity. When Proposition 209 abolished affirmative action in California's state university system, for example, most critics of the move didn't simply complain that the state was ending a generous policy. They said that getting rid of affirmative action was positively immoral. Affirmative action, on this view, isn't simply something that's nice to do, like a college campus sponsoring a free concert for the local community. Rather, affirmative action is something that it's positively wrong not to do.

Similarly, most people in the anti camp, those who oppose affirmative action, don't just think that affirmative action isn't such a great idea. They claim that it's positively unjust. If a state's universities practice affirmative action, for example, these critics don't simply say that the policy is imprudent. They say that it's positively immoral. Affirmative action, on this view, isn't simply unwise, the way that it would be unwise for a university's endowment to be invested in a portfolio that's too risky. Rather, affirmative action is something that's positively immoral.

Most critics of affirmative action think it's downright wrong to practice affirmative action, then, and most defenders of affirmative action think it's downright wrong not to. As a result, those who oppose affirmative action policies are often angry when such policies are applied to them. Those who support affirmative action policies are often angry at those who are angry at affirmative action. Both groups are quick to quote Martin Luther King Jr. and to claim that if he were alive today, he would agree with them.[3] And, perhaps most important, both groups are prone to write or speak as if the debate over affirmative action can only have these two sides. One popular anthology on the subject, for example, is called *Affirmative Action: Social Justice or Reverse Discrimination?* Another text, containing a debate on the issue between two philosophers, is called *Affirmative Action: Social Justice or Unfair Preference?*[4] These titles reflect the widespread assumption that affirmative action must either be demanded by justice or be prohibited by it.

The assumption that there's only room for these two sides in the affirmative action debate, moreover, is also frequently made explicit in the literature on the subject itself. The philosopher John Kekes, for example, introduces an article on the issue by saying that it sets out "to advance the claim that one side has it right and the other is mistaken."[5] The philosopher Alan Goldman writes that a middle ground on the subject is so hard to imagine that "[i]nterested persons coming to this literature for the first time may have no choice but to review its now extensive history and make an informed choice to come down on one side or the other."[6] Law Professor Mitchell H. Rubinstein begins a paper on the issue by writing that "The debate over affirmative action has generated two opposing viewpoints" one which views the practice as "unlawful" and one which views it as "necessary."[7] And in the opening paragraph of his recent book *Understanding Affirmative Action*, which is designed to provide a balanced and up-to-date introduction to the subject, Public Administration and Policy Professor J. Edward Kellough writes that "People disagree on whether affirmative action should be permitted or, if it is judged to be necessary, on the specific types of efforts that should be included," as if the only options are that affirmative action is impermissible or that it's obligatory.[8]

But this common assumption that affirmative action must be either morally required or morally prohibited is a mistake. Some things are forbidden by justice and some things are required by justice, but plenty of other things fall in between. Justice doesn't require you to put your left shoe on before your right, for example, but it doesn't forbid you from doing so either. Unlike most people who write about affirmative action these days, and unlike virtually everyone who protests for or against it, I think that affirmative action falls into this in between area.[9] So far as morality and justice are concerned, that is, schools and businesses and governments are free to practice affirmative action if they so choose and free to decline to practice it if they so choose. If a school, or business, or government practices affirmative action, that's not morally wrong. If a school, or business, or government doesn't practice affirmative action, that's not morally wrong either.

I'll give a preliminary reason for thinking that this is true in the section that follows and I'll then try to respond to a number of objections to my view in the remainder of this chapter and in the chapter that follows.

It's possible, of course, that in trying to stake out a middle ground between the view that practicing affirmative action is immoral and the view that not practicing it is immoral, I'm misunderstanding the extent to which my own view is out of step with that of most people who write and talk about this issue. Perhaps most people who oppose affirmative action don't really mean it when they use words like "unjust" or "immoral" or "morally heinous" to describe the practice or when they complain that affirmative action violates the "rights" of white applicants.[10] Perhaps these are just rhetorical flourishes that obscure the more mundane view that affirmative action, although not morally wrong, isn't a good idea. And perhaps most people who support affirmative action don't really mean it when they use words like "immoral" or "a grave injustice" to refer to initiatives like Proposition 209 that prohibit affirmative action or when they call affirmative action itself "morally mandatory."[11] Perhaps these, too, are just rhetorical flourishes, obscuring the more mundane view that even though it's not immoral to abandon affirmative action, it would be better not to abandon it. If most people already believe that it's not wrong to practice affirmative action and that it's not wrong not to practice it, then it will turn out that the goal of this chapter and the chapter that follows is to provide a justification for what most people already believe, rather than to defend an alternative to the views that most people currently believe. And since the goal of this book as a whole is to try to answer some controversial questions involving racial matters by developing positions that can be justified on grounds that most people accept, I'll be more than happy if it turns out that I'm simply making explicit what most people already tacitly think about affirmative action and providing a more careful and detailed defense of that position than has typically been made available.

I'm generally inclined to take people at their word, though, and to take the arguments they present at face value. And on the face of it, at least, most critics really do seem to be saying and trying to show that affirmative action is positively immoral, and most supporters really do seem to be claiming and attempting to show that not practicing affirmative action is positively immoral. If most of these people don't really mean what they clearly seem to be saying, moreover, it's somewhat difficult to understand what they're getting so worked up about. If you concede that affirmative action isn't really immoral and doesn't really violate anyone's rights, after all, you might still think it's a bad idea but why would you try to ban it? If you admit that no one has a right to the benefits of affirmative action and that declining to practice affirmative action isn't immoral, you might still think that getting rid of it's a mistake, but why would you accuse those who seek to do so of being immoral or racist? In any event, regardless of whether it's common to believe that neither practicing nor not practicing affirmative action is immoral, that is the view that I will attempt to defend in the discussion that follows.

CONFESSIONS OF A WHITE AFFIRMATIVE ACTION BABY

One of the most widely quoted works on the subject of affirmative action is Stephen Carter's thoughtful book, *Confessions of An Affirmative Action Baby*. In it, Carter discusses the fact that he was admitted to the Yale Law School under an affirmative action program that gave priority to qualified black applicants like him over white candidates who had even higher grades and test scores. Describing his admission under such circumstances as a "mixed blessing," Carter poignantly depicts the various psychological costs that can burden those who are meant to benefit from affirmative action policies.[12]

I have something in common with Stephen Carter. I got into Yale under an affirmative action policy, too. The policy that I benefited from helped me get into Yale College rather than Yale Law School, and it benefited me because of my geographical identity rather than because of my racial identity. But I'm inclined to think that the similarities between the two cases are more important than the differences and more important than most people have recognized. Indeed, the more deeply I've looked into the literature on race-based affirmative action, the more firmly I've come to believe that the similarities between geography-based and race-based affirmative action can help point the way to a resolution of the debate over race-based affirmative action, a kind of middle ground between the pro and anti camps that appeals to considerations that people in both groups already accept.

Let me start by explaining what I mean by geography-based affirmative action. When a student applies to a school like Yale, the admissions office puts a good deal of weight on things like the student's grades, test scores, extracurricular activities, teacher recommendations, and so forth. But schools like Yale typically care about more than this. They want, among other things, to ensure that their students are exposed to people who come from backgrounds that are different from their own. One way to do this is to try to bring together students from as many parts of the country as possible. And one way to make this happen is to give some preference to applicants from parts of the country that are underrepresented on campus. If there are virtually no students from North Dakota in the current student body, for example, and if there are already a very large number of students from New York, then an applicant with very good grades and test scores from North Dakota might well be admitted ahead of an applicant with somewhat better grades and test scores from New York. Like Stephen Carter, I can't be sure that affirmative action helped make the difference in my admission to Yale. But I do know this: I was admitted to every college I applied to on the East Coast and was not admitted to the one school I applied to on the West Coast. Having grown up in a Western state, geography-based affirmative action counted in my favor when I applied to schools on the East Coast and counted against me when I applied to schools on the West Coast. This is the reality of geography-based affirmative action.

Setting aside the issue of race-based affirmative action for a moment, let's consider the moral status of geography-based affirmative action. I think that most people, regardless of what they think about race-based affirmative action, would agree about two things. First, morality allows organizations to practice geography-based affirmative action. Geography-based affirmative action, that is, is morally permissible. If Yale admits a slightly less qualified student from North Dakota over a slightly better qualified student from New York, for example, the student from New York can't really complain that his moral rights have been violated. So far as I can remember, I've never heard anyone claim that a policy such as Yale's is positively unjust.[13] Nor, for that matter, have I heard anyone complain about the geography-based affirmative action policies employed by the U. S. Military Academies. In order to be admitted to West Point, for example, students must first secure a nomination to be considered, and most of the nominations that are available are distributed by congressional district. This makes it considerably easier to get into West Point if you grow up in some parts of the country than if you grow up in others. But, again, virtually everyone seems to agree that, morally speaking, West Point has the right to make its admissions decisions in this way if it thinks it important that future military leaders be drawn from, or learn to work alongside people who are drawn from, all parts of the country. And while some white applicants who were rejected by the University of Michigan famously sued the university over its policy of adding points to the admissions scores of black applicants, there have been no comparable lawsuits filed over the fact the university also adds points to the admissions scores of applicants who are residents of Michigan's Upper Peninsula.[14] So geography-based affirmative action, whether practiced by a private organization or by a state institution, strikes nearly everyone as morally permissible. It's not forbidden by considerations of morality or justice.

The second thing I think most people would agree about with respect to geography-based affirmative action is that it isn't required by considerations of morality or justice, either. Organizations have no moral duty to engage in it or, to put it another way, geography-based affirmative action is non-obligatory. If Yale or West Point decided to eliminate its geography-based affirmative action policy, that is, and if it therefore decided to admit a slightly better qualified student from New York over a slightly less qualified student from North Dakota, the student from North Dakota couldn't really complain that his moral rights had been violated, either. Neither the slightly better qualified student from New York nor the slightly less qualified student from North Dakota has a moral right to be admitted to West Point or Yale ahead of the other. Morally speaking, the schools are free to admit whichever of the two qualified candidates they prefer. Geography-based affirmative action, in short, is permissible but non-obligatory. It's morally optional.

Virtually everyone, regardless of their view of race-based affirmative action, recognizes that geography-based affirmative action is permissible but non-obligatory. This is what's made it possible for geography-based affirmative action to be employed by so many schools for as long as there have been formal admissions policies without generating any real controversy and why it's also been possible for many other schools not to practice geography-based affirmative action without generating any real controversy either.[15] If an organization practices geography-based affirmative action, that's fine. If an organization doesn't practice it, that's fine, too. Either way, virtually no one complains about it or files lawsuits about it.

But geography-based affirmative action seems to have the morally significant features that people on both sides of the debate over race-based affirmative action typically point to when they argue for or against it. Defenders of race-based affirmative action, for example, typically appeal to the fact that some races have been historically disadvantaged relative to others, that some races are currently disadvantaged relative to others, or that adding members of underrepresented races to an organization can benefit it by increasing the diversity of perspectives it can make use of. All of these things are also true of geography-based affirmative action: some parts of the country have long been disadvantaged relative to others, some parts of the country are currently disadvantaged relative to others, and schools where all the students are from the same area provide a less stimulating learning environment than schools whose students come from all across the country. Opponents of race-based affirmative action typically point out that you can't control what race you're born into, that generalizations about racial groups aren't true of each individual member of those groups, and that race-based affirmative action takes group membership into account rather than judging people solely on their individual merits. All of these things are true of geography-based affirmative action, too: you can't control what part of the country you're born and raised in, generalizations about people from different parts of the country aren't true of each individual in those parts, and geography-based affirmative action takes group membership into account rather than judging people solely on their individual merits. Race-based affirmative action, at least as far as these considerations go, seems to be morally on a par with geography-based affirmative action. What morality says about one it seems it should also say about the other.[16]

These considerations suggest a simple two-step argument in support of the view that race-based affirmative action is permissible but non-obligatory. In fact, they suggest two such arguments. One argument takes as its first step the claim that geography-based affirmative action is permissible but non-obligatory and adds as its second step the claim that race-based affirmative action is morally on a par with geography-based affirmative action. If both steps of this argument are accepted, it follows that race-based affirmative action is permissible and non-obligatory, too. The second argument also takes as its first step the claim that geography-based affirmative action is permissible but non-obligatory but it adds as its second step the more modest claim that we have *some reason* to think that race-based affirmative action is morally on a par with geography-based affirmative action. If both steps of this second argument are accepted, it doesn't follow that race-based affirmative action really is permissible and non-obligatory. It simply follows that we have some reason to think that it is.

After having spent a good deal of time trying to work my way through the literature on race-based affirmative action, I find myself inclined to accept the stronger of these two arguments. Although there are clearly differences between race-based and geography-based affirmative action, and although in the case of at least some of the differences there is certainly some initial force behind the thought that the difference in question is morally significant, in the end I've come to believe that none of the features that distinguish race-based from geography-based affirmative action are important enough to render its race-based form impermissible if its geography-based form is permissible or to render its race-based form obligatory if its geography-based form is non-obligatory.

But while the stronger version of the argument seems right to me, I don't expect it to seem right to most readers, certainly not right away, because I don't expect the stronger version of the second step to seem right to most readers without first considering a number of objections that might be raised against it. For the purposes of this chapter and the chapter that follows, then, I simply want to appeal to the weaker version of the argument. The second step of the weaker version merely maintains that we have *some reason* to think that the two forms of affirmative action are morally on a par, and I think I've already shown that we have some reason to think this by showing that the morally relevant features that appear most conspicuously in arguments for and against race-based affirmative action are also features of geography-based affirmative action. The conclusion of this more modest argument isn't that race-based affirmative action is permissible and non-obligatory, but simply that it's reasonable to start with an initial presumption in favor of the view that race-based affirmative action is permissible and non-obligatory. With that presumption established, then, the question is whether there are any arguments on either side of the issue that are strong enough to overcome it. I don't think that there are, and that's what I'll try to show over the course of the discussion that follows.

Before turning to the details of the various arguments that can be given for and against affirmative action, though, it's worth noting one possible source of confusion that may arise at this point. For it may seem that I've already insisted that there really is an argument strong enough to overcome this presumption and that, in particular, I've already committed myself to the view that affirmative action, far from being morally optional, is really morally obligatory. In Chapters 2 and 3, after all, I presented and defended an argument in favor of slave reparations. The reparations position maintains that black Americans are entitled to be benefited today because of the wrongful harms that were inflicted on Africans and African Americans in the past. Race-based affirmative action is designed to benefit black Americans. Because race-based affirmative action benefits black Americans and because the reparations position that I've already defended maintains that black Americans are entitled to be benefited, it may seem that I've already argued in defense of the claim that black Americans are entitled to race-based affirmative action. And if black Americans are entitled to race-based affirmative action, then race-based affirmative action is morally obligatory, not morally optional. For me to argue in these two chapters that race-based affirmative action is not, in fact, morally obligatory might therefore seem inconsistent with what I maintained in the previous two chapters.

While this diagnosis of my position is understandable, and while most people who support slave reparations probably do also support affirmative action, there's nothing inconsistent about maintaining that slave reparations are obligatory while denying that affirmative action is obligatory. There's nothing inconsistent, for that matter, about maintaining that slave reparations are obligatory while denying that affirmative action is even morally permissible. Saying that the government has an obligation to provide some sort of benefit to a group of people, after all, isn't the same as saying that the government has an obligation to provide every kind of benefit that it could provide to that group, nor is it the same as saying that it has an obligation to provide any one particular kind of benefit to it. Providing free toothpaste to every black American would clearly benefit them, for example, but believing in the reparations position doesn't entail believing in an obligation to provide free toothpaste to all black Americans. Stealing money from the Queen of England and distributing it to black Americans would clearly benefit them, too, but believing in the reparations position doesn't entail that doing so would be morally permissible, let alone morally obligatory. The fact that affirmative action is one kind of benefit that black Americans could be offered, then, isn't enough to show that an obligation to provide reparations for slavery and its aftermath entails an obligation to engage in race-based affirmative action. There's nothing inconsistent about believing that there's an obligation to provide some kind of benefit or other without believing that there's an obligation, or even a right, to provide this kind of benefit in particular.

None of this, of course, shows that affirmative action isn't morally obligatory. But it should be enough to show that a commitment to the reparations position isn't enough by itself to justify a commitment to the claim that affirmative action is morally obligatory. There's nothing inconsistent about maintaining that the former is obligatory while maintaining that the latter isn't. And so whether one accepts or rejects the arguments that I offered in Chapters 2 and 3, we are left in the same position with respect to the question of the moral status of affirmative action that we started with: the case of geography-based affirmative action gives us at least some reason to start with a presumption in favor of the view that race-based affirmative action is permissible but non-obligatory, and we must now consider the question of whether there are any arguments strong enough to overcome this initial presumption. I haven't yet tried to show that there aren't any. But I've at least tried to show that accepting the slave reparations position doesn't mean that there are.

My claim about race-based affirmative action is a moderate one. It says that morally speaking, organizations may practice affirmative action if they so choose, but that morally speaking, they aren't required to do so. Because my position attempts to occupy a kind of middle ground in the debate over affirmative action, it can be attacked from two very different sides. Those who support affirmative action will welcome my claim that affirmative action is permissible, but most of them will reject my claim that it isn't obligatory. Those who oppose affirmative action will welcome my claim that it isn't obligatory, but most will reject my claim that it's permissible. I'll try to address these two sets of complaints in turn, beginning in the rest of this chapter with the arguments most commonly presented by defenders of affirmative action and then turning in the next chapter to the arguments most commonly presented by opponents of affirmative action.

Before starting in on the arguments in defense of affirmative action, though, two preliminary points should be made clear. First, in maintaining that affirmative action isn't obligatory, I don't mean to be insisting that no institution has or could have a moral obligation to practice affirmative action. If a business makes an explicit promise to practice affirmative action, for example, then that might well make it impermissible for it to refrain from doing so. If a university commits itself to achieving a certain goal and achieving the goal requires it to practice affirmative action, then that might also underwrite an obligation to practice affirmative action. Just as the special mission of a women's college commits it to adopting an admissions policy that excludes men, for example, a school's special mission might include the promotion of certain goals that would in turn commit it to adopting affirmative action as part of its admissions policy.[17] Such considerations, though, wouldn't do anything to show that affirmative action itself is morally obligatory unless there was a reason to think that it was morally obligatory to make the promise or the commitment that gave rise to the obligation in the first place. At most, they would simply establish that some policies that are not otherwise obligatory can become obligatory when promises or commitments of a certain sort are made. Since my concern in the remainder of this chapter is with the question of whether there's something about affirmative action itself that makes it wrong not to engage in it, I will simply set these sorts of considerations to the side. As long as it's morally permissible not to make the sorts of promises or commitments that might require a particular organization to practice affirmative action in order to live up to the special mission it has established for itself, these sorts of considerations will be irrelevant to trying to determine the moral status of affirmative action itself.

The second point to make clear is this. Some of the arguments that have been offered in defense of affirmative action explicitly aim to show that affirmative action is morally obligatory. Others are somewhat ambiguous between claiming to show that affirmative action is morally obligatory and merely claiming to show that it's a good (but morally optional) thing to do. And still others, perhaps, are offered as an attempt to identify something good about affirmative action without really trying to justify a moral conclusion about it at all. Whatever the intentions behind the various arguments that have been made in defense of affirmative action have been, though, they pose a challenge to my claim that affirmative action is permissible and non-obligatory only if they can do something to show that it's positively immoral not to practice affirmative action. For the purposes of the discussion in the rest of this chapter, then, I'll focus on the question of whether any of them can.

THE UNFAIR DISADVANTAGE ARGUMENT

One kind of argument in favor of affirmative action is essentially backward-looking. This kind of argument points to the many harmful injustices committed against black Americans in the past and claims that the lingering effects of these historical wrongs ground an obligation to use affirmative action as a means of benefiting black Americans in the present. This is the kind of justification that defenders of affirmative action originally provided for such policies in the 1960s.

The most familiar version of this backward-looking kind of argument appeals to a principle of fairness. The argument is often motivated by appealing to the example of runners competing in a race, and it goes back at least as far as an early speech on the subject by President Lyndon Johnson, who famously declared in 1965 that "You do not take a person who, for years, has been hobbled by chains and liberate him, bring him up to the starting line of a race and then say, 'You are free to compete with all others,' and still just believe that you have been completely fair."[18] This appeal to fairness as a justification for affirmative action has a good deal of intuitive force behind it, and the argument based on it has been picked up on more recently by a number of people. The philosopher James Sterba, for example, defends affirmative action for those candidates who "have the potential to be as qualified or more qualified than their peers, but [whose] potential has not yet been actualized because of past discrimination and prejudice." His claim is that it isn't fair to reject a candidate who would have won a position had he not been hampered by the effects of previous injustices. And, echoing Johnson's famous words, he attempts to support his position by appealing to the case of a runner who is unfairly hampered in a race: "persons who receive preferential treatment are like runners in a race who for a time are forced to compete at a disadvantage with other runners, e.g., by having weights tied to their legs, but then after are allowed to transfer those weights to the runners in the race who had previously benefited from the unfair competitive advantage so that the results of the race will now be fair."[19]

This unfair disadvantage argument for affirmative action depends on two claims. The first is the claim that black Americans who apply for jobs and admission to schools in the present are unfairly disadvantaged by the effects of unjust discrimination that took place in the past. White Americans today enjoy an unfair competitive advantage, in other words, because of the misdeeds of white Americans of yesterday. The second is the claim that if black applicants really are unfairly disadvantaged relative to white applicants in the hiring and admissions process, then it would be morally wrong for those who evaluate such applications to fail to adjust for this fact in making their final decisions about which applications to accept. Knowing that some entrants in a competition have been unfairly disadvantaged, in other words, those who sponsor the competition are morally obligated to take this fact into account before deciding on the winners.

Perhaps not surprisingly, I think that the first claim made by the unfair disadvantage argument should be accepted. The first claim, after all, is essentially the same as the third step in the compensation argument for slave reparations that I endorsed in Chapters 2 and 3, and I defended that claim in that context at some length. But I think that the second claim made by the unfair disadvantage argument should be rejected, and that it should be rejected on grounds that virtually everyone on both sides of the affirmative action debate already accepts. And that's why I think that the unfair disadvantage argument itself should be rejected.

The second claim needed in order to sustain the unfair disadvantage argument maintains that those who evaluate applications are morally required to take unfair disadvantage into account when making their final decisions. At first glance, this seems to be an uncontroversial assumption. What could be more reasonable than requiring people to be fair? But on reflection, this claim turns out to have implications that virtually everyone, regardless of their view of affirmative action, will reject as unacceptable.

The easiest way to see this is to begin by looking at a simpler case that focuses on just a single pair of applicants and that doesn't presuppose any views about the moral relevance of race in particular. So consider the case of Bill and Ted, two white students who go to the same high school. During their freshman and sophomore years, Bill got somewhat better grades than Ted and did somewhat better on practice SAT tests. There was therefore every reason to believe that Bill was going to be somewhat more qualified and better prepared for college than Ted was going to be by the time they both graduated. Over the summer between their sophomore and junior years, though, Bill's father was unjustly framed and convicted for a crime that he didn't commit. As a result, Bill's life was seriously disrupted. His father's being sent to prison was emotionally painful for Bill. Bill was forced to get a job working after school. He had less time to spend on his homework and even when he worked on it he had more difficulty concentrating. His study habits declined somewhat because he no longer had a father at home to keep after him, his grades went down a bit as a result, and he didn't end up doing as well on the SAT as his earlier practice scores would have predicted. By the time that college applications came around, in fact, Ted had a somewhat better overall academic record than Bill and was somewhat better prepared to succeed in college.

Now let's suppose that you're the admissions officer at a college to which Bill and Ted have both applied. Both Bill and Ted are suitably qualified for admission to your school. Ted's academic preparation and record are somewhat better than Bill's. But you know from reading their letters of recommendation that Bill's preparation and record would almost certainly have been somewhat better than Ted's had Bill's father not been unjustly convicted of a crime he didn't commit. You only have room to admit one more student. And now ask yourself this question: Would it be okay for you to admit Ted on the grounds that he is the better prepared and better qualified candidate or must you instead take into account and adjust for the fact that Bill has been unfairly disadvantaged by the wrong that was done to his father?

Note that the question is not whether you *should* admit Ted. A reasonable case might be made for admitting either candidate. The question is whether it would be *okay* for you simply to admit the white student who in fact has the better academic preparation and qualifications rather than give preferential treatment to the white student who almost certainly would have had the better academic preparation and qualifications had the world been a more fair place. And in this case, at least, the answer seems quite clear: you would have every right to admit Ted to your school over Bill. Although it would be considerate of you to take Bill's misfortune into account, you do nothing morally wrong if you decide simply to admit the white student who is, in fact, better prepared and qualified for admission over the white student who is, in fact, less prepared and qualified. Surely most people, regardless of their views about race-based affirmative action, would accept this judgment.

But if I'm right about this,[20] an important conclusion follows, and this conclusion undermines the second claim made by the unfair disadvantage argument. It's clear in the case of Bill and Ted, after all, that Ted enjoyed an "unfair competitive advantage" over Bill. Ted was able to spend more time on his homework than Bill because he didn't have to get a job after school, he was able to concentrate more when he did his homework than Bill because he had a more stable family life than Bill had, and he continued to reap the benefits of having a father in the house to help keep him in line, an asset whose value Bill never fully appreciated until he lost it. All of this is true because Bill's father, but not Ted's, was unjustly convicted of a crime that he didn't commit. And this is clearly unfair. But while it's clear that Bill therefore suffers an unfair disadvantage relative to Ted, it's equally clear that morality permits a school to admit Ted over Bill without adjusting for this fact. And this means that the schools that Bill and Ted apply to are not morally obligated to adjust for the fact that Bill suffers an unfair disadvantage relative to Ted in making their final decision about which application to accept. Knowing that some entrants in the competition for admission to their school have been unfairly disadvantaged relative to others, in other words, they are not morally obligated to take this fact into account before deciding on the winners. The second claim needed to sustain the unfair disadvantage argument for race-based affirmative action is therefore shown to be false on terms that virtually everyone on both sides of the debate over affirmative action will accept.

And, indeed, when the attempt to look at affirmative action through the lens of an unfair race is carried out with this important point in mind, the same lesson about the requirements of morality and fairness emerges from the very sort of example that defenders of affirmative action have so frequently appealed to. For suppose, instead, that Bill and Ted had each been preparing to try out for the last available slot on the track team. In previous years, they trained for the same amount of time each week and Bill had been a little bit faster and more consistent than Ted. After Bill's father was sent to prison and Bill had to get a job after school, though, Bill gained weight from overeating as a coping mechanism, had less time to practice running because of his job, and missed the firm but loving discipline his father had always provided. As a result of this, by the time the day of the tryouts arrived, Ted was a little bit faster and more consistent than Bill. Virtually everyone, regardless of their view of race-based affirmative action, will agree that the track coach would do nothing morally wrong in this case if he simply gave the slot on the team to the white runner who in fact is a bit faster and more consistent rather than to the white runner who in fact is a bit slower and less consistent but who would have been a bit faster and more consistent had he not been unfairly disadvantaged by the unjust harm that was inflicted on his father. And so in this case, too, it should be clear that it's morally acceptable simply to select the person who is in fact better prepared and qualified over the person who would have been better prepared and qualified if the world has been a fairer place.

In cases where two white students compete for a position, then, it should be clear that the fact that one is better prepared and qualified than the other only because the other has been unfairly disadvantaged by a past injustice doesn't mean that it's wrong to accept the better prepared and qualified applicant without taking the effects of the past injustice into account. But this means that the second claim needed to sustain the unfair disadvantage argument must be rejected, and along with it the argument itself, on grounds that people on both sides of the affirmative action debate already accept: the fact that black applicants are unfairly disadvantaged by past injustice relative to white applicants doesn't mean that those charged with evaluating the applications are morally obligated to take the effects of the past injustice into account. And, more specifically, the fact that a particular black applicant would have been better prepared and qualified than a particular white applicant had the black applicant not been unfairly disadvantaged by the legacy of slavery and its aftermath doesn't show that it would be wrong to admit the better prepared and qualified white applicant over the less well prepared and qualified black applicant without taking the effect of these past injustices into account.

Now a defender of the unfair disadvantage argument might well complain that this conclusion is premature. There are, after all, some fairly conspicuous differences between the unfair disadvantage involved in the case of Bill and Ted and the unfair disadvantage involved in the case of race-based affirmative action. And it might well be thought that these differences can be used to undermine the objection to the unfair disadvantage argument that I've raised here. If the differences turn out to be morally relevant, on this account, then they might explain how it could be morally acceptable to ignore the unfair disadvantage and select Ted over Bill in the first case but not morally acceptable to have a policy of ignoring the unfair disadvantage and admitting slightly better prepared and qualified white applicants over slightly less prepared and qualified black applicants in the case of race-based affirmative action.

One difference between the two cases, of course, is that the Bill and Ted case involves comparing two candidates of the same race while race-based affirmative action programs involve comparing candidates of different races. But while it might be tempting for a defender of affirmative action to complain that this feature of my example is enough to render it irrelevant, this response would be unsatisfactory. The defender of race-based affirmative action can't simply assume that race is morally relevant in this context because the claim that race is morally relevant in this context is precisely what the defender of race-based affirmative action is trying to establish. The unfair disadvantage argument at first seems to provide the defender of affirmative action with a way of doing this. The argument seems to show that the difference between being black and being white should matter in the context of evaluating applications for competitive positions because the difference in race corresponds to a difference in terms of unfair disadvantage and because there is a moral obligation to take unfair disadvantage into account. To argue in this way is not to assume that race is morally relevant, but, rather, to try to show that it is. But the case of Bill and Ted shows that there isn't a general moral obligation to take unfair disadvantage into account. And so unless the defender of the argument can appeal to some difference between the two cases other than the fact that one involves race and the other doesn't, there will be no way to avoid the conclusion that the case of Bill and Ted undermines the unfair disadvantage argument for race-based affirmative action.

A second difference between the two cases is that the case of Bill and Ted involves a single, isolated incident, while race-based affirmative action involves a great many cases in which a slightly less qualified black candidate has been unfairly disadvantaged relative to his slightly better qualified white rival. It might be thought that this difference in numbers makes a difference. This response strikes me as unsatisfactory for two reasons. First, it's hard to see why the numbers involved should be morally relevant. In trying to figure out whether it's okay to select one particular candidate over another candidate who's a bit less qualified as a result of some unfair disadvantage, why should it matter how many other people find themselves in a similar situation? Why would it be okay to select the better qualified candidate if the situation is rare but not okay to do so if the situation is common? Why should the merits of Bill's plea to have his family's misfortune taken into account be made to depend on whether other families have suffered a similar injustice?

Second, this suspicion that the difference in numbers is irrelevant seems to be vindicated if we change the case of Bill and Ted to make it more like the case of race-based affirmative action in terms of the number of people involved. Suppose, for example, that Bill isn't the only white person in the country to have been hindered by his father having been wrongfully convicted of a crime he didn't commit. Suppose it turns out that there are a great many such white people, all of whom find themselves a bit less prepared and qualified for a position they apply for than some other white candidate who has not suffered a similar misfortune. Does the existence of this large number of other unfairly disadvantaged white candidates change your intuition about the case of Bill and Ted? It doesn't change mine. It seems just as clear to me in this version of the story as in my initial version that it's morally acceptable to select Ted over Bill even though Bill would have been better prepared and qualified than Ted had Bill's father not been unjustly imprisoned. It's hard to believe that many people on either side of the debate over race-based affirmative action would disagree. And so it's hard to see how this second response to my objection to the unfair disadvantage argument could be accepted.

A third difference between the two cases, though, does seem to pose a bigger problem for my argument. The point isn't just that there are a large number of unfairly disadvantaged black candidates while there's only one unfairly disadvantaged Bill, a critic of my position might say, but rather that the black candidates have been disadvantaged systematically, while Bill has been disadvantaged as the result of a more or less random act of wrongdoing. Indeed, this may well prove to be the most common complaint about my argument to this point: that my appeal to the intuitive reaction to individual cases, even if we stipulate that there are a great many of them, obscures the systematic nature of racial disadvantage in this country.

Although I realize that many people are inclined to put a great deal of weight on this point, however, I have to admit that I don't find this third objection to be any more compelling than the second. Indeed, the same two considerations that lead me to reject the second objection to my argument lead me to reject this third objection as well. First, at a general level, it just isn't clear why the difference between being a victim of systematic harm and being a victim of non-systematic harm should be considered morally relevant in this context. In trying to figure out whether it's permissible to select one particular candidate over another candidate who's a bit less qualified as a result of some unfair disadvantage, why should it matter how the unfair disadvantage was caused? It's not hard to understand why it might matter whether the disadvantage was caused fairly or unfairly. If one candidate is disadvantaged as a result of some harm that was caused fairly, after all, then presumably no one will think that we're obligated to select him over another better qualified candidate. If Bill had been forced to work long hours after school instead of doing his homework or training for the track tryouts because of something that was clearly his own fault, for example, then it's not hard to see how that would make things importantly different from the case of black candidates who are disadvantaged relative to white candidates due to no fault of their own. But given that the disadvantage that Bill suffers in the original version of the case is just as unfair to him as the disadvantage that unfairly disadvantaged black candidates suffer is unfair to them, why should it matter that the unfair disadvantage is caused systematically in the latter case and nonsystematically in the former? Why would it be permissible to select the better qualified white candidate over the white candidate who would have been better qualified had he not been unfairly disadvantaged by a nonsystematically caused harm but not permissible to select the better qualified white candidate over the white candidate who would have been better qualified had he not been unfairly disadvantaged by a systematically caused harm?

Second, this suspicion that the difference between systematic and nonsystematic harm is irrelevant to the issue at hand seems, at least to me, to be vindicated if we again change the case of Bill and Ted to make it more like the case of the black and white candidates involved in affirmative action cases. The black candidates in question are hindered by harms that were inflicted systematically on many black families because they were black. So suppose that we change the story about Bill and Ted and make it the case that when Bill's father was framed, this wasn't a random act of wrongful prosecution, but was part of a systematic, large-scale enterprise. The government, let's suppose, had deliberately targeted Bill's father and many others like him, and it had organized the prosecutions because it didn't like something that all of the families had in common: they were all Mormons, let's say, or Irish. I, at least, find that this change in story doesn't change my intuition about the admissions office's moral obligations: if it's morally permissible for the admissions office to admit Ted over Bill when Bill's father was one of many people who were targeted randomly, it seems clear to me that it should be morally permissible for the admissions office to admit Ted over Bill when Bill's father was one of many people who were targeted systematically.

I have to admit, though, that a number of people don't seem to share this intuition. They find that when this change is made in the story of Bill and Ted, their intuition about the case changes, too. Simply appealing to people's responses to a suitably modified version of the original case of Bill and Ted, then, may not be enough to help us assess the objection to my argument that arises from the distinction between random and systematic harms. What can we do, then, if there really isn't a sufficiently strong consensus at this point in the discussion? I think we can do two things. First, we can try to decide which side in the dispute can most reasonably be taken to have the burden of proof. Second, we can consider the ways in which they might try to meet that burden.

With respect to the first task, there are two reasons to conclude that the burden of proof lies with the critic who maintains that the difference between nonsystematic and systematic harm undermines my objection to the unfair disadvantage argument. The first reason is that this critic has already conceded that there's no general obligation to take unfair disadvantage into account. The critic has conceded, for example, that it would be morally permissible for the admissions officer to admit Ted over Bill in the original version of the story. Since the critic agrees that, in general, the fact that Bill has been disadvantaged by unjust acts committed against his father isn't enough to make it obligatory that Bill be admitted ahead of Ted, the burden is on the critic to explain why the fact that he's been disadvantaged as a result of a systematic form of harm in particular should be enough to make his admission obligatory. The second reason to place the burden of proof on the critic is more general. It seems reasonable, as a general matter, to start with the presumption that any controversial distinction is morally irrelevant unless there's a reason to think it's relevant rather than to start with the presumption that any controversial distinction is morally relevant unless there's a reason to think it's morally irrelevant. For both of these reasons, then, it seems fair to proceed by asking whether there's a good reason to think that the difference between systematic and nonsystematic forms of harm is relevant enough to undermine my objection to the unfair disadvantage argument.

One reason that might be given for thinking that the distinction poses a problem for my objection is that harming someone because they're Irish or because they're Mormon might in itself seem to be worse than harming someone randomly. Indeed, as we'll see in the discussion of hate crime laws in Chapters 8 and 9, there's good reason to think that claims such as this are true. But even if it's more objectionable to harm someone because of their group membership than to harm someone randomly, this would not be enough to undermine my objection to the unfair disadvantage argument. The relevant question is not how wrong the injustice committed against Bill's father was, but whether the admissions officer is morally obligated to take the resulting unfair disadvantage into account when deciding which candidate to admit. If Bill's father was intentionally convicted despite his innocence, for example, this would be morally worse than if he were negligently convicted. But if the admissions officer wouldn't be obligated to admit Bill over Ted in the latter case, then it isn't at all clear why he'd be obligated to admit him in the former case even though a greater moral wrong was committed against Bill's father in the former case. In the same way, and for the same reason, even if we agree that it's morally worse to target Bill's father systematically rather than to target him at random, it isn't at all clear why this would mean that the admissions officer would be obligated to admit Ted over Bill in the former case if it he wouldn't be obligated to admit him in the latter.

A second reason that might be given for thinking that the distinction between random and systematic harm undermines my objection to the unfair disadvantage argument appeals to the possibility that the difference is relevant in a different way: not in terms of how morally objectionable a given action is, but in terms of the kinds of responses that would be necessary in order to compensate for a given action's harmful effects. Systematic harms require systematic solutions, on this account, while random harms don't. But even if it's true that systematic harms require systematic solutions in a way that random harms don't, this account of the distinction wouldn't be enough to undermine my objection to the unfair disadvantage argument either. The relevant question isn't what kind of policy would best make up for the particular kind of unfair disadvantage that Bill suffers as a result of his father's mistreatment, but whether the admissions office is morally obligated to take the unfair disadvantage into account in deciding which candidate to admit in the first place. To appeal to the claim that Bill's disadvantage must be taken into account in the systematic harm case because doing so is the best or only way to make up for the unfairness in that case would therefore simply beg the question that is at issue: whether or not there really is a moral obligation to make up for the unfairness in the first place.

It's quite possible, of course, perhaps even likely, that even after rejecting these possible justifications, a number of readers will continue to feel that Bill really does have a right to be admitted over Ted when Bill's father was harmed as part of a systematic plot against Mormons or Irish people even though they agree that Bill would not have a right to be admitted over Ted when Bill's father was the victim of a nonsystematic plot to commit a comparable number of unjust acts at random. On this response, the change from random to systematic harms is enough to generate a moral obligation to take the resulting unfair disadvantage into account, and the claim that it's enough to generate this obligation is justified not by appealing to any further considerations, but simply by maintaining that it seems intuitively obvious that that claim is true. To readers who have this sort of reaction, I must admit that I have no further argument to offer and that I have no further reason to provide for rejecting the unfair disadvantage argument. But this concession should be of little comfort to defenders of that argument. It amounts, after all, to little more than saying that some people find the claim that affirmative action is morally obligatory to be intuitively obvious and in need of no further support and that there is little that can be said in response to their reaction. This fact can do little to support the argument because the same can be said of the claim that affirmative action is morally impermissible. Some people, for example, find the claim that affirmative action violates the rights of white male applicants to be intuitively obvious and in need of no further support and continue to believe this even if they can't provide a clear explanation of precisely what right is being violated. The question I've been concerned with here is whether there's any reason that can be given to reject my objection to the unfair disadvantage argument that doesn't simply start with the assumption that affirmative action is morally obligatory. And when all is said and done, it seems that the appeal to the possible relevance of the distinction between systematic and nonsystematic harm fails to provide such a reason.

Finally, a critic of my argument might point to the fact that the case of Bill and Ted involves an admissions officer making a decision about what to do in a particular instance while affirmative action involves a school making a decision about what sort of admissions policy to adopt and then apply to a large number of cases. And the critic might maintain that there's an important difference between the moral judgments we're inclined to make about particular cases involving particular people and the moral judgments we're entitled to make about what sorts of general policies should be adopted. Indeed, I suspect that a number of people who believe that affirmative action is morally obligatory will be wary of my attempt to argue from assessments of particular cases to conclusions about general policies for precisely this reason.

But while I do appreciate this further difference between the two cases, it's once again difficult to see how the difference could be morally relevant. If it would be morally acceptable for a particular worker within a particular organization to behave in a particular way, after all, then why wouldn't it be morally acceptable for the organization itself to adopt a policy that would permit the worker to behave in that way? If it would be morally unacceptable for the worker to behave in a certain way, why wouldn't that make it morally unacceptable for the organization to adopt a policy that would permit it? The critic of my argument at this point concedes that it would be morally acceptable to simply admit Ted rather than Bill in the original version of the story but denies that this judgment can be used to reach a conclusion about what sorts of admissions policies it would be morally permissible for a school to adopt. But if it would be morally acceptable to admit Ted without adjusting for the fact that Bill has been unfairly disadvantaged, then it would be morally permissible for a school to adopt a policy that would allow its admissions officers to act in such a way in such cases. If it would be morally permissible for a school to adopt such a policy, then it's morally permissible for a school to adopt a policy that doesn't require its admissions officers to take unfair disadvantage into account. And if it's morally permissible for a school to do this, then it's morally permissible for a school to decline to take unfair disadvantage into account when deciding whether or not to practice race-based affirmative action.

When we set aside the divisive subject of race for a moment, I think that virtually everyone on both sides of the affirmative action debate agrees that we aren't morally obligated to favor a slightly less qualified white candidate over a slightly more qualified white candidate simply because the slightly less qualified white candidate has been disadvantaged by past injustices. But given that this is true in the case where both candidates are white, it must be true in the case where one candidate is white and one is black. We therefore have good reason to reject the unfair disadvantage argument for race-based affirmative action on grounds that most people on both sides of the affirmative action debate already accept. The fact that black American candidates are unfairly disadvantaged by the legacy of slavery and its aftermath may make it desirable and even commendable for an organization to practice affirmative action. But it's not enough to make it morally obligatory.

THE (OTHER) COMPENSATION ARGUMENT

A second kind of backward-looking argument for an obligation to practice affirmative action appeals instead to a principle of compensation. The argument begins with a basic principle that most people are likely to accept. Suppose, for example, that Larry vandalizes Moe's car. It costs Moe $3,000 to fix the damage and he has to spend $250 renting a car while his is in the shop. Virtually everyone will agree that Larry owes Moe at least $3,250 in compensation. This is because virtually everyone accepts the principle that when you wrongfully harm someone, you're morally obligated to compensate them for the harm. This means that you're obligated to restore your victim to the level of well-being that he would have enjoyed had you not wrongfully harmed him. But on the assumption that black Americans who apply for jobs and admission to schools have been disadvantaged by the legacy of slavery and its aftermath, this might well mean that such applicants are entitled to preferential treatment as a matter of compensatory justice. If a black job candidate would have been the best qualified for the job had he not been unjustly harmed, after all, then it would seem that giving him the job would be required in order to restore him to the level of well-being he would have enjoyed had he not been harmed in the first place. This appeal to compensation is perhaps less widespread than the appeal to fairness, but it provides a second backward-looking argument for the obligation to practice affirmative action nonetheless, and one that at least some supporters of affirmative action have defended. In *Racism and Justice: The Case For Affirmative Action*, for example, the philosopher Gertrude Ezorsky maintains that "blacks have a moral claim to compensation for past injury" and argues that affirmative action is thereby justified as "an appropriate method of compensation for blacks."[21]

Like the unfair disadvantage argument, this compensation argument depends on two claims: the claim that black applicants for positions in the present are owed compensation for the harms that black Americans have suffered in the past, and the claim that if this is so, then they are entitled to preferential treatment when their applications are considered. As with the unfair disadvantage argument, I'm inclined to accept the first claim. Indeed, as with the unfair disadvantage argument, the first claim of this compensation argument is essentially the same as one of the claims that I appealed to in my defense of slave reparations in Chapters 2 and 3. But, again as with the unfair disadvantage argument, I'm inclined to reject the second claim that this compensation argument depends on. That's why, although I eventually found myself convinced by the compensation argument for slave reparations, I remain unconvinced by this other compensation argument for affirmative action.

To see what's wrong with the second claim needed to make the compensation argument for affirmative action work, it's important to begin by noticing an important difference between the unfair disadvantage argument and the compensation argument. The unfair disadvantage argument applies to every organization that accepts applications for some sort of position. That argument, after all, rests on the claim that if you hold a competition for a position, you're obligated to ensure that the results of the competition are fair. If the unfair disadvantage argument works, then, it will show that every organization should practice affirmative action. But the compensation argument, even if it turns out to be successful, can at most establish that an organization is obligated to engage in affirmative action if the organization itself can legitimately be held responsible for having caused the wrongful harm that rendered its black applicants a bit less qualified than they would otherwise be. If Larry vandalizes Moe's car, after all, then it's Larry that owes compensation to Moe, not Curly or Shemp. Similarly, if black candidates today are continuing to suffer the lingering consequences of slavery and its aftermath, then it is those who are responsible for causing slavery and its aftermath who would owe them compensation. Those schools or businesses that can't legitimately be held responsible for having caused these wrongful harms in the past can't be said to owe such compensation. And thus any argument for affirmative action that rests on a claim about such compensation can't apply to them.

With this limitation on the scope of the argument in mind, let's return to the case of Bill and Ted. But this time, let's say that both have submitted applications to be admitted to an educational institution run not privately, but by the federal government. If the compensation argument for affirmative action will work anywhere, it should at least work in this kind of case, since if any organization can be said to owe compensation to black Americans as a result of the legacy of legalized slavery, discrimination, and segregation it's the federal government. So let's say that Bill and Ted have applied to West Point, that both of them are suitably prepared and qualified to be admitted, and that you're the head of the admissions office. Ted is a bit better prepared and qualified than Bill, but let's start by supposing that you know nothing about the circumstances that brought this about. Since Ted is somewhat better prepared and qualified, you're about to offer him the final slot in the entering class. But at the last minute, you receive an additional piece of information: Bill's father was sent to prison a few years ago, and Bill's academic and athletic record was actually better than Ted's up to that point. It seems clear to you, in other words, that Bill would have been somewhat better prepared and qualified for admission to West Point than Ted if Bill's father hadn't been sent to prison.

As in the case of the unfair disadvantage argument, I think it's clear that most people, regardless of their views of race-based affirmative action, will agree that it's permissible for you simply to admit Ted over Bill under these circumstances rather than to adjust your decision by taking Bill's misfortune into account. The fact that Bill would be mentally and physically sharper than Ted today if his father hadn't been sent to prison doesn't mean that West Point is obligated to give him preference over Ted given that Ted is, in fact, mentally and physically sharper than Bill. But now let's add the fact that Bill's father was innocent and that he was unjustly framed and imprisoned by the federal government in particular. Does this change in the story produce a change in your moral intuitions?

In some respects, of course, the change in the story does make a difference. You will now think that the government owes Bill's father compensation for the wrongful harm that it inflicted on him, and may well agree that it would also owe compensation to Bill himself for the harm that he suffered as an indirect result of the harm that was inflicted on his father. But as the head of admissions at West Point, that's not the question that you have to answer. The question you have to answer is whether West Point should be obligated to admit Bill ahead of Ted. And with respect to this question, at least, it's hard to see how this change in the story could change your answer. If it's okay for you to admit Ted over Bill if Bill's father is guilty, why wouldn't it be okay to admit Ted over Bill if Bill's father is innocent? If you weren't obligated to admit Bill over Ted in the first place, then you aren't obligated to admit him now that you've discovered that it's the government's fault that his father was unjustly imprisoned. And since it seems clear that you weren't obligated to admit Bill in the first place, this means that you're still not obligated to admit Bill. It's true that Bill would have been somewhat better prepared and qualified for West Point than Ted were it not for the terrible injustice committed by the government against his father. And it's true that this may well generate an obligation on the part of the government to provide some kind of compensating benefit to Bill. But from the fact that the government would owe some kind of compensation to Bill it doesn't follow that just because West Point is run by the government, it would be morally obligated to admit Bill ahead of Ted.

Let's now assume that I'm right about that. If I am right, then an important lesson can be drawn from this version of the story of Bill and Ted: although offers of admission to a state-run university (or of employment at state agencies) are a valuable benefit to those who receive them, the government isn't obligated to distribute these benefits by giving them to the people who have been most harmed by the government. If Bill has suffered as a result of wrongful harms that the government inflicted on his father, then the government may well owe him some kind of compensation. But even if this is true, it doesn't mean that it's obligated to ensure that West Point admits him ahead of Ted. The compensation argument for affirmative action must therefore be rejected. A particular black student who's somewhat less prepared and qualified than a particular white student only because of the lingering effects of slavery and its aftermath, after all, is in precisely the same position that Bill was in with respect to Ted: he does not, in fact, have better grades and test scores than his rival but, by hypothesis, he would have had better grades and test scores were it not for the unjust harms that were committed by the government against members of previous generations of his family. Since this fact isn't enough to generate an obligation to admit the slightly less qualified Bill over the slightly more qualified Ted, it also isn't enough to generate an obligation to admit the slightly less qualified black student over the slightly more qualified white student.

My claim about this other compensation argument may at this point generate the same sort of confusion I tried to fend off near the beginning of this discussion. In Chapters 2 and 3, after all, I endorsed the claim that the federal government does have a moral obligation to make reparations to contemporary black Americans for the lingering harms caused by the legacy of slavery and its aftermath. But in this chapter, I'm denying that the federal government, or anyone else, has a reparations-based moral obligation to benefit contemporary black Americans by engaging in race-based affirmative action. This may seem to be inconsistent. So let me offer one final example, once again trying to take race out of the picture for a moment. Suppose that the state of California wrongfully harms a white teenager by negligently causing him to be injured. Suppose also that this injury has the same discouraging effect on his high school career as the injustice done to Bill's father had on Bill's high school career. The white teenager sues for damages and a jury determines that he's entitled to a substantial benefit from the state. Suppose that this teenager had applied to several campuses of the University of California (UC) school system. Based on his academic qualifications, he was rejected by Berkeley but admitted by a few of the other schools. In this case, it should be clear that it would be consistent to maintain that the state should pay for the student's room and board at one of the schools he was admitted to and to deny that it should direct the Berkeley campus to admit him to their undergraduate program. But if that's right, then it's just as consistent for me to maintain what I've maintained here and in the previous chapters. A black student who gets into another UC campus but not into Berkeley might have a right to receive room and board support from the state government as a form of reparations, but this wouldn't mean that he has a right to have the government ensure that he be admitted to a school that he would not otherwise be admitted to. Most people seem to view the slave reparations position as an extreme, radical position while they view the claim that affirmative action is obligatory as a kind of modest, run-of-the-mill opinion. But once the arguments about compensation are carefully sorted out and examined, we can see that just the opposite is true. The principle of compensation does provide a sound argument for the reparations position. But it doesn't provide a sound argument for the affirmative action position.

I conclude that backward-looking arguments for affirmative action are unsuccessful. They may succeed in identifying some respect in which things would be better if a somewhat less prepared and qualified black candidate were selected over a somewhat more prepared and qualified white candidate. But even if they do, they fail to establish that there's a moral obligation to make things better in this respect. It's true, of course, that if a school declines to adopt an affirmative action policy and instead makes its admissions decisions in a race-neutral manner, then its policy will tend to work to the advantage of those who have already been unfairly advantaged and to the disadvantage of those who have already been disadvantaged. And it might be thought that this fact provides one final way to ground a backward-looking defense of the claim that race-based affirmative action is morally obligatory. But to the extent that black Americans today are unfairly disadvantaged relative to white Americans on the whole, race-neutral policies which are uncontroversially permissible in all sorts of other contexts have this very same effect. Black Americans, for example, pay precisely the same tax rates that white Americans pay on income, property, purchases of goods, and so forth. They pay precisely the same fines for speeding, littering, and any other fineable offense that white people pay. The post office charges them the same amount for stamps. They are forced to comply with precisely the same burdensome licensing requirements that white people are forced to comply with in order to gain work as barbers, or doctors, or pilots, and so on. All of these race-neutral policies are better for white Americans and worse for black Americans than policies which take race into account by lowering the tax rates, fines, prices, licensing requirements, and so on for black Americans relative to those for white Americans. In all of these cases, then, the adoption of race-neutral policies perpetuates the currently existing inequities between black and white Americans. But in none of these contexts is this fact by itself thought to make such race-neutral policies unjust. In the same way, then, and for the same reason, the fact that race-neutral admissions policies are better for white applicants and worse for black applicants than are race-based affirmative action policies doesn't mean that affirmative action is morally required or that doing without it is morally unjust. In the end, there seems to be no successful backward-looking argument for the claim that race-based affirmative action is morally obligatory.

THE APPEAL TO DIVERSITY

Arguments for affirmative action that rest on considerations about compensation or fairness are essentially backward-looking. They appeal to claims about things that happened in the past as a way of trying to justify an obligation we are said to have in the present. I've explained why I don't find these arguments convincing. But there's also a very different kind of argument that many people now offer in defense of affirmative action. This more recent kind of argument is essentially forward-looking. It appeals to the claim that adopting affirmative action policies now will lead to valuable benefits in the future, and maintains that these benefits are sufficiently important to secure the case for affirmative action.

The most familiar version of this kind of argument involves an appeal to the value of diversity. Suppose, for example, that there are relatively few black students on a particular college campus. And suppose, also, that black students tend to come from backgrounds and have points of view that are different from those of typical white students. In that case, increasing the number of black students on the campus can reasonably be expected to help increase the extent to which both black and white students are exposed to others from different backgrounds and with different points of view. Since being exposed to people with different backgrounds and perspectives seems likely to be of significant educational value, this seems clearly to be the kind of thing that colleges should be doing. And so, according to this argument, it should seem pretty clear that affirmative action is the kind of thing that colleges should be doing as well. As Neil Rudenstine, the former president of Harvard, has put the point: diversity is "an educational resource comparable in importance to the faculty, library or science lab…. It is the substance from which much human learning, understanding, and wisdom derive. It offers one of the most powerful ways of creating the intellectual energy and robustness that lead to greater knowledge." University of Michigan President Lee Bollinger has argued that student diversity "is as essential as the study of the Middle Ages, of international politics and of Shakespeare" on the grounds that it "broadens the mind and the intellect – essential goals of education." And as Gerhard Casper, the former president of Stanford, put it a bit more bluntly, "We do not admit minorities to do them a favor."[22]

The appeal to diversity is perhaps the most common argument presented in defense of affirmative action on American campuses today. Not surprisingly, it's also one of the most controversial. Many people complain that the argument depends on the oversimplified and demeaning assumption that people of the same race all think alike. The philosopher Ellen Frankel Paul, for example, has objected that "the assumption that all blacks, all women, all Hispanics, and all members of other 'protected groups' share the same social philosophy is patronizing in the extreme and should be offensive to precisely those individuals it seeks to accommodate."[23] This worry strikes me as overblown. The argument from diversity doesn't have to assume that all black people think alike and that all white people think alike. It simply has to assume that there are, on average, some differences in life experiences and points of view so that, on the whole, a group made up entirely of white Americans is likely to contain a narrower range of experiences and points of view than is a group that contains a representative portion of black Americans. And it isn't clear, at least to me, that this is an unreasonable assumption.

Other people maintain that while the argument from diversity might work in some contexts, it doesn't work in others. Maybe it's important to seek ethnic diversity in a history department, they might say, but it's not important in a math department.[24] Different perspectives on the rise and fall of the Roman empire are useful, after all. Different perspectives on the square root of seven are not. This objection, too, strikes me as unconvincing. Part of the reason that diversity might prove useful in a university setting does have to do with the importance of having different perspectives on a given subject. And it's probably (although not obviously) true that math and physics aren't subject to such different perspectives in the valuable way that history and literature are.[25] But part of the reason that diversity might prove important has to do with its ability to foster innovative approaches to things other than the subject matter of a discipline itself: things like alternative approaches to teaching, to doing collaborative work with others, to resolving disputes with colleagues, to connecting the university to the larger community beyond, and so on. If, for example, black Americans on the whole are likely to have had different kinds of experiences interacting with authority figures than are white Americans, then they might, on average, be likely to come up with different approaches to understanding and responding to the authority that a teacher has over a student or an administrator over a teacher. There's no particular reason to think that a math teacher would benefit less from being exposed to more approaches to these issues than would a history teacher. And so even if racial diversity might prove to be more valuable to a history department than to a math department, this provides little reason to deny that it could be valuable to a math department at all.[26]

Understood as an argument for the claim that affirmative action has some positive consequences, then, I'm inclined to think that the appeal to diversity may well prove to be a reasonable one. And, indeed, its merits seem easy enough to apply to the world outside the university. In any kind of enterprise that benefits from innovation and the interplay of different ideas and approaches, some effort to create a more racially diverse population might prove capable of producing some tangible benefits.[27] When the University of Michigan was forced to defend its affirmative action policies in court, for example, sixty-five prominent

American corporations filed an *amicus* brief in its support. The brief, which was filed on behalf of such businesses as General Electric, Microsoft, and Coca-Cola, argued that "the need for diversity in higher education is indeed compelling" and that in virtue of "the increasingly global reach of American business," the companies "need the talent and creativity of a workforce that is as diverse as the world around it."[28] A similar brief was filed on behalf of a group of twenty-nine retired military and civilian leaders in support of affirmative action policies at the service academies and in ROTC programs.[29]

But it's important to remember that the supporters of affirmative action that I'm concerned with in this chapter don't simply make the relatively modest claim that affirmative action has some positive consequences. They don't even limit themselves to the considerably stronger claim that the positive consequences of affirmative action outweigh whatever negative consequences it might have. Rather, they make the much more robust claim that there's a moral obligation to engage in affirmative action, that it would be positively immoral for a school or business or government to decline to practice affirmative action. And understood as an argument for the claim that there is such an obligation, the argument from diversity proves to be considerably weaker, even if it's true that the diversity generated by affirmative action has some positive consequences and even if it's true that these positive consequences outweigh whatever negative consequences might accompany them.[30]

Perhaps the simplest way to see the problem with using the value of diversity as a basis for an obligation to engage in affirmative action is to look at other cases in which hiring someone would contribute to diversity. Suppose, for example, that a philosophy department is choosing between two finalists for a position teaching ethics. Both are white men who have very similar records, though one is somewhat better qualified because he has published a bit more, or in somewhat more impressive professional journals. The somewhat more qualified applicant is from Chicago, and the somewhat less qualified applicant was born, raised, and educated in Switzerland. The department currently has twelve members, all of whom have lived their entire lives in the United States. It seems clear in this case that the Swiss candidate would contribute an important and valuable kind of diversity to the department that the American candidate would not. People who were born and raised in other countries are, on average, likely to bring with them a distinctive set of life experiences and perspectives that can be beneficial to those who encounter them. And it seems plausible, at least to me, to think that this fact could count in favor of hiring him. But it's hard to believe that anyone would think that this means the department has a moral *obligation* to hire the Swiss candidate over the American, that it would be positively unjust for it to hire the somewhat better qualified American candidate instead.[31]

The same judgment, moreover, seems difficult to avoid in virtually every other context in which admitting or hiring someone would plausibly contribute to a valuable sort of diversity. Suppose, for example, that a department consists entirely of white male Christians and it's choosing between two white men, one of whom is also Christian, but the other of whom is Jewish or Muslim and a bit less qualified. Or suppose that a slightly less qualified candidate would bring diversity to a department by becoming the only member of the department to have been raised by a same-sex couple, or in an orphanage, or in extreme poverty, or to have served in the military, or in the Peace Corps, or in Congress, or in prison, or to be deaf, or blind, or in a wheelchair, and so on. In all of these cases, it seems plausible, at least to me, to think that the candidates who would add diversity really would bring something distinctive to the department in virtue of their unique background that would be of value to at least some of the students and faculty they would interact with. And so in all of these cases, it seems plausible, at least to me, to suppose that it could be appropriate to take diversity into account when making a final decision. But in none of these cases does it seem at all plausible to think that it would be positively unjust to refrain from doing so, and it's hard to believe that many people on either side of the race-based affirmative action debate would think otherwise. All of these cases, then, raise serious problems for the claim that the diversity that a black candidate would add to a department can provide the basis for an obligation to give preference to that candidate.

This problem with the argument from diversity, in fact, runs even deeper. For there are still further sorts of cases where it's even more clear that hiring someone would increase diversity in a way that's valuable to a university, and yet even in these cases, it seems clear that this fact doesn't ground an obligation to promote diversity. Consider, for example, a department of Asian Languages at a large university that's looking to hire another professor. The department already offers courses in Chinese and Japanese but offers no courses in Korean. The search produces two finalists: one who would offer some courses in Korean, and a slightly better qualified candidate who would offer courses in Chinese. In this case, it seems difficult to deny that the kind of diversity produced by hiring the Korean professor is a kind of curricular diversity that a university must place a high value on. Yet even here, it seems clear that this doesn't mean that the university has a moral obligation to hire the Korean teacher ahead of the Chinese one. If it decides to hire the slightly better qualified candidate rather than the one who would add more diversity to its curriculum, it doesn't act unjustly. It's difficult to imagine that any defenders of race-based affirmative action would disagree with this judgment. But if that's so, then even defenders of race-based affirmative action must concede that the claim that it's good to promote diversity isn't enough to justify the claim that there's a moral obligation to promote diversity. And if there's no such obligation, then while the appeal to diversity may well help to establish that affirmative action has some positive consequences, it will prove unable to establish that it's morally wrong to refrain from practicing affirmative action.[32]

A defender of affirmative action, of course, could point to an obvious difference between promoting racial diversity and promoting the other sorts of diversity that the various examples that I've appealed to here involve. The lack of racial diversity in American institutions, after all, is often traceable to past acts of injustice in a way that the lack of these other forms of diversity typically isn't. That difference might well prove to be morally relevant. And so it could be perfectly consistent for a defender of race-based affirmative action to maintain that there's a moral obligation to promote racial diversity but no comparable moral obligation to promote, say, curricular or nation of origin diversity.

But while appealing to this distinction might be relevant in attempting to defend race-based affirmative action by means of the kind of backward-looking arguments that I considered in the previous two sections, it isn't available to the defender of affirmative action who seeks to provide an alternative kind of defense of the practice on forward-looking grounds. From that point of view, it doesn't matter whether an absence of diversity arose in a just or unjust manner. All that matters is that an increase in diversity now will bring about benefits in the future. It's possible, of course, that people who defend affirmative action by appealing to the value of diversity would ultimately agree that promoting diversity is only obligatory when it's done in response to past injustices. And so it may be that seemingly forward-looking arguments for affirmative action ultimately collapse into the kind of backward-looking arguments that I've already considered.[33]

If the diversity argument is just another form of these other arguments, though, then it should be rejected for the reasons that I presented in the previous two sections. And if it isn't, then the diversity argument remains subject to the counterexamples that I've employed in this section. And it will, in addition, have further implications that virtually every supporter of race-based affirmative action is likely to reject. If promoting diversity is obligatory even in cases where the current lack of diversity isn't a result of past injustice, for example, then historically black colleges such as Morehouse and Spellman will have an obligation to increase their white enrolment even if this means admitting some white students ahead of some otherwise better qualified black students.[34] But it's difficult to believe that many defenders of affirmative action would be willing to accept this result. Whether or not the argument from diversity amounts to another version of the argument from past injustice, then, it fails to provide a satisfactory justification for the claim that race-based affirmative action is morally obligatory.[35]

THE NEED FOR ROLE MODELS

Looking back at his lax study habits when he first arrived at college, President Obama has reflected on the important benefits he derived from having professors who were black like him:

> I remember some of my teachers saying, 'Man, why are you pretending that you're not smart? Why are you spending all your time on something not serious, instead of focusing on what your talents are?' And, coming from black professors, especially, that was important, because I couldn't throw back at them, 'Oh, you just don't understand'. That's a big part of the reason it is so important to have black teachers, especially black male

teachers. I'm not saying exclusively, but in many situations you need someone who can call you on your stuff and say ... that it's not 'acting white' to read a book.[36]

These considerations suggest a second and distinct way in which race-based affirmative action can be defended on forward-looking grounds. On this version of the argument, the important benefit that such policies can provide is a steady supply of role models who can inspire and motivate the younger black people who would look up to them. The philosopher Joel J. Kupperman, for example, has argued that disadvantaged minorities are often held back by things like fear of success and low expectations of what is possible. Seeing other people like themselves overcome such obstacles, he maintains, can help young black people follow suit. And so affirmative action programs are justified, on this account, by their ability to provide role models to those who really need them.[37]

One possible problem with the role model argument arises from the fact that it depends on the empirical claim that role models really do provide the important benefits that defenders of the argument claim they do. This claim can be called into question. Thomas Sowell, for example, has complained that there's no real empirical evidence to support it. If there are more black teachers at medical school, for example, will there eventually be more black doctors? Will there be better black doctors? It isn't easy to say.[38] And in a recent study on faculty diversity, Stephen Cole and Elinor Barber conclude that while having a professor as a role model can have a positive impact on a student's decision to pursue an academic career, the race of the faculty member is irrelevant: "For students in all ethnic groups, it makes no difference whether the role model is of the same gender, the same race, or the same gender and race."[39]

But even if the role model argument does succeed in proving that affirmative action produces some positive consequences, that would not be enough to show that affirmative action is morally obligatory. This is the same basic problem that prevented the diversity argument from justifying an obligation to engage in affirmative action. There are, after all, lots of things that a university could do that would benefit a number of its students. It could build a bigger library. It could build a new recreation center. It could hire more people to work at its health center. It could offer better food in the dining halls. It could offer smaller classes. All of these would be good things to do because they would be good for the students. But the fact that they would be good things to do doesn't mean that it would be immoral not to do them. And so the same goes for the provision of role models for black students and others. The fact that it would be good to provide them isn't enough to make it immoral not to provide them.[40]

Indeed, this feature of the role model and diversity arguments is ultimately a problem for the attempt to use any forward-looking argument as a justification for the claim that affirmative action is not simply good but obligatory. If the consequences of increasing the number of black students on campus are said to be good because of some other sort of positive result they would lead to, such as increasing black representation in elite institutions or decreasing the relationship between race and class,[41] the same basic problem will remain: there are all sorts of good things that a university can do that would have positive social consequences whether in terms of global warming, world hunger, or combating AIDS. It's praiseworthy when a university devotes some of its resources to such worthy causes, but not impermissible when it refrains from doing so. The same is true of the worthy causes that might be served by increasing the number of black students it admits by engaging in affirmative action.

THE BIAS-ELIMINATION ARGUMENT

Arguments for affirmative action that appeal to compensation or fairness are essentially backward-looking. Arguments that appeal to diversity or the value of having role models are essentially forward-looking. I've explained why I don't think either of these kinds of arguments can provide a satisfactory justification for an obligation to engage in affirmative action. But there's one final direction in which a supporter of affirmative action might look: the present. There are, in particular, two kinds of argument that attempt to show that facts about the present suffice to generate an obligation to engage in some form of affirmative action. I will conclude my discussion of the arguments in favor of affirmative action by considering them in turn.

The first kind of present-looking argument appeals to the claim that selection criteria that on the face of it may appear to be race-neutral are in fact biased against black candidates. If this is so, the argument maintains, then some form of affirmative action is required in order to compensate for this bias, regardless of its historical origins and regardless of its future consequences. Suppose, to take a familiar complaint, that the SAT is biased against black test takers.[42] Suppose, to be more specific, that the test is biased against them by fifty points. Perhaps the test includes vocabulary words that, on average, are more likely to be familiar to white students than to black students of comparable intelligence, or perhaps it makes use of analogies involving examples that white students are more likely to be familiar with than are comparably talented black students. A black student, on this account, is really just as academically talented as a white student who scores fifty points higher than him. And in that case, the argument maintains, a college admissions policy should add fifty points to the test score of each black student before making a final admission decision. Affirmative action is justified in such cases simply as a means of assuring that the better candidate really does get admitted.[43]

This particular version of the bias-elimination argument can apparently be strengthened by appealing to more general claims about currently existing biases against black Americans. The social psychologist Claude Steele, for example, performed a widely discussed experiment on two groups of students at Stanford University that seems to support the claim that what he calls "stereotype vulnerability" creates a general obstacle that black students confront, but white students don't, when their academic abilities are being measured by apparently unbiased tests.[44] Steele gave two groups of black and white students an identical set of verbal questions that had been used in the GRE, the standardized SAT-like test that undergraduates who plan to attend graduate school take as part of the application process. Before taking the tests, one group was told that the exercise was simply intended to examine "psychological factors involved in solving verbal problems" while the other was told that it was "a genuine test of your verbal abilities and limitations." In the first group, the black students scored as well as the white students. In the second group, the white students scored the same as the white students in the first group, but the scores of the black students were significantly lower. Steele takes this as evidence that when black students take tests such as the SAT, GRE, and LSAT, they feel burdened by their attempt to overcome negative stereotypes about black academic ability and their scores suffer as a result. If this is correct, then even if the content of the tests they take is completely unbiased, the environment in which the tests are administered renders the results of the tests biased against black students. And if this is correct, then it again seems that it is necessary to correct for the bias by giving black applicants some kind of compensating advantage and that some form of race-based affirmative action would therefore be morally obligatory.[45]

Finally, some defenders of the bias-elimination argument for affirmative action appeal to the claim that the people who do the evaluating of applicants may themselves be biased against black candidates, even if only at a subconscious level. The philosopher Laurence Thomas, for example, defends the claim that an "unintentional" bias against black people is still widespread in the United States and that affirmative action is therefore required as a means of "correcting for unfavorable moral head winds" of the sort that will otherwise unfairly bias a decision procedure in favor of white applicants over black applicants.[46]

The bias-elimination argument depends on the claim that the deck is currently stacked against black candidates and that affirmative action is necessary in order to correct for this fact. One reason for rejecting the argument is that even if the argument proves to be successful, the practice that it would justify isn't really what people on both sides of the debate mean by affirmative action. What people who oppose affirmative action typically oppose, for example, is the idea of selecting a black candidate over a white candidate when the white candidate is, all things considered, better qualified. They think, for example, that if a particular white student's SAT scores are a bit higher than a particular black student's, this is good evidence that the white student is a bit more academically skilled than the black student. And since they think that the more academically skilled student merits admission ahead of the academically less skilled student, they think that the white student merits admission ahead of the black student for that reason. If the bias-elimination argument is successful, it will show that schools should in fact choose the black student over the white student in such cases. But since it will do so only by establishing that the black student really is, in fact, all things considered better qualified and more academically skilled than the white student, the practice that the argument will justify isn't really the practice that opponents of affirmative action take themselves to be opposing.

Similarly, what people who support affirmative action typically support is the idea that sometimes a black candidate should be selected over a white candidate even if the white candidate really is, all things considered, better qualified. They think, for example, that even if a black applicant is deemed to be a bit less academically skilled or qualified after all the relevant facts about such things as the accuracy of the SAT have been taken into account, he's still entitled to be admitted ahead of a slightly more academically skilled or qualified white applicant because of the unfair circumstances that led him to be all things considered less skilled or qualified. If the bias-elimination argument is successful, it will show that schools should sometimes admit *seemingly* less qualified black applicants over *seemingly* more qualified white applicants. But since it will do so only in cases in which the seemingly less qualified black student proves, in fact, to be *actually* better qualified when all the relevant facts about such things as the accuracy of the SAT are taken into account, the practice that the argument will justify isn't really the practice that supporters of affirmative action take themselves to be supporting. Even if the bias-elimination argument proves to be successful in justifying the adoption of practices designed to take into account current biases against black candidates, then, it can't succeed as a justification of what I described at the outset of this chapter as strong affirmative action.[47]

This first problem is a good enough reason to reject the bias-elimination argument, at least when it's presented as an argument in defense of affirmative action. But let's go ahead and suppose that it makes sense to refer to the bias-elimination procedures that the argument would justify as a form of affirmative action even in cases where the procedures are simply designed to ensure that the best qualified candidate really is selected, regardless of race. Even if we assume for the sake of the argument that such policies should count as a form of affirmative action, there's a second reason to reject the bias-elimination argument: it fails to show that there's a moral obligation to engage in such bias elimination in the first place.

Suppose, for example, that Joe Black and Jack White are competing for the last remaining spot in a particular graduate program. Suppose that Jack's GRE scores are a bit higher, that his letters of recommendation are a bit stronger, and that the (all-white) group of professors from the department who meet with him find him a bit more impressive than they find Joe. But suppose also that Jack's modest edge over Joe in all of these respects is entirely due to subtle biases against black people: if the GRE were perfectly objective and administered in a perfectly race-neutral environment, then Joe would have outscored Jack. If their professors hadn't harbored vague and tacit stereotypical assumptions about black academic ability, they would have gotten to know Joe better during his college days and would have written more enthusiastic letters for him than for Jack. If the professors in the graduate program didn't share the same sorts of racial prejudices, they would have found Joe to be a bit more impressive than Jack when they met with him.

Given all of these suppositions, we can conclude that Joe Black is, in fact, a better candidate for admission than Jack White. We can also conclude that a variety of subtle biases against black people are preventing the graduate program's admissions committee from recognizing this fact. And we can even conclude that a bias-elimination policy that gave preference to a black candidate who seemed a bit less qualified over a white candidate who seemed a bit more qualified might well produce a better outcome as a result. We could agree, that is, that a graduate program that adopts such a policy under such conditions is more likely to end up admitting the better student than is a graduate program that doesn't. Assuming for the sake of the argument that it makes sense to refer to such a policy as a form of affirmative action, then, we could say that affirmative action, when practiced in a society that's biased against black people, could be understood as acting like a set of corrective lenses that simply help to produce the results that an admissions or hiring committee would be able to produce without such a policy if its vision of things were not corrupted in various important respects. Affirmative action of this sort, in short, might be needed in order to make sure that the best candidate really does prevail.

Even if we were to accept all of this, though, it would still fail to establish that there's a moral obligation to practice affirmative action. The reason for this is simple: there's no moral obligation to select the best candidate in the first place. Thus, even if affirmative action really is needed in order to ensure that the best candidates are selected, this can't show that there's anything immoral about a program or company or government that does not practice affirmative action. At most, it can show that there may be something unwise or imprudent about their declining to engage in affirmative action. And the fact that a policy is unwise does not mean that it is unjust.[48]

I'll try to defend my claim that there's no moral obligation to select the best candidate in just a moment. But before I do, it's worth stressing that defenders of affirmative action should be quick to embrace this claim anyhow. In most other contexts, after all, it's precisely the defenders of affirmative action who are prone to insist that it really would be okay to admit or hire a somewhat less qualified black person over a somewhat more qualified white person. But if they're right about this, then it clearly follows that there's no general moral obligation to select the most qualified candidate. If there really were such an obligation, after all, then it would always be wrong to hire a less qualified black person over a more qualified white person. But while defenders of affirmative action seem clearly to recognize this point when they talk about the importance of compensation or fairness or about the value of diversity, they seem also to forget about it when something like the bias-elimination argument comes up. In the context of that argument, they uncharacteristically appeal to the claim that we have to engage in affirmative action because we have to make sure that the best candidate is selected. But if the fact that a particular white candidate is the best qualified doesn't mean that we're morally obligated to select him, then the fact that a particular black candidate is really the best qualified doesn't mean that we're morally obligated to select him either. Either way, if we want, morality allows us to choose to settle for less. And so, either way, morality won't require us to engage in affirmative action even if affirmative action really is needed in order to select the best candidates overall.

So the defender of affirmative action, at least upon reflection, is already committed to the claim that I'm using here to undermine the bias-elimination argument, the claim that there's no moral obligation to select the best qualified candidate. Since the claim that it's okay not to select the best candidate will also play an important role in some of my responses to the arguments made by opponents of affirmative action in the next chapter, though, it's important to see that this claim can also be supported by appealing to other cases about which defenders and opponents of affirmative action alike will almost certainly agree.

Here's a simple case to start with. A tree blows over and makes a hole in the roof of my house. The hole is clearly visible from the street. Within a day, a number of roof repair companies have stopped by, taken a look, and left binding estimates for me explaining exactly what they would do to fix my roof, when they would do it, how much they would charge me, what their qualifications are, how many years of experience they have, testimonials from satisfied customers, and so forth. Now suppose it turns out that they will all charge me the same price and that they're all available on the same day. Would I be morally obligated to select the company that is the very best qualified? Or would morality permit me to just pick one at random from the Yellow Pages? Even if I knew that one company was better qualified, would it be morally permissible for me to select another company instead simply because I liked its name better? From a self-interested point of view, of course, it might well make sense for me to carefully select the company that is best suited for the job. But morally speaking, it's hard to believe that I'd be doing anything wrong if I just selected a company at random or chose the company with the name I liked the most. And I think that virtually everyone, regardless of their view of affirmative action, would agree with this judgment. But this judgment clearly means that there's no moral obligation to select the best qualified person for the job.[49]

A critic of my argument here might agree with my assessment of this particular case, but wonder whether it would hold in cases involving education or publicly funded organizations. So suppose, instead, that I'm the chair of a philosophy department at a state university. The department suddenly finds that it is in need of an extra person to teach a logic class that begins in a few weeks, and I'm inundated with applications from over a hundred people. Am I morally obligated to carefully examine every detail in every application file so that I can pick the very best applicant, or is it okay if I simply offer the job to the first person I come across who's clearly qualified and clearly available? Again, it seems clear that morality doesn't require me to make sure that the very best candidate gets the job and so, again, it seems clear that even if affirmative action is necessary to make sure that the best candidate gets the job, this isn't enough to make affirmative action morally obligatory.

A final example is a bit more complicated, but worth considering because it's so widespread and so universally accepted. This is the practice that a number of colleges and universities have of making their admissions decisions on a rolling basis. When a school uses a standard admissions decision procedure, it operates on a deadline. If its applications for a given year's entering class are due on January 15, for example, then it waits until that date has passed, goes through all of the applications that it has received for that year, and picks out what it takes to be the best of all of them to make offers of admission to. When a school uses a rolling admissions policy, however, it has no such deadline. It evaluates each application as it comes in and makes a decision about whether or not the application seems good enough. As the year goes by, the number of available slots at the school goes down and so it typically becomes more and more difficult to get into that school. This means that a student who's admitted to the entering class of a school with a rolling admissions policy near the start of its admissions cycle may well have a weaker academic record than that of many of the students who are rejected for the very same entering class by the very same school near the end of the very same admissions cycle. Indeed, guidebooks for students applying to colleges frequently suggest that high school seniors with somewhat mediocre academic records deliberately seek out schools that have rolling admissions policies and apply to them as early in the application cycle as possible for this very reason.

A school that adopts a rolling admissions policy does not, in fact, end up admitting the very best of the students who apply to it in a given year. If there's a moral obligation to admit only the best students who apply for admission to a given school in a given year, then rolling admissions policies are immoral. But while defenders and opponents of affirmative action may disagree about many things, I've never heard any of them maintain that rolling admissions policies are immoral. Nor does it seem plausible to think that they are. A rolling admissions policy enables a school to exercise more precise control over the exact number of students who end up enrolling in a given year than does a policy on which a school admits a group of students all at once and then sits back and waits to see how many people accept its offer. If a school wishes to put more weight on retaining this sort of predictability than on admitting only the very best students who apply in a given year, it seems clear that morality permits it to do so. This, again, means that it's morally okay to adopt a policy that leads one to select less than the best. And this, in turn, once again means that the bias-elimination argument is unsuccessful. There's no moral obligation to select the very best people who apply for any given position, and so even if existing biases against black people make it necessary to use affirmative action in order to accurately select the very best people, this fact provides no reason to believe that there's a moral obligation to engage in affirmative action.

A defender of affirmative action, of course, could once again appeal to the claim that the case of race is different because the history of racial injustice in this country makes it different. We have a moral obligation to correct for biases that arise from past injustices, on this account, but no moral obligation to correct for other factors that might lead us to select less than the best. But while this kind of response would be relevant to those arguments that attempt to ground an obligation to engage in affirmative action in backward-looking considerations about compensation or fairness, it isn't available to those who seek to provide an alternative to such arguments. If the fairness- or compensation-based arguments are successful, then there's no need to appeal to claims about currently existing biases. And if those arguments are unsuccessful, then the fact that current racial biases are rooted in the past will prove to be irrelevant. If there's no obligation to take unfair disadvantage into account in the first place, for example, then the fact that currently-existing biases cause an unfair disadvantage to black candidates won't be relevant. And so, either way, the bias-elimination argument will fail to provide, or to support, a reason to conclude that race-based affirmative action is morally obligatory.

RACE AS A QUALIFICATION

A second kind of present-looking argument for affirmative action appeals to the claim that race itself can be a positive qualification for a position. Suppose, for example, that black students respond better to black teachers, or that black police officers can more effectively patrol predominantly black neighborhoods because they can elicit a higher degree of cooperation and trust from the people who live there. If this is so, then it may well make sense to hire a black teacher or a black police officer with somewhat less experience or fewer credentials over an otherwise more qualified white applicant for the same position. Race-based affirmative action, in other words, might be called for in such cases to make sure that the candidate who is hired is the one who really is the best qualified in the broadest and most important sense of the term.[50]

There are several reasons to be wary of the argument based on the claim that race can be a qualification. First, while it seems to be somewhat plausible in some cases, it seems clearly implausible in many others. Black students might well respond better to black teachers, for example, but it's hard to see why black pilots, or black computer programmers or black assembly-line workers, would do their jobs any more effectively than their white counterparts simply by virtue of their being black. Since most supporters of affirmative action for teachers and police officers are also supporters of affirmative action for such other positions as well, it's hard to believe that the argument from race as a qualification can really serve as a satisfactory basis for their position.

A second and more worrisome problem with the view that race should be used as a qualification for a position is that it cuts both ways. Indeed, on the whole, putting this view into practice might well do at least as much to harm black applicants as it would do to help them. Many schools in this country, for example, have virtually no black students. Imagine a black applicant for a job teaching kindergarten, or middle school, or college chemistry at such a school being told "I'm sorry, you were the smartest and best trained candidate we had, but we just don't have enough black students for you to teach here." Surely defenders of affirmative action would find this outrageous. But if race can be used as a qualification to justify hiring a black teacher because it's claimed that black students learn better from black teachers, then it's hard to see how we could avoid using race to justify hiring a white teacher on similar grounds in similar circumstances. And since there are more white students in this country than there are black students, this kind of reasoning would tend to favor white teachers over black teachers more often than it would favor black teachers over white teachers.

The same kind of problem, moreover, seems to arise from the other sorts of cases that proponents of the race as a qualification argument tend to give. If it's true that people who live in predominantly black neighborhoods are more likely to trust black police officers or black doctors, for example, then it seems at least as plausible to suppose that there are places where most of the people are white and are more comfortable around white people. It would then follow that white candidates should always be favored over black candidates for jobs that involve providing services in such areas. It's hard to believe that any advocate of affirmative action could accept this result. But if they're unwilling to accept it, then they should be unwilling to rely on the argument that race should be used as a qualification when trying to defend forms of affirmative action that would benefit black applicants.

These two objections to the race as a qualification argument strike me as pretty significant. In addition, the argument seems to have the same basic problem that the bias-elimination argument has: even if it succeeds, it isn't at all clear that the practice it would justify is the one that defenders and opponents of affirmative action take themselves to be arguing about in the first place. Consider, for example, a case in which it seems clearly reasonable to treat sex, rather than race, as a qualification: a summer camp is hiring counselors who will, among other things, need to supervise young boys and girls while they're changing in and out of their swimsuits in the locker rooms at a public swimming pool. If there are going to be an equal number of boys and girls at the camp, it seems reasonable to ensure that there are a roughly equal number of male and female counselors. If most of the people who apply for those positions are male, then the camp may be forced to hire a qualified female counselor with fewer years of experience and less glowing letters of reference over a more experienced and highly recommended male applicant. This is simply a case in which the logic of the race as a qualification argument is applied to the case of sex. But hiring an otherwise less qualified female counselor because the camp needs another person to supervise the girls while they're in the locker room isn't the kind of thing that opponents of gender-based affirmative action take themselves to be opposing. And giving preferential treatment to female applicants only in cases where sex is clearly relevant in this way – the camp, let's say, gives no priority to female over male applicants when filling its administrative positions – isn't the kind of policy that defenders of gender-based affirmative action take themselves to be defending. Even if the race as qualification argument succeeds, then, it won't justify the claim that supporters of race-based affirmative action are trying to justify or entail the claim that opponents of race-based affirmative action are trying to resist. In this sense, the race as a qualification argument seems to be largely irrelevant to the debate over affirmative action.

But even if all of these concerns can be overcome, there's a much more fundamental problem with using the race as a qualification argument as a means of justifying an obligation to engage in race-based affirmative action. The problem is that, at most, the argument shows only that sometimes a black candidate who initially appears to be less qualified than a white candidate is, in fact, more qualified once all of the relevant considerations are taken into account. But even if this is true, this can be used as grounds for an obligation to hire the black candidate over the white candidate only if there's a general obligation to always hire the most qualified candidate. And as I pointed out in the previous section on the bias-elimination argument, it's implausible to suppose that there is such an obligation. There's nothing morally wrong with choosing to admit a less qualified student or to hire a less qualified worker. And so even if the race as a qualification argument could show that affirmative action is needed in order to identify the most qualified applicants, it still couldn't show that there's a moral obligation to engage in affirmative action.[51]

I've now examined those justifications for affirmative action that focus on the past, the future, and the present. There's nowhere else to look. I conclude that while affirmative action may prove to have some desirable features and some beneficial consequences, there's no reason to believe that it's morally obligatory. As far as morality and justice are concerned, if a school or business or government declines to practice affirmative action, that's okay.

5

Two Cheers for Affirmative Action

Why There's Nothing Wrong with Not Abandoning Racial Preferences, Either

I argued in Chapter 4 that race-based affirmative action isn't morally obligatory. Many people will agree with me about this. But most of those who do agree will insist that I haven't yet gone far enough. Not only is affirmative action not obligatory, they'll say, it's not even permissible. It's not just that it's not immoral not to practice affirmative action on their view. It's that it's positively immoral to practice it. But I think these people are mistaken, too. Having explained in the previous chapter why I'm not convinced by arguments for the claim that affirmative action is obligatory, then, I'll try in this chapter to explain why I'm not convinced by arguments for the claim that it's unjust or impermissible either.

Before turning to the many arguments that have been offered against affirmative action, though, two preliminary points should be made. These points parallel the two preliminary points I made before discussing the arguments in favor of affirmative action in the previous chapter. First, in maintaining that affirmative action is not morally impermissible, I don't mean to be insisting that no institution has or could have a moral obligation to refrain from practicing affirmative action. If a school or business makes an explicit promise not to practice affirmative action in its admissions or hiring decisions, for example, then that might well make it impermissible for the school or business in question to practice affirmative action. If the management of a publicly traded corporation does not reasonably believe that practicing affirmative action will be in the corporation's financial interests, and if it fails to notify its shareholders that it plans to practice affirmative action despite the fact that doing so will not be in the corporation's financial interests, then its fiduciary obligations to the corporation's shareholders might well make it impermissible for that particular corporation to practice affirmative action.[1] Such considerations, though, wouldn't do anything to show that affirmative action itself is morally impermissible unless there was a reason to think that it was morally obligatory to promise not to practice it, in the first sort of case, or to fail to notify the shareholders that it would be practiced, in the second. At most, they would simply establish that some policies that are not otherwise impermissible can become impermissible when promises of a certain sort are made or information of a certain sort is concealed. Since my concern in this chapter is with the question of whether there's something about affirmative action itself that makes it wrong to engage in it, I will simply set these sorts of considerations to the side. As long as it's morally permissible not to make the sorts of promises or commitments that might in turn require an organization not to practice affirmative action in order to live up to the expectations it has reasonably generated in other people, these sorts of considerations will be irrelevant to trying to determine the moral status of affirmative action itself.

The second point to make clear is that, as with the case of the many arguments that have been offered in defense of affirmative action, it isn't always clear just what, precisely, the many arguments that have been offered against affirmative action are trying to establish. Some arguments against affirmative action clearly aim to demonstrate that affirmative action is positively immoral. Others are somewhat ambiguous between claiming to show that affirmative action is immoral and merely claiming to show that it's a bad (but morally acceptable) idea. And still others, perhaps, are offered as an attempt to identify something undesirable about affirmative action without really trying to show that it's wrong to practice it at all. Whatever the intentions behind the various arguments that have been made against affirmative action have been, though, the arguments pose a challenge to my claim that affirmative action is permissible and non-obligatory only if they can do something to show that it's positively immoral to practice affirmative action. For the purposes of the discussion in this chapter, then, I'll focus on the question of whether any of them can do this.

THE RIGHT TO BE JUDGED ON ONE'S INDIVIDUAL MERITS

One kind of argument against affirmative action involves rights. If affirmative action violates somebody's rights, then that's a good reason to conclude that the practice is unjust. And many people believe that affirmative action does, in fact, violate somebody's rights, namely the rights of the better qualified applicants who are passed over in the selection process by means of affirmative action policies. But while it's easy to find people who claim that selecting a less qualified black applicant over a more qualified white applicant violates the white applicant's rights, it's often less easy to determine exactly what right they're talking about. Early in his book *Ending Affirmative Action: The Case for Colorblind Justice,* for example, Terry Eastland claims that affirmative action policies always come "at the expense of individual rights."[2] But while the rest of his book spends plenty of time maintaining that affirmative action is a bad idea, at no point does it actually identify a specific individual right that white applicants have and that's violated when they're passed over in favor of less qualified black applicants.

I'm inclined to think that there's a good reason for this common omission. That's because I'm inclined to think that there is no such right. But since many people seem to think that there is such a right, and since if there is such a right, it would certainly ground a powerful argument against the permissibility of affirmative action, I'll begin my survey of the arguments that people have made against affirmative action with this question: does affirmative action violate anyone's rights?

One common answer to this question is that affirmative action violates people's rights because people have the right to be judged on their individual merits.[3] The argument for this position typically goes like this: each person has the right to be judged as an individual, not merely as part of a group. When a person is judged as an individual, all that matters is that person's particular qualifications. So if each person is judged on their individual merits, the best qualified candidate will be selected. This means, in turn, that if each person truly does have a right to be judged on their individual merits, then the best qualified candidate really does have a right to be selected for the position he applies for. It follows from this that any decision procedure that deliberately selects a less qualified black applicant over a more qualified white applicant violates the better qualified white applicant's rights. And if that's true, then affirmative action is unjust and must be rejected for that reason.

Although this is one of the most common arguments against affirmative action, it's always struck me as one of the least plausible. This is because if the best qualified candidates really do have a right to be selected because their individual qualifications are the best, then all sorts of practices that virtually everyone accepts as morally permissible would turn out to be grossly immoral. Hardly anyone, for example, as I pointed out near the beginning of the last chapter, believes that geography-based affirmative action is unjust. If Yale or West Point admits a slightly less qualified candidate from North Dakota over a slightly more qualified candidate from New York, virtually no one believes that the New Yorker has had his moral rights violated. Even the famous Rhodes Scholarship program, a paradigm of rewarding academic merit, practices a form of geography-based affirmative action. Each year, it offers up to thirty-two scholarships to send students from the United States to Oxford University in England. But rather than picking the thirty-two best students who apply from across the country, it divides the country into sixteen "Districts" and selects up to two students from each District. In the most recent round of competition, for example, District 3 consisted of New York while District 6 consisted of Georgia, North Carolina and South Carolina. If in that year there were more highly competitive applicants from District 2 then from District 6, then, a Columbia University undergraduate who grew up in New York and who just missed winning a scholarship might well have had better credentials than a less qualified Duke student who grew up in North Carolina but who nonetheless won a Rhodes Scholarship from District 6. But if the New Yorker really does have the right to be judged solely on his individual qualifications, then it will turn out that his rights really are violated if he is passed over by Yale, or West Point, or the Rhodes Scholarship program for a slightly less qualified person from North Dakota or North Carolina. Virtually no one, regardless of their view of race-based affirmative action, really believes that the New Yorker has had his moral rights violated in these sorts of cases. And this provides a good reason to reject the claim that people have a right to be judged solely on their individual merits.

In addition to the example of geography-based affirmative action, the various cases that I cited as problems for the bias-elimination argument in defense of affirmative action in the previous chapter pose problems for the argument against affirmative action that is based on a right to be judged solely on one's individual merits as well, and for the same reason. If I decide to hire a particular company to fix my roof simply because I like the company's name, for example, virtually everyone would agree that I've done nothing morally wrong. If a college or university decides to admit students who seem good enough to it on a rolling admissions basis until all its slots are filled, rather than setting a deadline and then picking the very best of all the people who apply, virtually everyone will agree that it's acting within its rights. But if the very best candidate really does have the right to be selected, then I would violate the best roofing company's rights by not selecting it and the school would violate the rights of those candidates rejected late in the admissions cycle who are better qualified than some of those who were accepted earlier in the same cycle. Since virtually everyone on both sides of the affirmative action debate will reject these claims, we again have good reason to deny that people have the right to be selected when they are the best candidate. And if the best candidate does not, in fact, have a right to be selected simply because he's the best candidate, then the argument against affirmative action that's based on an appeal to the right to be judged on one's individual merits must be rejected.

I'm inclined to think that these examples are sufficient to justify rejecting the argument against affirmative action that's based on the claim that people have a right to be judged and selected exclusively on their individual merits. But in case none of what I've said so far seems convincing, here's one final example. My neighborhood supermarket employs a number of people whose sole responsibility is to bag the customer's groceries. The qualifications for this position seem pretty straightforward: you are good at this job to the extent that you put things in the bags quickly, arrange them so that nothing breaks, do so without wasting too many bags, and are pleasant to the customers. Virtually all of the people who work in the store do very well in all of these respects. One of the women who holds this position, though, doesn't do nearly as well. She's significantly slower than the rest, often puts just one or two things in a bag before getting out another bag, isn't as selective about which things go together in a bag, and isn't particularly social with the customers, often failing to even make eye contact with them. This woman has Down syndrome.

Now, it's perfectly clear that this woman was hired ahead of other people who were better qualified for this position and who would have done a considerably better job. But it's hard to believe that anyone really thinks that the store acted immorally in hiring her because of this. If anything, I suspect that most people, regardless of their view of affirmative action, would admire the store for giving this woman a break despite the fact that she really wasn't the most efficient bagger that it could have hired. And yet, if the best qualified candidate really does have the right to be selected because people have a right to be judged exclusively on their individual merits, then my neighborhood supermarket acted unjustly by hiring this woman. Since it should be clear to virtually everyone on both sides of the affirmative action debate that the store did not, in fact, act unjustly in this case, it should be clear, once again, that the best qualified candidate for a position doesn't have the right to that position. And if that's so, then, once again, a white applicant who's passed over for a less qualified black applicant can't complain that his rights were violated simply because he was better qualified.

A critic of race-based affirmative action who agrees that it's permissible for a store to hire an inefficient bag checker with Down syndrome, of course, might try to account for this judgment by insisting that the woman really was the best qualified candidate overall. The critic might do this by arguing that efficiency is just one relevant qualification. If, for example, helping the store to maintain good relations with the local community is another qualification, and if occasionally hiring people with disabilities will help the store to do that, then perhaps the woman with Down syndrome really was the best qualified candidate after all and hiring her therefore didn't violate the rights of any of the other candidates.

But there are two problems with this attempt to fend off the case of the bag checker with Down syndrome. The first problem is that its justification of the store's right to hire her depends on the claim that the store in fact benefits from hiring her rather than a more efficient bag checker. This means that the store wouldn't have the right to hire her if doing so would be genuinely altruistic, and virtually no one on either side of the affirmative action debate would accept this result. The second problem is that if it's acceptable to insist that the woman with Down syndrome really was the best qualified candidate in this case, then it will be just as acceptable to insist that the seemingly less qualified black candidate really is the best qualified candidate in cases involving affirmative action. As long as the institution in question can point to some respect in which it thinks it will benefit by hiring or admitting the black candidate – increasing diversity, improving its relationship with the local black community, or feeling good about contributing to the rectification of past injustices for example – then it will turn out that the otherwise less qualified black applicant is in fact better qualified and that hiring or admitting him won't violate anyone else's rights after all, even if people do have the right to be judged exclusively on their individual qualifications. In the end, then, there seems to be no credible way to reject affirmative action by appealing to the claim that the best qualified applicant has a right to the position.

THE RIGHT TO EQUAL TREATMENT

A second and distinct right that critics of affirmative action frequently appeal to is the right to be treated equally with others. The argument based on this right is typically restricted to cases involving affirmative action as practiced by some branch of the government: affirmative action for police officers, postal workers, and so forth, or for students and employees at state universities. So understood, the argument appeals to the claim that there is a right to equal treatment (or equal protection) under the law, and leaves open the possibility that it might be permissible for private companies and organizations to engage in affirmative action. California's fiercely debated Proposition 209, for example, prohibited public schools like UCLA and Berkeley from practicing affirmative action in admissions and hiring, but didn't interfere with the right of private schools like Stanford and Pomona to do so. Ward Connerly, one of the most vocal leaders of the movement to pass Proposition 209, declared in his election night victory speech that those who had voted for it had reaffirmed an inalienable "right" by proclaiming "the sanctity of the principle of equal treatment for all people."[4] And Carl Cohen, one of the most prominent philosophers to have argued against the practice, has written that "Every applicant to a state university has a right under the U.S. Constitution to the equal protection of the laws. Where goods are in short supply – as are admissions to a fine state university – advantages given to some by race inevitably result in disadvantages imposed upon others by race. To give by color is to take by color. That is a denial of the equal protection of the laws."[5] Following the position taken by such writers and by those who supported Proposition 209 in California and similar movements in Texas and elsewhere, I will therefore limit my focus in this section to state-sponsored affirmative action. I want to consider the question of whether the appeal to a right to equal treatment or equal protection can justify the claim that affirmative action is unjust at least in cases where it's practiced by the government.

The answer to this question depends on what's involved in having a right to equal treatment or equal protection in the first place. So let's suppose that you're a white student who didn't get into the local campus of your state university. And let's suppose that you've since discovered that a number of black applicants were admitted to the campus during the same year you applied even though they had lower grades and test scores than you did. You're wondering if the fact that the black applicants were given preferential treatment because of their race means that the state violated your right to equal treatment under the law. In order to answer this question, we first have to distinguish between a stronger and weaker sense in which you might be thought to have this right. And once we draw this distinction, we'll see that the claim that affirmative action violates the right to equal treatment has implications that virtually everyone on both sides of the debate will reject as unacceptable.

Let's start with a strong version of the right to equal treatment. On this understanding, it means the right to be treated in the same way as members of other races regardless of the circumstances. If you have a right to equal treatment in this strong sense, then it would always be wrong, and under any circumstances, for the government to take your race into account in deciding how to treat you. Clearly a state university policy of giving preferential treatment to black applicants because they're black is inconsistent with this right. And so, if people really do have a right to equal treatment in this strong and unconditional sense, then that right is clearly violated whenever a state university engages in affirmative action. And if such policies violate rights, they are unjust and impermissible for that reason.

But it's implausible to believe that anyone has a right to equal treatment in this strong sense. Suppose, for example, that the CIA is considering two candidates for an undercover assignment in an overwhelmingly black African country. One of the candidates has a bit more experience and a bit more knowledge of surveillance techniques than the other, but the somewhat more experienced and knowledgeable agent is white while the somewhat less experienced and knowledgeable agent is black. Or suppose that a national park is auditioning two actors to portray Abraham Lincoln in an educational program for visiting school children. One of the candidates is a somewhat better actor with more performing experience, but he is black while the somewhat less talented and experienced candidate is white. Or the National Institutes of Health is looking for participants in a study to determine whether a particular drug is especially effective in treating hypertension in African Americans. Virtually everyone, regardless of their view about race-based affirmative action, will agree that it's morally permissible for the state to take race into account in these cases when deciding how to treat the people in question. But if the government has the right to take race into account in these cases, then there's no right to equal treatment in the strong sense in which you have a right to be treated in the same way as members of other races regardless of the circumstances. Any argument against affirmative action that requires the existence of the right in this strong sense must therefore be rejected.

Those who support the equal treatment argument against affirmative action, of course, might not be particularly worried by these examples. "It's fine to take race into account in those cases," they might say, "because in those cases, the difference between black people and white people is relevant. When we said there was a right to equal treatment under the law, we didn't mean that it was *always* wrong for the state to take race into account. We just meant that it was wrong for the state to take race into account when race is irrelevant. But race isn't irrelevant in the cases you've presented. And so those cases don't refute our claim that there's a right to equal treatment."

This seems like a perfectly reasonable response. On this account, the right to equal treatment doesn't mean the right to be treated in the same way as members of other races regardless of the circumstances. Rather, it means the right to be treated in the same way as members of other races except in circumstances where differential treatment is justified. The claim that there's a right to equal treatment in this weaker sense is therefore immune to these counterexamples. But now there's a new problem. In the case of the strong version of the right to equal treatment, it's clear that if there is such a right, then affirmative action violates it. But in the case of the weak version of the right to equal treatment, this isn't so. A policy violates someone's right to equal treatment in the weak sense if it treats race as relevant in circumstances in which race shouldn't be treated as relevant. And so affirmative action will violate the right to equal treatment in the weak sense only if it treats race as relevant when race shouldn't be treated as relevant.

But whether or not race should be treated as relevant in the kinds of circumstances in which affirmative action programs exist is precisely the question at issue. Defenders of affirmative action maintain that race should be viewed as relevant in such cases while opponents of affirmative action maintain that race should not be viewed as relevant. In order to argue against affirmative action by appealing to the claim that affirmative action violates the right to equal treatment in the weak sense, then, the opponent of affirmative action must first assume the very thing he is trying to prove: that affirmative action takes race into account when it shouldn't. The claim that there's a right to equal treatment in the strong sense would help to justify this assumption: if there is a right to equal treatment in the strong sense, then it's always wrong to take race into account, and so wrong to view race as relevant in the case of affirmative action in particular. But the claim that there's a right to equal treatment in the weak sense does nothing to help justify this assumption: the claim that it's wrong to take race into account when race should be viewed as irrelevant does nothing to tell us whether race should be viewed as relevant in the case of affirmative action in particular. In the end, then, the argument based on the right to equal treatment is impaled on the horns of a dilemma. If the right is strong enough to do the job of opposing affirmative action, it's too strong to be plausible. If it's weak enough to be plausible, it's too weak to do any independent work in opposing affirmative action.

These worries strike me as good enough reasons to reject the equal treatment argument against affirmative action. Before moving on to consider other arguments that have been raised against affirmative action, though, I'd like to briefly consider two responses that might be made to the objection I've raised against this one, press one additional concern about the argument as I've presented it, and then say something about a somewhat different version of the argument.

The two responses I have in mind both appeal to the claim that there might be a still further interpretation of the right to equal treatment that's stronger than the weak version but weaker than the strong version and that might help the opponent of affirmative action to overcome the objection that I've raised against the equal treatment argument. The first version of this response maintains that the objections I raised against the strong version aren't strong enough to force a retreat to the weak claim that the right to equal treatment is a right not to have race taken into account except when race is relevant. Rather, this response argues, my examples are only strong enough to justify weakening the right so that it becomes a right not to have race taken into account except when race is relevant in a very specific kind of way, namely, when it's relevant to a person's ability to perform the tasks required by the particular position they are applying for. The reason that it's okay for the CIA to take race into account in deciding which agent to hire, for example, isn't simply that race is relevant in just any old way, but rather that it's relevant in particular to the agent's ability to carry out his assignment successfully. But if the right to equal treatment only permits race to be taken into account when it's relevant to the performance of a particular task, the critic might then claim, then it's still strong enough to do the job of rendering affirmative action positively unjust. Affirmative action, after all, seeks to treat race as relevant for other sorts of reasons.

There are two problems with appealing to this intermediate version of the right to equal treatment. The first is that, like the weak interpretation it seeks to improve upon, it ultimately begs the question against the defender of affirmative action. The argument, that is, depends on the claim that race isn't relevant to a person's ability to carry out their assigned role, but a defender of a diversity-based argument for affirmative action will simply deny that this is the case. Second, and more importantly, this intermediate interpretation, like the strong interpretation it seeks to improve upon, has implications that virtually everyone on both sides of the affirmative action debate will reject as unacceptable. Suppose, for example, that a man names an executor in his will and directs him to disperse his considerable assets as he sees fit among organizations that give money to black Americans. And suppose a dispute arises over whether or not the money is being distributed in a manner consistent with the terms of the will. A judge steps in to resolve the dispute. In this case, at least, it should be clear to everyone on both sides of the affirmative action debate that it would be perfectly appropriate for the government to treat the race of the people getting the money as relevant in deciding what to do. But the proposed intermediate version of the right to equal treatment would be unable to account for this judgment. That version says that race may be considered only when it is relevant to the performance of a particular job. But in this case, race is relevant for a very different reason: it's relevant because a certain action in the past generated an obligation to give preference to black Americans over white Americans in distributing the money in question. In order to account for the appropriateness of taking race into account in this case, then, the defender of the equal treatment argument must acknowledge that the right is a right not to have race taken into account except in cases where something has happened in the past to make race relevant in the present. And at that point, we are right back to the problem that undermined the argument based on the weak interpretation: the argument will simply beg the question against the defender of affirmative action who maintains that events in the past have, indeed, rendered race relevant in the present.

A second way that a defender of the equal treatment argument might try to find an interpretation of the right that falls between the strong and the weak interpretation would be to appeal to the doctrine of "strict scrutiny" that's been developed by the United States Supreme Court over the last few decades. According to this approach to understanding the rights guaranteed by the Fourteenth Amendment, the state can treat people differently according to race without violating the right to equal treatment only if the state can establish that doing so serves a "compelling state interest" and that it does so in a way that's necessary to serve that interest. It's plausible to think that this approach represents a reasonable middle ground between the weak and strong interpretations of the right that my objection appealed to, and plausible, too, to think that affirmative action fails to meet the test established by the strict scrutiny standard. If people have a right to equal treatment in this intermediate sense, and if affirmative action would violate the right in that sense, then the objection to affirmative action based on the existence of a right to equal treatment will prove to be successful after all.

The problem with this response to my objection, though, is that the strict scrutiny standard, too, has implications that virtually everyone on both sides of the affirmative action debate will reject.[6] Consider, again, the case of the national park that wants to hire an actor to portray Abraham Lincoln in an educational program for school children. Or perhaps it wants to hire someone to portray Frederick Douglass, or to reenact scenes involving slaves and their masters. Virtually everyone would agree that it's morally permissible for the organizers of the event to take race into account when deciding which actors to cast in which roles. But it's clearly implausible to say that doing so is necessary for serving some compelling state interest. If people have a moral right not to have the state take their race into account unless doing so is necessary to serving some compelling state interest, then people have a moral right not to have race taken into account in this case. But virtually everyone, regardless of their view of affirmative action, will agree that people don't really have a moral right not to have race taken into account in this case. And so virtually everyone should agree that people don't really have the moral right to equal protection under the law in the way that the legal doctrine of strict scrutiny would interpret that right. And since people don't really have that right, the right can't be used to ground an argument against affirmative action.

The additional concern I want to raise about the equal treatment argument is this: if everyone really does have a right to equal treatment that can't be violated, and if taking race into account in hiring and admissions decisions really does turn out to violate this right, then why do people like Connerly think that private universities should still be allowed to engage in affirmative action? Consider, for example, a white student graduating from high school in California who applies to Stanford and to Berkeley. If Berkeley can't take his race into account because his right to equal treatment is simply inalienable, then why should Stanford be allowed to take his race into account? Either the right is inalienable or it isn't. If it's inalienable, then it seems that neither school should be allowed to violate it. If it isn't inalienable, then it seems that both schools should be allowed to violate it. Either way, it seems that if the kind of argument that people like Connerly have in mind is successful, then they should want the government to ban affirmative action in private schools and businesses as well. Some critics of affirmative action may accept this implication, of course, and so they won't see this as a further difficulty with the equal treatment argument.[7] But many people who make this kind of argument seem unwilling to have the government interfere with the marketplace by banning affirmative action in the private sphere. For those critics of affirmative action, at least, this provides one further reason to reject the equal treatment argument against affirmative action.

There is, however, a different way of understanding the argument based on a right to equal treatment. It seems to be less common in the academic literature on affirmative action, but nonetheless quite popular in the public debate on the subject.[8] On this second version of the argument, the reason that the difference between public and private institutions matters so much is that tax dollars go to support public institutions in a way that they don't go to support private institutions. Suppose, for example, that I'm a white high school senior in California and that I've applied both to Stanford and to Berkeley. Stanford isn't funded by my tax dollars and so, on this account, I don't have any particular right to have Stanford makes its admissions decisions in one way rather than another. But Berkeley is supported by my tax dollars and so, the argument maintains, I have a right that I be given exactly the same amount of consideration as anyone else when Berkeley makes its decisions. I have to pay my taxes that go to Berkeley just like anyone else, and so Berkeley should have to treat me just like it would treat anyone else. If Berkeley gives preferential consideration to black applicants over white applicants, that is, then it violates my right to equal treatment in a way that Stanford's giving such preferential consideration wouldn't.

This second version of the right to equal treatment argument does seem able to avoid one potential difficulty with the first version, the difficulty of explaining why affirmative action should be banned at state but not at private universities. But in doing so, the second version of the argument creates an additional difficulty that the first version seems to avoid. The new problem arises when we compare cases involving students who apply to Berkeley from within California with cases involving students who apply to Berkeley from out of state. So suppose that Cal White and Cal Black are high school seniors in California and Kent White and Kent Black are high school seniors in Kentucky. Cal White is a bit better qualified than Cal Black and Kent White is a bit better qualified than Kent Black. All four apply to Berkeley.

This second version of the equal treatment argument implies that while it would be wrong for Berkeley to admit the slightly less qualified Cal Black over the slightly more qualified Cal White, it wouldn't be wrong for Berkeley to admit the slightly less qualified Kent Black over the slightly more qualified Kent White. This is because the case that this version of the argument makes against affirmative action in public but not private institutions is grounded in the claim that the white candidates who are disadvantaged by such forms of affirmative action have been paying taxes to support public but not private institutions. Cal White has been paying taxes in California and that's why he's supposed to have a right to equal consideration relative to Cal Black when Berkeley makes its admissions decisions. But Kent White and Kent Black haven't been paying any taxes in California, and so the argument provides no reason to think that Berkeley does something wrong if it admits the slightly less qualified Kent Black over the slightly more qualified Kent White. The second version of the equal treatment argument, in short, implies that state universities may not practice race-based affirmative action with respect to their in-state applicants, but may practice race-based affirmative action with respect to their out-of-state applicants. Very few opponents of affirmative action would be willing to accept this result. So for most opponents of affirmative action, the fact that the second version of the equal treatment argument has this implication should count as a good reason to reject it.

This first problem with the second version of the equal treatment argument strikes me as a pretty serious one. But there is, in any event, a second and much deeper problem with this version of the argument. The problem is that the argument neglects the distinction between having a right to equal treatment in two importantly different contexts: the context in which the government to which one pays taxes is deciding what kind of decision procedure one of its public institutions should adopt, and the context in which one of its public institutions is using such a decision procedure. As with many of the other problems that I've noted to this point, the importance of this distinction can be made clear by looking first at a case that doesn't involve race. And, again as with many of the other problems that I've noted to this point, once we look at such a case, it becomes clear that the argument in question has implications that are unacceptable to virtually everyone regardless of their views about race-based affirmative action.

Suppose, for example, that the federal government is trying to decide what sort of admissions policy the military academies should have. And suppose, in particular, that someone makes the following proposal: "people who live in the South aren't as important as people who live in the North, so we should have the military academies adopt the admissions policy that would best enable the military to serve the interests of people in the North." Clearly, in this case, the proposal would be unacceptable. The taxpayer in Alabama has a right to have his interests treated equally with those of the taxpayer in Maine when the government is deciding how to organize its military academies. But now suppose that everyone agrees that in deciding what sort of admission policy the military academies should have, the government must consider the interests of all Americans equally. And suppose that someone makes the following proposal: "since our military officers will eventually be forced to work and fight alongside people from all over the country, it's important that they be exposed to people from all over the country during their training and education. Therefore, it's in the interest of all Americans, regardless of where in the county they live, that the military academies practice some form of geography-based affirmative action." This second proposal is clearly very different from the first. The first proposal involved justifying the adoption of a certain decision procedure by appealing to the claim that adopting the procedure would be good for people in one part of the country rather than in another. The second involves adopting a decision procedure that will give preference to applicants from some parts of the country rather than other parts, but it justifies adopting the procedure by showing that adopting it will be good for everyone, where each part of the country is valued equally. This is why virtually everyone would agree that the first proposal violates each American's right to equal treatment while the second proposal doesn't.

I think that virtually everyone on both sides of the race-based affirmative action debate would agree that the right to equal treatment that we have is a right that would protect us from the first kind of proposal but not from the second. But if I'm right about that, then the second version of the equal treatment argument against race-based affirmative action should be rejected on grounds that virtually everyone on both sides of the debate already accepts. To see this, simply take the two proposals I just described and change them to proposals involving a state university's decision to practice race-based affirmative action. Suppose, first, that someone made the following proposal: "black people are more important than white people, so Berkeley should choose the admissions policy that will best enable it to serve the interests of black people rather than white people." Clearly this proposal would violate the right of white Californians to have their interests treated equally when deciding how the state should spend some of their tax money. But now suppose that everyone agrees that in deciding what admissions policy to have its public universities use, the state should treat the interests of black and white Californians equally. And suppose that someone then makes the following proposal: "since we want all of our students to learn as much as possible, and since on average a racially diverse campus will provide a wider variety of viewpoints and thus a more enriching learning environment than will a more racially homogenous campus, Berkeley should practice some form of race-based affirmative action." If we agree that the second of the two proposals doesn't violate the right to equal treatment in the case of geography-based affirmative action, then we must agree that the second of the two proposals here doesn't violate the right to equal treatment in the case of race-based affirmative action.

If West Point admits a slightly less qualified candidate from North Dakota over a slightly better qualified candidate from New York, this doesn't violate the New Yorker's right to equal treatment despite the fact that some of his tax money goes to fund West Point. He has a right to have his interests considered equally when the decision is made about what kind of admissions policy West Point should have, but this doesn't mean that West Point must have an admissions policy that treats him equally with the student from North Dakota. In the same way, and for the same reason, if Berkeley admits a slightly less qualified black Californian over a slightly more qualified white Californian, this doesn't violate the white Californian's right to equal treatment despite the fact that some of his tax money goes to fund Berkeley. He has the right to have his interests considered equally when the decision is made about what kind of admissions policy Berkeley should have, but this doesn't mean that Berkeley must have an admissions policy that treats him equally with black Californians. In the end, then, no version of the right to equal treatment argument provides a plausible reason to believe that race-based affirmative action is morally impermissible.

THE OVERGENERALIZATIONS ARGUMENT

A related but distinct argument against affirmative action appeals to the claim that affirmative action depends on making overgeneralizations about people. Suppose, for example, that a university admits some black students with grades and test scores that are lower than the grades and test scores of some of the white students that it rejects. And suppose that the school attempts to justify its right to do so by appealing to some claim such as "black students have had to overcome race-based obstacles that white students have not had to overcome" or "black students would bring a distinctive point of view to campus that adding more white students would not." In response to such claims, the argument against affirmative action that I want to focus on in this section complains that they rest on overgeneralizations. Yes, the critic of affirmative action will agree, many black students have had to overcome race-based obstacles, but not all of them have. And yes, they will continue, many black students would bring a distinctive point of view to campus, but not all of them would. And furthermore, they will add, some white students have had to overcome race-based obstacles, and some would bring a distinctive point of view to campus, too. So while having been racially disadvantaged or having a distinctive point of view may in themselves prove to be relevant considerations, these critics will conclude, it would be wrong to give preference to black students over white students on such grounds because this will provide a benefit to some students who don't really merit the benefit and will withhold a benefit from some students who really do merit the benefit. This argument is sometimes put in terms of the familiar language of rights – "I have the right to be judged as an individual, not as a member of a group" – and sometimes put simply in terms of justice or fairness – "it isn't fair to lump me together with those other students just because of the color of my skin." But no matter how, exactly, the argument is formulated, it ultimately appeals to the claim that affirmative action rests on overgeneralizations and that this makes affirmative action wrong.[9]

The problem with the overgeneralizations argument is that it depends on an overgeneralization – an overgeneralization, moreover, about overgeneralizations. The argument, that is, depends on the claim that it's wrong to distinguish between two groups of people based on generalizations about the members of the groups. But while it does seem to be wrong to do this sort of thing in some cases, there are other cases where it doesn't seem to be wrong at all. Geography-based affirmative action, for example, rests on generalizations about people in different parts of the country. But even though the generalizations it appeals to aren't true in each and every instance, virtually no one, regardless of their view of race-based affirmative action, really believes that this renders geography-based affirmative action unjust or immoral. Or consider the case of the many distinctions that the law makes based on age. Most people below the age of eighteen fall below a certain level of maturity and most people eighteen and older meet that level or exceed it. So the state says that those who are not yet eighteen don't have the right to vote and those who are eighteen and older do. This rule clearly rests on a generalization: there are plenty of seventeen-year-olds who are mature enough to vote responsibly, and plenty of eighteen-year-olds who aren't. And the same is true of the many other laws that take age into account: laws regarding driving, smoking, drinking, marrying, engaging in sexual activity, serving in the military, and so forth. In all of these cases, the state draws a line between two groups based on generalizations about them. And, at least so far as I am aware, in none of these cases have opponents of affirmative action complained that the state's acting on these generalizations is impermissible. Critics of affirmative action don't complain that the voting age violates the rights of mature seventeen-year-olds, for example, or argue that it's unfair for the law to allow immature fifty-year-olds to buy alcohol just because most fifty-year-olds are mature enough to drink responsibly.

But if it's permissible to act on group generalizations in all of these cases, then why should the fact that affirmative action also involves acting on group generalizations render it morally impermissible? If anything, the generalization that black students are more likely than white students to have suffered race-based obstacles in their upbringings is a far more reliable one than the generalization that teenagers one day past their eighteenth birthday are more likely to be mature enough to vote or responsibly than are people one day before their eighteenth birthday. And the generalization that black Americans on average are likely to have viewpoints and life experiences that are different from those of the average white American seems at least as plausible as the generalization that North Dakotans on average are likely to have viewpoints and life experiences that differ from those of the average New Yorker. So far as acting on generalizations is concerned, then, it should be much harder to justify acting on age-based generalizations than to justify acting on the sorts of race-based generalizations that defenders of affirmative action typically appeal to, and at least as easy to justify race-based affirmative action as to justify geography-based affirmative action. But since critics of affirmative action seem content to accept policies that generalize about age and geography, even when the policies are adopted by the state, they can't consistently appeal to the fact that affirmative action also relies on generalizations as a reason for rejecting affirmative action whether it's practiced by a private institution or by the government.[10]

I'm inclined to think that this problem is serious enough to warrant rejecting the overgeneralizations argument. There's simply no general moral obligation to make sure that all and only those who deserve to be benefited are benefited, and so nothing particularly unjust about a policy that sometimes benefits those who don't deserve to be benefited and that sometimes overlooks those who do. Before moving on to other arguments against affirmative action, though, it's important to acknowledge that there's a way for the overgeneralizations argument to be reinforced. This involves appealing not simply to the claim that affirmative action fails to benefit some of those who deserve to be benefited, but to the stronger claim that it tends to benefit the least disadvantaged members of the groups that it does benefit and to do nothing for the most disadvantaged members of those groups. This is one of the central complaints about affirmative action made by some of its most prominent critics, including the economist Thomas Sowell and Law Professor Stephen Carter, and it's also one of the most common complaints about affirmative action contained in the literature as a whole.[11] So the overgeneralizations argument can't be fully dismissed without saying something about this further claim.

The first thing to say about this further claim is that it's not at all clear that it's true. Proponents of this complaint typically point to cases involving affirmative action at elite universities and graduate schools. In order for affirmative action to help a black student get into Yale Law School, for example, the student must still have a very strong undergraduate record. And, these critics point out, it's much more likely that a black student from a middle- or upper-class background will have attained such a record than that a black student raised in crushing poverty will have done so. Therefore, they conclude, affirmative action mostly benefits the best-off black candidates and does relatively little for the worst-off black candidates.

But this argument is unconvincing. It's true that if affirmative action is only practiced by elite schools, then it's likely to provide most of its benefits to students from relatively privileged backgrounds.[12] But that's just a reason to make sure that affirmative action is more widely practiced, not a reason to think that it's wrong to practice it at all. If schools that admit less advanced students to begin with and companies that hire workers with relatively few skills also practice affirmative action, that is, then it seems plausible to suppose that more black people from more seriously disadvantaged backgrounds will get diplomas and jobs as a result. When affirmative action policies were adopted by parts of the southern textile industry in the late 1960's, for example, the black workers who were hired generally came from seriously disadvantaged backgrounds.[13] And there's no reason to doubt that this would be true today.

In addition, and perhaps more importantly, it's not at all obvious that affirmative action policies benefit only the particular people who actually end up getting admitted or hired as a result of their being implemented. Affirmative action policies, after all, make things easier for every black applicant than it would otherwise be for that particular applicant, and so they increase the chances of success for every black person. And, in general, it seems plausible to think that providing you with something that increases your chances of success is a benefit to you even if you don't end up succeeding. If using sunscreen increases your chances of successfully avoiding skin cancer, for example, then it seems clear that someone benefits you by giving you free sunscreen to use even if you still end up getting skin cancer. Everyone who's given free sunscreen is better off for receiving it, because everyone benefits from reducing their odds of getting skin cancer, and this remains true even if only some of the people who get the sunscreen end up successfully avoiding skin cancer. In just the same way, it seems to me, every black person whose chances of success are increased by the existence of an affirmative action policy is better off because of the policy, even if only some of them end up successfully getting a job or a diploma as a result. So it seems to me that the popular claim so frequently used to prop up the overgeneralizations argument, the claim that affirmative action mostly benefits the least disadvantaged black people, is simply false.[14]

But let's go ahead and assume that it's true. Let's suppose that the practice of affirmative action mostly benefits people who are already relatively well off. Even if this claim does turn out to be true, it's hard to see how it could count as a reason to think that affirmative action is immoral. It doesn't seem immoral in general, after all, to do things that primarily benefit people who are already doing very well. Consider, for example, an engineer who works for Rolls Royce, helping to make their cars run a little bit better. It seems plausible to suppose that most of the people who will benefit from what he does are already quite well off. But I doubt that anyone, regardless of their view of affirmative action, would conclude that what he does is therefore unjust. Or suppose that a federal law is passed that imposes stricter safety standards on the construction of luxury yachts. Again, it seems plausible to suppose that most of the people who would benefit from the law are already quite well off. And, again, it seems unlikely that anyone, regardless of their view of affirmative action, would consider this a reason to deem the law unjust. The fact that doing something is likely to primarily benefit people who are already doing very well isn't a reason to think that doing it would be wrong. And so even if it's true that affirmative action primarily benefits people who are already doing very well, this isn't a reason to think that affirmative action is unjust or immoral.

IF DISCRIMINATION WAS WRONG THEN, THEN IT'S WRONG NOW

The strongest arguments start with the weakest assumptions. An assumption is weak if the claim it makes is so modest that virtually nobody would reject it. The weakness of an assumption makes an argument strong because it makes the argument's conclusion more difficult to resist. If you find yourself forced to accept an argument's starting point, after all, then you may find yourself unable to avoid accepting its ending point, too.

Here's an example of a very weak assumption: the racial discrimination that favored white Americans over black Americans in the past was morally wrong. Virtually everyone now agrees that this is true. Virtually no one today thinks that black people should be excluded from state universities, forced to drink from separate water fountains, or actively prevented from voting. If there were an argument that started from the assumption that these past forms of discrimination were wrong and that ended by showing that affirmative action today is wrong, it would be a very powerful argument indeed.

Many people seem to think that there is just such an argument. It goes like this: if it was wrong for racial discrimination to favor white people over black people in the past, then it's wrong for racial discrimination to favor black people over white people in the present. It was, in fact, wrong for racial discrimination to favor white people over black people in the past, so it is, in fact, wrong for racial discrimination to favor black people over white people in the present. Affirmative action is a form of racial discrimination that favors black people over white people in the present. Therefore, affirmative action is wrong. As Supreme Court Justice Clarence Thomas has put it in advancing this kind of argument, "government-sponsored racial discrimination based on benign prejudice is just as noxious as discrimination inspired by malicious prejudice. In each instance, it is racial discrimination, plain and simple."[15] As the philosopher Lisa Newton has put it, addressing affirmative action not just as practiced by the state but as practiced by schools and businesses, "When the southern employer refuses to hire blacks in white-collar jobs, when Wall Street will only hire women as secretaries with new titles, when Mississippi high schools routinely flunk all black boys above ninth grade, we have examples of injustice... But, of course, when the employers and the schools *favor* women and blacks, the same injustice is done. Just as the previous discrimination did, this reverse discrimination violates the public equality which defines citizenship and destroys the rule of law for the areas in which these favors are granted."[16] And as Virginia Black has put it even more forcefully, "If it is irrational and unjust and cruel to fire someone because he is a black or she is a woman – cases whose absurdity seems obvious – then it is equally irrational and unjust and cruel to hire someone because he is a black or she is a woman. To appreciate the parallel, one has only to remember that to hire X *because* of color is, ipso facto, *not* to hire Y because of color. When inscribed in law, this is racism."[17]

This is a very common argument against affirmative action. I don't find it convincing. The reason for this is simple. It assumes that if an act is wrong in one kind of context, then it must be wrong in all other contexts. But that assumption is clearly false. Suppose, for example, that I asserted that a black person has the right to kill a white person in self-defense. If a white person has started shooting at a black person, and if the only way for the black person to survive is to kill the white person who is attacking him, then the black person has the right to do so. I assume that virtually everyone, regardless of their views of affirmative action, would agree with this claim. But now imagine that a critic of my assertion raised the following objection "if it's permissible for a black person to kill a white person in self-defense today, then it must have been permissible for white people to kill black people by lynching them in the past. In both cases, it's killing, plain and simple. But everyone now agrees that it wasn't permissible for white people to kill black people by lynching them in the past. Therefore, your claim that it's permissible for a black person to kill a white person in self-defense in the present must be mistaken."

In the case of this argument about the right to kill in self-defense, I suspect that virtually everyone would immediately spot the problem with the critic's objection. My claim that it's permissible for a black person to kill a white person in one particular kind of situation does commit me to something. It commits me to the claim that it would also be permissible for a white person to kill a black person in the same kind of situation. But just because it's permissible to kill in cases that involve self-defense doesn't mean that it's also permissible to kill in cases that don't involve self-defense. And so the critic would be wrong to maintain that my claim that black people may kill white people in self-defense in the present implies that it was permissible for white people to kill black people by lynching them in the past.

In the case I've just described, virtually everyone would see the flaw involved in the critic's reasoning. But many people nonetheless fail to recognize that the same flaw is involved in the reasoning about affirmative action that appeals to the wrongness of past discrimination. When we all agree that the racial discrimination that favored white people over black people in the past was wrong, that is, this does commit us to something. It commits us to the view that it would also be wrong for racial discrimination to favor black people over white people in the same sorts of circumstances. Discrimination against black people in the past took place in a specific context: it was used as a means of expressing the white majority's contempt for and feelings of superiority to the black minority. And so our rejection of this objectionable form of behavior does commit us to something: it commits us to the view that it would also be wrong for black people to use racial discrimination as a means of expressing contempt for or feelings of superiority to white people. But no one seriously believes that contemporary race-based affirmative action does anything of the sort. When the governor of Alabama stood at the doors of his state's university and prevented black citizens of his own state from entering, his actions expressed the view that black people were incapable of, or unworthy of, higher education, that their presence would contaminate the environment in which their white counterparts were learning. But if a state university today admits a somewhat less qualified black applicant over a somewhat more qualified white applicant, it's perfectly clear that the university's act in no way expresses contempt for or disapproval of the white applicant in particular or white people in general. And so the recognition that what was done by white people to black people in the past was seriously wrong provides no support for the conclusion that what is done to white people by affirmative action today is wrong.[18]

I'm inclined to think that this is enough to show that the argument from the wrongness of past discrimination to the wrongness of present affirmative action is simply a bad argument. But since it seems to be such a popular argument against affirmative action, it may also be worth noting that the same reason for rejecting the argument can clearly be detected by looking at things from the other direction as well. The claim that discrimination that favors black people over white people today is morally permissible, that is, does commit defenders of affirmative action to something. But what it commits them to is not the claim that discrimination that favors white people over black people would also be permissible under any circumstances whatsoever. Rather, it commits them only to the claim that discrimination that favors white people over black people today would also be permissible in the same sorts of circumstances. And this is an implication that proponents of affirmative action would surely find acceptable. If there were an African nation that had enslaved and persecuted a white minority for a substantial period of time, for example, and if the current generation of white people living there were significantly disadvantaged relative to the black population as a result, then a defender of the kind of affirmative action that favors black applicants over white applicants in the United States would have to agree that it would be permissible to practice a form of affirmative action that favored white applicants over black applicants in that country. If there's an academic discipline in this country in which white people are significantly underrepresented relative to black people, then, again, the defender of affirmative action would have to accept the claim that it would be permissible to favor white candidates over black candidates in such a case. If hardly any white students enter programs in black studies, for example, then the claim that affirmative action that favors black applicants over white applicants is appropriate in other departments might very well mean that affirmative action that favors white applicants over black applicants would be appropriate in this department. But, again, it's hard to believe that defenders of affirmative action would find these implications to be a problem. If supporting affirmative action for black Americans in the present meant supporting the wrongs that were committed against black Americans in the past, then there would certainly be a powerful argument against affirmative action here. But it doesn't. So there isn't.

THE BAD TRACK RECORD ARGUMENT

A related but distinct argument against affirmative action appeals to the claim that this country has a bad track record when it comes to treating people differently according to race. In the past, the argument points out, policies that treated people differently along racial lines almost always resulted in injustice. And because this is so, the argument concludes, policies shouldn't treat people differently along racial lines today. Affirmative action policies do treat people differently along racial lines today. And so, according to this argument, affirmative action policies are wrong. This seems, for example, to be the primary argument against affirmative action in Terry Eastland's *Ending Affirmative Action: The Case for Colorblind Justice*. In responding to the claim that racial classifications can be used by governments in permissible and even praiseworthy ways, Eastland characteristically writes that "we need only consider the history of our country to see that when government makes racial distinctions, bad things do follow."[19]

The bad track record argument depends on the claim that if a distinction was frequently misused in the past, then it shouldn't be used today. But this claim is implausible. The fact that something used to be done incorrectly in the past provides no reason not to do it correctly today, though it may well provide reason to be cautious in attempting to do so. And the fact is that our government has a pretty bad track record with respect to all sorts of distinctions. The law, for example, distinguishes between adult and child, citizen and non-citizen, innocent and guilty, mentally competent and incompetent. In all of these cases, the distinctions have sometimes been misused in the past. But in none of these cases does it seem plausible to conclude that the government should therefore never draw the distinctions in the present. And so the same goes for the distinction between black and white. The fact that this distinction was misused in the past can't, by itself, give us a reason to think it must be wrong to use it differently in the present. It may well give us reason to examine our thinking very carefully before we proceed, but if after examining all of the arguments about affirmative action soberly and dispassionately we can identify no other reason to believe that race-based affirmative action would be unjust, then the mere fact that in the past race-based distinctions were often misused shouldn't count as a reason to think that it would be wrong to practice race-based affirmative action today.

THE NEGATIVES OF AFFIRMATIVE ACTION

Many people who support affirmative action justify their support by appealing to the claim that affirmative action has positive consequences. As I argued toward the end of the previous chapter, this kind of approach may succeed in showing that affirmative action is a good idea, but it can't really show that an organization acts immorally if it decides not to engage in it. The fact that it would be good to do something is not by itself a reason to think that one has no right not to do it. Similarly, many people who oppose affirmative action justify their opposition by appealing to the claim that affirmative action has negative consequences.[20] My argument in this section will be similar, too: while this kind of approach might succeed in showing that affirmative action is a bad idea, it can't really show that an organization acts immorally if it decides to engage in it. I'll address each of the various negative consequences that critics of affirmative action appeal to one at a time. But the underlying problem with appealing to any of them is basically the same: the fact that an act will have some bad consequences isn't, in itself, a good reason to think that one has no right to do it.

Let's begin with perhaps the most common complaint of this sort: that affirmative action has a stigmatizing effect on the very people it's supposed to benefit.[21] If everyone on a given college campus knows that the black students there were admitted under a relaxed set of standards relative to the white students, for example, the argument maintains that two things are likely to happen. First, the white students are likely to think less of the black students. Second, the black students are likely to think less of themselves. Stephen Carter, for example, writes of the "terrible psychological pressure that racial preferences often put on their beneficiaries."[22] And many other authors have maintained that being admitted or employed as a black person under an affirmative action policy induces self-doubt.

Let's assume that affirmative action really does have this kind of stigmatizing effect on those it aims to benefit. Does this provide a good reason to conclude that it's unjust? Clearly, the answer is no. Consider, for example, the practice that many universities have of admitting athletes under academic standards that are relaxed relative to the standards that are applied to non-athletes. Just as the average SAT score of the black students at a given school might be considerably lower than the average SAT score of the white students, that is, so the average SAT score of the white players on the school's football team might be considerably lower than the average SAT score of the rest of the white students on campus. In the case of reduced admissions standards for athletes, it again seems quite plausible to suppose that this will have a stigmatizing effect. Just as a white student who meets a black student may assume that the black student got in only because he's black, so a white non-athlete who meets a white athlete may assume that the white athlete got in only because he's an athlete. These forms of affirmative action, that is, may increase the number of people who think that black people are dumb and the number of people who think that athletes are dumb. Virtually nobody, though, really thinks that it's literally unjust for a university to give preference in admissions to athletes, even if doing so does have this stigmatizing effect, though of course many people think it's a bad idea for other reasons. And the same is true for other commonly accepted forms of preferential treatment. Many universities, for example, give preference to so-called legacies, the sons and daughters of their graduates. This practice may lead their fellow students to assume that they were admitted only because of who their parents were. And the same sort of thing can also happen when schools practice geography-based forms of affirmative action. As all of these cases that don't involve race should make clear, the mere fact that an admissions policy may stigmatize the group it favors isn't enough to make it morally wrong. But if that's so, then the fact, if it is a fact, that race-based affirmative action also stigmatizes the group it favors isn't enough to make it morally wrong either.

A second kind of negative consequence that critics of affirmative action typically appeal to concerns the effects that such programs may have on race relations. The argument here is that affirmative action is wrong because it's divisive, creating rifts on campus, in the workplace, and throughout society in general.[23] This kind of argument strikes me as puzzling. Affirmative action is certainly a divisive subject.[24] But it seems strange to blame one side rather than the other for this fact. The debate over abortion rights, for example, is at least as divisive as the debate over affirmative action. But imagine a defender of abortion rights suggesting that pro-life protesters should abandon their cause because the abortion controversy is tearing the nation apart. Surely, in that case, it would be clear that the pro-life protesters would be entitled to reply by suggesting that the abortion rights advocates abandon their cause for precisely the same reason. It's true that if people stopped trying to outlaw abortion, the issue would no longer be so divisive. But it's equally true that if people stopped trying to prevent abortion from being outlawed, the issue would no longer be so divisive. The divisiveness of the abortion issue, in short, provides no reason to come down on one side of it rather than the other.

And yet while this seems to be clear to everyone in the context of the debate over abortion, many people seem to overlook it in the context of the debate over affirmative action. It's true that if supporters of affirmative action were to abandon their support, then many opponents of affirmative action would stop being so angry and resentful. But it's equally true that if opponents of affirmative action were to abandon their opposition, then many supporters of affirmative action would stop being so angry and resentful. Affirmative action programs make many people angry and resentful. Ending affirmative action programs makes many people angry and resentful. That's unfortunate. But it doesn't help to settle the controversy.

A third negative consequence that some critics of affirmative action appeal to is a reduction in efficiency. If a company fails to hire the best qualified candidate for any given position, on this account, then productivity will go down. If a college fails to admit the best students, then graduation rates – including black graduation rates – will go down.[25] If a country's affirmative action policies make it too difficult for the best qualified white applicants to find employment, then they will look elsewhere. And so on.[26] Not surprisingly, defenders of affirmative action have produced a set of counterarguments to this claim that try to show that affirmative action actually increases efficiency. These arguments tend to appeal to the claim that affirmative action increases diversity and that diversity in turn tends to generate new ideas, new approaches, and so on. As a backup response, they at least appeal to studies suggesting that affirmative action does not make things less efficient.[27]

I don't have much to say about whether or not affirmative action increases inefficiency. Sometimes it probably does, and sometimes it probably doesn't. But I do have something to say about whether or not increasing inefficiency would be enough to make affirmative action immoral. And what I have to say is this: it wouldn't. Indeed, once again, I think that this is already clear to most people on both sides of the affirmative action debate whenever they look at cases that don't involve race. When my neighborhood supermarket hired the grocery bagger with Down syndrome, for example, they failed to maximize the efficiency of their operation. But no one thinks that what the store did in hiring that worker was immoral for that reason because no one really thinks that there's a moral obligation to be as efficient as possible in the first place. And since it isn't immoral to fail to be as efficient as possible, the fact that affirmative action is inefficient, if it is a fact, isn't enough to make affirmative action immoral either.

Finally, it may be that some opponents of affirmative action consider the mere fact that such policies involve taking note of race itself to be a negative consequence of implementing them. Simply taking into account that one person is white and another person is black, after all, can be taken to reinforce the idea that there is indeed a difference between being white and being black and this, in turn, might be thought to impair our ability to work toward a world where all people are treated the same. It's a bit less clear whether critics of affirmative action really mean to be pressing this claim,[28] but whether there are people who mean to be asserting it or not, the claim itself certainly merits repudiation.

Virtually everyone, for example, agrees that it's permissible for the government to ensure that black people aren't excluded from serving on juries simply because they're black. In order to do so, the government must keep track of the number of white people and black people who live in a given area, the number of white people and black people who are called for jury duty, and the number of white people and black people who finally end up sitting on juries after they are called. In order to do all of this, the government clearly has to take note of who is white and who is black, as it must in cases where it attempts to enforce laws prohibiting racial discrimination in housing or employment. Virtually no one would say that the mere fact that the government must take note of who is white and who is black in these cases counts as a reason against its doing so. And the same is true of the uncontroversial cases I appealed to in the section discussing the right to equal treatment argument. Virtually everyone on both sides of the affirmative action debate agrees that it's acceptable for the government to take race into account when looking for someone to go undercover in an overwhelmingly black country, to portray Abraham Lincoln in a play, or to take part in research on the effectiveness of certain drugs on African American patients. These actions, too, involve the government taking note of who is black and who is white and, again, since the consideration of race involved seems appropriate, the mere fact that they involve taking notice of race seems appropriate too. And so no one should be convinced by the claim that the mere fact that affirmative action involves taking note of who is white and who is black counts as an argument against it.

Like most policies, in any event, affirmative action programs have some positive consequences and some negative consequences. And, as with most policies, the positive consequences aren't enough to make affirmative action obligatory and the negative consequences aren't enough to make it unjust.

When a white employer has his son come to work for him at the family business, no one complains that he violates the rights of the more qualified candidates he might otherwise have hired. When the son's promotion within the company creates resentment among those who are passed over, when his coworkers assume that he has only gotten where he is because of his last name, or when the son himself begins to have doubts about his abilities because of the policy under which he was hired, no one concludes that these unfortunate consequences are enough to render the policy unjust or immoral. This is because, when we set aside the anger and emotion that racial issues often provoke in this country and focus on a case where a white employer hires a white applicant, we can see that it's morally permissible to hire someone who isn't the best candidate, even when doing so has these sorts of negative consequences. When a white employer hires a black applicant over other white candidates who are better qualified, however, many people lose sight of this important lesson. This is an unfortunate mistake. Not practicing affirmative action isn't wrong. But neither is practicing it.

A QUICK WORD ABOUT AN IRRELEVANT WORD

Before concluding this discussion, it may be worth briefly noting the fact that I've managed to write two whole chapters about affirmative action without once using the word "quota." How did I do that? The answer is simple: quotas are an irrelevant distraction. Although clearly useful as a rhetorical device for rallying support among those who oppose affirmative action, the question of whether or not an affirmative action program employs numerical quotas makes no difference to the merit of any of the arguments that I've developed here.

That this is true can clearly be seen, as can so much else that's true in the debate over race-based affirmative action, by once again returning to the uncontroversial case of geography-based affirmative action. So suppose that two schools on the East Coast currently have no geography-based affirmative action program and suppose that both notice that they have very few students from North Dakota. Each decides that their overall academic mission would be better served if their students were exposed to people from a broader range of regional backgrounds, and so each decides to implement a geography-based affirmative action program. One school introduces an admissions policy that doesn't involve quotas: each qualified applicant from North Dakota has a few extra points added to the total score that the admissions office arrives at based on each student's grades, SAT scores, and other considerations. In some years, this results in two or three additional students being admitted from North Dakota. In some years, it results in seven or eight additional students being admitted. In some years, it turns out to make no difference at all. The other school introduces an admissions policy that does involve quotas. Since roughly two out of every thousand Americans live in North Dakota, and since the school admits roughly two thousand students each year, it sets a target of admitting four students from North Dakota each year: preference is given to qualified students from North Dakota over somewhat more qualified students from New York until four students from North Dakota have been admitted, at which point the rest of the applications from North Dakota are treated in the same way as the rest of the applications from elsewhere. In some years, the school doesn't receive enough qualified applications from North Dakota to fulfill its quota, in some years it receives so many qualified applications that it exceeds it, and in some years the applicants from North Dakota are so much weaker than the applicants from the New York that it ends up admitting no one from North Dakota at all.

In the case of these two schools and their geography-based affirmative action policies, two things should be clear. First, if the first school's policy is morally permissible, then so is the second school's. If a student from New York can't really complain that his rights are violated by the kind of geography-based affirmative action policy that doesn't involve quotas, that is, then there's no basis for complaining that his rights are violated by the kind of geography-based affirmative action policy that does involve quotas. When schools like West Point distribute the majority of the nominations needed to secure admission to their program by congressional district in a way that clearly does amount to a quota system, for example, no one really complains that this is unjust. And as noted earlier, the Rhodes Scholarship program operates on a very precise quota system on which rather than selecting the thirty-two best candidates in the country, up to two winners are selected from each of sixteen geographical districts. Again, virtually no one on either side of the affirmative action debate really thinks that this is unjust.

The second thing that should be clear is that if the first school's policy isn't morally obligatory, then neither is the second school's. If it would be morally permissible for the first school to abandon its nonquota program and revert to a policy on which it practices no geography-based affirmative action at all, that is, then it would be morally permissible for the second school to abandon its quota program and do the same. And, indeed, when schools refrain from practicing geography-based affirmative action, no one really complains that this is unjust, either. Surely no one would call it unjust if the Rhodes Scholarship program were to eliminate its geography-based quota policy and were instead to simply select the thirty-two best candidates from across the country. If a geography-based affirmative action program that doesn't employ quotas is permissible but non-obligatory, in short, then a geography-based affirmative action program that does employ quotas is permissible but non-obligatory, too. Whether or not the policy in question makes use of numerical targets or quotas simply makes no moral difference.

But if this is true in the case of geography-based affirmative action, then there's no reason for it not to be true in the case of race-based affirmative action. None of the features that distinguish race-based affirmative action from geography-based affirmative action would suffice to render quotas impermissible in one case but permissible in the other or obligatory in one case but non-obligatory in the other. And so if race-based affirmative action without quotas is permissible but non-obligatory, as I've argued it is, then so is race-based affirmative action with quotas. Either way, race-based affirmative action is morally optional.

AN UNEXCITING CONCLUSION

So what should we do? If either of the standard positions on affirmative action proved to be acceptable, this question would have a simple answer. If race-based affirmative action were unjust, then it would be wrong for any organization to practice it. If race-based affirmative action were morally obligatory, then it would be wrong for any organization not to practice it. But neither of these standard positions is acceptable. Race-based affirmative action, as I've argued, is permissible but non-obligatory. It's morally optional.

To say that something is morally optional, though, isn't necessarily to say that it's morally neutral. Sometimes something is morally optional but still morally good. Donating some of your money to Oxfam, for example, might not be morally required of you, but even if it isn't, it's probably a praiseworthy thing for you to do nonetheless. Other things might be morally optional but still be morally bad. Morally speaking, for example, you may be within your rights to engage in true though mean-spirited gossip, but it might still be objectionable for you to exercise that right. And, of course, some things that are morally optional really do seem to be morally neutral as well. It's neither impermissible nor obligatory to put your left shoe on before your right, and it doesn't seem to be particularly good or bad to do so either. So if we accept my conclusion that race-based affirmative action is neither impermissible nor obligatory, we might still try to determine if it's morally good (though not required), morally bad (though not forbidden), or morally neutral (and thus essentially morally irrelevant). And in this way, perhaps, the defenders of the two more extreme positions that I've argued against in these two chapters might still hold out some hope that, in the end, the truth will lie much closer to their own view than to the view of their opponents. Those who've sought to establish that affirmative action is obligatory, that is, might point out that what I said in the previous chapter is consistent with the claim that it's morally much better to practice affirmative action than not to practice it, even if practicing it isn't strictly speaking required by morality. And those who've tried to show that affirmative action is unjust might point out that what I've said in this chapter is consistent with the claim that it's morally much worse to practice affirmative action than not to practice it, even if practicing affirmative action isn't strictly speaking forbidden by morality.

While either of these final judgments must be accepted as possibilities, though, they strike me as remote possibilities. As with most things that are morally optional, it seems unlikely that there will prove to be a simple, uniform, across the board answer to the question of whether it's just plain good or just plain bad to practice affirmative action. In this respect, demanding a simple yes or no answer to a question like "should universities practice race-based affirmative action?" is like demanding a simple yes or no answer to the same question about any other morally optional practice. Should universities employ geography-based affirmative action? Should they have rolling admissions? Should they require students to learn a foreign language? Should they give preferential consideration to those who can play football or who are children of alumni?

In all of these other cases, the requirements of morality will not provide an answer. It's surely permissible for a university to take athletic ability into account if it wants to, for example, and it's just as surely permissible for a university not to take athletic ability into account if that's what it wants to do. And given this, it seems unlikely that there will be one generic answer to the question of what should be done that would apply equally to all forms of preferential consideration for athletes and to all schools and all circumstances, let alone to questions about rolling admissions or foreign language requirements. In some cases, admitting football players with lower grades and test scores than other applicants who are rejected might prove to do more good than harm. The effect on academic standards might be minimal, it might cause very little resentment or stigmatization of the students in question and at the same time it might significantly enhance the school's profile, substantially improve the size and quality of its applicant pool, have a major impact on alumni donations and generate a feeling of community and camaraderie across the campus. In such cases, giving preferential consideration to such athletes would probably be a good, though not obligatory, thing to do. In other cases, admitting football players with lower grades and test scores than other applicants who are rejected might prove to do more harm than good. The effects on academic standards and graduation rates might be more serious, the extra costs incurred in paying for the requisite tutors and other special resources might come at the expense of other, more worthy, programs, it might be a source of divisiveness rather than unity on campus, and in the end in might not produce any tangible benefits to compensate for all of these costs. In such cases, giving preferential consideration to such athletes would probably be a bad, though not unjust, thing to do. For these reasons, I doubt it would surprise anyone to conclude that there's no general answer to the question of whether a university should take athletic ability into account or to the question of what the best way to take it into account is for those schools that do take it into account, and that the only reasonable way of answering these questions would be to examine the relevant details on a case by case basis. Nor would anyone be surprised to reach a similar conclusion about geography-based affirmative action, rolling admissions, or preferential consideration for legacies.

But if what I've said about the morality of affirmative action in these two chapters is correct, then we should say precisely the same thing about race-based affirmative action: there's no general answer to the question of whether an organization should practice such affirmative action or to the question of what form of affirmative action it should practice if it does, and the only reasonable way of answering these questions would be to examine the relevant details on a case by case basis. In some cases, it might be good, but not obligatory, to have such policies. In other cases, it might be bad, but not unjust, to have them. Sometimes having such a policy may make no real difference at all and prove to be neither good nor bad.

So what should we do? We should resolve to accept that it's permissible for an organization to practice affirmative action and that it's permissible for an organization not to practice it. And we should direct our energies away from the often strident debate about whether affirmative action is obligatory or unjust and focus instead on the much more mundane, but much more important, task of trying to figure out which organizations would do more good than harm by having such a policy and which would do more harm than good, which forms of affirmative action would do more good than harm and which forms would do more harm than good.[29] I admit that this is a much less exciting answer to the question than the answers provided by the two dominant views on the subject of affirmative action. But sometimes, even for a philosopher, the least exciting answer to a question turns out to be the right one to accept.

6

Why I Used to Hate Hate Speech Restrictions

Appeals to Traditional Exceptions to Freedom of Expression and Why They All Fail

Two students are walking across different parts of the same campus. Each passes a fellow student that he strongly dislikes. The first insults the student he encounters by calling him a fat and ugly asshole. The second insults the student he encounters by calling him a fat and ugly nigger. Because the college in question has a policy prohibiting hate speech, the second student is punished for his use of offensive language while the first student isn't. Meanwhile, two arsonists are walking around different parts of the same state. Each is planning to burn down someone's house and each is trying to find a suitable house to target. The first ends up selecting a particular house because it's a bit more convenient to get to than others in the area. The second ends up selecting a particular house because the family who lives in it is black. Both are caught and are punished for their acts. Because the state in question has a hate crime law, the second arsonist receives a greater punishment than the first.

These two pairs of cases have a number of things in common. In both pairs of cases, each person does something objectionable. In both pairs of cases, the kind of objectionable thing that the first person does is the same as the kind of objectionable thing that the second person does. In both pairs of cases, what the second person does involves targeting someone by race while what the first person does doesn't involve targeting someone by race. And in both pairs of cases, there's a policy in place that results in the second person receiving a particular kind of sanction that the first person doesn't receive as a result of this fact.

In one obvious sense, the sorts of policies involved in these two pairs of cases are controversial. Many people strongly support hate speech restrictions and hate crime laws and many people strongly oppose them. But in a second and more subtle sense, there seems to be a fairly broad consensus on the subject: the similarities between the two pairs of cases strike many people as being more important than the differences. Those who support one of the two policies tend to support the other, that is, and those who oppose one of the two policies tend to oppose the other as well. While people tend to disagree quite sharply about whether hate speech restrictions and hate crime laws should be embraced or

rejected, then, many of them agree that the two sorts of policies should ultimately stand or fall together. As Dinesh D'Souza puts it in opposing both of
them, for example, "free speech is subordinated to the goals of sensitivity and
diversity, as in so-called hate speech and hate crimes laws."[1]

This common tendency to view hate speech restrictions and hate crime laws
as if they were philosophically joined at the hip is an understandable one. But I
think it's mistaken. The similarities between the two sorts of policy are important, but so are the differences. That's why I think that we can't reach a reasonable
position about either of them without investigating each of them separately. And
when we do this, I think we find that considerations that people on both sides
of both debates generally accept support the conclusion that we should oppose
hate speech restrictions but support hate crime laws. The goal of this chapter
and the one that follows is to explain why I oppose hate speech restrictions. The
goal of the two chapters after that is to explain why I nonetheless support hate
crime laws. The goal of the four chapters taken as a whole is to establish that
hate speech restrictions and hate crime laws shouldn't be thought to stand or
fall together.

The full set of reasons for holding different positions on these two issues will
emerge from the details of the various discussions that follow. But since the lingering suspicion that the two cases must go hand in hand may distract some
readers as they try to work their way through these details, it's worth briefly
addressing this suspicion up front before beginning our discussion of hate speech
restrictions in earnest and turning to a more detailed set of arguments. So consider two claims that virtually everyone on both sides of both of these debates
is likely to accept. The first claim maintains that if a certain kind of activity is
illegal, then it's generally appropriate for the state to inflict a greater penalty
on those who engage in it in a more harmful manner or with a more objectionable state of mind. Arson, for example, is illegal, and it's appropriate to place
arson that causes more than a million dollars in damage in a different category
from arson that causes less than a thousand dollars in damage and to punish the
former more severely than the latter. Breaking into someone's house is illegal,
and it's appropriate to treat the act of breaking into someone's house in order
to rob them as a greater crime than the act of breaking into someone's house in
order to get in out of the rain. The second claim maintains that if a certain kind
of activity is not prohibited, then it's generally not appropriate for a government
or a university to impose a penalty on some people for engaging in it simply
because they engage in the nonprohibited form of activity with a particularly
objectionable state of mind or in a way that will be particularly hurtful or upsetting to other people. If a state or college doesn't prohibit its citizens or students
from moving from one apartment to another, for example, then the fact that a
particular student was motivated to change apartments out of a vindictive desire
to make his ex-girlfriend angry wouldn't be enough to make it appropriate for
the state or the college to punish him for doing so. If a state or college doesn't
forbid its citizens or students from taking night jobs as strippers, then it wouldn't

be appropriate for either to penalize a particular citizen or student for doing so simply because if she took the job, it would break her parents' hearts.

These two claims by themselves, of course, can't do much to establish the case for hate crime laws or the case against hate speech restrictions. The support for those cases, as I've already indicated, will each require two chapters of their own. But the two claims should be enough to establish that there's nothing inconsistent about supporting hate crime laws while opposing both legal and academic hate speech restrictions. If defenders of hate crime laws can establish that the arsonist who targets by race causes more harm or acts with a more objectionable state of mind than does the ordinary arsonist, for example, then they can appeal to the first claim as a justification for punishing the arsonist who targets by race more severely than the ordinary arsonist. Arson, after all, is already illegal. And so the first claim would help support the conclusion that extra punishment is appropriate when arson is committed in an especially harmful or objectionable manner. But even if the supporter of state or campus hate speech restrictions can establish that targeting people by race for verbal abuse is similarly more hurtful or more objectionable than insulting people in other ways, the opponent of such restrictions who nonetheless supports hate crime laws can appeal to the second claim as a justification for opposing hate speech restrictions. Insulting people, after all, isn't prohibited as a general matter by law or by campus policies. And so the second claim would help support the conclusion that it would be inappropriate for a government or a university to impose a penalty on some people for insulting people because they insult people from a particularly objectionable state of mind or in a way that is particularly hurtful or upsetting to other people. With these brief considerations in mind, then, we should be able to set aside the worry that it must be inconsistent to support hate crime laws while opposing legal and academic hate speech restrictions and turn instead to the specific considerations that have led me, at least, to do precisely that.

WHAT HATE SPEECH RESTRICTIONS ARE

Let's start by getting clear about what hate speech restrictions are. "Hate speech" isn't a technical or legal term, so a precise definition is unlikely to prove acceptable to everyone. But as a rough approximation that should prove good enough for the purposes of this discussion, we can say that hate speech refers to verbal or written attacks on people that target them because of their group membership, where this at least includes their race or ethnicity and may well include other characteristics like religion, gender, and sexual orientation. A hate speech restriction is a rule or set of rules that prohibits such speech. Since my focus in this book is on moral problems involving race, I'll focus here on race-based hate speech in particular. For the purposes of this chapter and the chapter that follows, then, when I refer to a hate speech restriction, I'll mean a rule or sets of rules that prohibits verbal or written attacks that target people by race in particular.

This rough definition of hate speech restrictions leaves a number of questions open. Some people, for example, support hate speech restrictions that apply only to verbal attacks against minority groups, so that a white person aiming a racial epithet at a black person would be restricted in a way that a black person aiming a racial epithet at a white person wouldn't be. Others, though, think such restrictions should be neutral in this respect, treating all hate speech that targets by race in the same way. Thinking of hate speech in terms of a verbal or written "attack" leaves things ambiguous with respect to whether the speaker must intend his words to be an attack, some listener must construe the words as an attack, or both. Some hate speech restrictions might put more weight on the speaker's intent, while others might put more weight on the listener's reaction. The use of the word "niggardly" to describe someone as thrifty where no offense was intended but offense was nonetheless taken, for example, might be proscribed by some restrictions but not by others. Saying that hate speech involves attacking people because of their group membership, moreover, leaves it unclear whether attacks on groups of people as whole count or only attacks on particular members of such groups. Some hate speech restrictions might apply to statements like "all black people are stupid" as well as to statements that aim racial epithets at specific black individuals. Others might apply to the latter but not to the former. And by referring to rules or sets of rules, this general account of hate speech restrictions leaves it open whether they are propagated and enforced by governments or by colleges and universities and whether, if they are government rules, they are part of the civil or criminal law.

For the most part, we can set these further questions aside. The reasons for opposing hate speech restrictions arise from features that different forms of hate speech restriction have in common rather than from features that help to distinguish one particular hate speech restriction from another. When I say that the goal of this chapter and the chapter that follows is to argue against hate speech restrictions, then, I mean that the goal is to argue against all restrictions of this general sort whether they are legal or academic, public or private, narrow or broad.[2]

It's important to emphasize, though, that this doesn't mean that the goal of these chapters is to argue against every policy that would have, as an indirect consequence, the prohibition of hate speech of a certain sort or in a certain context. If a city or college library has a policy that says that there's no talking in the reading room, for example, this would include a prohibition on uttering racial epithets in the reading room, too. If a city has a noise ordinance that forbids producing sounds above a certain number of decibels in residential neighborhoods, this will as a consequence forbid the uttering of racial epithets above that number of decibels in those areas. These two rules would effectively ban at least some forms of hate speech, but they wouldn't ban them in virtue of the fact that they are forms of hate speech. Similarly, if a professor has a rule that forbids name calling in her classroom, the rule would forbid the use of race-based name calling as a result, but would not forbid it in virtue of the fact that it was race-based. Nothing that I will say in this chapter or the one that follows will count against rules and policies such as these. A policy that just happens to restrict some forms of hate speech as the predictable consequence of its much broader restriction on expression, after all, isn't really a hate speech restriction. A monastery that requires its monks to take a vow of silence, for example, can't plausibly be described as imposing hate speech restrictions on them. A hate speech restriction, rather, is a policy by which a government or university singles out a set of verbal or written attacks that target people by race and prohibits them *because* they are verbal or written attacks that target people by race. This is what people mean by a hate speech restriction when they argue about such restrictions. Those who oppose hate speech restrictions don't oppose rules requiring silence in a library's reading room, and those who support hate speech restrictions don't want the uttering of racial epithets to be restricted only in cases where uttering words in general is restricted. For the purposes of the discussion here, then, a hate speech restriction is a policy by which a government or university singles out a set of verbal or written attacks that target people by race and prohibits them *because* they are verbal or written attacks that target people by race. Defenders of such restrictions maintain that there's something about race-based hate speech itself that warrants such restrictions. Opponents of such restrictions deny that this is so. I'm an opponent.

Finally, when I say that I'll be opposing both government hate speech restrictions and hate speech restrictions imposed by colleges and universities, I don't mean to imply that the two cases are fully on a par. It may well be considerably more objectionable for the state to punish one of its citizens for using hate speech than for a college to punish one of its students for doing so, just as it's presumably true in many other cases that it would be considerably more objectionable for a government to adopt a given policy then for a college to adopt it. It would be objectionable for a college to ban interracial dating, for example, but even more objectionable for the government to do so. Nor, for that matter, do I mean to be insisting that state and campus hate speech restrictions are on a par with respect to the issue of whether, strictly speaking, the institutions in question have a right to adopt such restrictions. One might well hold, for example, that if the government were to ban interracial dating, this would not only be morally objectionable, but would in addition be something it simply had no right to do. But many who hold this view might still be inclined to think that even though it would also be morally objectionable for a college to ban interracial dating, the college would nonetheless have the right to do so, at least if it were a private school and all the students who were admitted to it were made aware of the policy before they decided whether or not to attend. I'm certainly open to the conclusion that governments have no right to impose hate speech restrictions while schools, or at least private schools, do. The problem I'm concerned with here is not the question of whether either kind of institution has the right to impose such restrictions, but rather the question of whether it would be morally objectionable for either kind of institution to impose such restrictions, regardless of whether it has the right to do so. While there may well be a number of important differences between legal and academic hate speech restrictions, then, I will be focusing here on an assessment that in my view applies equally to both of them: morally speaking, they are objectionable and should be opposed for that reason.

In the United States, at least, when people think of hate speech restrictions, they tend to think of prohibitions that are imposed by colleges and universities rather than by the government. This is because while there are no laws against hate speech in this country, and while attempts to pass such laws have been consistently rejected by the courts, there are many colleges and universities that have hate speech codes. A little over two decades ago, there were virtually no hate speech codes of this sort on American campuses. That began to change in 1987 when a few prominent universities, including the University of Michigan and Stanford, adopted hate speech codes in response to racial incidents that had occurred on their campuses. Just five years later, over three hundred schools had adopted similar sets of rules.[3] The scope of these policies varied enormously from campus to campus. Some policies explicitly excluded words spoken in the classroom. Others deliberately included them. Some were very broad. A policy at the University of Connecticut, for example, prohibited among things "inappropriately directed laughter [and] inconsiderate jokes" as well as the "conspicuous exclusion" of people from discussions. Others were intentionally narrow. Stanford, for example, became known for having a particularly modest code that focused exclusively on insults aimed directly at a particular individual and using epithets that could be construed as "fighting words."[4] Many other campus codes lay somewhere in between.

Since most Americans associate hate speech restrictions with college campuses, there has been a tendency in recent years to treat the controversy they generated as somewhat passé, a debate that had its moment in the late 1980s and early 1990s, but which has since been overtaken by more timely (or, at least, more trendy) subjects like racial profiling. This is because at the end of that period, campus hate speech restrictions of virtually every type were struck down as unconstitutional in a series of rulings in such states as California, Michigan, Wisconsin, and Ohio, and the view that campus hate speech restrictions are unconstitutional was ultimately confirmed by the United States Supreme Court in the 1992 case of *R.A.V. v. the City of St. Paul*.[5]

But treating the debate over hate speech restrictions as one that has come and gone is an important mistake for two reasons. First, as Jon B. Gould convincingly argues in his provocative 2005 book, *Speak No Evil: The Triumph of Hate Speech Regulation*, the fact that campus hate speech restrictions were rejected by the courts doesn't mean that they were rejected by the campuses themselves. And, in fact, Gould's book offers a detailed and persuasive case for the conclusion that the court rulings against such restrictions have largely been ignored and that the number of colleges and universities with hate speech codes has actually increased significantly in the years since the courts rejected them.[6] To the extent that campus hate speech restrictions raise a moral question, then, that question is actually more pressing now than it was then despite the fact that the courts seem to have rendered it moot. Second, while there are no laws against hate speech in the United States, and while the courts here seem clearly to have closed the door on their arising in the foreseeable future, there are hate speech laws of one sort or another on the books in most other countries that have roughly similar legal systems, including Canada, Australia, and New Zealand, and much of Western Europe. As a 1992 policy paper from Human Rights Watch put it, "The United States stands virtually alone in having no valid statutes penalizing expression that is offensive or insulting on such grounds as race, religion or ethnicity."[7] And several prominent international human rights declarations implicitly or explicitly endorse hate speech restrictions as well. Article 20 of the 1966 International Covenant on Civil and Political Rights, for example, declares that "Any advocacy of national, racial or religious hatred that constitutes incitement to discrimination, hostility or violence shall be prohibited by law."[8] Far from being a settled matter, then, the debate over the moral status of hate speech restrictions remains a contentious issue, not just in America, but around the globe.[9]

WHY I HATE HATE SPEECH RESTRICTIONS

The source of my opposition to legal and academic hate speech restrictions is simple. Such policies prohibit people from saying certain sorts of things. I think it's morally objectionable to prohibit people from saying certain sorts of things unless there's a sufficiently good reason for the prohibition. And I don't think there's a sufficiently good reason for the prohibitions enacted by hate speech restrictions in either the legal or the academic context. So I think that both forms of hate speech restrictions are morally objectionable.

While the basic structure of my argument against hate speech restrictions is therefore a simple one, though, the details can get a bit complicated. This is because the argument is indirect. It begins by establishing a moral presumption against restrictions on freedom of expression in general and then maintains that none of the arguments that have been offered in defense of hate speech restrictions in particular are strong enough to overcome this presumption in either the legal or the academic context. The presumption arises from the thought that if someone proposes to impose a restriction on people's freedom of expression, the burden of proof is on them to justify the appropriateness of the imposition, rather than on the people to justify the appropriateness of their being free of it. People should be allowed to express themselves unless there's a reason for them not to be, that is, rather than prevented from expressing themselves unless there's a reason for them not to be. Since virtually everyone, regardless of their view of hate speech restrictions, seems to agree that there should be a general presumption in favor of freedom of expression, this starting point should prove to be acceptable to virtually everyone on both sides of the hate speech debate. And, indeed, virtually everyone who has attempted to defend hate speech restrictions has done so not by denying that such restrictions stand in need of a positive defense, but precisely by trying to provide an argument to ground such a defense. The only real point of contention, then, is whether any of these arguments is sufficiently powerful to warrant our assent.

The many arguments that have been offered in defense of hate speech restrictions can be broken down into two types. The first type of argument builds from the fact that virtually everyone already agrees that it's morally unobjectionable to restrict at least some kinds of expression. This type of argument begins by identifying a particular kind of case in which virtually everyone already agrees that speech may justifiably be restricted, and then attempts to show that if restrictions are morally unobjectionable in the uncontroversial case, then they are morally unobjectionable in the case of hate speech as well. The second type of argument attempts to justify adding a new and previously unrecognized category to the traditional list of kinds of speech that may unobjectionably be restricted, and then argues that hate speech belongs in this further category. When I first became aware of the controversy over hate speech restrictions, I was only aware of the first sort of strategy for defending them. I was opposed to hate speech restrictions because I didn't think that any of the arguments of this sort were satisfactory. After I looked into the literature in some detail, I discovered that some of the most prominent and potentially powerful arguments for restricting hate speech are of the second type. But I don't think that any of these arguments prove to be satisfactory either. That's why I'm still opposed to legal and academic hate speech restrictions. I'll focus on the first kind of argument in the rest of this chapter, and will turn to the second kind of argument in the chapter that follows.

WORDS THAT THREATEN

Suppose that I walk up to you and utter the following words: "I have a gun in my pocket and if you don't give me all of your money right now, I'm going to shoot you in the head." Strictly speaking, all I've done is said something to you. But even the most zealous advocate of freedom of expression will agree that it's morally unobjectionable for the government, not to mention a college or university, to prohibit me from saying this sort of thing.[10] Virtually everyone, that is, regardless of their view of hate speech restrictions, agrees that speech may legitimately be restricted in the sort of case in which uttering certain words amounts to threatening to harm someone unjustly.

Some defenders of hate speech restrictions claim that this exception can be exploited to vindicate such restrictions.[11] Suppose, for example, that a group of white students are walking across campus late at night and they encounter a black student holding hands with his white girlfriend. Angry at this sight, one of them yells "damn nigger!" at him. Given the shameful history of this word in particular and of the treatment of black people in America by the sort of people who would utter it in general, it might be perfectly reasonable for the black student to construe this utterance as a threat. But, then, if it's morally unobjectionable to prohibit me from saying "give me your money or I'll shoot you in the head," it should also be morally unobjectionable to prohibit the white student from yelling "damn nigger!" at the black student, and unobjectionable for the same reason. Legal and academic hate speech restrictions might both be justified, then, simply by appealing to this already uncontroversial limitation on freedom of expression.

There are three problems with this attempt to justify hate speech restrictions by appealing to the right to prohibit threats. The first is that even if we agree that it's reasonable to construe the words "damn nigger!" as a threat in this particular context, it isn't reasonable to generalize from this case to all cases involving the use of race-based hate speech. If a frail, old wheelchair-bound white woman encounters a group of young, healthy black men and utters the very same words as she passes them in the street, it may be perfectly clear both to her and to them that while she is contemptuous of their presence, she intends and poses no threat to their well-being. And one can easily imagine many other sorts of cases in which the sorts of utterances that hate speech restrictions seek to forbid could be made in an insulting, demeaning, humiliating but clearly nonthreatening manner. The attempt to justify hate speech restrictions by appealing to the uncontroversial case of forbidding the use of threatening words depends on the claim that hateful speech is always threatening speech. But this claim is not sufficiently plausible to warrant endorsing the argument that depends on it.

A defender of hate speech restrictions could respond to this objection by appealing to the additional claim that even nonthreatening instances of hate speech indirectly contribute to an environment in which threatening hate speech is able to flourish. Even if a student's saying that black people are lazy can't reasonably be construed as making a threat against anybody, for example, it might still be thought to provide some kind of support or motivation that could inspire other people to say things to black people that clearly are threatening and, indeed, to carry out threats against black people.[12] But this response would require the defense of hate speech restrictions to rest on the claim that it's legitimate to restrict nonthreatening speech that indirectly contributes to other people engaging in threatening speech. And this claim, in turn, has implications that virtually everyone on both sides of the hate speech debate would surely reject. A student's saying that abortion is morally on a par with murder can't reasonably be construed as making a threat to anybody, for example, but could just as reasonably be thought to provide some kind of support or motivation that could inspire other people to make threats, and indeed to carry out threats, against those who provide abortions. But while virtually everyone would agree that it's appropriate to restrict speech of the form "stop performing abortions or I'll shoot you in the head," virtually no one would agree that it's morally unobjectionable to restrict speech of the form "abortion is morally on a par with murder," regardless of whether the restriction was enforced by a college or by a government.[13]

This first problem with the threat-based defense of hate speech restrictions strikes me as sufficient to warrant rejecting it. The history of racism and of racial violence in this country may well make it reasonable to construe some instances of race-based hate speech as threatening that would not otherwise count as threatening. The words "go home, moron" for example, might not by themselves constitute a threat even if the words "go home, nigger" does, and the difference between the two might be traceable to facts about our nation's history. But even if this is true, it's simply implausible to insist that every instance of race-based hate speech can be construed as a threat.

Let's suppose, though, that I'm mistaken about this. Let's suppose, for example, that the words "black people are lazy" really can be reasonably construed as threatening words. Even if this is true, it will still fail to provide support for hate speech restrictions. Even without rules that prohibit hate speech, after all, there are already laws and campus policies against threatening to unjustly harm other people. If uttering the words "black people are lazy" really should be understood as being on a par with uttering the words "give me all your money or I will shoot you in the head" in this respect, then uttering the words "black people are lazy" should be understood as being covered under the rules that already exist against threatening other people. Using the fact that the words are threatening as a justification for enacting hate speech rules would be like using the fact that uttering them makes noise as a justification for enacting a rule against uttering racial epithets in a library where uttering words of any kind was already prohibited. And this points to two additional reasons for rejecting the threat-based defense of hate speech restrictions.

First, it would clearly be pointless to enact a ban on the uttering of racial epithets in a room where uttering any words is already prohibited. Since the uttering of racial epithets would already be prohibited by the ban on uttering words, the fact that uttering racial epithets makes noise would provide no reason to enact the additional policy. Second, even if the library decided to go ahead and pointlessly add a second rule banning the uttering of racial epithets in particular, it would be banning them as forms of noise, not as forms of group-based expressions of animus or hostility. But as I noted at the outset of this chapter, a hate speech restriction isn't simply a rule that happens, as an indirect consequence, to forbid hate speech. Rather, it is a rule that forbids hate speech because it is hate speech. If the library adds a ban on the utterance of racial epithets in the reading room to its already existing ban on uttering any words at all in the reading room, and it does so because uttering racial epithets makes noise, it doesn't identify anything distinctive about uttering hate speech in particular that justifies its prohibition. And so even if it did end up adopting the policy, it couldn't really be understood as enacting a hate speech restriction. Since the structure of the situation in this case is identical to the structure in the case where a ban on threats turns out to include within its scope a ban on hate speech, the same must be said in that case, too. Not only would the adoption of a second ban specifically aimed at hate speech prove to be superfluous, but it wouldn't really amount to a hate speech restriction in the first place since it would be banning certain forms of speech because they are threatening, not because they are hateful.

In the end, then, the appeal to the appropriateness of state and campus prohibitions on threatening people as a means of justifying hate speech restrictions is
impaled on the horns of a dilemma: either the appeal is unconvincing because not
all forms of hate speech are threatening, or it's unnecessary precisely because all
forms of hate speech are threatening and are therefore already prohibited. Either
way, it provides no justification for academic or legal hate speech restrictions.

THEM'S FIGHTING WORDS

A second relatively uncontroversial restriction on freedom of expression involves
so-called "fighting words". In the United States, the fighting words doctrine as a
legal doctrine arises from the 1942 Supreme Court ruling in *Chaplinsky v. New
Hampshire*. Walter Chaplinsky, one of several Jehovah's Witnesses who had
gathered in a New Hampshire town to proselytize on behalf of their religion,
became involved in a confrontation with local authorities. In the heated discussion that followed, Chaplinsky called a police officer "a God-damned racket-
eer" and "a damned Fascist." He was arrested, charged, and convicted under a
state law that made it a crime to "address any offensive, derisive or annoying
word to any other person who is lawfully in any street or other public place"
or to "call him by any offensive or derisive name."[14] The Supreme Court unani-
mously upheld Chaplinsky's conviction. Justice Frank Murphy, writing for the
Court, noted that "There are certain well-defined and narrowly limited classes
of speech, the prevention and punishment of which have never been thought
to raise any Constitutional problem," and among these, he included "the insulting or 'fighting' words." He then went on to distinguish between two kinds of
fighting words: those that "by their very utterance inflict injury," and those that
"tend to incite an immediate breach of the peace."[15] I want to set aside the first
kind of case for discussion in a later section, and will focus here on the second.
So for purposes of this section, "fighting words" refers to the kind of expression
that has the tendency to "incite an immediate breach of the peace." Understood
as a legal matter, the "fighting words" doctrine is the claim that restrictions on
speech that has this kind of tendency are Constitutional. But for the purposes of
this section, I want to focus on the moral question rather than the Constitutional
question. So for the purposes of this section, the fighting words doctrine will be
understood as the claim that such restrictions are morally unobjectionable, and
the "fighting words"-based argument for hate speech restrictions will refer to the
argument that is grounded in two claims: that it is morally unobjectionable to
restrict speech of this sort and that hate speech restrictions can be shown to be
morally unobjectionable by appealing to this fact.

I have serious reservations about the first of these two claims. One problem
with saying that it's morally unobjectionable to restrict fighting words understood in this way is that such restrictions seem to permit people to render otherwise protected expression forbidden simply by making themselves available to
be incited by it. Suppose, for example, that a group of racists is planning to hold

a picnic on a small, rarely used lawn in a large city park or a large university campus, and that they intend to say horrible things about black people while they are there. If no one else shows up at the lawn during their picnic, then their racist words won't tend to incite an immediate breach of the peace because no one present will be offended by them. But if a sufficiently large number of people who are strongly opposed to racism make a point of gathering on the lawn at just that time, then the uttering of the very same words will have such a tendency, and so will no longer count as protected speech according to the fighting words exception. Those who would be incited by the racists' expression if they were present, in other words, can effectively censor the racists by making themselves present, a troubling implication that has sometimes been referred to as the "heckler's veto."[16] It seems morally problematic to give people the right to engage in such selective censorship: imagine being forced to cancel your egalitarian picnic because a bunch of racists made a point of showing up just so that they could be incited to violence by your proclaiming the virtues of racial equality. And this provides one reason to be skeptical of the claim that it's morally unobjectionable to restrict fighting words.

A second worry about the moral claim that I'm referring to here as the fighting words doctrine concerns its implications for attributions of personal responsibility. As Law Professor Randall Kennedy has put this concern: "Rather than insisting that the target of the speech control himself, the doctrine tells the offensive speaker to shut up. This is odd and objectionable."[17] This worry, moreover, seems especially acute when the fighting words doctrine is applied to the case of race-based hate speech in particular. In the 1997 case of *In Re: Jerry L. Spivey*, for example, the North Carolina Supreme Court explicitly appealed to the *Chaplinsky* ruling in grounding its decision in the legal version of the fighting words doctrine. And in applying the legal doctrine to a case in which a man had repeatedly referred to a black man in a bar as a "nigger," it wrote that "No fact is more generally known than that a white man who calls a black man a 'nigger' within his hearing will hurt and anger the black man and often provoke him to confront the white man and retaliate."[18] But by treating the word "nigger" as having this almost hypnotic power, the fighting words doctrine in both its legal and its moral formulation seems to deprive the black man in question of the responsibility to respond peacefully, and to reinforce worrisome stereotypes about black men being innately prone to violence.

Finally, and perhaps most important, the claim that it's morally unobjectionable to prohibit speech when it has a tendency to "incite an immediate breach of the peace" has implications that on reflection, I suspect, most people on both sides of the hate speech debate would find unacceptable. Consider, for example, anti-abortion protesters who rally outside an abortion clinic and yell "baby killer" at the women and doctors who enter. Given the extremely heated nature of the abortion debate in this country and the emotional situation that most women with unwanted pregnancies already find themselves in, it's hard to deny that screaming such words in such a context would have a tendency to incite an immediate breach of the peace. But while people may disagree about the propriety and details of laws that limit how far back from the clinic the protesters must stand, virtually everyone on both sides of the hate speech debate would morally object to legal or university restrictions that forbid the protestors from using such words even if they were standing behind the designated line. And the same would presumably be true of many other forms of protest that might well incite disturbances. Tempers often flare when pro- and antiwar demonstrators meet, for example, but it's hard to believe that many people would accept as morally unobjectionable a ban on using such words as "murderer" or "traitor" in the context of such gatherings. And they would find such restrictions morally objectionable, moreover, regardless of whether the demonstrations took place in a public park or on a college campus. A city or college might have a legitimate reason to deny a permit to hold a particular demonstration on its property, but it's hard to believe that many people would find it morally unobjectionable for the city or college to grant the permit but prohibit the protestors from uttering these particular words.

A defender of hate speech restrictions, of course, might claim that there's an important difference between calling a black man a "nigger" on the one hand, and calling a woman getting an abortion a "baby killer" or a returning soldier a "murderer" on the other. The latter two cases, it might be argued, amount to the expression of social or political opinions while the former merely amounts to name calling. And so, it might be claimed, banning the use of the word "nigger" on grounds that using it involves the use of fighting words wouldn't have to entail banning the use of such terms as "baby killer" and "murderer" in the context of protests about abortion and war.

There are two problems with this response to my third concern about the fighting words doctrine. The first problem is that the point of the doctrine was supposed to be to explain how speech that should otherwise be protected can come to be unprotected in virtue of the fact that it constitutes an immediate threat to public order. If being likely to incite an imminent breach of the peace is something that can make otherwise protected speech unprotected, then it shouldn't matter that expressions like "baby killer," "murderer" and "traitor" are otherwise protected speech in virtue of the fact that they involve the expression of social or political opinions. If the doctrine of fighting words justifies banning otherwise protected words because of their tendency to incite an imminent breach of the peace, then it will justify banning these words at these protests regardless of why they would otherwise have been protected. The unprotected words "give me your money or I'll shoot you in the head" don't become protected when they are changed to "give me your money so that I can donate it to the poor or I'll shoot you in the head because I believe that wealthy capitalists like you don't have a right to so much money while other people are starving." And if threatening words don't become protected when they express social and political views, there's no reason to think that fighting words should either.

But second, and more fundamentally, it strikes me as disingenuous to allow that terms like "baby killer," "murderer," and "traitor" involve the expression of social or political opinions while denying that the same is true of the term "nigger." Calling a black person a nigger is so offensive and hurtful in the first place precisely because it involves expressing the view that black people are inferior, contemptible, and unworthy in virtue of their being black. And so if the fighting words doctrine is said not to apply in the case of words like "baby killer," "murderer" and "traitor" on the grounds that these terms express social or political opinions, then it shouldn't be applied to the case of the word "nigger" and other instances of race-based hate speech for the same reason. Either way, then, the doctrine can't justify a ban on race-based hate speech that's likely to incite others without at the same time justifying a ban on provocative political speech that's as likely to provoke the same sort of consequences. Since most people, regardless of their view of restricting race-based hate speech, will think it morally objectionable to restrict these forms of provocative political speech, this provides a third reason to be wary of the fighting words doctrine.

I've been arguing against the fighting words justification for hate speech restrictions so far by arguing against the fighting words doctrine itself. But let's now suppose that the doctrine is perfectly acceptable and that it really is morally unobjectionable for a government or school to forbid the use of words in contexts in which they would tend to incite an immediate breach of the peace. Even if this is so, the attempt to justify hate speech restrictions by appealing to this doctrine is still unsuccessful, and for the same basic reasons that turned out to undermine the threat-based argument for such restrictions. First, even if it's reasonable to construe the use of the word "nigger" as fighting words in some contexts, it's unreasonable to insist on doing so in all contexts. Even if calling a young, physically powerful black man a nigger is too likely to prompt a violent retaliation, for example, there's no reason to think that aiming the epithet at a frail, old black woman would be. And the same would be true of many other sorts of cases in which we had particular reason to think that the person being insulted would be unlikely to respond with violence: known pacifists, members of the clergy, people who had been called the word many times before without responding violently, and so on. Kennedy suggests that this feature of the fighting words doctrine provides yet another reason to object to the doctrine itself. It strikes him as problematic that the doctrine "gives more leeway to insult a nun than a prizefighter since the nun is presumably less likely to retaliate."[19] I'm inclined to agree that this is a further problem with the doctrine. Certainly it's hard to justify granting greater protection to powerful, young black men than to frail, old black women, and that's what the fighting words doctrine seems to do. But regardless of whether this limitation on its scope is an additional defect of the doctrine itself, it's clearly a reason to deny that the doctrine could be used to justify the claim that hate speech restrictions are morally unobjectionable. Since the doctrine only applies in particular contexts where the use of particular words generates a significant risk of an immediate breach of the peace, and since hate speech doesn't always take place in this context, legal and academic restrictions that forbid hate speech can't be grounded in the fighting words doctrine. A defender of hate speech restrictions might appeal to the claim that even hate speech that's unlikely to incite an immediate breach of the peace may contribute to bringing about an environment in which other people will later be more likely to incite such a breach. But, as with the parallel response in the case of the threatening words argument, this response has implications that virtually everyone on both sides of the debate would surely reject. A student's claiming that abortion is morally on a par with murder is unlikely to incite an immediate breach of the peace, but it, too, could contribute to bringing about an environment in which other people will later be more likely to incite such a breach.

Finally, even if I'm wrong in claiming that many instances of hate speech can't reasonably be construed as fighting words, the fighting words argument for hate speech restrictions must still be rejected. If it turns out that every single instance of hate speech is also an instance of fighting words, after all, then there's no reason to adopt hate speech restrictions: hate speech will already be left unprotected in virtue of the fact that it's a form of fighting words and so will already be indirectly restricted by laws and policies that restrict the utterance of fighting words. In the end, then, the appeal to the fighting words doctrine as a means of justifying hate speech restrictions is impaled on the horns of the same dilemma that undermined the threat-based argument for such restrictions: either the appeal is unconvincing or it's unnecessary. Either way, it provides no justification for adopting legal or academic hate speech restrictions.

LIBELOUS WORDS

A third kind of case in which restrictions on freedom of expression have traditionally been accepted involves libel. Virtually everyone, no matter how firm their commitment to freedom of speech in general and regardless of their views of hate speech restrictions in particular, agrees that it's morally unobjectionable for the state to restrict or prohibit speech when it's libelous. Libel is standardly understood as a form of speech that harmfully defames a particular individual,[20] but if it's reasonable to restrict libel against individuals, it may well seem reasonable to restrict libel against groups of individuals as well. And since it may also seem reasonable to think of hate speech as a kind of libel against groups of individuals, it may well seem that the uncontroversial case of restricting libelous speech can provide a firm foundation for justifying the claim that restrictions on expression are morally unobjectionable in the controversial case of hate speech. The attempt to justify hate speech restrictions by understanding hate speech as a form of group libel isn't a particularly popular one in the contemporary legal literature on the subject. But it did enjoy favor for a brief period in the middle of the last century and it's been at least tentatively endorsed by a few formidable thinkers since then, including the distinguished law professor Catherine A. MacKinnon.[21] It therefore merits consideration as a further argument.[22]

In the 1952 case of *Beauharnais v. Illinois*, the United States Supreme Court considered a challenge to a 1917 Illinois law that made it a crime for anyone "to manufacture, sell, or offer for sale, advertise or publish, present or exhibit in any public place ... [anything that] portrays depravity, criminality, unchastity, or lack of virtue of a class of citizens, of any race, color, creed or religion," where doing so would expose "the citizen of any race, color, creed, or religion to contempt, derision, or obloquy or which is productive of breach of the peace or riots."[23] The latter part of the second clause points to part of the fighting words justification for restricting speech discussed in the previous section, but in his majority opinion in the narrow 5–4 decision to uphold the Illinois law, Justice Felix Frankfurter made it clear that it was the concept of group libel that carried the day. Frankfurter noted that in the *Chaplinsky* case, Justice Murphy had included libel in the set of "certain well-defined and narrowly limited classes of speech" that were not protected by the First Amendment. And he argued that the Illinois law at issue simply took the traditional law of libel and extended it from individuals to "designated collectivities" in a manner that was reasonable and appropriate.[24]

The Illinois statute amounted, in effect, to a very early form of hate speech law. And the legal doctrine maintaining that laws restricting libelous speech are not unconstitutional seems to have an equally plausible parallel in the moral doctrine that laws restricting libelous speech are not morally objectionable. So if Frankfurter's reasoning in defense of the claim that the Illinois law is constitutional is accepted, it would seem to provide a model for defending the claim that at least some modern-day hate speech restrictions are morally unobjectionable. As it turns out, the reign of the group libel approach as a legal doctrine in America was short-lived and without influence. The *Beauharnais* decision itself was not well received, the most prominent advocates of the idea of group libel soon repudiated it, the Court's minority position eventually developed into its majority position and by 1961, the state of Illinois repealed the 1917 law that had prompted the original case.[25] Still, since there does seem to be some surface appeal to a moral version of the group libel argument for hate speech restrictions, and since the group libel approach in general has had some important and accomplished defenders, it's worth stepping back for a moment to consider the merits of the position itself.[26]

The best way to examine the merits of the group libel case for hate speech restrictions is to start with a clear, uncontroversial case in which restricting libel at the individual level is morally unobjectionable and then to consider what would be involved in extending such libel law to the case of groups like racial minorities. So suppose that you own and manage a small restaurant and I write and publish a review of it in the local paper in which I deliberately fabricate the charge that you've been using dog meat in your hamburgers. A public outcry erupts, followed by a well-organized boycott, and you lose thousands of dollars in revenue. In this case, virtually everyone, regardless of their view of hate speech restrictions, will agree that it's morally unobjectionable for the state to permit you to sue me for libel, and to collect damages from me to compensate for the income my libelous review caused you to lose. But, a defender of the group libel approach might then say, if it's morally unobjectionable to permit you to sue me for libel under such circumstances, then it must also be morally unobjectionable to permit a corporation to sue me under similar circumstances. If I deliberately fabricate and publish the charge that McDonald's routinely uses dog meat in its hamburgers, for example, then morally speaking, the McDonald's Corporation should be permitted to sue me for libel and to collect damages for the very same reasons. The McDonald's Corporation is group of people rather than a single individual. If it can be morally unobjectionable for me to be sued for libeling McDonald's, then, it can be morally unobjectionable for me to be sued for libeling a group of people and not just for libeling an individual. A race, like a corporation, is also a group of people. And so, on this account, it can be morally unobjectionable for me to be sued for libeling a race as well. Race-based hate speech, in effect, amounts to libel against a race. And so, the argument concludes, it can be morally unobjectionable for the state to sanction those who use hate speech in the same way, and for the same reason, that it's morally unobjectionable to sanction those who use libelous speech against individuals. This, at its core, is the group libel argument for the moral acceptability of hate speech restrictions.

The group libel argument for hate speech restrictions rests on two claims: the claim that the content of the expression in a typical case of hate speech is relevantly similar to the content of the expression in a typical case of libelous speech, and the claim that the subject of the expression in a typical case of hate speech is relevantly similar to the subject of the expression in a typical case of libelous speech. If both of these claims can be sustained, then it may well prove reasonable, as Justice Frankfurter took it to be, to move from the uncontroversial case of restricting libelous speech to the controversial case of restricting hate speech. And this may well prove reasonable not only as a means of using the constitutional acceptability of libel laws to show that hate speech laws are constitutional, but as a means of making the move that I want to focus on in this section: from the claim that libel laws are morally unobjectionable to the conclusion that hate speech restrictions are morally unobjectionable. In the end, though, both of the claims needed to sustain the argument should be rejected, and on grounds that virtually everyone on both sides of the hate speech debate already accepts.

The principal problem with the first claim made by the group libel argument arises from the fact that there are important differences between the content of the statements involved in clear, uncontroversial cases of libel and the content of the utterances involved in clear, paradigmatic cases of hate speech. The main difference is that libel cases involve assertions about factual matters while hate speech typically involves assertions of opinions or feelings or the uttering of epithets that are not really assertions about anything at all.[27] If I say that you're using dog meat in your restaurant's hamburgers, I'm making a factual claim that is either true or false. But if a bigot tells a black person to "go back to Africa" or that he hates black people, or if he utters the words "damn nigger" at him, the bigot isn't making a factual statement that is either true or false because he's not making a factual assertion at all.[28] This difference between libelous speech and hate speech is crucial because in order for a statement to be libelous it must be false. Publishing the claim that you're using dog meat in your restaurant's hamburgers, for example, can be libelous. But publishing the statement that you should shut your restaurant down or that I hate your restaurant or uttering the words "damn carnivore" at you can't be libelous. Nor does the claim that it's morally unobjectionable for the state to permit you to sue when I falsely state that you're using dog meat in your hamburgers provide support for the claim that it would also be morally unobjectionable for the state to permit you to sue when I state that you should shut your restaurant down or that I hate your restaurant or when I utter the words "damn carnivore" at you. Most forms of hate speech consist of utterances such as these that are neither true nor false. And so most of the forms of hate speech that proponents of hate speech restrictions seek to restrict can't be covered by an argument for hate speech restrictions that appeals to the uncontroversial case of libel.

This first problem with the first claim made by the group libel argument arises for most forms of hate speech. But it doesn't arise for all of them. Some forms of hate speech, after all, do seem to involve factual assertions. And in these cases, at least, it might seem that the group libel approach could justify the sort of restrictions that proponents of hate speech restrictions seek to justify. Even in the case of hate speech that seems to involve making factual assertions, though, there are often important differences between the assertions in question and the kinds of assertions that are involved in clear, uncontroversial cases of libel. Many of the most conspicuous forms of hate speech, for example, arise from some sort of religious convictions. The claim that "God hates fags," for example, makes an assertion that something is true, as do the claims that the Bible endorses white supremacy and that white people with black spouses will burn in hell. But while these statements do make factual assertions, they are fundamentally different from the sorts of factual assertions that are involved in uncontroversial cases of libel. If I were to publish a review of your restaurant maintaining that God hates meat eaters, for example, that the Bible endorses vegetarianism, or that your restaurant's customers will burn in hell, virtually no one would think it morally acceptable for the state to get involved. Having the state determine that certain claims about the content of your hamburger meat are false is one thing. Having it determine that certain claims about the content of God's commands are false is quite another.

And even in the case of hate speech that seems to make factual assertions about the natural world, the objectionable expressions are often so vague or subjective that it's difficult to say in the end just what, precisely, would render them true or false. If a bigot declares that "black people are lazy" or that "black people don't respect the law," for example, it isn't clear what, exactly, is meant and so it isn't clear what, exactly, would have to be established to show that the statements were false. How do we measure laziness? How lazy do people have to be to count as lazy? Is the statement meant to be true of all black people, or just a significant proportion of them? If the latter, how significant? And so on. Such statements, which are representative of the type of expression that advocates of hate speech restrictions typically seek to suppress, are more like my writing that your waitresses are rude and unfriendly than like my writing that your hamburgers contain dog meat. Again, having the state determine whether or not your hamburgers contain dog meat is one thing. Having it determine whether or not your waitresses are rude or unfriendly is quite another. So even in many of the cases of hate speech that do seem to involve the assertion of factual claims, the differences between hate speech and libelous speech will prove more important than their similarities.

None of this is to insist that there can never be hate speech whose content is relevantly similar to the content of libelous speech. The claim made by Herrnstein and Murray in *The Bell Curve* that the IQ of black people is, on average, approximately 15 points lower than that of white people and that there is a substantial genetic component to the explanation for this gap, for example, makes an assertion that might well be clear and specific enough to be factual and testable. So statements of this sort might plausibly be included in the range of cases covered by a group libel approach to hate speech restrictions. But once we find ourselves limited to such cases, several additional problems arise for the defender of the group libel argument.

In the first place, the sort of restrictions that the argument will be able to produce will now turn out to be precisely the opposite of those that most advocates of hate speech restrictions seek to justify. Most advocates of such restrictions, for example, want to restrict such utterances as "I hate black people" or "damn nigger" but don't want to ban books like *The Bell Curve* from public or university libraries. But once we take note of the essential role that contested factual assertions play in uncontroversial cases of libel, we can see that the group libel argument would potentially justify taking action against people for writing books like *The Bell Curve*, since it does make such assertions, but could not be used to justify taking action against people for making such utterances as "I hate black people" or "damn nigger," since they don't. Second, the kind of factual assertions that are specific and empirical enough to be potentially defamatory to a race of people are typically more complex and contestable than those involved in clear cases of libel. Determining whether or not there's dog meat in your restaurant's hamburgers, for example, is a considerably simpler task than determining whether or not there are group differences in intelligence and whether or not, if there are, genetic differences play a significant role in accounting for them.

Finally, and perhaps most important, being false isn't enough to make a statement libelous. In addition, the statement must be made knowing that it's false or at least with a reckless disregard for its truth. If I write that your restaurant's hamburgers contain dog meat and I know this to be false or take no real care to confirm its truth, then I can be sued for libel. But if I write this only after undertaking a reasonably thorough investigation, then even if the conclusion I reach turns out to be mistaken, I can't be sued for libel as a result of my honest mistake. The range of cases to which the group libel approach might legitimately be made to apply, then becomes smaller still. Even if claims made in such books as *The Bell Curve* turn out to be false, after all, it would be hard to establish that the authors knew they were false or made the claims with a reckless indifference to the truth.

Before moving on to consider the group libel argument's second claim, it's worth briefly mentioning a few final concerns about its first claim. First, in order for a defamatory statement to be libelous, it must be made publicly. If I publish my scurrilous charge about your hamburgers in the local newspaper, I may be sued for libel. But if I happen to see you walking down the street and tell you that your hamburgers taste so awful that I've concluded they must be made from dog meat, I can't. No matter how distressing you may find our one-on-one encounter, my statement can't be libelous if it's addressed only to you. Yet many of the most important kinds of cases that proponents of hate speech restrictions are concerned with are precisely those in which a person aims a racial epithet directly at another individual. Indeed, the Stanford policy, which is often cited as one of the most narrowly focused and defensible examples of a campus hate speech code, focuses exclusively on this kind of case. Since these sorts of cases don't involve the public dissemination of a defamatory statement, they can't be covered by the group libel argument even if the other difficulties with the argument's first claim can be overcome.

Second, even if I publicly proclaim that your hamburgers contain dog meat, you can't sue me for libel unless you can demonstrate that you've suffered some monetary harm. If you don't lose any customers as a result of my review, for example, then even if what I said was false and I knew it was false, you'd be unable to collect any damages from me even if my words hurt your feelings. This additional feature of libel law points to yet another respect in which uncontroversial libel cases differ even from many of those instances of hate speech that do involve factual assertions. If a bigoted student publishes a piece in the campus newspaper in which he maintains that the leader of a black student group plagiarized a term paper, for example, then even if this allegation proves to be demonstrably false and the writer was indisputably reckless with the facts, the student group leader still can't sue the bigoted author for libel unless he can demonstrate that he has suffered some kind of monetary loss as a result of the publication. But in the vast majority of the cases that proponents of hate speech restrictions are concerned with, there's no particular reason to think that the person who uttered the hateful speech has caused the subject of his utterance any monetary losses. And so, once again, the attempt to move from uncontroversial cases of libel to typical cases of hate speech proves to be unsuccessful.

In the end, then, very few instances of hate speech prove to be relevantly similar in content to the sorts of clear, uncontroversial examples of libel that are needed to ground the group libel argument in cases about which people on both sides of the hate speech restrictions debate generally agree. In order for an instance of hate speech to prove suitable for such an argument, it must involve a public assertion of an empirically false claim, the person asserting it must know it to be false or be recklessly indifferent to whether it's false, and its public assertion must cause someone a monetary loss sufficient to grant them standing to sue the person for asserting it. Relatively few instances of hate speech are like this. And so relatively few instances of hate speech could be covered by the group libel argument's first claim. In those cases in which hate speech doesn't have all of these features, the argument will provide no justification for imposing restrictions on it. And in those relatively rare cases in which an instance of hate speech does prove to have all of these features, the argument will provide no justification for imposing restrictions beyond those that already exist. The law already permits a person to be sued if his speech is genuinely libelous, after all, and so in those cases there will be no justification for introducing an additional hate speech restriction. As far as the first claim made by the group libel argument is concerned, then, hate speech restrictions again turn out to be either unjustified or unnecessary.

The first claim needed to sustain the group libel argument for hate speech restrictions maintains that the content of hate speech is relevantly similar to the content of libelous speech. Although this claim has some initial surface appeal, I've argued that it's false in the vast majority of cases, and that the relatively few cases to which it might apply can be handled without recourse to adopting hate speech restrictions. But let's now suppose that I've been mistaken about this. Let's suppose that the content of typical hate speech utterances like "I hate black people" and "damn nigger" really is sufficiently similar to the content of uncontroversially libelous statements like "your restaurant uses dog meat in its hamburgers." Even if this is true, the group libel argument is still unsuccessful. This is because the argument also requires a second claim, the claim that the subject being defamed in typical cases of hate speech is relevantly similar to the subjects that are defamed in uncontroversial cases of libel. And this claim, too, turns out to be objectionable on terms that people on both sides of the hate speech debate are already committed to.

To see what the problem with the argument's second claim is, it may help to begin by asking why you are an appropriate subject to be protected from my libelous statements in the first place. The answer to this question is straightforward: you are an individual whose welfare is affected by your public reputation, and when your welfare is unjustly damaged by others, you are entitled to seek compensation as a result. This answer suggests that part of what makes you a suitable subject of libel is that you are an individual with your own welfare, and this in turn suggests a simple rebuttal to the second claim made by the group libel argument: a person who is defamed by a libelous statement is an individual with his or her own welfare, but a race that's defamed by hate speech is not an individual with its own welfare. Since a race is not an individual in this sense, and since being an individual in this sense is relevant to being a suitable candidate for protection from libel, the second claim made by the group libel argument must be rejected. From the fact that it's appropriate to protect individuals like you or me from libelous speech, it doesn't follow that it would be appropriate to protect races from hate speech, even if it turned out that the content of hate speech was relevantly similar to the content of libelous speech.

This simple rebuttal is too simple. As I noted at the outset of this discussion, if it's morally unobjectionable for the state to permit you to sue me when I publish false claims about your restaurant's hamburger meat, then it seems just as morally unobjectionable for the state to permit a corporation like McDonald's to sue me under similar circumstances. But McDonald's isn't an individual like you or me, either. It's a collection of such individuals. The case of corporations, then, seems to establish that you don't have to be an individual in order to be a suitable subject for a morally unobjectionable libel claim. And if the fact that a corporation isn't an individual doesn't rule it out as a suitable subject for a libel claim, then the fact that a race isn't an individual doesn't rule it out as a suitable subject for a libel claim, either. The second claim needed to sustain the group libel argument for hate speech restrictions, then, seems to be back on track.

There's something to this response. A corporation isn't an individual; it's a collection of individuals. But while there's therefore something to this response, there's not enough. A corporation is a collection of individuals, but it isn't just any old collection of individuals. A corporation is a very specific kind of collection of individuals. And once we get clear about the conditions that make a collection of individuals a corporation, it becomes clear that the reasons for thinking that it's appropriate to permit corporations to sue for libel don't carry over to the case of hate speech directed against specific races.

A corporation is a group of individuals who have elected to associate themselves with a joint enterprise through a voluntary action like signing a contract of employment, accepting a position on the board of directors, or purchasing a share of stock. Typically, choosing to become a part of a corporation in one of these ways involves agreeing to abide by an explicit set of rules that includes, among other things, specific job descriptions, procedures for electing members of the board of directors, conditions for the reselling of stock, and so on. As a result of their freely chosen consent, the people who constitute a corporation have bound themselves to the corporation's fate in various ways and have agreed to participate, in one way or another, in its common endeavor. This is the reason that it makes sense, from a legal and moral point of view, to think of a corporation as a kind of artificial person and to treat it that way. A corporation, for example, can break the law. It can make a generous donation to the local community. It can develop a new treatment for depression. It can acquire another company or agree to be acquired by one. It can sue a distributor for failing to live up to its contractual obligations. It can be sued by a customer for selling a defective product. And so on. A corporation can perform and be subject to these particular kinds of actions not because every single individual who is a part of it causes them to occur or is subject to them, but rather because the individuals who together constitute it have agreed to a set of rules and principles that enable them to coordinate their behavior in a unified manner. If McDonald's announces that it's donating a million dollars to a children's charity, for example, this doesn't mean that every single person associated with McDonald's decided to chip in some money. It means that the relevant governing body that represents all of those people decided to spend some of the assets that it controls on their behalf in this manner. If you successfully sue a large corporation for selling you a defective product, to take another kind of case, it may be that only a handful of the people who work for the company were actually involved in the design and production of that particular item. Still, you wouldn't sue those particular people as private individuals. You would sue the company itself. And it isn't those particular people who would be ordered to pay you damages. The money would come from the assets of the corporation as a whole. All of the people who have voluntarily associated themselves with the corporation's common enterprise would bear the cost of the corporation's mistake, and not just the particular people who designed and produced the defective product, because their voluntary association with the corporation renders all of them responsible in this sense for the corporation's behavior. This is why corporations can have rights and responsibilities. This is why they can sue and be sued. And this is why, in particular, they can sue for libel.

With this understanding of why a corporation is the kind of group that's capable of being libeled, we can now see the problem with the second claim needed to sustain the group libel argument for the moral acceptability of hate speech restrictions. That claim maintains that the subject of hate speech, such as a race, is relevantly similar to the subject of libelous speech, such as a corporation. But to ask whether a race of people is relevantly similar to a corporation, we can now see, is to ask whether a race of people has the sorts of features that render a corporation the kind of body that can properly be taken to be the subject of libel. And once we see that this is the question, we can see that the answer is no. The race of black people, for example, is not a group of people who have voluntarily agreed to join together in a common endeavor. They have no official representatives, job descriptions, or board of directors. They do not act as one. If a number of black Americans make a generous donation to a children's fund, we don't praise black America; we praise the particular black Americans who contributed to the fund. If you're wrongfully harmed by a small number of black Americans, you don't sue black America; you sue those particular black Americans as individuals. You can libel individual black Americans, then, but you can't libel black America or the black race.

The content of most hate speech is relevantly different from the content of libelous speech. Most hate speech doesn't involve the deliberate or reckless assertion of false and harmful empirical claims. But even in those cases in which the content of hate speech does seem to be suitably similar to the content of libelous speech, the group libel argument still breaks down because a race is relevantly different from a person or a corporation. In the end, then, the group libel argument for hate speech restrictions merits the fate that history has assigned to it: an intriguing idea that deserved a fair hearing, but that doesn't deserve to be endorsed.

OBJECTION FOUR: HARASSMENT WITH WORDS

A fourth kind of case in which restrictions on of freedom of expression have
come to be widely accepted in recent years involves sexual harassment. Title
VII of the 1964 Civil Rights Act reads in part as follows: "It shall be an unlawful
employment practice for an employer ... to fail or refuse to hire or to discharge
any individual, or otherwise to discriminate against any individual with respect
to his compensation, terms, conditions, or privileges of employment, because of
such individual's race, color, religion, sex, or national origin." Although the statute itself doesn't use the term "harassment," a series of important court decisions
have held that, as a legal matter, the terms of Title VII can be violated by a sexually hostile work environment, at least in cases where the environment, in effect,
discriminates against some employees with respect to the conditions of their
employment because of their sex. In the 1982 case of *Henson v. City of Dundee*,
for example, the Eleventh Circuit ruled that Title VII protects women from a
sexually hostile work environment, and it spelled out the conditions required for
such a violation to take place. In order to establish a successful sexual harassment claim as a legal matter, the Court ruled, the harassment in question "must
be sufficiently pervasive so as to alter the conditions of employment and create
an abusive working environment," where "abusive" means that the harassment is
severe and persistent enough to "affect seriously the psychological well-being of
the employees."[29] And a few years later, in the 1986 case of *Meritor v. Vinson*, the
U.S. Supreme Court affirmed the claim that sexually hostile work environments
are prohibited by Title VII. While many of the cases in which the hostile workplace doctrine was developed involved physical as well as verbal abuse, moreover, the Supreme Court's decision made it clear that purely verbal behavior
could be enough by itself to trigger a legally valid Title VII claim.[30] As a legal
matter, then, sexual harassment in the workplace provides a further example in
which many people now agree that it's acceptable to restrict people's freedom of
expression. For the purposes of this section, I will assume that such restrictions
are morally unobjectionable.

Since Title VII refers to race as well as sex, it's natural to wonder whether the
claim that laws against sexual harassment in the workplace are morally unobjectionable could be used as a foundation for justifying the claim that race-based
hate speech restrictions are morally unobjectionable as well. And since a university environment may well seem sufficiently similar to a workplace environment,
it seems natural to suppose that such restrictions could be justified at least as a
matter of campus policy, even if not as a matter of law governing people's interactions throughout society.[31]

But there's a problem with the attempt to use currently accepted sexual harassment doctrine to justify hate speech restrictions in this way. The problem
arises from the fact that the part of currently accepted sexual harassment law
that deals with hostile workplace complaints specifically requires the harassment
to be pervasive and persistent while hate speech restrictions apply to individual

instances of abusive speech. This important limitation on the scope of sexual harassment claims, moreover, has been clear since the 1971 Fifth Circuit case of *Rogers v. EEOC*. And, indeed, in the paragraph cited earlier from the Eleventh Circuit's more recent *Henson* decision, the court explicitly notes this very fact. In the sentence just before its affirmation that the harassment in question must be "sufficiently pervasive" to create an "abusive" environment, the *Henson* court wrote that "The court in *Rogers* made it clear ... that the 'mere utterance of an ethnic or racial epithet which engenders offensive feelings in an employee' does not affect the terms, conditions, or privileges of employment to a sufficiently significant degree to violate Title VII."[32] When sexual harassment law applies to sexist speech, in short, it applies to patterns of such speech that are extensive and pervasive enough to create serious harms. When hate speech restrictions apply to hate speech, on the other hand, they apply to it in each of its specific instances.

This difference between sexual harassment law as it is currently accepted and hate speech restrictions as proponents of those restrictions would like to see them adopted undermines the attempt to justify the acceptability of the latter by appealing to the acceptability of the former. It does so because the appropriateness of prohibiting a certain pattern of behavior isn't enough to justify the appropriateness of prohibiting individual instances of such behavior. Consider, for example, the case of stalking. The legal definition of stalking varies somewhat from state to state but what stalking laws tend to have in common is that they prohibit some forms of behavior only when they are done repeatedly. If on a single occasion you leave a flower on your neighbor's doorstep, for example, or call her and tell her that you like her, or stand on the sidewalk outside of her house for a few minutes, or send her an admiring letter or postcard or e-mail, it's unlikely that you will have broken any laws. If you do this every day, though, it's likely that at some point you will have. This feature of the laws regarding stalking strikes most people, regardless of what they think of hate speech restrictions, as perfectly reasonable. Persistent repetition of legally acceptable behavior can have cumulative consequences that justify rendering their persistent repetition legally unacceptable. This is the logic underlying laws regarding stalking and the widely accepted laws regarding sexual harassment in the workplace. And this is the reason that the laws regarding sexual harassment as they are currently accepted fail to provide support for restrictions regarding hate speech. Just as the acceptability of a law that prohibits repeatedly leaving a flower on your neighbor's doorstep doesn't entail the acceptability of a law that prohibits leaving her a flower on a single, isolated occasion, the acceptability of a law that prohibits the pervasive and persistent use of certain forms of speech in the workplace doesn't entail the acceptability of a policy that prohibits each particular instance of using such speech. The claim that sexual harassment law as it's currently understood is morally unobjectionable, then, fails to provide a way to justify the claim that legal or academic hate speech restrictions would be morally unobjectionable too.

A defender of hate speech restrictions might respond to this problem with the argument based on sexual harassment law in one of two ways. One would be to concede that sexual harassment law as currently interpreted by the courts is limited in precisely the way that I've said it is, but to insist that morally speaking, this is a mistake. As it now stands, for example, the law might justify taking action against a worker who talks during every coffee break about how much he likes pornography and who does so within the hearing distance of the women who work in the office. But it would not justify taking action against such a worker for doing this a single time, or for doing it infrequently over a period of several years. A defender of hate speech restrictions might acknowledge that this is in fact how the law currently operates, but maintain that morally speaking the law should step in and sanction the worker after a single infraction. This would help to make the argument based on sexual harassment law apply to the kinds of cases that proponents of hate speech restrictions generally have in mind when they attempt to justify the moral acceptability of such restrictions.

The problem with this response, though, is that the resulting argument for hate speech restrictions would no longer be grounded in a widely accepted assumption. The assumption that it's morally unobjectionable for the law to intervene in cases involving patterns of expression that are persistent and perva- sive enough to generate a hostile work environment is relatively uncontroversial. The assumption that it's morally unobjectionable for the law to intervene every time someone makes a sexist comment in a work place is not. A defender of hate speech restrictions, of course, could attempt to give an argument for this much stronger claim. But in the absence of such an argument, this response must be deemed unsuccessful.

The other way that a defender of hate speech restrictions might respond to the problem I've identified here would be to bite the bullet and simply concede that such restrictions are justified only when they apply to patterns of hateful expression that are persistent and pervasive enough to generate a hostile envi- ronment. A campus hate speech policy of this sort, for example, wouldn't punish a student for an isolated incident in which he directed a racial epithet at a black student, but it might render the student subject to punishment if he persisted in harassing his victim, or other black students on campus, for a sufficiently long period of time. In this way, a defender of hate speech restrictions might attempt to salvage his ability to rest his position on the presumed acceptability of con- temporary sexual harassment law by narrowing the scope of the restrictions he attempts to defend.

But there are two problems with this response to the difficulty posed by the difference between sexual harassment law and hate speech restrictions. The first problem is that if the proposed restrictions are limited in this manner, they no longer really qualify as hate speech restrictions. A prohibition on stalking that forbids you from sending your neighbor an admiring letter every day isn't a prohibition on writing admiring letters, after all. It's a prohibition on stalking. Similarly, a campus policy that forbids a student from aiming a racial epithet at a black student who lives in his dorm every day isn't a prohibition on using racial epithets. It's a prohibition on harassment. The antistalking law, that is, kicks in when sending an admiring letter to someone becomes more than just sending them an admiring letter, and the proposed campus policy kicks in when aiming a racial epithet at someone becomes more than just aiming a racial epithet at them. But the whole point of hate speech restrictions in the first place was supposed to be that aiming a racial epithet at someone was already, in and of itself, something that merited prohibition in a way that sending an admiring letter to someone is not. A defender of hate speech restrictions, then, can't rest his case on an appeal to the appropriateness of prohibiting harassment, sexual or otherwise.

The second problem with restricting the scope of hate speech restrictions to cases in which the hate speech amounts to harassment is that it renders the restrictions unnecessary. States and universities, after all, already have policies that prohibit harassment, and so if the claim is that hate speech should be prohibited but only in cases where it amounts to harassment, then such hate speech has already been prohibited. A person who repeatedly insults someone by aiming racial epithets at them, therefore, would already be covered by existing laws and policies forbidding harassment.[33] In the end, then, the attempt to justify hate speech restrictions by appealing to the widely accepted laws governing sexual harassment runs into the same kind of problem that undermines the other attempts to ground a new kind of restriction on freedom of expression in an already existing doctrine about the limits of such expression: either the appeal to existing law is unconvincing or it's unnecessary. Either way, it provides no reason to adopt hate speech restrictions.

There are, of course, a number of other kinds of restrictions on freedom of expression that are by and large accepted as morally unobjectionable. There are laws prohibiting the publication of works that would violate copyrights, academic rules against plagiarism, restrictions on the dissemination of military secrets, ordinances governing the place, time and volume at which people are permitted to make noise, and so on. But none of these seem relevantly similar to restrictions on hate speech, and so none of them seem capable of providing a plausible basis for justifying the claims that such restrictions are morally unobjectionable either.[34] In the end, then, the attempt to justify the claim that legal or academic hate speech restrictions are morally unobjectionable by grounding them in some other kind of restriction on freedom of expression that most people on both sides of the hate speech debate already accept as morally unobjectionable proves to be unsuccessful. If there is to be a satisfactory defense of the moral acceptability of hate speech restrictions, it will have to rest on an argument that tries to carve out a new and previously unrecognized category of speech that may legitimately be restricted. It is to the subject of this second kind of argument in defense of hate speech restrictions that I will turn in the next chapter.

7

Why I Still Hate Hate Speech Restrictions

New and Improved Exceptions to Freedom of Expression and Why They Fail, Too

One way to try to justify hate speech restrictions is to argue from categories of expression that most people already accept as legitimate subjects of constraint. I argued in Chapter 6 that such arguments are unsuccessful. The kinds of cases in which most people agree that it's morally unobjectionable to restrict people's freedom of expression can't be used to show that hate speech restrictions are morally unobjectionable. The lesson I'm inclined to draw from this analysis is: so much the worse for hate speech restrictions. But a defender of hate speech restrictions might instead draw a very different lesson: so much the worse for the traditional limits on legitimately restricting freedom of expression. Rather than trying to justify hate speech restrictions by appealing to an already existing category of unprotected speech, that is, supporters of such restrictions might instead try to justify them by carving out a new category of speech that may unobjectionably be restricted and by showing that hate speech belongs in this new category. And, in fact, three of the most prominent and potentially powerful arguments for restricting hate speech in the contemporary literature have precisely this structure. I want to conclude my discussion of hate speech restrictions in this chapter, then, by considering these three arguments in turn and by explaining why they, too, strike me as unsuccessful.

WORDS THAT WOUND

One argument of this sort appeals to the simple claim that hate speech hurts. In one sense, this isn't really a new argument. As I noted in the previous chapter in the section on the "fighting words" doctrine, the opinion that Justice Murphy wrote for the United States Supreme Court in the 1942 *Chaplinsky* case included as a class of unprotected speech words that "by their very utterance inflict injury." But as time went by, the Supreme Court came to ignore this element of the *Chaplinsky* ruling, and even though it was never officially overturned, it eventually became obsolete. A 1991 Supreme Court decision striking down a University of Wisconsin hate speech code as unconstitutional, for example, referred to this part of *Chaplinsky* as "defunct."[1] In this sense, endorsing hate speech restrictions now on the grounds that hate speech hurts is a case of something old being new all over again.

And, in fact, a number of important writers have recently pressed just this case. Law Professor Charles Lawrence, for example, has referred to the use of the word "nigger" and other racial epithets as an "assaultive" act and "a form of violence by speech."[2] Law Professor Richard Delgado argues that hate speech is "like a slap in the face" while writer Anthony Cortese compares it to "a breathtaking punch to the stomach, a quick stiff jab to the nose, or a forcible slap in the face."[3] Delgado refers to such language as "words that wound,"[4] and Lawrence, Delgado, and others have come to refer to it as "assaultive speech."[5] Each of these writers, and a number of others as well, have argued that hate speech restrictions can be justified because hate speech causes not merely offense, but injury.[6]

Part of the justification for this claim rests on simple empathetic identification with those who are on the receiving end of hate speech. A black person who is called a "nigger" or who is told that "black people are stupid" or that "black people should go back to Africa," on this account, does not experience the words as a simple conveyance of information, upsetting as the information may be. Rather, the words are experienced in the same way that a slap in the face is experienced – as a sharp, unexpected, unmediated pain. In addition, some defenders of this approach have attempted to back their position up by citing empirical studies indicating that hate speech does, in fact, cause a variety of harmful consequences for those who find themselves on the receiving end of it, including feelings of humiliation, isolation, self-hatred, mental illness, heightened blood pressure, hypertension, rapid pulse rate, difficulty breathing, nightmares, even psychosis and suicide, as well as financial harms that result from quitting school or performing poorly in academic or professional settings.[7] While the claim that hate speech should be banned because it harms the people it targets had fallen out of favor for quite some time as a legal doctrine, then, it has now become one of the most important parts of the contemporary case for hate speech restrictions.

Like the arguments discussed in the previous chapter, the harm-based argument for hate speech restrictions can be rendered in moral rather than constitutional terms as a simple two-step argument: one step identifies a category of speech and claims that it's morally unobjectionable to restrict speech that falls into this category and a second step claims that hate speech falls into this category. Unlike those other arguments, though, the harm-based argument's first step involves putting forward a new category of unprotected speech, a category defined in terms of the harm it causes to those who are exposed to it. And this, in the end, is why the argument should be rejected.

The problem with the introduction of an unprotected category of words that wound is that it would leave unprotected too many forms of expression that virtually everyone on both sides of the hate speech debate believes should remain protected. As noted in the context of my discussion of the fighting words doctrine in Chapter 6, for example, most people on both sides of the hate speech debate agree that anti-abortion protesters should be allowed to yell "baby killer" at women and workers entering an abortion clinic, and that pro- and anti-war protesters should be permitted to use such words as "traitor" or "murderer" when they engage each other at rallies. They agree, moreover, that it would be morally objectionable to restrict the people in question from using such words at protest rallies regardless of whether they take place in public parks or on college campuses. But these, too, are hurtful words, and it's hard to deny that they, too, have the ability to cause pain to those they are aimed at, to be experienced as a sharp slap in the face, just as hateful epithets do.[8] People with strong religious convictions, moreover, are often led to say things that are hurtful to those who don't share their views. Virtually no one thinks that a theist should be prevented from calling someone he disagrees with a "heretic" or a "traitor" to his religion, whether in a public park or on a campus quad, but, again, it's hard to deny that such words can be extremely painful to hear. In the context of personal and family relationships, moreover, people often say things that are tremendously hurtful without anyone thinking that their words could therefore permissibly be restricted. A student who tells his brother that he hates him and never wants to see him again surely causes him a tremendous amount of pain. But he just as surely has the right to tell him this, whether they're talking on the telephone, on a city street, or in a campus dorm. In the end, then, the claim that it's morally unobjectionable to restrict words that wound is too implausible to underwrite a defense of legal or campus hate speech restrictions.

There's a reason, moreover, that the category of words that wound generates so many powerful counterexamples to the harm-based argument. The reason is that virtually everyone agrees that, as a general matter, forms of behavior that it would be objectionable to prevent people from engaging in don't become behavior that it would be unobjectionable to prevent people from engaging in simply because the people in question engage in them in ways that will cause these kinds of harm to others. Virtually everyone, for example, would agree that competent adults should be permitted to have consensual sexual relationships with other competent adults as they choose. Even those who object very strongly to sexual promiscuity as a moral or theological matter rarely think that secular authorities should get involved in restricting it. But a man who cheats on his girlfriend surely causes her a tremendous amount of grief, and the claim that she will experience his cheating like a sharp slap in the face seems just as reasonable as the claim that someone on the receiving end of race-based hate speech will do so. Since virtually everyone agrees that it would be morally objectionable for the legal or academic authorities to restrict the man's freedom to cheat on his girlfriend,[9] virtually everyone agrees that this protected form of behavior doesn't become unprotected simply because it's done in ways that will cause great distress to some people. If a state or college permits adults to engage in consensual sexual behavior within its borders, that is, it would be objectionable for it to forbid such behavior in some cases on the grounds that the behavior in those instances would cause distress to other people.

And the same is true of many other forms of behavior. If people should be free to move from Florida to Alaska, for example, then a man should be free to do so even if doing so will leave his girlfriend distraught. If people should be free to practice whatever religion they choose, then Jews should be free to convert to Christianity and Christians should be free to convert to Judaism, even if doing so will cause tremendous anguish to the families involved. If a state permits its citizens to work as topless dancers and a college permits its students to do so as well, then neither should prevent a particular woman from doing so simply because it will break her parents' hearts. In all of these cases, virtually everyone on both sides of the hate speech debate will agree that the right to behave in a certain way doesn't disappear simply because exercising the right will cause significant mental pain to others. But virtually everyone on both sides of the debate will also agree that the right to freedom of expression is at least as fundamental and important as these other rights. The fact that the reasoning underlying the harm-based argument is clearly unacceptable in the case of these other rights provides further evidence that it's unacceptable in the case of the right of freedom of expression as well. And this provides a second reason to reject the harm-based argument for legal or academic hate speech restrictions.

Three objections might be raised against my argument at this point. First, a defender of the harm-based approach might complain that intentions mark an important difference between hate speech, on the one hand, and the examples that I've appealed to here on the other. When a racist calls a black person a "damn nigger," it isn't just that his use of these words happens to turn out to cause harm to someone. It's that the words are uttered with the intention of causing the harm. But while moving from one state to another, or changing religions, or choosing certain professions might also end up causing significant grief to other people, these are not the sorts of things that are done in order to cause such grief. And that, a critic might maintain, explains why it's appropriate to restrict hate speech because of the harm it (intentionally) causes but inappropriate to restrict these other forms of behavior even when they (unintentionally) cause comparable amounts of harm.

This first attempt to rescue the harm-based argument for hate speech restrictions is unsuccessful because the examples I used can simply be modified. Suppose, for example, that a man sleeps with a woman solely in order to upset his girlfriend, or an Orthodox Jewish student starts eating pork precisely because he knows it will cause his parents great anguish. Regardless of whether this affects our moral assessment of their behavior, it's extremely unlikely to affect our assessment of whether it would be acceptable for their government or their college to prevent them from engaging in it. In the case of these other fundamental rights, that is, we think that people should remain free to exercise the right in question even when they do so with the intention of causing grief to others. But if this is so in the case of these other rights, then it should be so in the case of hate speech and the right to freedom of expression as well.

A second objection to the position I've taken here points to another kind of difference between the use of racial epithets and the other kinds of harmful speech I've pointed to. As Richard Delgado puts the point, "Racial insults are different qualitatively because they conjure up the entire history of racial discrimination in this country." And as a result, he maintains, they have a "unique, powerfully evocative nature," that accounts for "the insidious harms they inflict."[10] I have to admit that I'm sympathetic to this concern. There does seem to be something truly distinctive, and distinctively terrible, about calling a black person a nigger, and it seems right to say that none of the examples that I've pointed to are really just like it. But there are two problems with appealing to this fact as a way of trying to overcome my objection to the harm-based defense of hate speech restrictions.

The first problem is that my objection doesn't depend on the claim that my examples are exactly like the case of calling a black person a nigger. It depends only on the claim that the examples are like the case of calling a black person a nigger in one particular respect: that of being experienced by others as being akin to having the wind knocked out of you by a sharp jab to the stomach or being on the receiving end of a sharp slap in the face. Since this is the feature of race-based hate speech that the defender of the harm-based argument appeals to in supporting the claim that it's morally unobjectionable to restrict such speech, the fact that this is also a feature of being called a baby killer or a traitor, or of having your boyfriend tell you he's cheating on you or your son tell you that he's leaving your religion or your brother tell you that he hates you is enough to show that the argument would justify restrictions in these cases as well. Since virtually no one on either side of the hate speech debate will be willing to accept these implications, this is enough to sustain my objection. It doesn't matter that there are many other differences between race-based hate speech and these other examples. What matters is what they all have in common.

The second problem with appealing to the uniqueness of race-based hate speech as a basis for rejecting my objection to the harm-based argument is that the other sorts of harmful speech that I've appealed to also have their own unique and powerful natures that account for the distinctive ways in which they can inflict serious harms. If you're not a black person, for example, there's probably little you can do to truly grasp how painful it can be to be called a nigger. But if you're not an Orthodox Jew, there's probably just as little you can do to appreciate how painful it can be to have your son tell you that he's going to start eating pork, or marry a Catholic woman, or convert to Islam. And if you don't have any siblings, you probably can't understand how painful it can be to have a brother or sister tell you that they hate and can no longer stand the sight of you. These sorts of cases are all unique in various ways, but this provides no reason to think that racially motivated hate speech is more harmful than the others, or is harmful in a way that is sufficiently different to justify restricting it without restricting the others. And the mere fact that it's unique can't by itself help to justify restricting race-based hate speech because the fact that the other forms of hurtful speech are also unique would justify restricting them as well. Given that this is so, this second attempt to defend the harm-based argument from my critique must also be deemed unsuccessful.

A third objection maintains that my objection to the harm-based argument has an unacceptable implication. It seems to imply that no matter how severe the resulting mental suffering is, it's always morally objectionable to intervene on the sufferer's behalf. But one can imagine at least some sorts of cases in which the speech is so horrific and the grief that follows so devastating that many people, including many who strongly value freedom of expression, would approve of something being done in response, even by the government. In these sorts of cases, at least, it may strike many people as perfectly appropriate and morally unobjectionable for the state to do something about those whose hateful expressions caused so much grief. And if my objection to the harm-based justification for hate speech restrictions is unable to accommodate this judgment, this may well strike them as a serious problem with my position.

But my response to the harm-based defense of hate speech restrictions is neutral with respect to the question of what, if anything, should be done in such extreme cases. It's consistent with saying that the state shouldn't get involved in such cases, but it's also consistent with saying that the state should get involved in such cases. This is because my response to the harm-based argument is consistent with accepting, and also consistent with rejecting, a legal doctrine known as the "tort of intentional infliction of emotional distress." This relatively recent but now widely recognized legal principle enables people to sue and collect civil damages when they are the victims of "extreme and outrageous conduct" that "intentionally or recklessly" causes "severe emotional distress" even in cases where no physical harm results. If, for example, a person played an extremely cruel and vicious practical joke on you by fabricating compelling evidence that your spouse had been brutally murdered, the tort of intentional infliction of emotional distress might enable you to sue for damages based on the intense emotional suffering this caused you.[11]

Those who believe that the state should intervene in cases of hate speech that involve extreme emotional distress, then, can't take this as grounds for concluding that the state should adopt hate speech restrictions. Instead, they can simply appeal to the claim that the tort of intentional infliction of emotional distress should be applied to such cases. Rather than helping to reinforce the case for hate speech restrictions, then, such extreme cases demonstrate that hate speech restrictions are unnecessary even if one believes that the state should intervene in such cases.

A proponent of the harm-based argument for hate speech restrictions, of course, might try to argue that every instance of hate speech involves extreme and outrageous conduct that intentionally or recklessly causes severe emotional distress. But there are two problems with this response. First, it's simply implausible

to insist that every instance of hate speech rises to this level of outrage and severity.[12] And, second, even if it does, this still fails to provide a justification for hate
speech restrictions. If every instance of hate speech really does involve extreme
and outrageous conduct that intentionally or recklessly causes severe emotional
distress, after all, then every victim of hate speech should already be able to collect damages under the already existing tort of intentional infliction of emotional
distress. Whether or not we think that people should be able to collect damages
in some or all such cases, then, in the end they provide no reason to accept the
harm-based argument for hate speech restrictions. And, either way, the many
strongly counterintuitive implications of the argument give us many good reasons to reject it.[13]

WORDS THAT SUBORDINATE

A second attempt to justify hate speech restrictions by going beyond the traditionally recognized categories of unprotected speech appeals to a claim about
the relationship between hate speech and the subordination of those it attacks.
This subordination-based argument for hate speech restrictions arises from a
parallel argument that a number of people have developed in favor of restrictions on pornography, and it can perhaps best be explained in terms of that argument. The subordination-based argument for restricting pornography, in turn,
can perhaps best be explained by first attending to the distinction between the
claim that something is a *depiction* of subordination, the claim that something is
a *cause* of subordination, and the claim that something is a *form* of subordination.
Subordination involves putting someone in an inferior position. And so we might
say, for example, that rape is a *form* of subordination of women, that if anger
toward women leads a man to commit rape then such anger can be a *cause* of the
subordination of women, and that if a story includes a scene in which a man rapes
a woman then the story contains a *depiction* of the subordination of women.

With this three-part distinction in mind, we can now get clear about just what,
precisely, the subordination-based argument amounts to. One claim that a critic
of pornography might make is that pornography depicts the subordination of
women. If a pornographic story or image portrays a man raping a woman, for
example, or depicts the woman in a submissive or servile position relative the
man, the critic might claim that it depicts the subordination of women. A second
claim that a critic of pornography might make is that pornography causes the
subordination of women. If a story or image inspires or encourages a man to
mistreat women, for example, the critic might claim that it is a cause of the subordination of women. Both of these claims are fairly common, and while they
may in the end prove to be false, it's at least fairly clear what it would mean for
them to be true and why someone might think that, if they are true, they provide
a reasonable basis for restricting pornography.

But the subordination-based argument for restricting pornography doesn't
depend on either of these claims. Instead, it's grounded in the claim that

pornography is itself a form of the subordination of women. The famous Indianapolis anti-pornography ordinance that was developed by Catherine MacKinnon and Andrea Dworkin, for example, began with the words: "We define pornography as the graphic sexually explicit subordination of women in pictures or words" – not the explicit *depiction* of such subordination, but rather the subordination itself.[14] And in her provocative 1993 book *Only Words*, which first brought this approach to the public's attention, MacKinnon was explicit in maintaining "that 'subordination' is something pornography does, not something it just says."[15]

On the face of it, at least, this claim strikes many people as implausible if not simply absurd. There's a difference, they want to insist, between speech, on the one hand, and acts, on the other. Speech can certainly depict subordination, they agree, and perhaps it can even cause it. But to literally place someone in a subordinate position, you have to actually do something to them, and to do something, you need actions, not mere words. Just as a story can depict a woman being raped but can't literally rape a woman, so pornography can depict, and perhaps cause, the subordination of women, but it can't literally be an instance of the subordination of women. Or so, at least, it seems to many people.

The key to understanding the subordination-based argument for restricting pornography, and thus to understanding the parallel argument for restricting hate speech, is understanding how proponents of the argument respond to this natural concern about their position. They do so by denying that the distinction between speech and act is as clear and precise as their critics seem to presume. And they do this by making use of an insight widely associated with the philosopher J. L. Austin: that sometimes, under some conditions, people can literally do things with words.[16] Consider, for example, a judge who stands before a man and woman and utters the words "I now pronounce you man and wife." One way to think of what the judge has done is that he has conveyed some information to those in attendance: that it is this particular man and this particular woman who are now married and not, say, a man and a woman who happen to be walking by outside at the time, that they are being married and not, say, divorced, or deported, and so on. A second way to think of what the judge has done is in terms of the effects that his utterance may have. If some people in the room start to cry as a result of his statement, for example, then we might say that by uttering the words he has caused some tears to flow. But if all we say about what the judge did by uttering the words he uttered is that he conveyed some information and caused some tears to flow, we will clearly omit something crucial that he did by uttering those words: he *married* them. Before he uttered the words, they were not married; in virtue of his uttering the words, they became married. Simply by saying some words, then, the judge *did* something: he married them. This kind of phenomenon, moreover, arises in other contexts as well. By uttering the word "guilty," for example, a judge can make a defendant a felon. By calling a runner out, an umpire can make one team a loser and the other a winner. And so on.

Although it's easy to overlook this fact, once it's noticed it becomes difficult to deny: some acts are speech acts. Defenders of the subordination-based argument try to make use of this fact to thwart those critics who maintain that pornographic expression can't literally subordinate women because it's only speech and not action. If some forms of expression, like the judge uttering the words "I now pronounce you man and wife," can literally do things that alter the status of people, after all, then perhaps pornographic expression can as well. Felons, for example, are subordinated to nonfelons in a variety of ways including, in at least some states, by permanently losing their right to vote. If a judge's speech act can make some people subordinate to others by making them into felons, then perhaps a pornographer's speech act can render women subordinate to men in a similar sort of way. And if pornographic speech has the power to literally subordinate, then hate speech may, too.

The main challenge that confronts proponents of this subordination-based argument is that there seems to be a crucial difference between judges and umpires, on the one hand, and the purveyors of pornographic and hate speech, on the other. A judge, for example, is an elected or appointed official who has been duly authorized to pass judgment on society's behalf when people are tried in his courtroom. It seems clearly to be in virtue of this fact that his words can literally make someone a felon. If he utters the words "I hereby declare the defendant to be guilty," for example, then his words can change an accused person into a convicted person. If a defendant is officially found innocent and someone in the courtroom then shouts out "he's gulity" as the defendant is hugging his lawyer, the words "he's guilty" can't have a comparable effect. Similarly, an umpire is a duly authorized official who has been assigned the task of making final judgments about balls and strikes. It seems clearly to be in virtue of his official position that his words can make the difference between a team winning and losing a game while a fan's words can't. If the umpire declares a pitch to be a strike, for example, that may be enough to end the game and result in one team's winning. If a fan yells "strike," at a pitch in the very same situation, his words can't do the same thing.

But the publisher of a pornographic magazine, by contrast, is not an elected or appointed official who has been duly authorized to pass judgment on society's behalf when young men have questions about their sexual interactions with women. If his magazine publishes stories or images that urge men to treat women in ways that would render them subordinate to men, then, while his words or pictures might have subordinating effects, it seems that they can't in themselves constitute a literal act of subordinating women because he doesn't occupy the kind of official position of authority that a judge or an umpire does. And the same seems to be true of those who utter the kinds of words that hate speech restrictions seek to target. To the extent that the subordination-based argument for restricting pornography or hate speech depends on an analogy with relatively uncontroversial cases like those of the judge or the umpire, then, the argument seems to be in serious trouble.

Defenders of the subordination-based approach, though, aren't ready to give up at this point. Instead, they maintain that, in a morally relevant sense, pornographers are, in fact, authorities on sexual matters. The claim here is not that they've literally been vested with authority in the way that a judge or an umpire has, but rather that they're nonetheless viewed as having authority over their subject matter by their target audience. If young men who buy pornographic magazines treat the messages conveyed by their words and images as speaking more authoritatively about sexual relationships than they treat the words of their parents, teachers or religious leaders, for example, then on this account the pornographer really is an authority in the relevant sense in this context and so really does have the power to subordinate women with his words and images. And, once again, if this is so, then the same may be true in the context of hate speech. Restrictions on such speech may prove to be justified not because such speech may encourage others to subordinate the groups of people it is aimed at, that is, but because uttering such speech is itself literally an act of subordination. If the words of white people are treated more authoritatively than are the words of black people, for example, then a white person uttering the words "black people don't belong in this country – they should go back to Africa" may literally be putting black people in a subordinate position. This would provide a novel justification for hate speech restrictions, and one that goes well beyond the various kinds of justifications that have been given for more traditionally recognized limits on freedom of expression.

The problem with this attempt to defend the subordination-based argument for hate speech restrictions, though, is that, like other attempts to defend such restrictions, it has implications that virtually everyone on both sides of the hate speech debate will reject as unacceptable.[17] Consider, for example, a Catholic priest who addresses his congregation and utters the words "God does not want women to be priests." If all it takes to be an authority in the relevant sense is to be someone whose words are viewed as such by its target audience, then the priest is surely at least as much an authority on spiritual matters for his audience as a pornographer is an authority on sexual matters for his audience. If it's morally unobjectionable to restrict the pornographer's expression on the grounds that it literally subordinates women, then it must be morally unobjectionable to restrict the priest's expression on the same grounds. But virtually everyone on both sides of the debates over hate speech and pornography, including those who strongly disagree with the priest's statement, agrees that it would be wrong to forbid him from uttering it simply because his subordinating words are taken to be authoritative by his congregants. And they agree that it would be wrong to forbid him from uttering it, moreover, regardless of whether he's leading services in a private church, or addressing a group of Catholic students on a college campus.

Or consider the case of popular radio and television personalities such as Rush Limbaugh and Bill O'Reilly. Both men have large audiences which include many people who consider what they say about social and political matters to be authoritative. If a political commentator in such a position says "women should stay at home and raise children" or "women don't belong in the military" or "biological differences explain why women don't do as well as men in math and science," they, too, on this account, won't simply be encouraging the subordination of women, but actually engaging in it. The subordination-based argument will therefore justify restricting their expression as well. This implication, too, will strike nearly everyone as unacceptable, regardless of their view of hate speech restrictions. And it will strike them as unacceptable, moreover, regardless of whether the restriction in question involves the government punishing Rush Limbaugh or a college punishing a student who hopes to be the next Rush Limbaugh and who broadcasts on the campus radio station.

The subordination-based argument also has the troubling implication that whether or not a given instance of expression may permissibly be prohibited depends on whether or not enough people take the person who utters it seriously enough. As I noted in Chapter 3, for example, Charles Murray and Richard J. Herrnstein argued that genetic differences between black and white people play a significant role in the average IQ gap between them in their controversial book, *The Bell Curve*. To place black people genetically below white people in terms of general intelligence is clearly to place them in a lower position. And so the content of *The Bell Curve* seems clearly to fit the analysis provided by the subordination-based argument for restricting hate speech. The only question that remains is whether Murray and Herrnstein would count as "authorities" for the purposes of the argument. And this feature of the argument, in turn, seems to entail that if they were generally viewed as cranks, then there would be no justification for prohibiting their work, since it couldn't actually subordinate black people, but that if they were viewed as sufficiently well qualified by a sufficiently large number of people, then their work could permissibly be restricted, since in that case it really could subordinate black people and not simply depict or cause such subordination. Or perhaps the decision would have to be based on their institutional affiliations: Herrnstein was a psychologist at Harvard and Murray a fellow of the American Enterprise Institute. Even if many people had never heard of either of them, they had at least heard of Harvard. The result might then be that the book could permissibly be banned if one of its authors was associated with Harvard, but not if they were both unknown, independent scholars. The same would be true of a college's right to censor the campus newspaper. Whether it had the right to punish a student for defending *The Bell Curve* in an op-ed piece would depend on whether the student was a popular class leader or a widely ignored loner. To the extent that this implication, too, should strike people on both sides of the hate speech restrictions debate as unacceptable, this result provides an additional reason to reject the appropriateness of the analysis appealed to by the subordination-based argument.

Finally, it's worth returning for a moment to the example of judges and jurors for a case that helps to illuminate more clearly why the subordination-based argument is unacceptable in the case of hate speech restrictions in particular. When a judge utters the words "I find the defendant guilty," she thereby transforms an accused person into a convicted person. In the case of people convicted of a felony, at least, this involves subordinating the person in a variety of ways. When a judge finds a defendant not guilty, though, it doesn't matter how many other people insist that he's guilty: their saying that he's guilty can't make him a felon and so can't subordinate him in this sense. If enough people publicly insist that an acquitted defendant was guilty, though, and if the people doing the insisting are taken sufficiently seriously by the public at large, there may well still be some sense in which their insisting that he's guilty renders him a second-class citizen: his right to vote won't be taken away, but he may still be shunned, ostracized, blacklisted, avoided, ridiculed, publicly condemned, and so on. In this sense, perhaps, it's possible for people to literally subordinate others by their words even if they aren't officially authorized to do so. And so in this sense, at least, we might still be able to accept the claim that private acts of hate speech can literally subordinate others despite the important difference between judges and umpires on the one hand and pornographers and bigots on the other.

But while this analogy with people who persist in calling an acquitted defendant guilty may help to salvage the claim that private acts of hate speech can literally subordinate in some sense, in the end it also helps to show that this sense of subordination is too weak to do the work that proponents of the subordination-based argument for hate speech restrictions need it to do. Virtually no one, for example, regardless of their view of hate speech restrictions, believes that people should be prevented from, or penalized for, publicly maintaining that O. J. Simpson was guilty of the two murders he was officially found not guilty of committing.[18] And virtually no one thinks this, moreover, regardless of whether it would be the state punishing one of its citizens for saying this or a college punishing one of its students. But if hate speech can justifiably be legally or academically restricted because it subordinates in this relatively weak sense of subordinating, then so can speech that involves publicly affirming Simpson's guilt. In the end, then, the subordination-based argument for hate speech restrictions is unacceptable. Introducing words that subordinate as a new class of unprotected speech might help to justify restrictions on some forms of hate speech, but since it would also justify restrictions on so many other forms of speech that virtually no one on either side of the hate speech debate thinks should be restricted, the support for hate speech restrictions that it would provide is itself unacceptable. And so, therefore, is the argument that is based on it.

WORDS THAT SILENCE

A third attempt to justify hate speech restrictions by going beyond the traditionally recognized categories of unprotected speech involves an appeal to the value of free speech itself. The central claim behind this further argument for such restrictions is that, at least in some kinds of contexts, one person's exercising his right to free speech can deprive other people of their right to free speech. If this is so, then the mere fact that a restriction would infringe on a person's right to freedom of speech will not, in itself, suffice to establish that the restriction would be morally unacceptable even if we agree that the right to freedom of speech is an extremely important one. If doing without the restriction would result in an even greater number of people having their right to freedom of speech infringed upon, after all, then we may be compelled to accept the restriction, at least as the lesser of two evils, no matter how important we think the right to freedom of speech is. Indeed, the more important we think the right is, the more important it may seem that we enact the restriction in order to minimize the extent to which people are deprived of it. If freedom of expression is especially important to the mission of a university because of the role that free expression plays in the generation and transmission of knowledge, for example, then the argument may show that it's especially important to establish the restriction in an academic environment. Like the subordination-based argument for hate speech restrictions, this kind of argument has been developed by a number of thinkers in the context of the debate over pornography. The claim there is that the propagation of pornography infringes on the freedom of expression of those women who are negatively affected by it, and the question here is whether or not a similar argument can be made in the case of hate speech restrictions. If hate speech directed at black people infringes on the freedom of speech of black people, for example, then this may suffice to justify legal or campus restrictions on such speech not by showing that hate speech falls into an already recognized category of unprotected speech, but rather by showing that its restriction is necessary to prevent an even greater encroachment on the kind of freedom of speech that nations and colleges already value in the first place.

This freedom-based argument for restrictions on certain forms of expression is often put in terms of the claim that pornography or hate speech has a kind of silencing effect. This claim can be understood in one of two ways, and so the argument itself can be understood in one of two ways.[19] One thing that might be meant by the claim that hate speech has a silencing effect is that it discourages those it's aimed at from speaking up for themselves. Cass Sunstein, for example, has argued that "People confronted by hate speech may experience a form of 'silencing' in the sense that they are reluctant to speak."[20] On this account, hate speech restrictions are justified because hate speech inhibits its victims from expressing themselves.

But if this is the feature of hate speech that proponents of hate speech restrictions mean to appeal to, then the "silencing" argument for such restrictions will have implications that virtually everyone on both sides of the hate speech debate will surely reject as unacceptable. Consider, for example, a minister who preaches from his pulpit in the strongest possible terms that abortion is a mortal sin on a par with the murder of an adult human being. If there's a woman in the congregation who would otherwise be inclined to make public her belief that abortion is morally permissible, the minister's fiery words will surely make her more reluctant to do so. If a student on a campus where most of his peers support abortion rights adamantly insists that only religious zealots oppose abortion, his sharp proclamation will surely render the small minority of students there who oppose abortion less comfortable in sharing their opinions. Or consider how difficult it would be for you to express your opposition to a given war in the face of a passionate defense of it offered by a decorated, injured veteran of the conflict, or to express your support for the war in the face of a passionate objection to it raised by the grieving parent of a fallen soldier. Finally, consider the effects of calling someone a racist because of their opposition, say, to affirmative action. In all of these cases, the powerful expression of strongly felt views is likely to have an intimidating effect on many people who would otherwise be inclined to express their rival opinions. In this sense, the speech in question is likely to have a "silencing" effect on those it is aimed at. But in all of these cases, nonetheless, virtually everyone on both sides of the hate speech debate will agree that it would be morally objectionable to restrict the speech in question. And they will agree about this, moreover, regardless of whether the restrictions are imposed by the government or by a college campus. The decorated, injured veteran should be free to express his passionate support for the war, for example, and the grieving parents who lost a child to the war should be free to express their passionate opposition to it, no matter how powerfully their speeches might intimidate others from expressing their opposing views and regardless of whether their speeches take place in a city park or a campus auditorium. And so the claim that hate speech has a silencing effect in this sense can't be used to ground a satisfactory argument for legal or academic hate speech restrictions.[21]

This first interpretation of what it means for speech to have a silencing effect focuses on the direct effects that speech can have on those it attacks. I've argued that this interpretation fails to generate a plausible argument for either governmental or academic hate speech restrictions. A second interpretation focuses instead on the indirect effects that such speech can have on those it attacks by exerting an influence on how others are inclined to view them. In the case of those who argue for restrictions on pornography, for example, the claim that pornography has a silencing effect on women is often understood as the claim that the prevalence of pornographic images leads many men to view women primarily in sexual terms and thus to take what women say less seriously than they otherwise would, or not to listen to them at all. Even if pornography doesn't render women less likely to speak, that is, it might still be thought to render them less likely to be heard. And this prospect has struck a number of people as providing a satisfactory foundation for developing a case for restricting pornography. In the same sort of way, the claim that hate speech has a silencing effect on those it attacks can be understood as the claim that, for example, hate speech aimed at black people tends to make white people less likely to take what black people say seriously. Even if it doesn't prevent black people from speaking, it may still prevent them from being heard.

This second interpretation of the silencing effect results in a different version of the silencing argument. But if the feature of hate speech that proponents of hate speech restrictions mean to appeal to is its ability to silence people in this second sense, then the silencing argument for such restrictions will still have implications that virtually everyone on both sides of the hate speech debate will reject as unacceptable. There are, after all, many other forms of speech that aim to make us take some people's words less seriously. In the case of these other forms of speech, virtually everyone agrees that this fact isn't enough to justify prohibitions on their expression. Even if it turns out that hate speech has the same sort of silencing effect that these other forms of speech have, then, this fact can't be used to generate a satisfactory justification for hate speech restrictions.

Consider, for example, speech that's designed to attack another person's credentials. Suppose a group takes out an ad in a city or campus newspaper maintaining that global warming is a hoax, and at the bottom of the ad it lists a number of professors who have endorsed this claim along with their institutional affiliations. A second group then takes out an ad in response to the first ad in which it points out that the professors listed in the first ad aren't scientists. The goal of this second ad is to encourage people not to take what the professors in the first ad say seriously, but virtually no one thinks that this fact warrants a restriction on the second ad's being published. Or consider speech that aims to attribute ulterior motives to people. This kind of speech, too, is designed to make us take their words less seriously. If a defender of abortion rights insists that abortion opponents are really motivated by a desire to punish women for being sexually active, for example, or if an opponent of abortion maintains that Planned Parenthood's defense of abortion rights is really motivated by its desire to make a profit by providing abortions, the purpose of the speech in question is to make us take what's said by the targets of its attack less seriously. But, again, virtually everyone on both sides of the hate speech debate agrees that it would be morally objectionable to restrict these forms of expression. And, once again, virtually everyone agrees about this regardless of whether the restrictions would be imposed by the government or by a university. It would be wrong for either institution to censor the ad that attacks the professors' credentials, and wrong to suppress the speech attributing ulterior motives to defenders or opponents of abortion regardless of whether the speech takes place in a public parking lot or a campus dining hall.

Indeed, virtually everyone will think that this is so even in cases where the speech attributing ulterior motives is aimed at undermining the influence of prominent black figures like Supreme Court Justice Clarence Thomas or Harvard Law School Professor Randall Kennedy when they address issues involving race on campus or off. Critics have frequently maintained that Justice Thomas's public opinions are simply designed to help him win white approval, or are the product of his being in denial about the benefits he's received from affirmative action programs, for example, and when Kennedy published a book in 2003 called *Nigger: The Strange Career of a Troublesome Word*, he was attacked by Martin Kilson, himself a black professor at Harvard and the first to have been tenured there, who wrote that Kennedy's "core purpose ... [is] to assist White Americans in feeling comfortable with using the epithet 'nigger.'"[22] But no one really thinks that such expression should be subject to legal or campus prohibition. Or take the case of speech that attempts to tar its opponent by means of guilt by association. An opponent of gun control or of vegetarianism, for example, may try to press his case by claiming that Hitler was a vegetarian or a supporter of gun control. As in the other cases raised here, his motivation for making such statements is to try to get people to dismiss the claims made by defenders of gun control or of vegetarianism, in this case by means of guilt by association. But while this technique of argumentation is clearly suspect, virtually no one thinks that it should be restricted in the public market or the college bookstore. In these ways and many others, people frequently attempt to make us take the words of other people less seriously. Since this fact about these other forms of speech fails to justify legally or academically restricting them, it fails to justify legal or academic restrictions on hate speech as well. While there may well prove to be a significant sense in which hate speech has a silencing effect, then, there's no sense strong enough to justify restricting it.

WORDS THAT WOUND, SUBORDINATE, AND SILENCE

There's a strong and widely accepted presumption in favor of a citizen's and a college student's right to freedom of expression. If legal or academic hate speech restrictions are to be justified, then, there must be some feature that hate speech has that's important enough to overcome this powerful presumption. A number of defenders of hate speech restrictions have taken on the challenge of identifying this feature. I've now completed the task of critically surveying all of the suggestions of this sort that I'm aware of, and I've argued that, in each case, the feature that the defender of hate speech restrictions appeals to fails to do the trick. A defender of hate speech restrictions might attempt to respond to all of this, though, by turning to one final strategy: even if none of the features that have been appealed to are powerful enough to justify hate speech restrictions when taken individually, the defender of such restrictions might suggest, several of them could prove to be sufficiently powerful when suitably combined. If each objectionable feature of hate speech counts at least a little bit in favor of restricting it, that is, then if enough of the objectionable features are added together, they may collectively do enough to justify restricting it. Hate speech restrictions on this account won't be justified because of some particular fact about hate speech. Rather, they'll be justified because of a set of facts about it.

This final strategy for justifying hate speech restrictions is unavailable in the case of the objections I considered and responded to in Chapter 6. In that chapter, I focused on features of some forms of speech that most people already agree justify limiting freedom of expression, like the fact that a certain utterance would be threatening, or inciting, or libelous. In arguing against attempts to justify hate speech restrictions by appealing to such features, I pointed out that in the case of each feature, there were important instances of hate speech that lack the feature in question: hate speech that isn't threatening, for example, or that isn't libelous.

But if a defense of hate speech restrictions based on the right to suppress threatening speech is unsuccessful for this reason, and if a defense of hate speech restrictions based on the right to suppress libelous speech is, too, then a defense of hate speech restrictions that requires speech to be both threatening and libelous in order for it to be legitimately restricted will be unsuccessful as well. If some cases of hate speech aren't threatening, after all, then those cases of hate speech fail to be both threatening and libelous. If other cases of hate speech aren't libelous, then those cases, too, fail to be both threatening and libelous. Any attempt to justify hate speech restrictions by appealing to the claim that it's permissible to restrict speech so long as it's both threatening and libelous will therefore fail for precisely the same reason that each of the arguments I discussed in Chapter 6 failed: it won't cover all of the cases that a defender of hate speech restrictions needs to cover. And assuming that there isn't perfect overlap between each of the different features, as more features are added to the argument, the argument will become weaker rather than stronger. If speech can be restricted only when it's threatening and inciting and libelous and harassing, after all, then very few instances of hate speech will be capable of permissibly being restricted because very few instances of hate speech will be all of these things. And even in those few instances, the cases themselves will do nothing to justify restricting them as hate speech since there are already restrictions against the use of threatening, inciting, libelous, and harassing speech. So the attempt to justify restricting hate speech by adding together different objectionable features that are only features of some cases of hate speech fails in the case of the features I covered in the previous chapter.

When I considered the various features discussed in this chapter, though, my strategy was different. When I responded to the objections based on the claim that hate speech involves words that wound, or that subordinate, or that silence, I didn't depend on the claim that some forms of hate speech fail to have these particular features. Instead, I appealed to the claim that these features provided an unacceptable basis for restricting hate speech even if hate speech has these features because appealing to such features would also justify restricting other forms of speech in cases where virtually everyone on both sides of the hate speech debate would reject the restrictions as morally objectionable. This leaves open the possibility that every instance of hate speech is an instance of speech that wounds and subordinates and silences. And this, in turn, seems to leave an opening for the defender of hate speech restrictions to exploit: perhaps the claim that words can be suppressed simply because they wound has unacceptable implications, and perhaps this is also so of the claim that they can be suppressed simply because they subordinate or simply because they silence, but perhaps all of these unacceptable implications can be avoided by appealing to the more heavily qualified claim that words may be suppressed provided that they wound and subordinate and silence. If it's reasonable to think of hate speech as having all three of these objectionable features, then the strategy of combining objectionable features may succeed in justifying hate speech restrictions after all.

Even though this approach to justifying hate speech restrictions is much more heavily qualified than the approaches that rely on a single feature, though, in the end it's unacceptable for the same basic reason that those other approaches are: it still has implications that virtually everyone on both sides of the hate speech debate will reject as unacceptable. Suppose, for example, that a black student publishes an op-ed in the campus newspaper defending affirmative action and a white student then tells him, in the presence of a number of other students, that he thinks he only wrote the column to rationalize the fact that he himself has benefited from affirmative action and calls the black student a "stupid nigger." And suppose a defender of hate speech restrictions justifies sanctioning the white student in this case on the grounds that his words wound, subordinate, and silence. If these features of the case suffice to justify restrictions on the white student's freedom of expression, then they will also justify restrictions in cases where virtually everyone will reject them as morally unacceptable.

Suppose instead, for example, that a Catholic student publishes an op-ed in the campus newspaper defending abortion, contraception, and gay rights and a fellow Catholic student then tells him, in the presence of a number of other students, that he's a "dangerous heretic" and that he doesn't deserve to call himself a Catholic or to take communion. It's very hard to believe that anyone would accept the claim that the state or the college would be justified in interfering with this student's right to express his disapproval of the op-ed in this way. But if the white student's words to the black student really are wounding, subordinating, and silencing in the first case, then it's just as hard to see why the student's words to his fellow Catholic student in the second case wouldn't be wounding, subordinating, and silencing as well. And since all of these features combined fail to justify restrictions on freedom of speech in the second case, they fail to justify it in the first case as well.

A defender of hate speech restrictions, of course, might complain that there's an important difference between these two cases: when the student calls his fellow Catholic a "heretic," he's expressing a social or political opinion, but when the white student calls the black student a "nigger," he isn't. And that, the defender of hate speech restrictions might say, is why it's permissible to punish the student in the second case but not in the first. But there are three reasons to reject this response to my argument. First, the "heretic" example can easily be modified so that no discernible social or political opinion is involved. Suppose, for example, that the president of a fraternity on a campus where fraternities dominate student life laughingly rejects a candidate's application to join his house by saying "you're too geeky to be a member of my fraternity" in front of all of the other applicants. It seems just as plausible to suppose that the words in question are wounding, subordinating, and silencing as it does in the other cases, and just as wrong to think that it should be subject to legal or campus restrictions in virtue of this fact. Yet the fraternity president in this example isn't expressing any social or political opinions.

Second, the difference between political and non-political speech isn't relevant to the kind of argument the defender of hate speech restrictions is seeking to defend. The argument maintains that otherwise protected speech becomes unprotected when it's wounding, subordinating, and silencing. If this is true, then it shouldn't matter why the otherwise protected speech would otherwise be protected. The words "give me all your money or I'll shoot you in the head," as I noted in a different context in Chapter 6, don't change from unprotected to protected when they're changed to "give me all your money or I'll shoot you in the head because you're a greedy capitalist pig and my deeply held political convictions dictate that I take your money and redistribute it among the working poor." Either the fact that the words are threatening justifies restricting them or it doesn't. The same should be true of words that wound, subordinate, and silence.

Finally, and perhaps most importantly, it's simply a mistake to maintain that calling the black student a "nigger" doesn't involve the expression of a social or political belief. When a white person aims a racial epithet at a black person, they are expressing a belief about the social and political significance of racial differences: that black people are inferior to white people, that they are contemptible, uncivilized, or something else to that effect. That's precisely why the words are so hurtful to begin with. If a white person calling a black person a "nigger" was a purely descriptive statement, like saying "the majority of your ancestors migrated out of sub-Saharan Africa more recently than did the majority of my ancestors," then the words wouldn't be objectionable precisely because they wouldn't be conveying any objectionable social or political opinions. And so if the Catholic student's wounding, subordinating, and silencing words should be protected because they convey some of his social or political views, then the same should be true of the white student who calls the black student a "nigger". While the strategy of combining the particular objections that I've considered and rejected in this chapter into a new objection is certainly worth examining, then, in the end it too must be rejected.

FREE SPEECH NONABSOLUTISM

I began this discussion of hate speech restrictions in Chapter 6 with what strikes me as a modest presumption in favor of freedom of expression: people shouldn't be prohibited from expressing themselves unless there's a good reason for the prohibition. Most people, regardless of their view of hate speech restrictions, accept this presumption. I then considered two ways in which defenders of hate speech restrictions have attempted to overcome this presumption: arguments that try to justify such restrictions by establishing that hate speech is relevantly similar to other forms of speech that we already accept as legitimate subjects of restriction, and arguments that try to justify hate speech restrictions by establishing that there are reasons to restrict expression that go beyond those that are already widely accepted. I tried to show that none of these arguments are successful, and that they can be shown to be unsuccessful on terms that virtually everyone on both sides of the debate already accepts.

While the result of this chapter and the chapter preceding it is therefore that we should be opposed to legal and campus hate speech restrictions, though, it's important to emphasize in conclusion that this doesn't mean that every particular instance of hate speech should be protected. As I noted in Chapter 6, for example, it seems perfectly appropriate to restrict speech that involves threatening others. Those particular instances of speech that threaten others can therefore appropriately be restricted, not because they are instances of hate speech, but because they are instances of threatening speech. The same may also prove true for hate speech that amounts to fighting words or that falls into some other already uncontroversially restricted category. In addition, it's important to emphasize that nothing said in either of these chapters implies that the fact that an insult is a racial insult is irrelevant to whether or not it may appropriately be restricted. Because of the terribly violent history associated with the word "nigger," for example, there may well be contexts in which the statement "go home, you moron" is not reasonably interpreted as a threat while the statement "go home, you nigger" is. The substitution of a racial epithet, that is, may well make the difference between speech that's hostile but not-threatening and speech that's genuinely threatening, and this difference in turn may well make the difference between speech that may legitimately be restricted and speech that may not be. But, again, in cases such as this, the speech that may be restricted may be restricted because it's threatening speech, not because it's hate speech.

A free speech absolutist would oppose all restrictions on speech, including speech that falls into categories that most people accept as unprotected. A proponent of hate speech restrictions, on the other hand, supports restrictions on hate speech even when it falls into none of those categories. Both of these positions, in the end, strike me as extreme and indefensible. The position that I've defended in these two chapters as an alternative to those positions, by contrast, rests on claims that virtually everyone on both sides of the debate already accepts as moderate and reasonable. And, perhaps more importantly, it permits us to acknowledge that some hate speech may justly be restricted without lapsing into the untenable position that all of it should and enables us to affirm that legal and academic hate speech restrictions should be rejected without committing us to the untenable position that all restrictions on speech should be rejected.

8

How to Stop Worrying and Learn
to Love Hate Crime Laws

Why Objections to Hate Speech Restrictions
Don't Work as Objections to Hate Crime Laws

Two arsonists are walking around town looking for a suitable house to burn down. One ends up selecting a particular house because it is a bit more convenient to get to than those nearby. The other ends up selecting a particular house because the family who lives in it is black. Both are caught, convicted, and punished for their acts. The men live in a state that has a hate crime law. Such laws treat what the second arsonist does as worse than what the first arsonist does. As a result, the second arsonist receives a greater punishment than the first.

Many people are troubled by hate crime laws. And many of those who are troubled by them are troubled for largely the same reasons that they're troubled by hate speech restrictions. As Dinseh D'Souza has put it in lumping the two cases together, for example, "free speech is subordinated to the goals of sensitivity and diversity, as in so-called hate speech and hate crimes laws."[1] These are people who will largely agree with what I said about hate speech restrictions in Chapters 6 and 7, but who will think that I haven't yet gone far enough. The reasons for rejecting hate speech restrictions, they'll say, are also reasons for rejecting hate crime laws.

I think these people are mistaken. In this chapter, I'll explain why. I'll start by explaining what hate crime laws are, why they've always struck me as perfectly appropriate, and I'll then consider and respond to the objection that claims that hate crime laws are objectionable for the same basic reason that hate speech restrictions are. In the chapter that follows, I'll then consider a variety of additional objections that can be raised against hate crime laws and will explain why I don't find any of them convincing either. The result of all of this is that while I've always hated hate speech restrictions, and continue to hate them, I've never hated hate crime laws and still don't.

WHAT HATE CRIME LAWS ARE

Hate crime laws are relatively new. While most states currently have them and the federal government does as well, they were virtually nonexistent a mere thirty years ago.² Before considering the merits of such laws, then, it's important to start by getting clear about what exactly a hate crime law is and to take care to avoid a few popular misconceptions. For the purposes of this chapter and the one that follows, then, a hate crime law is a law that takes an ordinary crime, like arson or assault, and adds an extra amount of punishment to the crime when the crime is committed not simply as a crime, but as a hate crime. The best way to get clear about what a hate crime law is, therefore, is to get clear about how hate crimes differ from the ordinary crimes that they otherwise resemble. So consider first the arsonist who has decided that he would like to burn down a building and who selects a particular house to burn because of its convenient location. This is a crime, but it's not a hate crime. What changes would have to be made to the story in order to make what the arsonist does not simply a crime, but a hate crime?

At a minimum, the arsonist would have to select his victim for a reason that, at least in part, has something to do with his beliefs about the victim's group membership. A case in which the victim is selected because he's black would be a clear example of this. Virtually all hate crime laws cover cases in which a victim is selected because of facts about race, religion, ethnicity, or national origin. Some also include considerations about gender, disability, or sexual orientation. For the purposes of this discussion, I'll stick to considerations having to do with race. When I say that hate crime laws are justified, then, I'll mean that they're justified at least in cases in which the law treats race as a relevant group. A case in which an arsonist targets a particular house because a black family lives in it is a clear example of this. It's almost certainly true that if race-based hate crime laws are appropriate then the same will be true of laws that make reference to other categories as well, but I'll leave that issue for others to consider.

So suppose that our arsonist selects a particular house to burn down not because he thinks its location is convenient, but rather because he thinks a black family lives in it. Does it matter if his belief turns out to be mistaken? If he burns the house down because he believes that it belongs to a black family but it turns out that it belongs to a white family, is his crime still a hate crime? Existing state laws don't seem to be entirely consistent on this point. Wisconsin's hate crime law, for example, specifically focuses on cases in which the offender "intentionally selects the person against whom the crime ... is committed or selects the property that is damaged or otherwise affected by the crime ... in whole or in part because of the actor's belief or perception regarding the race, religion, color, disability, sexual orientation, national origin or ancestry of the person or the owner or occupant of that property, *whether or not the actor's belief or perception was correct.*" Delaware's hate crime statute, by contrast, simply refers to cases in which the offender "selects the victim because of the victim's race, religion, color, disability, national origin or ancestry,"³ which seems to mean because of the victim's actual membership in such a group. Our arsonist at this point, then, might be guilty of committing a hate crime in Wisconsin but not in Delaware.

It's not clear what hate crime laws should say about cases in which the offender's belief about his victim's group membership turns out to be mistaken. On the one hand, it seems right to say that if there's something distinctly troubling about a person who would choose a house to burn down because a black family lives in it, then there's something distinctly troubling about that person regardless of whether or not his belief about who lives in the house turns out to be correct. On the other hand, there seems to be something puzzling about saying that such an arsonist has, in fact, committed a hate crime when he has not, in fact, done what he thought he was doing. If I hand the clerk at a store what I firmly believe to be a counterfeit twenty dollar bill but which in fact turns out to be a genuine twenty dollar bill, after all, I may be intending to commit a crime or attempting to commit a crime, but it seems that I'm failing to commit a crime nonetheless. So it also seems plausible to say that the arsonist who thinks he's targeted a black family but has not in fact done so is intending or attempting to commit a hate crime but is not, in fact, committing one, although he's still committing the ordinary crime of arson. Since I want to focus here on clear, paradigmatic cases of hate crimes, I'll set aside cases in which the offender acts on a mistaken belief. When I say that race-based hate crime laws are justified, then, I'll mean that they're justified at least in the case where they focus on offenders who in fact succeed in targeting their victims by race.

So let's now suppose that our arsonist has selected a house to target because he believes that a black family lives in it and let's also suppose that he's correct about this. Is this enough to make his act a hate crime? A few more complications remain. First, does the race of the arsonist matter? You've probably been assuming that the arsonist in this case is white, but I didn't say that he was. Perhaps he's a black person with an inferiority complex about black people. Should that make a difference? As far as I can tell, hate crime laws as they're written never specify that the offender must be a member of a different group from the victim. But there's certainly a popular understanding of the concept of a hate crime on which this requirement must be satisfied. In a high-profile case in New York City a few years ago, for example, a lawyer attempted to defend his client from the charge that his part in the death of a gay man implicated him in a hate crime by claiming that his client himself was gay.[4] And does it matter that the case involves a member of a majority group attacking a member of a minority group rather than the other way around? Again, there seems to be nothing about hate crime laws as actually written that would require this. And, in fact, the important case of *Wisconsin v. Mitchell*, in which the U.S. Supreme Court upheld that state's hate crime law, involved a group of black teenagers who had specifically set out to find and attack a white victim. But the popular understanding of hate crime laws, at least among its detractors, often does seem to include this additional requirement. In any event, for purposes of simplicity, I'll focus on cases like the one in which a white arsonist targets his victim (at least in part) because the victim is black. If hate crime laws are ever justified, they're at least justified in these kinds of cases.

Finally, there's an important though frequently neglected distinction between two kinds of case in which a white arsonist might select his victim because of the fact that his victim is black. One kind of case involves the arsonist targeting black families because he has some kind of negative attitude toward black people. He thinks that black people deserve to suffer, for example, or he takes pleasure in causing black people to suffer, and this is why he targets them. A second kind of case involves the arsonist targeting black families not because he has a negative attitude toward black people but rather because he believes, correctly or incorrectly, that selecting a black victim will be useful to him as a means to promoting some other end that he cares about. Suppose, for example, that the arsonist believes that if he burns down the house of a white family, the police will take the case seriously and will investigate it thoroughly, but that if he burns down the house of a black family, the police will fail to dedicate any real resources to investigating it. Or suppose that the arsonist believes that a house owned by a black family is less likely to have a security system than a house owned by a white family and he's concerned that a security system may thwart his plans. In this second kind of case, the arsonist will also target his victims because they're black. But while the first kind of arsonist targets black victims because of a negative attitude that he has toward black people, the second kind of arsonist doesn't. Should hate crime laws focus on both kinds of cases, what might be called the tactically biased arsonist as well as what might be called the bigoted one, or should they focus exclusively on cases that involve some kind of negative attitude toward black people on the arsonist's part?[5]

As with the question of whether or not the offender's belief about the race of his victim must be correct in order for his crime to count as a hate crime, currently existing hate crime laws don't provide a simple or uniform answer to this question. The hate crime laws in some states seem clearly to include both sorts of cases. The Wisconsin law cited earlier, for example, simply requires that the offender "intentionally selects" his victim because of his belief about the victim's group membership but says nothing about why the offender cares about the victim's group membership. The tactically biased arsonist and the bigoted arsonist both intentionally select their victims because they believe that their victims are black, and so the Wisconsin law would clearly count what both of them do as hate crimes. The same is true of the corresponding laws in some other states such as Delaware and Virginia.[6] A few other states have laws that define hate crimes in ways that would clearly exclude the tactically biased arsonist. Florida's law, for example, states that "The penalty for any felony or misdemeanor shall be [enhanced] if the commission of such felony or misdemeanor evidences *prejudice* based on the race, color, ancestry, ethnicity, religion, sexual orientation, or national origin of the victim," and the tactically biased arsonist is not prejudiced against black people. Similarly, the Massachusetts statute refers to actions "motivated by bigotry and bias," the New Hampshire law picks out cases in which the offender "was substantially motivated to commit the crime because of hostility towards the victim's" group,[7] and New Jersey's law enhances sentences for crimes that are at least partly motivated by "ill will, hatred, or bias due to race, color, religion, sexual orientation or ethnicity."[8] The tactically biased arsonist feels no bigotry, bias, hostility, ill will or hatred toward black people, and so he would not be guilty of a hate crime under those laws either. The laws in many states, moreover, are not completely clear about this question and in many cases have not yet been definitively interpreted by the relevant courts. And so in some states it may simply not be clear whether the tactically biased arsonist commits a hate crime.[9]

It might seem that while hate crime laws as a whole don't clearly and consistently address the case of the tactically biased arsonist, they at least clearly and unambiguously include the case of the bigoted arsonist. But even this does not seem to be quite correct. There can be more than one kind of bigoted arsonist, and the hate crime laws in some states seem to include only one kind but not the other. Since I want the discussion of hate crime laws here to be as clear and unambiguous as possible, it's therefore worth taking a moment to note and address this further possible source of confusion as well.

So consider the fact that there are, broadly speaking, two different kinds of negative attitudes that the bigoted arsonist might have toward black people. One attitude is a purely emotional one. A person might simply dislike black people, for example, without claiming that there's a good reason for other people to dislike them, in the same way that some people simply dislike cats without claiming that there's a good reason to dislike them. The other attitude is a purely cognitive one. A person might believe that black people are inferior to and have fewer moral rights than white people without disliking black people, for example, in the same way that a person might believe that cats are inferior to and have fewer moral rights than humans do without disliking cats. The first kind of bigoted arsonist has ill will or hostility toward black people, but he has no biased or prejudiced beliefs about them. People who don't like cats aren't prejudiced against them; they just don't like them. The second kind of bigoted arsonist does have a biased or prejudiced belief about black people, but he has no ill will or hostility to them. Someone who thinks that people are more important than cats need not have any ill will or hostility toward cats. Some of the state laws that I mentioned earlier would seem to include both kinds of bigoted arsonist. The New Jersey law, for example, refers to "ill will, hatred, *or* bias." The first two clauses cover the emotional kind of case and the third arguably covers the cognitive kind.[10] But some of the other laws don't seem to include both. The Florida law, for example, refers only to "prejudice," which might pick out the cognitive bigot but not the emotional bigot. People who simply don't like cats, after all, aren't really "prejudiced" against them. The New Hampshire law requires that the criminal act be motivated by "hostility" toward the victim's group, and Pennsylvania's law requires that the act be "motivated by hatred toward"[11] the victim's group, both of which seems to pick out the emotional bigot but not the cognitive bigot. People who think it's okay to eat beef, for example, aren't really "hostile" toward cows and don't really "hate" them.

The result of all of this is as follows. Some hate crime laws are clearly quite general: they would include every case in which an arsonist selected his victim because the victim was black: the tactically biased arsonist, the emotional bigot, and the cognitive bigot. Some would clearly exclude the tactically biased arsonist and clearly include both kinds of bigoted arsonists. Some seem to include only one kind of bigoted arsonist but not the other. And some, perhaps many, are not clear enough to determine exactly what they include. In addition, not all hate crime laws provide for the same result to occur in those cases that they do clearly identify as a hate crime. Some hate crime laws provide for a mandatory increase in the criminal's punishment, but others simply render such enhancement permissible. As a result of all of this, it's difficult to make an unequivocal judgment about hate crime laws in general. Some objections to such laws might apply only to laws that punish the bigoted arsonist without punishing the tactically biased arsonist, while others might apply only to laws that punish one kind of bigoted arsonist without punishing the other. In addition, some objections might apply to laws that make penalty enhancement mandatory but not to laws that make them permissible, while laws that permit but do not require such enhancements might pose problems of their own.

Rather than attempting to arrive at a specific assessment of every particular kind of hate crime law, then, my goal in this chapter and the one that follows will be to explain why I believe that hate crime laws are perfectly appropriate as a general matter. I'm inclined to think that the best arguments for hate crime laws justify laws that include every case of selecting a victim because of race within their scope: the tactically biased, emotionally bigoted and cognitively bigoted criminal. For that reason, I will frame my defense of hate crime laws as a defense of laws that cover all three categories. But if it turns out that there's a good reason for hate crime laws to be more narrowly defined, that won't pose a problem for my claim that hate crime laws, in some form or other, are morally justified. Since all hate crime laws at the very least permit penalty enhancement even if they don't require it, I'll try to defend the appropriateness of at least allowing penalty enhancement for such crimes if not positively mandating them. And even though of the three kinds of cases that I've discussed – the tactically biased, emotionally bigoted and cognitively bigoted criminal – only one can accurately be described as acting out of "hate," I'll nonetheless continue to use the term "hate crime" to refer to all three categories since the term "hate crime law" has become the most familiar way of referring to the laws that involve penalty enhancement in all three kinds of case.

For the purposes of the discussion that follows, then, a hate crime is a crime that falls under any of these three categories, and a hate crime law is a law that permits, and possibly requires, an extra penalty *at least* in cases where a white person who commits an ordinary crime like arson or assault[12] deliberately and successfully selects a black victim at least in part because the victim is black. It's almost certainly true that if such laws are justified then they will also be justified in cases where a black criminal deliberately targets a white victim for the same sorts of reasons and in cases in which the victim is targeted on the basis of such additional forms of group membership as religious or ethnic identity. It's probably also true that if such laws are justified then they're justified in cases in which the criminal and victim are members of the same group (a case in which an anti-Semitic Jew vandalizes a synagogue, for example). But I'll leave some of these questions about identifying the very best form for hate crime laws to take for others to consider and will focus here on the claim that such laws are justified at least as a general matter.

WHY I (STILL) DON'T HATE HATE CRIME LAWS

Hate crime laws so understood have been controversial from the very beginning. I have to admit, though, that for a long time I had difficulty understanding what all the fuss was about. I never thought much about the issue, but whenever I did think about it, it always seemed to me that there was a fairly simple justification for such laws: hate crimes are worse than ordinary crimes, worse crimes merit greater punishments, so hate crimes merit greater punishments. I don't think it ever occurred to me that either step in this simple two-part argument would need much support, but if I'd been pressed to justify the two steps in the argument, I suppose I would have said that both steps are justified because they provide the best explanation of a wide variety of judgments that I assumed virtually everyone would already be inclined to make.

Step one of my simple argument for hate crime laws, for example, maintains that hate crimes are worse than ordinary crimes. If I'd been asked to justify this step in the argument, I would probably have said that it seems to follow from the judgments that most people are already likely to make about a variety of cases. Consider, again, the arsonist who chooses a house to target because of its convenient location and the arsonist who chooses to target a particular house because the family who lives in it is black. I suspect that most people would respond to this example by thinking that while what the first arsonist does is clearly wrong, what the second arsonist does is even worse. If they discovered that one of their neighbors had been arrested for committing one of these crimes, for example, most people would be shocked in either case, but even more appalled in the second case than in the first. If they themselves were victims of such a crime, most would feel wronged in either case, but more deeply wronged in the second than in the first. But the only difference between what the first arsonist does and what the second arsonist does is that the first arsonist commits an ordinary crime while the second arsonist commits a hate crime that otherwise resembles the ordinary crime. And so if we agree that what the second arsonist does is worse than what the first arsonist does, this must be because hate crimes are, in fact, worse than the ordinary crimes that they otherwise resemble. When all the other facts about a pair of cases are equal, that is, the fact that one is a hate crime and the other isn't makes the hate crime a worse crime. And so, if I'd been pressed to try to justify this first step in my simple argument for hate crime laws, I would have said that the step is grounded in specific judgments that most people on both sides of the debate over hate crime laws already make.

The second step of my simple argument for hate crime laws maintains that the magnitude of a punishment should reflect the magnitude of the crime that it's a punishment for. The greater the crime, that is, the greater the deserved punishment. If asked to justify this step in the argument, I would again have said that accepting the truth of this principle seems to be necessary in order to account for the judgments that most people routinely make about the appropriate severity of the punishment for most crimes. Assuming that the practice of punishment itself is justified,[13] for example, virtually everyone agrees that the punishment for murder should be greater than the punishment for assault and that the punishment for assault should be greater than the punishment for shoplifting. And virtually everyone also agrees that murder is a worse crime than assault and that assault is a worse crime than shoplifting. But surely this isn't a mere coincidence. Virtually everyone believes that the punishment for one of these crimes should be greater than the punishment for another because they believe that one of these crimes is a worse crime than the other. It's hard to deny that the punishment for murder should be greater than the punishment for shoplifting, for example, and equally hard to see why the punishment for murder should be greater than the punishment for shoplifting if not because murder is a greater crime than shoplifting. So, if I'd ever taken the time to think about it, I would probably have said that the second step of my simple two-step argument for hate crime laws also seems to be well grounded in specific beliefs that most people already accept.

If both steps in my simple argument are accepted, moreover, there seems to be no way to avoid accepting hate crime laws as well. If hate crimes really are worse crimes than ordinary crimes, after all, and if worse crimes really do merit greater punishments than lesser crimes, then hate crimes clearly merit greater punishment than ordinary crimes. And since it always seemed clear to me, at least, that both steps in the argument really should be accepted, it always seemed clear to me that hate crime laws should be accepted as well. As a result, I never really understood why such laws were so controversial.

After looking more carefully into the literature on the subject, though, I can now see that things aren't as simple as my simple argument led me to believe. I can see that there's more to be said on the subject because I can see that more has been said on the subject. But while I now have a better understanding of why many people are opposed to hate crime laws, including many people who are motivated by the sorts of concerns that lead me to oppose hate speech restrictions, I remain unconvinced by the reasons that they've given for their opposition. Some potentially powerful objections can be raised in response to my simple argument. But I think that all of them can be overcome. That's why I still hate hate speech restrictions but still don't hate hate crime laws. I'll focus in the rest of this chapter on addressing the objection that claims that hate crime laws are wrong for the same basic reason that hate speech restrictions are wrong. In the next chapter, I'll address a variety of additional objections.

RETURN OF THE THOUGHT POLICE

Step one of my simple argument for hate crime laws maintains that hate crimes are worse than the ordinary crimes that they otherwise resemble. I'll consider objections that can be raised against this step of the argument at the start of Chapter 9, but let's suppose for now that that step one is correct. That would just leave step two. Step two maintains that worse crimes merit worse punishments. This step seems uncontroversial. Virtually everyone, regardless of their views about hate crime laws, agrees that punishments should be proportionate to the crimes for which they are imposed. The punishment for murder should be greater than the punishment for assault, for example, because murder is a worse crime than assault. And so it might seem that if step one of my argument is accepted, then the argument itself would have to be accepted, too.

On closer examination, though, it turns out that accepting step two of my simple argument isn't such a simple matter. A number of critics of hate crime laws have argued that whether the fact that one crime is worse than another makes it appropriate to punish it more severely than another can depend on why the one crime is worse than the other in the first place. And, in particular, they've claimed that if a crime is made worse simply because of the thoughts of the criminal committing it, then the fact that it's worse isn't enough to make it permissible, let alone appropriate, to punish it more severely. Punishing a hate crime more than a parallel ordinary crime because the hate crime is a worse crime, on this account, would amount to punishing the criminal who commits a hate crime for his objectionable thoughts. And that would be objectionable even if the criminal's objectionable thoughts really did make the crime worse. As Susan Gellman put this point in her influential law journal article, "Hate Crime Laws are Thought Crime Laws": "The only substantive element of most hate crimes statutes is that the defendant had a bias *motive* for committing the base offense. As motive consists solely of the defendant's thoughts, the additional penalty for motive amounts to a thought crime which offends the First Amendment."[14]

The complaint that hate crime laws illegitimately punish people for their objectionable thoughts has been pressed by a number of other writers,[15] and it's made its way into various legal opinions as well. When the Ohio State Supreme Court struck down that state's hate crime statute in the 1992 case of *Ohio v. Wyant*, for example, it ruled that "Enhancing a penalty because of motive ... punishes the person's thought, rather than the person's act or criminal intent." And when the Wisconsin Supreme Court issued a similar ruling in the case of *Wisconsin v. Mitchell* that year, it declared that "The hate crime statute violates the First Amendment directly by punishing what the legislature has deemed to be offensive thought.... Without a doubt, the hate crime statute punishes bigoted thought."[16] Since this objection to hate crime laws appeals to the fundamental value of freedom of expression, its popularity also helps to explain why so many people who oppose hate speech restrictions oppose hate crime laws as well. Hate crime laws, to put the concern in terms of the case of the two arsonists discussed earlier, mean that the arsonist who targets by race gets a longer sentence than the ordinary arsonist. Since the only difference between the two arsonists seems to be the racially biased thought that one but not the other of them acted on in selecting their victim, the extra part of the sentence for the arsonist who targets by race is, in effect, a punishment for his bad thoughts rather than for his bad deeds. And since virtually everyone agrees that the government shouldn't punish people simply for having bad thoughts, the objection concludes, virtually everyone should agree that the government shouldn't punish the arsonist who targets by race more for committing a hate crime than it would punish an ordinary arsonist for committing an ordinary crime.

There seems at first to be a clearly decisive response to this objection. The response points out that the law takes thoughts into account when determining levels of punishment all the time. This includes many cases in which virtually everyone on both sides of the hate crime laws debate agrees that doing so is perfectly appropriate. Consider, for example, the distinction that the law draws between first-degree murder and negligent homicide. Two people are each found to have dropped a heavy rock off of the top of a tall building with the result that the rock hit a pedestrian on the head and killed him. In the first case, the person who dropped the rock had been planning for weeks to kill his business rival. He followed him around every day until he knew his victim's routine, carried the rock to the top of a building that he knew he walked by every day, and waited patiently for hours until his business rival finally walked by. Then, at precisely the right moment, he carefully dropped the rock so that it would hit his rival on the head. In the second case, by contrast, the person who dropped the rock was just playing around on the top of the building when he came across a large rock that someone had left there. He wanted to hear the loud noise that the rock would make if he dropped it off the building, and he dropped it without first looking carefully enough to see if anyone was walking by beneath him. Both people killed someone by dropping a rock off the top of a building, and virtually everyone agrees that both of them should be punished for having done so. But virtually everyone also agrees that the first rock dropper should receive a much greater punishment than the second, and that this is because of a difference between what was going on in their minds at the time that they dropped the rock. In this case, at least, defenders and opponents of hate crime laws seem to agree that it's perfectly appropriate for the state to take mental states into account when deciding how much punishment to mete out to someone who has done something illegal.

Or suppose that two men are arrested for growing marijuana. One is growing it in order to smoke it in the privacy of his own home while the other is growing it in order to sell it in the alley behind the local high school. Again, the law draws an important distinction – in this case between possession with intent to consume and possession with intent to distribute – again, the distinction involves a difference in the state of mind of the two lawbreakers, and, again, virtually everyone on both sides of the hate crime laws debate agrees that it's perfectly appropriate for the state to do so. Even those who are skeptical about the merits of laws against marijuana agree that if there are going to be such laws it makes sense to punish people more severely for possession with intent to distribute and, again, this involves conceding that when someone has done an illegal act it can be perfectly reasonable and appropriate to take his state of mind when doing the act into account in determining how much punishment he should receive.

Or picture a group of tough guys sitting around a kitchen table looking over a copy of publicly available blueprints to the local bank. An assortment of tools, all of them legally purchased at a number of local hardware stores, lie scattered on the floor nearby. They're talking about exit routes, backup scenarios, places to lay low for a few days until the heat dies down. By planning to knock over the bank, these guys are committing a crime, but what makes their behavior illegal lies entirely in their minds. There's nothing the least bit illegal, after all, about sitting around a table and looking at some pictures. What makes them guilty of criminal conspiracy arises from what they are thinking, not what they are doing. And yet, once again, virtually everyone, regardless of their views of hate crime laws, agrees that it's perfectly appropriate for the state to take their mental states into account in deciding to punish them for what they are doing. Indeed, since this is a case in which the punishment seems to be entirely for the thought and not at all for the action, it seems to provide an especially strong basis for rebutting what I'll refer to in this section as the "thought police" objection to hate crime laws. If we can punish these guys for their thoughts when they haven't even done anything to act on them yet, after all, why shouldn't we take the thoughts of the arsonist who targets by race into account when deciding how much to punish him for burning down a black family's house because they're black?

This initial response to the thought police objection isn't as decisive as it might at first appear to be. Or, at least, it isn't as decisive as it at first appeared to be to me. This is because it turns out that many critics of hate crime laws believe that there's an important difference between two different kinds of mental states that the law might take into account when determining sentencing: motive and intent. Gellman is again a forceful representative of the hate crime law opponent's position on this point: "*motive* is the reason why the offender forms the *intent* to commit the act. Intent and purpose affect *what* the offender is doing; motive is *why* he or she is doing it."[17] An intention, on this account, refers to a goal or aim, the reason one has in mind for performing an action and that in part contributes to the action's having the character it has. Intentions are captured by the "in order to" that leads someone to do something. When one person drops a rock in order to make a loud noise and another drops a rock in order to kill someone, they do the same thing from an external point of view but they do it with different intentions and their different intentions have an effect on how we understand their acts: what the first person is doing is playing around while what the second person is doing is committing murder. A motive, on the other hand, refers to the desire that leads someone to form and act on a given intention in the first place. When two people each drop a rock from the top of a building in order to kill the person walking by below, on this account, they both act with the same intention – the intention of killing someone – but they may be motivated by very different desires that lead them to form and act on this intention. One may be motivated to kill his victim because the victim is a business rival, for example, while the other may be motivated to kill his victim because the victim had an affair with his wife. In the first pair of cases, two people do the same act with different intentions, while in this second pair of cases, two people act with the same intention but have different motives for forming and acting on that intention.

This distinction between motive and intention can be used to try to respond to the problem cases that I've raised for the defender of the thought police objection. Those cases, the critic may argue, involve taking the criminal's intentions into account, while hate crime laws instead involve taking the criminal's motives into account. It's the fact that a rock was dropped in order to kill someone rather than in order to make a loud noise, for example, that makes the difference between first-degree murder and negligent homicide. It's the fact that a person possesses a drug in order to sell it rather than in order to consume it that makes it a more serious offense. And it's only because the people looking at the blueprints of the bank are doing so in order to rob it that they can be charged with conspiracy. Hate crime laws, by contrast, involve the law taking into account someone's motive rather than their intention. If two people spray gasoline on a house and set a match to it, for example, both act with the same intention. They do what they do in order to burn the house down. If one targets a house because it's ugly and the other targets a house because a black family lives in it, then they act with the same intention – the intention of burning down a house – but they are led to form and act on this intention by different motives. A law that punished the second arsonist more severely than the first, then, would be taking motive into account rather than intention, while the uncontroversial examples that I appealed to in my initial response to the thought police objection all involve the law taking intention into account rather than motive. And so, the critic of hate crime laws concludes, the thought police objection succeeds in defeating my simple argument for hate crime laws after all. It isn't that hate crime laws are objectionable because they take into account just any kind of mental state at all. It's that they're objectionable because they take into account the criminal's motive in particular. And since none of the examples that I appealed to show that it's ever okay for the law to take motive into account when determining the amount of punishment that's appropriate, nothing that I've said so far really rescues my simple argument for hate crime laws from the thought police objection.

There are several problems with this attempt to use the distinction between motive and intention as a means of rescuing the thought police objection to hate crime laws. The first problem is that it isn't clear that the distinction itself is a meaningful one.[18] Consider, for example, the case of growing marijuana. Let's suppose that Larry, Moe, and Curly each do the very same act: they plant some marijuana seeds. Larry plans to smoke the pot that will result from his act, Moe plans to sell the pot that will result from his act so that he can buy a flashy new car, and Curly plans to sell the pot that will result from his act so that he can buy some expensive medicine for his ailing mother. One way to describe this set of cases is like this: Larry does the act that he does because he intends to smoke his pot, while Moe and Curly do the acts that they do because they each intend to sell theirs. On this understanding, Moe and Curly have different motives for their acts but their different motives have led both of them to form precisely the same intention: the intention to sell marijuana. And so, on this description of the cases, there are three different motives – wanting to get high, wanting a new car, wanting a healthy mother – and two different intentions: the intention to sell pot (Moe and Curly) and the intention to smoke pot (Larry). A second way to describe the same set of cases is like this: Larry, Moe, and Curly each do the act that they do because they intend to produce mature marijuana plants. On this understanding, they each have different motives for producing mature marijuana plants but their different motives have led all three of them to form precisely the same intention: the intention to produce mature marijuana plants. And so, on this second description of the cases, there are again three different motives – wanting to get high, wanting a new car, wanting a healthy mother – but only one intention: the intention to produce mature marijuana plants.

Now if there really is a genuine distinction between motives and intentions, there must be a correct answer to this question: is the difference between Larry and Moe simply a difference in motive or is it also a difference in intention? According to the first description of the cases, Larry and Moe have different motives and different intentions. According to the second description of the cases, Larry and Moe have different motives but the same intention. On the first description, the difference between growing pot to smoke it and growing pot to sell it marks a difference in intentions, and so punishing Moe more than Larry because Moe is growing pot in order to sell it would involve punishing him more for having a different intention. But on the second description, the difference between growing pot to smoke it and growing pot to sell it marks a difference in motives, and so punishing Moe more than Larry because Moe is growing pot in order to sell it would involve punishing him more for having a different motive.

If there's a real distinction between motives and intentions, then one of these descriptions must be correct and the other must be incorrect. But I, at least, find it hard to believe this. Each description seems like an equally accurate way of conveying the mental states that lead the three men to do what they do. What basis could there be for saying that one of the descriptions is right and the other one is wrong? I, at least, find it hard to see what it could be. But if there really is no rational basis for preferring one description to the other, then there's no rational basis for choosing between the claim that Larry and Moe have the same intention and the claim that they have different intentions. Rather than marking a real distinction between two different ways that the world could be, saying that they have different intentions and saying that they have the same intention but different motives seems to simply represent two equally accurate ways we might choose to describe the very same situation.

This result undermines the attempt to salvage the thought police objection for the following reason. The attempt to save the objection depends on the claim that there's a principled distinction between an intention and a motive and that while it's appropriate to take a person's intention into account in determining the extent of their deserved punishment, it's inappropriate to take their motive into account when doing so. It maintains that hate crime laws are unacceptable because they really punish people for their motives rather than for their intentions while laws that punish growing marijuana for distribution more than growing it for personal use are acceptable because they really punish people for their intentions rather than for their motives. But if the distinction between motive and intention amounts to no more than a difference between two equally legitimate ways of describing one and the same situation, then there will be no justification for saying that hate crime laws "really" punish for motive while drug distribution laws "really" punish for intention. The attempt to rescue the thought police objection to hate crime laws by appealing to the distinction between motive and intention will therefore fall apart.

I'm inclined to be satisfied with this first response to the motive versus intention argument. But let's suppose that I'm wrong. Let's suppose that, although it's quite subtle and difficult to pinpoint, there really is a difference of some sort between a motive and an intention and that the difference between Larry and Moe really is a difference in intention while the difference between the ordinary arsonist and the arsonist who targets by race really is a difference in motive. Even if this is true, it will only pose a problem for the second step of my simple defense of hate crime laws if the difference is a morally relevant one. There would have to be something about the difference between a motive and an intention, that is, that would explain why it's perfectly appropriate to take people's intentions into account when they break the law but morally unacceptable to take their motives into account. But even if there does turn out to be some kind of genuine difference between intentions and motives, it's hard to see how the difference could be so morally significant. What motives and intentions have in common seems far more important than anything that might turn out to render them distinct.

That this is so can perhaps most easily be seen by considering a simple case where virtually everyone, regardless of their view of hate crime laws, will surely agree that it's appropriate for the law to take intentions into account. So return for a moment to the case of the two people who each drop a rock off the top of a tall building with the result that a pedestrian below is killed. One drops the rock in order to hear a loud noise without first looking carefully enough to see if there are any people below, while the other deliberately drops the rock in order to kill his business rival. Virtually everyone will agree that the second person should receive a greater amount of punishment than the first. But there seem to be only two plausible explanations for why the difference in intention should matter, and both of these explanations seem to apply just as well to cases involving differences in motive.

One explanation appeals to the claim that the mental state of the person who deliberately kills is simply more objectionable than the mental state of the person who negligently kills. The other explanation appeals to the claim that the total social costs generated by intentional killing are greater than the total social costs generated by negligent killing. But both of these explanations for why it's appropriate for the law to take intentions into account apply equally to the question of whether it's appropriate for the law to take motives into account, even if we assume that motives and intentions really are two different things. Just as we find the mental state of the murderer more abhorrent than the mental state of the person whose negligence inadvertently leads to someone's death, for example, so we find the mental state of the arsonist who targets by race more abhorrent than the mental state of the ordinary arsonist. And just as the overall social costs imposed by the murderer are greater than the overall social costs imposed by the negligent person, so the overall social costs imposed by the arsonist who targets by race are greater than those imposed by the ordinary arsonist, at least if we assume, as I'm assuming for now, that step one of my simple argument for hate crime laws is true: hate crimes cause more harm to their immediate victims than do ordinary crimes and hate crimes cause harm to the broader community of members of the targeted group in a way that ordinary crimes don't.[19] Even if there turns out to be a difference between intentions and motives, then, there's no good reason to think that the difference is morally relevant. The reasons for thinking that intentions matter morally are reasons to think that motives matter morally, too.[20]

I've argued so far that there doesn't seem to be a clear difference between intentions and motives and that, even if there does turn out to be a difference, there's no reason to think that the difference is a morally relevant one. But now let's suppose that I've been mistaken on both of these points: there really is a difference between intentions and motives and the difference between them really is a morally relevant one. Even if both of these claims are true, they're still not enough to vindicate the thought police objection to hate crime laws. The objection doesn't merely maintain that we have *more* moral reasons to take intentions into account than we have to take motives into account. It maintains that we have no moral reason to take motives into account at all: that while taking intentions into account is perfectly appropriate, taking motives into account is positively inappropriate. But even if we agree that motives and intentions are different and that there is some morally relevant difference between them, it doesn't follow from this that taking motives into account is objectionable. There might still be good reasons to take motives into account even if there also happen to be even stronger reasons to take intentions into account as well. And, in fact, when we step back from the debate over hate crime laws in particular, we find that there are a number of cases in which taking motive into account strikes most people as perfectly appropriate. If this is so, then the fact that hate crime laws, too, take motive rather than intention into account, if it is a fact, can't be a reason to reject them even if in general it's easier to justify taking intentions into account than it is to justify taking motives into account.[21]

One kind of case that makes this clear involves the death penalty. When deciding whether someone should be convicted of first-degree murder rather than negligent homicide, a crucial consideration involves intention: did the accused intend to cause the death in question, or did the death arise as the result of recklessness or negligence? But once someone has been duly convicted of first-degree murder, judges have traditionally taken a number of additional factors into account when deciding whether or not to apply the death penalty. And one of these further factors has uncontroversially been the murderer's motive in killing his victim. A murder motivated by financial opportunism, for example, has typically been viewed as worse than one motivated by revenge.[22] But giving a criminal a greater punishment than he would otherwise receive because he acted out of an especially objectionable motive is precisely what hate crime laws do, at least on the assumption that critics like Gellman are right in distinguishing between motives and intentions in the way that they do. If the fact that murder sentencing standards take motive into account doesn't count as an objection to them, then the fact, if it is a fact, that hate crime laws take motive rather than intentions into account doesn't count as an objection to them either.

The reasons for taking intention into account may well turn out to be considerably stronger reasons than the reasons for taking motive into account. It may well prove much more important, for example, to distinguish between murder and negligent homicide than to distinguish between murder brought about by one motive and murder brought about by another. But even if this is so, it doesn't follow that there aren't good reasons to take motive into account, too. And, in fact, this very feature of capital punishment cases was one of the considerations that the U.S. Supreme Court appealed to when it ultimately overturned the Wisconsin State Supreme Court and upheld that state's hate crime statute in the 1993 case of *Wisconsin v. Mitchell*. Writing for a unanimous court, Chief Justice Rehnquist noted that in the case of *Barclay v. Florida* ten years earlier, the United States Supreme Court had already ruled that it's not unconstitutional for a judge to take "racial animus" into account in deciding to impose the death penalty in a murder case rather than life in prison.

In one sense, of course, appealing to claims about the appropriateness of the death penalty must inevitably remain controversial. Many people support capital punishment, but many others oppose it. In the more limited sense in which I'm making use of it here, though, the claim is one that most people on both sides of the hate crime laws debate will surely accept: if it's appropriate for the state to execute the worst of its murderers, then it's appropriate for the state to take motive into account when determining which murderers should receive the more severe sentence. The case of capital punishment for murder, then, provides one instance in which virtually everyone already agrees that taking motive into account is perfectly appropriate even if there proves to be a morally significant difference between motives and intentions and even if it turns out that taking intentions into account is more important than taking motives into account.

A second case in which most people agree that it's appropriate for the law to take motives into account arises in the context of civil antidiscrimination law. Consider, for example, Title VII of the 1964 Civil Rights Act. Among other things, that law makes it illegal to fire or refuse to hire someone because of the person's race. As one commentator on the law has noted, "If an employer fires someone because she does not like his taste in music, it violates no law. If she fires him because of his race, it does."[23] This means that, again assuming that something like Gellman's distinction between motive and intention proves to be vindicated, it's motive and not intention that the law takes into account in deciding whom to punish. If two bosses each sign a document authorizing the termination of one of their workers, they act with the very same intention: they do what they do in order to get rid of the worker in question. If the law punishes the boss who wants to do this because she doesn't like black people but doesn't punish the boss who wants to do this because she doesn't like people who listen to country music, then the law takes action against the first boss but not against the second boss because of a difference between their motives, not between their intentions.

Virtually everybody today, regardless of their view of hate crime laws, agrees that what the 1964 Civil Rights Act does is perfectly appropriate. Even people who generally oppose policies that are designed to benefit black Americans on the grounds that the law should be color blind almost always agree that the government should at least enforce antidiscrimination laws. Since virtually everyone accepts that it's appropriate for the government to enforce antidiscrimination laws, and since such laws take motive into account in deciding whether or not someone who fires an employee should be sanctioned, such laws provide a second reason to conclude that taking motive into account is acceptable even if there proves to be a morally important difference between motives and intentions.[24]

I'm inclined to think that these two cases are good enough. But since some people may well think that motives shouldn't be taken into account in death penalty cases and since some people disagree with the 1964 Civil Rights Act, I'll go ahead and provide one final example. This is a further case in which the government clearly takes differences in motive into account in determining sentences and in which, as far as I can tell, absolutely no one seems to think it should do otherwise. This is the practice of allowing for mitigating excuses. Suppose, for example, that two guys walk into a bar and that each subsequently punches someone in the nose. The first guy goes into the bar because he's following a long-standing business rival whom he's been trying to attack for months. When he finally has his rival cornered in the bar, he punches him in the nose. The second guy just goes into the bar to have a drink but is immediately confronted by a stranger who starts shouting horribly obscene things at him about his mother. He keeps his emotions in check for a long time, but finally gives in to the temptation to punch his antagonist in the nose.

In this pair of cases, both people do something illegal: they assault someone. And in this pair of cases, both people act with the same intention: they each do what they do in order to harm the person that they punch. But the law clearly distinguishes between an unprovoked attack and a provoked attack and it imposes a greater punishment on the person who's convicted of the first kind of attack than it does on the person who is convicted of the second kind. This practice, moreover, is about as uncontroversial as a legal practice can get. Virtually everyone, regardless of their view of hate crime laws, agrees that the law should punish the first guy in the bar more severely than the second guy. But on reflection, it should be clear that this kind of case, too, involves taking motives into account, again assuming that we follow critics of hate crime laws who distinguish between intentions and motives in the way that people like Gellman do. Each of the two nose punchers does what they do with the very same intention, that is, but the motives that drive them to form and act on their intentions are different. One is motivated by a long-standing animosity toward his rival, the other is motivated by his suddenly generated burst of anger, and this in the end is why virtually everyone agrees that the first attacker should be given a more severe sentence than the second.[25] But, once again, if it's perfectly appropriate for the law to take differing motives into account when determining the sentences in these sorts of cases, then the fact that hate crime laws also involve taking motives into account when determining the relative severity of sentences can't be held against them. Whatever truth there is to the claim that hate crime laws punish people for their motives rather than their intentions, it's equally true of laws that take motive into account in capital murder cases, federal antidiscrimination cases, and cases involving mitigating excuses. Since virtually everyone will agree that this isn't enough to justify opposing these other practices, virtually everyone must concede that it can't be enough to justify opposing hate crime laws either, even if there proves to be a difference between motives and intentions and even if the difference proves to have some moral significance.

I've argued to this point that there isn't really a clear difference between motives and intentions, that even if there is such a difference it isn't a morally relevant one, and that even if it is a morally relevant one, it's not important enough to render it inappropriate to take motives into account when determining sentences. But now let's assume that I've been mistaken about all three of these claims: there is such a difference, it is morally relevant, and it's important enough to make it inappropriate to take motives into account. Even if all of this is true, there's still one final reason to reject the attempt to sustain the thought police objection to hate crime laws by appealing to the distinction. The reason is that hate crime laws don't really take motive into account in the first place. In responding to the motive versus intention argument so far, I've been following hate crime law critics like Gellman in assuming that if there proves to be a clear distinction between motives and intentions then it will be clear that hate crime laws fall on the motive side of that divide. But, in fact, to the extent that the distinction can be successfully unpacked, there's good reason to believe that hate crime laws fall on the intentions side of the divide, that they really punish people for acting with certain sorts of intentions rather than for acting because of certain sorts of motives. Since even critics like Gellman agree that taking intentions into account is perfectly appropriate, this provides a final reason to reject her defense of the thought police objection to hate crime laws.

Gellman, remember, maintains that there's a clear line between motive and intent because intent is about *what* a person is doing while motive is about *why* they are doing it. If two people each do the same kind of act but do so with different intentions, on this account, then they really are doing two different things. And since it's appropriate to punish people differently for doing different things, it's appropriate to take differences in intention into account. But if two people are prompted by different motives to do the very same kind of act, then they should receive the very same punishment because they're doing the very same thing. Return, for example, to the case of the two men who drop a rock off the top of a tall building with the result that a pedestrian walking by below is killed. The difference between murder and negligent homicide, on this account, is clearly a difference in intentions. One is dropping a rock in order to kill someone while the other is dropping a rock in order to produce a loud noise. Dropping a rock in order to kill someone is a different activity from dropping a rock in order to produce a loud noise. And so it makes sense to take this difference into account in deciding on a suitable amount of punishment. But if one person drops a rock in order to kill someone he wants to kill because his target is a business rival and another drops a rock in order to kill someone he wants to kill because his target had an affair with his wife, then the two rock droppers are engaging in exactly the same activity: committing murder. They simply have different motives for engaging in it. And in that case, on this account, differences in punishment would be unjustified.

Let's now assume that this account of the difference between motives and intentions is correct. If it is correct, then the best explanation of why it's correct seems to involve a certain kind of counterfactual test. If Larry and Moe each drop a rock off the top of a building with the result that a pedestrian is killed and a loud noise is produced, that is, we can determine the nature of their intentions by asking them the following two questions: would you have dropped the rock if you knew that it would kill the person and that it would not make any noise? And would you have dropped the rock if you knew that it would not kill the person and that it would make a loud noise? Suppose that Larry answers yes to the first question and no to the second, while Moe answers no to the first question and yes to the second. Larry that is, would drop the rock if it would silently kill the victim but not if it would harmlessly make a loud noise, while Moe would drop the rock if it would harmlessly make a loud noise but not if it would silently kill the pedestrian below. It seems reasonable to take these answers to mean that what Larry was really aiming at was the death of the person below while what Moe was really aiming at was the loud noise he was hoping to produce. Larry, that is, was dropping the rock in order to kill someone while Moe was dropping a rock in order to make a loud noise. And this seems to be just another way of saying that Larry acted with the intention of killing his victim while Moe did not act with such an intention. This counterfactual test, moreover, successfully illuminates the more mundane sorts of choices that people make all the time. If you decide to fly rather than drive on your next vacation, for example, you may know that this will cause you to arrive at your destination more quickly and that it will cause you some airsickness, but you'll have no doubt that in making the decision to fly rather than drive, you act with the intention to arrive more quickly rather than with the intention to cause yourself some airsickness. The counterfactual test provides an intuitively satisfactory explanation of why this is so: you would still fly rather than drive if it got you there sooner and without causing airsickness, but you would not fly rather than drive if it would cause you airsickness without getting you there any sooner. If there really is a good way of getting at what makes a particular mental state an intention rather than something else, then, the counterfactual test seems to be it.

But now consider what the counterfactual test implies about hate crime laws. Suppose that Larry, Moe, and Curly each burned down the house of a black family and we asked the following question of each: would you still have burned down the house in question if the family living in it had been white? Suppose that Larry answers yes to this question while Moe and Curly each answer no. In this case, the counterfactual test reveals that the difference between Larry, on the one hand, and Moe and Curly, on the other, is a difference in intentions. Larry's intention was simply to burn down a house, while Moe and Curly each intended not just to burn down a house, but to burn down a black family's house. And now suppose further that we asked Moe and Curly why they each acted with the intention of burning down a black family's house. And suppose that here they gave different answers. Suppose that Moe formed and acted on the intention to burn a black family's house because he dislikes black people and feels animosity toward them while Curly formed and acted on the intention to burn a black family's house because he believes that the police will do less to investigate a crime if it's committed against a black family. In this case, the result would be that Moe and Curly had different motives for forming and acting on their intentions, but the intentions they acted on would nonetheless remain the same: the intention not just to burn down a house, but to burn down a black family's house.

Yet if the jurisdiction where Larry, Moe, and Curly live has a hate crime law of the sort that I've set out to defend here, the law will apply to Moe and Curly but not to Larry. Larry, after all, didn't burn down a house because of the fact that a black family lived in it while Moe and Curly each did. And this means that the difference that such hate crime laws pick out is ultimately a difference in intentions rather than a difference in motives. What the counterfactual test shows, that is, is that what makes the arsonist who targets by race different from the ordinary arsonist is that the arsonist who targets by race has an additional, and objectionable, intention that the ordinary arsonist doesn't have: the intention not just to harm someone, but to harm someone because of their race. Even if critics such as Gellman are right in thinking that there's a difference between motives and intentions and that the difference is a decisive one, then, their claims will still fail to support the thought police objection to hate crime laws. Such critics all concede that it's perfectly appropriate for the state to take differences in intention into account when determining sentencing and the analysis that I've developed here shows that, in the end, that's all that hate crime laws do.

I've now responded to the motives versus intentions defense of the thought police objection in a number of different ways. The result may seem a bit confusing if not outright inconsistent. I began by maintaining that there isn't really a difference between motives and intentions, after all, and ended by maintaining that hate crime laws really focus on intentions rather than on motives. But if there isn't really a difference between motives and intentions in the first place, then hate crime laws can't really focus on one rather than the other. And so my response to the attempt to defend the thought police objection by means of the distinction between intentions and motives may seem a bit incoherent.

And it is a bit incoherent. That's the nice thing about attacking an argument rather than defending one. When you're constructing an argument of your own, consistency is absolutely essential: the smallest little contradiction that slips in can cause the entire edifice to collapse. But when you're objecting to someone else's argument, consistency becomes irrelevant. You can try out one objection, and if that one doesn't work, you can try another. It doesn't matter whether the two objections are compatible with each other because all it takes is one to bring down the argument you've targeted. And that's the best way to understand what I've attempted to do in this section. I'm inclined to be skeptical about the distinction between motives and intentions. If my skepticism proves to be justified, then the defense of the thought police objection developed by such critics of hate crime laws as Gellman will have to be rejected for that reason. If my skepticism proves to be unjustified, then I will indeed turn out to be wrong in thinking that there's no clear distinction between motives and intentions. But if I'm wrong about that, the argument will still be subject to the further concern that the distinction is irrelevant. If I'm wrong about that, the argument will still be subject to the still further concern that it isn't relevant enough, and if I'm wrong about that, the argument will still be subject to the even further concern that hate crime laws fall on the morally acceptable side of the divide. As long as at least one of the four objections that I've developed in this section proves to be successful, the motives versus intentions strategy will be defeated and so, along with it, will be the thought police objection to hate crime laws.

Before concluding this discussion, though, it's important to note that there's still one final response available to the defender of the thought police objection. I've been proceeding up to this point on the assumption that the objection's central complaint is that hate crime laws enhance punishment for motive rather than for intention. That's certainly the most prominent way in which the objection has been developed. But the objection can be focused more narrowly as the complaint that hate crime laws enhance punishment for one kind of motive in particular, the kind that involves ideological beliefs. If ideological motivations merit special protection from the law above and beyond that accorded to other kinds of motivations, then perhaps the thought police objection can be sustained after all. In a spirited and insightful paper called "Susan Gellman Has It Right," for example, Ralph S. Brown argues that while motive might not necessarily have to be kept off the table in all cases involving sentence determination, "when the motive's kernel is exposed, and it reveals a political or social belief system that we are compelled to tolerate, then: not so fast!"[26] Martin H. Redish makes a similar point in his own defense of Gellman's position. "The unique defect of [hate crime] laws under the First Amendment," he argues, is not that they take into account just any kind of motive, but rather that "they penalize the holding of a particular political or social attitude."[27] And Gellman herself raises this point as a kind of back-up response that's meant to hold regardless of whether we analyze such laws in terms of intentions or in terms of motives: "In punishing a 'purpose' that is nothing more than the defendant's beliefs on a social issue, the government is still punishing the defendant's viewpoint and opinion. By contrast, a purpose such as the purpose to commit a felony (which changes trespass to burglary) does not implicate the exercise of First Amendment rights. It has no ideological content, expresses no disapproved viewpoint, and has no relationship to communications. The same cannot be said of bigotry, whether we characterize it as a 'motive' or as a 'purpose'."[28] If this response is correct, then hate crime laws succumb to the thought police objection after all, not because such laws take motive into account, but because by doing so, or even instead of doing so, they take ideology into account.

This supplementary defense of the thought police objection may well be telling against one particular kind of hate crime law. Suppose, for example, that a hate crime law is written in such a way that it clearly includes the cognitively bigoted arsonist but clearly excludes the emotionally bigoted arsonist as well as the tactically biased arsonist. It enhances punishment for the arsonist who targets a black family's house because he believes that black people are inferior, that is, but doesn't enhance punishment for the arsonist who targets a black family's house because he simply dislikes black people or because he thinks the police will be likely to investigate the case less thoroughly if a black family is the victim. In this kind of case, the cognitively bigoted arsonist might plausibly complain that he is being punished because of his racial ideology since it's only his beliefs about black people that distinguish him from the emotionally bigoted and tactically biased arsonists who also target their victims by race. Even here, it's not clear that the complaint would be fully justified. Strictly speaking, the cognitive bigot is punished for acting on that ideology rather than just for having it. If he broke a law while believing in this ideology but broke the law for reasons having nothing to do with his ideology – if he grew marijuana for reasons unrelated to his beliefs about black people, for example – he wouldn't receive an extra punishment simply because he believed in this objectionable ideology. Still, the objection would at least have some traction in the case of this particular kind of hate crime law.

But whatever the merits of this version of the thought police objection to this particular kind of hate crime law, it's clearly unsuccessful when aimed at the broad sort of hate crime law that I set out to defend at the start of this chapter.

That sort of law simply focuses on cases in which the arsonist targets a black family because they're black. Such laws enhance punishment for the emotionally bigoted arsonist and the tactically biased arsonist as well, and neither of them have any racial ideology at all.[29] Hate crimes laws that enhance punishment in the case of the arsonist who targets by race, then, do so not because the arsonist who targets by race has objectionable ideological beliefs – although he may well have such beliefs – but because he selects his victims in a manner that is objectionable regardless of whether the selection is grounded in such beliefs. It's true, of course, that some people who fall within the scope of such laws will fall within it because of their ideological beliefs, but this is true of many laws that take mental states into account. The difference between simple trespass and the more serious crime of burglary, for example, is that burglary involves the intent to commit a felony. And while some burglars may form this intention for reasons having nothing to do with ideology, others may form it for reasons having to do with their beliefs about private property laws, the rich having too much money, and so on. Punishing these ideological criminals for burglary and not just for trespassing in such cases doesn't amount to punishing them for their political beliefs even if it's their political beliefs that led them to form the intention that distinguishes burglary from simple trespass. In the same way, then, and for the same reason, the sort of hate crime law that I've been trying to defend here doesn't amount to punishing the cognitively bigoted arsonist for his racist ideology even if it's his racist ideology that led him to form the intention that distinguishes the arsonist who targets by race from the ordinary arsonist.

In the end, I suspect, it doesn't really matter what we call the mental states that distinguish the ordinary criminal from the one who commits a hate crime. Laws that take such mental states into account when determining sentences don't really punish people for having these mental states. Rather, they punish people for acting on them. In the context of capital punishment, for example, virtually everyone agrees that the fact that a murder was done for hire should count as an aggravating circumstance. And as Law Professor Paul H. Robinson has nicely put the point in that context, "killing for a fee may suggest an extreme indifference to the value of human life. It is not that the law punishes an actor for his or her greed or indifference but, when such aspects of character are *exercised* in performance of the offense conduct, they may alter our assessment of the blameworthiness of the actor for that conduct."[30]

The same is true in the case of hate crime laws. Whether we think of the character trait manifested by the arsonist who targets by race as an objectionable motive or an objectionable intention or an objectionable mental state of some other sort, the result is the same: when that character trait is exercised in committing a crime, it affects our assessment not simply of the person himself, but of what the person does. The difference between the criminal who commits ordinary arson and the hate criminal who targets by race when he commits arson isn't just about people with two different mental states, then, but about people who have done two different sorts of things. And so just as it's perfectly consistent to punish murder for hire more severely than other murders without punishing people just for being greedy, so is it perfectly consistent to punish arsonists who target by race more severely than ordinary arsonists without punishing people just for having racially biased mental states, whether they be, or be called, motives or intentions or purposes or something else. In the end, then, we can retain our support for hate crime laws while agreeing that people shouldn't be punished for having, or for expressing, racist thoughts. While the specter of the thought police remains a good reason to reject hate speech restrictions, then, it provides no good reason to reject hate crime laws. The question that remains is whether there is any other good reason to reject hate crime laws. I will turn to that question in the chapter that follows.

9

How to Keep on Loving Hate Crime Laws

Why Other Objections to Hate Crime Laws Don't Work, Either

In Chapter 8, I presented a simple, two-step argument in defense of hate crime laws: hate crimes are worse than ordinary crimes, worse crimes merit greater punishment, so hate crimes merit greater punishment. I noted that many people who oppose hate speech restrictions are led to oppose hate crime laws for the same sorts of reasons, acknowledged that this "thought police" objection to hate crime laws is considerably stronger than it may at first appear to be, but argued that in the end the objection fails to undermine the case for hate crime laws. Let's now suppose that I was right about this. Even if I was right, hate crime laws might still be objectionable for some other reason. So in this chapter, I'll consider and respond to other objections that people have raised against such laws. I'll conclude that none of them are successful, either.

WHAT'S HATE GOT TO DO WITH IT?

Step one of my simple argument for hate crime laws maintains that hate crimes are worse than the ordinary crimes that they otherwise resemble. A number of people have raised doubts about this step of the argument. It isn't necessarily that their intuitions about such crimes are different from mine. As far as I can tell, even many critics of hate crime laws have the same sort of fundamental response that I have: the arsonist who targets a house because a black family lives in it does something worse than the arsonist who strikes at random. But while they may share my intuitive reaction to such cases, these critics aren't satisfied with letting a case for hate crime laws rest on such reactions. Instead, they demand a further argument of some sort, an argument that doesn't simply establish that we tend to think that hate crimes are worse than ordinary crimes, but that explains why they are worse. More specifically, they demand an argument that identifies some property that distinguishes hate crimes from ordinary crimes and that can plausibly be used to show that hate crimes are worse in a manner that's consistent with other things we commonly believe about the relative severity of crimes. For a variety of reasons, these critics are skeptical about the viability of such an argument. And, for a variety of reasons, I'm not. In fact, I think there are two distinct arguments that can plausibly be given to justify the conclusion that hate crimes are worse than the ordinary crimes that they otherwise resemble.

The simplest argument for the conclusion that hate crimes are worse than ordinary crimes appeals to the claim that hate crimes are more harmful than ordinary crimes.[1] Virtually everyone, regardless of their view of hate crime laws, agrees that, all else being equal, one crime's being more harmful than another makes it a worse crime. And so virtually everyone should agree that if hate crimes are more harmful than the ordinary crimes that they otherwise resemble, then hate crimes are worse crimes than those ordinary crimes. This argument, in turn, can be broken down into an argument about the effect of such crimes on their immediate victims and an argument about the effect of such crimes on the larger relevant communities.

Let's start with the effects of a typical, ordinary crime on its immediate victim. So suppose that you're a black homeowner and that when you return from work one day, you discover that an arsonist has randomly burned down your house. Take a moment to consider the total magnitude of the harm that you would suffer in such a case: the financial loss, the emotional harm involved in the destruction of items of sentimental value, the inconvenience of having to find and furnish a new place to live, the hurt and anger you would feel toward the arsonist for what he had done to you, and so on. Now, after you have a good sense of the total amount of harm that you'd suffer in such a case, change the story so that the arsonist targeted your house in particular because you're black. It's hard to believe that you'd be completely indifferent to this change in the story, that this added feature wouldn't make things at least a little bit worse for you, that you wouldn't feel at least a bit more hurt, angry, insecure, and so on. Just as you'd feel worse if your house was torched by a random arsonist than you would if it were struck by lightning, you'd feel worse if it was torched as the result of a hate crime than if it was torched by a random arsonist.

This judgment about the relative harm in the two cases is partly a matter of common sense. It's just hard to believe that a racially biased motive would make absolutely no difference to the victim at all. But there also seems to be empirical support for this conclusion. A study sponsored by the National Institute Against Prejudice and Violence, for example, found that those who had been victimized by ethnically motivated violence had suffered 21 percent more trauma symptoms than had victims of otherwise comparable violence.[2] Another study, this one focusing on workplace violence, concluded that "victims of bias-motivated violence reported a significantly greater level of negative psychophysiological symptoms than did victims of nonbiased-motivated violence."[3] As a result, it seems reasonable to say that hate crimes cause more total harm than ordinary crimes. And since it's reasonable to say that when all else is equal more harmful crimes are worse crimes, it's perfectly reasonable to say that when all else is equal, hate crimes are worse than ordinary crimes.

A critic of this kind of argument, though, might respond by complaining that it rests on an overgeneralization about hate crimes. One way to press the point would be to complain that not all hate crimes are more harmful than ordinary crimes. The philosopher Claudia Card, for example, complains that a "hate crime can inflict almost any kind and degree of harm. That it was a hate crime does not tell us what kind or how much harm was inflicted, only what the motive was or the intention behind the selection of a victim. Nor is it clear that hatred makes crimes more harmful than crimes that are characteristically committed without hatred. Enormous damage can be done by sheer criminal negligence (polluting the natural environment, with contaminants that are uncontainable once let loose) and by greed (a common enough motive for murder)."⁴

This claim about the difference between hate crimes and ordinary crimes is certainly true. A murder that's motivated by a desire for profit or a serious beating that's aimed at a randomly selected victim surely causes more total harm than does an act of minor vandalism or petty theft that's driven by racial bias. But this particular comparison is irrelevant to evaluating the merits of hate crime laws. A hate crime law doesn't say that every hate crime merits a hasher punishment than every ordinary crime. It doesn't say, for example, that a racially motivated vandal merits a longer prison sentence than a greedy murderer. Rather, it says that every hate crime merits a harsher punishment than would be given for an ordinary crime that in all other respects was exactly like that particular hate crime. And once this feature of hate crime legislation is taken into account, it should be clear that Card's objection is beside the point. It doesn't matter that negligent polluting can cause more harm than racially motivated spray painting. What matters is that racially motivated polluting causes more harm than negligent polluting. And, again, it's hard to believe that anyone would deny this if they were on the receiving end of the wrongful treatment. As angry as you would probably be if a company negligently or intentionally dumped toxic waste in your neighborhood, you'd almost certainly be even angrier if the company targeted your neighborhood in particular specifically because most of its inhabitants were black.

A second way to press the concern about overgeneralizations is more modest and more plausible. It maintains that even if we limit our focus to pairs of cases in which all else is equal, it still isn't always the case that the hate crime will cause more harm than the ordinary crime. Even if most black Americans would feel a greater total loss if their house were destroyed by a racially motivated arsonist than by a random arsonist, that is, a critic might suggest that some black Americans might not feel that way. I'm left-handed, for example. If an arsonist targeted my house because I'm left-handed, I'd think that was peculiar, but I don't really think I'd feel any worse than I'd feel if an arsonist targeted my house at random. Perhaps there are some black Americans who feel about their blackness the way I feel about my left-handedness.⁵ If this is so, then this more modest version of the overgeneralization objection might still succeed. While it would remain the case that most hate crimes are more harmful than the ordinary crimes they otherwise resemble, it again would not always be the case. And that might be good enough to undermine the defense of the first step of my simple argument for hate crime laws that appeals to the claim that hate crimes are worse because they're more harmful.

In one important respect, this more modest version of the overgeneralization objection represents an improvement over the initial version. The initial version responds to a misleading picture of what hate crime laws involve, and this version is at least aimed at an accurate account of such laws. But while this modest version of the objection is correct in maintaining that hate crime laws may sometimes end up adding extra punishments in particular cases where no extra harm was caused by the fact that a crime was a hate crime and not just an ordinary crime, it's unreasonable to take this fact as a genuine problem for hate crime laws. In the case of many other reasonable rankings of the relative severity of crimes, after all, it can also sometimes be the case that no more harm is caused by a generally more harmful offense. In those other cases, we don't take that fact to be a good enough reason to reject our ranking of the offenses in general and so we shouldn't do so in the case of hate crimes either.

Consider, for example, the relative severity of assaulting a person and vandalizing a person's car. Virtually everyone, regardless of their view of hate crime laws, would agree that assault is a more serious crime than vandalism. And it seems plausible to suppose that at least part of a satisfactory explanation of this assessment would involve appealing to the fact that assault is a more harmful crime than vandalism. Most people, surely, would rather have their car destroyed than suffer even a relatively minor beating. But some people, of course, might not. They might be so emotionally attached to their cars or so indifferent to their physical well being that, on the whole, they would feel worse off having their car destroyed than being physically assaulted. This seems true enough. But now suppose that someone made the following argument: "since assaulting someone doesn't *always* harm them more than vandalizing their car, the standard punishment for assault shouldn't be greater than the standard punishment for vandalizing a car." In this case, it should be clear, virtually no one, regardless of their view of hate crime laws, would find the argument convincing. If assault is generally more harmful than vandalism, it's reasonable to count that in favor of making the punishment for assault greater than the punishment for vandalism. But if that's so in the case of this particular comparison, then it must be so in the case of the comparison between hate crimes and the ordinary crimes that they otherwise resemble. Even if hate crimes don't always cause more harm than their ordinary counterparts, it's hard to deny that they generally do. And as long as they generally do, that's enough to provide a reasonable basis for concluding that hate crimes are worse than the ordinary crimes they otherwise resemble.

Indeed, the case for hate crime laws on this point is even stronger than this. The comparison between assault and vandalism, after all, is a bit like comparing apples and oranges: it involves saying that one kind of behavior is generally more harmful than a second and very different kind of behavior. But the comparison between a hate crime and the ordinary crime that it otherwise resembles is more like comparing an apple not to an orange, but rather to the very same apple plus something extra. And since that something extra creates a significant (even if not certain) probability of increasing the total amount of harm that's caused, it's even easier to conclude that hate crimes are worse than ordinary crimes than to conclude that assault is worse than vandalism. Assault is not simply vandalism plus an extra bad thing, but a hate crime just is a parallel ordinary crime plus an extra bad thing.

In this respect, a second and more forceful analogy makes the case for hate crime laws on this point even more difficult to resist. This is the case of robbery versus armed robbery. When all else is equal, the punishment for armed robbery is considerably greater than the punishment for unarmed robbery. And virtually everyone, regardless of their views of hate crime laws, seems to accept that this is perfectly appropriate. But armed robbery is simply robbery plus something extra, the use of a weapon. And so the only explanation for this judgment must be that the presence of this something extra makes the crime worse.

It's easy to see why this would be so in general. The presence of a gun is likely to cause more psychological stress to the victim of a robbery, and to increase the chances that more harm on the whole will result. But while these seem to be good reasons to think that armed robbery is more harmful and dangerous than unarmed robbery in general, it doesn't follow that this is so in every instance. In some cases, for example, a victim of an unarmed robbery might be emboldened to attack the robber, with disastrous results, and the stress of deciding whether or not to attack might itself be painful. In such cases, the victim of an unarmed robbery might well have been better off if the robber had instead been using a gun. But the possibility that this may sometimes happen generates no real doubt about the fact that armed robbery is generally more harmful than unarmed robbery, nor does it generate any real doubt about the fact that this is a good enough reason to consider armed robbery a worse crime than unarmed robbery.[6] For the very same reasons, then, the fact that a hate crime may sometimes prove to be no more harmful than the ordinary crime that it otherwise resembles provides no reason to doubt that hate crimes are generally more harmful or that hate crimes are therefore worse crimes than ordinary crimes.

I'm inclined to think that the fact that a hate crime is so likely to cause more harm to its immediate victim is a good enough reason to conclude that hate crimes are worse than the ordinary crimes that they otherwise resemble. Before moving on to see how the argument for this conclusion can usefully be supplemented, though, it's worth considering one further objection that might be raised at this point. For a critic of the argument might concede that people generally do care about their racial identity in a way that they don't care about their left- or right-handedness and he might admit that this shows that hate crimes are generally more harmful than the ordinary crimes that they otherwise resemble, but the critic might nonetheless maintain that it's irrational to care more about one's race than about one's left- or right-handedness and that the law shouldn't put any extra weight on the harms caused by racial bias precisely for this reason.

The fact that someone irrationally cares about something, on this view, doesn't mean that the law should take the harms that are traceable to their irrational beliefs or desires into account when determining the severity of the crimes that caused the harms.

The rationality of racial pride and self-identification strikes me as a tricky subject. But for the purposes of this discussion, we can simply assume that the critic is correct: although most black Americans would, in fact, feel worse being targeted by a racist arsonist than by a random arsonist, let's suppose that this is ultimately irrational of them. If people were more rational, they would treat race as just another irrelevant fact about themselves and care no more about it than they care about the color of their eyes or the shape of their toes. Even if this is true, though, it doesn't follow that it's inappropriate for the state to take the extra harm generated by what we're now assuming to be their irrational feelings into account in assessing the severity of hate crimes. What matters is not whether their feelings can be rationally justified, but whether it's reasonable to expect that the typical, generally reasonable, citizen will have such feelings. And once it becomes clear that this is the relevant question, it should become clear that there's nothing inappropriate about the state's taking the extra harm caused by hate crimes into account even if the extra harm turns out to rest on people having an irrational concern with their race and their racial identity.

Consider, for example, the case of public nudity. Most Americans would be offended or disturbed by the sight of grown adults walking around in public spaces with no clothing on. In some cultures, though, public nudity might prove completely innocuous. Members of those cultures might argue that the dominant attitude toward the human body in this country is irrational. And they might be right. Perhaps if we were more rational, we would recognize that our hangups about nudity are completely unfounded. But even if it's true that the common attitude toward nudity in this country is ultimately irrational, this doesn't mean that the state has no business taking the harms that public nudity can cause into account when deciding how to treat those who break the law. Suppose, for example, that two men are arrested on a charge of disturbing the peace. Each was walking down the street of a public pedestrian mall while screaming obscenities and throwing rotten vegetables at people. Assuming that all else was equal in the two cases, one would expect that there is some just amount of punishment that both of them would deserve.

But now suppose that all else was not equal in the following respect: one of the men was fully clothed while he was disturbing the peace and the other man was completely naked. There is little doubt that the second man would receive a greater amount of punishment than the first and little doubt that virtually everyone, regardless of their view of hate crime laws, would view this as an appropriate result. This case is admittedly not perfectly symmetric with that of hate crime laws: public nudity is an additional offense to be added on top of the charge of disturbing the peace while the racial targeting component of a hate crime is not by itself an independent crime. Nonetheless, the basic point remains the same: in both cases, one person is penalized more than another because he did what he did in a manner that would be likely to cause additional distress to others as a result of their (we are assuming) irrational attitudes toward their body or their racial identity. As long as it's reasonable to expect that the typical, generally reasonable, citizen will be disturbed or offended by the sight of public nudity, it's reasonable for the state to take the harms that public nudity causes into account in this way even if the harms only arise because the average reasonable American has irrational attitudes about the human body. In the same way, then, and for the same reason, as long as it's reasonable to expect that the typical, generally reasonable, victim of a hate crime will be more disturbed or offended than he would be by being the victim of an otherwise comparable ordinary crime, it's reasonable for the state to take the extra harms that the racial motivation causes into account even if the harms only arise because the average American has irrational attitudes about the importance of racial identity. In the end, then, there seems to be no good reason to deny that hate crimes generally cause more harm to their victims than do the ordinary crimes they otherwise resemble, and no good reason to deny that this supports the claim that hate crimes are therefore worse crimes than those ordinary crimes.

My first argument for the claim that hate crimes are worse than ordinary crimes can usefully be supplemented by considering the fact that, on average, hate crimes are also more likely to cause extra harm to people other than their immediate victim: those members of the victim's community who are likely to feel degraded and threatened by the crime. If an ordinary arsonist burns down someone's house, after all, his act is an assault against his particular victim, but it's not really an affront against anyone else. If an arsonist deliberately sets out to burn down a particular house because a black family lives in it, on the other hand, his act is reasonably taken to be an affront not just against the victim, but against other black families in the community as well.[7] It also seems plausible to suppose that it increases the chances of retaliatory violence and rioting.[8] And, perhaps most disturbingly, it reinforces the belief that black people are particularly suitable targets for such acts, which may encourage even further criminal acts that target them.[9] Since increased harm and risk of harm to secondary victims seems just as relevant to determining the overall seriousness of a crime as does increased harm and risk of harm to primary victims, this provides a second reason to conclude that hate crimes are worse than ordinary crimes.

As with the case of the appeal to the increased harm that hate crimes cause to their immediate victims, it's open to a critic of such laws to complain that this appeal to the increased harm that hate crimes cause to others in the community need not hold in every case. Perhaps some black neighbors of a hate crime victim view their being black in the way that I view my being left-handed, for example, and so feel no particular impact as a result of such attacks. But, again as with the case of the appeal to the increased harm that hate crimes cause to their immediate victims, the fact that in some cases a hate crime proves no more harmful to the larger community than the ordinary crime that it otherwise resembles poses no real problem for the claim that hate crimes are worse crimes than those ordinary crimes. Armed robbery may in some cases prove no more harmful than unarmed robbery, after all, but this fact doesn't undermine the claim that armed robbery is appropriately treated as a worse crime. In the same way, and for the same reason, the fact that hate crimes may in some particular instances prove no more harmful than the ordinary crimes that they otherwise resemble doesn't undermine the claim that hate crimes are nonetheless appropriately treated as worse crimes than those ordinary crimes.

Being prone to cause more harm to innocent people is one way that one criminal act can be worse than another. Virtually everyone, regardless of their view of hate crime laws, agrees with this claim. And when we take care to compare a hate crime not just to any ordinary crime, but to the ordinary crime that it otherwise resembles, it becomes clear that hate crimes are, in fact, prone to cause more harm to innocent people. This provides one good reason to conclude that hate crimes really are worse crimes than ordinary crimes.[10] A second way that one criminal act can be worse than another is if it's done with a worse state of mind. The mental state involved in the killing carried out by a professional hit man, for example, is more objectionable than that involved in the killing carried out to avenge a serious wrong, and this also contributes to the fact that the former is a worse crime than the latter. The claim that worse mental states make for worse crimes is also generally accepted by people on both sides of the hate crime laws debate. And this claim, too, ultimately provides support for the conclusion that hate crimes are worse than the ordinary crimes that they otherwise resemble.

Consider, again, the ordinary arsonist and the arsonist who deliberately targets a particular house because the family that lives in it is black. Setting aside questions about whether the second arsonist's act is, at least on average, likely to result in a greater amount of overall harm, it's difficult to avoid the feeling that his act is done with a more objectionable state of mind. And since it seems clear that acting from a more objectionable state of mind can make a crime worse than it would otherwise be, this fact provides a second and distinct justification for the claim that hate crimes are worse than the ordinary crimes that they otherwise resemble.[11]

A critic might object at this point that while this claim about the mental state involved in a hate crime applies to the emotionally bigoted and cognitively bigoted criminal, it doesn't apply to the tactically biased criminal. Since the tactically biased criminal has nothing against black people himself, it might be thought that the mental state he acts from is no worse than that of the ordinary criminal. But there are two problems with this objection. First, a defender of hate crime laws could simply concede the point and limit hate crimes to those that involve racial animus of one sort or another. As I noted near the start of Chapter 8, after all, many hate crime laws already do this either explicitly or at least as a matter of practice. But second, and more importantly, the mental state of the tactically biased criminal can't be let off the hook so easily. When the tactically biased criminal deliberately targets black victims out of the belief that the police are less likely to take such cases seriously, after all, he deliberately takes advantage of the fact that the people he's targeting are particularly vulnerable to such exploitation. As a general matter, what's involved in intentionally preying on the most vulnerable members of society strikes most people as particularly objectionable. And in a variety of other contexts, virtually everyone on both sides of the hate crime laws debate agrees that this fact warrants a greater amount of punishment than would otherwise be deserved. Federal sentencing guidelines, for example, as well as those of many states include a provision for sentencing enhancement in the case of crimes in which the defendant "knew or should have known that a victim of the offense was a vulnerable victim." And while the federal guidelines define a "vulnerable" victim in part as someone who is "unusually vulnerable due to age, physical or mental condition" they also include those who are "otherwise particularly susceptible to the criminal conduct."[12] In those cases where a person's race makes it tactically advantageous to target them, they are for that very reason particularly susceptible to criminal conduct. And so the claim that most people already accept, the claim that those who deliberately target the vulnerable are especially despicable, supports the claim that what the tactically biased hate criminal does is especially despicable, too. Whether because he himself dislikes or disapproves of black people or because he's willing to exploit the racism of others indirectly in order to advance his own interests, then, the racial attitude the hate criminal acts with betrays an objectionable state of mind lacking in the case of the ordinary criminal.[13]

Critics of hate crime laws typically respond at this point by raising doubts about whether hate crimes really are worse in this respect. Philosopher David A. Reidy, for example, asks "is it obvious that the mental state of a criminal who selects his victims out of racist animosity is more culpable than that of the criminal who selects his victims out of a desire to see the weak suffer, or to impose the greatest harm possible on a nonvictim third party, or to display his superiority to the ordinary run of humanity, or to salve an ego all to easily bruised?"[14] But this response to the second reason for taking hate crimes to be worse than ordinary crimes suffers from the same defect as the parallel response to the first reason that I discussed earlier: hate crime laws don't say that every hate crime is worse than every ordinary crime. Rather, they say that hate crimes are worse than those ordinary crimes that they otherwise resemble. And when that feature of hate crime laws is kept in mind, it becomes clear that Reidy's complaint, like that of Card, is beside the point. It doesn't matter that some other mental states are also extremely objectionable. What matters is that a crime committed from a racially biased mental state is a worse crime than one that isn't but that resembles the first crime in all other respects. In order to defend the claim that hate crimes are worse than ordinary crimes, that is, it isn't necessary to claim that racial animus is worse than, say, sadism toward the weak. It's merely necessary to claim that a hate crime that betrays such animus is worse than an otherwise parallel ordinary crime that doesn't. An arsonist who singles out poor black people as part of his campaign to make the weak suffer, that is, does something even worse than an arsonist whose otherwise parallel campaign picks out poor people at random.

To defend hate crime laws on this point, for that matter, it isn't even necessary to claim that racial bias is worse than simple greed. Consider, for example, a man who goes around stealing from people so that he can afford a flashy new car. Now compare him to a man who goes around deliberately targeting black people to steal from so that he can afford a flashy new car. The defender of the claim that hate crimes are worse than ordinary crimes doesn't have to insist that every racially biased crime involves a worse mental state than every greedy crime. He must simply maintain the mental state of the second greedy thief is worse than the mental state of the first greedy thief. This is an extremely modest claim and one that most people on both sides of the hate crime laws debate will surely accept. And so, once again, it's hard to resist the claim that hate crimes are worse than the ordinary crimes they otherwise resemble.

If the first step in my simple two-step argument for hate crime laws maintained that every hate crime is worse than every ordinary crime, then neither the appeal to greater harm nor the appeal to more objectionable mental states would provide a satisfactory defense of it. But since hate crime laws depend only on the claim that hate crimes are worse than those particular ordinary crimes that they otherwise resemble, the appeal to greater harm and the appeal to more objectionable mental states each suffice to defend the first claim made by my simple argument for hate crime laws: in the only sense that's needed in order for the argument to succeed, hate crimes really are worse crimes.

THE DEVIL MADE ME (WANT TO) DO IT

A further objection to hate crime laws appeals to a general principle that virtually everyone on both sides of the debate clearly accepts: people shouldn't be punished for what's beyond their control. If I deliberately punch you in the nose, for example, then it's fair to hold me responsible for my behavior. But if a sudden seizure irresistibly forces my fist into your nose, then while the resulting damage my hand causes you might be just as great, it would be wrong to hold me culpable for having caused it.

On the face of it, at least, it's hard to see how this uncontroversial moral principle could pose a problem for the defender of hate crime laws. It's not as if the difference between the ordinary arsonist and the hate crime arsonist is a difference between someone who has control over whether he sets a house on fire and someone who doesn't. But at least a few critics of hate crime laws have argued that such laws violate this fundamental principle nonetheless.[15] Their claim is not that those who commit hate crimes have no choice but to break the law, but rather that when they do freely choose to break the law, they have no control over the facts that render their crime not just an ordinary crime, but a hate crime. The extra punishment they receive for committing a hate crime rather than an

ordinary crime, that is, turns out on this account to be punishment for something
over which they have no, or at least not enough, control.

Law Professor Heidi M. Hurd, for example, asks us to consider the case of an
anti-Semitic vandal: "At the moment that a defendant is about to throw a rock
through his neighbor's window, we are reasonably sure that he can will to do
otherwise; but at that moment, can he will away his hatred of his neighbor as a
Jew?"[16] Hurd answers this question, plausibly enough, by suggesting that while
it may be possible for people to indirectly influence their bigoted attitudes in the
long run – deliberately seeking out experiences that might not fit the stereotypes
they hold, for example – it isn't really possible for a person to simply decide to
change such a deep-seated attitude at a moment's notice. But this seems to pose
a problem for the defender of hate crime laws. Suppose, after all, that two van-
dals are each about to throw a rock through one of their neighbor's windows. The
first is an ordinary vandal who doesn't like his neighbor because he thinks he's
obnoxious. The second is the anti-Semitic vandal who doesn't like his neighbor
because he's Jewish. If both follow through with their plans, and if there's a hate
crime law in their jurisdiction, then the anti-Semitic vandal will receive a greater
punishment than will the ordinary vandal.

But while all of the punishment that the ordinary vandal would receive would
be for something that was fully within his control – he could easily have refrained
from throwing the rock if he had wanted to – the extra amount of punishment
that the anti-Semitic vandal would receive would be for something that was not
within his control: he could not have simply decided to stop hating Jews. This
seems to show that such a law, in Hurd's words, "targets things that are not fully
or readily within defendants' immediate control. And if law ought not to punish
us for things that we cannot autonomously affect, then hate and bias crime legislation is suspect for doing just that."[17] This is not to insist that the anti-Semitic
vandal should receive no punishment at all. It is just as much within his control to refrain from throwing the rock as it is within the control of the ordinary
vandal. And so, on this account, the hate crime vandal should be punished for
throwing the rock just as the ordinary vandal should. But since it's not within the
hate crime vandal's control to simply choose to abandon his hatred for Jews, the
enhanced punishment that the hate crime vandal receives for committing a hate
crime rather than an ordinary crime amounts to punishing him for something
that's beyond his control. And since it seems wrong to punish someone for something that's beyond his control, it seems wrong to punish him more for committing a hate crime than for committing an ordinary crime.

There's something right about this objection. People shouldn't be punished
for doing something that was beyond their control. Virtually everyone, regardless
of their view of hate crime laws, accepts this fundamental principle. But there's
something wrong about this objection, too.[18] It's wrong to think that when someone freely chooses to break the law, this uncontroversial moral principle is violated if the law provides extra punishment based on factors that were beyond
the offender's control at the time that he freely chose to break the law. There

are, in fact, a variety of cases in which the law adds extra amounts of punishment for factors that are beyond the offender's control at the moment that he freely chooses to violate the law. These practices are widely accepted by people on both sides of the hate crime laws debate, and widely understood to be consistent with the ideal of punishing people only for doing things that are within their control. And once we understand why this form of penalty enhancement is accepted in the cases where it is uncontroversially accepted, we can see why the rule against punishing people for things that are beyond their control, when properly understood, provides no reason to reject hate crime laws.

Virtually everyone on both sides of the hate crime laws debate, for example, agrees that repeat offenders should receive harsher punishments than first-time offenders who commit the same crime under the same circumstances. But at the time that someone is freely choosing whether or not to break the law, they have no control over whether it would be their first offense. The practice of giving harsher punishments to repeat offenders, then, involves the law's considering in favor of penalty enhancement a factor that is not under an offender's control at the time that he chooses to break the law. The same is also true of the practice of taking mitigating excuses into account. As was also noted in the discussion of the thought police objection in the previous chapter, virtually everyone agrees that the punishment for an unprovoked assault should be greater than that for a provoked assault. But at the moment that a person is free to choose whether or not to punch a stranger in the nose, he has no control over whether or not the stranger had previously provoked him.[19] Finally, the amount of punishment for many offenses varies, sometimes considerably, from state to state. The punishment for selling a certain amount of marijuana, for example, may be quite a bit higher in one state than in another. But at the moment that a person is free to choose whether or not to sell that amount of marijuana to someone, he has no control over which state the sale will take place in.

With these cases in mind, we're now in a position to see that Hurd's objection to hate crime laws must be rejected. The objection maintains that it's wrong to impose a greater punishment on the anti-Semitic vandal than on the ordinary vandal because the extra punishment arises in virtue of the anti-Semitic vandal's hatred of Jews and at the time that he chooses to throw the rock through his neighbor's window, he has no control over whether or not he hates Jews. But if the way that hate crime laws generate penalty enhancements were rejected for this reason, we would also have to reject penalty enhancement in a wide range of cases in which virtually everyone on both sides of the hate crime laws debate clearly accepts it. The hate crime vandal has no control over the fact that if he throws the rock he will have committed a hate crime rather than an ordinary crime, but the hit man has no control over the fact that if he pulls the trigger he will have committed murder for hire rather than ordinary murder. The person who already has a prison record has no control over the fact that if he breaks the law it will be as a repeat offender rather than as a first-time offender, the bar patron who hasn't been provoked has no control over the fact that if he punches someone he will have committed unprovoked assault rather than provoked assault, and the person passing through a state in which selling a certain amount of marijuana is a felony rather than a misdemeanor has no control over the fact that if he sells that amount right now he will have committed a felony rather than a misdemeanor. In all of these other cases, virtually everyone agrees that this feature of the penalty enhancement in question isn't enough to render it morally unacceptable. The same must therefore be said about the penalty enhancement involved in hate crime laws.

The fact that these other cases are so uncontroversial, moreover, doesn't just show that Hurd's objection is unfounded; it also helps to explain why it's unfounded. Suppose, for example, that a convicted hit man were to complain about the enhancement of his sentence. And suppose his complaint was that at the time that he pulled the trigger he had no choice but to be killing for money rather than to be killing for some other reason. In that case, virtually everyone would immediately see the flaw in his argument. In one sense, it's true that he had no choice but to be killing for money: if he killed at that moment, it was going to be for money and not for something else. But in another sense, he did have a choice: he could choose whether or not to kill in the first place, and if he chose not to kill, then he wouldn't be guilty of killing for money. In the hit man case, moreover, it should be clear that it's the second sense of choice that's morally relevant. If murder for hire is worse than ordinary murder, then it's permissible to impose a more severe penalty on the hit man than on the ordinary murderer because the hit man freely chooses to be guilty of this worse crime by freely choosing to kill. This is why penalty enhancement is permissible in the cases where it is uncontroversially permissible and why such enhancement doesn't violate the important moral principle that says that people shouldn't be punished for doing something that was beyond their control. In the morally relevant sense, committing a murder for hire wasn't beyond the hit man's control because he could have freely chosen not to pull the trigger.

But in the same way, then, and for the same reason, we must say the same thing about the anti-Semitic vandal who receives a greater punishment than the ordinary vandal receives because of the existence of a hate crime law. Hurd's complaint about such laws is that at the time that the anti-Semitic vandal threw the rock through his neighbor's window, he had no choice but to be committing a hate crime rather than an ordinary crime. In one sense, it's true that he had no choice but to be committing a hate crime: if he went ahead and threw the rock, it was going to be because he hates Jews and not for some other reason. But in another sense, he did have a choice: he could choose whether or not to throw the rock in the first place, and if he chose not to throw it, then he wouldn't be guilty of a hate crime. As the uncontroversial case of the hit man clearly demonstrates, it's the second sense of choice that matters in such circumstances rather than the first. And since in the second sense of choice the anti-Semitic vandal was free to choose – he wasn't free to choose not to be anti-Semitic, but he was free to choose not to be an anti-Semitic vandal – punishing him more than the ordinary vandal is punished doesn't violate the important moral principle that says that people shouldn't be punished for doing something that was beyond their control. In the morally relevant sense, committing a hate crime wasn't beyond the anti-Semitic vandal's control because he could have freely chosen not to throw the rock. And so, in the end, considerations about freedom and responsibility provide no reason to reject hate crime laws.

DOUBLE JEOPARDY

I've been characterizing hate crime laws up to this point as laws that add an extra amount of punishment when someone commits a crime like arson or assault as a hate crime rather than as an ordinary crime. In a typical case, for example, an ordinary arsonist might be sentenced to three years in jail while an arsonist who committed an otherwise comparable hate crime might be sentenced to five years. A different way of representing the same set of facts, though, would be to say that hate crime laws punish a person twice for committing a single crime. The arsonist who targets by race, on this understanding, receives a three-year sentence for burning down a black family's house and an additional two-year sentence for the very same act. This way of construing hate crime laws raises the possibility that such laws might violate a second fundamental principle: the Fifth Amendment guarantee against being exposed to double jeopardy. This possibility hasn't been explored in the literature on hate crimes as thoroughly as have the other objections that I've considered so far, but it's been forcefully pressed by at least one critic of such laws, Gregory R. Nearpass, in a 2002 law review article.

Nearpass begins by quoting the Fifth Amendment guarantee that "No person shall ... be subject for the same offence to be twice put in jeopardy of life or limb." And citing the 1969 case of *North Carolina v. Pearce*, he notes that courts have traditionally understood this to mean that the double jeopardy clause provides three distinct protections: it "protects against a second prosecution for the same offense after acquittal. It protects against a second prosecution for the same offense after conviction. And it protects against multiple punishments for the same offense."[20] The relevant part for our purposes here is the third: does punishing the arsonist who targets by race more than the ordinary arsonist amount to aiming multiple punishments at the arsonist who targets by race for one and the same offense? If it does, and if there really is a legitimate right against such multiple punishments, then it would seem that hate crime laws violate the rights of those who are punished according to their dictates and are objectionable for that reason. I'll assume, at least for the sake of the argument, that there's a moral right corresponding to the legal right against being exposed to double jeopardy. The question, then, is whether hate crime laws can reasonably be construed as violating this right.

In order to answer the question of whether hate crime laws expose those who break them to an objectionable form of double jeopardy, Nearpass explains how the United States Supreme Court understood the double jeopardy clause in the

1993 case of *United States v. Dixon*.[21] Dixon had been arrested for second-degree murder and then released from jail on bond. A condition of his release required that he not commit "any criminal offense" while on bond, and specified that failing to meet this requirement would result in his being prosecuted for contempt of court. While on conditional release and awaiting trial, Dixon was then arrested and charged with possession of cocaine with intent to distribute. He was found guilty of contempt of court. His lawyer then moved to dismiss the drug charge. His argument was that the punishment for contempt of court was already a punishment for the drug possession and so to charge him now with violating drug laws would be to punish him twice for one and the same act.

The Supreme Court agreed that prosecuting Dixon for the possession charge violated his right not to be exposed to double jeopardy. And in analyzing their decision as a way of laying a foundation for his case against hate crime laws, Nearpass emphasizes that they reached that decision by applying what has come to be referred to as the "*Blockburger* test," named after an earlier 1932 decision. The Blockburger test is designed to answer the question of whether two charges that are brought against a defendant really are two distinct charges, in which case there's nothing objectionable about bringing both of them, or whether they're really just two different ways of charging someone for one and the same act, in which case prosecuting a defendant on both charges violates his right against being exposed to double jeopardy. Nearpass cites the Court's characterization of the Blockburger text as it was described in the *Dixon* decision. In that opinion, the test is presented as one that asks "whether each offense contains an element not contained in the other."[22] If there's something about charge one goes beyond what's involved in charge two and something about charge two goes beyond what's involved in charge one, that is, then the two charges pass the Blockburger test and both can legitimately be brought against the defendant. But if at least one of the charges contains nothing that isn't already contained in the other charge, then adding the redundant charge to the original one would amount to charging the defendant twice for one and the same offense. The pair of charges would therefore fail the Blockburger test and bringing both charges against the defendant would violate his right against being exposed to double jeopardy.

In the *Dixon* case, the Court concluded that the prosecution on both charges failed the Blockburger test. The charge of contempt did include an element not included in the drug charge: it included the element of being in violation of the conditions of his release from jail on bond. But the drug charge didn't include any element not already included in the contempt charge. The contempt charge was filed because Dixon had violated a condition of his release by committing a "criminal offense," and the criminal offense was precisely the possession of cocaine with intent to distribute. In being found guilty of contempt of court, that is, Dixon had already been convicted for possession of cocaine with intent to distribute. And so to prosecute him for the drug charge after having already prosecuted him for the contempt charge would be to prosecute him twice for one and the same act. As the Court put it in its ruling, because "Dixon's drug offense did not include any element not contained in his previous contempt offense, his subsequent prosecution violates the Double Jeopardy Clause."[23]

Having explained how the Blockburger test is used to determine whether a state action objectionably exposes a defendant to double jeopardy, Nearpass then argues that hate crime laws can be shown to be objectionable for precisely the same reason by showing that they, too, fail the Blockburger test. Punishing the assaulter who targets by race more than the ordinary assaulter, he argues, "effectively puts the defendant on trial for assault twice – once for his *acts* [where he gets one punishment, the one that the ordinary assaulter gets] and again for his *intent* behind the acts [where he gets a second punishment, one that the ordinary assaulter doesn't receive]."[24] Hate crime laws, on this analysis, effectively bring two charges against the defendant for one and the same offense. One charge involves assault and the other involves assault with a certain kind of intention. But while the second charge thus contains an element that the first charge lacks, the first charge contains no element that the second charge lacks. The Blockburger test, as Nearpass emphasizes, requires that each charge contain some element that the other lacks. And so, he concludes, hate crime laws are structurally identical to the *Dixon* case, and must be rejected for that reason.[25]

There are two problems with Nearpass's argument. The first is that it misconstrues the nature of hate crime laws. Hate crime laws don't punish the assaulter who targets by race once for assault and then a second time for biased assault. They simply punish him once, for biased assault rather than for ordinary assault, and they punish him more for biased assault than he would be punished for ordinary assault because biased assault is worse than ordinary assault. It's therefore inaccurate to picture such laws as violating the Blockburger test. They would violate the test if they punished for assault and then for biased assault, since if they did that the first charge would contain no element not contained in the second. But they don't do that, and so they don't fail the test. Indeed, Nearpass himself seems to recognize this fact when he characterizes hate crime laws as putting the defendant on trial "once for his *acts* and again for his *intent* behind the acts." On this characterization of such laws, they clearly pass the Blockburger test: the charge for acting in a certain way contains an element that a charge for having a certain kind of intention doesn't include, and the charge for having a certain kind of intention includes an element that the charge for acting in a certain way doesn't include. So Nearpass's argument is impaled in the horns of a dilemma: either it depends on a misrepresentation of what hate crime laws do or it fails to establish that such laws fail the Blockburger test. Either way, the argument fails to show that hate crime laws, properly understood, objectionably violate the right that defendants presumably have against being subject to double jeopardy.

The second problem with Nearpass's argument is that it has implications that virtually everyone on both sides of the hate crime laws debate will surely reject as unacceptable. For suppose that Nearpass were correct in maintaining that hate crime laws violate the right against being exposed to double jeopardy because they punish someone for committing a certain kind of act and then punish them again for doing the act with a certain kind of intention. If this feature of hate crime laws really were enough to render them morally unacceptable, then we'd also have to reject a wide range of further practices that virtually everyone on both sides of the hate crime laws debate clearly accepts.

One example of this problem, ironically enough, comes from the crime that Dixon himself was charged with in the very case that Nearpass appeals to in developing his argument: possession with intent to distribute. As I noted in the discussion of the thought police objection toward the end of Chapter 8, virtually everyone agrees that if it's appropriate to ban the use of a certain drug, then possession of the drug with the intent to distribute it should be punished more severely than possession of the drug with the intent to consume it. But if Nearpass's argument shows that hate crime laws violate the right against double jeopardy, then it will also show that such drug laws do as well, and for the same reason. Such laws, after all, punish the drug offender a certain amount for possessing the drug, and then add a greater amount of punishment if he possesses it with the intent to distribute it. If taking intent into account in this way is enough to make hate crime laws violate the right against double jeopardy, then it will be enough to make such drug laws violate that right as well. But virtually everyone on both sides of the hate crime laws debate agrees that if such drugs are to be illegal, it's perfectly appropriate for the decisions about how much to punish people to take intention into account in this way. And so virtually everyone should reject Nearpass's parallel complaint against hate crime laws.

A second example of this problem was also noted in the context of the thought police objection: the practice of treating the fact that a murder was done for hire as an aggravating circumstance. Again, virtually everyone on both sides of the hate crime laws debate agrees that this practice is perfectly appropriate. But, again, Nearpass's argument would entail that it violates the murderer's right not to be exposed to double jeopardy. Such laws, after all, permit the state to charge the defendant with murder and then to seek to add a greater penalty for the objectionable mental state the murderer acted on. Since virtually everyone agrees that this feature of such laws isn't enough to make them violate the right against double jeopardy, virtually everyone should agree that the fact that hate crime laws have this feature isn't enough to make them violate the right either. Finally, consider the case of burglary. A person who breaks into a house with the intent to commit a crime such as theft is guilty of burglary, while a person who breaks into a house in order to get out of the rain isn't. Virtually everyone on both sides of the hate crime laws debate agrees that the first trespasser should receive a greater sentence than the second. But, yet again, Nearpass's argument against hate crime laws is unable to account for this judgment. Such laws, after all, punish the burglar for illegally entering the house and then add some additional punishment for his illicit intention. If these facts about the laws regarding burglary aren't enough to make them violate the right against double jeopardy, then the fact that hate crime laws do the same thing isn't enough to make them violate the right either. In the end, then, while appealing to the right against being subject to double jeopardy may help to generate a novel objection to hate crime laws, it fails to generate a compelling one.

JUST CHILLING

The first two objections I've considered in this chapter maintain that hate crime laws are objectionable because they violate an important moral right of those who are charged under them: the right not to be punished for what is beyond one's control and the right not to be subject to double jeopardy. In both cases, I've tried to show that the objections are misguided. But there's a final set of worries that critics of hate crime laws have also raised and that focus on more pragmatic concerns. I'll conclude my defense of hate crime laws in these last few sections, then, by explaining and responding to them.

Suppose, first, that a law is such that in theory, at least, it doesn't violate anyone's rights, including their right to freedom of speech or freedom of thought, but in practice it will likely be used in ways that do infringe on such freedoms. In cases of this sort, a court may well strike the law down on the grounds that it is "overbroad." As Law Professor James Weinstein explains it, the "rationale of the overbreadth doctrine is that the very existence of a statute with a real potential for application to protected speech unconstitutionally 'chills' the exercise of First Amendment rights."[26] Even if hate crime laws don't violate the First Amendment in principle, then, they might still be objectionable on the grounds that, in practice, they would have this worrisome chilling effect. And, in fact, a number of critics have raised this worry as an additional objection to such laws.

Gellman is an important representative of the hate crime law critic's position on this point as well. "A person genuinely wondering about ethnic differences or subjects such as intermarriage, genetic differences, affirmative action, or integration," she argues, "might think twice about airing his or her thoughts, knowing that they could be marched out as damning (or at least embarrassing) evidence" if they were ever charged with a crime that could be construed as a hate crime.[27] And the Wisconsin Supreme Court invoked the overbreadth doctrine in the *Mitchell* case as one of several grounds for rejecting that state's hate crime law as unconstitutional.[28] Even if enhancing punishment for a hate crime would not in itself involve punishing someone for expressing their objectionable ideas, then, as the thought police objection discussed in the previous chapter maintained, it might still be the case that the enforcement of such laws would inhibit people from exercising their right to express those ideas. It would do this not by counting their expression of such ideas as a violation of the law in itself, but rather by treating their expression of such ideas as evidence that in violating a law against such acts as arson or assault they were guilty of a hate crime rather than of an ordinary crime. And that prospect itself might be deemed sufficiently worrisome to warrant rejecting such laws.

There are two reasons to reject this "chilling effect" objection to hate crime laws. The first is that the objection has implications that virtually everyone on both sides of the debate over such laws already rejects. As noted earlier, for example, most people, regardless of their view of hate crime laws, accept the legitimacy of antidiscrimination laws such as that embodied by Title VII of the 1964 Civil Rights Act. They agree, for example, that the law may permissibly forbid an employer to fire or refuse to hire someone simply because they're black. But if hate crime laws should be rejected on the grounds that they may discourage people from expressing certain sorts of unpopular views, then antidiscrimination laws should be rejected for precisely the same reason. Indeed, if anything, the worry about possible chilling effects generates a far more powerful objection to antidiscrimination laws than it does to hate crime laws. Suppose, to take one of Gellman's examples, that I believe that interracial marriage is immoral and am considering expressing my view publicly. Since I think it's extremely unlikely that I'll ever assault someone or burn down someone's house, the thought that my expressing this view might one day be used to justify charging me with a hate crime if I did would be unlikely to occur to me, and unlikely to carry much weight in my deliberations even if it did. The existence of a hate crime law, then, would do virtually nothing to deter me from expressing my view about interracial marriage. But if I'm an employer, I'll know that it's quite likely that I'll sometimes have to fire people and virtually inevitable that I'll frequently have to decline to hire people who apply for positions working for me. Some of these people will probably turn out to be black. And as an employer, it's likely to occur to me that if and when I find myself firing or declining to hire a black person, I might be accused of violating an antidiscrimination law. So the thought is very likely to occur to me, and very likely to worry me, that if I publicly express my view about interracial marriage it may one day be used to justify charging me with firing or not hiring someone because they're black. The existence of antidiscrimination laws, then, will do far more to chill my freedom of expression than will the existence of any hate crime law. So if the prospect of such a relatively powerful chilling effect is not sufficient to warrant rejecting antidiscrimination laws, then the prospect of a relatively weaker chilling effect is surely not sufficient to warrant rejecting hate crime laws.

Not everyone, of course, will find this first example convincing. They may be inclined to oppose the existence of antidiscrimination laws in the first place and so find the implication that such laws should be rejected to be perfectly acceptable, though even here it's hard to believe that they would reject antidiscrimination laws merely on the grounds that they might have a chilling effect. It's much more likely that they would oppose them on the grounds that they violate the employer's right to freely decide who to hire and fire. But there are other, even less controversial, aspects of the law that would presumably also have a chilling effect of the sort that critics of hate crime laws appeal to. And in these cases it's hard to imagine that anyone would really be willing to accept the implication that these parts of the law should therefore be rejected. As was also noted earlier, for example, the law draws a sharp distinction between intentional homicide and negligent homicide, and virtually everyone agrees that this is perfectly appropriate. But just as prior expressions of controversial racial views might later be held as evidence that someone committed a hate crime rather than an ordinary crime if they were later charged with arson or assault against a black victim, so might such expressions later be held as evidence that an act that harmed a black victim was intentional rather than negligent. Similarly, the law uncontroversially aims more punishment at those who commit unprovoked assault than at those who commit an assault after being provoked. And just as prior expressions of controversial racial views might later be held as evidence that someone committed a hate crime rather than an ordinary crime if they were later charged with arson or assault against a black victim, so might such expressions later be held as evidence that an attack against a black victim was unprovoked rather than provoked. But no one really thinks that these possibilities are worrisome enough to warrant rejecting such laws. The same should therefore be said about the corresponding worry about hate crime laws.

I'm inclined to think that this first response to the chilling effect objection to hate crime laws is strong enough to warrant rejecting it. The worry that some people will be deterred from exercising their right to express their ideas about race because it might come back to haunt them if they one day find themselves accused of having committed a crime that could be construed as a hate crime simply strikes me as too remote to warrant rejecting such laws. But even if the prospect of people having such statements later held against them really does seem to be sufficiently worrisome, there's a second response to the objection that can be invoked, and this second response seems to be decisive: the law could simply adopt a rule that renders evidence of such previous statements inadmissible in court. Weinstein, for example, describes a case in which the defendant is charged with having attacked someone who is Jewish and in which the only evidence that the crime might have been a hate crime is that in previous conversations with friends the defendant had sometimes called Jews "kikes" and had on multiple occasions said that Jews were "cheap' and "subversive."[29] If inhibiting people from making such statements is deemed too great a cost to pay, then as Weinstein suggests, the evidence that the defendant made such statements can simply be excluded from the trial. It's possible, of course, that this will often make it difficult to successfully prosecute a case as a hate crime case. But the fact that it's often difficult to prove that a law has been broken isn't by itself a good objection to the law itself. And so, in the end, the chilling effect objection doesn't provide a good reason to reject hate crime laws.

THE CASE OF THE MIND-READING JURY

A further objection maintains that inflicting a greater amount of punishment on criminals who target by race renders hate crime laws unacceptable as a practical matter. This objection claims that even if we agreed that extra punishment for hate crimes was a good idea in theory, the empirical problems involved in determining the mental states of criminals would still be sufficiently great to warrant rejecting such laws in practice. As columnist George Will has put the concern, hate crime laws "mandate enhanced punishments for crimes committed because of thoughts that government especially disapproves. That is, crimes committed because of, not merely accompanied by, those thoughts. Mind-reading juries are required to distinguish causation from correlation."[30]

Will is correct in maintaining that hate crime laws require juries to make a determination about the thoughts that a criminal acted on in deciding, say, which person to attack or whose house to burn down. And in a certain sense, he's also correct to maintain that this requires them to be mind readers. But the law requires juries to be mind readers in this sense in the case of many other laws. This fact doesn't lead people to oppose these other laws. And so it shouldn't lead them to oppose hate crime laws either. As has already been noted in the context of the thought police objection, for example, the law imposes a greater punishment for possession of marijuana with intent to distribute than for possession with intent to consume. And it imposes a greater punishment for breaking into a person's house with the intent to steal than for breaking in with the intent to get in out of the rain. Virtually everyone, regardless of their view of hate crime laws, agrees that the laws that determine the relative severity of punishment in these cases are perfectly appropriate. These cases, too, require a jury to determine the intention that led the defendant to behave in the way that he did. Since this fact doesn't lead people to oppose such laws, the fact that hate crime laws also require juries to determine the intention that led the defendant to behave in the way that he did shouldn't lead them to oppose hate crime laws either. And since most people, regardless of their view of hate crime laws, accept the legitimacy of antidiscrimination laws, such laws pose a further problem for the "mind reading" objection. Antidiscrimination laws, after all, are just like hate crime laws in that they focus on whether or not a person was selected for a certain kind of unwelcome treatment because of their race. If the need to determine the intent of the person who fires a black employee isn't enough to warrant rejecting antidiscrimination laws, then the need to determine the intent of the person who burns down a black person's house isn't enough to warrant rejecting hate crime laws either.

None of this is to insist, of course, that prosecuting people for committing hate crimes is a simple matter. It may well often prove difficult for prosecutors to make a convincing case against someone charged with a hate crime, just as it may well often prove difficult to make convincing cases against people accused of other crimes that include intention as a component. Proving conspiracy, for example, is an inevitably tricky matter. But in these other cases, virtually everyone recognizes that the practical difficulty doesn't mean that the laws themselves should be rejected. And so, in the end, the same should be said about hate crime laws.

As I noted at the outset of the previous chapter, virtually every hate crime law includes race as a protected category, along with religion, ethnicity, and national origin. A number also include some additional categories, such as gender, disability, and sexual orientation. I've been focusing here exclusively on the case of race, and if what I've said is correct, then hate crime laws are justified at least in that case. But it might be thought that by focusing so narrowly on one particular category, I've neglected one final objection that might be raised against hate crime laws. This objection maintains that they fall prey to a kind of line-drawing problem: if we're going to enhance punishment for crimes that involve targeting people by race, that is, then it seems hard to deny that we should also include, at the least, some of these additional categories. But once we start increasing the number of protected groups, where will we stop? What principle will be used to determine which groups merit special treatment and which ones don't? Gellman, yet again, is a forceful critic of hate crime laws on this point. Drafting such laws, she worries, "requires a series of difficult to near-Solomonic decisions."[31]

In one sense, this objection to hate crime laws is simply implausible. If the reasoning behind such laws is sound, then in a great many kinds of cases it will be sufficiently clear that a certain kind of category shouldn't be included. It doesn't take the wisdom of Solomon, for example, to see that burning down someone's house because they have an odd number of letters in their last name, or because their address ends with an even number, or because they are allergic to grapes, wouldn't qualify as a hate crime in the morally relevant sense. These sorts of groups plainly lack the sorts of features that make crimes that target people by race particularly worrisome. People don't identify with their names, addresses, or allergies in the way that most people do identify with their racial make-up, for example, and there's no comparable history and legacy of discrimination based on these kinds of groupings of the sort that would tend to make such self-identification relatively common. So it would be implausible to take these kinds of crimes to be especially objectionable or harmful in the way that race-based hate crimes are plausibly taken to be.

In another sense, though, the line-drawing objection does point to a legitimate concern about hate crime laws. For there will just as clearly be at least some cases in which it really isn't so clear whether or not the category in question should be included. Consider, for example, a thug who attacks a person simply because he's homeless, or a high school bully who selects his victims based on their being identified by their peers as geeks. Here it may not be so clear whether the crimes in question should count as hate crimes.[32] And even within

the relatively clear and uncontroversial categories that such laws pick out, difficult line-drawing problems can emerge. Most people, for example, would agree
that if hate crime laws are justified at all, then religion is one of the categories
that they should recognize. But what, precisely, is a religion? Does Scientology
count? What about atheism?[33]

These are good questions. But a defender of hate crime laws need not answer
them. The reason for this is simple: comparable line-drawing problems persist
throughout the law. Since such problems arise even in the case of laws that virtually everyone on both sides of the hate crime laws debate accepts as just and
reasonable, the fact that they also arise in the case of hate crime laws provides no
reason to reject such laws.

One example that poses a problem for the hate crime law critic here should
come as no surprise at this point in the discussion: antidiscrimination laws such
as those embodied in Title VII of the 1964 Civil Rights Act. As has already been
noted in a few different contexts in this chapter, most people today, regardless
of their view of hate crime legislation, agree that it's appropriate for the state
to forbid employment discrimination based on race. But laws that forbid race-
based employment discrimination raise precisely the same line-drawing problem
that laws enhancing penalties for race-based hate crimes raise: where, precisely,
should we draw the line between those groups that should be recognized by such
laws and those that should not? In the uncontroversial case of antidiscrimination law, virtually everyone would respond to this question by saying two things:
that the question doesn't have a clear and obvious answer, and that the fact that
it doesn't is not a good reason to reject such laws. Instead, we should simply do
the best we can to draw the line between the groups that the law recognizes and
those that it doesn't in as reasonable a manner as possible. And so in order to
remain consistent, we must say the same thing about the parallel question raised
by hate crime laws: it, too, lacks a clear and obvious answer, but this lack, too,
fails to provide a good reason to reject such laws. Some groups should clearly be
included in the scope of hate crime laws, some groups should clearly be excluded,
some groups fall into a fuzzy gray area, but no group poses a problem big enough
to warrant the rejection of such laws.

Antidiscrimination laws thus provide one powerful rebuttal to the line-drawing objection. Since not everyone today endorses the appropriateness of such
laws, though, it's worth noting that equally difficult line-drawing problems arise
even in the case of laws that virtually everyone accepts as just and reasonable.
Virtually everyone, for example, agrees that the law should forbid rape and murder. If any laws are morally uncontroversial, these are. Yet even laws against rape
and murder raise line-drawing questions that can't be easily answered. Rape, for
example, involves having sex with another person without that person's consent. In some cases, it's clear that consent has been given, and in other cases, it's
clear that consent has not been given. But in some cases, unfortunately, it just
isn't clear whether the words or behaviors in question can reasonably be construed as constituting genuine consent. And self-defense is almost universally

acknowledged as a legitimate defense against a charge of murder. But while virtually everyone agrees about this much, the question of what counts as justified self-defense again raises difficult line-drawing problems. If I kill you in order to avoid a one hundred percent chance of your killing me, for example, then it's clear that I shouldn't be convicted of murder. If I kill you in order to avoid a tiny chance of your stepping on my big toe, then it's just as clear that I should be. But in between these extremes lie a variety of fuzzy gray cases: how much lower than one hundred percent can the risk of imminent harm to me drop before my killing you is no longer justified as self-defense? How much less severe than death can the prospective harm to me drop before my action is no longer justified in this way? These are all difficult questions that have no clear answer. But the fact that they have no clear answer doesn't mean that we shouldn't have laws against rape and murder. In the same way, then, and for the same reason, the fact that the line-drawing questions raised by hate crime laws have no clear answer doesn't mean that we shouldn't have hate crime laws either.

A MODEST CONCLUSION

Hate crimes are worse than the ordinary crimes they otherwise resemble. Worse crimes merit worse punishments. Hate crime laws enhance the punishment for hate crimes and so support for hate crime laws follows from these two claims. Since these two claims strike me as reasonable, and since support for hate crime laws follows from these two claims, support for hate crime laws strikes me as reasonable, too. It's worth noting, though, that some hate crime laws are more severe than others. And so it's worth emphasizing, in conclusion, that nothing that I've said here in defense of hate crime laws in general commits me to endorsing the more extreme forms that such laws can sometimes take.

One way that hate crime laws can vary quite significantly has to do with how much extra punishment they specify. A hate crime law adds at least some amount of extra punishment for crimes that are committed as hate crimes, but this amount can range from very small to very large. Some hate crime laws are quite severe in this respect. They might add two or three years in prison for a crime that would ordinarily call for little more than three years to begin with. In some cases, the relative magnitude of the enhancement can even be much greater. In the New York case of *People v. Grupe*, for example, Grupe was charged with striking a Jewish man in the face and chest while shouting ethnic slurs including "I'll show you, Jew bastard." Setting aside the issue of enhancing the punishment for committing the crime as a hate crime, the maximum penalty for his offense given the relatively minor nature of the assault was fifteen days in jail. New York's hate crime law, though, raised it to a year, making the punishment more than twenty-four times greater.[34]

This kind of result strikes me as unreasonably extreme. While hate crimes do seem worse than the ordinary crimes that they otherwise resemble, it's hard to believe that they're more than twenty-four times worse. It's difficult, of course, to say just how much worse they are. But it seems plausible to suppose that most of what's wrong about burning down a black family's house is that it involves burning down someone's house. So, at least in typical cases, it seems plausible to suppose that the amount of additional punishment that will be warranted for committing a crime as a hate crime will be on the relatively modest side. None of the arguments that I offered in defense of hate crime laws or in response to the various objections that have been raised against them depended on the claim that the enhanced punishments should be severe. And so nothing that I've said in this chapter or the previous chapter commits me to anything beyond a relatively mild form of hate crime law in this respect.

A second way that hate crime laws can vary concerns whether they render the amount of enhanced punishment in question obligatory or merely permissible. Some hate crime laws automatically add a given amount of punishment when a crime of a certain sort is committed as a hate crime. But others simply increase the maximum sentence that a judge is permitted to impose while leaving the final decision at the judge's discretion. Hate crime laws that mandate additional punishment strike me as more severe than those that simply render it permissible because their inflexibility prevents judges from responding to all of the details of a particular case. But what is potentially objectionable about such laws is not that they are hate crime laws, but rather that they are inflexible laws. Nothing about the defense of hate crime laws that I've offered in this chapter or the previous one commits me to this sort of inflexibility. Indeed, to the extent that my defense of the claim that hate crimes are worse than ordinary crimes rested on the claim that they tend to cause more harm as a general matter, it may well be better suited to a defense of flexible hate crime laws rather than inflexible ones. Either way, the fact that hate crime laws that inflexibly require additional punishments in every case may be objectionable poses no problem for the defense of hate crime laws that simply permit such enhanced punishments when they are called for.

Finally, and perhaps most important, hate crime laws can differ quite dramatically in terms of the form of additional punishment that they permit or require. In some states, enhanced punishment for hate crimes means little more than extra jail time for those who commit them. But a number of hate crime laws instead contain provisions for alternative forms of additional sentencing, including various forms of community service.[35] Having the arsonist who targets by race serve the same sentence as the ordinary arsonist but then, in addition, having him perform some sort of community service relevant to the black American community in particular strikes me as a more reasonable, enlightened, and fruitful approach than simply sticking him in prison for a longer period of time.[36] Nothing that I've said in this chapter or the previous chapter commits me to saying otherwise. And to the extent that adding some compulsory community service rather than extra jail time is more likely to help to repair some of the damage done by such crimes and to educate the offender about the distinctive nature of his wrongful acts, favoring this form of hate crime law follows naturally from the central claim made in these two chapters that hate crimes are particularly objectionable.

In the end, then, while some forms of hate crime law may well prove to be extreme and indefensible, the view that such laws should be abolished entirely is extreme and indefensible, too. Laws that require judges to add exorbitant amounts of jail time every time someone commits a hate crime should be rejected. But so should laws that prevent judges from adding a modest amount of community service in such cases. The best way to advance the debate over hate crime laws, then, is to commit ourselves to the conclusion that such laws are perfectly justified and appropriate as a general matter, and to devote ourselves to the remaining project of determining the most just and reasonable form that they can take.

10

Is Racial Profiling Irrational?

The Answer Isn't Black and White

A young man is driving on the New Jersey Turnpike. Like most people on the road, he's going a bit over the speed limit. Unlike most people on the road, he's pulled over by a cop. The cop is hoping that if he pulls over enough people, he'll catch some drug traffickers, either because their drugs will be clearly visible when they roll down their window or because they'll consent to a search of their vehicle when they're pulled over and incriminating evidence will be discovered as a result. The cop explains his decision to pull over this particular driver by pointing out that the young man was exceeding the posted speed limit and that he had changed lanes at least twice without first engaging his turn signal for the required amount of time. And this is, indeed, part of the story. If the cop hadn't seen the driver commit these moving violations, he wouldn't have pulled him over. But, as every police officer knows, it's virtually impossible to drive for any sustained period of time without committing at least some sort of moving violation. And the fact is that the cop saw a number of other drivers exceeding the posted speed limit and changing lanes without using their turn signals at all. He didn't pull them over, but he did pull this particular driver over. And the reason he pulled this one over rather than the others is that this particular young man is black and the cop believed that he was therefore more likely to be carrying illegal drugs. In deciding which speeding drivers to pull over, in other words, the cop targeted the drivers by race. Has the cop done something wrong?

Americans as a whole seem to agree about very little when it comes to the debate about racial matters in this country. But if there's one opinion that they do by and large seem to share, it's that the answer to this question is yes. President Clinton referred to such racial profiling as "morally indefensible" and "wrong," and President Bush after him said "It's wrong, and we will end it in America."[1] Al Gore is on the record as opposing racial profiling, and so is Dick Cheney.[2] Indeed, the conviction that such racial profiling is wrong may be one of the few things that unite liberals like Ira Glasser of the ACLU, conservatives like Dinesh D'Souza of the Hoover Institution, and libertarians like William Anderson and Gene Callahan of the Ludwig von Mises Institute.[3] A 1999 Gallup poll, moreover, found that fully 81 percent of Americans disapproved of racial profiling, and it's hard to find an opinion about anything that 81 percent of Americans can agree about, let alone an opinion about anything relating to race.[4] Since the events of September 11, 2001, of course, a number of people have become more open to the use of racial profiling in the context of preventing terrorist attacks. But, at least in the more mundane kinds of cases that I'll be concerned with in this chapter and the chapter that follows, where in the context of ordinary crimes like shoplifting or drug trafficking a police officer subjects a young man to a greater degree of scrutiny and investigation because he's black, there remains a powerful and striking consensus in this country: this sort of racial profiling is simply unacceptable.

I used to be a part of this consensus. It wasn't that I thought I had a good argument against racial profiling. I didn't really know of any arguments about racial profiling one way or the other. It's just that the idea of racial profiling struck me as repellant. When I started to look into the literature on the subject, then, I expected to find arguments that would help to clarify and justify my intuitive revulsion at the practice. What I discovered, though, was surprising and disappointing. The literature on racial profiling certainly contains a number of complaints about the practice. Indeed, most of the literature about racial profiling is really literature against racial profiling. But while I came to the literature against racial profiling with a desire to be convinced by it, and while some of the arguments it contains initially seemed to be quite compelling, in the end I found that none of them were persuasive.

This has left me in an uncomfortable position. I still feel the force of the thought that racial profiling is wrong. And I empathize with those who find the claim that it isn't wrong to be distressing and even offensive. But the more I've examined the arguments against racial profiling, the less convinced I've become that there's really anything wrong with it. So while I certainly wouldn't characterize myself as a fan of racial profiling, I find that I can no longer in good conscience represent myself as an opponent of it either. My goal in this chapter and the chapter that follows, therefore, is to explain how I've been reluctantly led to the conclusion that racial profiling isn't as objectionable as most people seem to think it is.

WHAT RACIAL PROFILING IS, AND WHAT IT ISN'T

Let's start by getting clear about what racial profiling is. Many works on the subject focus on real-life examples of racial profiling, and many of the real-life examples they appeal to involve behavior by the police that's clearly abusive.[5] They are cases, that is, in which cops treat the people they pull over in ways that would be objectionable regardless of the reason they had for pulling them over. But while abusive behavior may or may not be common in cases involving racial profiling, abusive behavior can't be taken to be part of the definition of what racial profiling is. Racial profiling is a practice that governs questions about which people should be investigated and how thoroughly they should be investigated. It's not a policy about how people should be treated, or mistreated, during the course of such investigations. A state trooper might employ racial profiling in deciding who to pull over and still treat everyone he pulls over with great politeness and respect, or he might not employ racial profiling in deciding who to pull over but still treat everyone he pulls over with great callousness and cruelty. So while stories involving abusive behavior may provide a powerful way to illustrate what can happen in the course of racial profiling, they provide a poor basis for examining the moral status of racial profiling itself.

Similarly, discussions of racial profiling often proceed as if such profiling involves treating people in certain ways solely on account of their race.[6] But this is also a mistake. A cop who pulls over a young black man under circumstances in which he wouldn't pull over a young white man is clearly engaging in racial profiling. But that same cop might not have pulled the black driver over either if the black driver had instead been a little old black lady. The cop's decision in such a case is not made entirely on grounds of his race, therefore, but he clearly engages in racial profiling nonetheless. What makes an act an act of racial profiling, then, is the use of race as at least one factor in determining whether or not to investigate someone or in determining how thoroughly to investigate them. Typically, at least, race will be used as just one factor among many others, including sex, age, physical appearance (style of clothes and jewelry, presence of tattoos, etc.), demeanor, and so on. This stipulation, though, shouldn't be taken to trivialize the role that race plays in racial profiling. In many cases, after all, there may prove to be no other conspicuous differences for a police officer to turn to in deciding, say, which of two speeding motorists to pull over, and so race may well make the final difference between someone's being pulled over or not in a good number of instances. Still, if we're going to try to develop a reasonable position on this most inflammatory of racial topics, it's important at the outset not to exaggerate the role that race actually plays in racial profiling. Racial profiling involves targeting by race, but it need not involve targeting exclusively by race.

It might be objected that by characterizing racial profiling in this somewhat abstract way – the use of race as at least one factor in determining whether or not to investigate someone or in determining how thoroughly to investigate them, independent of any questions about how they're treated when they're investigated – I'm framing the discussion in a manner that's too far removed from the way that racial profiling operates in the real world. Out on the streets, it might be complained, racial profiling is cruel and abusive, and to think of it so theoretically and artificially is to do a disservice to the real, live people who are its daily victims. In the comfort of the philosopher's armchair, that is, racial profiling might be conceived of as something much more simple and abstract, but thinking of it in this rarefied manner can do nothing to illuminate the debate about racial profiling in the world as it really is, dirty and specific.

I must admit that I have a great deal of sympathy for this complaint. It's impossible to read the real-life accounts of racial profiling that feature prominently in many works on the subject without being deeply disturbed by the cruel and sadistic treatment that they often involve: forcing people to sit in their cars for hours in the blazing sun with the air conditioning off and the windows up, making them abandon their vehicles in the middle of a busy highway with no way to get home, deliberately vandalizing their automobiles in the process of searching them, directing vile and inexcusable language at the drivers, humiliating them in front of their children, and worse. It may well be that racial profiling, in the world as it really is, is so tightly intertwined with such abusive behavior that we can't have one without the other. And if that does turn out to be case, then that will provide a very good reason to oppose racial profiling in the world as it really is. But while all of this is true, it doesn't really diminish the value of trying to examine the issue in a more abstract manner. Virtually any kind of policy will be objectionable if it's carried out in a cruel and abusive manner, after all, and if we want to know whether there really is something distinctively wrong with racial profiling in particular, as opposed to whether there's something wrong with carrying out policies in a cruel and abusive manner in general, we must force ourselves to think about racial profiling from a point of view that is more theoretical and less empirical, a perspective that focuses on the essence of racial profiling – its use of race as at least one factor in determining whether or not to investigate someone or in determining how thoroughly to investigate them – rather than on the details that contribute to the nature of the way it is actually put into practice in the real world.

Since this kind of approach to the issue may seem to stand in need of justification, and since it may well seem to pose a serious problem for the relevance of this entire chapter and the chapter that follows, it's worth briefly considering an analogy before moving on to the details of the discussion. So consider for a moment the debate over capital punishment. It would be relatively uncontroversial, I suspect, to define capital punishment as the intentional execution of a person carried out because they have been convicted of a crime. This definition omits many questions about how capital punishment is actually practiced. It may well be, for example, that the methods of execution that are typically used are needlessly painful, that the standards of evidence used in determining guilt are insufficiently reliable, that the decisions about who should receive the death penalty and who should receive life in prison are made capriciously, and so on. Some people who oppose capital punishment do so only because of these sorts of particular details about capital punishment as it is actually practiced. If they were convinced that the methods of execution were sufficiently humane, the jury system sufficiently reliable, and the sentencing decisions sufficiently even-handed, they would see nothing at all wrong with the death penalty. But most people who oppose the death penalty think that capital punishment would be wrong even if these practical issues could be effectively resolved. They think that capital punishment is wrong because they think that it's wrong to execute people for breaking the law. In order to test their position successfully, it would be important to focus on the more abstract account of capital punishment that treats it simply as the execution of those who have been sentenced to death for a crime they've been convicted of rather than to allow the various specific features that the death penalty may have in practice to creep into the discussion. Getting bogged down in questions about whether or not lethal injection as currently practiced causes an unnecessary amount of physical pain, for example, can't help to determine whether or not there's something wrong with capital punishment itself.

All of this should be fairly clear and uncontroversial in the case of the debate over capital punishment. But what's true of the debate over the death penalty is equally true of the debate over racial profiling. Some people who oppose racial profiling might oppose it only because they believe that it's carried out in an objectionably abusive or capricious manner. They would think that there's nothing wrong with racial profiling so long as those who engage in it do so carefully, politely, and respectfully. But most people who think there's something wrong with racial profiling think that it would be wrong to engage in it even if it were done in a perfectly cautious, friendly, and cordial manner. They think that racial profiling is wrong because it involves targeting people by race when determining who to investigate or who to investigate more thoroughly and they think that this form of targeting by race is wrong. In order to test their position successfully, then, it's important to focus on the more abstract understanding of racial profiling that I've presented here: the use of race as at least one factor in determining whether or not to investigate someone or in determining how thoroughly to investigate them, independent of any questions about how they are treated when they are investigated. So that is what I will try to do in this chapter and the chapter that follows.

Finally, it's important to note two additional features that stories about racial profiling often have in common and that must also be set aside in order to carry out a fruitful inquiry into the status of racial profiling itself. One is that many stories about racial profiling involve the police using it as a means of enforcing laws that are themselves open to moral criticism. Many stories about racial profiling, for example, involve the police looking for illegal drugs. And many people oppose the laws that make the possession and distribution of such drugs illegal in the first place. Their belief that the laws in question are unjust may lead them to conclude that the use of racial profiling in enforcing such laws is unjust as well and to associate the practice of racial profiling with the practice of enforcing unjust laws. But the question of whether there's something wrong with racial profiling is a question about which law enforcement techniques are acceptable, not a question about which laws should be enforced by whatever enforcement techniques prove to be acceptable. In order to carry out an accurate assessment of the status of racial profiling itself, therefore, we must set the latter sort of question to the side and focus exclusively on the former. For the purposes of this discussion, then, I'll simply assume for the sake of the argument that the laws that are being enforced are themselves just and reasonable ones. The question will be whether, given this assumption, it's wrong for the police and other security officials to target by race as a means of enforcing the laws, either in determining which people to investigate or in determining which people to investigate more thoroughly.

The other feature that needs attending to in this context often appears in some of the most disturbing incidents that are reported in works on racial profiling. These are cases that involve the police harassing black people in contexts in which they have no independent right to be investigating anyone – black or white – in the first place. A young black man is simply sitting on his front porch, for example, and a cop walks by and grabs the man's backpack and empties its contents in the street, perhaps hoping to find weapons or drugs. Or a young black man is peacefully walking along the sidewalk in a wealthy, predominantly white, neighborhood, and a cop approaches and demands that he empty his pockets. But while these kinds of abusive behavior, too, may or may not be prevalent among police departments that practice racial profiling, they too must be set aside if we are to engage in a fruitful inquiry into the status of racial profiling itself. If the police have no right to simply grab and empty the backpack of someone who is sitting on his front porch or to demand that someone peacefully walking along a public sidewalk empty his pockets, after all, then they have no right to do so regardless of whether race plays a role in their decision about whom to target for their unlawful treatment. Such behavior is wrong regardless of whether its target is selected by race in the same way that burning down someone's house is wrong regardless of whether the victim is targeted by race.

If the cop's use of race in deciding which people to harass makes his act worse than it would be if he simply harassed innocent people at random, moreover, this will be for the reasons that I defended in Chapters 8 and 9 as reasons for concluding that hate crimes are worse than the ordinary crimes that they otherwise resemble. If my argument in those chapters was correct, then a cop who engages in racially motivated harassment will merit a more severe sentence than a cop who engages in randomly targeted harassment. If my argument was mistaken, then a cop who engages in racially motivated harassment will merit the same sentence as a cop who engages in randomly targeted harassment. But either way, the claim that it's wrong for a cop to use race to select people to investigate in contexts in which he has no independent right to investigate anyone does nothing to show that it's wrong for a cop to use race to select people to investigate in contexts in which he does have an independent right to investigate people. As we saw in the discussion of hate speech restrictions in Chapters 6 and 7, after all, the fact that adding race to one kind of example can make already illegal behavior even more illegal doesn't mean that adding race to another kind of example is enough to make legal behavior illegal. And so recognizing that the cop's behavior is wrong in the sorts of cases in which he uses race to target for investigation people he has no right to investigate in the first place can provide no insight into whether or not the cop on the New Jersey Turnpike who lets several white drivers speed by before pulling over a speeding black driver has done something wrong by using race to decide which driver to pull over out of those who he does have an independent right to pull over.

In order to focus on the possible wrongness of racial profiling itself, then, we'll have to focus on contexts in which it's already generally accepted that the police or other security officials have the right to investigate people. It's generally accepted, for example, that the police have the right to pull over people who are speeding and to look into the car when they talk to the driver, and it's generally accepted that security officials have the right to search the contents of people's luggage when they're entering the boarding area of an airport. Given the assumption that pulling over speeding drivers or searching the luggage of traveling passengers is permissible as a general matter, but given also that it's practically impossible to pull over or search everyone who could permissibly be searched or pulled over, racial profiling can therefore be understood as the practice on which race is taken into account when deciding which people, from among those one could permissibly investigate, to focus one's limited enforcement resources on. If a state trooper or airport security official targets by race when deciding which people to pull over or search out of all those people he has an independent right to pull over or search, then he is engaging in racial profiling as I will use that term in this chapter and the chapter that follows. If a cop or security worker targets by race when deciding which people to harass out of all those people that he has no right to harass in the first place, then he's simply committing harassment. And while his use of race in deciding which people to mistreat would be relevant to the issue of hate crime laws discussed in the previous two chapters, it isn't relevant to the issue of racial profiling to be discussed in this chapter and the chapter that follows.

For the purposes of these two chapters, then, I will set aside questions about which laws should be enforced, what contexts are appropriate ones for investigating people, and how people should be treated when they're being investigated. The question will be whether there's something wrong with racial profiling itself, not whether there's something wrong with the laws it's sometimes used to enforce or with the way people are typically treated when it's used or with targeting people by race for searches in contexts where it's wrong to subject anyone to searches in the first place. Assuming that a police officer is attempting to enforce a just and reasonable law, that is, and that he's looking for people to search in a place where it's just and reasonable for him to look for people to search, and that he treats the people he decides to search in a just and reasonable manner, then the question is whether it's wrong for him to target by race in deciding which particular people to search, or to search more intensively, out of all of those he could permissibly search if he had unlimited time and resources. And the conclusion that this chapter and the chapter that follows reluctantly arrives at is that the answer to this question is no.

It's possible, of course, that once the heavily qualified and deliberately narrow focus of these two chapters has been made clear in this way, the thesis that they aim to defend will seem substantially less controversial or surprising. Perhaps some readers will think that there's really little to disagree with here if all I'm saying is that there's nothing wrong *in principle* with targeting by race to determine which people to investigate and how thoroughly to investigate them, in contexts where it's independently acceptable to investigate people, given that I'm also acknowledging that targeting by race in law enforcement as it currently exists *in practice*, may well prove to be unacceptable for any number of reasons. I, for one, will not be disappointed if this turns out to be the case. My purpose here is to examine the normative status of racial profiling itself, not to provoke, and I certainly don't relish the thought that the conclusions that I've reached about the subject will be viewed as offensive and upsetting by many people.

I suspect, though, that most people who are opposed to racial profiling – and most people are opposed to racial profiling – do think that there's something wrong with racial profiling in principle and not simply that there's something wrong with the way that it's currently put into practice. They think that it's wrong for the police to focus more on pulling over speeding black motorists than on pulling over speeding white motorists, for example, even if the police are doing so as a means of enforcing just and reasonable laws, even if they treat the people they pull over in a perfectly decent and polite manner, and even if, as the United States Supreme Court ruled in the 1996 case of *Wren v. United States*, they have the right to pull people over for speeding when their real motive is to try to investigate the driver for some other offense like drug trafficking.[7] Certainly most of the arguments that have been made against racial profiling attempt to show that there's something objectionable about the way that it targets by race even given these sorts of assumptions. And so it is to the question of whether there really is anything wrong with such racial profiling that I will now turn.

KEEPING IT REAL

I've been writing about racial profiling so far as if it actually exists. This shouldn't be surprising. Racial profiling is a controversial subject and nonexistent social practices don't tend to generate a lot of attention. But it's one of the striking features of the debate over racial profiling that one of the main arguments made by its defenders seems to be precisely that racial profiling doesn't exist in the first place. One of the pieces most frequently cited as a defense of racial profiling, for example, is a 2001 essay called "The Myth of Racial Profiling," by Heather Mac Donald of the Manhattan Institute. In this essay, Mac Donald seems to argue in defense of the following three claims: (1) engaging in racial profiling is rational because black Americans commit a disproportionate amount of a number of serious criminal offenses, (2) American cops are generally rational, nonracist people and (3) American cops don't really engage in racial profiling anyhow, hence the "myth" of racial profiling. In response to the complaint that a disproportionately large percentage of consent searches on the southern end of the New Jersey Turnpike between 1994 and 1998 involved black motorists, for example, Mac Donald responds as follows: "If blacks in fact carry drugs at a higher rate than do whites, then this search rate merely reflects good law enforcement" and provides no evidence that the police engage in racial profiling.[8]

This is a puzzling strategy for a so-called defender of racial profiling to adopt. If there really are significant differences between black and white rates of drug trafficking, after all, and if these differences really do make it rational – and not racist – for police to focus their attention disproportionately on black motorists, then instead of insisting that police officers in fact do no such thing, one should either acknowledge that they do and praise them for doing it or, if such profiling really turns out to be a myth, one should complain that the police are irrational and ineffective for that very reason. If one really means to provide a defense of racial profiling, that is, then one shouldn't draw a distinction between racial profiling, on the one hand, and "good law enforcement," on the other. Certainly one shouldn't attempt to establish that the practice is defensible by denying its existence. And so, for the purposes of this discussion at least, I'm simply going to assume that racial profiling as I have defined it really does exist.[9] The question I will be concerned with here is not whether racial profiling exists, but whether it's wrong. Most people think it is. I used to think so, too. But the question of what, exactly, is wrong with it turns out to be much harder to answer than most people seem to realize.

WHY RACIAL PROFILING SEEMS TO BE RATIONAL

Generally speaking, there are two kinds of reasons that might be given for concluding that there's something wrong with racial profiling: it might turn out to be irrational, or it might turn out to be immoral. To say that racial profiling is irrational, at least as I'll be using that term in this discussion, is to say that it fails to produce the positive results that it aims to produce. If racial profiling is irrational in this sense, then it fails on its own terms and should be opposed for that reason. To say that racial profiling is immoral, on the other hand, is to say that even if it would prove to be an effective public policy, and so in that sense a rational one, it would be unethical nonetheless and would merit rejection for that reason. Not everything that's rational in the sense of being instrumentally useful, after all, is morally acceptable. Some potentially powerful arguments have been made to try to establish that racial profiling is wrong for both of these reasons. I'll focus in the rest of this chapter on the question about its prudential rationality before moving on in the next chapter to the question about its moral status. Racial profiling is often referred to, even by people who oppose it, as "rational discrimination." But is it?

On the face of it, at least, the case for the prudential rationality of racial profiling seems to be simple and straightforward. What I'll call the "rationality argument" consists of two steps, each of which seems to be difficult to deny. Step one maintains that members of some races in the United States are more likely, on average, to commit certain kinds of criminal offenses than are members of other races. This claim seems to be well supported by a variety of statistical studies, though some potentially serious concerns about whether the support really is sufficient will be considered below. The most recent figures available from the FBI compilation of statistics taken from state and local police agencies, for example, show that while black Americans make up approximately 13 percent of the population, they account for 27.9 percent of all arrests, including 36.8 percent of all arrests for weapons violations and 34.5 percent of all arrests for drug abuse violations.[10]

It may seem impolitic or even offensive to publicly acknowledge the uncomfortable state of affairs represented by step one of the rationality argument, but there's really nothing amiss about doing so. Indeed, given the long history of slavery and discrimination in this country and the many respects in which black Americans today remain, on average, considerably behind white Americans in terms of such important predictors of criminal activity as education and income levels, it would be surprising if black Americans were not disproportionately responsible for certain sorts of crimes. If people who are less wealthy and less educated tend to be more prone to commit certain kinds of crimes, after all, and if black Americans on average tend to be less wealthy and less educated than white Americans, then one would expect that black Americans would on average be more prone to commit those offenses than would white Americans. And, in any event, to point out that one group of people is disproportionately responsible for a certain kind of criminal activity relative to a second group isn't to say that the members of the first group are worse than or inferior to or less important than members of the second. It's widely believed that white Americans commit serial murder at a higher rate than do black Americans, for example, but no one thinks that publicly affirming this belief means saying that white people are worse than or inferior to or less important than black people. And men clearly commit a wide range of serious criminal offenses at a much higher rate than women, but no one thinks that saying so means saying that men are worse than or inferior to or less important than women. While we should certainly check our facts before maintaining that step one of the rationality argument is true, then, and while we should certainly subject the arguments in its favor to critical scrutiny, there's no good reason to refrain from asserting the step if it survives such scrutiny.

Step two of the rationality argument maintains that it's rational for police departments to adopt those policies that will enable them to apprehend a larger number of offenders. This is an evaluative claim rather than a factual one, so it can't be supported simply by appealing to statistics. Still, at least on the face of it, and assuming as I'm assuming in this discussion that the laws being enforced are just and reasonable ones, it seems hard to imagine that anyone would deny it. Why do we have cops, after all, if not to catch the criminals who break such laws? And if the point of having cops is to have them catch such criminals, then it clearly seems rational to have them catch more of them rather than fewer.

Both claims made by the rationality argument, then, should seem at least initially convincing to people regardless of their view of racial profiling. But if both claims are accepted, then the rationality of racial profiling seems to follow pretty straightforwardly: if cars transporting illegal drugs are disproportionately driven by black drivers, after all, then a policy that disproportionately targets black drivers will, at least on average, result in more arrests and convictions than will a policy that scrutinizes black and white drivers with equal care. And if it's rational to adopt a policy that will, at least on average, result in more arrests and convictions, then it's rational to adopt a drug offense policy that disproportionately targets black drivers. That's just what racial profiling does. And so assuming that laws against transporting illegal drugs are themselves rationally acceptable, we seem to be entitled to conclude that racial profiling is rationally acceptable, regardless of whether it proves to be morally acceptable.[11]

GROUPS VERSUS INDIVIDUALS

Not everyone, though, finds this argument convincing. One common objection maintains that the rationality argument ignores the important difference between making judgments about groups and making judgments about individual members of those groups. It's one thing, for example, to claim that black Americans on average are more prone to commit drug offenses than are white Americans, but it's quite another to claim of some specific black American that he, in particular, is more likely to commit such an offense than is some specific, particular white American. The former claim seems to be well documented by a variety of statistical studies, but the latter claim is clearly false in a great many cases. If a black Sunday School teacher and a white drug dealer are heading down the turnpike, for example, the white driver is more likely to be carrying illegal drugs than the black driver.

Probabilistic differences between groups, then, don't automatically translate into probabilistic differences between specific members of the groups. And yet, this first objection to the rationality argument points out, racial profiling is a policy that directs police officers to behave in a certain way when they are confronted with a choice about how to treat individuals, not when they are confronted with a choice about how to treat groups. Racial profiling doesn't say that if black America is driving one car and white America is driving another, then the cop should be more inclined to pull over black America than to pull over white America. Rather, it says that if a specific, individual black American is driving one car and a specific, individual white American is driving another, then all else being equal, the cop should be more inclined to pull over the specific, individual black American than to pull over the specific, individual white American. But the fact that black Americans as a group are on average more likely to commit such an offense than are white Americans as a group on average, assuming that it is a fact, doesn't mean that the specific black American driving past a particular police officer is more likely to commit such an offense than the specific white American driving past that police officer. And so, the objection concludes, the rationality argument is unsound. It would be sound only if the first step maintained that every particular, individual black American is more likely to commit such a crime than is every particular, individual white American. But if the step maintained that, then it would clearly be false. As a 2003 fact sheet on racial profiling released by the Department of Justice put this point in justifying the Bush Administration's opposition to racial profiling, "Racial profiling rests on the erroneous assumption that any particular individual of one race or ethnicity is more likely to engage in misconduct than any particular individual of other races or ethnicities."[12]

There's something right about this objection: the difference between probabilistic judgments about groups and probabilistic judgments about particular individuals within those groups is an important one. But there's something wrong about this objection, too: this important difference doesn't, in fact, undermine the rationality argument. The reason it doesn't undermine the argument is that the objection itself ignores an important further difference: the difference between making a judgment about probabilities when you have complete information and making a judgment about probabilities when you have incomplete information. And once this further difference is taken into account, it should be clear that step one of the rationality argument in defense of racial profiling doesn't have to insist that there's a probabilistic difference between every member of one race and every member of the other. In order for the argument to work, step one has to claim only what it does claim, that there's a difference between the two groups on average.

To understand this problem with the "groups versus individuals" objection to the rationality argument, it's important first to be clear about the distinction between judging probabilities based on complete and incomplete information. So consider a case in which a large number of people have been exposed to a potentially harmful virus and you're a doctor with a limited supply of the only known vaccine. You have to decide who to give the vaccine to before anyone begins to show any symptoms, because once the symptoms occur it's too late for the vaccine to be effective. You know the following facts about the virus: women are, on average, significantly more likely to be infected than men, older people are, on average, significantly more likely to be infected than younger people, and obese people are, on average, significantly more likely to be infected than people who aren't obese. In addition, you're aware that some people are genetically prone to be more susceptible to the disease than others and that there are long and complicated blood tests that can be done to determine a person's level of susceptibility. You come across a man and a woman walking down the street. Both rush up to you and tell you that they were exposed to the virus. They appear to be about the same age and the same weight, and you don't have time to perform the long and complicated blood tests. You have only one dose of the vaccine remaining, and splitting it into two would render both half-doses completely ineffective.

In this case, the rational choice is clear: since women are significantly more likely to get the disease on average than are men, and since you don't know of any other relevant differences between the two people, the rational thing for you to do is to give the vaccine to the woman. While some people might argue that the ethical thing to do would be to flip a coin, it's hard to imagine that any-one, regardless of their view of the rationality of racial profiling, would deny that the rational thing to do is nonetheless to give the vaccine to the person who, based on all the information available to you, is more likely to benefit from it. Now suppose it turns out that this particular woman is genetically disposed to be extremely resistant to the virus and that this particular man is genetic-ally disposed to be extremely susceptible to it. In that case, even though women are more likely to contract the disease than men on average, this particular man is more likely to contract the disease than this particular woman. But even if this turns out to be true, it would clearly remain rational for you to give the vaccine to the woman in the story as I described it. That's because, in the circumstances under which you must make your decision, you don't have information about the genetic differences between the two people and you don't have time to acquire that information. When you're forced to make a decision with less than complete information about the relevant options, that is, the rational thing for you to do is to pick the option that's most likely to produce the best overall results given the information that you have. Choices take place in particular contexts, that is, and in order to judge them as rational, we have to take the contexts into account. Again, it's hard to imagine that anyone, regardless of their view of racial profil-ing, would disagree.

But given all of this, the flaw in the "groups versus individuals" objection to the rationality argument should be clear. If a black Sunday School teacher and a white drug addict both speed past a cop who's pulled over on the side of the road, the cop can see which one is white and which one is black, but he can't see which one is a Sunday School teacher and which one is a drug addict. Like the doctor who can only give a dose of the vaccine to one of two people and who must make a decision based on the information available at the time, the cop who can only pull over one of the two drivers must make a decision about which driver to pull over based on the information available at the time. When the doctor knows that one of the people is a woman and one is a man but doesn't know more specific facts about them, the rational thing to do is to base the decision on the difference between men and women when it comes to contracting the disease on average. In the same way, and for the same reason, when the cop knows that one of the driv-ers is black and one of the drivers is white but doesn't know more specific facts about them, the rational thing to do is to base the decision about which driver to pull over on the difference between black and white drivers when it comes to carrying illegal drugs in their car on average.

Step one of the rationality argument, then, doesn't have to insist that every particular black driver is more likely to be carrying illegal drugs than every par-ticular white driver. The charge made by the "group versus individual" objection is mistaken. It is enough for step one to claim that there is such a difference between the two groups on average. As long as step one is true in this much more modest sense, and as long as step two is true, too, we really seem to have no choice but to admit that racial profiling is rational.

RUNNING IN CIRCLES

Step one of the rationality argument is more plausible than the "individuals versus groups" objection makes it out to be. But this doesn't mean that it's true. And in his important 2002 book *Profiles in Injustice: Why Racial Profiling Cannot Work*, Law Professor David A. Harris offers two distinct arguments against it. Harris's book can be understood as a defense of the claim that black Americans as a group, even on average, are no more likely to be guilty of breaking the law than are white Americans as a group, and thus as a challenge to even the more modest version of step one of the rationality argument: the version that maintains not that every black American is more likely to break the law than is every white American, but rather that black Americans as a group, on average, are more likely to be guilty of breaking the law than are white Americans as a group, on average, at least with respect to certain sorts of crimes. If either of Harris's arguments for this position is successful, then we'll have good reason to reject even the more modest version of step one of the rationality argument and thus good reason to reject the argument itself.

Harris's first argument against step one of the rationality argument maintains that appeals to the fact that black Americans are disproportionately arrested for a number of serious types of crime are unconvincing because they are circular. Black people are arrested at a disproportionately higher rate, on this account, precisely because police investigate black people at a disproportionately higher rate, and the police then use the fact that they arrest black people at a disproportionately higher rater to justify the claim that they should investigate black people at a disproportionately higher rate.[13] If the police looked more carefully elsewhere they would find more evidence of criminality elsewhere, and so in the end there's no reason to accept the first step of the rationality argument even in its more modest formulation.

There's probably something to this complaint. But it seems unlikely that there's enough to it to justify rejecting the first step of the rationality argument. It's probably true, for example, that if the police pulled over many more white drivers and many fewer black drivers than they currently do, the number of white arrests would go up and the number of black arrests would go down. Black people, as a result, would make up a smaller proportion of those arrested than they currently do. But it's also probably true that even if the police ignored race entirely in deciding who to investigate, there would still be a sizeable disparity between the rate at which black people are arrested and convicted for certain sorts of offenses and the rate at which white people are arrested and convicted for those sorts of offenses. The reason for this has to do with data taken from studies of crime reports made by victims of offenses such as robbery, assault, and rape, cases where the victim is able to provide a description of the offender.

According to one recent National Crime Victimization Survey, for example, 24.6 percent of such criminals are black. Since black people make up only 13 percent of the U.S. population, this means that the rate at which black people are identified by victims as the perpetrator of a crime in these sorts of cases is roughly twice what it would be if black Americans committed such crimes at the same rate as the population as a whole.[14] This result is very close to the results of studying arrest reports. And this, in turn, suggests that the circularity problem with arrest report data is minor at best. While the decisions that police officers make about who to investigate will obviously have an impact on who they end up arresting, after all, there seems to be no corresponding worry about relying on victim identification reports. A victim of a crime has no reason to lie about the racial identity of his or her attacker and, assuming they would like to see their attacker brought to justice, every reason to tell the truth. It's possible, of course, that in some cases a victim may mistakenly believe that a white attacker was black, and there have been some notorious instances in which white people have been caught inventing a story about a black criminal in order to cover up their own crimes, but these seem clearly to be relatively isolated incidents and news-worthy precisely because they are relatively unusual. As a result, there seems to be no good reason to doubt that, in general, victim identification reports provide a roughly accurate representation of the racial composition of the criminal popu-lation in question and thus a powerful confirmation of the general reliability of the data taken from FBI arrest report statistics. As Law Professor Michael Tonry, a scholar who has been described as a "leading liberal expert on sentencing" puts it, "The main reason that black incarceration rates are substantially higher than those for whites is that black crime rates for imprisonable crimes are substan-tially higher than those for whites."[15] There seems, then, to be no reason to accept the circularity argument and thus no reason to accept Harris's first objection to step one of the rationality argument.

THE PROBLEM OF EQUAL HIT RATES

Harris has a second objection to the rationality argument that appears to be far more powerful than the first. This objection appeals to data about what are com-monly referred to as "hit rates": the rate at which evidence of a crime is uncov-ered when members of a given group are searched. A study of stops and searches conducted by the Maryland state police in 1995 and 1996, for example, revealed that black drivers made up only 17 percent of those on the road but accounted for over 70 percent of those searched. Yet the rate at which police actually found drugs, guns, or other pieces of incriminating evidence were virtually identical for searches of black drivers and searches of white drivers during that period of time.[16] This, Harris argues, shows that black drivers and white drivers are really offending at the same rate. And if this is so, then the first step of the rationality argument is mistaken, and racial profiling isn't rational. If black drivers and white drivers are offending at the same rate, after all, then there's no reason to focus disproportionately on one group rather than the other. And, indeed, in other cases that Harris cites, the hit rates turn out to be somewhat higher when white people are searched than when black people are searched, suggesting that, if anything, racial profiling should rationally be directed against white Americans.[17] Certainly the hit rate data seem to provide no justification for focusing disproportionately on black Americans.

When I first encountered Harris's hit rates argument, it struck me as a virtually decisive objection to racial profiling. If the hit rates for black and white Americans are essentially the same, after all, then what would be the point of racial profiling? Indeed, the argument struck me as so unexpected and so convincing that the question of whether racial profiling is morally wrong – the question that first got me interested in the subject – started to seem almost irrelevant. If racial profiling accomplishes nothing useful in the first place, after all, it hardly seems to matter if it would be morally wrong to engage in it if did accomplish something useful. After doing some more reading and some further reflecting on the subject, however, I've come to see that even if we accept the accuracy of the data that Harris relies on, there are several reasons to question the conclusions that he draws from the data.

One reason to be dissatisfied with Harris's argument is that it depends on studies in which evidence of offending at any level at all is found at roughly equal rates between searches of black and white drivers. But this kind of equal hit rate is consistent with the claim that black drivers offend at a higher rate than do white drivers when it comes to the sorts of serious offenses that police are most concerned with and that are most likely to result in an actual conviction. From the claim that black and white drivers are equally likely to have at least some amount of an illegal drug in their car, for example, it doesn't follow that black and white drivers are equally likely to have a significant amount of an illegal drug in their car. And, indeed, a number of writers have pointed to studies indicating that the hit rates are not, in fact, equal in this more straightforwardly relevant sense.

In an article entitled "Racial Bias in Motor Vehicle Searches: Theory and Evidence," for example, the economists John Knowles, Nicola Persico, and Petra Todd report that "In our data, vehicles of African-American motorists are searched much more frequently than those of white motorists. However, the probability that a searched driver is found carrying *any amount* of contraband is very similar across races.... When we look at the probability that a searched driver is carrying contraband *in excess of a high threshold*, this probability is higher for African Americans."[18] Indeed, when the threshold is set so that possession of amounts exceeding the threshold constitutes a felony rather than a simple misdemeanor, the results of their study indicate that the hit rate for black drivers is in fact more than four times higher than the hit rate for white drivers: 13 percent compared to 3 percent.[19]

The same sort of result occurs, moreover, when some of the important data from Maryland is examined more carefully. A frequently cited study by Illya Lichtenberg, for example, looked at information collected by the Maryland State Police in the context of 1,914 consent searches that followed traffic stops. The study found that the rate at which black and white drivers were determined to be in possession of illegal substances were nearly identical, with just a single percentage point separating the two, again seeming to support Harris's argument. But in those cases in which drugs were found, there was on average a very significant difference in terms of the amount that was recovered from black and from white drivers. In the case of cocaine in its powder form, for example, the average search of a black driver yielded 111 grams while the average search of a white driver produced only one-tenth of one gram. The numbers were similar for crack cocaine and marijuana.[20]

And as yet another recent analysis of the Maryland data emphasized, the significance of this difference in average amounts of drugs seized per search becomes conspicuous when it's considered side by side with evidence about the amount of profiling taking place at any given point in time. One of the two main empirical conclusions that Law Professor Samuel R. Gross and statistician Katherine Y. Barnes reached from their study was that when comparing black and white drivers, a larger percentage of the black drivers were found to have had "substantial quantities of illegal drugs."[21] And the implications of this statistical difference were significant:

In the 1–95 corridor we find a sharp break [in the difference between the rates at which black and white drivers were pulled over] between 1996 and 1997, possibly in response to the anti-racial profiling litigation focusing on that section of highway. Racial profiling did not stop after 1996, but it became considerably less pronounced; at the same time, the total quantities of drugs seized in the 1–95 corridor decreased markedly.[22]

In fact, the percentage of drivers pulled over who were white increased from approximately 21 percent in the period 1995–96 to over 40 percent from 1997 to 2000. The percentage of drivers pulled over who were black decreased from over 70 percent in the first period to just over 50 percent in the second period.[23] And at the same time, they report,

The total proportion of big dealers arrested dropped by half from 1996 to 1997, and declined further after that.... The totals fluctuate, and are heavily affected by small numbers of large seizures. For heroin and especially cocaine, however, the picture is unambiguous. Total and average seizures both dropped sharply after 1996 and never recovered. For cocaine the change is stark: over 90% of all the cocaine found by the [Maryland State Police] was seized in the first two years of this five-and-a-half year period. This is particularly significant since cocaine is easily the most important drug of the four, accounting for more than half of the medium and large dealers arrested, and perhaps 60% of the total retail value of the drugs seized.[24]

Since it seems rational for police to be concerned with the total amount of illegal drugs they capture and not just the total amount of stops that result in the capture of at least some drugs, the nearly-equal hit rates that at first seem to support Harris's claim again turn out to undermine it.

Similarly, Harris cites studies indicating that black and white drivers are equally likely to exceed the speed limit. This kind of equal hit rate is particularly relevant given that speeding is often cited as the pretext justification for pulling a particular driver over, which in turn can often lead to a search of some sort. But, again, the claim that black and white drivers are equally prone to offend at a minimal level doesn't mean that they're equally prone to offend at a more serious level. People typically don't get pulled over for going five miles over the speed limit, for example, but it's not unusual to get pulled over for going fifteen miles over the speed limit. And, again, there are studies that conclude that at the more serious levels of law violation, the levels that typically attract the attention of the police regardless of race, the hit rates of black and white drivers are not so equal. A study that was commissioned by the New Jersey Attorney General in the wake of the uproar over racial profiling in that state, for example, focused on 40,000 photo radar pictures of people caught exceeding the speed limit by at least 15 miles per hour, and concluded that black drivers were in fact guilty of this offense at a disproportionately higher rate.[25] While these sorts of studies can't conclusively establish that black drivers are offending at a higher rate than are white offenders when it comes to the more serious levels of these sorts of offense, they do illustrate the flaw in arguing from an equal hit rate at all levels of a form of behavior to an equal hit rate at the sort of level that law enforcement is typically concerned with. And this flaw provides one reason not to be convinced by Harris's hit rates argument.

A second reason to be skeptical about the inferences we can draw from Harris's hit rate data is that police officers may well be more selective about which white drivers they pull over than about which black drivers they pull over.[26] Suppose, for example, that they pull over young black men more or less at random whenever they see them, but only pull over young white men when there are several suspicious indicators that the white men may be engaged in criminal activity. If that's the case, then an equal hit rate for black and white drivers who are pulled over doesn't mean an equal offending rate among black and white drivers as a whole. Rather, it means that the average young male black driver offends at about the same rate as the average young suspicious-looking or suspiciously behaving white driver. On the assumption that such white drivers turn out to be offending at a higher rate than white drivers as a whole, which again seems reasonable, the equal hit rate between black and white drivers who are searched would be consistent with a higher offending rate by black drivers than white drivers. Indeed, given these plausible assumptions, the equal hit rates cited by Harris are not simply consistent with a higher black offending rate, but actually count as evidence for a higher black offending rate. And so, again, when the argument is examined more carefully, it fails to provide a reason to deny step one of the rationality argument.

Finally, and most importantly, there's a much more fundamental problem with the kind of inference that Harris's hit rates argument depends on. The problem is that the equal hit rates data that he appeals to all come from studies involving racial profiling. As a result, it may well be that the hit rates that he cites are equal, if they are equal, precisely because of racial profiling. If this is so, then rather than providing an argument against the rationality of racial profiling, Harris's hit rates argument will end up inadvertently providing a powerful argument in its defense.

Suppose, for example, that on a certain highway over a certain period of time, a black driver is five times more likely to be pulled over by the police than is a white driver, and that the hit rate for finding a certain amount of illegal drugs in a driver's car is ten percent for both black drivers and white drivers who are pulled over. One way to think about this situation is the way that Harris wants us to think about it: it's irrational to disproportionately target the black drivers because pulling over black drivers is producing precisely the same number of arrests per driver as is pulling over white drivers. But a second and importantly different way of looking at the very same set of numbers is this: when white drivers know that they're unlikely to be pulled over, they offend at a ten percent rate. But even when black drivers know that they're much more likely to be pulled over, they still offend at a ten percent rate. White drivers offend at this level when relatively little is being done to try to actively deter them, that is, but black drivers persist in offending at this rate even when it is clear that a great deal is being done to actively deter them. Imagine, then, how much higher the rate of offending among black drivers would be if they weren't being profiled. If a significant number of black drivers are willing to run the risk of getting caught with illegal drugs in their car even when the police are known to be disproportionately focusing their attention on black drivers in particular, after all, then an even greater number of black drivers would presumably be willing to run the risk of getting caught if the risk were made significantly smaller by the elimination of racial profiling.

These are two different ways of looking at the same set of numbers. But they are not two equally legitimate ways. The first way of looking at the numbers ignores the context in which the numbers are generated. It focuses on the fact that black and white drivers have the same hit rate when they are pulled over, but doesn't look at the circumstances under which they are pulled over. The second way of looking at the numbers takes this context into account. Like the first way, it looks at the fact that black and white drivers have the same hit rate when they are pulled over, but unlike the first way, it takes into account the effect that the circumstances in which they are pulled over can have on the hit rates. The second way of looking at the numbers is therefore more illuminating. And when we make use of it, it provides a final reason to reject Harris's second argument. Once again, the equality of the black and white hit rates among motorists who are actually pulled over will fail to establish that black Americans and white Americans offend at the same rate and will thus fail to provide a reason to reject the first step of the rationality argument.

Indeed, a number of economists have looked at just the sort of hit rate data that Harris appeals to in arguing against the rationality of racial profiling and have used it to justify precisely the opposite conclusion: if black drivers have to be pulled over at a disproportionately higher rate in order to get their hit rates down to the level of white drivers, then it's rational – though, again, not necessarily ethical – to target them disproportionately for just this reason. In the absence of such profiling, that is, the black drivers would presumably offend at a higher rate. In moving from a policy of no racial profiling to a policy of racial profiling, therefore, the police would on average apprehend a greater number of people breaking the law.[27] This is not to insist, of course, that every policy that disproportionately targets black drivers would be rationally justified under such circumstances. A policy that focused so much attention on black drivers that it drove the black offending rate down below the white offending rate would clearly be irrational. This seems to have been the case recently in Los Angeles, for example, according to a report issued by the ACLU of Southern California in October 2008. The study, conducted by Law Professor Ian Ayres and examining data from over seven hundred thousand cases in which LAPD officers stopped pedestrians and/or drivers between July 2003 and June 2004, found that, among other things, black people who were stopped were 127 percent more likely to be frisked than were white people, but were nonetheless 42.3 percent less likely to be found with a weapon and 25 percent less likely to be found with drugs. But while Ayers is clearly right to characterize such an approach as one on which black residents are "over-stopped, over-frisked, over-searched and over-arrested,"[28] it would be a mistake to conclude from this that every level of racial profiling would amount to overdoing things in these respects. When black people who are stopped are 127 percent more likely to be frisked and yet the amount by which they are less likely to be found with drugs is only 25 percent, for example, it remains quite plausible to suppose that a policy on which they are more likely to be frisked than white people but by a considerably smaller margin would produce something closer to equal hit rates. Certainly the figures don't suggest that equal hit rates would result from the absence of profiling altogether. And so, once again, arguments appealing to equal hit rates – or even to rates in which the black hit rate is lower than the white hit rate – fail to undermine step one of the rationality argument and thus fail to undermine the claim that racial profiling is rational. Arrest report data and victim report data consistently and strongly support the conclusion that, at least with respect to some forms of criminal activity, black Americans are on average more likely than white Americans to break the law. And the available hit rate data, while intriguing and certainly meriting careful scrutiny, in the end do little to rebut this conclusion. If anything, they serve to reinforce it.

THE ELASTICITY ARGUMENT

In the end, then, step one of the rationality argument proves to be difficult to deny. The best understanding of the available evidence seems clearly to indicate that, at least as things currently stand in this country, members of some races are more likely to commit certain kinds of criminal offenses than are members of other races. What about step two of the argument? This is the step that claims that it's rational for police departments to adopt those policies that will enable them to apprehend a larger number of offenders. This step seems, if anything, even harder to deny than the first step. The reason we have police departments in the first place, after all, is to help us minimize the number of people who get away with breaking the law, and if we want to minimize the number of people who get away with breaking the law, the rational thing to do seems clearly to be to maximize the number of people we catch breaking the law. A police department that selectively engages in racial profiling can reasonably expect to catch more lawbreakers than a police department that doesn't. And so, while continuing to set aside the question of whether racial profiling is morally acceptable, it should seem clear that racial profiling is at the very least rationally acceptable, at least on the assumption that the laws it helps to enforce are themselves rationally acceptable.

But things are not as simple as they appear. In fact, while Harris aims all of his criticism at the first step of the rationality argument, in the end it's the second step in the argument that actually seems to pose the bigger problem for the rationality of racial profiling. The reason for this is straightforward enough once you notice it, but it's easy not to notice it: minimizing the number of people who get away with something is not the same as maximizing the number of people who get caught doing it. It's the same if the number of people committing the offense in question remains constant, but it's not the same if the number of people committing it can be influenced by the way in which we try to catch people for doing it. For this reason, while the first step in the rationality argument turns out to be considerably less problematic than it might at first seem, the second step in the rationality argument turns out to be far more problematic than it might at first seem.

Suppose, to take a simple example, that the number of drug offenses committed in a given town each month is one hundred, and that this is true regardless of what methods are used to try to catch people in the act. Clearly, any method that increases the number of people caught committing a drug offense will at the same time decrease the number of people who get away with committing a drug offense. If a method increases the number of people caught per month from twenty to thirty, for example, then it will at the same time decrease the number of people who get away with it each month from eighty to seventy. But suppose instead that the number of people who commit such offenses each month is determined, at least in part, by the kind of policy that's used to try to catch people committing such offenses. In that case, it would be possible for a policy to increase the number of people who are caught committing a drug offense each month but at the same time increase the number of people committing such offenses in the first place. And depending on how the numbers work out, this in turn means that a particular change in policy might increase the number of people who are caught committing a drug offense and yet increase the number of people who get away with committing a drug offense at the very same time.

Suppose, for example, that under the police department's current policy, one hundred people commit a drug offense each month and the police succeed in catching twenty people doing so each month. Suppose that if it implemented a different policy, the department would increase the number of people it caught breaking the law each month by ten but would also increase the number of people breaking the law each month by twenty. In that case, adopting the new policy would increase the number of people caught breaking the law but would also increase the number of people getting away with breaking the law. The number of people getting caught per month would go up from twenty to thirty, but instead of going down, the number of people getting away with breaking the law each month would go up, too, from eighty to ninety.

When the goal of decreasing the number of people who get away with breaking the law diverges from the goal of increasing the number of people who get caught breaking the law, moreover, it should be clear that the rational thing to do would be to pursue the former goal rather than the latter. The point of having a police department, that is, is to reduce the level of crime, not to increase the number of crimes that are committed so that it can increase the number of people who get punished for committing them. And so in this sort of case, at least, it should be clear that while the department would increase the number of people it caught breaking the law by adopting the new policy, adopting the new policy would nonetheless be irrational. And this means that the fact that racial profiling increases the number of arrests and convictions that are made, if it is a fact, doesn't show that it would be rational to adopt a policy of racial profiling.

Now all of this might well seem to be of purely academic interest. The mere fact that it's logically possible for a policy to increase the number of lawbreakers who get caught while also increasing the number of lawbreakers who don't get caught isn't enough to warrant thinking that this would be likely to happen in the case of racial profiling in particular. But in his provocative and insightful 2006 book *Against Prediction: Profiling, Policing, and Punishing in an Actuarial Age*, Law Professor Bernard E. Harcourt makes an extremely powerful case for the claim that there's a particular feature of racial profiling that makes it likely to suffer from precisely this problem.[29]

The key to Harcourt's argument is the "elasticity" of a group's rate of offending: the extent to which the group's crime rate is influenced by changes in policing techniques. Suppose that the police introduce a significant change in their behavior and that as a result, one group continues offending at about the same rate as before, but a second group's rate of offending changes dramatically. In this case, the second group's rate of offending is more elastic than the first's. This kind of phenomenon is quite widespread, and it poses a potential problem for step two of the rationality argument for the following reason. Suppose it turns out that the white crime rate is more elastic than the black crime rate. Suppose, that is, that the rate at which white Americans break the law is more significantly affected by changes in policing techniques than is the rate at which black Americans break the law. If this is so, then if the police move from a race-neutral policy to a policy that targets black people for special scrutiny, the total number of law breakers may well go up rather than down *even if it's true that black Americans on average commit more of certain sorts of offenses than do white Americans*. While the increased scrutiny of black people will discourage some black people from breaking the law who would otherwise have broken the law, the corresponding decreased scrutiny of white people will encourage an even greater number of white people to break the law who would otherwise have not broken the law. Even if more people get caught breaking the law than before, then, the overall crime rate may well go up rather than down. If the white crime rate is more elastic than the black crime rate, that is, then racial profiling may well turn out to be irrational after all, even if the black crime rate is higher than the white crime rate for certain sorts of criminal offenses.

And here's the kicker: there seems to be good reason to suspect that the white crime rate is, in fact, more elastic than the black crime rate. Black Americans on average, after all, aren't doing as well as white Americans in terms of such relatively uncontroversial measures of human well-being as income, education, health, and life expectancy. It therefore seems plausible to suppose that, on average, black Americans who break the law are more likely to do so because they see themselves as having relatively few attractive alternatives. If black law breakers tend to turn to crime because they see themselves as having relatively few alternatives, then many of them may well continue to break the law even when the police subject black people to extra scrutiny. The black crime rate, that is, may well prove to be relatively inelastic: considerations that would deter people with better prospects from breaking the law may tend not to deter them from doing so. But if, again on average, white Americans tend to have more to lose by breaking the law, then their rate of law breaking will be more sensitive to changes in police policy: a given level of risk of arrest that would have some deterrent effect on black Americans would tend to have an even greater deterrent effect on white Americans, but the flip side is that a given reduction in the level of risk of arrest that would tend to increase the crime rate of black Americans by a modest amount would tend to increase the crime rate of white Americans by an even greater amount. If all of this is true, then racial profiling may well prove to be irrational after all. A police department that moves from a race-neutral policy to a policy of targeting by race may well increase the number of people that it arrests, but at the same time it may well also increase the number of people who get away with breaking the law. This would plainly be irrational, and a powerful reason to reject racial profiling.

Harcourt's objection to the second step of the rationality argument strikes me as persuasive. Because of the phenomenon of differential elasticity rates, we can't simply assume that increasing arrests decreases crime, and if a policy increases arrests but also increases crime, then it's clearly not rational to adopt that policy. So the second step of the rationality argument turns out to be unjustified. Does this mean that racial profiling turns out to be irrational after all? Not exactly. While the second step of the rationality argument proves to be unwarranted, a defender of the rationality of racial profiling can simply modify the second step by changing it to this: it's rational for police departments to adopt those policies that will enable them to apprehend a larger number of offenders except in cases where apprehending a larger number of offenders would also increase the over-all level of crime. Nothing about Harcourt's argument suggests that this modified version of the second step is mistaken and, indeed, the whole thrust of his argu-ment proceeds from the assumption that it isn't. And while Harcourt's analysis provides reasons for thinking that there will often be a sufficiently large diffe-rence between black and white elasticity rates to render racial profiling irrational, it doesn't provide a reason to think that this will always be the case. Nor, for that matter, does Harcourt himself claim that it does. He repeatedly characterizes his thesis as the claim that this is something that "may"[30] happen when police engage in racial profiling, but this is consistent with the conclusion that it is also some-thing that may not happen. And this, in the end, seems to me to be the most rea-sonable conclusion that we can draw about Harcourt's argument: racial profiling is rational when the difference in elasticity rates is sufficiently small and irrational when the difference in elasticity rates is not sufficiently small. Sometimes the difference will be sufficiently small and sometimes it won't be. And so sometimes racial profiling will prove to be rational, and sometimes it won't.

MINIMIZING MISTAKES

At this point, it might well seem that there's nothing left to say about the ration-ality, as opposed to the morality, of racial profiling. If there's a difference between black and white crime rates for some sorts of criminal offenses, and if the diffe-rence between black and white elasticity rates for those sorts of offenses is suf-ficiently small, then it seems clear that racial profiling for those offenses will increase arrests and decrease crime. And since it seems clear that increasing arrests and decreasing crime would be a rational thing to do, it should seem clear that racial profiling would be a rational thing to do under such circumstances, even if it turns out to be morally objectionable.

Before turning in the next chapter to the question of whether racial profil-ing would be morally acceptable under such circumstances, though, I want to consider one final objection that might be raised against the claim that racial profiling is rational. To conclude that it would be rational to adopt a policy of racial profiling under such circumstances requires assuming that the people who would carry out the policy would carry it out rationally. And that assumption itself can be called into question. Suppose, to turn for a moment to the case of racial profiling in the context of airport security, that being an Arabic-looking male is one of a large number of factors that correlate positively with the prob-ability that someone is a terrorist. And suppose also that some of the other fac-tors that correlate positively include a nervous demeanor, lack of frequent flyer membership, a last-minute purchase of ticket paid for with cash, and an absence of check-in luggage. Under these circumstances, a security policy that dispropor-tionately singles out Arabic-looking men for closer scrutiny would seem to be more rational than a policy that treats racial appearances as irrelevant. But now suppose that it also turns out that if race is included in the profile that airport security officers are told to follow, they will tend to focus on race even more exclusively than the probabilities justify. Suppose, for example, that they would stop and search Arabic-looking male passengers who had no other suspicious characteristics while overlooking nervous white or Asian passengers who bought their tickets at the last minute with cash and who had only carry-on luggage. Under these circumstances, it might well be rational to adopt a policy that prohibits racial profiling despite the fact that racial profiling would be rational if it were practiced rationally. It would be rational to prohibit the use of race in deciding who to search if permitting the use of race would lead to more overemphasis on race than forbidding it would lead to underemphasis. And as Frederick Schauer has pointed out in raising this kind of concern about racial profiling in the kind of case I've just described, there does seem to be good reason to suspect that this would sometimes be the case: "from what we know about the social psychology of race and ethnicity, it is quite possible that these attributes would be treated as the most important among many attributes of these factors even if they were not."[31]

This objection to the rationality of permitting racial profiling is grounded in a perfectly rational assumption: if race is going to be misused whether we permit it to be considered or not, then the rational thing to do is to adopt the policy that will minimize the degree to which race will be misused. If it will be misused to a greater degree by overusing it if its use is permitted than by underusing it if its use is forbidden, then the rational thing to do is to forbid its use. And, again, it would be rational to forbid its use under such circumstances despite the fact that it would be perfectly rational to permit its use if doing so did not, irrationally, encourage people to overemphasize its importance to a dangerous degree. As Schauer again effectively puts the point, "it could well turn out that, in a world of nonideal [that is, not perfectly rational] employees inclined to overuse race and ethnicity even when they are statistically relevant, mandatory underuse or nonuse would actually be more effective, not because race and ethnicity are not relevant, but because dramatic overuse of race and ethnicity might detract from the ability to examine closely those passengers with an even larger number of properly suspicion-raising characteristics and behaviors."[32]

As with the case of Harcourt's objection based on differential elasticity rates, Schauer's objection based on people's tendency to overemphasize race when they're permitted to consider it at all strikes me as a convincing one. The people who actually carry out policing and security policies aren't perfectly rational. The fact that the differences in crime and elasticity rates would make it rational for perfectly rational beings to adopt a policy of racial profiling doesn't mean that it would be rational for imperfectly rational beings like us to do so. But, again as with the case of Harcourt's objection, the cogency of Schauer's argument doesn't mean that permitting racial profiling for beings like us is always irrational, either. It means that permitting it would be irrational in cases where permitting it would predictably result in a greater degree of misuse of race than would forbidding it. But it doesn't mean that permitting it would, in fact, always lead to a predictably greater degree of misuse. Race might be overused even if racial profiling is officially prohibited, for one thing, for the very same psychological reasons that Schauer worries it will often be overused if it's officially permitted. And indeed, again as was the case with Harcourt's objection, Schauer never insists that his objection to the rationality of racial profiling would hold in all cases. Rather, he says that it's "quite possible" that permitting racial profiling would increase overall inefficiency in particular cases and that it is a problem that "could well turn out" to arise in particular cases. And this, in the end, seems to be the most reasonable conclusion we can draw about Schauer's position: permitting racial profiling is rational when the expected degree of misuse of race is smaller when it's permitted than when it's forbidden and irrational when the expected degree of misuse of race is greater when it's permitted than when it's forbidden. Sometimes the expected degree of misuse will be smaller and sometimes it won't. And so sometimes permitting racial profiling is rational despite all of the objections that have been raised against it, and sometimes it isn't.

WHY SOME RACIAL PROFILING STILL SEEMS TO BE RATIONAL

The argument for the rationality of racial profiling contains two steps. The first step maintains that for some forms of criminal behavior there are differences between black and white crime rates, at least in the United States. The second maintains that it's rational for police departments to adopt those policies that will enable them to apprehend a larger number of offenders, at least (on the modified version of the step) when doing so won't increase the overall crime rate and at least (as I've been assuming in this chapter), when the laws themselves are worthy of being enforced. I'm not persuaded by the "groups versus individuals" objection that tries to show that these two steps don't suffice to establish the rationality of racial profiling. If both steps are correct, then racial profiling is rationally acceptable, even if it turns out to be morally unacceptable. And I'm not persuaded by either of Harris's arguments against the argument's first step. The best available understanding of the most widely accepted statistics seems to indicate that for some important forms of criminal activity, black Americans really do break the law at a higher rate than do white Americans. The first step of the argument seems to be correct, that is, and the conclusion that racial profiling is rational seems to follow if both steps of the argument are correct. The question, then, ultimately comes down to the second step.

The arguments of Harcourt and Schauer each raise a kind of concern about the second step in the argument, and each does so convincingly. But while both writers succeed in demonstrating that racial profiling would not be rational in some instances in which it would otherwise seem to be rational, neither succeeds, or even claims to succeed, in showing that racial profiling is never rational. And this, in the end, seems to be the most reasonable conclusion we can draw about the rationality of racial profiling as a whole. Supporters of the rationality argument, such as Heather Mac Donald, and the various writers who have endorsed racial profiling in the pages of conservative magazines, such as the *National Review* and the *Weekly Standard*, are far too quick to conclude that current crime statistics prove that racial profiling is rational. Opponents of racial profiling, such as David Harris, are far too quick to conclude that flaws in the argument prove that racial profiling is irrational. The truth almost certainly lies somewhere in between. When the difference in crime rates is sufficiently large, the difference in elasticity rates is sufficiently small, and the expected misuse of race is at least as great if consideration of race is prohibited as when it is permitted, then a policy of racial profiling can reasonably be expected to result in an overall decrease in crime. When the difference in crime rates is too small, the difference in elasticity rates too large, or the expected degree of misuse of race too great if consideration of race is permitted, then a policy of racial profiling can't reasonably be expected to result in an overall decrease in crime. So is racial profiling rational? Sometimes it isn't. But sometimes it is.

Is Racial Profiling Immoral?

A Reluctant Defense of America's Least Popular Form of Discrimination

I argued in Chapter 10 that racial profiling is sometimes rational. Let's now assume that this is correct. Rational racial profiling takes into account some uncomfortable and unfortunate but nonetheless apparently accurate claims about the differences between black and white crime rates in America, at least with respect to certain sorts of offenses, and uses those facts to make police work more efficient and more effective. By focusing more attention on those groups that are, on average, disproportionately responsible for committing certain kinds of crimes, rational racial profiling helps to keep the overall crime rate down. It may often be difficult, as a practical matter, to figure out which cases of racial profiling are rational and which are irrational, but at least in those cases where it turns out to be rational, it's more plausible to suppose that racial profiling may be worthy of our support.

But even if some racial profiling does prove to be rational, this doesn't mean that it would be okay to engage in it. A practice might be practically effective, after all, but still be morally objectionable. Performing painful, involuntary medical experiments on homeless people, for example, might turn out to be a fast and efficient means of testing some new drugs or surgical procedures. But even if it did turn out to be effective from a practical point of view, and so rational in this instrumental sense, virtually everyone would nonetheless reject it as morally unacceptable. Similarly, even if it turns out that some forms of racial profiling really are rational in this sense, there might still be a good reason to reject them as immoral. Assuming for the purposes of this chapter that some racial profiling is rational, then, I want now to consider whether rational racial profiling is nonetheless immoral.

WHY RATIONAL RACIAL PROFILING SEEMS TO BE MORALLY ACCEPTABLE

Morally speaking, rational racial profiling has at least two things going for it. First, it's bad when people are victimized by crime and so it's good when people are protected from crime. Rational racial profiling helps to protect people from crime. And so rational racial profiling, at least in this respect, is a morally good thing. Second, the kind of racial profiling that I'm concerned with here takes place when a police or security officer is deciding which people to investigate, or to investigate more thoroughly, among those people he is already permitted to investigate on independent grounds. It's generally agreed, for example, that a police officer has the right to pull over cars that are speeding and to look into the interior of the car when talking to the driver or ask for their permission to search the vehicle. And it's generally agreed that an airport security official has the right to search the luggage of people who wish to bring it onto an airplane. The question raised by the controversy over racial profiling is not whether the official in question can investigate people under such circumstances in general but rather, in cases where he can't investigate all of the people he would be permitted to investigate, or can't investigate them all with equal thoroughness, it's permissible for him to take race into account when deciding which subset of them to investigate or to investigate more thoroughly. The fact that the people he would select for investigation under a policy of rational racial profiling are people that on independent grounds it would be permissible for him to investigate anyway – because they are exceeding the speed limit on the highway, for example, or carrying baggage into the boarding area of an airport – seems to count in favor of the conclusion that it would still be permissible for him to investigate them even he selected them by taking their race into account. And if he uses racial profiling to select people to investigate in contexts where he has no independent right to investigate anyone – as in the case where he walks by people peacefully sitting on their porches minding their own business and grabs and empties the backpack of the one black person on the block – his act can be shown to be wrong simply because he has no independent right to investigate that person, or any of the others, in the first place, regardless of whether he takes race into account in deciding which person to harass.

These considerations alone, of course, can't serve as the final word on the question of whether or not rational racial profiling is morally acceptable. There might be other moral considerations that tell against racial profiling, after all, and they might be strong enough to override these preliminary moral considerations in its favor. But the fact that rational racial profiling helps to prevent bad things from happening, and the fact that it does so by helping to select more efficiently which people to investigate out of those it's already permissible to investigate on independent grounds does, at the least, establish an initial presumption in favor of the moral acceptability of rational racial profiling. Since rational racial profiling seems to have at least this much going for it morally speaking, that is, we're entitled to believe that rational racial profiling is morally acceptable unless we encounter a strong moral argument against it. The question, then, is whether there are any sufficiently powerful moral arguments against rational racial profiling. I used to assume that there were. Now, I think that there aren't.

UNREASONABLE SEARCHES AND SEIZURES

The most promising kind of moral objection to racial profiling maintains that racial profiling – even rational racial profiling – violates people's rights. If rational racial profiling violates people's rights, after all, then that's a good reason to reject it as immoral even if it would reduce crime rates overall. The question, then, is what right, exactly, we should think rational racial profiling violates.

Perhaps the most common answer to this question maintains that racial profiling violates the Constitutional right to be free from unreasonable searches and seizures.[1] This objection appeals to the Fourth Amendment guarantee that "The right of the people to be secure in their persons, houses, papers, and effects, against unreasonable searches and seizures, shall not be violated, and no Warrants shall issue, but upon probable cause, supported by Oath or affirmation, and particularly describing the place to be searched, and the persons or things to be seized." Understood as a Constitutional right, the right to be free from unreasonable searches and seizures is a legal right rather than a moral right. But it seems plausible to suppose that we have a moral right that corresponds to this legal right, and so I want to assume, at least for the sake of the argument, that we have a moral right to be treated in the way that the Fourth Amendment specifies. The question, then, is whether rational racial profiling violates this moral right.

The right at issue is a right against searches and seizures that are "unreasonable," and so whether or not rational racial profiling violates this right depends on what's meant by that term. One thing that might be meant is that it's unreasonable to pull over or search a particular person if there's no good reason to think that that particular person is guilty of anything.[2] If this is what's meant by "unreasonable," then rational racial profiling does seem to violate the right against unreasonable searches and seizures. Even if the chances that the average black driver on the New Jersey Turnpike has illegal drugs in his car really do turn out to be greater than the chances that the average white driver does, after all, the mere fact that a particular driver is black doesn't mean there's a good reason to think that he, in particular, is guilty of drug possession or of anything else. As Law Professor Tracey Maclin has put it in pressing this objection to racial profiling, "The black motorist who is stopped for speeding and subjected to investigative practices designed to discover narcotics does not receive such treatment because there is good reason to believe he is transporting narcotics." And as a result, she concludes, such conduct "violates the guarantees embodied in the Fourth Amendment because the black motorist has been seized (and sometimes searched) without good cause."[3]

But this interpretation of what it is for a search to be "unreasonable" has implications that virtually everyone, regardless of their view of racial profiling, will find unacceptable. An argument against the moral permissibility of rational racial profiling that depends on the claim that we have a right not to be subject to "unreasonable" searches in this sense, therefore, is itself unreasonable. Consider, for example, the case of airport security. The last time I traveled by air, my bags were sent through an X-ray machine, I had to remove my shoes, and I was made to walk through a metal detector. But the security officials who compelled me to undergo this search had no particular reason to think that I was guilty of anything. Indeed, they didn't pick me out for any particular reason at all: they did this to everyone. If it's unreasonable to search someone without a specific reason to think that they, in particular, are guilty of something, then making everyone go through airport security is a violation of our moral right against unreasonable searches. But as irritating as it can be to have to wait in a long line at the airport, I doubt that many people believe that being made to do so really violates our moral rights. At least on the assumption that such screening is rational and really does make airport travel safer, virtually everyone on both sides of the racial profiling debate agrees that it's morally permissible. So the claim that a particular person has a right not to be searched unless there's a good reason to think that that particular person is guilty of something must be rejected.

Indeed, the case of widely accepted airport security practices generates a second and even deeper problem for this first interpretation of the right against unreasonable searches and seizures. Many airports, after all, have a policy of not simply making everyone pass through a security checkpoint, but of randomly picking out a select subset of the people passing through and subjecting them to a substantially more thorough search. Virtually everyone agrees that this policy, too, is morally acceptable, at least on the assumption that it, too, is a rational way of making airports safer, and that it's practically impossible to subject everyone passing through the airport to a search of this degree of thoroughness. And, in particular, people who oppose racial profiling in determining which passengers to subject to greater scrutiny in airports often explicitly present random searches as a morally acceptable alternative. But if the right against unreasonable searches and seizures means that a particular person has a right not to be singled out for scrutiny unless there's a good reason to think that that particular person is guilty of something, then random airport searches will also turn out to be morally impermissible. If a person has been selected for a search randomly, after all, then he hasn't been selected for any particular reason at all. But virtually everyone agrees that such random searches can be morally permissible. And so, again, this first interpretation of the right against unreasonable searches and seizures must be rejected as unreasonable.

It may be tempting to respond to these problems with the first interpretation by appealing to a claim about tacit consent. Perhaps, a critic of racial profiling might suggest, people really do have a right not to be searched in these ways, but they tacitly consent to waive their rights when they voluntarily agree to enter the airport. This would help to reconcile the claim that we really do have such rights with the claim that commonly accepted forms of airport searches are nonetheless morally permissible. But this response can't salvage the objection to racial profiling for a few reasons. First, it isn't clear why the same argument wouldn't also apply to people who drive on the New Jersey Turnpike. If freely choosing to enter a public airport is enough to make you waive your right against unreasonable searches, that is, then why isn't freely choosing to drive on a public highway enough to do the same thing? The critic might say that everyone knows your luggage will be searched if you enter an airport and that's why it's reasonable to infer their consent. But this would only show that racial profiling is wrong if the government fails to clearly inform everyone that if they drive on a public highway they will be subject to racial profiling. And surely everyone who opposes racial profiling thinks that it's wrong even if everyone it clearly informed that it's happening. In addition, even if there does turn out to be a difference between the driving case and the airport case, this wouldn't show that there's anything wrong with racial profiling itself. It would just show that there's something wrong with using racial profiling in some contexts and not in others. And that's true of plenty of policies.

Finally, and perhaps most importantly, even in the case of driving on a public highway, there are at least two cases in which virtually everyone on both sides of the debate over racial profiling already agrees that it can be permissible for the police to pull someone over even if there's no particular reason to think that that person in particular is guilty of anything. One is the case of random sobriety checkpoints, in which the police pull people over at random in an attempt to crack down on drunk driving. Since the drivers are pulled over at random, they are not pulled over because there is some particular reason to think that they, in particular, are guilty of anything. The other is the case of cars that are entering the country at the Canadian or Mexican border.[4] It's widely accepted that the Border Patrol may subject every car entering the country to a search but, as with the case of searching passengers in an airport, if everyone is searched, then each individual who is searched is not searched because there is any particular reason to think that he in particular is guilty of anything. The cases of random sobriety checkpoints and border searches, then, show that even in the context of driving on public highways, it can be permissible for a security officer to search a person without any specific reason to think that that particular person is guilty of anything. And together with the cases of universal and random airport security searches, these cases therefore undermine the first interpretation of the right against unreasonable searches and seizures.

There's a natural enough explanation, of course, for why we don't think that airport security checks and random sobriety stops violate a person's right against unreasonable searches. The explanation is that we think that the policies themselves are reasonable ones. This suggests a second and importantly different thing that might be meant by saying that a particular search of a particular person is unreasonable. It's reasonable to search a particular person, on this second account, if – but only if – searching him is entailed by a policy that itself is reasonable. Since it seems reasonable to have a policy of searching every car that enters the county and every person in an airport who's ticketed to board an airplane, reasonable to sometimes subject a random subset of the airline passengers to additional searches, and reasonable at times to employ random sobriety checkpoints on public roads, this second account of what makes a search an unreasonable one won't objectionably entail that it's wrong to search a passenger in an airport, or a car at a border crossing, or to stop a driver at a sobriety checkpoint without first establishing that there's a particular reason to think that the person being searched is guilty of something. And so this second account of what it means for a search to be an unreasonable one isn't subject to the counterexamples that undermine the first account.

The problem for the critic of racial profiling at this point, though, is that this second account of the right against unreasonable searches can't be used to show that rational racial profiling violates that right. The right against unreasonable searches, on this revised account, means the right not to be searched unless the search is entailed by a policy that itself is reasonable. But the requirement that the policy that justifies the search be reasonable can, in turn, be understood in one of two ways, and neither one can be used to secure a moral case against rational racial profiling.

One thing that might be meant by a "reasonable" policy is what I've been referring to in this discussion as a "rational" policy: one that successfully achieves the objectives it's designed to fulfill. On this purely instrumental interpretation of a reasonable policy, the second account of the right not to be subject to an unreasonable search is the right not to be searched unless the search is justified by a policy that's rational in this sense. But by definition, rational racial profiling refers to those forms of racial profiling that are rationally justified in precisely this sense. Since by its very nature a policy of rational racial profiling isn't unreasonable if unreasonable means irrational, the searches that a policy of rational racial profiling would justify wouldn't violate the right against unreasonable searches on this understanding of that right.

On the other hand, the term "reasonable" is sometimes used more broadly to mean something like "all things considered acceptable." In this broader sense of the term, a policy might be rational in the narrow sense of being effective or efficient but still be unreasonable because it's unacceptable for some other reason. If we apply this broader conception of reasonableness to the second account of the right against unreasonable searches, the result is that we have the right not to be searched unless the search can be justified by a policy that's all things considered acceptable. This version of the right seems perfectly reasonable. It amounts, after all, to the claim that it's objectionable to subject people to objectionable policies. But the problem for the critic who claims that rational racial profiling is immoral is that on this interpretation of the right against unreasonable searches we now need an independent reason to believe that rational racial profiling is an objectionable policy. Appealing to the claim that racial profiling violates the right against unreasonable searches was supposed to provide a reason for thinking that racial profiling is objectionable. But on this final account of what the right amounts to, we can't conclude that racial profiling violates the right against unreasonable searches unless we first have an independent reason to believe that racial profiling is objectionable – a reason not grounded in the claim that it violates that right. The objection, in short, will get stuck in a vicious circle: racial profiling is objectionable because it violates the right against unreasonable searches and it violates the right against unreasonable searches because it's objectionable. There's no way to escape this vicious circle without providing an independent reason to think that racial profiling is objectionable – a reason other than the claim that it violates the right against unreasonable searches. And if such a reason is in fact identified, then that will be the reason that racial profiling is wrong. The existence of a right not to be subjected to unreasonable searches will prove to be irrelevant.

In the end, then, the appeal to a right against unreasonable searches fails to show that rational racial profiling is immoral. If the right is understood as a right not to be searched unless there's a good reason to think that the person being searched is guilty of something, then rational racial profiling violates the right but the claim that such a right exists has implications that virtually everyone on both sides of the debate already rejects. If the right is understood as a right not to be searched unless the search is entailed by a policy that itself is a reasonable one, then either this means that profiling is permissible if the policy is a rational one – in which case rational racial profiling doesn't violate the right – or it means that profiling is permissible if the policy that authorizes it is an unobjectionable one – in which case we need some independent reason to believe that racial profiling is objectionable in order to show that it violates that right, and the existence of a right against unreasonable searches won't be able to provide such a reason. Although the appeal to a right against unreasonable searches represents one of the most common objections to racial profiling, then, the right ends up proving to be implausible, ineffective, or irrelevant.

EQUAL PROTECTION UNDER THE LAW

A second rights-based objection to rational racial profiling appeals to the Fourteenth Amendment guarantee of equal protection under the law. Section I of that Amendment stipulates that no state shall "deny to any person within its jurisdiction the equal protection of the laws." And while this again is a legal right rather than a moral right, it again seems plausible to suppose that there's a genuine moral right that corresponds to it. As Law Professor George C. Thomas III puts it in defending the claim that racial profiling is immoral, "even if racial profiling produces a positive utilitarian outcome – more arrests of more guilty people – it is a violation of a serious right: the right to equal concern and respect."[5] So let's assume, at least for the sake of the argument, that there's a moral right to be treated equally in the way that the Fourteenth Amendment specifies that there's a legal right. The question is whether, as critics like Thomas have charged, rational racial profiling violates this right.[6]

The answer, as was the case with the right against unreasonable searches and seizures, depends on what exactly is meant by this right. On one interpretation, the right to equal protection under the law includes the right not to have the government take race into account under any circumstances at all. This seems to be what Dinesh D'Souza has in mind when he argues that racial profiling is wrong even when it's rational: "police officers, who are agents of the state, should not be permitted to use race in deciding whether to question potential muggers or stop suspected drug dealers. The reason: We have a constitutional right to be treated equally under the law, meaning the government has no right to discriminate on the basis of race or color."[7] Racial profiling clearly does involve the state's taking a person's race into account when deciding how to treat him. And so if there's a moral right against the state's taking a person's race into account when deciding how to treat him, then racial profiling – even when it's rational – is clearly immoral.

But as we saw in considering the parallel argument against state-practiced affirmative action in Chapter 5, the claim that there's a moral right to equal treatment or equal protection in this strong sense is implausible. There are a variety of cases in which virtually everyone, regardless of their view of racial profiling, will agree that it's morally permissible for the state to take a person's race into account when deciding how to treat him. Suppose, for example, that a national park wishes to hire some actors to portray Abraham Lincoln and Frederick Douglass, or to reenact scenes involving slaves and their masters, as part of an educational program for young school children. Virtually everyone will agree that it's morally acceptable for the state to take race into account when deciding which actors to cast in which roles. Or suppose that a police department or federal agency is trying to hire an officer or agent to go undercover in a predominantly black neighborhood or country. Or a federal research facility is looking for subjects to participate in an experiment to determine whether or not a particular treatment for hypertension is especially effective for African Americans. Again, virtually everyone on both sides of the racial profiling debate will agree that the state violates no moral rights if it takes race into account in making its final decisions. But if this is so, then there's no moral right to equal treatment or equal protection in the strong sense that the critic of racial profiling appeals to here.[8]

As was the case with the problem that airport searches, Border Patrol searches, and random sobriety checkpoints posed for the strong version of the right against unreasonable searches, these problems with the strong version of the right to equal protection suggest a second and more reasonable interpretation of that right. On this more modest version, the state may not take race into account when deciding how to treat people unless race is relevant. In the case of the actors, undercover officers, and medical research subjects, race is clearly relevant to the decision about which people should be selected. And so this more modest version of the right to equal protection or equal treatment won't have the objectionable implication that the state may not take race into account in these cases.

The problem for the critic who claims that rational racial profiling is immoral, though, is that this more modest version of the right to equal treatment isn't violated when the state engages in rational racial profiling. The right, on this weaker version, isn't a right never to have race taken into account. Rather, it's the right not to have race taken into account except when race is relevant. But, by its very nature, rational racial profiling refers to those instances of racial profiling in which racial differences do prove to be relevant. And so while the right to equal treatment or equal protection would suffice to show that irrational racial profiling is immoral, it fails to show that there's anything immoral about rational racial profiling. The objection based on the right to equal protection under the law, then, like the objection based on the right against unreasonable searches and seizures, is ultimately impaled on the horns of a dilemma: either the right is construed in a reasonable manner, in which case rational racial profiling doesn't violate the right, or it's construed in a way that would be violated by racial profiling, but which is objectionable on independent grounds that virtually everyone, regardless of their view of racial profiling, already accepts. Either way, the argument fails to identify a reasonable moral principle that's violated by rational racial profiling.

As we saw in the discussion of affirmative action in Chapter 5, there's a third and potentially more promising option available to the critic of racial profiling at this point. Over the last few decades, the U.S. Supreme Court has developed a complex, multitiered approach to interpreting the legal rights guaranteed by the Fourteenth Amendment, and when it comes to racial distinctions, in particular, it has come to apply the standard of "strict scrutiny": the state may treat people differently according to race without violating the Constitutional right to equal protection, on this understanding, as long as the state can establish that doing so "serves a compelling state interest" and does so in a way that is "necessary to serve that interest." This third understanding of the right to equal treatment, then, is weaker than the right never to have race taken into account, but stronger than the right not to have race taken into account only when race is irrelevant. If racial differences are relevant, on this third account, but taking them into account isn't strictly speaking necessary to serving a compelling state interest, then the right to equal protection under the law will still forbid the law from taking those differences into account when deciding how to treat people.

A defender of racial profiling, of course, could insist that rational racial profiling really is necessary to serve the compelling interest that the state has in protecting its citizens from serious harm. But even if such profiling fails to satisfy this very strict standard, this doesn't really pose a problem for the claim that rational racial profiling is morally acceptable. This is because, whatever merits strict scrutiny may have as a legal doctrine, it's unacceptable as a moral principle. Consider, again, the case of the national park that wants to hire some actors to portray Abraham Lincoln and Frederick Douglass, or to reenact scenes involving slaves and their masters. Virtually everyone would agree that it's morally permissible for the organizers of the event to take race into account when deciding which actors to cast in which roles. But it's clearly implausible to say that doing so is necessary for serving some compelling state interest. Putting on the show hardly serves a compelling state interest, and it isn't strictly speaking necessary to cast actors by race, even though doing so will make the presentation more effective. If people have a moral right not to have the state take their race into account unless doing so is necessary to serving some compelling state interest, then people have a moral right not to have race taken into account in this case. But virtually everyone, regardless of their view of racial profiling, will agree that people don't really have a moral right not to have race taken into account in this case. And so virtually everyone should agree that people don't really have the moral right to equal protection under the law in the way that the legal doctrine of strict scrutiny would interpret that right. And since people don't have that right, it doesn't matter whether rational racial profiling would violate that right if they did have it.

Finally, there's one last kind of case that poses a problem for both kinds of rights-based objections to rational racial profiling. Virtually everyone, regardless of their views about racial profiling, agrees that it's morally permissible for the police to take race into account in cases where a physical description of a specific suspect has been given in the context of a specific crime. Suppose, for example, that a bank has just been robbed and that while the sole witness to the crime didn't see the car the robber drove away in, he did see that the robber was a young, black man. In this kind of case, virtually everyone agrees that it would be permissible for the police to set up roadblocks along the various possible get-away routes, and for them to subject black male drivers who pass by to a greater degree of scrutiny in the process.

But if either the right against unreasonable searches and seizures or the right to equal protection under the law are interpreted in a way that would render rational racial profiling immoral, they would also render taking race into account in this kind of case immoral. Since virtually no one thinks that taking race into account in this kind of case would be immoral, this problem provides one final reason to reject both of the rights-based objections to racial profiling. In order for the right against unreasonable searches and seizures to show that racial profiling is wrong, for example, it has to be interpreted as a right that a person has not to be searched unless there's a good reason to think that he, in particular, is guilty of something. But if the police start subjecting every black man who's driving away from the scene of the bank robbery to a heightened level of scrutiny, the fact that a given driver is black doesn't give them any reason to think that he, in particular, is the bank robber. If the right against unreasonable searches and seizures rendered racial profiling impermissible, it would therefore render taking race into account impermissible in this case as well. And in order for the right to equal treatment and protection under the law to show that racial profiling is immoral, it has to be interpreted as a right that a person has not to have race taken into account even when race is probabilistically relevant. But if the police start subjecting every black man who's driving away from the scene of the bank robbery to a heightened level of scrutiny, they would be violating this right as well. The fact that a single eyewitness described the robber as black, after all, doesn't mean that any particular black driver they pull over is guilty; it simply makes it more probable that he is guilty than that an otherwise comparable white driver is guilty and thus makes it reasonable for the police to focus their limited resources more intensively on the black drivers who pass by than on the white drivers. But if this difference in probabilities isn't enough to make taking race into account permissible in the case of racial profiling, then it can't be enough to make taking race into account permissible in this case either.

Virtually no critic of racial profiling is opposed to taking race into account in cases where a physical description has been given of a specific suspect in a specific crime. But the rights-based arguments against racial profiling entail that taking race into account in such cases is wrong. And this poses one final reason to reject the claim that rational racial profiling is immoral because it violates rights.

THE COSTS OF RACIAL PROFILING

If rational racial profiling doesn't violate anyone's moral rights, it could still be morally wrong for some other sort of reason. The most commonly cited such reason rests on the claim that racial profiling, even rational racial profiling, has negative consequences. Where racial profiling is practiced, after all, innocent black people may well feel distressed, upset, degraded, angry, and outraged at being targeted by race for investigation, at least in part, because of the color of their skin. These negative mental states would all count as direct costs of the practice. In addition, racial profiling may well have many indirect costs as a result of these direct costs. Many black people may feel discouraged from moving around in public for fear of being unjustifiably targeted by the police, for example.[9] They may be deterred from living in predominantly white neighborhoods, and so such policies may end up reinforcing patterns of residential segregation.[10] Racial profiling may have the effect of undermining people's trust in the legal system.[11] Black jurors, for example, may be less likely to believe the sworn testimony of police officers.[12] Black people may be less willing to get involved in police investigations.[13] Black lawyers may be less willing to join the prosecutor's office out of fear that they'd be accused of betraying their race, and the lack of black lawyers working for the government may make it even harder to regain trust in the system among black Americans.[14] And so on.[15] All of this makes for a potentially powerful further objection to rational racial profiling, one that doesn't depend on the claim that profiling violates anyone's rights.

The costs of racial profiling that this objection appeals to are all grounded, in one way or another, in the claim that racial profiling will generate a negative attitude of some sort toward the police and the legal system in general: innocent black Americans will feel resentment if they are pulled over, distrust of police testimony in court, estrangement from the legal system as a whole, and so on. As a white man, I can't really pretend to know how I would feel under such circumstances, but at the very least I can see that these sorts of responses are all perfectly understandable. Certainly I have no reason to believe that I would react differently. There are nonetheless two reasons to think that these sorts of responses, understandable as they are, can't really ground a satisfactory objection to racial profiling.

The first problem that arises from the fact that the objection depends on these kinds of reactions is simple. Since the objection depends on an assumption about how innocent black Americans will react when they know that racial profiling is taking place, the objection depends on the assumption that they will, in fact, know that racial profiling is taking place. The objection, that is, assumes that the policy of engaging in racial profiling won't be kept secret. If a cop engages in racial profiling but no one is aware of this fact, after all, then none of the negative consequences that the objection appeals to will occur. And if none of the negative consequences that the objection appeals to occur, then the objection will fail to count against the cop's engaging in acts of racial profiling.

Now this initial problem with the costs of racial profiling objection might at first seem to be the sort of thing that only an academic would worry about. In the real world, after all, it should seem clear how difficult it would be to keep such a policy a secret, especially if it were practiced on a large scale. But this first problem with the costs of racial profiling objection can't be dismissed so easily for a few reasons. First, it isn't so obvious which police departments, if any, practice racial profiling and which, if any, don't. Simply looking at statistics about which groups are being pulled over, investigated, or arrested at what rates can't provide an answer without knowing why, exactly, they're being pulled over, investigated, or arrested at those rates. Difficulties in reaching a consensus about the latter generate difficulties in reaching a clear answer about what, if anything, the former tell us about whether or not racial profiling is taking place in any given instance. It's hard, for example, to know precisely what percentage of drivers on a given highway are black and what percentage are white. It's hard to know what percentage of those drivers who speed are black and what percentage are white. And even if we can collect reliable data about the number of black and white drivers who are pulled over on any given road during any given period, it's virtually impossible to collect reliable data about why they were pulled over. Did the police officer see the race of the driver before he decided to pull the driver over? If he did, did he take the race of the driver into account when deciding to pull him over? At the time that he decided to pull the driver over, were there other speeding drivers he could instead have pulled over? If there were, what race were the other drivers? We would need to have reliable answers to all of these questions in order to know how best to interpret the numbers. Since it's hard to know if we ever have such answers, there's often genuine disagreement about whether there's good evidence that profiling is taking place in any particular jurisdiction.[16] And so it doesn't seem to require a scenario far removed from reality to imagine a case in which black drivers genuinely don't know whether or not they're being profiled.

Suppose, for example, that on a given stretch of highway, 20 percent of the drivers who speed are black and 80 percent of the drivers who speed are white. Now consider two black drivers who have each been pulled over for speeding. The cop who pulled over one of the drivers pulls over twenty speeding black drivers for every hundred speeding drivers he pulls over. The cop who pulled over the other driver pulls over forty speeding black drivers for every hundred speeding drivers he pulls over. Each cop pulls over more white drivers than black drivers, but the second cop is engaging in racial profiling while the first cop isn't. How could the two black drivers tell which cop was the cop that had pulled them over? There's no clear answer to this question, and so no clear reason to think that people can't be profiled without realizing that they're being profiled.

Second, even if the scenario in which racial profiling is carried out without people realizing it does turn out to be extremely artificial, this doesn't make it irrelevant to our moral assessment of racial profiling itself. Virtually everyone who believes that racial profiling is immoral, after all, believes that it would be immoral even if people didn't realize that it was taking place. Indeed, when it was first reported that some police departments had apparently been engaging in racial profiling for some time without being noticed, the reaction of critics wasn't to say that it would be wrong to continue the practice now that people knew about it and were being made to feel upset by it. Rather, the reaction was that what had been discovered was precisely the fact that the departments had been doing something that was immoral and that had been immoral even before anyone knew that it was happening. Since virtually everyone who opposes racial profiling believes that profiling would be immoral even if it could successfully be kept secret, consistency requires that they can appeal to an argument against racial profiling only if it is able to account for this judgment. If they offer an argument against racial profiling and the argument is unable to explain why racial profiling would be immoral even if it could successfully be kept secret, that is, then the argument would fail on their own terms even if it turns out that in practice it is or would be very difficult to keep the practice a secret.

A rights-based objection to racial profiling, if successful, would account for this reaction. If racial profiling is immoral because it violates people's rights, then it's immoral even if the people in question don't realize that it's happening. It's wrong to violate people's rights, after all, even if they don't realize that their rights are being violated. But the objection based on the negative feelings that innocent black people will have when they realize that profiling is occurring is incapable of justifying this belief. Since it depends on the assumption that the people who are being profiled are aware that they're being profiled, it can provide a reason to think that racial profiling is immoral only when it's practiced openly and overtly. A few critics of racial profiling, I suppose, might be willing to concede that it would be fine for police departments to engage in racial profiling as long as they successfully kept it a secret. But for those who would be unwilling to concede this – and this would presumably be virtually all of them – the costs of racial profiling objection must be rejected. It's simply incapable of supporting the moral claim that they seek to support.

A second and deeper problem with the costs of racial profiling objection can best be put in the form of a dilemma: either the outrage at being profiled that the objection appeals to is independently justified or it isn't.[17] Suppose first that the innocent black drivers who are pulled over under a policy of racial profiling are justified in their outrage at being profiled. If their outrage is justified, then there must be something about racial profiling that's genuinely outrageous, something that makes the practice wrong independent of the fact that people are outraged by it. If they're justifiably outraged because profiling violates their rights, for example, then it isn't that racial profiling is immoral because it causes them to be outraged by this fact. Rather, it's that racial profiling is immoral because it violates their rights, which in turn justifiably outrages them. In order for an objection based on the outrage caused by racial profiling to succeed on this first assumption, then, we must identify a reason to believe that racial profiling is immoral, a reason that's independent of the fact that people are outraged by it. But the objection based on the costs of racial profiling doesn't do this. It doesn't provide a reason to think that people would be justified in being outraged by racial profiling. Rather, it argues from the assumption that people will, in fact, be outraged by it.

But suppose, on the other hand, that the outrage caused by racial profiling is not independently justified. This, too, raises a problem for the objection. Suppose, for example, that a policy of disproportionately targeting young black male drivers on the New Jersey Turnpike violates no one's rights and helps to protect people from drug-related violence. Suppose, in short, that if no one were outraged by the policy, then there would be nothing morally wrong with it. In that case, while it's easy to see how the fact that many people will be outraged by the policy could make implementing the policy a bad idea under the circumstances, it's hard to see how it could show that there's something morally wrong with the policy itself. Many people are outraged by the prospect of cloning, or same-sex marriage, or pornography, for example, but in those cases we don't take the mere fact of the outrage itself to show that these practices are immoral. We instead want to know what reasons people have for finding the practices outrageous and then want to consider whether or not they are good reasons. If we are convinced, for example, that same-sex marriage would violate no rights, would not be unfair to anyone, and so on, then we should think that there's nothing morally wrong with it. If we then become aware that a great many people will be extremely upset, disturbed, distressed, and outraged if their government recognizes same-sex marriage, we should think of this as a reason to think that these people's opposition to same-sex marriage is mistaken, rather than as a reason to think that same-sex marriage itself is immoral.

The same should therefore be said in the case of racial profiling. A moral objection to racial profiling should give us a reason to be outraged by the policy, not a reason to think that people will be outraged by it. But the costs of racial profiling objection provides no such reason. If the outrage caused by racial profiling is independently justified, then the objection is superfluous; racial profiling will be wrong for whatever reason it is that independently justifies people's outrage at it. If the outrage it causes is not independently justified, then the objection is inert. The mere fact that people will unjustifiably object to a policy can't be enough to make the policy itself immoral. Either way, the objection fails to provide a good reason to believe that rational racial profiling is immoral.

If enough people oppose racial profiling strongly enough, of course, a policy of rational racial profiling will become problematic and perhaps even unworkable. And if the overall negative consequences of their being outraged by the policy are strong enough, then it may well become wrong to adopt the policy under those circumstances for those very reasons. But that's true of any policy – including a policy of not having racial profiling. If enough white people would be sufficiently outraged by affirmative action policies because they believed that such policies violated their rights, to take another example, then that might make it wrong to adopt such policies under those circumstances, even if they were mistaken in thinking that affirmative action violated their rights, but it would do nothing to show that affirmative action itself was immoral. When we ask if affirmative action is morally wrong, we want to know whether there's a good reason to oppose it, not whether there's a good reason to believe that it will have bad consequences if enough people will unjustifiably think that there's such a reason. And the same should be said of racial profiling: when we ask if racial profiling is morally wrong, we want to know if there's a good reason to oppose it, not if there's a good reason to believe that it will have bad consequences if enough people will unjustifiably think there's such a reason. In the end, then, the cost of profiling objection doesn't really give us any reasons to think that racial profiling is immoral. Instead, it simply presupposes that many people will think there are such reasons. And so, in the end, the objection gives us no real reason to reject the moral acceptability of racial profiling.

IS RACIAL PROFILING UNFAIR?

A related worry about the costs involved in racial profiling appeals not to the magnitude of the costs, but to the pattern of their distribution. In particular, this objection maintains that even if the overall benefits of racial profiling outweigh the overall costs, the practice must be rejected as immoral because the costs are distributed in a manner that disproportionately burdens black Americans.[18] If state troopers engage in pretext stops at random, for example, then the number of innocent black drivers who get pulled over will on average be proportionate to the number of black drivers on the road. Innocent black motorists, that is, will be incurring no more than their fair share of the burden involved in pretext stops. But if state troopers instead adopt a policy of disproportionately targeting black drivers, then the number of innocent black drivers who get pulled over will be disproportionately large. Black motorists, the objection maintains, will therefore end up incurring an unfairly large share of the burden involved in pretexts stops. And since the policy will be unfair, it will be morally unacceptable.

The fact that racial profiling disproportionately burdens black Americans is an undeniably disturbing feature of the practice. It no doubt plays a significant role in generating the intuitive disapproval of racial profiling that most Americans, myself included, are inclined to feel. But in the end, this consideration, too, fails to provide a satisfactory reason to reject racial profiling as immoral. One reason

for this is simple: the benefits of racial profiling are also disproportionately distributed to black Americans. Black Americans, after all, are disproportionately
victims of crime. When crime is reduced, therefore, black Americans on average
are disproportionately the beneficiaries. If a practice disproportionately benefits
black Americans, then it's not clear why it would be unfair for it also to disproportionately burden them. Of course, it may be that in some instances, perhaps
even in many, crime is reduced in a way that fails to disproportionately benefit
black Americans. If black Americans are disproportionately the victims of drug-
related violence, for example, a particular drop in such violence might still end up
occurring in a predominantly white neighborhood. But even if that's so, the disproportionate burden involved in racial profiling would show that racial profiling
is objectionable only in these particular sorts of cases, not that it's immoral as a
general matter. And since virtually every opponent of racial profiling thinks that
it's immoral as a general matter, this first problem with the unfairness objection
will remain a problem for them.

But let's suppose that while the burdens of racial profiling are disproportionately imposed on black Americans, the benefits are distributed roughly proportionately across the population as a whole. Even if that's so, the fairness-based
objection to racial profiling must still be rejected. This is because, again on the
assumption that the racial profiling in question is rational, shifting the costs from
disproportionately burdening black Americans to proportionately burdening
them would also require increasing the total number of people who would be
subject to such costs. And once this becomes clear, the principle underlying the
fairness-based objection can be seen to be unacceptable on terms that virtually
everyone on both sides of the debate over racial profiling already accepts.

Since this feature of the situation is easy to overlook, it may help to focus on
a specific example. So suppose, to keep things simple for the purposes of illus-
tration, that there's a city where 25 percent of the residents are black and 75
percent are white. Suppose also that engaging in racial profiling in the context
of illegal narcotics is rational in this city because currently, in the absence of
racial profiling, the black rate of committing drug offenses is twice as high as the
white rate. To keep the math simple, let's suppose that on average one in twenty-
five pretext stops of a white driver yields a drug-related arrest and that two in
twenty-five pretext stops of a black driver yield such an arrest. If the police continue to engage in random pretext stops, then for every one hundred stops they
make, they will on average pull over twenty-five black drivers and seventy-five
white drivers. Since on average twenty-five black drivers will yield two arrests
and seventy-five white drivers will yield three arrests, random stops will on average produce five drug-related arrests per one hundred drivers pulled over. Now
suppose, in this context, that the police decide to engage in racial profiling. Since
in this example black drivers are twice as likely to be transporting illegal drugs
as white drivers, the police decide to target them twice as intensively: although
they make up only 25 percent of the population, they will now make up 50 percent of the pretext stops. If the police proceed in this manner, then for every one

hundred stops they make, they will on average pull over fifty black drivers and fifty white drivers. Since on average fifty black drivers will yield four arrests and fifty white drivers will yield two arrests, this form of racial profiling will on average produce six drug-related arrests per one hundred drivers pulled over, rather than the five drug-related arrests per one hundred drivers pulled over in the absence of racial profiling. Racial profiling in this example will therefore increase efficiency by 20 percent.[19]

In this example, racial profiling clearly burdens black drivers disproportionately. But it also increases efficiency by 20 percent. If the police wanted to achieve the same overall level of security without engaging in racial profiling, therefore, they would have to increase the total number of drivers they pulled over by 20 percent. In order to make six arrests without engaging in racial profiling, for example, they would have to pull over 120 drivers (30 black and 90 white) rather than just 100 drivers (50 black and 50 white). If they return to a policy of pulling speeding drivers over at random, then for every 120 stops they make, they will on average pull over 30 black drivers and 90 white drivers. Since on average, 30 black drivers will produce 2.4 drug-related arrests and 90 white drivers will produce 3.6 arrests, this will result in six arrests without engaging in racial profiling.

What does all of this have to do with the fairness-based objection to racial profiling? The answer is this: the objection depends on a principle of fairness that maintains that a policy is unfair if it disproportionately burdens black Americans. This principle may be plausible in cases where the total number of people who will be burdened remains constant. If the choice is between burdening twenty-five black and seventy-five white residents of the city and burdening fifty black and fifty white residents of the city in order to produce a particular public good, then given the city's racial demography, it might well seem wrong to select the latter distribution over the former. But as the example developed here makes clear, that's not the choice. The choice, rather, is between burdening one hundred residents of the city in a racially disproportionate manner and burdening 120 of them in a racially proportionate manner. And in these sorts of cases, at least, the principle of fairness underlying the fairness-based objection to racial profiling can be seen to be implausible on terms that virtually everyone, regardless of their view of racial profiling, will surely accept.

To see this, it may help to begin by considering a kind of case that's far removed from the practice of racial profiling before turning to a case that more closely parallels it. So suppose, to begin with, that an underground pipe has developed a leak in this same city, and that workers are going to have to close down a street for a couple of days in order to repair it. Due to the nature of the problem, there are two different residential blocks it could choose as its point of entry. On one block, there are one hundred residents: fifty black and fifty white. On the other block, there are 120 residents; 30 black and 90 white. Virtually everyone, regardless of their views of racial profiling, would agree that in this case it's morally permissible for the city to simply close down the block with fewer total residents, thereby burdening only 100 innocent people rather than 120. It's true that the

city could instead ensure that it imposes the burdens in a more racially proportionate manner if it instead closed down the more heavily populated block. It
could burden twenty fewer innocent black residents by burdening forty more
innocent white residents. But it's hard to believe that morality would require it
to do this, and so hard to believe the moral principle that underlies the fairness-
based objection to racial profiling.

Indeed, this problem with the argument can be seen by looking at a second
kind of case, one that resembles the practice of racial profiling even more closely.
Suppose that you're a police officer in this same city and you've just arrived at the
scene of a riot where large-scale looting is taking place. You see two vans fleeing
the scene and, although you won't be sure until you pull them over and examine
their contents, you have equally good reason to think that both may have been
participating in the looting. The two vans are starting to head off in opposite
directions, so you can only chase after one of them. You see that the van heading
east has four people in it: one black and three white. The van heading west has
six people in it: three black and three white. Surely in this case, virtually everyone, regardless of their view of racial profiling, would agree that there's nothing
wrong with simply deciding to chase after the van with more people in it. Doing
so increases your efficiency, since if you catch one of the vans and it turns out to
contain looters, you'll catch six looters by heading west and only four looters by
heading east.

But if the principle of fairness underlying the fairness-based objection to
racial profiling shows that racial profiling is immoral, it will also entail that it
would be morally wrong of you to chase after the van with more people in it in
this case. The people in the eastbound van, after all, match the racial demographics of the city: 25 percent are black and 75 percent are white. But the people in
the westbound van are disproportionately black: the city is only 25 percent black
but the people in the westbound van are 50 percent black. This means that if you
pull over the westbound van and the people in it turn out to be innocent, you'll
be disproportionately burdening innocent black people, while if you pull over
the eastbound van and the people in it turn out to be innocent, the black and
white populations will each bear their proportionate share of the resulting burden. Virtually nobody would insist that you're morally obligated to pull over the
van with fewer possible looters in it just in order to ensure a racially proportionate burden to innocent people if they turn out not to be looters. But the choice
between chasing the van carrying more potential criminals with a disproportionately large number of black people in it and chasing the van carrying fewer
potential criminals with a perfectly proportionate number of black people in it is
structurally equivalent to the choice between capturing more criminals and burdening a disproportionately large number of innocent black people by engaging
in racial profiling and capturing fewer criminals and burdening a perfectly proportionate number of innocent black people by not engaging in racial profiling.
In both cases, you don't know if the people you pull over will be guilty, and in
both cases you can reasonably expect to end up catching more guilty people by

aiming at the group with a disproportionately large black membership. Choosing to target the disproportionately black group of possible offenders seems clearly to be permissible in the case of the two vans, and so the fact that racial profiling, too, disproportionately burdens black people can't be enough to make racial profiling impermissible either.[20]

Finally, the fairness-based objection to racial profiling is subject to the same problem that turned out to undermine both of the rights-based objections to racial profiling: the fairness-based objection entails that the use of race in circulating a physical description of a particular suspect in the case of a specific crime is morally impermissible. The problem here is that suspect descriptions themselves are disproportionately black. As was noted in the discussion of the circularity objection to the rationality of racial profiling in Chapter 10, for example, a recent National Crime Victimization Survey of crime reports made by victims of offenses such as robbery, assault, and rape in cases where the victim was able to provide a description of the offender showed that 24.6 percent of the suspect descriptions identified the suspect as black. Since black Americans make up only about 13 percent of the population, this means that the rate at which suspects are described by victims as black is roughly twice what it would be if suspects were described as black in a number proportionate to their representation in the population as a whole. And this, in turn, means that when the police inadvertently stop or pull over innocent people based on the racial component of a physical suspect description, the total number of innocent people burdened by this practice will be disproportionately black as well. Since the fairness-based objection to racial profiling maintains that racial profiling is wrong because it disproportionately burdens black people, and since the use of race in physical suspect descriptions disproportionately burdens black people in precisely the same way, the proponent of the fairness-based objection to racial profiling is committed to the conclusion that the use of race in physical suspect descriptions is morally impermissible as well. But virtually everyone, regardless of their view of racial profiling in cases like those involving pretext stops on the New Jersey Turnpike, agrees that the use of race in providing physical descriptions of suspects in the case of particular crimes is morally permissible. And so the case of physical suspect descriptions provides one final reason to reject the fairness-based objection to racial profiling.

I've provided several reasons to reject the fairness-based objection to racial profiling. Before moving on to consider one final objection, though, it's important to note that a critic of racial profiling might complain that I've failed to appreciate the full force of this one. Racial profiling is unfair, such a critic might insist, not simply because it disproportionately burdens black Americans, but because it reinforces an unfair pattern of incarceration. If the police engage in racial profiling, after all, they'll end up arresting a disproportionately larger number of black people than if they don't. If they arrest a disproportionately large number of black people, this will contribute to there being a disproportionately large number of black Americans in prison. But the disproportionately large number of black Americans in prison, this critic is likely to maintain, is itself largely due to the legacy of slavery and its aftermath. This renders the current distribution of black and white Americans in prison an unfair one, and so racial profiling is unfair, more specifically, because it contributes to this unfair distribution.

There are two reasons to reject this attempt to reinforce the fairness-based objection to racial profiling. The first is that this version of the objection, like the original version, entails that the use of race in providing physical suspect descriptions is impermissible. Since the rate at which suspects are described by victims as black is roughly twice what it would be if suspects were described as black in a number proportionate to their representation in the population as a whole, the use of race in providing physical suspect descriptions leads to a disproportionately large number of black arrests and convictions. If the police were not permitted to use race in providing physical suspect descriptions, that is, this would enable some white criminals to avoid capture, but would enable a disproportionately larger number of black criminals to avoid capture. The result would be that the overall ratio of black and white Americans in prison would be closer to the ratio of black and white Americans in society as a whole. But virtually no one thinks that this is a good reason to forbid the use of race in the provision of physical suspect descriptions. And so virtually no one should think that the fact that forbidding racial profiling would also make the overall ratio of black and white Americans in prison closer to the ratio of black and white Americans in society is a good reason to forbid the use of racial profiling either.

The second reason to reject the revised version of the fairness-based objection is that it mislocates the source of the unfairness in America's current prison demographics. The root of the problem is that with respect to certain important categories of criminal behavior, black Americans disproportionately break the law. The goal, therefore, should be to reduce the rate at which black Americans break these laws, not to reduce the rate at which black Americans who do break them are successfully apprehended and convicted. And once the problem is approached from this point of view, it becomes clear that racial profiling actually promotes the goal of making things fairer rather than hinders it.

The reason for this is simple, but, as we saw in the context of the elasticity argument about the rationality of racial profiling in Chapter 10, easy to overlook. When a police department moves from conducting random pretext stops to focusing its pretext stops disproportionately on black drivers, it increases the level of deterrence directed at potential black criminals and decreases the level of deterrence directed at potential white criminals. In cases where adopting such a policy is rational, the decrease in black crime will be sufficient to outweigh the accompanying increase in white crime. A policy of racial profiling can produce this result only if it reduces the rate at which potential black criminals break the law. Rational racial profiling, then, moves the ratio of black and white Americans who break the law closer to the ratio of black and white Americans in society as a whole. In doing so, it therefore helps to combat the problematic pattern in which black Americans disproportionately break the law. Rather than providing a reason to reject the claim that racial profiling is permissible, then, this further development of the fairness-based objection ultimately seems to provide a further reason to accept it.

Let's now suppose that whatever negative consequences rational racial profiling might have, their magnitude and distribution would not suffice to render it immoral, and that the practice itself wouldn't violate anyone's moral rights. Would this be enough to make rational racial profiling morally acceptable? Not quite. Sometimes, a practice that would otherwise be morally unobjectionable becomes morally objectionable because it's adopted for morally objectionable reasons. And so before we conclude that rational racial profiling is morally acceptable, we should consider whether this final sort of objection could be made to apply to it.

The objection based on ulterior motives is perhaps best approached by means of a particular example. So consider the form of geography-based affirmative action discussed in Chapters 2 and 3 on which college applicants from geographically underrepresented areas are given preference in admissions. A school that adopts such a policy, for example, might end up admitting a somewhat less qualified student from North Dakota over a somewhat more qualified student from New York if it already has a large number of students from New York and virtually none from North Dakota. Virtually everyone, regardless of their views of racial profiling, or of race-based affirmative action, for that matter, agrees that geography-based affirmative action is morally permissible.

But now suppose that a school adopted a geography-based affirmative action policy because it knew that doing so would help it to limit the number of students it admitted from some racial or ethnic group that it disliked. If a school started admitting fewer students from New York and more students from North Dakota, for example, this might well have the effect of reducing the number of Jewish students it admitted. So suppose a school wanted to admit fewer Jewish students out of an animosity toward Jews and adopted a policy of geography-based affirmative action for just that reason. In that case, many people would say that the school's action was morally objectionable. Indeed, there's evidence that some schools originally adopted such policies for precisely this reason, and in such cases the school's decisions have been subject to significant moral criticism as a result. But, a critic of racial profiling might then claim, police departments that adopt a policy of racial profiling should be subjected to the same kind of moral criticism. Even if such policies can be rationally justified on the grounds that they provide an efficient way to reduce crime, the critic might complain that this is not the reason that they are actually adopted. Instead, on this account, the efficiency of such policies is merely a smokescreen, a convenient excuse to harass innocent black people with impunity. Racial profiling policies, even when they're rational, are therefore as one writer has put the objection, "simply a pretense for racial harassment."[21]

It's hard to know why a particular police department adopts the policies it does. In some cases, of course, it's possible that there might be a written record of people having adopted a policy of racial profiling for explicitly racist reasons. In that sort of case, the ulterior motives objection would seem to be a fair one to raise. And if a particular department took race into account when deciding who to investigate but ignored other probabilistically relevant factors, that might count as indirect evidence that its racial profiling was motivated by racial animus rather than by rational considerations of efficiency. But regardless of whether a particular department can reasonably be subject to the ulterior motives objection, the objection itself fails to show that there's anything immoral about racial profiling itself. As in the case of geography-based affirmative action, the objection shows that the act of adopting a policy can be morally objectionable even if the policy itself is unobjectionable. But the question this chapter is concerned with is whether there's anything immoral about the policy of racial profiling itself. The ulterior motives objection fails to show that there is even in cases where the objection can reasonably be applied. And so, in the end, it provides no reason to reject the moral permissibility of racial profiling.

IS PERMISSIBLE RACIAL PROFILING MORALLY OBLIGATORY?

Let's now assume that some racial profiling is rational, and that rational racial profiling is morally permissible. If that's right, then one final question arises: is rational racial profiling also morally obligatory? If it isn't wrong to engage in rational racial profiling, that is, is it wrong not to? On the face of it, at least, it might seem that the most reasonable answer to this question is yes. The state, after all, has a special obligation to protect its citizens from crime. And if engaging in rational racial profiling would enable the state to provide a greater degree of such protection, then it might seem that doing so would be not merely permissible, but obligatory as well.[22] But there are two reasons to reject this further line of reasoning.

The first reason to deny that the state is morally obligated to engage in rational racial profiling arises from considering other cases in which someone has a special moral obligation to provide protection. If you're the parent of a young child, for example, you have a powerful obligation to protect that child from harm. If you take your child somewhere in your car, it would be wrong for you not to carefully strap him into a suitable car seat first. But the fact that you have a special obligation to protect your child from harm doesn't mean that you must do everything possible to maximize your child's safety. If you put a helmet on your child's head in addition to putting him in a car seat, after all, he would be even safer than if you merely put him in the car seat. But while most people would agree that it would be wrong for you not to put the child in a car seat, virtually no one would think it would be wrong for you to refrain from also putting a helmet on his head, even though doing so would make him even safer.

The lesson of the car seat and helmet case is that when you have a special obligation to protect someone, this doesn't mean that you must maximize their safety. It simply means that there's a high level of protection below which you must not let them fall. As long as you're doing a good job of keeping your children at that high level of protection, it isn't wrong for you to decline to protect them even further. And it therefore seems reasonable to say the same thing in the case of the government's special obligation to protect its citizens from crime. The state has a duty to protect its citizens, but this doesn't mean that it has a duty to maximize their safety. If it can provide a high level of protection without engaging in racial profiling, then even if adding racial profiling to its other practices would increase safety overall, this doesn't mean that it would be wrong for the state not to engage in it. And this provides one reason to think that the permissibility of rational racial profiling doesn't entail that rational racial profiling is morally obligatory. It will be morally obligatory if there's no other way for the state to provide a high level of protection to its citizens, but if it can provide a high level of protection without engaging in rational racial profiling, then engaging in such profiling won't be morally obligatory even if it would make its citizens even safer.

Second, and more importantly, it's misleading to frame the choice between permitting rational racial profiling and forbidding it as the choice between having more security and having less. It can just as easily be framed as the choice between achieving a certain level of security in part though the use of rational racial profiling and achieving the very same level of security by doing something else to compensate for the lack of rational racial profiling. This feature of the options we have to choose from is often overlooked in the debate over racial profiling.[23] But once it's noticed, it should become even clearer that racial profiling, even when it would permissibly increase security, need not be morally obligatory.

Suppose, for example, that there are currently twenty police cars regularly patrolling a particular stretch of the New Jersey Turnpike. Suppose also that the police in the state are currently employing a form of rational racial profiling, and that one hundred drug-related arrests are made on that part of the road each week as a result. And suppose, finally, that if the police were to abandon their practice of racial profiling and instead make their decisions about which drivers to pull over without putting any weight at all on the racial identity of the drivers, the number of drug-related arrests would drop to eighty per week. In this case, it might initially seem that abolishing racial profiling would mean a 20 percent drop in the number of drug-related arrests made each week. But this is misleading. If twenty patrol cars would catch eighty drug offenders each week without using racial profiling, then the state could still catch one hundred drug offenders each week without using racial profiling by paying to deploy a few extra patrol cars. If each car on average would make four arrests per week without using racial profiling, then adding five extra police cars would be enough to generate an extra twenty arrests per week. Twenty-five patrol cars not using racial profiling, in other words, would produce the same level of safety as twenty patrol cars using racial profiling. The state's choice, then, wouldn't have to be between arresting one hundred drug offenders each week and arresting only eighty drug offenders.

It could instead be the choice between arresting one hundred drug offenders using twenty police cars engaging in racial profiling and arresting one hundred drug offenders using twenty-five police cars not engaging in racial profiling. And when the choice is put this way, it becomes even clearer that permissible racial profiling need not be obligatory. Even if we believe that the state has an obligation to catch one hundred drug offenders each week rather than 80, it could meet its obligation without engaging in racial profiling by paying for a few extra patrol cars.

If the state abolished racial profiling and at the same time increased its patrols by 20 percent to compensate for the fact that racial profiling would be 20 percent more efficient, of course, there would be some sort of opportunity cost involved. Spending cuts would have to be made in other parts of the budget or taxes would have to be raised. Either way, sacrifices would have to be made in order to avoid engaging in racial profiling. Since rational racial profiling is morally permissible, the people in the state would not be obligated to make such sacrifices in order to do without racial profiling. But if they were willing to make such a sacrifice, it's hard to see any reason to think that it would be impermissible for them to do so. And this provides a second reason to conclude that while rational racial profiling is morally permissible, it need not be morally obligatory.

In the end, then, I've grudgingly come to the conclusion that racial profiling isn't as objectionable as most Americans think it is. In some instances, perhaps even in many, it would probably be ineffective. In other instances, though, it would probably be effective. In those instances in which it would probably be effective, it wouldn't be immoral for the state not to engage in it. But it wouldn't be immoral for the state to engage in it, either. I realize that this is not the most uplifting note to end on, and this is certainly not the concluding paragraph I envisioned writing when I first started thinking about working on a book about applied ethics and race several years ago. But, as with the other topics I've discussed here, the conclusion I've come to about racial profiling strikes me as the one that's best supported by considerations that virtually everyone on both sides of the debate already accepts. This approach to resolving the debates that I've discussed in this book has left with me a somewhat eclectic set of conclusions, one that lacks the unity and coherence that might arise by approaching the issues from the perspective of a single theory, and one that as a whole can't really be characterized as liberal or conservative, colorblind or color-conscious. Perhaps this suggests that there's something wrong with the approach that I've taken to these issues. But perhaps, as I think more likely, it shows that the set of moral problems raised by the use and misuse of race in America is itself an eclectic one that has no single or simple answer.

Notes

Chapter 1. Thinking in Black and White: An Introduction to the Moral
Questions that America's Past Raises about Its present

1. For a forceful defense of the view that the division of human beings into different races is a matter of social construction rather than of biology, see Graves Jr. (2005). For an equally forceful defense of the view that the division is grounded in facts about biology rather than social construction, see Sarich and Miele (2005). A useful recent discussion that is sympathetic to both sides of the debate can be found in Arthur (2007: chapter 2).
2. Graves (2005: xxv, 5).
3. Graves (2005: 162).
4. Sarich and Miele (2005: 207–8).
5. Graves (2005: 116).
6. Sarich and Miele (2005: 21–2).
7. See, for example, Malik (2008: 56–8).
8. Hacker (2003: 15). See also Kennedy (2008: 17–18).
9. The discussion of racial profiling may well also have implications for immigration policy. See Hernandez and Cuauhtemoc (2009) for a recent discussion of racial profiling in the context of enforcing immigration laws.
10. For three recent and extremely useful general surveys of this subject, all of which served as basic source material for this section, see Adams and Sanders (2003), Browne-Marshall (2007), and Klarman (2007). Another exemplary resource, though one that begins after slavery was abolished, is Thernstrom and Thernstrom (1997: Part I).
11. Adams and Sanders (2003: 3).
12. Quoted in Adams and Sanders (2003: 5).
13. Adams and Sanders (2003: 6).
14. Adams and Sanders (2003: 11).
15. Adams and Sanders (2003: 13).
16. Adams and Sanders (2003: 19). This was so despite the fact that England had officially abolished the practice four years earlier, when Lord Mansfield, chief justice of the King's Bench, ruled in the case of James Somersett, an African slave who had been brought by his master from Virginia to England, that "as soon as

any slave sets foot upon English territory, he becomes free" (Adams and Sanders (2003: 1)).

17. Strictly speaking, the Constitution continues to contain this clause, though it has since been superseded by the Thirteenth Amendment. Pedants might point out that the Constitution does not refer to slavery or African people at all. The clause in question reads: "No Person held to Service or Labour in one State, under the Laws thereof, escaping into another, shall, in Consequence of any Law or Regulation therein, be discharged from such Service or Labour, But shall be delivered up on Claim of the Party to whom such Service or Labour may be due." But it's clear what's meant.

18. Waldstreicher (2009: 6) emphasizes the role this clause played in helping the Constitution to feed "slaveholder power directly."

19. Adams and Sanders (2003: 160–1).

20. Adams and Sanders (2003: 49). See also Klarman (2007: 28).

21. Adams and Sanders (2003: 129).

22. Quoted by Adams and Sanders (2003: 143). See also Klarman (2007: 31).

23. Brooks (2004: 32).

24. Klarman (2007: 28).

25. Although it's worth noting that it did not bring an immediate end to some practices that resembled slavery in some important respects. Sharecropping, for example, which bears some similarity to indentured servitude, continued into the twentieth century. And the practice of peonage, on which an unemployed black man was arrested for "vagrancy" and jailed until he could afford to pay the corresponding fine, at times also came close to treating its victims as slaves: a plantation owner could pay the fine on behalf of the arrested person and then "hire" him until he earned enough money to pay it back, and this put the peon in a position not radically unlike that of a slave: forced to work, locked up at night, and captured if he tried to escape (Robinson 2000a: 226). For a meticulously documented study of what he refers to as "slavery by another name" from the period beginning after the civil war and ending at the start of the Second World War, see Blackmon (2008).

26. Quoted by Adams and Sanders (2003: 199).

27. Adams and Sanders (2003: 230–1).

28. Adams and Sanders (2003: 235–6).

29. Thernstrom and Thernstrom (1997: 31).

30. Thernstrom and Thernstrom (1997: 30–1).

31. Adams and Sanders (2003: 230).

32. Klarman (2007: 95).

33. Adams and Sanders (2003: 246).

34. Adams and Sanders (2003: 257).

35. Adams and Sanders (2003: 288).

36. Adams and Sanders (2003: 261–2). See also Klarman (2007: 129–31).

37. Frady (2002: 29–30).

38. Frady (2002: 36).

39. For a useful, concise, and recent treatment of *Brown*, see Klarman (2007: Chapter 9). See also Thernstrom and Thernstrom (1997: 98–107).

40. Adams and Sanders (2003: 242). See also Thernstrom and Thernstrom (1997: 37).

41. Klarman (2007: 86–7).

42. Wicker (1996: 92–3).

43. Wicker (1996: 95).
44. Wicker (1996: 96).
45. Adams and Sanders (2003: 277–9).
46. Frady (2002: 153).
47. Frady (2002: 154).
48. Thernstrom and Thernstrom (1997: 157).
49. See Thernstrom and Thernstrom (1997: 40–1).
50. See, for example, Browne-Marshall (2007: 199–200).
51. See, for example, Karlan (2008: 48), which argues that "Felon disenfranchise-ment has decimated the potential black electorate" and notes that in Alabama and Florida, almost one third of all black men are disenfranchised for life. See also Browne-Marshall (2007: 136), which reports that about 15 percent of all black men in the United States are currently disenfranchised because of their criminal records.
52. McShane and Tompson (2007: 2A).
53. Quoted in Adams and Sanders (2003: xi).
54. Oliver and Shapiro (2006: 225–6). Similarly, in 2000, 3 in 200 young white Americans were incarcerated while 1 in 9 young black Americans were (Loury (2008: 23)).
55. For an exhaustive treatment of the rise of the black middle class in America, see Thernstrom and Thernstrom (1997: part two, especially chapter 7). While they do much to emphasize the good news about racial progress in the United States and characterize their book as an "optimistic" one (1997: 544), even the Thernstroms acknowledge "the grim reality that disproportionately large numbers of African Americans do indeed live in poverty" (1997: 184). And while they emphasize that "a majority of blacks are not poor, and a majority of poor Americans are not black," they also acknowledge that the poverty rate for black Americans "is nearly triple the poverty rate for white Americans" (1997: 232).
56. Hacker (2003: 111). For some additional figures, see Oliver and Shapiro (2006: e.g., 88–9, 283).
57. Galster and Hill (1992: 8).
58. Blair and Fichtenbaum (1992: 78).
59. Brophy (2006: 56).
60. Thenstrom and Thernstrom (1997: 197).
61. Adams and Sanders (2003: 322).
62. Hacker (2003: 60). For more on mortality rates, see also Osei (1992).
63. Oliver and Shapiro (2006: 241). For more on disparities between black and white American levels of health and health care, see also Williams and Collins (2004).
64. In 1988, for example, the Detroit public schools spent $3,600 per student in pre-dominantly minority areas and $6,000 per student in the mostly white suburbs (Moore 2005: 83). See (Moore 2005: 93) for similar statistics involving Chicago and New York.
65. Moore (2005: 157)
66. The precise figure is 28 percent (Adams and Sanders (2003: 322)).
67. The precise figure is 4.3 percent, in figures taken from a 2003 report (quoted in Sabbagh 2007: 73).
68. Hacker (2003: 111).
69. Hacker (2003: 112). It should be noted, though, that things look much better in the case of black women. A black woman who finished high school earns $944 for

every $1,000 earned by a white woman who finished high school, and black women with bachelor's or master's degrees actually make more on average than do white women with comparable degrees ($1,117 and $1,030, respectively).
70. Klarman (2007: 202).
71. Quoted in Harmon (2001: 84).
72. Kinder and Sanders (1996: 17).
73. Kinder and Sanders (1996: 30).
74. Flaherty and Carlisle (2004: 1).
75. Brophy (2004: 1183–4).

Chapter 2. Repairing the Slave Reparations Debate: How I Got into an Argument with Myself about David Horowitz and Lost

1. Horowitz (2002: 9).
2. In a 2002 Gallup poll, for example, 90 percent of white Americans opposed slave reparations, as did half of black Americans. A 2001 Gallup poll also found that 70 percent of white Americans opposed an official government apology for slavery (both cited in Williams [2006: 80]).
3. See, for example, Chrisman and Allen (2001: 49).
4. Horowitz (2002: 13). In reproducing Horowitz's "Ten Reasons" in this chapter, I have followed the definitive version contained in his 2002 book. There seem to be some minor differences between this version and earlier versions that were published in some of the newspapers or that have since appeared online (e.g., some differences in capitalization and in terms of whether a number is spelled out or represented by a numeral) but nothing that should affect the substance of any of the discussion that follows.
5. It's worth noting, however, that to the extent that the other responsible parties were individuals or corporate entities who no longer exist, it may also be fair to insist that the government inherit their share of the debt as well. If a plaintiff is wrongfully harmed by the joint actions of three corporations, for example, and if one of the corporations would normally be judged as responsible for only a third of the total damages, it can still be sued for the entirety of the damages if the other two corporations no longer exist at the time a legal action is brought against it.
6. See, especially, Bittker (1973).
7. As Brophy puts it in his recent and very thorough survey of the reparations movement and its critics, "It is difficult to find reparations proponents who seriously propose direct payments to individuals" (2006: 175).
8. For some examples of the variety of forms of reparations that have been proposed, see, for example, Asante (2003: 12–15), Johnson (1999), Ogletree (2003a: 1071; 2003c: 261), Van Dyke (2003: 74–5), Westley (2003: 129), Forman (1969: 168–70), America (1993), Nzingha (2003: 312–13), Crawford, Nobles, and Leary (2003: 275–80), Brophy (2006: 167–79). See also Brooks (2004), which maintains that a formal apology is a necessary perquisite for meaningful reparations (e.g., 2004: 142–3) and suggests that redress for slavery should include the construction of museums about slavery (e.g., 2004: 157). Arthur, by contrast, defends the claim that the United States should apologize for slavery as an alternative to making reparations (2007: 222–7). Finally, it's worth noting Levmore (2004), which develops an intriguing model on which reparations for slavery could be, at least partially, privatized.

9. See, for example, Sebok (2004: 1416) for some examples.

10. Robinson (2000a), Boxill (1992: 37–8), McGary (1977–78: 95–6). Other appeals to the unjust enrichment argument can be found in Robinson (2000b: 622), Feagin (2000: 262–3), Armstrong (2002), Darrity and Frank (2003: 253), Ogletree (2003a: 1055–6, 1069; 2003b: 311–12), Van Dyke (2003: 58ff), Kelly (2003: 218–21), Westley (2003: 125–6), Outterson (2003: 136–7), Dagan (2004), Hitchens (2003: 175, 177), America (1993; 1997), Browne (1993), Gutmann (1996: 173–4), Secours (2003), Tutu (2003: 324), Brooks (2004: 144, 188), Block (2002), Paterson (2004: 19), Klimchuk (2004), Harvey (2007: 144, 157–8), Alson and Block (2008) (although Alson and Block defend the argument only as one that shows that private individuals have an obligation of reparation if they have inherited property that properly belongs to the descendants of slaves) and Stark (2004) (although Stark defends the argument specifically in the context of defending affirmative action as a form of reparations for slavery).

11. Robinson (2000a: 221).

12. Sherwin (2004: 1447).

13. Robinson (2000a: 221, emphasis added).

14. See, for example, Sherwin (2004: 1449), from which some of the examples that follow are borrowed.

15. For a further set of reasons for rejecting the unjust enrichment approach to slave reparations, see Sherwin (2004: esp. sec. III).

16. America (1990: xix). Nor, for that matter, is there much agreement on the magnitude of the overall enrichment if it does exist. For some useful discussions of some of the issues arising from attempts to carry out the relevant calculations, see the various papers collected in this anthology, but especially Bailey-Williams (1990), Browne (1990: 202–4), Feiner and Roberts (1990), Marketti (1990), Neal (1990), Ransom and Sutch (1990), and Vedder, Gallaway, and Klingaman (1990).

17. See, for example, Robinson (2000a: 3), Ogletree (2003b: 282; 2003c: 247).

18. See Kornweibel (2003).

19. Outterson, for example, reports that slave taxes were "a crucial source of revenue for improvements, wars, and government finance such as the Louisiana Purchase" (2003: 148–9).

20. See, e.g., Neal (1990: 92–3).

21. Arthur (2007: 205). It might be argued that the remaining forty percent of the wealth generated by slavery would suffice to justify reparations. This would be true if, on the whole, the remaining 40 percent was enough to outweigh all the costs of slavery that were passed down as well. My point here is simply that the less the concrete benefits of slavery survived the war, the less likely it is that on the whole America is better off today because it practiced slavery up until that point.

22. Masters (1990: 180).

23. Wise's book (2008), for example, focuses exclusively on arguing for the claim that white privilege gives contemporary white Americans a relative advantage over black Americans and does nothing to show that white Americans today would be worse off, in absolute terms, if slavery and its aftermath had never occurred. It might seem that the more modest claim that the legacy of slavery and its aftermath has harmed black Americans more than it has harmed white Americans would still be enough to justify slave reparations. But while that may be true on the compensation argument for reparations that I develop in the section that follows, it isn't

enough to help salvage the unjust enrichment argument I am considering here. That argument maintains that white Americans owe reparations in virtue of the fact that they are unjustly benefiting from the legacy of slavery. If they aren't benefiting, then the argument is unsound for that reason.

24. Masters (1990: 185), though later on the same page he seems to overlook the significance of this fact and treat an increase in relative well-being as in itself sufficient to ground a claim of reparations.

25. Two more problem cases that are worth considering are people who purchased slaves shortly before the Civil War broke out, and so spent money on the slaves but did not own them long enough to profit from them, and people whose slaves died before they had done enough work to recover the costs involved in purchasing and providing for them. In the context of this second kind of problem case, for example, it is worth noting the claim made by Robert William Fogel and Stanley L. Engerman that "Prior to age 26, the accumulated expenditures by planters on slaves were greater than the average accumulated income which they took from them" (quoted by Horowitz (2002: 129)). Schedler (2002: 389) makes a somewhat similar point.

26. For some further objections to the unjust enrichment argument, see also Sebok (2004: 1422–42).

27. Robinson (2000a: 9, emphases altered). See also Robinson (2000a: 204, 207, 221) for this analogy and passages such as (2000: 8), which talks in terms of black people suffering "at the hands of those who benefited" (e.g., 2000: 206–7; 208–9).

28. Robinson (2000a: 207).

29. It might at first seem that my comment here is inconsistent with part of what I said about the unjust enrichment argument in the previous section. In that section, I maintained that the unjust enrichment argument would fail if it turned out that white Americans today are not benefiting from the legacy of slavery and its aftermath, but here I am saying that I would still owe you compensation even if I did not benefit from stealing and destroying your car. But if that's true, then it seems that white Americans might owe reparations for slavery even if they are not benefiting from it either. The appearance of inconsistency, though, is misleading. My claim in the previous section was not that if white Americans are not benefiting from slavery and its aftermath then they can't owe reparations for it. Rather, my claim was that if they are not benefiting from slavery and its aftermath then the unjust enrichment argument in particular can't be used to justify the claim that they owe reparations. And rather than being inconsistent with what I am saying here, the car example instead reinforces what I said there: if I don't benefit from destroying your car, then the unjust enrichment argument in particular can't be used to justify the claim that I would owe you something for destroying it either.

30. There are also a few places in Robinson's book where he comes closer to the compensation argument than to the unjust enrichment argument (e.g., 2000a: 24), but it's clear that, on the whole, the book is meant to be a defense of the unjust enrichment argument. As Brody puts it in his careful study of the reparations movement and its critics, "Robinson's best-selling book had as its thesis the idea that African Americans contributed to the building of America, received minuscule compensation, and thus were owed compensation, hence the title, *The Debt*" and "Robinson represents one strand of reparations thought: that the basis for reparations is the degree to which African Americans have enriched American society" (2006: 70,

71). Simliarly, while Ogletree Jr. generally seems to have the unjust enrichment argument in mind (e.g., 2003a: 1055–6, 1069; 2003b: 311–12), at times he briefly seems instead to appeal to something more like the compensation argument (e.g., 2004: 22). See also Bittker (1973: ch. 2) for an argument that comes closer to the compensation argument. Valls seems explicitly to defend a version of the compensation argument in (1999: 305–6) but as soon as he turns to defending it from objections, the argument seems just as explicitly to turn into the unjust enrichment argument (1999: 307). Logue (2004: 1322) also starts with an argument that seems similar to what I am calling the compensation argument, but it quickly turns instead into an argument grounded largely in egalitarian concerns. Three essays that come much closer to defending what I'm calling the compensation argument are Fullinwider (2000) and Lyons (2004; 2007). See also Bolner (1968), Davis (2000), Sebok (2004) and, more tentatively, Brophy (2003: 423). And much of Loury (2008) can be interpreted as defending a version of the compensation argument in which reparations take the form of reforming the criminal justice system with an eye toward reducing the enormous gap between black and white incarceration rates.

31. Hackney Jr. develops the analogy between toxic waste, the legacy of slavery, and its aftermath in (2004: 1194–8).

32. Robinson (2000a: 8, 216, 216). See also Robinson (2004: 1, 5–6).

33. Robinson (2000a: 75).

34. The same is true of Robinson (2000b: 623) and Robinson (2004: 12).

35. A more detailed defense of what I am referring to as the causal claim can also be found in Brooks (2004: ch. 3).

36. Hacker (2003: 36). See also Graves Jr. (2005: 177, 191–2).

37. For a detailed discussions of the various clauses in the Constitution that directly or indirectly protected the practice of slavery, see Finkelman (1999) and Waldstreicher (2009).

38. This quote comes from his article in *The Nation* (Robinson [2000c: 373]), but at one point in his book he says virtually the same thing: "The life and responsibilities of a society or nation are not circumscribed by the life spans of its mortal constituents" (2000a: 230; see also 2000b: 623). Chrisman and Allen say something similar in their response to Horowitz: "As the government is an entity that survives generations, its debts and obligations survive the lifespan of any particular individuals" (2001: 51).

39. Adams and Sanders (2003: xiv–xv, 324) offer another useful analogy in suggesting a defense of this argument: stockholders in a company that in the past caused an environmental catastrophe. See also Fullinwider (2000; 2004) for a similar analysis.

40. Horowitz (2002: 12).

41. Horowitz (2002: 111–12).

42. Horowitz (2002: 112).

43. It's possible that Horowitz is also trying to make a third point here: that the United States government isn't solely responsible for facilitating even that portion of the practice of slavery that existed within its borders, since agents acting in other parts of the world also contributed to the ability of the American government to maintain the practice of slavery within its borders. But if this is Horowitz's point, then it is not really inconsistent with the reparations position. You can owe someone a debt in virtue of the role you played in wrongfully harming someone even if you were not the only person who played a role in wrongfully harming them.

44. Horowitz (2002: 12).
45. "How," he asks, "did a black worker in a tobacco state not benefit from the investment that slavers had made?" (2002: 81).
46. Horowitz (2002: 84–5).
47. In *Out of America: A Black Man Confronts Africa*, for example, Keith B. Richburg, a reporter for the *Washington Post* who spent three years on assignment in Africa, is repeatedly drawn back to the thought that he is grateful to be a black American rather than a black African. He complains about being "told by some of our supposedly enlightened, so-called black leaders that white America owes us something because they brought our ancestors over as slaves" and seems to think it obvious that the case for reparations is undermined by the fact that things are so much worse for black people in Africa than they are in America (Richburg [1997: xiii]). For some of his expressions of gratitude for the fact that he was born in America rather than Africa, see, for example, pp. 55, 160, 162, and perhaps most strikingly 233, where he finds himself "quietly celebrating the passage of my ancestor who made it out." Brophy (2003: 522) also reluctantly raises this objection, though unlike Horowitz he is explicit in presenting it only as an objection to the unjust enrichment argument in particular.
48. Horowitz (2002: 12).
49. Horowitz (2002: 120). See, more generally Horowitz (2002: 116–20), Flaherty and Carlisle (2004: 20–1, 32–4, 36–8), and Levin (1997: 273), who claims that white sacrifice by the North would at least reduce what is owed.
50. Horowitz (2002: 13).
51. I'm apparently not the only person who has been persuaded by this kind of consideration: Illinois Republican Henry Hyde, responding to the idea of Congress approving reparations for slavery, declared that: "The notion of collective guilt for what people did [over 200] years ago, that this generation should pay a debt for that generation, is an idea whose time has gone. I never owned a slave. I never oppressed anybody" (quoted in Williams (2006: 79)). Similarly, Kathleen Parker in a column in the *Chicago Tribune* writes: "So let's get this straight: We who have never owned a slave, who have never believed in or condoned slavery, who are not descended from anyone who ever owned a slave must pay people who have never been slaves? The search for logic in the reparations argument is futile" (quoted in Pettigrove [2003:334]). Flaherty and Carlisle (2004: 21–2) also appeal to the case of the recent immigrant, as does Block (2002: 60) and Alston and Block (2008: 381), at least in the context of objecting to the claim that reparations could be owed by the federal government
52. Brooks (2004: 190) also cites the example of recent immigrants finding that some of their tax money goes toward paying off the national debt. See also Brophy (2004: 1202–3) for other useful examples involving taxpayers having to pay when their city's police department is successfully sued and shareholders losing money when the corporations they own stock in are successfully sued. Brophy reiterates this point in (2006: 832). See also Arceneaux's response to Horowitz (2005: 144).
53. Horowitz (2002: 13).
54. The problem has also been noted by others. See, e.g., Fortson (2004: 106–11).
55. See, for example, Winbush (2003a: xi–xii), Winbush (2003b: 47), Assante (2003: 5–7), Flaherty and Carlisle (2004: 12–16).
56. This point is also noted by Chrisman and Allen (2001: 51).

57. Horowitz (2002: 13–14). Williams (2006: 72–3) also raises skeptical doubts about the causal claim underlying the reparations position.
58. Capaldi (1996: 102) raises the same objection and also appeals to the case of the West Indies in support of it (1996: 99).
59. Hitchens (2003: 177) points this out in his response to Horowitz, as do Chrisman and Allen (2001: 53).
60. See Engerman (1990: 24).
61. Chrisman and Allen make this point (2001: 53).
62. Horowitz (2002: 14).
63. See Horowitz (2002: 85), Armstrong Williams (2003), and Juan Williams (2006: 69, 84). As one descendant of slave owners puts her response to the reparations movement, "I think they ought to be glad they are Americans, living in a free country. The more of that stuff that gets stirred up, the more hate there will be on both sides" (Thompson [2001: 137]).
64. "We would show ourselves to be responding as any normal people would to victimization were we to assert collectively ... our demands for restitution.... We would begin a healing of our psyches were the most public case made that whole peoples lost religions, languages, customs, histories, cultures, children, mothers, fathers. It would make us more forgiving of ourselves, more self-approving, more self-understanding to see, really see, that ... survivors had little choice but to piece together whole new cultures from the rubble shards of what theirs had once been" (Robinson 2000a: 208). Robinson compares this to advice an analyst would give a patient damaged by childhood trauma – "If you're ever to get past this, it must be gotten out and dealt with. Whatever awful thing was done to you must be drawn out and exorcized.... You were caused to endure terrible things. The fault is not yours. There is nothing wrong with you. They did this to you" (2000: 242, original in italics). "The catharsis occasioned by a full-scale reparations debate could change all that, could launch us with critical mass numbers into a surge of black self-discovery" (2000: 243). See also McGary (1984: 121) and see Brooks for the claim that what he calls slave redress, at least when it includes a formal apology for past wrongs, is a key to racial reconciliation (e.g., 2004: x, 191–2; 2003: 112–13) and Paterson who says that "One of the reasons we pursue reparations cases is because they give us the power to make and change history" (2004: 19).
65. Hitchens (2003: 178).
66. Gutmann (1996: 137n30) puts this point nicely in responding to Shelby Steele: "We should not deny people otherwise justified benefits because of the paternalistic consideration that the benefits may demoralize them or enlarge their self-doubt."
67. At least one scholar who has argued in defense of slave reparations has recently suggested, although for different reasons, that black Americans might do better to "let reparations rest as a political agenda" (Outerrson [2009: 102]). But, again, this is consistent with saying that the reparations position is, in fact, justified.
68. Horowitz (2002: 14).
69. Horowitz (2002: 122). This concern is also raised by Epstein (2004: 1189).
70. Horowitz (2002: 124). In addition, it is worth noting that Horowitz is mistaken to construe welfare programs, in particular, as a form of race-based compensation. Such programs are designed to benefit poor Americans regardless of race and while many black Americans received such benefits so did many white Americans.

71. To recognize that Horowitz's eighth objection fails to undermine the compensation argument, I should add, is not by itself to answer the question that the objection in the end poses: if the approaches to improving the lot of black Americans that have been tried thus far have not been sufficiently effective, what precisely should be done instead? Horowitz also writes, "This reality poses questions that the reparations claimants do not even begin to address. If huge sums of government monies already expended have not made a dent in the solution to these problems, why should there be any cause to think 'reparations' might solve them in the future?" (2002: 124). This is, indeed, a good question. But while it is a good question, and while it does not have an easy answer, this fact does not pose a problem for the reparations position. The reparations position maintains that reparations are owed and the compensation argument gives us good reason to accept this claim even if it does not tell us how best to make reparations.

72. Danziger and Gottschalk (1990: 175, 177).

73. I owe this point to Kershnar (2004: 86–7).

74. Horowitz (2002: 15).

75. Capaldi (1996: 78) makes a similar claim, though in the context of compensatory arguments for affirmative action.

76. Horowitz (2002: 15–16).

77. Horowitz (2002: 112).

78. Horowitz (2002: 85).

Chapter 3. Advancing the Slave Reparations Debate: Bonus Objections, Bonus Responses, and a Modest Proposal

1. Quoted in Brooks (2004: 21).

2. Adams and Sanders (2003: 1).

3. Quoted in Waldstreicher (2009: 42).

4. Quoted in Waldstreicher (2009: 96).

5. Waldstreicher (2009: 46).

6. Horowitz (2002: 116). Waldstreicher (2009: 85) makes the same point, noting that delegate John Dickinson's notes for a speech to be given at the Constitutional Convention asked "What will be said of this new principle of founding a Right to govern Freemen on a power derived from Slaves.... The omitting the *Word* will be regarded as an Endeavour to conceal a principle of which we are ashamed."

7. Schedler (2002: 401).

8. See also Capaldi (1996: 79).

9. McWhorter (2001: 100).

10. McWhorter (2001: xiv).

11. Steele (1990: 27–8). I should note that the passage that I have cited in the text here continues as follows: "But the relevant question ... is why they *choose* to internalize this view of themselves. Why do they voluntarily perceive themselves as inferior?" Steele treats this as the important question because he is primarily concerned to demonstrate that such students are still ultimately responsible for their choices. It would be a mistake, that is, to embrace a version of the theory that black culture has a negative impact on black students if the theory "sees blacks only as victims, without any margin of choice. [Such a theory] cannot fully explain the poor performances of these black students because it identifies only the forces

that *pressure* them to do poorly. By overlooking the margin of choice open to them, this theory fails to recognize the degree to which they are responsible for their own poor showing" (Steele [1990: 27]). He then goes on to suggest that the best answer to this question is that "they choose to believe in their inferiority, not to fulfill society's prophesy about them, but for the comforts and rationalizations their racial 'inferiority' affords them" (1990: 28). But while this may be the relevant question from the point of view of Steele's project, it is not the relevant question from the point of view of mine. What matters in trying to develop an objection to the causal claim that is distinct from Horowitz's sixth objection is not the question of how American culture pressures blacks into failing but whether it does. Steele is in agreement with the claim that it does, in fact, exert this pressure, and this is enough to warrant treating him as a proponent of the objection I wish to discuss here.

12. D'Souza (1995: 24, 484). See also (1995: 526–7).
13. Subotnik (2005: 189).
14. Cited in Williams (2006: 100).
15. Subotnik (2005: 192).
16. Cited in Wicker (1996: 160–61). For a list of some relevant additional readings, see Kennedy (2008: 59).
17. The same is true, although in a somewhat different way, of the treatment of black culture in Arthur (2007: Chapter 5). One writer who has clearly recognized this point as a problem for those who blame black American culture for black American problems is Glen C. Loury (see, e.g., Loury [2002: 12, 104, 124]). Another is Bernard R. Boxill (see, e.g., 1992: 157).
18. McWhorter (2001: 213).
19. McWhorter (2001: 27).
20. McWhorter (2001: 83).
21. McWhorter (2001: 138).
22. Steele (1990: 68–9).
23. Steele (1990: 54).
24. Steele (1990: 133).
25. D'Souza (1995: 96). See also (1995: 100).
26. D'Souza (1995: 334).
27. D'Souza (1995: 500).
28. Steele (1990; 25).
29. McWhorter (2001: 91, 150).
30. D'Souza (1995: 476, 482).
31. D'Souza (1995: 478).
32. D'Souza (1995: 516).
33. Thenstrom and Thernstrom (1997: 240).
34. McWhorter (2005: 6).
35. McWhorter (2005: 63, 112 [original in italics]).
36. McWhorter (2005: 6).
37. McWhorter (2005: 70).
38. McWhorter (2005: 94, 378–9).
39. McWhorter (2005: 5, 6).
40. McWhorter (2005: 158, 269). See also, e.g., (2005: 112, 143, 154, 163, 265).
41. McWhorter (2005: 287–8, italics deleted).

42. Two final ways in which the cultural critic might continue to press the case against the reparations position despite what I have said here may also merit a brief comment. First, the critic might agree that the dysfunctional black culture in question is not biological in its origin but deny that it is therefore the product of the legacy of slavery and its aftermath. Instead, he might suggest, American black culture is simply the product of African culture (or cultures). If the counterproductive habits of the mind that the cultural critic appeals to originated in Africa, then it is Africa's fault, not America's, that African Americans today are impaired by black American culture (assuming that they are). But there are two problems with this response. The first is that it seems to simply push the problem back yet again: if the critic rejects the claim that black people are genetically disposed to anti-intellectualism, for example, then he will need an explanation for why African culture(s) was anti-intellectual in a way that caused problems when it was taken to the United States. But second, and more important, one of the most serious harms caused by the institution of slavery was precisely that it disrupted the transmission of African cultures from one generation to the next. Slaves were routinely, and deliberately, placed with other slaves from different cultures who spoke different languages for just this reason. The claim that African American culture is African rather than American, then, is simply implausible.

The other way to try to diffuse the analysis I've offered here would be to concede that contemporary black American culture did develop in reaction to slavery and its aftermath, but to blame black Americans for this result rather than the perpetrators of slavery and the various forms of racial segregation and discrimination that followed. If the dysfunctional features of contemporary black American culture are the faults of contemporary black Americans, after all, then the claim that it is this culture that is responsible for contemporary black American problems really will seem to show that the causal claim is false. But it's hard to see how black Americans could be faulted for responding to slavery and its aftermath in the way that they did, and so hard to see how this kind of response could be sustained, too.

43. By "average" I mean mean, and not median or mode. If a large number of randomly selected people take a particular intelligence test and the scores are added up and then divided by the number of people taking the test, the result should be very close to 100.

44. D'Souza (1995: 442).

45. Herrnstein and Murray (1994: 276–8).

46. Levin cites this report and a number of others in (1997: 34–7). The quotation from the report itself is taken from D'Souza (1995: 673fn54).

47. Quoted in D'Souza (1995: 442).

48. Hacker (2003: 167). See also D'Souza (1995: 456), Thernstrom and Thernstrom (1997: 19).

49. Levin (1997: 96–9ff.).

50. Herrnstein and Murray (1994: 107).

51. Identical twins are formed when an embryo divides into two at a very early stage of development, so that both twins arise from the same sperm and the same egg. Fraternal twins are formed when two different sperm fertilize two different eggs. Thus, the similarity between the DNA of a pair of fraternal twins is no different from the similarity between the DNA of any two siblings.

52. Cited in D'Souza (1995: 451). See also Kohn (1995: 101–2).

53. Levin cites some estimates putting the genetic component at around 70–75 percent (1997: 97, 109). Herrnstein and Murray report results of twin studies putting the figure at somewhere between 75 and 80 percent, although they also note a low estimate of 40 percent from other studies of siblings (1994: 107).

54. Herrnstein and Murray (1994: 309–10). See also D'Souza (1995 453–5). In a more recent article, Levin refers to adoption studies first when briefly referring to the evidence discussed in his book (2007: 31–2).

55. Levin (1997: 56–8, 104–5).

56. Herrnstein and Murray (1994: 283).

57. Herrnstein and Murray (1994: 283–4, 303).

58. D'Souza (1995: 442–3) points this out.

59. Herrnstein and Murray (1994: 321ff.).

60. Levin (1997: 262ff.).

61. Herrnstein and Murray (1994: 340). See also D'Souza (1995: 443).

62. Levin (1997: 251). See also Pojman (1998a: 104–5; 1998b: 170). When Levin refers to the "compensation argument" here, he is referring to an argument for affirmative action in particular, but the substance of the argument is essentially the same as the compensation argument for slave reparations that I have been defending in this chapter. When he refers to innate differences in "time preference," he is referring to the claim that black people tend to put more weight on short-term gratification than do white people and that there is a genetic basis for this difference as well. For the purposes of the discussion that follows, though, it makes no difference whether the genetic differences that are claimed to exist are cashed out exclusively in terms of intelligence or in terms of intelligence along with other mental traits.

63. Levin (1997: 10).

64. Levin (1997: 359).

65. Kohn (1995: 103–4) cites this argument of Gould's.

66. See also Appiah (1996: 71fn58), which also makes use of the example of differences in height within and between groups.

67. Herrnstein and Murray report that "the consistent story has been that men and women have nearly identical mean IQs" (1994: 275). It may also be worth noting that, strictly speaking, the studies in question really measure skull size, not brain size, and that it is possible that in bigger skulls, the brains just expand to fill the space: "The brain is a soft wet object that occupies a rigid container. As the volume of the container increases, the brain may expand to fill the space available, but that does not necessarily mean that the number of neurons or the connections between them is increased. It may simply be a less compressed organ" (Kohn 1995: 133).

68. Herrnstein and Murray (1994: 105).

69. Herrnstein and Murray (1994: 23).

70. Herrnstein and Murray (1994: 22).

71. Herrnstein and Murray (1994: 304).

72. Herrnstein and Murray (1994: 105). See also (1994: 390) where they emphasize that even those who make the strongest genetic claims still "leave 20 to 30 percent of cognitive ability to be shaped by the environment."

73. Levin (1997: 10, emphasis added).

74. Levin (1997: 359, emphasis added). See also Levin (1997: 272, emphasis added): "It cannot be proven beyond all doubt that intelligence is a valid construct measured by IQ, that the races differ with respect to it, that this difference explains race

differences in outcome, and that this difference is due *significantly* to genes. But certainty on these points is not required. All that is required to rebut the compensation argument is that these propositions, taken together, offer an account of the attainment gap at least as plausible as the racism hypothesis."

75. The passage continues: "'Environmentalism' attributes all race differences to environmental factors" (Levin (1997: 8, emphasis added)).

76. Levin (1997: 144, emphasis added).

77. Levin (1997: 91, emphasis added).

78. Levin (1997: 99, emphasis added).

79. Levin (1997: 272, emphasis added).

80. Levin (1997: 357, emphasis added).

81. Indeed, Herrnstein and Murray, at least, explicitly concede this much at one point: "The legacy of historic racism may still be taking its toll on cognitive development, but we must allow the possibility that it has lessened, at least for new generations" (1994: 293).

82. The study, conducted by Mark Snyderman and Stanley Rothman, asked the following question: "Which of the following best characterizes your *opinion* of the heritability of the black-white difference in IQ?" (emphasis in the original). The results, as reported by Herrnstein and Murray (1994: 295–6), were as follows:

> the difference is entirely due to environmental variation: 15 percent
> the difference is entirely due to genetic variation: 1 percent
> the difference is a product of both genetic and environmental variation:
>   45 percent
> the data are insufficient to support any reasonable opinion: 24 percent
> no response: 14 percent

83. It may also be worth noting, however, that surveys of the general public reveal a general decline in belief in genetically based racial differences in intelligence among the population at large. See, e.g., Kinder and Sanders (1996: 97). Levin (1997: 254) presses this objection. See also Waldron (1992: 12 [although in the context of New Zealand reparations toward the Maori]), Schedler (2002: 392–3), and Kershnar (2004: 58–60, 70, 73–6). D'Souza (1995: 113) also comes very close to making this objection explicit.

84. In tying the argument to claims about compensation rather than to claims about wrongness, I'm presenting the non-identity argument in a nonstandard way so that it can more directly be applied to the compensation argument. For a more detailed and conventional explanation of the problem, along with a critical survey of some of the solutions contained in the literature and an alternative solution, see Boonin (2008b).

85. For other ways of defending the reparations position from the non-identity problem, see also Simmons (1995: 178n41), Sher (2005), Sepinwall (2006: 226–8), Shiffrin (2009), and Herstein (2008a; 2008b).

86. For a useful discussion of some of the relevant tort cases, see Wenger (2006).

87. Quoted in Waldstreicher (2009: 96).

88. Kershnar (2009: 85).

89. Indeed, some opponents of reparations seem actually to *endorse* the surviving public obligation principle without realizing that the principle can be used to ground a case in favor of reparations. The philosopher Chandran Kukathas, for example,

has argued against the reparations position by construing it in terms of the unjust enrichment argument and the argument that runs along biological bloodlines (e.g., 2006: 334–5, 338–9). But he goes on to concede that just as "Coca-Cola today is the same entity as the Coca-Cola of fifty years ago," the "same might hold for governments, which do not change with each new administration but remain continuous for as long as the polity remains stable and the personnel change without affecting the regime" (2006: 339). This, in effect, is to admit the surviving public obligation principle. But because Kukathas also acknowledges that governments "can clearly be held responsible for rectifying past injustices when they themselves have committed them" (2006: 340), he inadvertently lays the foundation for the compensation argument for slave reparations without recognizing that it provides a much stronger case for reparations than the ones he argues against.

90. This is the feature that George Schedler appeals to in perhaps the most explicit defense of this objection by a philosopher (Schedler [1998: 117]). The objection is also raised by Hughs (2004: 252).

91. Sepinwall (2006: 208) also makes this point.

92. A similar response to the objection is also suggested by Corlett (2003: 203–4).

93. Some philosophers will deny that this follows. On their account, there might not be any thirty-year period between the founding of the country and today about which it is clearly true that the government at one end is not the same as the government at the other end, but a gradual enough change may have occurred over the country's entire history so that the government today is not the same as the government that existed at the outset. If this is thought to pose a problem for my response to the equivocation objection here, we can simply modify the example: the family bought hundreds of savings bonds at the very outset of the nation's existence and cashes one in every year. If the government today is literally not the same government as the one created by the Founding Fathers, then there must be some point at which the government would refuse to honor the savings bonds, just as the American government today would not honor a French savings bond issued a few years ago. But this result, too, is clearly unacceptable (the same goes in the case of using very old postage stamps) and so, again, is the equivocation objection that gives rise to it.

94. In addition to the objections that I have raised against the equivocation objection here, it is also worth noting one further problem: even if we were to agree that the U.S. government today is literally a different government from the government that ruled the United States prior to the Civil War, it would not immediately follow that the new government is not responsible for paying off the old government's debts. If the new government legitimately took over authority from the old government, then it seems plausible to suppose that it also took over whatever debts and assets the old government had. This, for example, is how it works in the case where one corporation takes over the powers of another. And so in addition to overcoming the objections I have raised in the text, a defender of the equivocation objection would have to explain how the supposedly new and different government could legitimately replace the old and now supposedly extinct government without taking over that government's obligations. (This point is nicely made by Kershnar [2004a: 89; 2004b: 157]).

95. Williams (2003: 170).

96. For a recent discussion of the problem, see David (2007).

97. Williams (2003: 170). See also Subotnik (2005: 257).

98. Some people might respond to this case by saying that the government would not be obligated to help them lower their cholesterol as long as it instead compensated them in some other sort of way, such as by giving them money. This response would not undermine the main point I am trying to make by means of this example: they would agree that the government would owe these people something and would agree that this is so despite the difficulty of determining precisely how much (either in terms of money or in terms of cholesterol lowering) it would owe.

99. This should also help to overcome the concerns about determining the magnitude of reparations owed that are raised by Arthur (2007: 215–21).

Chapter 4. One Cheer for Affirmative Action: Why There's Nothing Wrong with Abandoning Racial Preferences

1. Hobart Taylor, Jr., who drafted the Executive Order 10925 document that originated the practice chose the words "affirmative action" to lend it "a sense of positiveness" (Woo 1997: 514).

2. Missouri State Senator Steven E. Ehlmann's comments in this regard are typical: "The use of the term 'affirmative action' in the context of modern political debate is flawed, for the modern discussion is not truly about affirmative action, but rather about racial preference" (Ehlmann (1998: 93)). Similarly, University of Texas Law Professor Lino A. Graglia writes that "'Affirmative action' has become simply a deceptive label for racial preferences" (1998: 31).

3. Critics of affirmative action almost universally appeal to the line in King's famous "I Have a Dream" speech in which he dreams that his children "will one day live in a nation where they will not be judged by the color of their skin but by the content of their character." On the other hand, King also wrote the following: "Whenever this issue of compensatory or preferential treatment for the Negro is raised some of our friends recoil in horror. The Negro should be granted equality, they agree; but he should ask for nothing more. On the surface, this appears reasonable, but it is not realistic. For it is obvious that if a man is entering the starting line in a race three hundred years after another man, the first would have to perform some impossible feat in order to catch up with his fellow runner" (quoted in Moore 2005: 88).

4. Beckwith and Jones (1997) and Mosley and Capaldi (1996).

5. Kekes (1993: 144).

6. Goldman (1993: 299).

7. Rubinstein (1985–6: 112).

8. Kellough (2006: 3).

9. For examples of supporters of affirmative action who believe that affirmative action is required by morality, see Armour (1997), Moore (2005), Thomas (1993), Francis (1993), Turnbull (1993), Arneson (who calls it "morally mandatory") (1993: 164), and Sterba (1994). For examples of opponents of affirmative action who believe that affirmative action is prohibited by morality (typically calling it "unjust" or "immoral"), see Kekes (1993), Simon (1993), Hartle (1993), Quinn (1993), Olafson (1993: 211), and Sommers (1993). It's hard to find anyone who has explicitly tried to stake out the kind of middle ground I seek to occupy in this chapter, but one exception worth reading is Thomas Nagel's (1973) article. In this paper, Nagel argues that affirmative action is not required by justice but also argues that it is not "seriously unjust" either. But while the position he is led to is thus one of the few to come close

to the one I try to defend here (I say close because Nagel leaves it open that affirmative action might still be moderately unjust, and I don't think that's the case, either), the argument he presents in its defense is quite different from the sort of arguments I develop in this chapter and the chapter that follows.

10. Numerous critics of affirmative action have referred to it as unjust or immoral. The claim that it is "morally heinous" comes from Pojman (1998a: 98).

11. Arneson calls affirmative action "morally mandatory" (1993: 164). Mosley writes that initiatives to abolish affirmative action "would inflict a grave injustice on African Americans" (1996: 53).

12. Carter (1991: 71).

13. One possible exception that is worth noting could arise in cases where a school adopts a geography-based affirmative action program in order to discriminate against a disliked racial or ethnic group. And there is, in fact, some evidence that elite universities like Harvard, Yale, and Princeton originally adopted such policies for precisely this reason. The anti-Semitism then prevalent at such institutions led them to want to limit the number of Jewish students they admitted, and one way to do this was to limit the number of applicants accepted from cities that had large Jewish populations (see, e.g., Arthur [2007: 239] and Karabel [2005]). It seems plausible to me to think that if an otherwise morally acceptable policy is adopted in order to achieve a morally objectionable goal, then the act of adopting the policy for that reason is morally objectionable even though the policy in and of itself is not. Even if it can be wrong to adopt a geography-based affirmative action program in this way, however, this will have no bearing on the discussion of race-based affirmative action in this chapter. No one really thinks that affirmative action policies that favor black applicants over white applicants are adopted out of contempt for white people, and so while there might be a reason to think that some cases of geography-based affirmative are morally objectionable, there will be no comparable reason to think that any cases of race-based affirmative action are.

14. This is pointed out by James Sterba (2003a: 291).

15. Dartmouth became the first college to adopt a formal admissions policy in 1922, and one of its nine criteria for admissions was "the principle of geographical distribution." And Harvard can trace its geography-based affirmative action practices back even further, at least as far back as the tenure of President Charles W. Eliot, who presided over the University from 1896 to 1909. Eliot's approach to student admissions put weight on "the wholesome influence that comes from observation of and contact with" people from differing backgrounds and thus sought to bring to Harvard students "from North and South, from East and West" (quotes taken from Fullinwider and Lichtenberg [2004: 83–4, 165, 166]).

16. It might at first seem that there's an important difference between the two cases insofar as you can change your geographical location but not your race, but this appearance is misleading: a student whose parents choose to raise him in New York rather than in North Dakota can no more make it the case that he is raised in North Dakota than a student whose parents are white can make it the case that he is black. It's true, of course, that some students may credibly be able to present themselves as residing in more than one state. If a student's parents are divorced and have joint legal custody of him and one of them lives in New York and the other lives in North Dakota, for example, then the student may be able to choose which state to identify himself with when he applies to college. But, then again,

if a student's parents are of sufficiently mixed ancestry, he, too, may find that he can try to "pass" as either black or white depending on the circumstances; there is no real difference between the cases here. The analogy between race-based and geography-based affirmative action is sometimes used by defenders of race-based affirmative action to show that race-based affirmative action is morally permissible (e.g., Gutmann [1996: 126–8]), but I'm not aware of anyone who has tried to build from it the claim that it is also non-obligatory and therefore morally optional.

17. See, e.g., Raphael (2005), which argues that Jesuit Law Schools have an obligation to practice affirmative action because of the distinctive mission of Jesuit education.

18. Quoted in Moore (2005: 80).

19. Sterba (1993a: 287). Sterba defends this approach with a caveat – only in cases where the winner can, in effect, be expected to catch up with some extra help (1993a: 286–7). Sher also defends this kind of argument: "the key to an adequate justification" of affirmative action, he says, is "to see that practice, not as the redressing of past privations, but rather as a way of neutralizing the present competitive disadvantage caused by those past privations and thus as a way of restoring equal access to those goods which society distributes competitively" (1975: 53). For a more recent version of this kind of argument, though one that focuses more on the claim that an unfair disadvantage arises from present racism rather than from past discrimination, see Himma (2002). See also Hajdin (2002: 87–8) and Hill (1991: 126, 128). For a version of this kind of argument that also ties the obligation to take unfair disadvantage into account to the obligation to make reparations for slavery and its aftermath, see McGary (1977–8).

20. It may be worth noting that even if someone insists that it would be positively immoral for you to admit Ted rather than Bill, this response is unlikely to lend support to the claim that race-based affirmative action is morally obligatory. If you think that it's unfair for Bill to be penalized for the fact that his father went to jail, after all, then you'll probably think this regardless of whether or not Bill's father was guilty. Either way, after all, the fact that his father went to jail was not Bill's fault, and so, either way, you'll think that the university would be obligated to take this fact into account. You'll think that it's wrong to let Ted's financial advantage over Bill help Ted get admitted ahead of Bill not because Ted's financial advantage arose from some unjust action that took place in the past, that is, but simply because you'll think that it's wrong for any financial advantage to help one student get admitted ahead of the other. While this kind of reasoning might therefore help to defend some form of class-based affirmative action, then, it will not help to justify an obligation to engage in race-based affirmative action in particular, and my focus in this chapter and the chapter that follows is exclusively on race-based affirmative action.

21. Ezorsky (1991: 73, 75). The same sort of argument is also defended in Hughes (1968), Masters (1990), Groarke (1990: 210–11), Boxill (1992: 148ff), Delgado (1997), Malamud (1997), and Valls (1999). See also Stark (2004), who defends affirmative action as a form of reparations but who appeals instead to the unjust enrichment argument, and Mosley (1996: 23–38), whose version of the compensation argument for affirmative action appeals both to the compensation argument and the unjust enrichment argument. The objections I raised against the unjust enrichment argument in Chapter 2 would also count as objections to Stark's defense of affirmative action and to that part of Mosley's defense that appeals to claims about unjust enrichment.

22. Rudenstine and Casper both quoted in Moore (2005: 8), Bollinger quoted in Arthur (2007: 263). For other defenses of the diversity-based argument, see also Turnbull (1993: 139, 142), Murphy (1995), Gutmann (1996: 127, 131), Chemerinsky (1996: 1346–47), Cho (1997), Bowen and Bok (1998: 280), Sterba (2003b: Chapter 8), Cantor (2004), Gurin, Dey, Gurin, and Hurtado (2004), Card (2005), and Tabb (2005: 30–1). A useful brief account of the way the courts have treated this argument can be found in Krislov (2003–4).

23. Paul (1993: 250). For similar complaints, see also Hartle (1993), Collier (2005: 8), Cohen (1998: 49), and Wolf-Devine (1993: 230).

24. See, e.g., Simon (1993).

25. LeFevre (2003) argues that the benefits of diversity justify affirmative action even in the case of the natural sciences.

26. This reply also strikes me as a good reason to reject another objection that is sometimes raised against the diversity argument. Goldman, for example, complains that "proponents of [the argument from diversity] rely on correlations between race and gender and other factors such as diversity in academic viewpoints or expertise in such areas as feminism or African American studies. But when these other factors are easily measurable in themselves, as they are for potential faculty with written work to submit, then such statistical correlations should be irrelevant" (1993: 298). But this objection, too, unfairly limits the range of considerations that the diversity argument can appeal to. Whether or not a job candidate holds a certain view about the subject matter he teaches might be established by examining his written work, but whether or not his background and life experiences would lead him to approach his duties as a teacher, administrator, or colleague differently cannot.

27. For a useful list of empirical work on the question of whether or not diversity produces such benefits in different areas, see Kellough (2006: 165n10).

28. Quoted in Dworkin (2003–4: 886). For similar statements from the Chairman and CEO of The Coca-Cola Company and of the Chrysler Corporation, see Bowen and Bok (1998: 12).

29. Dworkin (2003–4: 886).

30. For the claim that the positive educational benefits of diversity are outweighed by various negative consequences, see Kershnar (2007: 440–55).

31. Someone who agrees with this assessment might still want to endorse some kind of negative judgment here. They might say, for example, that the members of the department have a kind of professional responsibility to promote the intellectual development of the students and faculty and that if giving preference to the Swiss philosopher would better achieve this goal, then even if it isn't strictly speaking immoral or unjust to hire the slightly better qualified American philosopher, they still have a certain kind of responsibility to do so.

    I have to admit that I'm a bit skeptical of this kind of argument. While I can see how it would be irresponsible for a department to allow its program to fall below a certain level of quality, it's less clear to me that it's irresponsible to decline to do everything one could do to maximize it. In this sense, there might be a professional responsibility to engage in affirmative action if the lack of diversity that would otherwise result would prevent the school from offering good quality programs, but no responsibility to do so if it could still offer perfectly good educational programs without doing so. And the burden would then be on the proponent of the argument not just to show that diversity can make things better, but that the absence of diversity prevents a school from meetings it professional duties to its students. It's much less clear that the argument could establish this.

But even if this kind of argument succeeds, it doesn't really undermine the main claim that I'm trying to advance in this chapter. It might help to show that the philosophers in a department that fails to promote diversity through affirmative action aren't doing their jobs very well, since they aren't fully living up to their professional responsibilities, but we don't generally think that it's immoral not to do your job well, and the main question I'm concerned with here is whether there's something immoral about not practicing affirmative action.

32. Some versions of the diversity argument appeal to benefits from diversity beyond those I've discussed here. An amicus brief in defense of affirmative action filed by the Black Law Students Associations of Harvard, Stanford, and Yale Law School in the case of *Grutter v. Bollinger*, for example, argues that racial diversity in the student body improves an elite law school's ability to train its students for future leadership roles (Gray and LeBlanc (2003: 45); see also the "Brief" itself, e.g. (2003: 2–4), Dworkin (2003–4: 887), Issacharoff (1998). Laycock (2004) appeals to these and still further benefits of diversity. But the fundamental problem that undermines the more familiar version of the diversity argument undermines these and all other versions as well: the mere fact that increasing diversity would produce such benefits is not enough to make it morally obligatory.

33. The philosopher George Sher, for example, argues that this is the case (1999), and some defenders of the diversity argument explicitly acknowledge that in the end their argument must appeal to such considerations as those having to do with compensation (e.g., Strike 2006: 190).

34. The claim that the case of historically black colleges poses a problem for the diversity argument is made by Levey (2003: 497), although not in the context of the claim that affirmative action is morally obligatory.

35. For some further objections to the argument from diversity, see Thomas (2003–4), Westmoreland (2003–4).

36. Quoted in Barkley (2005: 23–4). See also Thomas (1993).

37. See, e.g., Kupperman (1993: 184), Gutmann (1996: 128).

38. Sowell (2004: 144). Pojman (1998a: 99) raises similar doubts.

39. Quoted by Arthur (2007: 261–2) from the book *Increasing Faculty Diversity: The Occupational Choices of High-Achieving Minority Students* (Cambridge, MA: Harvard Univerity Press, 2003), p. 247.

40. The philosopher Judith Jarvis Thomson makes this point using the example of the recreation center (1973: 368–9). The same problem ultimately undermines any attempt to ground an obligation to engage in affirmative action in the claim that such policies have positive consequences. On the account endorsed by Fullinwider and Licthenberg (2004: 178, 208), for example, affirmative action is justified as a means of producing a greater amount of representation among black Americans as civic leaders, business leaders, educational leaders, and so on. But while this might again be a good state of affairs to bring about, the fact that it would be good cannot be enough to make it positively immoral not to bring it about.

41. See, e.g., Sabbagh (2007).

42. Although this is a fairly common claim, it has long been accepted in the literature on academic testing that the SAT overpredicts rather than underpredicts the grades

that black test takers go on to earn in the freshman year in college. On average, that is, the SAT actually overstates rather than understates the academic potential of the typical black test taker. Since colleges are primarily interested in the SAT to the extent that it provides a measure of how well a given student can reasonably be expected to perform in college, this suggests that, at least in terms of the way in which the test is actually used, the SAT is biased in favor of black students rather than against them (see Fullinwider and Lichtenberg [2004: 100]; Kershnar [2007: 455–6]). For claims about racial bias in the LSAT, see White (2001: 407–9).

43. For some examples of the bias-elimination argument, see Francis (1993: 26–30), Thomas (1993: 126–7), Beauchamp (1998), White (2001: 418–19), Kang and Banaji (2006), and Harris and Narayan (2007), though White, at least, argues only that bias-elimination makes affirmative action permissible, not that it makes it obligatory (2001: 418). Purdy has also defended the bias-elimination argument, most conspicuously in the context of affirmative action for women (1984; 1994: 135, 139–41).

44. Armour (1997: 154–5) presents a useful summary of Steele's research and appeals to it as support for the bias-elimination argument. See also White (2001: 414–17), though for some criticisms of Steele, see also Subotnik (2005: 193–5).

45. See also the intruiging preliminary report of a study providing evidence of an "Obama effect," on which the gap between black and white student performance on a twenty-question test adapted from the Graduate Record Exam was virtually eliminated in cases where the exam was administered right after Obama's acceptance speech at the Democratic National Convention or right after the presidential election (Dillon [2009: A15]).

46. Thomas (1993: 126–27). See also McMillian (1998: 41).

47. Some defenders of the bias-elimination argument come close to conceding this point. The title of Kang and Banaji (2006), for example, presents their argument as a revision of "affirmative action," but in the text of the article they often go on to employ the term "fair measures" and acknowledge that the two terms are not precisely synonymous (2006: 1067). As they go on to note, moreover, the point of the bias-elimination mechanisms they recommend is "to prevent present acts of inaccurate measurement" (2006: 1100) and to that extent their argument explicitly refrains from endorsing a process on which a black candidate who is actually less qualified would ever be selected over a white candidate who is actually better qualified.

48. A possible exception to this conclusion may be worth briefly noting: if a university has publicly committed itself to the claim that it only admits the very best students, then it may acquire an obligation to engage in a bias-correcting form of race-based affirmative action as a means of living up to its promise. A school that claimed to admit the smartest students but then knowingly ignored evidence that some of the black students it rejected were in fact smarter than some of the white students it accepted would therefore be guilty of acting in bad faith. While this kind of case is worth noting, however, its significance must remain limited in the context of the debate about affirmative action as a whole. The claim that a school could acquire an obligation to engage in affirmative action by acting in a certain way does not by itself provide any reason to think that there is an obligation to engage in affirmative action independent of such actions. After all, a school could clearly incur an obligation to engage in affirmative action simply by promising that it will engage

in affirmative action, but the fact that it can be obligatory to do something if you promise to do it provides no reason to think that it is obligatory to do it even if you don't promise to do it. And the claim I am concerned with here is the strong claim that schools and other organizations are obligated to engage in affirmative action whether they have already committed themselves to it or not.

49. Stephen Kershnar also notes that the permissibility of hiring people at random undermines the claim that the best qualified person has a right to the position (1999: 204).

50. This kind of argument is pressed by Shelton (1993: 235–8ff.).

51. This objection also undermines the related argument, defended by Law Professor Margaret Y. K. Yoo, that membership in a persecuted race should be considered a form of merit because overcoming discrimination is evidence of character and initiative (1997: 518–19). Again, even if this shows that affirmative action involves selecting the candidate who is more "meritorious," this isn't enough to show that it's morally wrong to refrain from engaging in it.

Chapter 5. Two Cheers for Affirmative Action: Why There's Nothing Wrong with Not Abandoning Racial Preferences, Either

1. Arnold (1998: 140), for example, defends this view.

2. Eastland (1997: 17).

3. See, e.g., Pojman (1998b: 177).

4. (Connerly 1996: 65).

5. Cohen (1998: 72). See also Cohen (1995: 19, 49, 96, 150, 164) and Cohen (2003a: 24, 39). Others who have endorsed the claim that affirmative action violates the principle of equal protection under the law include Capaldi (1996: 69, 73), Pojman (1998b: 177), Steele (2006: 35), Corry (1996a, 1996b), Pell (2003: 309, 317–18), Thernstrom and Thernstrom (1997: 419), and Mellott (2006: 1130–44). See also Gross (1978: 96) who puts the point in terms of a right to equal consideration.

6. It's also worth noting that it isn't clear that affirmative action would fail the strict scrutiny test. In the 2003 case of *Grutter v. Bollinger*, for example, the U.S. Supreme Court ruled (albeit in a 5–4 vote) that the goal of obtaining a diverse student body is a "compelling state interest," that can justify some forms of affirmative action (Sabbagh [2007: 164]).

7. And Connerly, of course, may be one of them. Perhaps he thinks that affirmative action should be illegal at Stanford, too, and refrains from making this part of his position for reasons of political expediency. Still, the movement for Proposition 209 as a whole leaves the impression that affirmative action is okay in private schools but not in public schools, and this can still seem difficult to reconcile with the claim that affirmative action violates some inalienable right that people have to be treated equally by race.

8. Though see Kershnar (2004: 36, 49–50) for a version of this kind of argument.

9. See, e.g., Bolick (1996: 79) and Justice Antonin Scalia quoted in Sabbagh (2007: 14).

10. As at least a few philosophers have pointed out, veteran's benefits provide another good example of this (see, e.g., Thomson (1973: 379–80), Ezorsky (1991: 75–6), Sterba (2003b: 266–7)). Virtually nobody complains if the state provides certain educational benefits to veterans that it does not provide to non-veterans, after all,

or if it adds some points to their civil service exam scores as part of their job applications, since it seems fair to repay people who make significant sacrifices for their country. But not every veteran ends up having a bad or dangerous experience in the military, and some non-veterans make significant sacrifices for their country in other ways.

11. See, e.g., Sowell (2004: 12, 48, 76, 120, 186, 195) and Carter (1991: 71–2ff., 80, 133, 233). For other examples of this complaint about affirmative action, see also Kekes (1993: 150), Simon (1993: 57), Kupperman (1993: 182, 183), and Bolick (1996: 4, 66).

12. Although it may be worth noting that when affirmative action enables a black student to enroll in an elite school that he might not otherwise have been admitted to, this means that he won't enroll at a less elite school that he would otherwise have ended up going to, and there will therefore be one more space at that less elite school for other black students to compete for, including students from less privileged backgrounds.

13. Ezorsky cites this example as a response to the claim that affirmative action disproportionately benefits those who need it least (1991: 64).

14. In addition, as Mosley (1996: 30) points out, the least well off black Americans are not necessarily the ones who have been the most seriously disadvantaged by the sorts of injustices that defenders of affirmative action often appeal to in justifying the practice. If, as Mosley suggests, past racial discrimination created even greater obstacles to black success in the more elite schools and professions, then it would seem to be perfectly appropriate that affirmative action disproportionately aim its benefits in those contexts.

15. Quoted in Kennedy (1997: 6). See also Capaldi (1996: 75). Thomas has also written that "under our Constitution, the government may not make distinctions on the basis of race," and so can also be understood as endorsing the strong (and, we saw earlier) implausible version of the right to equal protection argument (quoted in Fullinwider and Lichtenberg [2004: 179]).

16. Newton (1973: 310).

17. Black (1974: 106). See also Gross (1978: 102), Bolick (1996: 13), McGee (1998), Pojman (1998a: 110), Pell (2003: 310–11), and philosopher Carl Cohen: "The unfairness of preference is obvious when one asks what our response would be if white skins were systematically preferred. We would be outraged…. We would say, emphatically, that *no* preference by skin color is acceptable under *any* circumstances" (2003b: 301).

18. This point has been put nicely by the philosopher Thomas Nagel: "Traditional discrimination was as bad as it was not because it employed racial and sexual criteria, but because it told people they were despised or not taken seriously in light of their race or sex (1977: xii; see also 1973: 16). The philosopher Bernard R. Boxill makes the same point in (1992: 3), as do Thomas Hill, Jr. (1991: 114) and Albert Mosley (1998: 161).

19. Eastland (1997: 141). See also Bolick (1996: 123–4), Cohen (1998: 67).

20. For a useful recent presentation of these arguments, see Cohen (2003a: chs. 7–9), though Cohen himself also opposes affirmative action for a number of additional reasons and is careful to present these as reasons to think it is "bad" rather than "wrong."

21. See, e.g., Kekes (1993: 152–3), Paul (1993: 260), Capaldi (1996: 92), Subotnik (2005: 191), Cohen (1995: 20–1, 33–4, 211, 231; 2003a: 110; 2003b: 298–9), Bolick (1996: 64),

Eastland (1997: 9, 85–6, 141, 142), Steele (2006: 146; 2008: 13). For the related worry that it perpetuates the image of black people as victims, see also Pojman (1992: 188), and McWhorter (1996: 64ff.), which gives some evidence from the social sciences for this claim.

22. Carter (1991: 14). Though it is worth noting that Carter acknowledges that the self-doubts fade over time (1991: 24) and that Carter does not, in the end, oppose all forms of affirmative action (see, e.g., 1991: 84–5, where it is clear that he endorses at least a limited form of affirmative action in college admissions and perhaps even in some graduate programs).

23. See, e.g., Eastland (1997: 87), and Sowell, who argues that affirmative action has produced "Poisonous intergroup relations and real dangers to the fabric of society" in some countries Sowell (2004: 22). See also Sommers (1993: 292, 294), Bolick (1996: 63), and Cohen (1995: 102, 211, 231).

24. Note also that a 2000 *New York Times* poll asked "In order to make up for past discrimination, do you favor or oppose programs which make special efforts to help minorities to get ahead?" 46 percent of white respondents favored and 44 percent opposed, but for black respondents it was 76 percent in favor and only 11 percent opposed (Sack and Elder 2001: 372).

25. See, e.g., Arthur (2007: 277), Thernstrom and Thernstrom (1997: 405–9), Elder (2008: 179), Heriot (2008). Bowen and Bok cast doubt on this claim, at least in the context of elite colleges and universities (1998: 259–60).

26. The objection that affirmative action is inefficient has been pressed especially by Thomas Sowell in a number of works. See, e.g., Sowell (2004: 47–8). See also Bolick (1996: 60), Pojman (1998: 110–11).

27. See, e.g., Dieterle (2005: 90), citing a study that focused on doctors trained over a twenty-year period at the University of California, Davis, and that concluded that there were no significant differences between the postgraduate careers of those who had been admitted with special considerations given to such factors as race and ethnicity and the careers of those who had not. Similarly, the economist Steven N. Durlauf's recent study of the matter concludes "that there is little basis for regarding either meritocratic or affirmative action admissions as more efficient than the other" (2008: 133).

28. Thernstrom and Thernstrom, for example, write: "Race-conscious policies make for more race-consciousness; they carry American society backward" (1997: 539).

29. For a useful brief survey of some of the empirical work that has already been done on this question, see Kellough (2006: chapter 7). See also Kidder (2001: 221–30) and Alger (1998: 79–85) for useful brief surveys of recent work on the consequences of affirmative action in higher education in particular.

Chapter 6. Why I Used to Hate Hate Speech Restrictions:
Appeals to Traditional Exceptions to Freedom of
Expression and Why They All Fail

1. D'Souza (1995: 530). See also D'Souza (1995: 538): "Hate speech and hate crime laws that impose punishment or enhanced penalties for proscribed motives and viewpoints are inherently illiberal and destructive of intellectual independence and conscience."

2. One case that I will set to the side, though, is the adoption of hate speech restrictions in elementary and secondary schools. It may prove reasonable to maintain that the presumption in favor of freedom of expression is weaker in that context to begin with and some of the arguments for adopting such restrictions may prove stronger in the context of minors, especially given that up to a certain age their attendance in school is compulsory. For a thoughtful and nuanced discussion of hate speech restrictions in this context, see Bilford (2008).
3. Shiell (1998: 3).
4. Walker (1994: 133).
5. Gould (2005: 3).
6. See especially Gould (2005: ch. 5).
7. Quoted in Walker (1994: 4). See also Sudurski (1999: 179–80).
8. Quoted in Walker (1994: 5). For a particularly thorough discussion of international law as it pertains to hate speech, see Farrior (1996).
9. For a useful summary of how American hate speech law compares with hate speech law in much of the rest of the world, see Boyle (2001: esp. III).
10. Even Nadine Strossen, in explaining the official ACLU position, explicitly grants this much (1996: 455; 2001: 245)
11. For a defense of hate speech laws along these lines see, e.g., Knechtle (2005–6).
12. See, e.g., Tsesis (2000; 2002), who appeals in part to the case of the anti-Semitic speech that helped give rise to the Holocaust in defending this sort of approach to justifying hate speech restrictions. Farrior (1996: 4, 97–8) also suggests that this kind of argument underlies a significant portion of international law on the subject.
13. Desai (2003: 386) raises a similar objection, appealing to claim that the argument could be used to justify banning the teaching of Marxism.
14. Walker (1994: 70–1). See also Shiell (1998: 40–2) in a legal context.
15. Walker (1994: 71).
16. See, for example, Walker (1994: 105), Lawrence (1993: 710).
17. Kennedy (2002: 69).
18. Quoted by Kennedy (2002: 68).
19. Kennedy (2002: 69). Lawrence (1993: 710–11) also raises this objection.
20. Legally, libel refers to written or broadcast defamation while slander refers to oral defamation. Since this distinction isn't relevant to the discussion that follows, I'll use the term libel to cover all three cases for the sake of convenience.
21. See, e.g., MacKinnon (1993: 51–2, 81–2, 99). The group libel defense of hate speech restrictions has also been defended by Kenneth Lasson in a series of papers. See Lasson (1985: 298–320; 1986: 30–55; 1991: 60–89).
22. Though it's worth noting that the three main group libel laws that were on the books during this period (Illinois, New Jersey, and Massachusetts) were virtually never enforced (Walker (1994: 146–7)).
23. Quotations taken from Walker (1994: 93).
24. Walker (1994: 95).
25. Walker (1994: 77, 98–9). More generally, see Chapter 5. See also Shiell (1998: 42–5).
26. At least one more recent admirer of the decision is the Canadian Supreme Court. In its 1992 decision upholding a hate speech law in *Regina v. Keegstra*, the Court included a discussion of American case law on the subject and maintained that

Beauharnais had been correctly decided and was more consistent with Canadian values than were the subsequent U.S. Supreme Court decisions that later undermined it (Mahoney [1995: 283]).

27. This point is noted by Weinstein (1999; 57).
28. Strictly speaking, when the racist says "I hate black people," he is making a factual assertion: the factual assertion that it's the case that he hates black people. But that claim is (presumably) true, and truth is a defense against libel.
29. Cited in Leidholdt (1995: 219).
30. Gould (2005: 128–9), Leidholdt (1995: 219).
31. See, e.g., Cox (1995: 124–6), Brownstein (1994) and (in the context of anti-Semetic speech in particular) Marcus (2008).
32. http://www.altlaw.org/v1/cases/430789.
33. This is not to insist that harassing someone by using racial epithets is not worse than harassing them by using other sorts of insults. Racially motivated harassment may very well be more objectionable than ordinary harassment in which case it might well merit a greater degree of punishment. But this is relevant to the subject of hate crime laws, discussed in Chapters 8 and 9, rather than to the subject of hate speech restrictions, which is the subject of the present chapter.
34. One possible exception worth noting is that of obscenity. It's generally agreed that the use of obscene words can justifiably be restricted, at least in certain contexts, and a defender of hate speech restrictions might attempt to justify such restrictions by appealing to this fact. In the end, though, this approach, too, would suffer from the same two problems I've noted with the other proposals considered so far: while it may well be plausible to characterize the word "nigger" as obscene, for example, it isn't plausible to insist that every utterance of hate speech involves obscene language (e.g. "Go back to Africa where you belong"). And if every instance of hate speech really were plausibly construed as obscene, then hate speech restrictions would be unnecessary because they would already be indirectly included in existing restrictions on the use of obscenity. It may also be worth adding that treating hate speech as an instance of obscenity would have a further implication that even most defenders of hate speech restrictions would be unlikely to accept: it's generally agreed, for example, that it's appropriate to forbid broadcast television programs from using obscene language. But from this it would follow that it would be appropriate to forbid a television program from broadcasting an episode in which a racist character called a black person a "nigger."

Chapter 7. Why I Still Hate Hate Speech Restrictions: New and Improved Exceptions to Freedom of Expression and Why They Fail, Too

1. Walker (1994: 153). The case was *UWM Post v. Board of Regents of the University of Wisconsin.*
2. Quoted by Kennedy (2002: 79).
3. Delgado (2006: x), Cortese (2006: 1–2).
4. Quoted by Kennedy (2002: 79).
5. See, for example, Larwence, Matsuda, Delgado, and Crenshaw (1993: 1).
6. Lawrence (1993: 74), for example. In addition to the writers noted in the text, see also Matsuda (1993) and Mahoney (1996).

7. Shiell (1998: 32–3). See also, for example, Matsuda (1993: 24) and Delgado (1993: 93–6). Delgado, in particular, also emphasizes the negative consequences for others in society and the impact on parenting that can transmit harms to future generations. For an example of the use such writers also make of appeals to anecdotal evidence, see Delgado (1995).

8. Lawrence, for example, maintains that the two features of face-to-face racial epithets that render them beyond protection are that "[t]he injury is immediate" and that they run counter to the purpose of fostering dialogue (1993: 67–8). But the same is surely true of the cases I note here.

9. I'm setting aside the case of religious schools that might have sexual behavior codes for their students. But even in this case, it's unlikely that people would accept a rule in which a student was permitted to have sex with his girlfriend but was not permitted to have sex with other women.

10. Delgado (1993: 100).

11. See Kennedy (2002: 83–4). The words come from the commonly referred to *Second Restatement of Torts*, but the doctrine varies somewhat from state to state (see, e.g., Delgado [1993: 97]).

12. The courts have tended to rule this way as well. In *Bradshaw v. Swagerty*, for example, the Kansas Court of Appeals ruled that the use of the epithet "nigger" alone did not suffice to satisfy the requirements for a tort of intentional infliction of emotional distress (Delgado [1993: 99]).

13. For some additional objections that focus more on raising Constitutional objections to the proposal originally made in Delgado's "Words That Wound," see Heins (1983) and Delgado's response to Heins in Delgado (1983).

14. Quoted in Langton (1993: 294), who also stresses this point.

15. MacKinnon (1993: 92). See also, e.g., MacKinnon (1993: 11, 29, 90), Michelman (1995). Similarly, in his defense of hate speech restrictions, the philosopher Andrew Altman refers to the sorts of hate speech he thinks may justifiably be restricted as "speech acts of subordination" (1993: 317). See also Altman (1993: 310, 313, 315). For a brief but effective response to Altman, see Alexander (1996: 87–9).

16. See, for example, his famous and aptly titled *How to Do Things with Words*. The debt to Austin is sometimes explicit as in Langton (1993: 295ff) and Altman (1993: 309) and sometimes more subtle as in MacKinnon (1993: 121n31).

17. For further critical discussion see Sadurski (1999: 119–33). See also Baez (2002: 53–8). Kennedy (2002: 150–9) criticizes hate speech codes.

18. For the purposes of the example, we can ignore the fact that Simpson was later found liable for one of the deaths in a civil trial. I assume that even if there had never been a subsequent civil trial, virtually everyone would still agree that it would be wrong to prohibit people from publicly affirming their belief that Simpson was guilty.

19. The discussion that follows is heavily influenced by the illuminating discussion of this kind of argument in Sadurski (1999: 98–111).

20. Sunstein (1993: 186), although it's worth noting that Sunstein himself does not take this to be a compelling justification for hate speech restrictions and simply concludes from this that "there is nothing obvious or clear about the view that the First Amendment should ban laws prohibiting racial hate speech." See also Fiss (1995), Ma (1995: e.g., 696, 703, 713, 719).

21. For further examples of uncontroversially protected speech that would be rendered unprotected on this account, see Gelman (1995: 310–11).

22. Regarding Thomas, see Kennedy (2008: ch. 4). The Kilson quote is cited by Kennedy (2008: 188).

Chapter 8. How to Stop Worrying and Learn to Love Hate Crime Laws: Why Objections to Hate Speech Restrictions Don't Work as Objections to Hate Crime Laws

1. D'Souza (1995: 530). See also D'Souza (1995: 538): "Hate speech and hate crime laws that impose punishment or enhanced penalties for proscribed motives and viewpoints are inherently illiberal and destructive of intellectual independence and conscience."

2. The first hate crime statutes in the United States were passed around 1980, and two decades later they were on the books in at least forty-three states and the District of Columbia, and were a part of federal law as well (see Gerstenfeld [2004: 2]).

3. Lawrence (1999: 190, emphasis added).

4. Brick (2007). This misunderstanding of hate crime laws sometimes slips into even otherwise quite careful academic treatments as well (e.g., Blake [2001: 123–4]).

5. For a compelling defense of the claim that the tactically biased criminal, in particular, should be included within the scope of hate crime laws, see Wang (1997, 1999, 2000, 2001, 2002–3) and also Woods (2008).

6. Lawrence (1999: 190).

7. Lawrence (1999: 191, emphasis added).

8. Lawrence (1999: 35).

9. See Lawrence (1999: 29–39) for a very helpful discussion of this.

10. Emphasis added. An interesting further question would be whether laws that include both kinds should treat both equally. Sistare (2004: 246), for example notes that "coolness in the course of violence against members of despised groups has characterized some of the most heinous historical instances of hate crime" and suggests that "some might even regard the perpetrator carried away with hatred as less culpable than the one who acts on his prejudices with little feeling."

11. Woods (2008: 500).

12. Hate crime laws often include murder, but I'm deliberately setting that case aside. In the United States, at least, the main way to enhance a penalty for murder is to increase the punishment from life in prison to the death penalty. But the death penalty itself raises special problems because some people are opposed to it on principle. I don't want a defense of hate crime laws to have to require a defense of capital punishment, so I focus on the claim that hate crime laws are legitimate at least in the case of the other typical sorts of crimes to which they are applied. If capital punishment is permissible, then they are probably also justified in this case. But if it isn't, they are not justified in this case not because there is something wrong with hate crime laws but because there is something wrong with capital punishment.

13. As it turns out, I don't really accept this assumption (see Boonin [2008a]), but will do so for the purposes of this discussion. When I say that hate crime laws are appropriate, what I really mean is that if the state is going to punish people for breaking the law in the first place, then it's appropriate that it punish hate crimes more severely than the ordinary crimes that they otherwise resemble.

14. Gellman (1992/3: 514–15). See also Gellman (1995b: 869), Gellman (2005: 425–8), Riggs (1995: 954). Hurd presses this point, too (2001: 229–32). For some useful criticisms of the Gellman position see, e.g., Weinstein (1992a: esp 7–15) and (1992b: 61–2).
15. See, e.g., Jacobs and Potter (1998: 122–9). Goldberger (1992/3), Redish (1992: 30), Greve (1992/3), Crocker (1992/3), as well as other works by Gellman, especially Gellman (1991; 1992)
16. Gerstenfeld (2004: 40).
17. Gellman (1992/3: 515). See also Gellman (1991: 364; 2005: 426), Riggs (1995: 951–2).
18. Lawrence (1993: 720) presses this point effectively.
19. This claim will be developed in more detail at the start of the following chapter.
20. Murphy (1992) expresses a similar sort of skepticism about this distinction.
21. See, e.g., Robinson (1992/3: 605), Greenawalt (1992/3: 623–5).
22. Lawrence (1993: 717–18) notes this problem with appealing to the claim that hate crime laws punish for motive rather than for intention.
23. Gerstenfeld (2004: 40).
24. Lawrence (1993: 718–19) also makes this point.
25. A critic might object that it isn't really the difference in motive that does the work here, but rather the fact that the person who launches a premeditated attack is fully responsible for his behavior while the person who is provoked into attacking is not fully responsible for his. But even if we are inclined to explain the difference between the cases in terms of differences in the levels of responsibility, we'll still have to appeal to the difference between motives at some point: it's because the second person is motivated by taunting in a way that the first person isn't that we are inclined to say that the second person is less than fully responsible for his behavior. In the end, then, there seems to be no good way to account for the difference between the cases without conceding the claim that differences in motive can be relevant to differences in sentencing.
26. Brown (1992: 47).
27. Redish (1992: 38).
28. Gellman (1992/3: 516).
29. Margulies (1992: 44) notes this.
30. Robinson (1992/3: 607).

Chapter 9. How to Keep on Loving Hate Crime Laws: Why Other Objections to Hate Crime Laws Don't Work, Either

1. See, e.g., Sistare (2004: 254–6), Lawrence (2005: 423–4).
2. Cited by Card (2001: 206), though in the end she rejects this approach. For details of the study, see Ehrlich, Larcom, and Purvis (1995).
3. Larwence (1999: 40). Wang (1997: 112) also cites evidence that victim counselors report hate crime victims suffer more than do the victims of otherwise comparable crimes. Harrell and Parchomovsky, though, cite a study that concludes that hate crimes do not cause greater psychological harm than otherwise parallel crimes (1999: 515).
4. Card (2001: 209). Jacobs and Potter raise the same objection, noting for example that the racially motivated beating of an Asian store owner is not a worse act

than the ideologically motivated assassination of a political leader (1998: 80, 86–7). David A. Reidy also seems to press the same objection (2004: 259). And Baehr raises the same objection, though in the context of harms to secondary victims (142–3). See also Harrell and Parchomovsky (1999: 513).

5. A critic of hate crime laws might also, I suppose, appeal to the related claim that it would be better if everyone came to view their race as no more significant than their left- or right-handedness. But this claim, too, poses no real problem for the defender of hate crime laws. In the first place, the fact that it would be better if people didn't care about their race is irrelevant to the question of whether hate crimes tend to cause more harm given that people do, in fact, tend to care about their race. It might be better if people were not bothered by the sight of public nudity, after all, but it is perfectly reasonable to prohibit it given that most people, in fact, are. And if race consciousness is such a bad thing that it is worth striving for a world in which no one cares about race, then this fact would seem to support the central claim made by proponents of hate crime laws: that there is something distinctly objectionable about those criminals who select their victims in a race-conscious manner.

6. Lawrence (2005: 425) uses the same example. The same reasoning applies to the distinction between robbery without an accomplice and robbery with an accomplice. A number of states treat the latter as a form of aggravated robbery and attach a correspondingly greater sentence to it as a result and this, too, provides support for the claim that a crime can be worse than another because it is more likely to result in greater trauma and harm to the victim (see Woods [2008: 508–9]).

7. See, e.g., Lawrence (1999: 41).

8. See Wellman (2006: 70), Sistare (2004: 255). The United States Supreme Court also appealed to this consideration in *Wisconsin v. Mitchell*, noting that hate crimes "are more likely to provoke retaliatory crimes, inflict distinct emotional harms on their victims, and incite community unrest" (quoted in Crocker [1992/3: 486]). Steven M. Freeman, Director of Legal Affairs for the Anti-Defamation League, raises the same point (1992/3: 581–5).

9. Woods (2008: 492). Wang also raises this concern (2000: 1400; 2002: 14).

10. See also Altman (2001: 163–6) who defends the claim that hate crimes cause a special kind of harm by causing or reinforcing second class status for the targeted group.

11. See, e.g., Crocker (1992/3: 492–3).

12. Cited by Woods (2008: 509) in this context. Wang (2000: 1400–1, 1419) makes the same point. Two other examples from Woods are also worth noting: laws that make looting a worse crime than simple theft or burglary, on the grounds that the victims are particularly vulnerable during the events that prompted the looting, and the Emergency and Disaster Assistance Fraud Penalty Enhancement Act of 2007, which enhanced the punishment for fraud in connection with major disaster or emergency funds, and was a response to numerous allegations of fraudulent use of relief funds intended for victims of Hurricanes Katrina, Rita, and Wilma (2008: 510).

13. Harrell and Parchomovsky (1999) argue that the enhanced punishments recommended in the case of especially vulnerable victims are justified not because the criminal acts with a more depraved state of mind, but because the state has an obligation to provide extra protection to the most vulnerable. There's no reason for the latter explanation to preclude the former, though, and even if we accept

their alternative explanation, the result will still be, as they themselves maintain, a vulnerability-based justification of hate crime laws, though along different lines from the one I develop here.

14. Reidy (2004: 262–3).
15. Hurd develops this objection in (2001: 224–6). The objection is also endorsed by Jacobs and Potter (1998: 81).
16. Hurd (2001: 224)
17. Hurd (2001: 226).
18. For a different response, see Taslitz (1999: 755), who argues in part that it's permissible to hold the racist's character against him even if there's nothing he can do to change it now because it was open to him to attempt to change it in the past.
19. Kim (2006: 858) makes a similar point using an example at the opposite end of the culpability spectrum: if a man has been carefully planning to kill his wife for a long time, at the moment he must decide whether to carry out the plan he is free to choose not to kill her, but he has no control over the fact that, if he does kill her, it will be as a result of careful premeditation.
20. Nearpass (2002: 558).
21. Nearpass (2002: 560).
22. Nearpass (2002: 560).
23. Nearpass (2002: 560, again quoting from the *Dixon* case).
24. Nearpass (2002: 562).
25. Nearpass (2002: 563–4).
26. Weinstein (1992a: 15).
27. Gellman (1991: 361). See more generally Gellman (1991: 358–62), Gellman (1992: 28).
28. Weinstein (1992a: 15).
29. Weinstein (1992a: 16).
30. Will (2007: B7). See also Jacobs (1992: 55–7).
31. Gellman (1991: 383).
32. See Blake (2001) for an illuminating discussion of these cases.
33. Crocker raises some of these questions in (1992/3: 502).
34. Gellman (1991: 357)
35. Sistare (2004: 244).
36. See, e.g., Abramovsky (1992/3: 537).

Chapter 10. Is Racial Profiling Irrational? The Answer Isn't Black and White

1. Pampel (2004: 31).
2. Heumann and Cassak (2003: 3–4).
3. Glasser (2000); D'Souza (1999); Anderson and Calahan (2001).
4. Pampel (2004: 48).
5. See, e.g., ACLU (2005).
6. When he declared his opposition to racial profiling in a 2002 address to the Arab Community Center for Economic and Social Services in Detroit, for example, U.S. Secretary of Transportation Norman Y. Mineta characterized the practice he was opposing as "profiling based *solely* on race" that involved making decisions based on "race *alone*" (quoted in Schauer [2003: 334n13, emphases added]). Laney

reports that "The Fraternal Order of Police (FOP) opposes the practice of stopping someone based *solely* on race because it is wrong to believe a person is a criminal based on the color of his or her skin" (2006: 8, emphasis added) And Christina Fauchon begins her "Case Against Profiling" by writing that "Racial profiling can be defined as stopping and searching people passing through public areas *solely* because of their color, race, or ethnicity" (2004: 157, emphasis added).

7. Douard (2001: 2).

8. Mac Donald (2003: 18). Her argument is also endorsed by Frum (2003: 60).

9. For useful discussions of some of the problems involved in interpreting the relevant data, see Ramirez, McDevitt, and Farrell (2006) and U.S. General Accounting Office (2006). For a detailed treatment of such issues in the context of the police work in a single jurisdiction, that of Eugene, Oregon, see Gumbhir (2007).

10. Pampel (2004: 26).

11. The rationality argument, in one version or another, has been endorsed by several writers in the *National Review*, including Derbyshire (2001a: 38–9; 2001b: 44), Lowry (2002: 34), Buckley (2002: 63), and the unsigned pieces "Better Safe" (2002) and the *American Spectator* (Fund (2006)), though largely in the context of profiling Arabic-looking men in airports. Philip Terzian is quoted defending the argument in the *Weekly Standard* in Somin (2006: 53). See also Krauthammer (2002), Reddick (2004), and Reed (2006) for the same argument.

12. Department of Justice (2003: 1).

13. Harris (2002: 225). See also Harris (2001: 16). The objection has also been pressed by a number of other writers, including Fauchon (2006: 53), Cooper (2006: 28), Maclin (2001: 120–23), Wang (2001: 233), and Romero (2003: 378–9).

14. Pampel (2004: 26). Arlington, Virginia, for example, has a ten percent black population, but robbery victims there identify nearly 70 percent of their attackers as black; in New York City in 1998, victim report data indicated that black residents were 13 times more likely than white residents to commit violent assault (Mac Donald [2003: 24–5]). For further statistics along these lines, see also Meeks (2000: 54), Thernstrom and Thernstrom (1997: 271–2), Subotnik (2005: 216).

15. The description of Tonry and the quote from him are both taken from Kennedy (1997: 23). Similarly, Alfred Blumstein concludes his statistical analysis of the causes of racial disparities in prison populations by writing: "Any significant impact on the racial mix in our prisons will have to come from addressing the factors in our society that generate the life conditions that contribute to the different involvement between the races in serious … crimes" (1982: 52).

16. Harris (2002: 79–80). See also Harris (2001: 14), Pampel (2004: 35). The hit rates objection is also endorsed by Davies (2003: 58), ACLU (2006: 19) Fauchon (2004: 157; 2006: 53), Maclin (2001: 123), and Carter (2004: 27).

17. According to data taken from the southern end of the New Jersey Turnpike in 2000, for example, troopers found evidence of crimes in searches of white drivers 25 percent of time and only 13 percent of the time in the case of black drivers (Harris 2002: 80). A 1999 New York Attorney General study of stops and frisks of pedestrians in New York City reported that police arrested 12.6 percent of white pedestrians stopped and 10.5 percent of black pedestrians (Harris 2002: 81). The same study also reported that among those stopped on suspicion of weapons violations, arrests resulted 1 out of 15 times in white cases and 1 out of 17.4 times in black cases (Harris 2002: 82).

18. Quoted by Harcourt (2006: 120, emphasis added). Most of my worries about Harris's argument derive from Harcourt's book.
19. Harcourt (2006: 120).
20. Thomas (2001: 41–2).
21. Gross and Barnes (2002: 660).
22. Gross and Barnes (2002: 661).
23. Gross and Barnes (2002: 715).
24. Gross and Barnes (2002: 717).
25. 16 percent of the drivers in the study were black, but 25 percent of those going 15 or more miles per hour over the speed limit were black (Pampel [2004: 26–7]), Mac Donald [2003: 28, 31]).
26. See Harcourt (2006: 136–8) who also points out there may be differences in how thoroughly searches are conducted in the two cases.
27. See, e.g., Harcourt (2006: 120), Subotnik (2005: 233–4).
28. Ayres (2008). The full study can be found in Ayres and Borowsky (2008).
29. Harcourt (2006: 123–5ff). A 2006 statement by the Leadership Conference on Civil Rights Education Fund makes the same point in the context of airport security (2006: 31–2). See also McGary (1996: 172–3).
30. See, e.g., Harcourt (2006: 3, 145).
31. Schauer (2003: 186–7). The list of suspicion-heightening characteristics comes from Schauer (2003: 184). See also Lund (2003: 331, 335–41), though also see London's reply to Lund (2003: esp. 345).
32. Schauer (2003: 188–9). See Muller (2003: 109, 125, 129, 131–2) for a slightly different version of this objection.

Chapter 11. Is Racial Profiling Immoral? A Reluctant Defense of America's Least Popular Form of Discrimination

1. This argument seems to be endorsed by Ira Glasser, Executive Director of the ACLU (Glasser 2003: xiii).
2. In one of her articles arguing against racial profiling, for example, the philosopher Annabelle Lever, writes that "we generally suppose that the police are entitled to stop and search only people whose behavior supports the belief that they have committed, or are about to commit, a crime" (Lever 2007: 20–21).
3. Maclin (2001: 124). See also Colb (2001: 209).
4. In the case of *United States v. Martinez-Fuerte*, the United States Supreme Court "held that the Border Patrol could stop all cars, without individual suspicion, at a fixed checkpoint 60 miles from the Mexican border" Gross and Barnes (2002: 733).
5. Thomas (2001: 40, see also 43).
6. Others who endorse this argument include Maclin (2001: 124–5), Buckman and Lamberth (2001), Gross and Barnes (2002: 740, 744), Davies (2003: 97), Ellman (2003: 676–8 [though he allows for exceptions in the case of combating terrorism]), and Pollack (2009: 4–5).
7. D'Souza (1999: 15A). ACLU: racial profiling is in every instance inconsistent with this country's core constitutional principles of equality and fairness" (2006: 19). Also Fauchon (2004: 158): "To single out a group of people by race violates equal protection." See also Lund (2003: 331–2).

8. In addition, as Andrew C. McCarthy has pointed out, this argument against racial profiling would entail that affirmative action is impermissible, making it unavailable to those who support affirmative action (2006: 23).

9. Harris (2002: 98–9).

10. Harris (2002: 102), Kennedy (1997: 153).

11. Harris (2002: 117). This point is also made on page 1 of the June 17, 2003, Department of Justice fact sheet on racial profiling, and has been endorsed by the International Association of Chiefs of Police (Laney [2006: 7]). See also Taylor, Jr. (2006: 37–8), Kennedy (1997: 151–2).

12. Harris (2002: 121–2), Kennedy (1997: 4).

13. Kennedy (1997: 4). A 2006 statement by the Leadership Conference on Civil Rights Education Fund makes the same point in the context of airport security (2006: 32–3).

14. Kennedy (1997: 4).

15. Forman (2001: 26) also makes a point about profiling lowering black cooperation with police and another subtle point: it reduces the stigma in the black community of being arrested since it makes it less clear that having been arrested means you broke the law. For more objections along the same lines, see also Amnesty International (2006), Carter (2004: 28), Lever (2007: 23), Harris (2001: 17–19), Wang (2001: 231–3; 2002: 20–1).

16. For a useful discussion of some of these issues, see Holbert and Rose (2006).

17. Readers familiar with the scant philosophical literature on racial profiling are likely to have read the complex and challenging article "Racial Profiling" by Mathias Risse and Richard Zeckhauser (2004), which also offers a qualified defense of the moral acceptability of the practice. Since an important and controversial part of their argument turns on a claim about discounting the feelings of resentment, hurt, and distrust associated with racial profiling, and since the argument that I offer here turns on a similar kind of claim, it's worth stressing that the reasoning I provide here is fundamentally different from that offered by Risse and Zeckhauser.

Risse and Zeckhauser argue that most of the mental harm associated with racial profiling is caused by underlying racism and social inequality rather than by the profiling itself, with the result that relatively little of the harm should be taken into account when weighing the various costs and benefits of the practice. I'm inclined to be skeptical of this line of argument. Even if it's true that racial profiling would cause no real offense if there were no history of racism in this country (Risse and Zeckhauser point out, for example, that when profiling is directed toward white people in the context of serial killers it doesn't seem to cause any real resentment, hurt, or distrust among white Americans [2004: 151]), it doesn't seem to follow that all of the hurt it causes shouldn't be counted against it. Suppose, for example, that you know that a neighbor of yours is extremely sensitive to loud noises only because of a great trauma that he suffered as a child. If you cause a loud noise that predictably causes him to be tremendously upset, it seems implausible to say that you aren't responsible for most of the harm and for you to appeal to the fact that the noise by itself wasn't particularly harmful. Given that his history understandably causes him to be predictably upset by your behavior, the full cost of his distress seems to count against your choosing to make the loud noise. In the same way, it seems to me, even if it's true that black Americans are upset by racial profiling primarily because of underlying facts about the social context in which it takes place, it seems implausible to say that the full costs of their distress shouldn't enter the equation for that reason.

The argument I develop in this section, by contrast, does not require this assumption. It appeals not to the claim that racial profiling doesn't cause all of the mental harm but, rather, to the claim that even if it does cause all of the mental harm, there is a dilemma involved in appealing to it as an objection to racial profiling. If the argument put forth by Risse and Zeckhauser turns out to be vindicated, that will provide additional support for the position I take in this section, but it's important to see that the position can be sustained even without it (for more on the debate over the Risse and Zeckhauser argument, see Lever (2005), Risse's response to Lever in (2007: esp. 10–15) and Lever's response to Risse's response in (2007)).

18. See, e.g., Maclin (2001: 123–4). Carter (2004: 86–7). Carter frames the argument as a legal argument for the claim that racial profiling violates the Thirteenth Amendment because he believes that that Amendment can be understood to condemn policies that have a disparate impact in this sense. But, as with my previous discussions of arguments based on the Fourth and Fourteenth Amendments, I will consider the argument here as a moral argument independent of its possible legal merits.

19. Of course, if the police instead decided to target black drivers exclusively, the expected yield would go up to eight arrests per one hundred drivers pulled over. But, as the discussion in the section on elasticity should make clear, this would in turn dramatically increase the rate of offending among white drivers. For the purposes of the example, then, I'll simply assume that something like a fifty-fifty ratio turns out to be the most sensible balance for the police to aim for.

20. A critic of my argument here might complain that I've overlooked an important difference between the case of the two vans and the case of racial profiling. In the case of the two vans, the police officer has a race-neutral reason for choosing to chase the westbound van. That van happens to contain a greater proportion of black people, but he doesn't chase the van because more of its occupants are black. He simply chases it because it has more people in it. The cop on the New Jersey Turnpike who engages in racial profiling, by contrast, chooses to pull over a particular driver (in part) precisely because he's black. The racial profiling case, that is, seems to involve an act of intentional discrimination while the case of the two vans involves at most a kind of inadvertent discrimination. And this might seem to show that the fact that it's okay to chase the westbound doesn't show that it's okay to engage in racial profiling.

But this appearance is misleading. If the reason it's okay to chase the west-bound van despite the fact that doing so will disproportionately target black people is that there is a race-neutral justification that can be given for the decision (it increases the number of successful arrests that will be made on average to choose in this way), then racial profiling will also be okay and for the very same reason. The cop who pulls over a disproportionate number of black drivers, after all, can give the very same race-neutral reason for his decision: assuming that the racial profiling he is engaged in is rational, it increases the number of successful arrests that will be made on average to choose in this way.

21. The quote comes from Schauer (2003: 159). Schauer does not explicitly endorse the objection, though he does not explicitly reject it either.

22. Defenders of racial profiling are not always clear in distinguishing between the claim that profiling is permissible and the claim that it's obligatory. Typically, they argue that the state "should" engage in profiling, which entails that it is at the very least morally permissible. But to say that the state should profile could mean either that it would be a good thing to do but not positively immoral not to do (i.e., that it would go above and beyond the state's duty) or that it is obligatory to do and thus positively immoral not to do (i.e., that it is part of the state's duty). Thus, it is usually not clear whether a particular defender of racial profiling believes that such profiling is obligatory.

One of the few defenders of racial profiling who recognizes this distinction explicitly is Michael Levin, who is also one of the few philosophers to have written on the subject (1991). But while Levin is clear that he is endorsing the claim that racial profiling is permissible, his attitude toward the question of whether it is obligatory is somewhat more tentative. At some points, he seems to argue that it is (e.g., [1991: 10], where he maintains that taking racial differences into account is "permitted and indeed required by the state's protective function") but at others, he seems less certain (e.g., [1991: 9], where he says that the rationality of taking race into account would "sanction and possibly mandate" something like racial profiling). For some responses to Levin's paper, see Adler (1993; 1994), Cox (1993), Pojman (1993), and Thomas (1992). For Levin's responses to some of these, see Levin (1994a; 1994b).

23. Although for an important exception, see Schauer (2003: 190, 197).

Sources

Abramovsky, Abraham. 1992/3. "Bias Crime: Is Parental Liability the Answer?" *Annual Survey of American Law*, no. 4, pp. 533–40.

ACLU. 2005. "Racial Profiling Exists." In David Erik Nelson, ed., *Racial Profiling*. Farmington Hills, MI: Greenhaven Press, pp. 20–35.

——. 2006. "U.S. Policies Sanction Racial Profiling." In Kris Hirschmann, ed., *Racial Profiling*. Farmington Hills, MI: pp. 16–20.

Adams, David M. 2005. "Punishing Hate and Achieving Equality." *Criminal Justice Ethics*, vol. 24, no. 1 (Winter/Spring), pp. 19–30.

Adams, Francis D. and Barry Sanders. 2003. *Alienable Rights: The Exclusion of African Americans in a White Man's Land, 1619–2000*. New York: HarperCollins Publishers, Inc.

Adler, Jonathan. 1993. "Crime Rates by Race and Causal Relevance: A Reply to Levin." *Journal of Social Philosophy*, vol. 24, no. 1, pp. 176–84.

——. 1994. "More on Race and Crime: Levin's Reply." *Journal of Social Philosophy*, vol. 25, no. 2, pp. 105–14.

Alexander, Larry. 1996. "Banning Hate Speech and the Sticks and Stones Defense." *Constitutional Commentary*, vol. 13, pp. 71–100.

Alger, Jonathan R. 1998. "Unfinished Homework for Universities: Making the Case for Affirmative Action." *Journal of Urban and Contemporary Law*, vol. 54, pp. 73–92.

Allen, Ernest, Jr. and Robert Chrisman. 2001. "Ten Reasons: A Response to David Horowitz." *The Black Scholar*, vol. 31, no. 2, pp. 49–55.

Alston, Wilton D. and Walter E. Block. 2008. "Reparations, Once Again." *Human Rights Review*, vol. 9, pp. 379–92.

Altman, Andrew. 1993. "Liberalism and Campus Hate Speech: A Philosophical Examination." *Ethics*, vol. 103 (January), pp. 302–17.

——. 2001. "The Democratic Legitimacy of Bias Crime Laws: Public Reason and the Political Process." *Law and Philosophy*, vol. 20, pp. 141–73.

America, Richard F. 1990. "Introduction." In America, ed., *The Wealth of Races: The Present Value of Benefits from Past Injustices*. New York: Greenwood Press, pp. xvii–xix.

——. 1993. *Paying the Social Debt: What White America Owes Black America*. Westport, CT: Praeger.

387

——. 1997. "The Theory of Restitution: The African American Case." In Michael T. Martin and Marilyn Yaquinto, eds., *Redress for Historical Injustices in the United States: On Reparations for Slavery, Jim Crow, and Their Legacies*. Durham, NC, and London: Duke University Press, pp. 160–69.

Amnesty International. 2006. "Racial Profiling Has a Heavy Social Cost." In Hirschmann, ed., *Racial Profiling*, pp. 83–91.

Appiah, K. Anthony. 1996. "Race, Culture, Identity: Misunderstood Connections." In Appiah and Amy Gutmann, *Color Conscious: The Political Morality of Race*. Princeton: Princeton University Press, pp. 30–105.

Arceneaux, Taniecea. 2005. "Reparations for Slavery: A Cause for Reparations, a Case Against David Horowitz." *The Review of Black Political Economy*, vol. 32, no. 3–4, pp. 141–8.

Armour, Jody David. 1997. *Negrophobia and Reasonable Racism: The Hidden Costs of Being Black in America*. New York and London: New York University Press.

Armstrong, Margalynne. 2002. "Reparations Litigation: What About Unjust Enrichment?" *Oregon Law Review*, vol. 81, pp. 771–82

Arneson, Richard. J. 1993. "Preferential Treatment Versus Purported Meritocratic Rights." In Steven M. Cahn, ed., *Affirmative Action and the University: A Philosophical Inquiry*, pp. 157–64. Philadelpia: Temple University Press.

Arnold, N. Scott. 1998. "Affirmative Action and the Demands of Justice." *Social Philosophy and Policy*, vol. 15, no. 2, pp. 133–75.

Arthur, John. 2007. *Race, Equality, and the Burdens of History*. Cambridge: Cambridge University Press.

Asante, Molefi Kete. 2003. "The African American Warrant for Reparations: The Crime of European Enslavement of Africans and Its Consequences." In Raymond A. Winbush, ed., *Should America Pay?: Slavery and the Raging Debate on Reparations*. New York: HarperCollins Publishers, Inc., pp. 3–13.

Ayres, Ian. 2008. "The LAPD and Racial Profiling." *The Los Angeles Times*, October 23.

Ayres, Ian and Jonathan Borowsky. 2008. *A Study of Racially Disparate Outcomes in the Los Angeles Police Department*. ACLU of Southern California. Available online at: http://islandia.law.yale.edu/ayers/Ayres%20LAPD%20Report.pdf.

Baehr, Amy R. 2003. "A Feminist Liberal Approach to Hate Crime Legislation." *Journal of Social Philosophy*, vol. 34, no. 1 (Spring), pp. 134–52.

Baez, Benjamin. 2002. *Affirmative Action, Hate Speech, and Tenure: Narratives about Race, Law and the Academy*. New York and London: Routledge Falmer.

Bailey-Williams, Sheryl. 1990. "An Appraisal of the Estimated Rates of Slave Exploitation." In Richard F. America, ed., *The Wealth of Races*, pp. 55–63.

Baker, Houston A., Jr. 2008. *Betrayal: How Black Intellectuals Have Abandoned the Ideals of the Civil Rights Era*. New York: Columbia University Press.

Barkley, Charles (edited and with an introduction by Michael Wilbon). 2005. *Who's Afraid of a Large Black Man?* New York: The Penguin Press.

Beauchamp, Tom L. 1998. "In Defense of Affirmative Action." *The Journal of Ethics*, vol. 2, pp. 143–58.

Becker, Lawrence C. 1993. "Affirmative Action and Faculty Appointments." In Cahn, ed., *Affirmative Action and the University*, pp. 93–121.

Beckwith, Francis J. and Todd E. Jones, eds., 1997. *Affirmative Action: Social Justice or Reverse Discrimination?* Amherst, New York: Prometheus Books.

Beinert, Peter. 2002. "Off-Color." *The New Republic*, vol. 227, nos. 2/3 (July 8–15), p. 8.

"Better Safe." 2002. *National Review*, vol. 54, no. 5 (March 25) p. 17–18.

Bilford, Brian J. 2008. "Harper's Bazaar: The Marketplace of Ideas and Hate Speech in Schools." *Stanford Journal of Civil Rights and Civil Liberties*, vol. 4, no. 2, pp. 101–27.

Bittker, Boris I. 1973. *The Case for Black Reparations*. New York: Random House.

Black, Virginia. 1974. "The Erosion of Legal Principles in the Creation of Legal Policies," *Ethics*, Vol. 84, No. 2 (January), pp. 93–115.

Blackmon, Douglas A. 2008. *Slavery by Another Name: The Re-Enslavement of Black Americans from the Civil War to World War II*. New York: Doubleday.

Blair, John P. and Rudy H. Fichtenbaum. 1992. "Changing Black Employment Patterns." In George C. Galster and Edward W. Hill, eds., *The Metropolis in Black & White: Place, Power and Polarization* (New Brunswick, NJ: Center for Urban Policy Research), pp. 72–92.

Blake, Michael. 2001. "Geeks and Monsters: Bias Crimes and Social Identity." *Law and Philosophy*, vol. 20, pp. 121–39.

Blum, Lawrence. 2002. *"I'm Not a Racist, But ...": The Moral Quandary of Race*. Ithaca, NY, and London: Cornell University Press.

Blumstein, Alfred. 1982. "On the Racial Disproportionality of United States' Prison Populations." In Shaun L. Gabbidon and Helen Taylor Greene, eds., *Race, Crime, and Justice*. New York: Routledge, 2005, pp. 39–54.

Block, Walter. 2002. "On Reparations to Blacks for Slavery." *Human Rights Review*, vol. 3, no. 4, pp. 53–73.

Bolick, Clint. 1996. *The Affirmative Action Fraud: Can We Restore the American Civil Rights Vision?* Washington, DC: the Cato Institute.

Bolner, James. 1968. "Toward a Theory of Racial Reparations." In Martin and Yaquinto, eds., *Redress for Historical Injustices in the United States*, pp. 134–42.

Boonin, David. 2008a. *The Problem of Punishment*. Cambridge: Cambridge University Press.

———. 2008b. "How to Solve the Non-Identity Problem." *Public Affairs Quarterly*, vol. 22, no. 2 (April), pp. 127–57.

Bowen, William G. and Derek Bok. 1998. *The Shape of the River: Long-Term Consequences of Considering Race in College and University Admissions*. Princeton: Princeton University Press.

Boxill, Bernard R. 1992. *Blacks and Social Justice*, rev. edn. Lanham, MD: Rowman & Littlefield Publishers, Inc.

Boyle, Kevin. 2001. "Hate Speech – The United States Versus the Rest of the World?" *Maine Law Review*, vol. 53, no. 2, pp. 488–502.

Brick, Michael. 2007. "Lawyer Claims Defendant in Hate Crime Is Gay, Too." *New York Times* (September 18).

———. 2003. "Brief of the Harvard Black Law Students Association, Stanford Black Law Students Association and Yale Black Law Students Association as *Amici Curiae* Supporting Respondents." *Harvard BlackLetter Law Journal*, vol. 19, pp. 55–92.

Brooks, Roy L. 2003. "Reflections on Reparations." In John Torpey, ed., *Politics and the Past: On Repairing Historical Injustices*. Lanham, MD: Rowman & Littlefield Publishers, Inc., pp. 103–14.

——. 2004. *Atonement and Forgiveness: A New Model for Black Reparations.* Berkeley: University of California Press.

Brophy, Alfred L. 2003. "Some Conceptual and Legal Problems in Reparations for Slavery." *NYU Annual Survey of American Law*, vol. 58, no. 4, pp. 497–556.

——. 2004. "The Cultural War Over Reparations For Slavery." *DePaul Law Review*, vol. 53, pp. 1181–1213.

——. 2006. "Reconsidering Reparations." *Indiana Law Journal*, vol. 81, pp. 811–49.

Brown, Ralph S. 1992. "Susan Gellman Has it Right." *Criminal Justice Ethics*, vol. 11, pp. 46–48.

Browne, Robert S. 1990. "Achieving Parity through Reparations." In Richard F. America, ed., *The Wealth of Races*, pp. 199–206.

——. 1993. "The Economic Basis for Reparations to Black America." In Martin and Yaquinto, eds., *Redress for Historical Injustices in the United States*, pp. 238–48.

Browne-Marshall, Gloria. 2007. *Race, Law and American Society: 1607 to Present.* New York: Routledge.

Brownstein, Alan E. 1994. "Hate Speech and Harassment: The Constitutionality of Campus Codes that Prohibit Racial Insults." *William and Mary Bill of Rights Journal*, vol. 3, pp. 179–217.

Buckley, Jr. William F. 2002. "Watch the Red-Haired Man." *National Review*, vol. 54 no. 11 (June 17) pp. 62–3.

Buckman, William H. and John Lamberth. 2001. "Challenging Racial Profiles: Attacking Jim Crow on the Interstate." *Rutgers Race and the Law Review*, vol. 3, pp. 83–115.

Butler, Paul. 1997. "Affirmative Action and the Criminal Law." *University of Colorado Law Review*, vol. 68, pp. 841–889.

Canedy, Dana. 2001. "The Hurt Between the Lines." In Correspondents of *The New York Times, How Race is Lived in America: Pulling Together, Pulling Apart.* New York: Henry Holt and Company, pp. 171–87.

Cantor, Nancy. 2004. "Introduction." In Gurin, Patricia, Jeffrey S. Lehman and Earl Lewis, *Defending Diversity: Affirmative Action at the University of Michigan.* Ann Arbor: University of Michigan Press, pp. 1–16.

Capaldi, Nicholas. 1996. "Affirmative Action: Con." In Albert G. Mosley and Nicholas Capaldi, *Affirmative Action: Social Justice or Unfair Preference?* Lanham, MD: Rowman & Littlefield Publishers, Inc., pp. 65–109.

Card, Claudia. 2001. "Is Penalty Enhancement a Sound Idea?" *Law and Philosophy*, vol. 20, pp. 195–214.

Card, Robert F. 2005. "Making Sense of the Diversity-Based Legal Argument for Affirmative Action." *Public Affairs Quarterly*, vol. 19, no. 1, pp. 11–24.

Carter, Stephen L. 1991. *Reflections of an Affirmative Action Baby.* New York: Basic Books.

Carter, Jr., William M. 2004. "A Thirteenth Amendment Framework for Combating Racial Profiling." *Harvard Civil Rights-Civil Liberties Law Review*, vol. 39, no. 1, pp. 17–93.

Chemerinsky, Erwin. 1996. "Making Sense of the Affirmative Action Debate." *Ohio Northern University Law Review*, vol. 22, pp. 1343–51.

Cho, Sumi K. 1997. "Multiple Consciousness and the Diversity Dilemma." *University of Colorado Law Review*, vol. 68, pp. 1035–63.

Cohen, Carl. 1995. *Naked Racial Preference.* New York: Madison Books.

——. 1998. "Preference by Race in University Admissions and the Quest for Diversity." *Journal of Urban and Contemporary Law*, vol. 54, pp. 43–72.

——. 2003a. "Why Race Preference is Wrong and Bad." In Carl Cohen and James P. Sterba, *Affirmative Action and Racial Preference: A Debate.* Oxford: Oxford University Press, pp. 3–188.

——. 2003b. "Reply to James P. Sterba." In Cohen and Sterba, *Affirmative Action and Racial Preference*, pp. 279–304.

Colb, Sherry F. 2001. "Stopping a Moving Target." *Rutgers Race and the Law Review*, vol. 3, pp. 191–222.

Collier, Charles W. 2005. "Affirmative Action and the Decline of Intellectual Culture." *Journal of Legal Education*, vol. 55, nos. 1–2, pp. 3–15.

Connerly, Ward. 1996. "The Sweet Music of Equal Treatment." In Beckwith and Jones, eds., *Affirmative Action*, pp. 64–69.

Conti, Joseph G. and Brad Stetson. 1997. "A Conversation With Shelby Steele." In Stan Faryna, Brad Stetson and Joseph G. Conti, eds., *Black and Right: The Bold New Voice of Black Conservatives in America.* Westport, CT: Praeger, pp. 143–51.

Cooper, Steve. 2006. "A Closer Look at Racial Profiling." In Steven J. Muffler, ed., *Racial Profiling: Issues, Data and Analyses.* New York: Nova Science Publishers, Inc., pp. 25–9.

Corlett, J. Angelo. 2003. *Race, Racism and Reparations.* Ithaca, NY, and London: Cornell University Press.

Corry, Robert J. 1996a. "Affirmative Action: An Innocent Generation's Equality Sacrificed." *Ohio Northern University Law Review*, vol. 22, pp. 1177–89.

——. 1996b. "Quotas, Special Privileges and Affirmative Action." *Ohio Northern University Law Review*, vol. 22, pp. 1305–14.

Cortese, Anthony. 2006. *Opposing Hate Speech.* Westport, CT: Praeger.

Cox, Chana Berniker. 1993. "On Michael Levin's 'Responses to Race Differences in Crime.'" *Journal of Social Philosophy*, vol. 24, no. 1, pp. 155–62.

Cox, Philip N. 1995. "The Disputation of Hate: Speech Codes, Pluralism, and Academic Freedoms." *Social Theory and Practice*, vol. 21, no. 1, pp. 113–44.

Crawford, Jewel, Wade W. Nobles and Joy DeGruy Leary. 2003. "Reparations and Health Care for African Americans: Repairing the Damage from the Legacy of Slavery." In Winbush, ed., *Should America Pay?*, pp. 251–81.

Crocker, Lawrence. 1992/3. "Hate Crime Statutes: Just? Constitutional? Wise?" *Annual Survey of American Law*, issue 4, pp. 485–507.

Dagan, Hanoch. 2004. "Restitution and Slavery: On Incomplete Commodification, Intergenerational Justice, and Legal Transitions." *Boston University Law Review*, vol. 84, pp. 1139–76.

Danziger, Sheldon and Peter Gottschalk. 1990. "Income Transfers: Are They Compensation for Past Discrimination?" In Richard F. America, ed., *The Wealth of Races*, pp. 169–77.

Darrity, Jr., William and Dania Frank. 2003. "The Political Economy of Ending Racism and the World Conference against Racism." In Martin and Yaquinto, eds., *Redress for Historical Injustices in the United States*, pp. 249–54.

Davies, Sharon. 2003. "Profiling Terror." *Ohio State Journal of Criminal Law*, vol. 1, pp. 46–101.

Davis, Adrienne D. 2000. "The Case for United States Reparations to African Americans." In Martin and Yaquinto, eds., *Redress for Historical Injustices in the United States*, pp. 371–78.

Davis, Angelique M. 2007. "Multiracialism and Reparations The Intersection of the Multiracial Category and the Reparations Movements." *Thomas Jefferson Law Review*, vol. 29, pp. 161–87.

Delgado, Richard. 1993. "Words That Wound: A Tort Action for Racial Insults, Epithets and Name Calling." In Mari J. Matsuda, Charles R. Lawrence III, Richard Delgao, and Kimberle Williams Crenshaw, *Words That Wound: Critical Race Theory, Assaultive Speech, and the First Amendment*. Boulder, CO: Westview Press, pp. 89–110.

——. 1995. "One Man's Dignity: An Interview with Emmit E. Fisher." In Laura J. Lederer and Richard Delgado, eds., *The Price We Pay: The Case Against Racist Speech, Hate Propaganda, and Pornography*. New York: Hill and Wang, pp. 23–6.

——. 1997. "Why Universities Are Morally Obligated to Strive for Diversity: Restoring the Remedial Rationale for Affirmative Action." *University of Colorado Law Review*, vol. 68, pp. 1165–72.

——. 2006. "Introduction." In Cortese, *Opposing Hate Speech*, pp. ix-xiii.

Derbyshire, John. 2001a. "In Defense of Racial Profiling," *National Review*, vol. 53, no. 3 (February 19), pp. 38–40.

——. 2001b. "At First Glance." *National Review*, vol. 53, no. 20 (October 15) pp. 42–4.

Desai, Anuj C. 2003. "Attacking *Brandenburg* with History: Does the Long-Term Harm of Biased Speech Justify a Criminal Statute Suppressing It?" *Federal Communications Law Journal*, vol. 55, no. 2, pp. 353–94.

Dieterle, J. M. 2005. "Affirmative Action and Desert." *Public Affairs Quarterly*, vol. 19, no. 2, pp. 81–94.

Dillon, Sam. 2009. "Study Sees an Obama Effect As Lifting Black Test-Takers." *New York Times* (national edition), Friday, January 23, p. A15.

Douard, John. 2001. "Racial Profiling: A New Road Hazard." *Rutgers Race and the Law Review*, vol. 3, pp. 1–7.

D'Souza, Dinesh. 1995. *The End of Racism*. New York: The Free Press.

——. 1999. "Sometimes Discrimination Can Make Sense." *USA Today*, Wednesday, June 2, p. 15A.

Durlauf, Steven N. 2008. "Affirmative Action, Meritocracy, and Efficiency." *Politics, Philosophy and Economics*, vol. 7, no. 2, pp. 131–58.

Dworkin, Ronald. 2003–04. "The Court and the University." *University of Cincinnati Law Review*, vol. 72, pp. 883–97.

Eastland, Terry. 1997. *Ending Affirmative Action: The Case for Colorblind Justice*. New York: Basic Books.

Egan, Timothy. 2001. "When to Campaign with Color." In Correspondents of *The New York Times, How Race is Lived in America*, pp. 115–31.

Ehlmann, Steven E. 1998. "Another Approach to Racial Preferences." *Journal of Urban and Contemporary Law*, vol. 54, pp. 93–106.

Ehrlich, Howard J., Barbara E. K. Larcom, and Robert D. Purvis. 1995. "The Traumatic Impact of Ethnoviolence." In Lederer and Delgado, eds., *The Price We Pay*, pp. 62–79.

Ellman, Stephen J. 2003. "Racial Profiling and Terrorism." *New York Law School Law Review*, Vol. 46, p. 675–730.

Engerman, Stanley L. 1990. "Past History and Current Policy: The Legacy of Slavery." In Richard F. America, ed., *The Wealth of Nations*, pp. 17–29.

Epstein, Richard A. 2004. "The Case *Against* Black Reparations." *Boston University Law Review*, vol. 84, pp. 1177–92.

Ezorsky, Gertrude. 1991. *Racism and Justice: The Case For Affirmative Action*. Ithaca and London: Cornell University Press.

Farrior, Stephanie. 1996. "Molding The Matrix: The Historical and Theoretical Foundations of International Law Concerning Hate Speech." *Berkeley Journal of International Law*, vol. 14, no. 1, pp. 1–98

Fauchon, Christina. 2004. "Counterpoint: The Case Against Profiling." *International Social Science Review*, vol. 79, nos. 3–4, pp. 157–9.

———. 2006. "The Benefits of Racial Profiling Cannot Justify Any Loss of Civil Liberties." in Hirschmann, ed., *Racial Profiling*, pp. 51–6.

Feagin, Joe R. 2000. *Racist America: Roots, Current Realities, and Future Reparations*. New York and London: Routledge.

Feiner, Susan F. and Bruce B. Roberts. 1990. "Slave Exploitation in Neoclassical Economics: Criticism and an Alternative Direction." In Richard F. America, ed., *The Wealth of Races*, pp. 139–49.

Finkelman, Paul. 1999. "Affirmative Action for the Master Class: The Creation of the Proslavery Constitution." *Akron Law Review*, vol. 32, no. 3, pp. 423–70.

Fish, Stanley. 1993. "Reverse Racism, or How the Pot Got to Call the Kettle Black." In Beckwith and Jones, eds., *Affirmative Action*, pp. 142–51.

Fiss, Owen. 1995. "The Supreme Court and the Problem of Hate Speech." *Capital University Law Review*, vol. 24, pp. 281–91.

Forman, James. 1969. "Black Manifesto." Reprinted as Appendix A in Bittker, *The Case for Black Reparations*, pp. 159–75.

Forman, Jr. James. 2001. "Arrested Development." *The New Republic*, vol. 225, no. 11 (September 10), pp. 24–7.

Fortson, Ryan. 2004. "Correcting the Harms of Slavery: Collective Liability, the Limited Prospects of Success for a Class Action Suit for Slavery Reparations, and the Reconceptualization of White Racial Identity." *African-American Law & Policy Report*, vol. VI, pp. 71–127.

Frady, Marshall. 2002. Martin *Luther King, Jr.* New York: Viking Penguin.

Francis, Leslie Pickering. 1993. "In Defense of Affirmative Action." In Cahn, ed., *Affirmative Action and the University*, pp. 9–47.

Freeman, Steven M. 1992/3. "Hate Crime Laws: Punishment Which Fits the Crime." *Annual Survey of American Law*, no. 4, pp. 581–5.

Frum, David. 2003. "Support Your Police." *National Review*, vol. 55 no. 6 (April 7) p. 60.

Fullinwider, Robert. 2000. "The Case for Reparations." *Philosophy and Public Policy Quarterly*, vol. 20, nos. 2/3 (Summer).

———. 2004. "The Reparations Argument: A Reply." *Journal of Social Philosophy*, vol. 35, no. 2, pp. 256–263.

Fullinwider, Robert K. and Judith Lichtenberg. 2004. *Leveling the Playing Field: Justice, Politics and College Admissions*. Latham, MD: Rowman & Littlefield Publishers, Inc.

Fund, John H. 2006. "Profiling Encouraged." *The American Spectator*, vol. 39, no. 8 (October), pp. 52–3.

Galster, George C. and Edward W. Hill. 1992. "Place, Power, and Polarization: Introduction." In Galster and Hill, eds., *The Metropolis in Black & White*, pp. 1–18.

Gates, Henry Louis, Jr. 1997. *Thirteen Ways of Looking at a Black Man*. New York: Random House.

Gellman, Susan. 1991. "Sticks and Stones Can Put You in Jail, but Can Words Increase Your Sentence?: Constitutional and Policy Dilemmas of Ethnic Intimidation Laws." *UCLA Law Review*, vol. 39, no. 2 (December), pp. 333–96.

——. 1992. "'Brother, You Can't Go to Jail for What You're Thinking': Motives, Effects, and 'Hate Crime' Laws." *Criminal Justice Ethics*, vol. 11, pp. 24–9.

——. 1992/3. "Hate Crime Laws Are Thought Crime Laws." *Annual Survey of American Law*, pp. 509–31.

——. 1995a. "Hate Speech and a New View of the First Amendment." *Capital University Law Review*, vol. 24, pp. 309–17.

——. 1995b. "Hate Crime Laws After *Wisconsin v. Mitchell.*" *Ohio Northern University Law Review*, vol. 21, pp. 863–70.

——. 2005. "The Case Against Bias-Crimes Laws." In Susan B. Gellman and Frederick M. Lawrence, "Agreeing to Agree: A Proponent and Opponent of Hate Crime Laws Reach for Common Ground." *Harvard Journal on Legislation*, vol. 41, pp. 425–33.

Gerstenfeld, Phyllis B. 2004. *Hate Crimes: Causes, Controls, and Controversies*. Thousand Oaks, CA: Sage Publications.

Glasser, Ira. 2000. "Introduction." In Meeks, *Driving While Black*, pp. xi–xiv.

Graglia, Lino A. 1998. "The 'Affirmative Action' Fraud." *Journal of Urban and Contemporary Law*, vol. 54, pp. 31–8.

Gray, Danielle C. and Travis LeBlanc. 2003. "Integrating Elite Law Schools and the Legal Profession: A View from the Black Law Students Associations of Harvard, Standord, and Yale Law Schools." *Harvard BlackLetter Law Journal*, vol. 19, pp. 43–54.

Gross, Barry R. 1978. *Discrimination in Reverse: Is Turnabout Fair Play?* New York: New York University Press.

Gross, Samuel R. and Katherine Y., Barnes. 2002. "Road Work: Racial Profiling and Drug Interdiction on the Highway. *Michigan Law Review*, vol. 101, No. 3, pp. 653–754.

Golab, Jan. 1999. "Probable Cause." *Los Angeles Magazine,* vol. 44 no. 8 (August), p. 28.

Goldberger, David. 1992/3. "Hate Crime Laws and Their Impact on the First Amendment." *Annual Survey of American Law*, no. 4, pp. 569–80.

Goldman, Alan H. 1979. *Justice and Reverse Discrimination*. Princeton: Princeton University Press.

——. 1993. "Comments on Compromise and Affirmative Action." In Cahn, ed., *Affirmative Action and the University*, pp. 295–99.

Gould, Jon B. 2005. *Speak No Evil: The Triumph of Hate Speech Regulation*. Chicago: University of Chicago Press.

Graves, Joseph L., Jr. 2005. *The Race Myth: Why We Pretend Race Exists in America*. New York: Penguin Books.

Greenawalt, Kent. 1992/3. "Reflections on Justifications for Defining Crimes by the Category of Victim." *Annual Survey of American Law*, no. 4, pp. 617–28.

Greve, Michael S. 1992/3. "Hate Crimes and Hypocrisy." *Annual Survey of American Law*, no. 4, pp. 563–8.

Groarke, Leo. 1990. "Affirmative Action as a Form of Restitution." *Journal of Business Ethics*, vol. 9, no. 3, pp. 207–13.

Gumbhir, Vikas K. 2007. *But Is It Profiling?: Policing, Pretext Stops, and the Color of Suspicion*. New York: LFB Scholarly Publishing LLC.

Gurin, Patricia with Eric L. Dey, Gerald Gurin, and Sylvia Hurtado. 2004. "The Educational Value of Diversity." In Gurin, Lehman and Lewis, *Defending Diversity*, pp. 97–188.

Gutmann, Amy. 1996. "Responding to Racial Injustice." In Appiah and Gutmann, *Color Conscious*, pp. 106–78.

Hacker, Andrew. 2003. *Two Nations: Black & White, Separate, Hostile, Unequal*, rev. and updated ed. New York: Simon & Schuster.

Hackney, James R., Jr. 2004. "Ideological Conflict, African American Reparations, Tort Causation and the Case for Social Welfare Transformation." *Boston University Law Review*, vol. 84, pp. 1193–1207.

Hajdin, Mane. 2002. "Affirmative Action, Old and New." *Journal of Social Philosophy*, vol. 33, no. 1, pp. 83–96.

Hanson, Karen. 1993. "Facing Facts and Responsibilities: The White Man's Burden and the Burden of Proof." In Cahn, ed., *Affirmative Action and the University*, pp. 174–80.

Harrell, Alon and Gideon Parchomovsky. 1999. "On Hate and Equality." *Yale Law Journal*, vol. 109, pp 507–39.

Harris, David A. 2001. "Law Enforcement's Stake in Coming to Grips with Racial Profiling." *Rutgers Race and the Law Review*, vol. 3, pp. 9–38.

———. 2002. *Profiles in Injustice: Why Racial Profiling Cannot Work*. New York: The New Press.

Harris, Luke Charles and Uma Naryan. 2007. "Affirmative Action as Equalizing Opportunity: Challenging the Myth of 'Preferential Treatment.'" In Hugh LaFollette, *Ethics in Practice: An Anthology*. Malden, MA: Blackwell Publishing, pp. 492–503.

Hartle, Ann. 1993. "Who 'Counts' on Campus?" In Cahn, ed., *Affirmative Action and the University*, pp. 132–3.

Harmon, Amy. 2001. "A Limited Partnership." In Correspondents of *The New York Times*, *How Race is Lived in America*, pp. 79–95.

Harvey, Jennifer. 2007. *Whiteness and Morality: Pursuing Racial Justice through Reparations and Sovereignty*. New York: Palgrave Macmillan.

Heriot, Gail. 2008. "Affirmative Action in American Law Schools." *The Journal of Contemporary Legal Issues*, vol. 17, pp. 237–80.

Hernandez, Garcia and Cesar Cuauhtemoc. 2009. "La Migra in the Mirror: Immigration Enforcement and Racial Profiling on the Texas Border." *Notre Dame Journal of Law, Ethics and Public Policy*, vol. 23, no. 1, pp. 167–96.

Herrnstein, Richard J. and Charles Murray. 1994. *The Bell Curve: Intelligence and Class Structure in American Life*. New York: Free Press.

Herstein, Ori. 2008a. "Historic Injustice, Group Membership and Harm to Individuals: Defending Claims for Historic Justice From the Non-Identity Problem." *Columbia Law School Public Law and Legal Theory Working Paper Group*, Paper Number 08–174 (version of March 3).

———. 2008b. "Historic Injustice and the Non-Identity Problem; The Limitations of the Subsequent-Wrong Solution and Towards a New Solution." *Law and Philosophy*, vol. 27, pp. 505–31.

Heumann, Milton and Lance Cassak. 2003. *Good Cop, Bad Cop: Racial Profiling and Competing Views of Justice.* New York: Peter Lang.

Hill, Thomas, Jr. 1991. "The Message of Affirmative Action." *Social Philosophy and Policy*, vol. 8, no. 2, pp. 108–29.

Himma, Kenneth Einar. 2002. "It's the Rationale that Counts: A Reply to Newton." *Journal of Business Ethics*, vol. 37, no. 4, pp. 407–12.

Hitchens, Christopher. 2003. "Debt of Honor." In Winbush, ed., *Should America Pay?*, pp. 172–79.

Holbert, Steve and Lisa Rose. 2006. "It Is Difficult to Establish Whether Racial Profiling Is Occurring." In Nelson, ed., *Racial Profiling*, pp. 43–51.

Holmes, Steven A. 2001. "Which Man's Army." In Correspondents of *The New York Times, How Race is Lived in America*, pp. 41–55.

Horowitz, David. 2002. *Uncivil Wars: The Controversy Over Reparations For Slavery.* San Francisco: Encounter Books.

Hughes, Graham. 1968. "Reparations for Blacks?" *New York University Law Review*, vol. 43, no. 6, pp. 1063–74.

Hughs, Paul M. 2004. "Rectification and Reparation: What Does Citizen Responsibility Require?" *Journal of Social Philosophy*, vol. 35, no. 2, pp. 244–55.

Hurd, Heidi M. 2001. "Why Liberals Should Hate 'Hate Crime Legislation.'" *Law and Philosophy*, vol. 20, no. 2 (March), pp. 215–232.

Issacharoff, Samuel. 1998. "Can Affirmative Action Be Defended?" *Ohio State Law Journal*, vol. 59, pp. 669–95.

Jacobs, James B. 1992. "Rethinking the War Against Hate Crimes: A New York City Perspective." *Criminal Justice Ethics*, vol. 11, pp. 55–61.

Jacobs, James B. and Kimberly Potter. 1998. *Hate Crimes: Criminal Law and Identity Politics.* Oxford: Oxford University Press.

Johnson, Jr., Robert. 1999. "Repatriation as Reparations for Slavery and Jim Crow." In Martin and Yaquinto, eds., *Redress for Historical Injustices in the United States*, pp. 402–10.

Kahan, Dan M. 2001. "Two Liberal Fallacies in the Hate Crimes Debate." *Law and Philosophy*, vol. 20, pp. 175–93.

Kang, Jerry and Mahzarin R. Banaji. 2006. "Fair Measures: A Behavioral Realist Revision of 'Affirmative Action.'" *California Law Review*, vol. 94, pp 1063–1118.

Karabel, Jerome. 2005. *The Chosen: The Hidden History of Admission and Exclusion at Harvard, Yale and Princeton.* New York: Houghton Mifflin.

Karlan, Pamela S. 2008. Untitled. In Loury, et. al., *Race, Incarceration and American Values*, pp. 41–54.

Kekes, John. 1993. "The Injustice of Strong Affirmative Action." In Cahn, ed., *Affirmative Action and the University*, pp. 144–56.

Kellough, J. Edward. 2006. *Understanding Affirmative Action: Politics, Discrimination, and the Search for Justice.* Washington, DC: Georgetown University Press.

Kelly, Robin D. G. 2003. "A Day of Reckoning." In Martin and Yaquinto, eds., *Redress for Historical Injustices in the United States*, pp. 203–21.

Kennedy, Randall. 2002a. *Nigger: The Strange Career of a Troublesome Word.* New York: Pantheon Books.

——. 2002b. "Blind Spot," *Atlantic Monthly*, vol. 289, no. 4 (April) p. 24.

——. 2008. *Sellout: The Politics of Racial Betrayal.* New York: Pantheon Books.

Kershnar, Stephen 1999. "Strong Affirmative Action Programs and Disproportionate Burdens." *The Journal of Value Inquiry*, vol. 33, pp. 201–209.

Kershnar, Stephen. 2004a. *Justice for the Past*. Albany: State University of New York Press.

———. 2004b. "The Case against Reparations." In Ronald P. Salzberger and Mary C. Turck, eds., *Reparations for Slavery: A Reader*. Lanham, MD: Rowman & Littlefield Publishers, Inc., pp. 151–61.

———. 2007. "Race As a Factor in University Admissions." *Law and Philosophy*, vol. 26, no. 5 (September), pp. 437–463.

Kidder, William C. 2001. "Affirmative Action in Higher Education: Recent Developments in Litigation, Admissions and Diversity Research." *Berkeley La Raza Law Journal*, vol. 12, pp. 173–230.

Kim, Janine Young. 2006. "Hate Crime Law and the Limits of Inculpation." *Nebraska Law Review*, vol. 84, pp. 846–94.

Kinder, Donald R. and Lynn M. Sanders. 1996. *Divided by Color: Racial Politics and Democratic Ideals*. Chicago and London: University of Chicago Press.

Klarman, Michael J. 2007. *Unfinished Business: Racial Equality in American History*. Oxford: Oxford University Press.

Klimchuk, Dennis. 2004. "Unjust Enrichment and Reparations for Slavery." *Boston University Law Review*, vol. 84, pp. 1257–75.

Knechtle, John C. 2005–6. "When to Regulate Hate Speech." *Penn State Law Review* vol. 110, no 3, pp. 539–78.

Kohn, Marek. 1995. *The Race Gallery: The Return of Racial Science*. London: Jonathan Cape, Random House.

Kornweibel, Jr., Theodore. 2003. "Railroads, Race, and Reparations." In Martin and Yaquinto, eds., *Redress for Historical Injustices in the United States*, pp. 294–304.

Krauthammer, Charles. 2002. "The Case for Profiling." *Time*, vol. 159, no. 11 (March 18), p. 104.

Krislov, Marvin. 2003–04. "Affirmative Action in Higher Education: the Value, the Method, and the Future." *University of Cincinnati Law Review*, vol. 72, pp. 899–907.

Kukathas, Chandran. 2006. "Who? Whom? Reparations and the Problem of Agency." *Journal of Social Philosophy*, vol. 37, no. 3, pp. 330–41.

Kupperman, Joel J. 1993. "Affirmative Action: Relevant Knowledge and Relevant Ignorance." In Cahn, ed., *Affirmative Action and the University*, pp. 181–88.

Laney, Garrine P. "Racial Profiling." In Muffler, ed., *Racial Profiling*, pp. 1–23.

Lasson, Kenneth. 1985. "In Defense of Group-Libel Laws, or Why the First Amendment Should Not Protect Nazis." *Human Rights Annual*, vol, 2, pp. 289–320.

———. 1986. "Racial Defamation as Free Speech: Abusing the First Amendment." *Columbia Human Rights Law Review*, vol. 17, no. 1, pp. 11–55.

———. 1991. "To Stimulate, Provoke, or Incite?: Hate Speech and the First Amendment." *St. Thomas Law Forum*, vol. 3, no. 1, pp. 49–89.

Lawrence III, Charles R. 1993. "If He Hollers Let him Go: Regulating Racist Speech on Campus." In Matsuda, et. al., *Words That Wound: Critical Race Theory, Assaultive Speech, and the First Amendment*. Boulder, CO: Westview Press, pp. 53–88.

Lawrence III, Charles R., Mari J. Matsuda, Richard Delgado, and Kimberle Williams Crenshaw. 1993. "Introduction." In Matsuda, et. al., *Words That Wound: Critical*

Race Theory, Assaultive Speech, and the First Amendment. Boulder, CO: Westview Press, pp. 1–15.

Lawrence, Frederick M. 1993. "Resolving the Hate Crimes/Hate Speech Paradox: Punishing Bias Crimes and Protecting Racist Speech." *Notre Dame Law Review*, vol. 68, pp. 673–721.

——. 1999. *Punishing Hate: Bias Crimes under American Law.* Cambridge, MA: Harvard University Press.

——. 2005. "The Case for Bias-Crimes Laws." In Susan B. Gellman and Frederick M. Lawrence, "Agreeing to Agree: A Proponent and Opponent of Hate Crime Laws Reach for Common Ground." *Harvard Journal on Legislation*, vol. 41, pp. 422–5.

Laycock, Douglas. 2004. "The Broader Case for Affirmative Action: Desegregation, Academic Excellence, and Future Leadership." *Tulane Law Review*, vol. 78, pp. 1767–1842.

Leadership Conference on Civil Rights Education Fund. 2006. "Profiling Muslims Hinders the War on Terror." In Hirschmann, ed., *Racial Profiling*, pp. 27–34.

LeFevre, Joseph. 2003. "The Value of Diversity: A Justification of Affirmative Action." *Journal of Social Philosophy*, vol. 34, no. 1, pp. 125–33.

Leidholdt, Dorchen. 1995. "Pornography in the Workplace: Sexual Harrassment Litigation under Title VII." In Lederer and Delgado, eds., *The Price We Pay*, pp. 216–32.

Lever, Annabelle. 2005. "Why Racial Profiling Is Hard to Justify: A Response to Risse and Zeckhauser." *Philosophy and Public Affairs*, vol. 33, no. 1 (Winter), pp. 94–110.

——. 2007. "What's Wrong with Racial Profiling? Another Look at the Problem." *Criminal Justice Ethics*, vol. 26, no. 1 (Winter–Spring), pp. 20–28.

Levey, Curt A. 2003. "Racial Preferences in Admissions: Myths, Harms, and Alternatives." *Albany Law Review*, vol. 66, pp. 489–503.

Levin, Michael. 1993. "Responses to Race Differences in Crime." *Journal of Social Philosophy*, vol. 23, no. 1, pp. 5–29.

——. 1994a. "Reply to Adler, Cox, and Corlett." *Journal of Social Philosophy*, vol. 25, no. 1, pp. 5–19.

——. 1994b. "Reply to Adler's 'More on Race and Crime: Levin's Reply.'" *Journal of Social Philosophy*, vol. 25, no. 2, pp. 115–18.

——. 1997. *Why Race Matters: Race Differences and What They Mean.* Westport, CT: Praeger.

Levmore, Saul. 2004. "Privatizing Reparations." *Boston University Law Review*, vol. 84, pp. 1291–1318.

Lewin, Tamar. "Growing Up, Growing Apart." In Correspondents of *The New York Times, How Race is Lived in America*, pp. 151–69.

Liptak, Adam. 2008. "Outside U.S., Hate Speech Can Be Costly." *New York Times* (national edition), Thursday, June 12, pp. A1, A20.

Logue, Kyle D. 2004. "Reparations as Redistribution." *Boston University Law Review*, vol. 84, pp. 1319–1374.

London, Herbert. 2003. "Profiling as Needed." *Albany Law Review*, vol. 66, no. 2, pp. 343–47.

Loury, Glen C. 2002. *The Anatomy of Racial Inequality.* Cambridge, MA: Harvard University Press.

Loury, Glen C. with Pamela S. Karlan, Tommie Shelby, and Loic Wacquant. 2008. *Race, Incarceration, and American Values*. Cambridge, MA: MIT Press.

Lowry, Richard. 2002. "Profiles in Cowardice," *National Review*, vol. 54, no. 1 (January 28), pp. 32–6.

Lund, Nelson. 2003. "The Conservative Case Against Racial Profiling in the War on Terrorism." *Albany Law Review*, vol. 66, pp. 329–42.

Lyons, David. 2004. "Corrective Justice, Equal Opportunity, and the Legacy of Slavery and Jim Crow." *Boston University Law Review*, vol. 84, pp. 1375–1404.

———. 2007. "Racial Injustices in U.S. History and Their Legacy." In Martin and Yaquinto, eds., *Redress for Historical Injustices in the United States*, pp. 33–54.

Ma, Alice K. 1995. "Campus Hate Speech Codes: Affirmative Action in the Allocation of Speech Rights." *California Law Review*, vol. 83, pp. 693–732.

Mac Donald, Heather. 2003. *Are Cops Racist?* Chicago: Ivan R. Dee.

MacKinnon, Catharine A. 1993. *Only Words*. Cambridge, MA: Harvard University Press.

Maclin, Tracey. 2001. "The Fourth Amendment on the Freeway." *Rutgers Race and the Law Review*, vol. 3, pp. 117–89.

Mahoney, Kathleen E. 1995. "Recognizing the Constitutional Significance of Harmful Speech: The Canadian View of Pornography and Hate Propaganda." In Lederer and Delgado, eds., *The Price We Pay*, pp. 277–89.

———. 1996. "Hate Speech: Affirmation or Contradiction of Freedom of Expression. *University of Illinois Law Review*, pp. 789–808.

Malamud, Deborah C. 1997. "Affirmative Action, Diversity, and the Black Middle Class." *University of Colorado Law Review*, vol. 68, pp. 939–1000.

Malik, Kenan. 2008. *Strange Fruit: Why Both Sides are Wrong in the Race Debate*. Oxford: Oneworld Publications.

Marcus, Kenneth L. 2008. "Higher Education, Harassment, and First Amendment Opportunism." *William and Mary Bill of Rights Journal*, vol. 16, pp. 1025–59.

Margulies, Martin B. 1992. "Intent, Motive, and the *R.A.V.* Decision." *Criminal Justice Ethics*, vol. 11, pp. 42–6.

Marketti, James. 1990. "Estimated Present Value of Income Diverted during Slavery." In Richard F. America, ed., *The Wealth of Races*, pp. 107–23.

Markie, Peter J. 1993. "Affirmative Action and the Awarding of Tenure." In Cahn, ed., *Affirmative Action and the University*, pp. 275–85.

Masters, Stanley H. 1990. "The Social Debt to Blacks: A Case for Affirmative Action." In Richard F. America, ed., *The Wealth of Races*, pp. 179–89.

Matsuda, Mari J. 1993. "Public Response to Racist Speech: Considering the Victim's Story." In Matsuda, et. al., *Words That Wound: Critical Race Theory, Assaultive Speech, and the First Amendment*. Boulder, CO: Westview Press, pp. 17–51.

McCarthy, Andrew C. 2006. "Profiling Muslims is Essential in the War on Terror." In Hirschmann, ed., *Racial Profiling*, pp. 21–26.

McGary, Howard. 1977–78. "Justice and Reparations." In McGary, *Race and Social Justice*. Malden, MA: Blackwell Publishers, 1999, pp. 93–109.

———. 1984. "Reparations, Self-Respect, and Public Policy. In McGary, *Race and Social Justice*, pp. 110–24.

———. 1996. "Police Discretion and Discrimination." In McGary, *Race and Social Justice*, pp. 165–80.

McGee, Robert W. 1998. "Does Adoption of an Affirmative Action Policy Constitute an Act Discreditable to the Profession?: A Philosophical Look at a Practical Ethical Question." *Journal of Accounting, Ethics & Public Policy*, vol. 1, no. 2, pp. 275–8.

McMillian, Theodore. 1998. "In Defense of Affirmative Action." *Journal of Urban and Contemporary Law*, vol. 54, pp. 39–42.

McShane, Larry and Trevor Tompson. 2007. "Survey: Young whites happier than minorities." *The Denver Post*, Tuesday, August 21, p. 2A.

McWhirter, Darien A. 1996. *The End of Affirmative Action: Where Do We Go From Here?* New York: Birch Lane Press.

McWhorter, John. 2001. *Losing the Race: Self-Sabotage in Black America* (edition with author afterword) New York: HarperCollins.

———. 2005. *Winning the Race: Beyond the Crisis in Black America*. New York: Gotham Books.

Meeks, Kenneth. 2000. *Driving While Black – Highways, Shopping Malls, Taxicabs, Sidewalks: How to Fight Back If You are a Victim of Racial Profiling*. New York: Broadway Books.

Mellott, Jared M. 2006. "The Diversity Rationale for Affirmative Action in Employment After *Grutter*: The Case for Containment." *William & Mary Law Review*, pp. 1091–1158.

Michelman, Frank I. 1995. "Civil Liberties, Silencing, and Subordination." In Lederer and Delgado, eds., *The Price We Pay*, pp. 272–6.

Moore, Jamillah. 2005. *Race and College Admissions: A Case for Affirmative Action*. Jefferson, NC, and London: McFarland & Co.

Moskos, Peter. 2006. "Driving While Black." *New York Times* (July 13), p. 13.

Mosley, Albert G. 1996. "Affirmative Action: Pro." In Mosley and Capaldi, *Affirmative Action*, pp. 1–63.

———. 1998. "Policies of Straw or Policies of Inclusion?: A Review of Pojman's 'Case against Affirmative Action." *International Journal of Applied Philosophy*, vol. 12, no. 2, pp. 161–68.

Muller, Eric L. 2003. "Inference or Impact? Racial Profiling and the Internment's True Legacy." *Ohio State Journal of Criminal Law*, vol. 1, pp. 104–32.

Murphy, Jeffrie G. 1992. "Bias Crimes: What do Haters Deserve?" *Criminal Justice Ethics*, vol. 11, no. 2 (Summer/Fall), pp. 20–23.

Murphy, Tanya Y. 1995. "An Argument for Diversity Based Affirmative Action in Higher Eduction." *1995 Annual Survey of American Law*, pp. 515–64.

Nagel, Thomas. 1973. "Equal Treatment and Compensatory Discrimination." Reprinted in Marshall Cohen, Thomas Nagel, and Thomas Scanlon, eds., *Equality and Preferential Treatment*. Princeton: Princeton University Press, pp. 3–18.

———. 1977. "Introduction." In Cohen, et al, eds., *Equality and Preferential Treatment* pp. vii–xiv.

Navarro, Mireya. 2001. "Bricks, Mortar and Coalition Building." In Correspondents of *The New York Times*, *How Race is Lived in America*, pp. 251–67.

Neal, Larry. 1990. "A Calculation and Comparison of the Current Benefits of Slavery and an Analysis of Who Benefits." In Richard F. America, ed., *The Wealth of Races*, pp. 91–105.

Nearpass, Gregory R. 2002. "The Overlooked Constitutional Objection and Practical Concerns To Penalty-Enhancement Provisions of Hate Crime Legislation." *Albany Law Review* vol. 66, no. 2, pp. 547–73.

Newton, Lisa. 1973. "Reverse Discrimination as Unjustified." *Ethics*, vol. 83, no. 4 (July), pp. 308–12.

Nzingha, Yaa Asantewa. 2003. "Reparations + Education = The Pass to Freedom." In Winbush, ed., *Should America Pay?*, pp. 299–314.

Ogletree, Charles J., Jr. 2003a. "The Current Reparations Debate." *U.C. Davis Law Review*, vol. 36, no. 5, pp. 1051–72.

———. 2003b. "Repairing the Past: New Efforts in the Reparations Debate in America." *Harvard Civil Rights-Civil Liberties Law Review*, vol. 38, pp. 279–320.

———. 2003c. "Reparations for the Children of Slaves: Litigating the Issues." *The University of Memphis Law Review*, vol. 33, pp. 245–64.

———. 2004. "Tulsa Reparations: The Survivors' Story." *Boston College Third World Law Journal*, vol. 24, pp. 13–30.

Olafson, Frederick A. 1993. "'Affirmative Action' in the Cultural Wars." In Cahn, ed., *Affirmative Action and the University*, pp. 206–11.

Oliver, Melvin L. and Thomas M. Shapiro. 2006. *Black Wealth/White Wealth: A New Perspective on Racial Inequality*. New York: Routledge.

Osei, Akwasi. 1992. "The Persistence of Differing Trends in African-American Mortality and Morbidity Rates." In Galster and Hill, eds., *The Metropolis in Black & White*, pp. 128–42.

Outterson, Kevin. 2003. "Slave Taxes." In Winbush, ed., *Should America Pay?*, pp. 135–49.

———. 2009. "The End of Reparations Talk: Reparations in an Obama World." *Kansas Law Review*, vol. 57, pp. 101–14.

Paterson, Eva Jefferson. 2004. "And Still We Rise." *African-American Law & Policy Report*, vol. 6, pp. 15–20.

Paul, Ellen Frankel. 1993. "Careers Open to Talent." In Cahn, ed., *Affirmative Action and the University*, pp. 250–63.

Pampel, Fred C. 2004. *Racial Profiling*. New York: Facts on File.

Pell, Terence J. 2003. "Racial Preferences and Formal Equality." *Journal of Social Philosophy*, vol. 34, no. 2, pp. 309–25.

Pettigrove, Glen. 2003. "Apology, Reparations, and The Question of Inherited Guilt." *Public Affairs Quarterly*, vol. 17, No. 4 (October), pp. 319–48.

Pojman, Louis P. 1992. "The Moral Status of Affirmative Action." In Beckwith and Jones, eds., *Affirmative Action*, pp. 175–97.

———. 1993. "Race and Crime: A Response to Michael Levin and Laurence Thomas." *Journal of Social Philosophy*, vol. 24, no. 1, pp. 152–54.

———. 1998a. "The Case Against Affirmative Action." *International Journal of Applied Philosophy*, vol. 12, no. 1, pp. 97–115.

———. 1998b. "Straw Man or Straw Theory?: A Reply to Albert Mosley." *International Journal of Applied Philosophy*, vol. 12, no. 2, pp. 169–80.

Pollak, Joseph D. 2009. "Racial Profiling is Wrong: A Doctrinal Comparison of Counter-Terrorism Racial Profiling in Europe and the United States." Available at SSRN: http://ssrn.com/abstract=1390269.

Purdy, Laura. 1984. "In Defense of Hiring Apparently Less Qualified Women." *Journal of Social Philosophy*, vol. 15, no. 2, pp. 26–33.

———. 1994. "Why Do We Need Affirmative Action?" *Journal of Social Philosophy*, vol. 25, no. 1, pp. 133–43.

Quinn, Philip L. 1993. "Affirmative Action and the Multicultural Ideal." In Cahn, ed., *Affirmative Action and the University*, pp. 197–205.

Rachels, James. 1993. "Are Quotas Sometimes Justified?" In Cahn, ed., *Affirmative Action and the University*, pp. 217–22.

Ramirez, Deborah, Jack McDevitt and Amy Farrell. 2006. "A Resource Guide on Racial Profiling Data Collection Systems: Promising Practices and Lessons Learned." In Muffler, ed., *Racial Profiling*, pp. 57–108.

Ransom, Roger L. and Richard Sutch. 1990. "Who Pays for Slavery?" In Richard F. America, ed., *The Wealth of Races*, pp. 31–54.

Raphael, Alan. 2005. "Affirmative Action and Admissions at a Jesuit Law School." *Loyola University Chicago Law Journal*, vol. 36, pp. 579–89.

Reddick Sharon R. 2004. "Point: The Case for Profiling." *International Social Science Review*, vol. 79, nos. 3–4, pp. 154–6.

Redish, Martin H. 1992. "Freedom of Thought as Freedom of Expression: Hate Crime Sentencing Enhancement and First Amendment Theory." *Criminal Justice Ethics*, vol. 11, pp. 29–43.

Reed, Fred. 2006. "All Police Officers Practice Racial Profiling." In Hirschmann, ed., *Racial Profiling*, pp. 57–61.

Reidy, David A. 2004. "Hate Crimes Laws: Progressive Politics or Balkanization?" In Christine T. Sistare, ed., *Civility and Its Discontents: Essays on Civic Virtue, Toleration, and Cultural Fragmentation*. Lawrence: University of Kansas Press, pp. 258–82.

Richburg, Keith B. 1997. *Out of America: A Black Man Confronts Africa*. New York: Basic Books.

Riggs, Robert R. 1995. "Punishing the Politically Incorrect Offender Through 'Bias Motive' Enhancements: Compelling Necessity or First Amendment Folly?" *Ohio Northern University Law Review*, vol. 21, pp. 945–57.

Risse, Mathias. 2007. "Racial Profiling: A Reply to Two Critics." *Criminal Justice Ethics*, vol. 26, no. 1 (Winter-Spring), pp. 4–19.

Risse, Mathias and Richard Zeckhauser. 2004. "Racial Profiling." *Philosophy and Public Affairs*, vol. 32, no. 2 (Spring), pp. 131–70.

Robinson, Paul. H. 1992/3. "Hate Crimes: Crimes of Motive, Character, or Group Terror?" *Annual Survey of American Law*, no. 4, pp. 605–16.

Robinson, Randall. 2000a. *The Debt: What America Owes to Blacks*. New York: Penguin Putnam.

——. 2000b. "Restatement of the Black Manifesto." In Martin and Yaquinto, eds., *Redress for Historical Injustices in the United States*, pp. 621–4.

——. 2000c. "America's Debt to Blacks." In David Boonin and Graham Oddie, eds., *What's Wrong?, Second Edition*. Oxford: Oxford University Press, pp. 372–73.

——. 2004. "What America Owes to Blacks and What Blacks Owe to Each Other." *African-American Law & Policy Report*, vol. 6, no. 1, pp. 1–13.

Romero, Victor C. 2003. "Critical Race Theory in Three Acts: Racial Profiling, Affirmative Action, and the Diversity Visa Lottery." *Albany Law Review*, vol. 66, pp. 375–86.

Rubinstein, Mitchell H. 1985–6. "The Affirmative Action Controversy." *Hofstra Labor and Employment Law Journal*, vol. 3, no. 1, pp. 111–36.

Sabbagh, Daniel. 2007. *Equality and Transparency: A Strategic Perspective on Affirmative Action in American Law*. New York: Palgrave Macmillan.

Sack, Kevin. 2001. "Shared Prayers, Mixed Blessings." In Correspondents of *The New York Times*, *How Race is Lived in America*, pp. 3–21.

Sack, Kevin and Janet Elder. 2001. "Appendix: The *New York Times* Poll on Race: Optimistic Outlook But Enduring Racial Division." In Correspondents of *The New York Times, How Race is Lived in America*, pp. 365–94.

Sadurski, Wojciech. 1999. *Freedom of Speech and Its Limits*. Dordrecht: Kluwer Academic Publishers.

Sarich, Vincent and Frank Miele. 2005. *Race: The Reality of Human Differences*. Boulder, CO: Westview Press.

Schauer, Frederick. 2003. *Profiles, Probabilities and Stereotypes*. Cambridge, MA: Harvard University Press.

Schedler, George. 1998. *Racist Symbols and Reparations: Philosophical Reflections on Vestiges of the American Civil War*. Lanham, MD: Rowman & Littlefield Publishers, Inc.

———. 2002. "Principles for Measuring the Damages of American Slavery." *Public Affairs Quarterly*, Vol. 16, No. 4 (October), pp. 377–404.

Sebok, Anthony J. 2004. "Two Concepts of Injustice in Restitution for Slavery." *Boston University Law Review*, vol. 84, pp. 1405–42.

Secours, Molly. 2003. "Riding the Reparations Bandwagon." In Winbush, ed., *Should America Pay?*, pp. 286–98.

Sepinwall, Amy J. 2006. "Responsibility for Historical Injustices: Reconceiving the Case for Reparations." *Journal of Law & Politics*, vol. XXII, pp. 183–229.

Sharp, Andrew. 1997. *Justice and the Maori: The Philosophy and Practice of Maori Claims in New Zealand since the 1970s, Second Edition*. Auckland, NZ: Oxford University Press.

Shelton, La Verne. 1993. "An Ecological Concept of Diversity." In Cahn, ed., *Affirmative Action and the University*, pp. 233–49.

Sher, George. 1999. "Diversity." *Philosophy and Public Affairs*, Vol. 28, No. 2, pp. 85–104.

Sherwin, Emily. 2004. "Reparations and Unjust Enrichment." *Boston University Law Review*, vol. 84, pp. 1443–65.

Shiell, Timothy C. 1998. *Campus Hate Speech on Trial*. Lawrence: University Press of Kansas.

Shiffrin, Seana Valentine. 2009. "Reparations for U.S. Slavery and Justice Over Time." In Melinda A. Roberts and David T. Wasserman, eds., *Harming Future Persons: Ethics, Genetics and the Nonidentity Problem*. London: Springer, pp. 333–39.

Simon, Robert. 1974. "Preferential Hiring: A Reply to Judith Jarvis Thomson." *Philosophy and Public Affairs*, Vol. 3, No. 3, pp. 312–20.

Simon, Robert L. 1993. "Affirmative Action and the University: Faculty Appointment and Preferential Treatment." In Cahn, ed., *Affirmative Action and the University*, pp. 48–92.

Simmons, A. John. 1995. "Historical Rights and Fair Shares." *Law and Philosophy*, vol. 14, no. 2, Special Issue on Rights (May, 1995), pp. 149–184

Sistare, Christine. 2004. "Hate Crime and Social Fragmentation." In Sistare, ed., *Civility and Its Discontents*, pp. 244–57.

Smith, Errol. 1997. "My Experience with the California Civil Rights Initiative." In Faryna, Stetson, and Conti eds., *Black and Right*, pp. 77–80.

Somin, Ilya. 2006. "How Affirmative Action is Like Racial Profiling." In Nelson, ed., *Racial Profiling*, pp. 52–6.

Sommers, Fred. 1993. "Saying What We Think." In Cahn, ed., *Affirmative Action and the University*, pp. 291–94.

Sowell, Thomas. 2004. *Affirmative Action Around the World: An Empirical Study*. New Haven, CT, London: Yale University Press.

Stark, Susan. 2004. "Taking Responsibility for Oppression: Affirmative Action and Racial Injustice." *Public Affairs Quarterly*, vol. 18, no. 3, pp. 205–21.

Steele, Shelby. 1990. The *Content of Our Character: A New Vision of Race in America*. New York: St. Martin's Press.

——. 1998. *A Dream Deferred: The Second Betrayal of Black Freedom in America*. New York: HarperCollins Publishers.

——. 2006. *White Guilt: How Blacks and Whites Together Destroyed the Promise of the Civil Rights Era*. New York: HarperCollins Publishers.

——. 2008. *A Bound Man: Why We Are Excited About Obama and Why He Can't Win*. New York: Free Press.

Sterba, James P. 1993. "The Case for Preferential Treatment." In Cahn, ed., *Affirmative Action and the University*, pp. 286–90.

——. 2003a. "Defending Affirmative Action, Defending Preferences." *Journal of Social Philosophy*, vol. 34, no. 2, pp. 285–300.

——. 2003b. "Defending Affirmative Action, Defending Preference." In Cohen and Sterba, *Affirmative Action and Racial Preference*, pp. 191–278.

Strike, Kenneth A. 2006. "Discussion of Fullinwider and Lichtenberg's *Leveling the Playing Field*." *Theory and Research in Education*, pp. 185–99.

Strossen, Nadine. 1996. "Hate Speech and Pornography: Do We Have to Choose Between Freedom of Speech and Equality?" *Case Western Reserve Law Review*, vol. 46, pp. 449–78.

——. 2001. "Incitement to Hatred: Should There Be a Limit?" *Southern Illinois University Law Journal*, vol. 25, pp. 243–80.

Subotnik, Dan. 2005. *Toxic Diversity: Race, Gender, and Law Talk in America*. New York: New York University Press.

Sunstein, Cass. 1993. *Democracy and the Problem of Free Speech*. New York: Free Press.

Tabb, William M. 2005. "Reflections on Diversity." *Journal of Legal Education*, vol. 55, nos. 1–2, pp. 28–34.

Taslitz, Andrew E. 1999. "Condemning the Racist Personality: Why the Critics of Hate Crimes Legislation Are Wrong." *Boston College Law Review*, vol. 40, pp. 739–85.

Taylor, Jr., Stuart. 2006. "Airlines Should Screen Passengers Who Match Terrorists' Racial Profiles." In Hirschmann ed., *Racial Profiling*, pp. 35–41.

Thernstrom, Stephan and Abigail Thernstrom. 1997. *America in Black and White: One Nation, Indivisible*. New York: Simon & Schuster.

Thomas, George C. III. 2001. "Blinded by the Light: How to Deter Racial Profiling – Thinking About Remedies." *Rutgers Race and the Law Review*, vol. 3, pp. 39–59.

Thomas, Laurence. 1992. "Statistical Badness." *Journal of Social Philosophy*, vol. 23, no. 1, pp. 30–41.

——. 1993. "What Good Am I?" In Cahn, ed., *Affirmative Action and the University*, pp. 125–31.

——. 2003–04. "Equality and the Mantra of Diversity." *University of Cincinnati Law Review*, vol. 72, pp. 931–59.

Thompson, Ginger. 2001. "Reaping What Was Sown on the Old Plantation." In Correspondents of *The New York Times, How Race is Lived in America*, pp. 133–49.

Thomson, Judith Jarvis. 1973. "Preferential Hiring." *Philosophy and Public Affairs*, vol. 2, no. 4, pp. 364–84.

Tsesis, Aleander. 2000. "The Empirical Shortcomings of First Amendment Jurisprudence; a Historical Perspective on the Power of Hate Speech." *Santa Clara Law Review*, vol. 40, pp. 729–86.

———. 2002. *Destructive Messages: How Hate Speech Paves the Way for Harmful Social Movements*. New York: New York University Press.

Turnbull, Robert G. 1993. "Reflections of Affirmative Action in Academia." In Cahn, ed., *Affirmative Action and the University*, pp. 134–43.

Tutu, Nontombi. 2003. "Afterward." In Winbush, ed., *Should America Pay?*, pp. 321–25.

United States Department of Justice. 2003. "Fact Sheet: Racial Profiling." http://www.usdoj.gov/opa/pr/2003/June/racial_profiling_fact_sheet.pdf

United States General Accounting Office. 2006. "Racial Profiling: Limited Data Available on Motorist Stops." In Muffler, ed., *Racial Profiling*, pp. 109–53.

Valls, Andrew. 1999. "The Libertarian Case for Affirmative Action." *Social Theory and Practice*, vol. 25, no. 2, pp. 299–323.

Van Dyke, Jon M. 2003. "Reparations for the Descendants of American Slaves Under International Law." In Winbush, ed., *Should America Pay?*, pp. 57–78.

Vedder, Richard, Lowell Gallaway and David C. Klingaman. 1990. "Black Exploitation and White Benefits: The Civil War Income Revolution." In Richard F. America, ed., *The Wealth of Races*, pp. 125–37.

Waldron, Jeremy. 1992. "Superseding Historic Injustice." *Ethics*, vol. 103, no. 1 (Oct., 1992), pp. 4–28.

Waldstreicher, David. 2009. *Slavery's Constitution: From Revolution to Ratification*. New York: Hill and Wang.

Walker, Samuel. 1994. *Hate Speech: The History of an American Controversy*. Lincoln: University of Nebraska Press.

Wang, Lu-in. 1997. "The Transforming Power of 'Hate': Social Cognition Theory and the Harms of Bias-Related Crime." *Southern California Law Review*, vol. 71, pp. 47–135.

———. 1999. "The Complexities of 'Hate.'" *Ohio State Law Journal*, vol. 60, no. 3, pp. 799–900.

———. 2000. "Recognizing Opportunistic Bias Crimes." *Boston University Law Review*, vol. 80, pp. 1399–1435.

———. 2001. "'Suitable Targets'?: Parallels and Connections Between 'Hate' Crimes and 'Driving While Black.'" *Michigan Journal of Race and Law*, vol. 6, pp. 209–36.

———. 2002. "Hate Crime and Everyday Discrimination: Influences of and on the Social Context." *Rutgers Race and the Law Review*, vol. 4, pp. 1–31.

———. 2002–3. "Unwarranted Assumptions in the Prosecution and Defense of Hate Crimes." *Criminal Justice*, vol. 17, pp. 5–11.

Weinstein, James. 1992a. "First Amendment Challenges to Hate Crime Legislation: Where's the Speech?" *Criminal Justice Ethics*, vol. 11, pp. 6–20.

———. 1992b. "Some Further Thoughts on 'Thought Crimes.'" *Criminal Justice Ethics*, vol. 11, pp. 61–3.

———. 1999. *Hate Speech, Pornography, and the Radical Attack on Free Speech Doctrine*. Boulder, CO: Westview Press.

Wellman, Christopher Heath. 2006. "A Defense of Stiffer Penalties for Hate Crimes." *Hypatia*, vol. 21, no. 2 (Spring), pp. 62–80.

Wenger, Kaimipono David. 2006. "Causation and Attenuation in the Slavery Reparations Debate." *University of San Francisco Law Review*, pp. 279–326.

Westley, Robert. 2003. "Many Billions Gone: Is It Time to Reconsider the Case for Black Reparations?" In Winbush, ed., *Should America Pay?*, pp. 109–34.

Westmoreland, Robert. 2003–04. "A New and Improved Affirmative Action?" *University of Cincinnati Law Review*, vol. 72, pp. 909–29.

White, David M. 2001. "The Requirement of Race-Conscious Evaluation of LSAT Scores for Equitable Law School Admissions." *Berkeley La Raza Law Journal*, vol. 12, pp. 399–427.

Wicker, Tom. 1996. *Tragic Failure: Racial Integration in America*. New York: Willam Morrow and Company, Inc.

Will, George F. 2007. "A Bustling Hate-Crime Industry." *The Washington Post*, Sunday May 13, p. B7.

Williams, Armstrong. 2003. "Presumed Victims." In Winbush, ed., *Should America Pay?*, pp. 165–71.

Williams, David R. and Chiquita Collins. 2004. "Reparations: A Viable Strategy to Address the Enigma of African American Health." In Martin and Yaquinto, eds., *Redress for Historical Injustices in the United States*, pp. 305–330.

Williams, Juan. 2006. *Enough: The Phony Leaders, Dead-End Movements, and Culture of Failure That Are Undermining Black America – and What We Can Do About It*. New York: Crown Publishers.

Winerip, Michael. 2001. "Why Harlem Drug Cops Don't Discuss Race." In Correspondents of *The New York Times*, *How Race is Lived in America*, pp. 231–49.

Winbush, Raymond A. 2003a. "Introduction." In Winbush, ed., *Should America Pay?*, pp. xi–xix.

———. 2003b. "And the Earth Moved: Stealing Black Land in the United States." In Winbush, ed., *Should America Pay?*, pp. 46–54.

Wise, Tim. 2008. *White Like Me: Reflections on Race from a Privileged Son* (rev. and updated ed.). Brooklyn, NY: Soft Skull Press.

Withrow, Brian L. 2006. *Racial Profiling: From Rhetoric to Reason*. Upper Saddle River, NJ: Pearson Prentice Hall.

Woods, Jordan Blair. 2008. "Taking the 'Hate' Out of Hate Crimes: Applying Unfair Advantage Theory to Justify the Enhanced Punishment of Opportunistic Bias Crimes." *UCLA Law Review*, vol. 56, pp. 489–541.

Wolf-Devine, Celia. 1993. "Proportional Representation of Woman and Minorities." In Cahn, ed., *Affirmative Action and the University*, pp. 222–32.

Yoo, Margaret Y. K. 1997. "Reaffirming Merit in Affirmative Action." *Journal of Legal Education*, vol. 37, no. 4, pp. 514–23.

Index